T0396239

Renaissance Music

The Library of Essays on Music Performance Practice.
Series Editor: Mary Cyr

Titles in the Series:

Medieval Music
Honey Meconi

Renaissance Music
Kenneth Kreitner

Baroque Music
Peter Walls

Classical and Romantic Music
David Milsom

Renaissance Music

Edited by

Kenneth Kreitner

University of Memphis, USA

ASHGATE

Published by
Ashgate Publishing Limited
Wey Court East
Union Road
Farnham
Surrey GU9 7PT
England

Ashgate Publishing Company
Suite 420
101 Cherry Street
Burlington
VT 05401-4405
USA

www.ashgate.com

British Library Cataloguing in Publication Data
Renaissance music. – (Music performance practice)
  1. Performance practice (Music)–History–To 1500.
  2. Performance practice (Music)–History–16th century.
  3. Music–Performance.
  I. Series II. Kreitner, Kenneth.
  781.4'3'09031-dc22

Library of Congress Control Number: 2010931200

ISBN 9780754629634

MIX
Paper from responsible sources
FSC
www.fsc.org FSC® C013056

Printed and bound in Great Britain by
TJ International Ltd, Padstow, Cornwall.

Contents

PART IV INSTRUMENTAL MUSIC

PART V NOTATION

PART VI PERSPECTIVE

Acknowledgements

The editor and publishers wish to thank the following for permission to use copyright material.

American Musical Instrument Society for the essay: Howard Mayer Brown (1986), 'Notes (and Transposing Notes) on the Transverse Flute in the Early Sixteenth Century', *Journal of the American Musical Instrument Society*, **12**, pp. 5–39.

Cambridge University Press for the essays: David Fallows (1983), 'Specific Information on the Ensembles for Composed Polyphony, 1400–1474', in Stanley Boorman (ed.), *Studies in the Performance of Late Mediaeval Music*, Cambridge: Cambridge University Press, pp. 109–59; Margaret Bent (1984), 'Diatonic *ficta*', *Early Music History*, **4**, pp. 1–48.

Claremont Graduate University for the essay: Noel O'Regan (2009), 'What Can the Organ *Partitura* to Tomás Luis de Victoria's *Missae, Magnificat, motecta, psalmi et alia quam plurima* of 1600 Tell Us about Performance Practice?', *Performance Practice Review*, **14**, pp. 1–14. Copyright © 2009 Claremont Graduate University.

Koninklijke Vereniging voor Nederlandse Muziekgeschiedenis for the essay: David Fallows (1985), 'The Performing Ensembles in Josquin's Sacred Music', *Tijdschrift van de Vereniging voor Nederlandse Muziekgeschiedenis*, **35**, pp. 32–64.

Oxford University Press for the essays: Lloyd Hibberd (1946), 'On "Instrumental Style" in Early Melody', *Musical Quarterly*, **32**, pp. 107–30; Christopher Page (1992), 'Going Beyond the Limits: Experiments with Vocalization in the French Chanson, 1340–1440', *Early Music*, **20**, pp. 447–59; William F. Prizer (1975), 'Performance Practices in the Frottola', *Early Music*, **3**, pp. 227–35; Tess Knighton (1992), 'The *a cappella* Heresy in Spain: An Inquisition into the Performance of the *cancionero* Repertory', *Early Music*, **20**, pp. 561–81; Stephen Keyl (1992), '*Tenorlied, Discantlied*, Polyphonic Lied: Voices and Instruments in German Secular Polyphony of the Renaissance', *Early Music*, **20**, pp. 434–45; Rinaldo Alessandrini (1999), 'Performance Practice in the *Seconda prattica* Madrigal', *Early Music*, **27**, pp. 633–39; Richard Sherr (1987), 'Performance Practice in the Papal Chapel during the 16th Century', *Early Music*, **15**, pp. 453–62; Graham Dixon (1994), 'The Performance of Palestrina: Some Questions, but Fewer Answers', *Early Music*, **22**, pp. 667–75; Noel O'Regan (1996), 'The Performance of Palestrina: Some Further Observations', *Early Music*, **24**, pp. 145–54; Kenneth Kreitner (1992), 'Minstrels in Spanish Churches, 1400–1600', *Early Music*, **20**, pp. 533–46; Keith Polk (1990), 'Voices and Instruments: Soloists and Ensembles in the 15th Century', *Early Music*, **18**, pp. 179–98; Andrew Johnstone (2006), '"High" Clefs in Composition and Performance', *Early Music*, **34**, pp. 29–53. Copyright © Andrew Johnstone 2006. Published by Oxford University Press. All rights reserved; Donald Greig (1995), 'Sight-Readings: Notes on *a cappella* Performance Practice', *Early Music*, **23**, pp. 125–48; Bonnie J. Blackburn (1997), 'For Whom Do the Singers Sing?', *Early Music*, **25**, pp. 593–609.

Series Preface

The four volumes that comprise the *Library of Essays on Music Performance Practice* are divided according to the traditional boundaries of the historical periods in music: Medieval, Renaissance, Baroque, and Classical/Romantic. Musical style and common approaches to composition within these four periods offer a way of unifying the writings, and each volume features a coherent selection of essays about how music was performed before the modern era of recorded sound. The essays are arranged within topics that draw readers' attention to areas of special interest and facilitate investigating a specific line of inquiry through several related essays. The topics vary according to the contents of each volume, but some areas of investigation also cross the temporal boundaries of individual volumes, making the series as a whole well worth consulting for anyone who wishes to understand more about how music of the past was performed. Issues such as the size and configuration of performing forces (choral versus solo voices and small versus large instrumental ensembles), pitch, vibrato, inexact rhythmic notation, and improvisation have often given rise to scholarly debate and revisionist thinking that has changed the direction of future research and performance. Many of the essays chosen for inclusion here demonstrate methods and approaches that have proven especially valuable as models for future research. The repertoire represented ranges broadly across Western art music, both secular and sacred, and each volume addresses issues that arise in both vocal and instrumental music. The geographical area covered also extends well beyond Europe.

Each volume includes a substantial introduction written by an editor who is a recognized authority in the field of performance practice and who has made significant contributions to research, teaching, and performing early music within the period in question. The editor's introduction offers an authoritative overview of the issues and controversies that have dominated performance practice research within a particular historical period and how the results of that research have changed the way the music is now performed and understood. Drawing on his or her own extensive research and personal experience, the editor is well-situated to provide a context for readers and to assist them in gaining a deeper understanding of the issues and controversies that hold particular importance. A select bibliography in each volume directs readers toward additional essays and books that amplify topics represented within the volume and also identifies other issues that warrant further study.

One of the paradoxes within the field of performance practice is that the desire of scholars, performers, and listeners today to understand how old instruments sounded, how music was sung and by whom, and how musical symbols were interpreted is itself a relatively new concept. Whether one investigates how music was performed in the past in order to create an 'authentic' performance (this term now having been generally abandoned in favour of descriptors such as a 'historically-informed' or 'historically-inspired' performance), the quest to understand more about the past can be traced to a revival of interest in early instruments that began about a hundred years ago. Since that time, the field has expanded greatly to include vocal as well as instrumental techniques and to embrace not only scholarly research and editing but also the practical knowledge that instrument builders, performers, and conductors are able to contribute. The results of research in performance practice, especially essays written within the past thirty years or so, have fundamentally changed the way that early music is performed today. *The Library of Essays in Music Performance Practice* offers fertile ground for students, scholars, performers, instrument builders, and listeners who wish to review these research results and for anyone who wishes to gain new insights about how studies in performance practice have brought about greater understanding and appreciation for music of the past and the directions that such research may take in the future.

MARY CYR,
Series Editor
University of Guelph, Canada

Introduction

When I first moved to Memphis, I had a neighbour who was an exterminator. One afternoon he asked what sort of doctor I was, and when I told him, he mentioned that he had a friend with a PhD in entomology, who taught courses to his fellow exterminators. How interesting, I said ... but what I thought was, How awful. I mean, presumably you become an entomologist because in some way you love bugs; what, I wondered, would it be like to spend your days teaching people how to kill them? Not for the first time, I was glad I was a musicologist instead of something else.

But in the years since, I have had plenty of occasion to reconsider my smugness. Is the lot of the performance-practice scholar really all that different? It was my hobby as an early-wind player, and the sound in my mind's ear of cornetts and sackbuts behind the great polyphony of the fifteenth and sixteenth centuries, that drew me to musicology in the first place; and once I got there, I have indeed ended up being part of killing off the thing I loved. And maybe, on reflection, that is as it must be: it is often the job of performance practice to deliver what sounds at the time like bad news.[1]

To back up a bit: the musicians of the nineteenth and twentieth centuries knew a thing or two about sacred choral music, about secular partsongs, about chamber music and about the solo music of keyboard and plucked-string instruments. And so, as more and more music from the fifteenth and sixteenth centuries came to light and into modern print over those years, it all dropped comfortably onto long-established and familiar archetypes. This is the way the human mind works: we all learn history by grafting it, consciously or unconsciously, onto our own experience. But it means that the study of Renaissance performance practice is in part a process of unlearning – of shedding the assumptions we bring to musical notation, whether we be aware of them or not, in the face of historical data.

For a vivid case in point, consider the voices-and-instruments debate that began in earnest in the 1970s and has not quite died down even yet. Here three basic facts were abundantly clear: (1) that apart from tablatures and so forth, the polyphonic music of the late Middle Ages and Renaissance almost never specifies its performing forces; (2) that most songs and a fair number of sacred pieces before 1500 leave one or more of their lines untexted in their sources; and (3) that musical instruments were available in a gratifying number and variety during this period. And for a long time, these three things seemed to go easily and obviously together: clearly, it seemed, the texted lines were to be sung and the untexted lines played on instruments. It is a conclusion that is hard to dissuade undergraduates from even now. But it proves to be, in large part, wrong. A lot of music that looks as though parts should be played on instruments, and a lot of music that to us sounds wonderful when accompanied by cornetts and sackbuts, was apparently meant to be done by voices alone. There are exceptions and refinements and there were compromises, of course; but the general trend of the last few

---

[1]   For my earlier essay on this and related subjects, see Kreitner (1998), from which I have borrowed freely for the present Introduction.

decades – and yes, the sackbuttist in me is a little sad to have been a part of it – has been to take instruments out of music where we used to imagine them.[2]

The voices-and-instruments debate is not explicitly the subject of this collection, but the alert reader will see it everywhere just the same. It has been in the foreground of a good deal of recent research on performance practice in the fifteenth and sixteenth centuries, and in the background of a great deal more: much current thinking on pitch standards and *musica ficta*, for example, has revolved around the behaviour of singers in an *a cappella* world. So it is possible, maybe inevitable, to see issues of what we might broadly call instrumentation everywhere in this book. Beyond and behind it all, however, is one eternal, inexhaustible, irresistible mystery. We know what, say, a Josquin mass looks like – *but what did it sound like?*

Method

I begin the collection with two essays in a part by themselves, partly because they cross generic boundaries so freely and thus do not fit well under the other headings, but also because, after years of reading and rereading, I find them still set apart in my mind. To call the part 'Method' is an injustice – both are full of useful data, original observations and elegant writing – but the title will do its job if it emphasizes that both of these essays got people in their day thinking in a different way about how to go about things, about what certain kinds of evidence actually mean and do not mean.

I was not around when Lloyd Hibberd's essay 'On "Instrumental Style" in Early Melody' (Chapter 1) appeared in the *Musical Quarterly* in 1946, but its revolutionary character is still evident at sixty years' remove. Its ostensible target, stated in the first sentence, is a series of books and essays from earlier in the century by Arnold Schering, who had died a few years before; but its real impact has been on the whole process of supposing that we understand the difference between vocal and instrumental music. Schering is no mere straw man for Hibberd: everything he is summarized as saying seems, even now, unexceptionably logical and humane. And point by point, Hibberd answers these assumptions with hard and wide-ranging evidence from the theorists and the surviving music of the Middle Ages and Renaissance. For calm and orderly refutation of everything its audience probably believed, this essay remains for me a model.

The other, 'Specific Information on the Ensembles for Composed Polyphony, 1400–1474' (Chapter 2), was read by David Fallows at a conference in New York in 1981 and published in its proceedings two years later. This one I do remember, and I remember the sensation it caused among my fellow graduate students, principally because it seemed to prove that just about all the polyphony of Dufay's time, sacred and secular alike, was written for voices alone. Fallows was careful not to say that exactly, and his argument is much more nuanced than what we immediately took away from it – though it should perhaps be said that in the years since, unaccompanied vocal performance has continued to be seen as the default for just

---

[2]   The most thorough and thoughtful evaluation of this period, though aimed (as many of these general discussions are) more at the Middle Ages than the Renaissance, is Leech-Wilkinson (2002); see also some of the essays in Kenyon (1988) for bits of early commentary, though this book is largely concerned with the performance baroque music and after.

about all polyphony from the fifteenth century. (It also helped that he happened to be writing at exactly the time when groups like the Hilliard Ensemble, Gothic Voices and Pro Cantione Antiqua were showing how much potency small groups of unaccompanied voices could pack – a classic case of symbiosis between scholarship and performance.)

But beyond the observations, negative and positive, Fallows made in this essay, three more general features have managed to stick in the imagination: first, the remarkable collection of evidence, in official records, pictures, descriptions, theoretical treatises, and the musical sources themselves, that he brought to bear on his questions; second, the discipline with which he marshalled all this evidence, concentrating on sources that were unambiguous in referring to written polyphony and on situations that reflected the ideals, and not the compromises, of the time; and third, the conversational tone of his essay and especially its last sentence, 'I also now think that much of the music sounds better that way' (Chapter 2, p. 62). Fallows's 'Specific Information' set the rules, and the style, for much of what would follow.

Songs

'Specific Information' remains in many ways the central statement on the performance of songs in the fifteenth century, the work that scholars and musicians keep coming back to, the work that we continue to react to. It was itself in some sense a reaction to an essay by Howard Mayer Brown, entitled 'Instruments and Voices in the Fifteenth-Century Chanson' published in a collection of essays in 1976, which made a still intriguing case, under less restrictive rules than those followed by Fallows, for a variety of combinations of voices and instruments in the courtly chanson (Brown, 1976a). But the *a cappella* argument proved to have very strong roots, not only in the pieces of evidence assembled by Fallows[3] but in work that was being done, and would continue to be done, on the courtly songs of the middle ages, some of which is reprinted in Honey Meconi's medieval volume of this series, *Medieval Music* (for a few examples see Page, 1977, 1982 [Chapters 15 and 16 in *Medieval Music*] Huot, 1989 [Chapter 5 in *Medieval Music*]; Earp, 1991 [Chapter 17 in *Medieval Music*]; Slavin, 1991).

This line of thought was dubbed the 'new secular *a cappella* heresy' by Brown in a record review of 1987 (Brown, 1987, p. 278), and the term was taken up gladly by the heretics themselves in the coming years.[4] But even the most impassioned among them had to concede one practical difficulty: how to sing a line that was untexted in the manuscript. Sometimes it is possible simply to add the text to the lower lines – but not always, and if that was what singers did, why did scribes leave the text out? It is a question that awaits a definitive solution; for now, the best effort I have seen to stop the gap is Christopher Page's 'Going Beyond the Limits: Experiments with Vocalization in the French Chanson, 1340–1440' (Chapter 3), which appeared in *Early Music* in 1992 and suggested that the vowel [y], the French *u* as in *tu*, was a good sound, easy to produce and unobtrusive to hear, and worked well for untexted parts in this repertory. Page was frank about this being a series of practical 'experiments' not based in historical evidence of the sort we want; but as the results of his experiments with

---

[3]   And here I should also mention Wright (1981), which anticipates some of Fallows's conclusions in, obviously, shorter form.

[4]   See the title of Slavin's (1991) essay, and for example Page (1992).

his ensemble Gothic Voices began to appear on disk,[5] the usefulness of [y] for untexted lines became abundantly clear. In the years since, the practice (with certain modifications) has quietly become a standard among performers of fifteenth-century music.

Next in our collection are three essays dealing with song repertories of the Josquin and post-Josquin generations: William Prizer on the Italian frottola (Chapter 4), Tess Knighton on the Spanish villancico (Chapter 5) and Stephen Keyl on the German lied (Chapter 6). The first of these preceded the heresy debate and shows a repertory that was not governed by the normal courtly rules, and the others essentially extend the heresy, with some modifications, into related song repertories outside the Franco-Flemish mainstream. Both Knighton and Keyl show a basic picture of their songs being sung *a cappella*, appropriated by purely instrumental ensembles, and 'arranged' for solo voice and an instrument like the lute or harp – but not normally performed by groups of voices and instruments as they were so often, and at the time persuasively, done in the mid-twentieth century.

The performance of sixteenth-century songs, in comparison, has been much less passionately debated in the musicological literature, probably because of a general sense that things tended to be freer: repertories like the Parisian chanson and the early madrigal, for instance, were published with text in all voices, showing that they could be and were sung, but in prints that were aimed at amateurs and often gave suggestions for instrumental performance on their title pages.[6] All these repertories have been well covered by general reference works like Kite-Powell (2007; see also Brown and Sadie, 1989), even if they have not inspired the kind of intense performance-practice research we have seen for the fifteenth-century chanson; what we learn about them is often found alongside something else we are reading about, as in, for example, the two essays by Howard Mayer Brown in the part on 'Instrumental Music' below (Chapters 15 and 16).

I have, however, chosen to include one short essay by Rinaldo Alessandrini about the performance of the late madrigal (Chapter 7), which is nominally concerned with the situation just after 1600, but which also has valuable data and insights about the situation just before – a useful reminder that in the late sixteenth century the madrigal was largely (though not exclusively) the province of professional singers with different priorities from those of amateurs.

Sacred Music

On the performance of sacred polyphony in the mid-to-late fifteenth century, David Fallows's 'Specific Information' (Chapter 2) is once again a good place to start. Part of his message was, as it were, negative – that the participation of instruments besides the organ was rare in European churches[7] – but he also managed to tease, from the documents and little hints (particularly ranges) in the music itself, three positive, concrete suggestions for chapel choirs

---

[5]   Notably in Gothic Voices, dir. Christopher Page, *The Medieval Romantics: French Songs and Motets, 1340–1440*, Hyperion CDA66463 (1991); see especially p. 9 of the liner notes.

[6]   For example, Pierre Attaingnant's two chanson prints of 1533 whose title pages explain which of their contents are suitable for flutes, recorders or both: see Howard Mayer Brown (Chapter 16).

[7]   In this contention, his most important immediate predecessors were McKinnon (1978) (Chapter 12 in the Medieval volume of this series) and, though it is aimed a little later, Wright (1978).

under ideal conditions in Dufay's time: for four-part music, an ensemble of fourteen adult, intact men, disposed (SATB) 6/2/3/3; for three-part music, a group of nine, 5/2/2; and, in institutions that had them, a situation in which a group of choirboys was accompanied by their masters taking the lower parts as soloists. The small size of these ensembles was perhaps no big surprise (though it did fly in the face of the twentieth-century choral ideal), but their apparent topheaviness, for want of a better word, is a puzzle that awaits a really convincing explanation and hints at the gulf, which we should never forget, between how they sang then and how we sing now.

'Specific Information' was published in 1983, and two years later Fallows produced a kind of sequel, entitled 'The Performing Ensembles in Josquin's Sacred Music' (Chapter 8), which reflected on all the discussion that the original essay had inspired – including, near the end, the issue of balance – and brought some of its arguments forward a couple of generations. The two essays are best read together: together they remain the most thorough and clear exposition of how sacred music was done in the fifteenth and early sixteenth centuries.

By the middle of the sixteenth century, the music printing industry had brought sophisticated polyphony into churches large and small all over the Continent, and such a broad comprehensive picture becomes much more elusive. Instead, modern scholarship has tended to extrapolate from the situation at the papal chapel and the other churches in Rome, partly because their records are voluminous and accessible, partly because the exceptionally famous and prolific Palestrina was there, and partly because, well, a lot of roads really did lead from Rome: these churches, and especially the papal chapel, took an active role worldwide in exploring and spreading the reforms of the Counterreformation. Three short, interrelated essays by Richard Sherr (Chapter 9), Graham Dixon (Chapter 10) and Noel O'Reagan (Chapter 11) will serve to show the kind of work that has been done on Roman performance practices of the mid- to late sixteenth century, and together they give an image rather different from that seen in the Fallows essays: it seems clear that Roman choirs tended to be more equally distributed SATB and not so topheavy, that one-on-a-part singing was more or less universal in some situations and surprisingly common in general, and that, outside the rarefied confines of the Sistine chapel, organs and trombones were not at all unheard of.[8]

What, then, about instruments in church towards the end of the sixteenth century? Probably the most celebrated Renaissance church band today is that of St Mark's basilica in Venice, an ensemble established permanently in 1568 but existing on a sporadic freelance basis for some time before, and which would grow to some sixteen cornetts, trombones, strings and organs by the time of the Gabrielis.[9] I have chosen, however, to look instead to Spain for my two specimens of scholarship on instrumentalists in church. The first (Chapter 12) concerns a book that had intrigued me at a distance for a long time before Noel O'Reagan's essay appeared in 2009: it is a collection, published in Madrid in 1600, of Victoria's polychoral works, all of which had already appeared in Italian prints as *a cappella* compositions, but

---

[8]   Sherr's essay of 1987 (Chapter 9) was actually, as he says in the opening paragraph, inspired by Lionnet (1987). I also recommend the entire Palestrina quatercentenary issue of *Early Music* (volume 22, number 4, November 1994), perhaps especially Sherr's (1994) essay, which, while not explicitly concerned with performance practice, gives an unforgettable insight into the not particularly enviable performing conditions in this very eminent choir.

[9]   A convenient overview of the Venetian situation in the Renaissance can be found in Fenlon (1989).

which here are supplied with organ partituras (short scores) that can essentially substitute for one of the choirs. O'Reagan's careful reading of these scores reveals much, not only about what organists did, but about issues like pitch standards, transpositions, instrumental doubling, positions of choirs within a church building and so forth; it is for me a model of how much can be learned from a single artefact.

Chapter 13 is one of mine, on the process by which loud bands were brought into and adopted by the cathedrals and parish churches of Spain over the course of the late fifteenth and sixteenth centuries. I shall avail myself of the editor's privilege here and add that there are a few details I would now change; in particular, I now believe these bands were not used to accompany singers in the way we used to think, but instead played for *alternatim* performances of psalms, canticles, hymns and so on, and to accompany processions, and at the elevation of the Host, and as spacers between liturgical events, and that most of them played from written music more often than they improvised (see Kreitner, 2003, 2009). But the central point is clear: Palestrina's works may have been written for voices alone, but Spanish churches, at least, were not an exclusively *a cappella* world by the end of the century.

Instrumental Music

Instrumental music in the Renaissance is harder to anthologize in a book like this. On the one side, much of what there is to say seems to be bound up with the individual instruments themselves,[10] and on the other, it proves difficult to trace the kind of continuous, evolving repertory that has structured our thoughts about songs and sacred music. A few general stories do, however, seem clear: that the medieval distinction between *haut* and *bas*, or loud and soft bands, persisted through the fifteenth century or so and remained as at least a practical consideration, if not a rigid habit, into the sixteenth;[11] that musical literacy among instrumentalists, relatively rare at the beginning of the Renaissance, reached some sort of threshold in the years around 1500, so that string and wind players took an active part in the growth of music publishing in Italy, France and the Low Countries;[12] that improvisation was the bread and butter of the professional instrumentalist in the fifteenth century and presumably remained an important if not indispensable skill to the end of the sixteenth;[13] that the sixteenth century saw an immense technological explosion of new musical instruments and various sizes of existing instruments, leading to another ideal of instrumentation, the consort of

---

[10]   See for example section 2 of Kite-Powell (2007, pp. 55–221), with its individual chapters on the various instruments.

[11]   The classic discussion is Bowles (1954).

[12]   The literature on this point is very extensive indeed. On the possibility that Ottaviano Petrucci's earliest prints (and a number of Italian manuscripts from the same era) were aimed at instrumental ensembles, see especially Litterick (1980), and more recently Fallows (2001). On the situation in the mid-sixteenth century, see for example Polk (2005b).

[13]   Again, a great deal has been written on this subject, of which it is perhaps sufficient to draw attention to Francisco Guerrero's instructions to the cathedral band of Seville, quoted and translated in my essay 'Minstrels in Spanish Churches, 1400–1600' (Chapter 13, pp. 233–34), and the profusion of ornamentation manuals published in the sixteenth century, evidently designed to help amateur musicians improvise ornaments on the tunes they played and sang; see for example Brown (1976b); Thomas (1992); and most recently Bass (2008).

matched recorders, viols, trombones (with cornett), crumhorns and so forth, analogous to the choral ideal that animated vocal music at the time; and that 'perfect' instruments like the lute, harp and keyboards, which could play several notes at once, led lives partly within, partly outside conventional ensembles (see for example Lawrence-King, 1992; Silbiger, 2004).

All of this, as I say, is hard to show in a few carefully selected essays. Instead, I have chosen to present three specimens of method, by two scholars who have done more than anyone else to bring the instrumental music of the Renaissance into our modern understanding. Keith Polk is probably best known for his doctoral dissertation on wind bands in the Low Countries (Polk, 1969) and his book on instrumental music in Germany (Polk, 1992), but he has been a prolific contributor to journals, collections and Festschriften over the years, almost all of it dealing with the problems of understanding these ensembles. His work is reasonably well represented, I hope, by an *Early Music* essay from 1990 (Chapter 14) in which he pulls together a staggering number of little bits of data, gathered from Germany and everywhere, about one of the most obvious but elusive questions – what instruments played (and did voices sing?) in these bands?

Howard Mayer Brown's lifelong fascination with early instrumental music is represented by two essays of contrasting styles. His 'Cook's Tour' essay (Chapter 15) begins with a wonderful document – a cookbook from 1529 that happens to include descriptions of the entertainments at various lavish feasts – and works out from there to paint an exceptionally rich and vivid image of what musicians (not just instrumentalists) did on these occasions and how they made it all work. And his 'Notes (and Transposing Notes) on the Transverse Flute ...' (Chapter 16) begins with a particular problem – Attaingnant's specification of flutes and/or recorders for some of his chansons – and goes down surprisingly deep into the dirty practicalities dealt with routinely by instrumentalists back then without our suspecting a thing.

Notation

It would be a beautiful world if editors and performers of Renaissance music agreed on everything and got happily out of each other's way; but anyone who has watched a rehearsal dissolve in recriminations over *ficta* or text underlay knows that we do not live in such a world. Here again, the anthologist's job could get seriously out of hand, for the overlap between editing and singing is substantial; so I have chosen just two examples to show what can happen at the intersection of music theory and practical performance. Both concern quite a basic question: what are the notes?

The rules of *musica ficta*, whereby performers back then would (in our modern terms) add sharps and flats to some notes as they sang or played along, are relatively simple, not dauntingly numerous and generally agreed on by contemporary theorists.[14] The problem (again, the problem for us, though it seems to have been at least an occasional problem for them) is that these rules often collide in the music, forcing the editor and the performer to choose between them based on priorities that few of us are really comfortable with. Margaret Bent's 'Diatonic *ficta*' of 1984 (Chapter 17) remains for me a classic not only of deep original thinking but of clear, patient expository prose. Bent lays bare the presuppositions we all grew

---

[14] A classic and accessible outline is in Lowinsky (1964); see also for example Berger (1987) and Wegman (1992).

up with, from the difference between modern scores and part- or choirbooks, to our keyboard-addled visual image of a scale with white keys and black, to the whole idea of written notes equalling frequencies, and replaces them with evidence from the theorists and commonsense observations about what it was like to read the music they had with the training they had. The result has been a profound new perspective on how to order our *ficta* priorities – even if it has not quieted all the arguments.

And then there is the problem of Renaissance pitch – not only what pitch standards were in use (and where, and when, etc.), but the whole issue of whether, in the *a cappella* environment that most polyphonic singers inhabited, the notion of consistent pitch standards has any meaning at all. It is a complex question,[15] and I have thought best to stick here to one small but important corner of it. Chapter 18, by Andrew Johnstone, is a recent exploration of the debate over clef-codes – briefly, the contention that sixteenth-century singers took certain high clef combinations (treble clef on top rather than soprano) as a signal to sing the music a certain interval below where it seems to be written.[16] The idea is now widely accepted in principle; the problem, as Johnstone shows, is in knowing precisely what they did, and when and how. And to this I would add a maybe more urgent concern for choirs today, and for all of us who depend on them: that in modern practice, among professionals and amateurs alike, it is much more common to sing high-clef pieces as written and transpose low-clef pieces up. It is easy to see why: most amateur choirs and some of the most eminent professional groups use women, not male falsettists, on the top lines, and low-clef pieces prove to be too low (especially the alto lines for female mezzos). But we should not forget that the consequences add up. How much of the general image of Renaissance music that is going out there, from your daughter's all-state chorus to the Tallis Scholars, is a systematic misrepresentation of what we believe it actually sounded like?

Perspective

Finally, I have included two essays that I have personally loved for a long time, under the vague but lofty heading 'Perspective'. Neither needs much introductory explanation. Donald Greig's essay (Chapter 19) is a long, thoughtful, fascinating meditation by one of the most eminent British ensemble singers of the last few decades on what the experience is like, and how it must resemble and not resemble the experience of singers back then, and what it all means. And Bonnie Blackburn's essay (Chapter 20), which was part of a special twenty-fifth-anniversary issue of *Early Music* devoted to 'Listening Practice', reminds us in elegant logic and lapidary words that this music was written by and for people whose lives, and whose need for music, were unimaginably different from our own, and that we must never forget the difference between music as performance and music as prayer.

***

---

[15] For my own essay on the subject, see Kreitner (1992); and more recently Haynes (2002).

[16] Johnstone's notes do a good job of recapitulating the previous work of scholars like Siegfried Hermelink, Andrew Parrott, Roger Bowers, Jeffrey Kurtzman and Patrizio Barbieri; I myself give a quick outline of the issue in Kreitner (1992, pp. 279–81).

Are we getting better at the performance of Renaissance music? I hope so, and certainly there is reason to think so in the wealth of fine recordings, of music from big names and small, that has been coming forward in the CD and mp3 eras. What a shocking luxury to live in a world where it is actually hard to keep up with all the new Renaissance polyphony coming out. Especially encouraging, at least to me, is the recent rise of a number of ensembles devoted to more or less specific repertories within the period and led by musicians who had already been well known as musicologists. Groups like the Binchois Consort, the Clerks, the Brabant Ensemble, the Ensemble Plus Ultra, Alamire and Ciaramella seem to be proving what many of us had long hoped – that if depth of scholarship in the repertory, immersion in the literature of performance practice and uncommon musicianship could be combined, the results would knock us out. Out, indeed, I have been knocked repeatedly in recent years. And on the other side, it is just as surprising to notice how many of the recordings that drew me with such force to the Renaissance thirty years ago are distressingly hard to listen to today. Those names I will not mention here; but let me say for the record that in their day they had a terrific power, worth our memory and respect, and that in particular the combination of voices with instruments, without which I honestly might have chosen a different period to study, now sounds not just dated but genuinely misguided. My early entomologically-based fears seem, I am happy to say, to have been for naught.

I write all this in 2010 and am aware that this book will be in libraries for a long time to come; and as hard as it is today to imagine a world where the Binchois Consort, the Clerks *et al.* will sound like quaint relics of a misguided time, I have no doubt that someday a reader will be shaking her head and smiling at this point. 'There is a standing dictum,' Thomas Hoving once said, 'about forgery: It will never last beyond one generation. The style of the maker is permeated by his generation. No matter how he tries, his own time will eventually show in what he does.'[17] And while art forgery may not be the kindest metaphor for what we do as students and performers of early music, it has to be admitted that we too are trying to create something new based on our best knowledge of something old, and trying to sell (or at least give) it to an audience that seeks contact with the old and genuine thing. And we are up against the same problem. Something is always missing from our knowledge, and we fill it in from ourselves; and like the forgers, we can never be completely conscious of what, and how much, we are filling in. All we know for sure is that one day it will show.

But we soldier on, scholars and musicians both, in the faith that we are not forging the works of Josquin Desprez when we sing them, but are simply doing our level best to understand them; and in the faith that our understanding of early performance will continue to grow and improve, generation by generation, just the way all spheres of human knowledge grow and improve – and in the faith, maybe as important as any other, that we will like what we hear.

It is, we should not forget, a matter of some urgency. Another quotation, this one from a very eminent historian, in a bestselling book, as recently as 1992:

> The vigor of the new age was not found everywhere. Music, still lost in the blurry mists of the Dark Ages, was a Renaissance laggard; the motets, psalms, and Masses heard each Sabbath – many of them by Josquin des Prés of Flanders, the most celebrated composer of his day – fall dissonantly on the ears of those familiar with the soaring orchestral works which would captivate Europe in the

---

[17] Quoted by John McPhee (1968, p. 24); McPhee's profile originally appeared in 1967 in *The New Yorker*, **43**, pp. 49–137.

centuries ahead, a reminder that in some respects one age will forever remain inscrutable to others. (Manchester, 1992, p. 88)

There is cause for despair in every word – what, for starters, was he listening to? – but the worst of them by far is *forever*. Forever inscrutable. Inscrutable forever.

And right there is the challenge for those of us who love Renaissance music and believe in what it still has to offer. Twenty years of teaching early music at a medium-large American public university have encouraged me to believe that the music of this period is actually very easy to like and to love. Sure, it holds some things at arm's length; but the sheer gorgeous shining human sound of it is hard for most of my undergraduates to resist, and its economy of means – so few people on stage, with no electronics and no instruments but what they were born with – has an elemental appeal to the rebellious post-adolescent spirit (and, I should perhaps not add, mine). Nobody so far has ever become a music major at the University of Memphis out of a passion for the works of Josquin; but once they are here and once they hear him, my students at least seem to catch on pretty quickly. To stand there once a year and watch thirty-five young musicians encounter the *Missa Pange lingua* for the first time is about enough to ask out of life. So it is somewhere between the music majors and the eminent historians that the message is apparently getting hung up. There is only one way out, and that will be through performances that we believe in and that may invite other people to hear what we hear.

Bibliography

Baroncini, Rodolfo (2005), 'Die frühe Violine: Form und Bauprinzipien: Zwei ikonographische Quellen aus der 1. Hälfte des 16. Jahrhunderts', *Basler Jahrbuch für historische Musikpraxis*, **29**, pp. 35–52.

Bass, John Burrell (2008), 'Rhetoric and Musical Ornamentography: Tradition in Sixteenth-Century Improvisation', PhD dissertation, University of Memphis.

Bent, Margaret (1996), 'The Early History of the Sign Ø', *Early Music*, **24**, pp. 199–225.

Berger, Anna Maria Busse (1993), *Mensuration and Proportion Signs: Origins and Evolution*, Oxford: Clarendon.

Berger, Karol (1987), *Musica Ficta: Theories of Accidental Inflections in Vocal Polyphony from Marchetto da Padova to Gioseffo Zarlino*, Cambridge: Cambridge University Press.

Berney, Boaz (2006), 'The Renaissance Flute in Mixed Ensembles: Surviving Instruments, Pitches and Performance Practice', *Early Music*, **34**, pp. 205–23.

Bonge, Dale (1982), 'Gaffurius on Pulse and Tempo: A Reinterpretation', *Musica Disciplina*, **36**, pp. 167–74.

Bonta, Stephen (1990), 'The Use of Instruments in Sacred Music in Italy 1560–1700', *Early Music*, **18**, 519–35.

Bowles, Edmund A. (1954), '*Haut* and *Bas*: The Grouping of Musical Instruments in the Middle Ages', *Musica Disciplina*, **8**, pp. 115–40.

Brown, Howard Mayer (1976a), 'Instruments and Voices in the Fifteenth-Century Chanson', in John W. Grubbs (ed.), *Current Thought in Musicology*, Austin, TX: University of Texas Press, pp. 89–137.

Brown, Howard Mayer (1976b), *Embellishing Sixteenth-Century Music*, London: Oxford University Press.

Brown, Howard Mayer (1987), Untitled review of Gothic Voices, *The Castle of Fair Welcome*, *Early Music*, **15**, pp. 277–79.

Brown, Howard Mayer (1989), 'Bossinensis, Willaert and Verdelot: Pitch and the Conventions of Transcribing Music for Lute and Voice in Italy in the Early Sixteenth Century', *Revue de Musicologie*, **75**, pp. 25–46.

Brown, Howard Mayer and Sadie, Stanley (eds) (1989), *Performance Practice: Music before 1600*, Norton-Grove Handbooks in Music, New York: Norton.

Bryan, John (2008), '"Verie sweete and artificiall": Lorenzo Costa and the Earliest Viols', *Early Music*, **36**, pp. 3–17.

Cyrus, Cynthia J. (2002), 'The Annotator of the Lorraine Chansonnier and His Taste in Accidentals', *Early Music*, **30**, pp. 189–200.

Dickey, Bruce (1978), 'Untersuchungen zur historischen Auffasung des Vibratos auf Blasinstrumenten', *Basler Jahrbuch für historische Musikpraxis*, **2**, pp. 77–142.

Duffin, Ross W. (1989), 'The *trompette des menestrels* in the 15th-Century *alta capella*', *Early Music*, **17**, pp. 397–402.

Earp, Lawrence (1991), 'Texting in 15th-Century French Chansons: A Look Ahead from the 14th Century', *Early Music*, **19**, pp. 195–210.

Edwards, Warwick (2006), 'Alexander Agricola and Intuitive Syllable Deployment', *Early Music*, **24**, pp. 409–25.

Elders, Willem (1989), 'The Performance of Cantus Firmi in Josquin's Masses Based on Secular Monophonic Song', *Early Music*, **17**, pp. 330–41.

Elias, Cathy Ann (1989), 'Musical Performance in 16th-Century Italian Literature: Straparola's *Le piacevoli notti*', *Early Music*, **17**, pp. 161–73.

Fallows, David (2001), 'Petrucci's *Canti* Volumes: Scope and Repertory', *Basler Jahrbuch für historische Musikpraxis*, **25**, pp. 39–52.

Fenlon, Iain (1989), 'Venice: Theatre of the World', in Iain Fenlon (ed.), *Man and Music: The Renaissance*, Englewood Cliffs, NJ: Prentice-Hall, pp. 102–32.

Gilbert, Adam Knight (2005), 'The Improvising alta capella ca. 1500: Paradigms and Procedures', *Basler Jahrbuch für historische Musikpraxis*, **29**, pp. 109–23.

Greenlee, Robert (1987), '*Dispositione di voce*: Passage to Florid Singing', *Early Music*, **15**, pp. 47–55.

Hadden, Nancy (2005), 'From Swiss Flutes to Consort: The Flute in Germany ca. 1500–1530', *Basler Jahrbuch für historische Musikpraxis*, **29**, pp. 125–43.

Harrán, Don (1986), *Word-Tone Relations in Musical Thought from Antiquity to the Seventeenth Century*, Musicological Studies and Documents 30, Neuhausen-Stuttgart: American Institute of Musicology and Hänssler-Verlag.

Haynes, Bruce (2002), *A History of Performing Pitch: The Story of 'A'*, Lanham, MD: Scarecrow.

Holman, Peter (2005), 'What Did Violin Consorts Play in the Early Sixteenth Century?', *Basler Jahrbuch für historische Musikpraxis*, **29**, pp. 53–65.

Houle, George (1990), *'Doulce memoire': A Study of Performance Practices*, Bloomington, IN: Indiana University Press.

Huot, Sylvia (1989), 'Voices and Instruments in Medieval French Secular Music: On the Use of Literary Texts as Evidence for Performance Practice', *Musica Disciplina*, **43**, pp. 63–113.

Kenyon, Nicholas (ed.) (1988), *Authenticity and Early Music: A Symposium*, Oxford: Oxford University Press.

Kirk, Douglas (1989), 'Cornetti and Renaissance Pitch Standards in Italy and Germany', *Journal de Musique Ancienne*, **10**, pp. 16–22.

Kite-Powell, Jeffery (ed.) (2007), *A Performer's Guide to Renaissance Music* (2nd edn), Bloomington, IN: Indiana University Press.

Knighton, Tess and Fallows, David (eds) (1992), *Companion to Medieval and Renaissance Music*, London: Dent.

Korrick, Leslie (1990), 'Instrumental Music in the Early 16th-Century Mass: New Evidence', *Early Music*, **18**, pp. 359–70.

Kreitner, Kenneth (1992), 'Renaissance Pitch,' in Tess Knighton and David Fallows (eds), *Companion to Medieval and Renaissance Music*, London: Dent, pp. 275–83.

Kreitner, Kenneth (1998), 'Bad News, or Not? Thoughts on Renaissance Performance Practice', *Early Music*, **26**, pp. 323–33.

Kreitner, Kenneth (2003), 'The Cathedral Band of León, and When It Played', *Early Music*, **31**, pp. 41–62.

Kreitner, Kenneth (2009), 'The Repertory of the Spanish Cathedral Bands', *Early Music*, **37**, pp. 267–86.

Kurtzman, Jeffrey G. (1994), 'Tones, Modes, Clefs and Pitch in Roman Cyclic Magnificats of the 16th Century', *Early Music*, **22**, pp. 641–65.

Lawrence-King, Andrew (1992), 'Perfect Instruments', in Tess Knighton and David Fallows (eds), *Companion to Medieval and Renaissance Music*, London: Dent, pp. 354–64.

Leech-Wilkinson, Daniel (2002), *The Modern Invention of Medieval Music: Scholarship, Ideology, Performance*, Cambridge: Cambridge University Press.

Lightbourne, Ruth (2004), 'Annibale Stabile and Performance Practice at Two Roman Institutions', *Early Music*, **32**, pp. 271–85.

Lionnet, Jean (1987), 'Performance Practice in the Papal Chapel during the 17th Century', *Early Music*, **15**, pp. 3–15.

Litterick, Louise (1980), 'Performing Franco-Netherlandish Secular Music of the Late 15th Century: Texted and Untexted Parts in the Sources', *Early Music*, **8**, pp. 474–85.

Lowinsky, Edward E. (1964), 'Foreword', in H. Colin Slim (ed.), *Musica Nova*, Monuments of Renaissance Music 1, Chicago, IL: University of Chicago Press, pp. v–xxi.

McGee, Timothy J. (2005), 'Florentine Instrumentalists and Their Repertory ca. 1500', *Basler Jahrbuch für historische Musikpraxis*, **29**, pp. 145–59.

McKinnon, James W. (1978), 'Representations of the Mass in Medieval and Renaissance Art', *Journal of the American Musicological Society*, **31**, pp. 21–52.

McPhee, John (1968), 'A Roomful of Hovings', in John McPhee, *A Roomful of Hovings and Other Profiles*, New York: Farrar, Straus and Giroux, pp. 1–64.

Manchester, William (1992), *A World Lit Only by Fire: The Medieval Mind and the Renaissance: Portrait of an Age*, Boston, MA: Little, Brown.

Meucci, Renato (1991), 'On the Early History of the Trumpet in Italy', *Basler Jahrbuch für historische Musikpraxis*, **15**, pp. 9–34.

Minamino, Hiroyuki (2004), 'The Spanish Plucked *viola* in Renaissance Italy, 1480–1530', *Early Music*, **32**, pp. 177–92.

Morehen, John (ed.) (1995), *English Choral Practice 1400–1650*, Cambridge: Cambridge University Press.

Myers, Herbert W. (1989), 'Slide Trumpet Madness: Fact or Fiction?', *Early Music*, **17**, pp. 383–89.

Myers, Herbert W. (2005), 'Evidence of the Emerging Trombone in the Late Fifteenth Century: What Iconography May Be Trying to Tell Us', *Historic Brass Society Journal*, **17**, pp. 7–35.

Page, Christopher (1977), 'Machaut's "Pupil" Deschamps on the Performance of Music: Voices or Instruments in the Fourteenth-Century Chanson?', *Early Music*, **5**, pp. 484–91.

Page, Christopher (1982), 'The Performance of Songs in Late Medieval France: A New Source', *Early Music*, **10**, pp. 441–50.

Page, Christopher (1992), 'The English *a cappella* Heresy', in Tess Knighton and David Fallows (eds), *Companion to Medieval and Renaissance Music*, London: Dent, pp. 23–29.

Polk, Keith (1969), 'Flemish Wind Bands in the Late Middle Ages: A Study of Improvisatory Instrumental Practices', PhD dissertation, University of California at Berkeley.

Polk, Keith (1989a), 'The Trombone, the Slide Trumpet and the Ensemble Tradition of the Early Renaissance', *Early Music*, **17**, pp. 389–97.

Polk, Keith (1989b), 'Vedel and Geige – Fiddle and Viol: German String Traditions in the Fifteenth Century', *Journal of the American Musicological Society*, **42**, pp. 504–46.

Polk, Keith (1989c), 'Augustein Schubinger and the Zinck: Innovation in Performance Practice', *Historic Brass Society Journal*, **1**, pp. 41–46.

Polk, Keith (1992), *German Instrumental Music of the Late Middle Ages: Players, Patrons and Performance Practice*, Cambridge: Cambridge University Press.

Polk, Keith (2005a), 'Instrumental Music ca. 1500: Performers, Makers, and Musical Instruments ca. 1500–1530', *Basler Jahrbuch für historische Musikpraxis*, **29**, 21–34.

Polk, Keith (2005b), 'Epilogue – Susato and the Repertory and Performance Practices of His Time', in Keith Polk (ed.), *Tielman Susato and the Music of His Time: Print Culture, Compositional Technique and Instrumental Music in the Renaissance*, Hillsdale, NY: Pendragon, pp. 191–99.

Praetorius, Michael (1986), Syntagma musicum II: De organographia, trans. David Z. Crookes, Oxford: Clarendon.

Roig-Francolí, Miguel A. (1995), 'Playing in Consonances: A Spanish Renaissance Technique of Chordal Improvisation', *Early Music*, **23**, pp. 461–71.

Rosselli, John (1988), 'The Castrati as a Professional Group and a Social Phenomenon, 1550–1850', *Acta Musciologica*, **60**, pp. 143–79.

Sachs, Klaus-Jürgen (1983), 'Arten improvisierter Mehrstimmigkeit nach Lehrtexten des 14. und 15. Jahrhunderts', *Basler Jahrbuch für historische Musikpraxis*, **7**, 166–83.

Savan, Jamie (2008), 'The Cornett and the "Orglische Art": Ornamentation in Early Sixteenth-Century Germany', *Historic Brass Society Journal*, **20**, pp. 1– 21.

Schroeder, Eunice (1982), 'The Stroke Comes Full Circle: ø and ¢ in Writings on Music, ca. 1450–1540', *Musica Disciplina*, **36**, 119–66.

Segerman, Ephraim (1996), 'A Re-Examination of the Evidence on Absolute Tempo before 1700', *Early Music*, **24**, pp. 227–48, 681–89.

Shaw, David J. (1990), 'A Five-Piece Wind Band in 1518', *The Galpin Society Journal*, **43**, pp. 60–67.

Sherr, Richard (1994), 'Competence and Incompetence in the Papal Choir in the Age of Palestrina', *Early Music*, **22**, pp. 607–29.

Silbiger, Alexander (2004), 'Performance Practice', in Alexander Silbiger (ed.), *Keyboard Music before 1700* (2nd edn), New York: Routledge, pp. 359–94.

Slavin, Dennis (1991), 'In Support of "Heresy": Manuscript Evidence for the *a cappella* Performance of Early 15th-Century Songs', *Early Music*, **19**, pp. 179–90.

Smith, Anne (1978), 'Die Renaissancequerflöte und ihre Musik – Ein Beitrag zur Interpretation der Quellen', *Basler Jahrbuch für historische Musikpraxis*, **2**, pp. 9–76.

Stewart, Rebecca (1985), 'Voice Types in Josquin's Music', *Tijdschrift van de Vereniging voor nederlandse Muziekgeschiedenis*, **35**, pp. 97–189.

Thomas, Bernard (1992), 'Divisions in Renaissance Music', in Tess Knighton and David Fallows (eds), *Companion to Medieval and Renaissance Music*, London: Dent, pp. 345–53.

Towne, Gary (1990/1991), 'A Systematic Formulation of Sixteenth-Century Text Underlay Rules', *Musica Disciplina*, (1990), **44**, pp. 255–87, (1991), **45**, pp. 143–68.

Tröster, Patrick (2001), *Das Alta-Ensemble und seine Instrumente von der Spätgotlk bis zur Hochrenaissance (1300–1550): eine musikikonografische Studie*, Tübingen: MVK.

Tröster, Patrick (2004), 'More about Renaissance Slide Trumpets: Fact or Fiction?', *Early Music*, **32**, pp. 252–68.

Vaccaro, Jean-Michel (ed.) (1995), Le concert des voix et des instruments à la Renaissance, Paris: CRNS Éditions.

Wagstaff, Grayson (2004), 'Morales's Officium, Chant Traditions and Performing 16th-Century Music', *Early Music*, 32, pp. 225–43.

Wegman, Rob C. (1989), 'Concerning Tempo in the English Polyphonic Mass, c. 1420–70', *Acta Musicologica*, **61**, pp. 40–65.

Wegman, Rob C. (1992), 'Musica ficta', in Tess Knighton and David Fallows (eds), *Companion to Medieval and Renaissance Music*, London: Dent, pp. 265–74.

Welker, Lorenz (1983), '"Alta capella": zur Ensemblepraxis der Blasinstrumente im 15. Jahrhundert', *Basler Jahrbuch für historische Musikpraxis*, 7, pp. 119–65.

Wickham, Edward (2002), 'Finding Closure: Performance Issues in the Agnus Dei of Ockeghem's *Missa L'homme armé*', *Early Music*, **30**, pp. 593–607.

Wright, Craig (1978), 'Performance Practices at the Cathedral of Cambrai 1475–1550', *Musical Quarterly*, **64**, pp. 295–328.

Wright, Craig (1981), 'Voices and Instruments in the Art Music of Northern France during the 15th Century: A Conspectus', in Daniel Heartz and Bonnie Wade (eds), *International Musicological Society Congress Report, Berkeley, 1977*, Kassel: Bärenreiter, pp. 643–49.

Part I
Method

[1]

ON "INSTRUMENTAL STYLE" IN
EARLY MELODY

By LLOYD HIBBERD

Some thirty years ago the late Arnold Schering of Berlin set forth his theories claiming a predominance of instrumental over vocal participation in the music of the 12th to 16th centuries.[1] In support of his contentions, he adduced specific features found in the music as criteria of its "instrumental style". These criteria were subjected at the time to at least one detailed criticism;[2] but although Schering's more extreme contentions have not been accepted by most scholars, the premises of his argument—and therefore the true significance of these criteria—have not been examined with sufficient care. As a result, the idea of a general "instrumental", as contrasted with a general "vocal", style has gained some currency and has been rather indiscriminately applied in present-day musicological writing.

It should be emphasized at the outset that just as Schering's criteria refer to the individual parts, so does the present article concern itself with instrumental style in melody alone. Especially must this be borne in mind where reference is made below to the music for harmonic or chordal instruments like the lute or the keyboard instruments; for the early music for such instruments does frequently bear the marks of a special instrumental style, not in the character of the parts so much as in their combination—that is, in the modifications of strict part-writing that are often necessitated by the rendering of several parts on a single instrument by a single performer. These modifications and the style that results from them must, however, await separate treatment at a future time.

[1] Principally in *Die Niederländische Orgelmesse im Zeitalter des Josquin*, Leipzig, 1912; *Studien zur Musikgeschichte der Frührenaissance*, Leipzig, 1914, and in *Aufführungspraxis alter Musik*, Leipzig, 1931, as well as in two articles, "Experimentelle Musikgeschichte" (*Zeitschrift der internationalen Musikgesellschaft*, XIV, May 1913, 234-40) and "Zur Orgelmesse" (*ZsdIMg* XV, October 1913, 11-16).

[2] Hugo Leichtentritt, "Einige Bemerkungen über Verwendung der Instrumente im Zeitalter Josquin's", *ZsdIMg* XIV, Sept. 1913, 359-65, as well as his brief reply (*ZsdIMg* XV, 17) to Schering's counterattack (*ibid.*, 11 ff.).

Schering's criteria of instrumental style are certain melodic, textual, and rhythmic features and may be summarized as follows:

A. *Melodic:*
  1) Unusual range (in excess of an octave or tenth)
  2) Violation of those traditional vocal principles that provide for the predominance of stepwise movement and for the avoidance of frequent, consecutive, or "awkward" leaps
  3) Rapidity of movement
  4) Continuous flow of tone, especially pedal points
  5) Fragmentary melodic lines, use of hocket
  6) Melodic sequences
  7) Coloratura passages

B. *Textual:*
  8) Absence of any text
  9) Temporary discontinuance of the text
  10) Irregular and arbitrary distribution of the text

C. *Rhythmic:*
  11) Frequent syncopations
  12) Tying of short notes to long ones
  13) Juxtaposition of very long and very short notes
  14) Use of dotted rhythms

Before examining these criteria, let us consider what we may properly call "instrumental style". The phrase necessarily implies a style of music possessing features that differentiate it from vocal music. The differences must have their origins in the very circumstance that the music is intended for instruments rather than for voices. Such differences would arise from either practical or esthetic considerations: that is, the writing of instrumental music would be influenced by the fact that some things are especially suitable and idiomatic for instruments and awkward or even impossible for voices, or at least by the fact that some effects, even though technically possible in either medium, are felt to be more apt and natural for instruments.

Now, from the practical standpoint, it becomes obvious with but little reflection that instruments vary so greatly among themselves in their capacity, range, agility, etc., that to compose music that (allowing, of course, for transposition) could

On "Instrumental Style" in Early Melody 109

be played on any instrument would constrain the composer to write melodies as simple as the simplest folksong. A general "instrumental style", then, possible for any and all instruments but not for voices, cannot really exist from a technical point of view—even in modern times when the various instrumental families have reached an advanced stage of mechanical development. Nevertheless, certain *particular* instruments or instrumental families do possess special potentialities, such as a very wide compass. Consequently it is possible to speak of music that exploits such potentialities as representing a *particular* instrumental style, such as the "violin style". It would be better (in recognition of the changes in technical resources and esthetic ideals occurring at different times and places) to speak of "the 18th-century Italian (or French) violin style", or, where possible, even more specifically, as "the Corelli violin style". On the other hand, the possession of special limitations by a particular instrument or instrumental family, which are considered in writing for them, may result in the creation of a particular instrumental style. A notable example is the style of writing for the early horn and trumpet families, whose inability to produce satisfactory chromatic tones led to the avoidance of such tones in their music.

From the esthetic point of view, it may be said that, on the whole, for the past four centuries the difference between what has been deemed suitable for instrumental music and not so for vocal music is a matter of degree rather than of kind. Thus it is indisputably true that instrumental music, by and large, contains a greater complexity of rhythm, more animation, a more continuous flow of tone, a greater use of leaps and chromaticism [3] than does vocal music taken as a whole. We may therefore legitimately speak of instrumental music that exhibits a preponderance of these characteristics as being more truly instrumental in style. We are not, however, justified in concluding that these features, when less frequent, always owe their presence in instrumental music solely to the fact that the music is written for instruments rather than for voices. Much less are we

---

[3] Schering's attribution of early chromaticism (*musica ficta,* or *falsa*) to the influence of instruments (*e.g. Studien,* 47-50) has already been criticized in the present writer's article "Musica Ficta and Instrumental Music *c.* 1250 — *c.* 1350", *The Musical Quarterly,* XXVIII (April 1942), 216-26.

permitted, with music that has a text and shows these features—even when they are fairly frequent—to assume as Schering does, either that the presence of the text is to be discounted and that the music is intended for instruments alone, or else that the voices are to sing a simplified version while instruments are performing the notated version. Nor is it often necessary, or even desirable, to regard text-equipped music of this sort as having been influenced by instrumental music.

It is true, also, that there are two features that are found in much instrumental music and in practically no vocal music, namely a) the continued repetition of the same interval several times in succession, and b) the persistence of the same note values (especially very short ones) or of the same rhythmic motives for more than, say, five measures. But even with these features, the distinction is one of degree, and such reiterations seem to be avoided in vocal music because their monotonous character is inimical to the "expressiveness" expected particularly of the human voice. As a matter of fact, even in instrumental music they are usually confined to compositions that are not primarily lyrical in character—such as dances, variations, and fast movements—or else to the instrumental accompaniments of melodies, vocal or instrumental. They owe their presence, really, not so much to the nature of the instruments as to the nature of particular forms and styles, which are often based on considerations other than the medium of performance. That these forms are universally employed for instruments rather than for voices makes these features "instrumental", but in a secondary rather than in a primary sense.

In the light of the foregoing remarks on the differences between instrumental and vocal music in general, we may now examine Schering's criteria of instrumental style given at the opening of this article. Those concerning the text may be dismissed on the grounds that in many cases they are open to question and that they necessitate the acceptance of the hypothesis that music may have a reasonably full text without being intended for singing, a hypothesis that is not accepted by all scholars.[4]

---

[4] The presence of what is evidently the first word or so of a *cantus firmus* at the beginning of a part (as in the case of the tenor incipits of 13th-century motets) may be accepted as intended merely for identification and as quite possibly indicating

On "Instrumental Style" in Early Melody 111

Of the melodic features assumed by Schering to be indicative of instrumental style, we may say that the range should exceed not merely an octave or tenth but the limits of even a virtuoso singer's voice in order to be accepted as *ipso facto* evidence of instrumental style. As regards "awkward" leaps, rapidity of movement, continuous activity, short melodic fragments, melodic sequences, and coloratura passages—the exclusive "instrumentalness" of all these becomes increasingly dubious on closer examination. The awkwardness of a melodic interval is far from absolute, since the difficulty may be mitigated by moderate tempo, by the anticipation of the second tone in another part, or by aid from supporting instruments (especially those where, as on the keyboard, the pitch is mechanically determined). It may also be mitigated by familiarity (as with the augmented second and augmented fourth in modern times), or by advanced technical skill on the part of the singer.

Nor is either rapidity of movement or the absence of convenient breathing-places always a sure indication of instrumental as distinct from vocal music; for both agility and the length of time over which the emission of a single tone, or of a continuous series of tones, can be maintained differs with the instrument, the wind instruments, for example, being dependent, like the voice, on the human breath. Moreover, with both wind instruments and the voice, skill in reserving the expenditure of breath, or in snatching quick breaths, enables the performer to avoid appreciably disturbing the continuity of the part. And finally—this is an important point—where two or more singers or wind instrumentalists are given a part in unison, even though they be not especially skilled, a more continuous activity (or, perhaps we should say, ostensible activity) may be given them (since brief respites for breathing may be obtained by each in turn) than if a single executant were called upon to perform it.[5]

purely instrumental performance, although as Leichtentritt has pointed out (*ZsdiMg* XIV, 364), it would have been a simple matter for contemporary singers to complete and correctly apply the texts of well-known melodies.

[5] Thus the high A sustained by the sopranos for 8½ measures in the last movement of the *Ninth Symphony* (mm. 718-26) can be executed by the chorus without a perceptible break, as they could not be by a soloist. Leichtentritt, *op. cit.*, 362, cites the "Patrem omnipotentem" and the "Sanctus" of Bach's *B minor Mass* as examples of continuous activity. It is noteworthy that these are for the chorus, not for soloists.

Schering's converse argument, namely that short melodic fragments are "unvocal" *per se*, rests largely on a question of taste. Such parts do not often, it is true, seem very expressive to modern ears, in vocal music, but earlier epochs may have felt quite otherwise about them. Schering makes the statement with regard to hocket that, at least where the distribution of the text is apparently careless or arbitrary, vocal performance cannot have been intended. In support of his point he quotes the following passage from Anonymus I in Coussemaker *Scriptores* III (p. 363): "Above all, take care that in songs [*cantilenae*] you do not interrupt the declamation by hocketing." But there is no indication that Anonymus I is referring to instruments. In fact three lines down the page in Coussemaker occurs the following description of hocket: "Let one person always sing while the other is silent" (*semper unus cantet dum alius tacet*). It is true that "*cantet*" might on occasion be freely used to denote instrumental performance, but since there is no mention of instruments in this passage, the reasonable presumption is that it here means singing. No doubt the device of hocket was abused, but properly managed it could at times give a charming effect without distorting the flow of the text. At all events there is no reason to suppose that hocket was primarily, much less exclusively, instrumental in origin or application.[6]

The device of sequence appears to have its origin as a means of varying the musical repetitions required by the repetitions of the steps in the dance, or as a means of modulation, or merely of prolonging the melodic line in either instrumental or vocal (especially solo) music. As regards coloratura and florid passages generally, there is no reason to think that these were primarily instrumental in character. Hugo Goldschmidt, it is true, has contended that 16th- and 17th-century vocal ornamentation was derived from instrumental ornamentation,[7] but this view has been opposed by other scholars such as Max Kuhn,[8] Johan-

[6] Marius Schneider ("Der Hochetus", *Zeitschrift für Musikwissenschaft*, XI [1928-29], 390-96) shows that hocket was employed in both vocal and instrumental music, and does not indicate priority for either medium.

[7] *Studien zur Geschichte der italienischen Oper im 17. Jahrhundert*, Leipzig, 1901, p. 7.

[8] *Die Verzierungskunst in der Gesangsmusik des 16. und 17. Jahrhunderts*, Leipzig, 1902, 28-30.

On "Instrumental Style" in Early Melody 113

nes Wolf,[9] Carl Krebs,[10] Wilhelm Fischer,[11] and most recently by Ernst Ferand.[12]

One sometimes encounters the notion that instrumental music is "more rhythmic" than vocal music. Thus C. H. H. Parry makes the statement that

voices are not adapted to rhythmic effects. For rhythm the means of producing the sound requires to have some capacity to give the effect of a blow, or to have a bite in the initiation of the sound. The effect of a shout (which approaches most nearly to the character of sound-production which lends itself to rhythmic effect) did not seem to enter into the [16th-century choral] composers' conception of music.[13]

Parry's use here of the term "rhythm" without qualification is unfortunate, for it is certainly incorrect to say that "voices are not adapted to rhythmic effects". Rhythmic effects, to exist, merely require the prominence of certain sounds above others —a prominence produced most clearly by greater length or greater intensity (usually both coincidentally)—arranged in some comprehensible order. This prominence may vary in degree, and does so vary in any expressive singing, so that all song may be said to have rhythm. Rhythm is, indeed, as natural to singing as to instrumental music, as anyone who recalls the sing-song of children's mysterious incantations realizes at once. What is *un*natural is to sing notes evenly without fitting them into some rhythmic pattern.

When Parry implies, as in the quotation just given, that the "shout" is the only vocal means of sound production that gives a rhythmic effect, he is obviously thinking of a special kind of rhythm produced by a strong ictus whereby a particular (short)

---

[9] *Handbuch der Notationskunde*, Leipzig, 1913-19, II, 147.

[10] "Girolamo Dirutas Transilvano", *Vierteljahrsschrift für Musikwissenschaft*, VIII (1892), 373-74.

[11] "Instrumentalmusik von 1450-1600" in Guido Adler, *Handbuch der Musik-geschichte*, 2d ed., Berlin, 1930, 383.

[12] *Die Improvisation in der Musik*, Zürich, 1938, 302 ff.

[13] *Style in Musical Art*, London, 1911, 29-30. Again on p. 35 he refers to the "absence of rhythm" in 16th-century polyphony, although he thereby seems to contradict his own statement on the preceding page that "the greater part of German sacred music of the sixteenth century is infused with a simple rhythmic character". In fairness to Parry, however, it should be pointed out that he is elsewhere more accurate, as when he remarks that "the separate voice-parts [of 16th-century polyphonic music] sometimes had rhythmic qualities of their own, but they were purposely put together in such a way as to counteract any obvious effect of rhythm running simultaneously through all the parts" (*Oxford History of Music*, III, 5). This confusion of statement in the work of a widely-read writer seems ample justification for the present remarks on the nature of rhythm.

tone is noticeably louder than those that surround it, or whereby the beginning of a (longer) tone is louder than the rest of the tone. With the human voice, a strong ictus of this sort is possible but requires effort, and its regular appearance in vocal music is, apart from especially stimulating circumstances such as those connected with dancing or other bodily movement, unnatural. The subtle effects of true vocal rhythm are too complicated for present discussion. One may point out, however, that the normal method of purely vocal performance is to begin a tone (or series of tones) with a slight ictus and to continue with small fluctuation at about the same dynamic level except when the effects of *crescendo, diminuendo, sforzando,* sudden *forte* and *piano,* are allowed to supervene for purposes of emotional intensity.

In instrumental music, on the other hand, a stronger contrast between the beginning and the continuation of a tone, and therefore a more obvious rhythmic character, is *sometimes* the natural—even unavoidable—result of the mechanical principles of tone production involved. Of no instruments is this more true than of the lute and clavier, where the sound is produced by a sharp plucking (harpsichord, lute) or by a blow (clavichord, piano), and, once emitted, instantly and inevitably begins to decrease in intensity. It is consequently such instruments that give the most pronounced rhythmic character to music performed on them. On bowed or wind instruments, however, a decided rhythm of this sort, though easily obtainable, is not a necessary concomitant of tone production, while on the organ it is practically impossible. In short, an incisive rhythm is not a criterion of all instrumental music.

A marked and regular rhythm appears to have at least three main sources not necessarily connected with instrumental performance: 1) the presence of a definitely metrical text; 2) the presence of an arbitrary prescription for the arrangement of note-values according to a simple and obvious recurrent scheme (as in the rhythmic modes evolved by the theorists of the 13th century and supposedly analogous to the meters of classical prosody); and 3) the dance. This last is the most important source of regular and strongly marked rhythm in music. And it is to be observed that in the history of the dance, the rhythmic reinforcement seems to have come at first not from instruments but from purely vocal noises (imitation of animal sounds), then

On "Instrumental Style" in Early Melody 115

from parts of the human body alone (clapping of hands) to which instruments (at first purely percussive ones) were eventually added. The earliest melodic accompaniment of the dance appears to have been always sung, and a melodic instrumental accompaniment comes quite late, with instrumental dance melody developing, not from instrumental rhythmic music, but from the "instrumentalizing" of dance songs, for which the words have been abandoned.[14] It would seem, then, that a strong and regular rhythm is not inherent in instrumental music as such, but is inherent in dance music, and had its source in the vocal rather than in the instrumental medium. That dance rhythm is found more often in later artistic instrumental music than in vocal music—and hence is more commonly associated with "instrumental style"—is accounted for by the fact that, in the course of time, the more complicated social dances branched off from the simple folksong-dances and became stylized. And it is the social dances (which came to dispense with singing), rather than the folk dances, that constitute so important a part of the instrumental repertoire from the 16th century on. A regular and pronounced rhythm is therefore primarily a feature of dance music, and only secondarily (through specially close association in later periods) a feature of (some) instrumental music.

As regards irregular or syncopated rhythms, and the tying of short notes to long ones, many of these instances appear as the result of modern methods of transcription with bar-lines. As with the juxtaposition of very long and very short notes, the ability to execute complicated rhythms depends upon the performer's rhythmic sense more than on his medium, and if they can be played, they usually can be sung. It should be sufficient to note that the earliest textbooks on vocal ornamentation— those of Bovicelli (1594), Conforto (1607), and Rognone (1620) among others—decidedly favored the employment of dotted rhythms, including those in which the shorter note comes first (♪♪. and ♪♩.),[15] and there is no evidence that they were adopting instrumental mannerisms.

Which of Schering's criteria, then, survive close examination? Actually only two: rapidity of execution, and range. And even

14 See Curt Sachs, *World History of the Dance*, New York, 1937, 175 ff.
15 See Max Kuhn, *op. cit.*, 79.

these are to a large extent matters of degree, and the superiority in agility and compass is true only of particular instruments. As for agility, it is of course quite true that some instruments can perform rapid florid passages more easily than the human voice —the modern violin comes to mind at once—but this is not true of all instruments, and in some instances it is true only at relatively recent stages of development, as in that of the clarinet since the improvements of Denner (*c.* 1690) and others. On the whole the notion of the superiority of instruments over voices in this respect has been greatly exaggerated, and is too frequently taken for granted.

Very little is known about the potentialities of particular instruments prior to the 16th century; what little instrumental music remains from the earliest times [16] rarely can be ascribed to a particular instrument, and is, moreover, no more florid than the contemporary vocal music. Nevertheless, it is interesting that in the late 13th century the stringed instruments (presumably above all the bowed *vielle*) were recognized by at least one theorist as superior to the voice in agility since they were able to execute as many as four rapid ornamental notes (*currentes*) to the *brevis*.[17] Yet this advantage is not revealed in the preserved musical documents of the time. It appears rather to have been the result of improvised ornamentation, whose existence in both vocal and instrumental music is known to us but not its details, since the earliest complete textbook on ornamentation does not come until the 16th century (Ganassi's *La Fontegara*, 1535).[18] It is true that, by the middle of the 16th century, the solo music for viola da gamba with keyboard accompaniment (in contrast to music for an unaccompanied ensemble) shows a certain individuality in the improvising of free fantasias as well as in the embellishing of motets, madrigals, etc., in such a way that, while the keyboard instrument plays the complete composition unadorned, the gamba employs its wide range in passing from one voice-part to any other at will, with added ornamentation.

[16] On the "instrumental style" of this music see the present writer's article "Estampie and Stantipes", *Speculum*, XIX (April 1944), 222-249.

[17] Four *currentes* to the *brevis* "are not used with the human voice but may be used with stringed instruments" (Anonymus IV in Coussemaker *Scriptores* I, 341). The *currentes* seem to be equivalent to the *semibrevis*, whose position was then only beginning to be recognized and whose value was still a variable fraction of the *brevis*.

[18] Facsimile reprint by the Bolletino Bibliografico Musicale, Milan, 1934.

On "Instrumental Style" in Early Melody 117

The ornamental figures in themselves, however, do not differ from those of contemporary vocal music.[19] It is also true that late in the century Zacconi (1592) speaks of the superiority of the keyboard instruments to the human voice in executing rapid leaps and in the performance of the smallest note-values (thirty-seconds and sixty-fourths).[20] Nevertheless the examples given by Max Kuhn from Ganassi (1535) to Rognone (1620) show no perceptible distinction between vocal and instrumental ornamentation with respect to frequency in occurrence of these values. Parry's statement that the 16th-century "canzone, ricercari, and fantasias were all adorned with strange runs and turns; and canti fermi were accompanied by new kinds of counterpoint, in which, though the parts were applied like the old voice-parts, the notes were too rapid to be sung",[21] and similar statements by other scholars, are largely the result of a failure to consider the question of notation, which will be discussed later.

So far we have dealt with the question of to what extent early instrumental music actually is more elaborate than vocal music, and we have found that there is much less difference between the two than has commonly been supposed. We may now consider whether the presence of Schering's "instrumental" features in vocal music can be attributed to the influence of instrumental music. In order to prove such an influence, it is necessary to establish the fact that these features appear earlier in instrumental than in vocal music. Priority in these matters is difficult to establish in the earliest centuries because so much of the elaboration was left to improvisation, and the details that would enable us to observe any differences are lacking. It must suffice to point out that the history of ornamental embellishment is a long and continuous one, and that we have more data about the vocal medium than about the instrumental.[22] And although we ought to assume that embellishment was employed by in-

---

[19] See the examples in Diego Ortiz, *Tratado de glosas . . . en la música de violones, Roma 1553* (ed. Max Schneider, Kassel, 1936), and discussion in Alfred Einstein, *Zur deutschen Literatur für Viola da Gamba im 16. und 17. Jahrhundert*, 1905.

[20] Friedrich Chrysander, "Ludovico Zacconi als Lehrer des Kunstgesanges", *Vierteljahrsschrift für Musikwissenschaft*, VII (1891), 354, and IX (1893), 265. The use of sixty-fourth notes is, at all events, quite rare in the 16th century. There are, for example, but two occurrences of them in the entire *Fitzwilliam Virginal Book*, one in a Farnaby duo (Breitkopf & Härtel edition, I, 202) and the other in Thos. Tomkins' *Grounds* (II, 92).

[21] *Oxford History of Music*, III, 67.

[22] The whole subject has been treated in Ferand, *op. cit.*

struments—to the extent permitted by their respective mecha-
nisms—about as freely as by voices, there is no reason whatever
to believe that the general practice or any specific devices of
melodic embellishment in early music originated upon instruments. Rather is the reverse the more likely, since the role of
instruments is, on the whole, subservient to that of the voice in
primitive and oriental cultures, and, until at least the 16th century, in Western Europe as well. The cases where instrumental
ornamentation differed from vocal ornamentation appear to have
been rare and of no demonstrable influence on vocal music.[23]
Among the earliest preserved examples wherein the process of
melodic embellishment may be observed through our possession
of both simple and ornamented versions of the same piece are
the keyboard adaptations (c. 1335) in the *Robertsbridge Codex*
(British Museum, Add. 28550) of motets from the slightly
earlier *Roman de Fauvel.* These are sometimes cited as examples
of peculiarly instrumental embellishment. This notion, however,
cannot be maintained in the light of the similarity between the
melodic ornamentation of the Robertsbridge pieces and those
shown in the contemporary treatise of *Petrus dictus Palma ociosa* (1336), who was certainly concerned primarily—and to all
appearances exclusively—with vocal ornamentation.[24]

Two more features that are found in early music and that
are occasionally alleged to be intrinsically instrumental in character claim our attention. One is organum, and the other the
bordunus, or drone bass.

Schering, to support his belief in the organ as the original
source and principal medium of organum, cites[25] the following
passages found in the treatise of Johannes Cotto (c. 1100) and
supported by a similar passage in the contemporary anonymous
treatise, *Ad Organum Faciendum:*

[23] In the late 13th century we encounter, in the treatise of Jerome of Moravia
(see Coussemaker, I, 91), a description of three varieties of the *flos armonicus* on
the organ, a form of trill in which the lower tone is held down while the upper tone
is vibrated against it—a procedure obviously impossible for the single human voice.
Even this, however, is an adaptation of the vocal *flos* rather than an ornament peculiar
to the organ. The same is true of the 16th-century mordent described by the organist
Hans Buchner (see *Vierteljahrsschrift für Musikwissenschaft,* V [1889], 33).

[24] This treatise is printed in *Sammelbände der internationalen Musikgesellschaft,*
XV (1914), 504-34. The ornamentations there may be compared with those of the
Robertsbridge Codex in J. Wolf, *Geschichte der Mensuralnotation,* Leipzig, 1904,
III, 191-99.

[25] *Studien,* 20.

On "Instrumental Style" in Early Melody 119

This manner of singing [i.e. note-against-note in contrary motion employing the consonances of 4th, 5th, and 8ve] is commonly called *organum*, since the "dissonant" human voice [i.e. the voice that does not have the plainchant] aptly imitates the likeness of the instrument which is called the organ.[26]

It is true that Cotto and the Milan Anonymous do say that organum took its name from, and imitated the effect of, the organ. On the other hand, the *Summa Musicae* attributed to Johannes de Muris (*c.* 1320) described not only the same type but also a later form (*diaphonia basilica*) in which the lower voice sustains a long tone against the more rapid tones of the upper voice; and of both Muris says that they "receive their name from that organ which is the instrument of singing since in this kind of music it exerts itself a great deal".[27] Although this quotation by itself does not preclude the possibility that the mechanical organ was the "instrument of singing" referred to, Muris later makes it quite clear (with the phrase "as has been said") that in the passage just quoted as well as in the following one, the vocal organ is the "instrument" in question: "*Organica* [*diaphonia*], as has been said, receives its name from the vocal organ."[28]

Of these two conflicting opinions one would be inclined to choose that of Cotto and the Anonymous as being earlier by two centuries and therefore nearer to the period of origin; but even they are still two centuries removed from the first use of the term, a circumstance that renders their authority hardly more weighty than that of later writers. Actually it is not a matter of great importance from the point of view of musical style, for while it is true that, in the 12th-century contrary-motion organum of Cotto and the Milan Anonymous, the wider and more frequent leaps in the organal voice distinguish it somewhat from the smoother line of the plainchant, this difference arises clearly from the desire to provide variety in harmonic intervals and not because the music was intended for an instrument. Of the later variety, where a difference arises between the character of the sustained tenor and that of the active melody of the upper parts, there is still no need to view either tenor or

---

[26] Quoted by Schering, *loc. cit.*, from Gerbert, *Scriptores*, II, 263.

[27] Gerbert, *op. cit.*, III, 239–40.

[28] *Ibid.*, 240.

[29] The word *organum*, without etymological reference and without any apparent connection with instruments, appears, for example, in the *Musica enchiriadis* (*c.* 900); see Gerbert, *op. cit.*, I, 169.

upper parts as representing a style of writing conceived for instruments rather than for voices. Friedrich Ludwig dismisses the necessity of supposing the florid upper parts to have been written for instruments by recalling the schooling in florid singing which church singers of the time received.[80] The other assumption—that the long notes of the tenor were impossible of performance by singers—falls to the ground if one considers the resources of trained breath control, the employment of short (unmarked) rests, or of the shared exertion possible to unison singing and mentioned earlier in this article.[81] Indeed the whole claim of the influence of the organ—or of other instruments—on the early polyphonic forms of organum, motet, and conductus should be, as Otto Ursprung says, rejected.[82] Even the textless tenors of the motets are usually derived from vocal music and their distortion by the schematic arrangements into rhythmic modes and *ordines* cannot be shown to have arisen from the circumstance that they were often, even perhaps usually, entrusted to instruments.

The original medium of the *bordunus*, or drone bass, cannot be traced. It is found in primitive music, vocal and instrumental,[83] and by the medieval period the presence of bourdon pipes on the organ and bagpipes and bourdon strings on the *vielle*,[84] as well as the (probably vocal) rendition of the same effect in the later organum already mentioned, makes it a device common to music both for voices and for certain instruments.

All in all, then, with the possible but unprovable exception of an originally instrumental source for the drone bass, one must conclude that there is no reason to see any primarily instrumental heritage among the general idioms of music handed down from the Middle Ages; and although the *vielle* has been recognized as possessing greater agility than the voice, neither the result of this superiority in instrumental music, nor its influ-

---

[80] Adler *Handbuch*, 223.

[81] Jacques Handschin, indeed, cites cases where the number of performers is recorded as exceeding the number of parts, and concludes that in the polyphonic music of the Notre Dame school, the extra singers were employed in doubling on the sustained tenor notes (J. Handschin, "Zur Geschichte von Notre Dame", *Acta Musicologica*, IV [1932], 8 ff.).

[82] *Katholische Kirchenmusik*, Potsdam, 1931, 117.

[83] See Ferand, *op. cit.*, 51-52; also Curt Sachs, *The Rise of Music in the Ancient World East and West*, New York, 1943, 50-51 and *passim*.

[84] See the description in the treatise of Jerome of Moravia (Coussemaker I, 153).

On "Instrumental Style" in Early Melody 121

ence on vocal music is apparent.[35] However, it must be said that by the end of the 14th century the music for instruments does occasionally show those devices of the reiterated interval and the persistence of the same short note values and rhythmic motives that were admitted early in this article to be frequent in instrumental music and practically non-existent in vocal music.[36] Moreover, in part-music, it occasionally happens about this time that one finds a single part whose restricted compass represents a modification of the writing to suit the limitations of a particular type of instrument, and therefore represents a contemporary instrumental style.[37]

The 15th century contributes nothing definite to our knowledge of differences between vocal music and music for an ensemble of melodic instruments (as contrasted with harmonic or chordal instruments like the organ, clavier, and lute). There is, however, an interesting remark in the *Tractatulus* of Arnulph of Saint Gilles, which is usually considered to refer to organ playing. Arnulph, who is decidedly conservative and concerned primarily with vocal liturgical music, notes that

we see some clerics who, by a sort of miraculous prodigy of inborn musical inventiveness, devise and teach on "organic instruments" extremely difficult musical passages which the human voice could scarcely undertake to render.[38]

The meaning of this passage is not entirely clear, but the context (too long and too involved in literary style for quotation here) shows that Arnulph is speaking of naturally talented but

[35] Passages in medieval treatises that refer to very high pitches (overtones) obtainable on the organ, on bells, and on stringed instruments, cannot, of course, be considered evidence of a special instrumental style, since these high pitches are not indicated and not considered in the writing of the music; they are mere simultaneous duplications which result from the nature of the means of tone production (see, for example, Anonymus IV, in Coussemaker I, 362).

[36] See the *estampies* etc., transcribed by Wolf in *Archiv für Musikwissenschaft*, I (1918-19), 19-42.

[37] See, for example, the momentary imitation (reiterated melodic interval of the fifth) of the "cornemuse" (bagpipe), mentioned in the text, in the anonymous 14th-century *virelai* partially transcribed in Besseler, *Musik des Mittelalters und der Renaissance*, 141-42. A more famous example, from the following century, is shown in the limitation of two canonic parts to the dominant and tonic, "in the manner of a trumpet", in Dufay's *Gloria ad modum tubae* (*Denkmäler der Tonkunst in Oesterreich*, VII, 145).

[38] ". . . nonnullos videmus clericos, qui in organicis instrumentis difficillimos musicales modulos, quod exprimere vix praesumeret vox humana, adinveniunt atque tradunt per miraculosum quoddam innatae in eis inventivae musicae prodigium." (Gerbert, *op. cit.*, III, 316.)

untrained musicians, and is to all appearances referring to instruments as aids or substitutes for singing rather than as independent media. The phrase *organicis instrumentis* may mean merely musical instruments in general, although it probably refers to the organ and perhaps to certain other instruments used for "organizing" (i.e., adding a second part to a *cantus firmus*), while *modulos* usually means passages or melodies (but certainly not "modulation" in the modern or harmonic sense of the term). The compass of the organ was at this time beginning to exceed the three octaves or so of the later Middle Ages, and the width of the keys on church organs was being gradually reduced until by the beginning of the 16th century it approximated that of the present day.[39] Yet any superiority of the organ over other instruments or over the human voice (save in range and in the possibility that the hands at the keyboard could, if desired, produce a melody with wide leaps which would be very awkward, if not impossible, for a singer) cannot be shown to have existed so early. It is true that the Van Eyck altarpiece at Ghent (1432) proves that a completely chromatic keyboard was not unknown in this century, but in the production of chromatic tones the organ must have been surpassed by instruments of more easily alterable pitch such as the *vielle*, as well as by the human voice. And it is more than doubtful if its agility at this epoch was greater than that of voices or some of the other instruments. We have, of course, from this period the earliest documents of a continuous school of organists (Paumann and others), documents that largely comprise keyboard adaptations of vocal music with added turns and other embellishments. The restriction of ornamentation among the 15th- and 16th-century German organists mainly to simple mordents and turns appears to have been the result of the limitations of their imagination rather than of the instrument, for contemporary Italian and English keyboard composers were doing immeasurably better. At all events, to what extent such melodic embroidery represents a peculiarly instrumental style is a moot question, and is at least partly a matter of the form of notation, a field into which a brief digression is necessary at this point.

Prior to about 1600 there were four forms of notation used

[39] G. Frotscher, *Geschichte des Orgelspiels und der Orgelkomposition*, Berlin, 1935, 39.

On "Instrumental Style" in Early Melody   123

for the setting down of music comprising more than a single line of melody.[40] These forms, based on the arrangement of the parts, were: *Choir-book Notation,* in which all the parts were contained in a single volume but were separately distributed on the page (or on two facing pages), each part by itself with no indication of how its notes coincided with those of the other parts; *Part-book Notation,* which differs from choir-book notation only in that the parts were distributed in different books, so that of a given collection the tenor book contained all (and only) the tenor parts, the altus book all (and only) the altus parts, etc.; *Score Notation,* in which the parts of a composition were written under each other, all in a single volume, each part on its own staff, so that the simultaneous tones appear vertically aligned with more or less exactitude; and *Tabulature,* in which the attempt to preserve the individuality of the parts, by means of separate staves for each, is sacrificed in favor of adjusting the writing to the convenience of the single player (especially one not very skilled), either by employing notes on a short score of only two staves (one for each hand of the keyboard player), or else by substituting, in place of notes, figures or letters which, in lute tablature, indicated the fret and string called for rather than the tone (tablature proper).

Choir-book notation is a type suitable for a small group (scarcely more than one performer to a part) gathered around the single choir-book; it was employed for almost all the examples of part-music from about 1250 to about 1450, after which it fell into disuse in practical music, though surviving, for reasons of expediency, in the illustrations in text-books. Part-book notation, which succeeded choir-book notation, is more suitable for a somewhat larger ensemble, vocal or instrumental; it was employed for most of the practical documents of printed music in the 16th century, and exists today in the separate parts of modern chamber and orchestral music. Neither of these types, however, was convenient for the single individual who had to direct or play all the parts, as, for example, performers on solo chordal instruments like the lute and the keyboard instruments. For these performers score or tablature was more suitable. Score notation had been employed for the very first at-

---

[40] For a detailed discussion of these forms of notation, see Willi Apel, *The Notation of Polyphonic Music 900—1600,* Cambridge, Mass., 1942.

tempts at part-music (from the text syllables of the 9th-century *Musica enchiriadis* to the organa, conductus, and clausulae of the 13th-century Notre Dame school), and was revived not only in ensemble music with the rise of orchestral music about 1600, but also in vocal music (de Rore's *Madrigali,* 1577) and in some documents of late 16th- and 17th-century keyboard music (Italy), especially those in which the strict part-writing of true contrapuntal style was observed (ricercari, etc.). Most keyboard music, however, as well as the music for other chordal instruments (principally the lute), was written in tablature of one type or another, especially music intended for students or for amateurs insufficiently skilled either at adapting the part-writing to suit the exigencies of fingering, etc., or at introducing improvised embellishments correctly and tastefully. This last point is one of considerable importance in comparing the style of music found in the tablatures with that of the music written in part-book or score notation, as we shall shortly see.

The 16th century is the one from which we possess the earliest repertoire of instrumental music in any appreciable quantity, and also it is the one from which we have the earliest instruction book in the art of improvised ornamentation for voices and instruments. One would suppose that any differences between contemporary instrumental and vocal styles in melody would be reflected in the instruction books as well as in the music documents. But such scholars as Wolf, Kuhn, Krebs, Ferand, and others, who have studied the instruction books in detail, find no general distinction between the two. On the other hand, it is a fact that in the practical documents of this period we do often find certain pieces for keyboard and lute (especially variations, toccatas, and free fantasias) that are more florid than are most other contemporary vocal or instrumental pieces (among the latter, especially the fugal ricercari). It is customary, in comparing the florid with the simpler examples, to call the former more "instrumental" and the latter more "vocal". But this viewpoint ignores the evidence of florid improvised ornamentation in the vocal as well as in the instrumental music of the time. As has been said, there is no reason to think that the vocal was derived from the instrumental ornamentation, either at that period or earlier. To the 16th century the human voice was the most perfect melodic instrument, not

On "Instrumental Style" in Early Melody 125

merely from the point of view of expressiveness, but also from that of technique.[41] Consequently, some better explanation of the presence of both a florid and simple style in 16th-century music must be found.

The truth is that the more florid appearance of many keyboard and lute pieces is less the consequence of this style being reserved for these instruments than it is a consequence of the form of notation. For, as has been said, lute and keyboard music, from the 15th to the 17th century, was almost always written in some form of tablature; and tablature, by its very practical nature, was much more explicit in presenting fully embellished versions of the pieces contained. Thus we find the German organist, Bernhard Schmid the Elder, announcing in the preface to his tablature of 1577:

> I have ornamented the motets and [the other] pieces incorporated in this work with modest coloraturas, [but] not with the intention of binding the trained organist to my coloraturas, for I would leave everyone free to better them, and, as I have said, I have added mine only on behalf of the beginners on the instrument, although for myself I would have preferred that the authority and art of the composer should remain undisturbed.[42]

On the other hand, part-book notation (as well as choirbook notation) was intended primarily for ensembles (vocal, instrumental, or mixed), and the ornamentation was left to the discretion of the director or performers. This was due no doubt partly to the fact that, when melodic instruments were used, the amount and type of ornamentation might be limited by the capacities of the instruments available at the moment, and partly to the fact that skilled musicians liked to express their own taste, while unskilled ones either had to be instructed in suitable ornaments, under the guidance of their director, or else

---

[41] All of the 16th- and 17th-century treatises on improvised ornamentation appear to be equally applicable to vocal and instrumental music—to judge from both examples and titles or prefaces. And although some treatises are especially recommended for one or another medium, there is no evidence that the ornamental figures there are especially designed for this medium. Occasionally one finds references to the human voice as the model which all instruments strive to imitate, as in the Breslau MS copy of Riccardo Rogniono's treatise, which gives ornaments "per cantare e suonare con ogni sorte de stromenti . . . cosa ancora utile a Suonatori per imitare la voce humana" (Kuhn, *op. cit.*, 18), or in Girolamo della Casa's recommendation of the *cornetto* as the most excellent of wind instruments "per imitare la voce humana" (*ibid.*, 31). On the other hand, to the present writer's knowledge, no theorist recommends that the human voice imitate an instrument.

[42] Quoted in Frotscher, *op. cit.*, 154.

had to confine themselves to the simplicity of the unembellished written version.

It is to be noted in passing that florid embellishment was not a mark of "secular style" and opposed to "sacred style"; it arises from an artistic impulse towards decoration rather than from one of religious devotion—for not only does Bernhard Schmid apply it to the motets in his volume, but in Giovanni Bassano's vocal collection of *Motetti, Madrigali et Canzoni Francesi Diminuti* (1591), we find Palestrina's motet, *In Festo Sanctae Trinitatis*, published with added "diminutions" during the composer's lifetime and, so far as we know, without any protest from him.[43] And by 1615, if not before, improvised ornamentation had made its appearance in church, even in Rome, as is attested by the title of Francesco Severi's work, *Salmi passeggiati per tutte le voci nella maniera che si canta in Roma ...*

Nor was the practice confined to a single country; in the 16th and 17th centuries at least, it seems to have been widespread in Europe. Although no treatises on diminution by the Netherlanders are preserved until that of Adrian Petit Coclicus (1552), there is evidence that they employed it earlier, and Kuhn places its origin in France and the Netherlands, whence it spread to Italy (Ganassi, 1535), Germany (Coclicus, 1552, and Finck, 1556), Spain (Bermudo, 1555), and, in the next century, England. Nor, again, may it be regarded merely as a degenerate license exercised only by popular performers or by egotistical virtuosi in violation of the practice and intention of serious composers. On the contrary, the practice was expounded by some of the most earnest and reputable musicians of the time, among them Josquin's pupil, Coclicus. Josquin himself, indeed, appears to have taught improvised ornamentation, for Coclicus' treatise contains examples headed "this is the first clausula [here meaning "cadential embellishment"] which Josquin taught his pupils",[44] and there is every reason to suppose he was merely continuing the medieval tradition of improvised ornamentation previously referred to. And Orlando di Lasso is mentioned as coaching singers in this practice of *gorgia* (as it was popularly

---

[43] This motet, with Bassano's ornamentation, is given in Kuhn, *op. cit.*, 100-09.
[44] Kuhn, *op. cit.*, 9.

On "Instrumental Style" in Early Melody   127

called), even in the Mass.[45] Nor was the diminution confined to any particular part. As Hermann Finck says:

> The art of employing coloratura depends on the skill, natural aptitude, and the originality of the individual. Everyone has his own method. Many think that the bass, others that the discant, ought to be embellished. My own view, however, is that all parts can and ought to be provided with coloratura; not continuously, however, but only at the places to be indicated, and also not in all parts at once, but each at the proper moment and the rest in their respective turns so that one embellishment can be heard and discriminated clearly and definitely from the rest, and thus the composition remain intact and undisturbed.[46]

Since the application of ornamentation was not limited to any part, form, country, or performing medium, and since it was highly regarded by the best practitioners of music of the time, one wonders not under what conditions it did take place, but rather under what conditions it did not. The answer is not clear, but, in addition to the use of the simple written version for unskilled musicians, we learn from Finck that

> Coloraturas cannot be introduced in choruses without deformation [of the music], for when one part is distributed to several voices for singing, there must arise very dissimilar coloraturas, by which the charm and the character of the melody is obscured.[47]

This passage, although unique among its fellows in distinguishing between one and several performers to a part, may perhaps be accepted as representing the general practice, and as showing that when a part was shared by more than one performer, it was sung or played as written. When, on the other hand, a single performer used the part, improvised embellishment seems to have been often, perhaps customarily, introduced.[48]

[45] Massimo Trojano, in his *Dialoghi* (1568), mentions "un Motetta [*sic*] che all hora il graduale della Messa grande con varii contrappunti Messere Orlando di Lasso dalli suoi fideli cantori a gorghizzare [i.e. embellish with *gorgia* or ornamentation] incominciar havea". (Quoted in Kurt Huber, *Ivo de Vento* . . . , Munich, 1918, 111.)

[46] A German translation of this passage is to be found in Raymond Schlecht, "Hermann Finck über die Kunst des Singens 1556", *Monatshefte für Musikgeschichte*, XI (1879), 139, and a portion of the original Latin in Ferand, *op. cit.*, 266.

[47] Quoted in Ferand, *op. cit.*, 266. A similar warning to avoid ornamentation when performing Gregorian chant in unison ("in multitudine personarum") had been given by Conrad von Zaubern in 1474 (see *Monatshefte für Musikgeschichte*, 1888, 98).

[48] A similar conclusion was reached by Manfred Bukofzer in a paper "On the Performance of Renaissance Music" read before the Music Teachers National Association at Minneapolis, December 1941, and published in the *Proceedings of the MTNA* (Pittsburgh, 1942), 225-35. The present writer expressed this view in his dissertation entitled *The Early Keyboard Prelude, A Study in Musical Style* (manuscript, Harvard University, 1941). His views were corroborated in Schering's *Aufführungspraxis*, 131.

The foregoing discussion of improvised ornamentation as it was employed by skilled soloists in vocal and instrumental ensemble music, as well as on a solo instrument, suggests that the distinction in early music between relatively florid and relatively simple types of melody is less often the result of their being intended for instruments or voices than it is the result of their being intended respectively for solo or for unison (or else amateur) performance of the parts. Even in Gregorian chant, as Otto Ursprung has pointed out,[49] we find that the *Alleluia* of the Mass was entrusted to a skilled soloist and consequently developed its florid *jubilus*, while the antiphon, which was performed in unison by the *schola* of ordinary singers, retained its modest range and simple melodic style throughout its career. And while we lack definite information regarding the extent to which unison or solo performance of melodic lines was intended in other forms of early music, we may assume it as probable that the most florid music was intended for a trained soloist or virtuoso rather than for amateur or unison rendition. In the course of time, however, with the gradual establishment of permanent bodies of trained musicians, the abilities of merely average performers increased enormously, through long and regular rehearsals, so that, at least from the 19th century on, the whole first violin section of a symphony orchestra often performs parts that are as elaborate as those for a soloist. The difference between unison and soloist melody then becomes one of timbre (solo or unison) rather than one of technique.

The present discussion rests its case on pointing out that the terms "instrumental style" and "vocal style" have been bandied about too carelessly, and on having shown that: 1) except that instrumental music frequently employs more immediate repetition of the same note-values and of melodic and rhythmic figures in certain forms of composition, a general and exclusively instrumental, as contrasted with a general vocal, style of melody cannot really be said to exist before the 17th century; 2) the various differences which Schering takes to be criteria of "instrumental style" are not common to all instruments (and therefore are not *generally* instrumental), and owe their existence to something other than the nature of the instrument as such (and therefore are not *intrinsically* instrumental), or are also charac-

[49] *Katholische Kirchenmusik*, 27.

On "Instrumental Style" in Early Melody   129

teristic of some vocal music as well (and therefore are not
peculiarly instrumental); and 3) in early music, a florid style
(which is what Schering's "instrumental style" largely reduces
to) is probably less often the result of its being intended for
instruments than of its being intended for soloists, vocal or
instrumental.

In addition, it is suggested that Schering (and those who
have consciously or unconsciously followed his thinking) has
taken too narrow a view of vocal style—specifically that of the
simplest plainchant[50]—and have used the term "instrumental
style" as a sort of glorified ash-heap for the disposal of all melodic and rhythmic features that do not fit this narrow concept,
instead of properly taking into account the full possibilities of
the human voice—as did for example those specialists in vocal
writing, the Italian opera composers of the Baroque period. It
is further suggested that this school of thought has erred in
assuming that where the style of the music has been modified
by the conditions of performance, it must necessarily have been
the *medium* of performance that produced the modification.
The performing medium, however, is only one of several factors
of performance that may affect the style, others being the social
purpose (e.g. dancing), and the degree of technical proficiency
required of the performers, an example of whose influence we
have just seen in the instance of improvised ornamentation.

The truth is that any features claimed as "instrumental" in
essence must be shown to be bound up either with instruments
in general (and such features, as we have seen, have not been
proved to exist) or else with the peculiarities of specific instruments. Of examples in melodic writing, with the exception of
such rare cases as the organ *flos armonicus*, no convincing instances have yet been revealed in music up to 1600, although a
more careful comparison of documents than has yet been made
might show a few. In the succeeding periods, in addition to an
increased use of persistent reiterations of the same note-values
and figures characteristic of much instrumental music, one may
expect to find certain melodic features involving very wide
leaps with rapid notes, awkward intervals, and sudden changes
of melodic direction, which are practically impossible even for

---

[50] For examples of so-called "unvocal" intervals in Gregorian chant, see Y.
Rokseth, *La Musique d'Orgue au XVe siècle et au début du XVIe*, Paris, 1930, 182.

a virtuoso singer but which are possible on certain instruments like the violin—and to a lesser extent on the rest of the strings, as well as on a few other very agile instruments, like the flute. In addition there are also to be found genuine examples of a particular instrumental (bowed string) style in those figures that employ an alternation of stopped and open-string tones of the same pitch.

Nevertheless, despite such indubitable developments in the direction of an individual melodic style for a special kind of instrument, one must bear in mind that not all of the changes to be observed in melody from the 17th century on are to be attributed to the nature of instruments per se. Some are due to a growing appreciation of vertical combinations of tones as musical entities in their own right rather than merely as the results of properly combined melodies. And the isolated arpeggio (as contrasted with persistent arpeggio figuration, which is instrumental because of its persistence rather than its arpeggiation) is a mark of harmonic or homophonic style rather than of instrumental style, because it is the harmonic concept, and not so much the nature of instruments, that gives such figurations birth.

[2]

Specific information on the ensembles for composed polyphony, 1400-1474

DAVID FALLOWS

Modern writers have repeatedly affirmed that composed polyphony was only a small part of mediaeval man's musical experience. Even in the grandest cathedrals and court chapels, plainchant was sung daily whereas polyphony was for the most part confined to special occasions; and simple improvised or semi-improvised polyphony now looks increasingly important in mediaeval Europe. Monophonic song remained a prominent musical embellishment to the rich courts just as it was ubiquitous in the towns.

So the searcher for information on how to perform written polyphony of the fifteenth century must search with caution. Lists of choirmen are now plentifully available, but there is virtually no evidence to say how many of these men could read mensural notation or were actually involved in any particular polyphonic performance. Pictures of music making survive in enormous quantity, but indications that they represent performances of composed polyphony are extremely rare.

My aim here is, therefore, to assemble the information that actually tells us something about the performing ensembles used in polyphony. Ideally, this information would specify a particular work, identify performers, and say what those performers did. But nothing quite so complete survives; and in the event almost any document that specifies polyphony and gives numbers or distributions is interesting. A further ideal requirement would be that the information should represent the highest aspirations of the time. Anyone who has examined the surviving sources of mediaeval music is likely to conclude that many institutions compromised; and the issue is surely not whether a particular kind of performance could conceivably have taken place in the middle ages so much as what was then considered the best performance. The social historian may be interested in all kinds of music making, but the student of the music that happens to survive needs to know what was thought to be the ideal performance, the one that is worth emulating in an attempt to revive the music today.

There are three items that come close to fulfilling these requirements, and all three concern sacred music. One is from the still unpublished Burgundian

110   David Fallows

court ordinances of 1469, and the other two are from Dufay's will of 1474. With these as a basis it becomes possible to reconsider certain other material and derive conclusions that reach back some distance towards the year 1400.

I. The Burgundian court chapel in 1469

Clearly the Burgundian court was in a position to expect performances that met the highest standards. And Duke Charles the Bold was in a particularly strong position: not only was he himself a composer and performer,[1] but there is considerable evidence to suggest that he took a special personal interest in composers, carefully cultivating the careers of Busnois and Hayne van Ghizeghem as well as receiving a substantial quantity of music from the hand of Dufay. He was probably the best educated, musically, of fifteenth-century patrons, and he inherited a court musical establishment that had counted for nearly a century as the most eminent in Europe.

Charles was a compulsive organiser, and, shortly after becoming duke, he promulgated a set of court ordinances giving detailed instructions for the running of his household. He was also, by all reports, an exceptionally devout man.[2] So there are several reasons why his chapel choir should occupy considerable space in the ordinances. Of the forty-eight folios that make up the single surviving copy of these ordinances no fewer than twelve are devoted to his chapel.

What makes the ordinances particularly interesting is the statement (f. 1) that in recent years the organisation of the household had become slack. For over ten years before he became duke, Charles had been increasingly impatient with his father, the ageing Philip the Good: it is easy to see that Charles would now want to establish a blueprint representing the ideal.

The Appendix to this article is a transcription of all the material in those ordinances that concerns music or musicians. But for the present enquiry the crucial passage is paragraph 11 of the chapel ordinances (ff. 13*r*-13*v*):

> Item pour le chant du livre y aura du moyns six haultes voix, troys teneurs, troys basses contres et deux moiens sans en ce comprendre les quatre chapelains des haultes messes ne les sommeliers lesquelz toutefoys s'ilz ne sont occupés a l'autel ou autrement raisonnablement seront tenus de servir avec les dessus ditz.

> Item: for singing polyphony there shall be at least six high voices, three tenors, three contrabasses and two *moiens* [presumably contratenors], excluding the four chaplains for High Mass [who must officiate, as detailed in paragraph 7, ff. 12*r*-12*v*] and the *sommeliers* who, however, must sing with the above-mentioned if they are not occupied at the altar or in some other reasonable way.

---

1 David Fallows, 'Robert Morton's songs: a study of styles in the mid-fifteenth century' (Ph.D. dissertation, University of California at Berkeley, 1979), pp. 303-24.
2 Richard Vaughan, *Charles the Bold: the last Valois Duke of Burgundy* (London, 1973), p. 161.

Ensembles for composed polyphony, 1400-1474 111

Clearly there is a special – indeed unique – interest in a fifteenth-century document that not only specifies a 6/3/2/3 distribution for the voices but also includes the vital words 'at least'. It does not tell us what music was to be performed in this way. But presumably we are right to translate *chant du livre* here as 'polyphony' and to conclude that four-part polyphony is intended because the names *teneur*, *basse contre* and *moien* can surely refer only to the voice-names in four-part polyphony.

By an unfortunate coincidence practically all the music that can be connected unambiguously with Charles the Bold's court is secular. On the other hand the paragraph quoted does imply that this four-voice polyphony was sung primarily during the Mass. This is no surprise since the surviving four-voice music of the time is confined largely to Mass Ordinary settings and to motets for special occasions – works like Compere's *Omnium bonorum plena*, Busnois' *In hydraulis* and Dufay's late *Ave regina celorum*. Service-music in four voices was still rare.

One group of pieces that apparently was sung at the court of Charles the Bold is the set of six anonymous *L'homme armé* Masses now in Naples.[3] The manuscript includes in its dedicatory poem the line 'Charolus hoc princeps quondam gaudere solebat' – Duke Charles [of Burgundy] used to take pleasure in this music. The voice-ranges for the first five Masses appear in Example 1a. Perhaps another work sung by this choir was the four-voice *L'homme armé* Mass of Busnois, for although the composer was not to join the chapel choir until slightly later, he was certainly a member of the court as a *varlet de chambre* and *chantre*; he had been in Charles's private household before that.[4] The ranges of the Busnois cycle are in Example 1b. In general, the ranges in Example 1 are characteristic of four-voice Mass cycles at the time: occasionally the written range was about a third lower,[5] but we cannot be far wrong in thinking of the relative ranges of the four voices intended by the ordinances as being as in Example 1.

---

3 The six cycles are edited by Laurence Feininger in Monumenta polyphoniae liturgicae sanctae ecclesiae romanae, 1st ser., iii (Rome, 1957, 1957, 1965, 1965, 1966, 1974); a new edition with the missing pages reconstructed has been prepared by Judith Cohen, *Six anonymous L'homme armé Masses in Naples, Biblioteca nazionale, MS VI E 40*, Corpus mensurabilis musicae, lxxxv (1981). Of many studies devoted to these works the most recent is Judith Cohen, 'Munus ab ignoto', *Studia musicologica Academiae scientiarum hungaricae*, xxii (1980), pp. 187-204.

4 Fallows, 'Robert Morton's songs', pp. 328-9.

5 All of Dufay's late four-voice Masses have this layout. Dating fifteenth-century Mass cycles is notoriously difficult, but a quick survey of the cycles in Trent, Museo Nazionale [*I-TRmn*] 88 and 89, Rome, Biblioteca Apostolica Vaticana [*I-Rvat*] S Pietro B 80 and Brussels, Bibliothèque Royale [*B-Br*] 5557 suggests that the earliest layer of four-voice cycles is represented by this layout with the clefs C1 C3 C3 C4 or C2 C4 C4 F4. In either case the total range is occasionally seventeen notes (*Veterem hominem*, *Christus surrexit*, Simon de Insula's *O admirabilis* and Frye's *Flos regalis*), most often eighteen or nineteen notes, and just occasionally twenty notes (*O rosa bella* and Faugues' *Le serviteur*). This could conceivably be at least a guide to chronology.

112   David Fallows

Example 1a. Ranges of Naples *L'homme armé* Masses I V

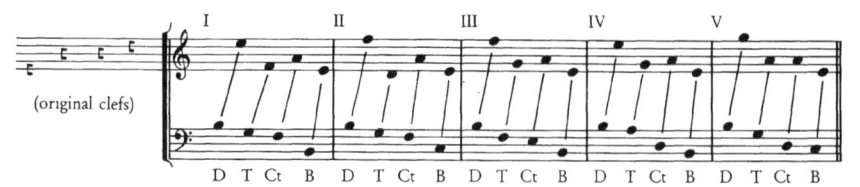

(original clefs)

D T Ct B   D T Ct B   D T Ct B   D T Ct B   D T Ct B

Key: D = discantus (supranus); T = tenor; Ct = contratenor (moien); B = bassus (contrabassus, basse-contre)

Example 1b. Ranges of Busnois, Mass *L'homme armé*

D T Ct B

Relative ranges are surely the issue here. There is no clear evidence concerning pitch standards in the fifteenth century, and current opinion seems to be that there was no general pitch standard.[6] It is therefore important to know whether the singers mentioned in Charles the Bold's ordinances were all men or whether children were involved for the top line.

Fortunately the court account books can answer that question beyond doubt if they are taken in conjunction with the ordinances. The ordinances are quite specific about the chapel staff. The first chaplain's duties were primarily administrative (ff. 19r-19v). The singers comprised twelve chaplains, six *clercs* and five *sommeliers*. In addition there was a *fourrier* who acted as verger during the services and arranged accommodation for the chapel members when they were on progress (ff. 22v-23r). The ordinances also state (f. 10v) that there can be chaplains who are not priests and there can be *clercs* and *sommeliers* who are priests; promotion from the one category to the next took place when there were vacancies and was made on the basis of singing ability and good service ('selon les merites disponibles de voix et bons services desdiz clercz et sommeliers'). The duties of the chaplains, *clercs* and *sommeliers* were therefore primarily concerned with singing; and all three categories could contain priests.

The chapel payment lists for January 1469 survive.[7] The numbers of singing-men do not quite tally with those required by the ordinances: there are four *clercs*, not six, and there are six *sommeliers*, not five. The numbers were

---

6   This assertion has yet to be argued for continental music, though for the next century remarkably similar conclusions emerge from Harold S. Powers, 'Tonal types and modal categories in renaissance polyphony', *Journal of the American Musicological Society*, xxxiv (1981), pp. 428-70. For English music of the fourteenth and fifteenth centuries, see Roger Bowers' contribution to the present volume and his pilot-article 'The performing pitch of English 15th-century church polyphony', *Early Music*, viii (1980), pp. 21-8.

7   Brussels, Archives Générales du Royaume, Chambre des Comptes, 1924, ff. 33r-35r.

rectified to agree with the ordinances over the next few months and were correct by the beginning of June.[8] But the payment list for January – the month of the ordinances – is useful because it shows beyond doubt that none of the chaplains or *clercs* can possibly have been a boy or even a youth. Those with the prefix 'Mr' were priests;[9] for each member I have added the approximate dates at which they are first recorded in the chapel.[10] The daily payments are included to stress the hierarchy of the groups.

First chaplains (36 *sous* per day)
  Mr Phelippe Siron (1441)

Chaplains (18 *sous* per day)
  1. Mr Robert de le Pele [= Robinet de la Magdelaine] (1450)
  2. Mr Anthoine Mauret (1462)
  3. Constans [Breuwe] de Languebrouc (1442)
  4. Mr Estienne de le Mote (1447)
  5. Mr Anthoine de Franceville (1453)
  6. Mr Gilles Brits (1453)
  7. Mr Robert Olivier (1456)
  8. Jehan [Lambert] de la Bassee (1452)
  9. Mathias Coquel (1461, but already a chaplain at the French royal court in 1452)
  10. Mr Pierre le Canonne (1461)
  11. Jehan Pintot dit Nicodemus (1461)
  12. Philippe de Passaige (1462)

Clercs (12 *sous* per day)
  1. Mr Glaude le Petit (1465)
  2. Mr Robert Moriton [= Morton] (1457)
  3. Mr Pasquier des Pres (1464)
  4. Johannes de Tricht (1453)

Sommeliers (11 *sous* or 7 *sous* per day)
  1. Jehan le Caron (1436)
  2. Mr Wautre Maes (1468)
  3. Gillet de Bousies (1461)
  4. Coppin Buckel (1465)
  5. Pierrequin du Wez (1467)
  6. Pierrequin Basin (1467)

Twelve of these twenty-three people were priests and therefore (barring special dispensations) at least twenty-five years old. Of those who were not

8 *Ibid.*, ff. 35*v*-37*r*.
9 Fallows, 'Robert Morton's songs', pp. 280-1.
10 Most of these dates are taken from Jeanne Marix, *Histoire de la musique et des musiciens de la cour de Bourgogne sous le règne de Philippe le Bon (1420-1467)*, Sammlung musikwissenschaftlicher Abhandlungen, xxviii (Strasbourg, 1939).

114   David Fallows

priests, the most recent arrival among the chaplains was Philippe de Passaige
who had arrived seven years earlier and could therefore hardly have been a boy
treble. The same goes for the *clercs* of whom only Johannes de Tricht was not a
priest and had been there for sixteen years.

Among the *sommeliers* there are three who could conceivably have been
boys: Coppin Buckel, Pierrequin du Wez and Pierrequin Basin. All three had
arrived within the previous four years and all three have diminutive forms in
their name which could suggest youth. But Basin had been *maître de chant* at
St Donatien, Bruges, in 1465-6, so he too was no boy.[11] And in any case the
ordinances state that the duties of the *sommeliers* were not primarily musical
(even though they would gain their promotion on the basis of singing ability).
Three of the *sommeliers* were to serve in the duke's private oratory (f. 20,
paragraph 1); the other two were to take turns serving at the altar in High Mass
(paragraph 2); and two (the youngest) were also to sleep near the chapel to
guard it (paragraph 3); moreover their main duties otherwise (paragraphs 4-16,
ff. 20*r*-22*v*) were in the service of the chapel. The passage from f. 13, quoted
above, clearly states that if the *sommeliers* were not occupied otherwise they
should sing with the choir, but it also implies (if I have understood correctly)
that the 6/3/2/3 distribution excludes the *sommeliers*.

The minimum fourteen singers required for polyphony were therefore all
grown men and were from among the twelve chaplains and the five *clercs*.
Moreover, the ordinances also state (paragraph 28, f. 18) that no more than
two men might be absent at any one time. Obviously if as many as four were
absent the numbers would have been insufficient for singing four-voice polyphony.

This particular paragraph continues:

> Ausi il [le premier chapelain] aura regard aux teneurs et contres tellement que le service
> soit tousjours fourny de deux teneurs et de deux contres.

> Also the first chaplain shall keep track of the tenors and contras so that there shall
> always be two tenors and two contras at a service.

That comment seems to conflict with the earlier statement that there must
always be at least three tenors and three contrabasses. It may well refer to less
festal occasions and to three-voice music; but we shall return later to that. What
is particularly important in the present context is the implication that the voices
were not interchangeable: a tenor was a tenor and a contra was a contra.

In his now fragmentary *De inventione et usu musicae* of around 1480,
Tinctoris similarly indicates that each voice was a specialist skill and a career.
He writes:[12]

11   The fullest information on Pierre Basin appears in Georges van Doorslaer, 'La chapelle musicale
     de Philippe le Beau', *Revue belge d'archéologie et d'histoire de l'art*, iv (1934), p. 29. For further
     details, see Fallows, 'Robert Morton's songs', p. 330.
12   Karl Weinmann (ed. Wilhelm Fischer), *Johannes Tinctoris (1445-1511) und sein unbekannter
     Traktat 'De inventione et usu musicae'* (Tutzing, 1961), p. 33.

> Enimvero: alii dicuntur tenoriste: alii contratenoriste: et alii supremi. Preterea: tenoristarum et contratenoristarum alii sunt imi hoc est vulgo bassi: et alii alti. Tenoristas vocamus: qui partes illas cantuum quos tenores appellamus canunt. Contratenoristas: qui contratenores: et supremos: qui supremas. Verum tenoriste et contratenoriste bassi denominantur: qui ad canendos tenores et contratenores bassos apti cognoscuntur: alti vero qui ad altos.

> Indeed: some [singers] are called *tenoristae*, some *contratenoristae* and some *supremi*. Moreover: among *tenoristae* and *contratenoristae* some are lowest, normally called basses, and some are high. *Tenoristae* we call those who sing the parts in music that are called tenor; *contratenoristae* those who sing the contratenor; and *supremi* those who sing the supremus. Some *tenoristae* and *contratenoristae* are called *bassi* when they are recognised as suitable for singing low tenors and contratenors; *alti* when for the high ones.

After that comes the famous passage in which Tinctoris names distinguished exponents of each voice, including Ockeghem as a low contra, Philippe de Passaige (whom we have encountered as the most recently arrived chaplain at the Burgundian court) as a low tenor, and Joannes de Lotinis Dinantinus as a supremus.

One piece of information from this passage merely confirms what would in any case be assumed: that different singers had different ranges and therefore specialised in singing the part that suited their range. Much more surprising, however, is the apparent assertion that *tenorista* and *contratenorista* were so firmly separate. In most surviving music of the time the tenor and the contratenor lines occupy the same range. Similarly, where there are two tenors, the lower tenor normally occupies the same range as the 'contratenor bassus'. An example of this (which can stand for many) is the sixth *L'homme armé* Mass in the Naples manuscript: its ranges are in Example 2.

Example 2. Ranges of Naples *L'homme armé* Mass VI

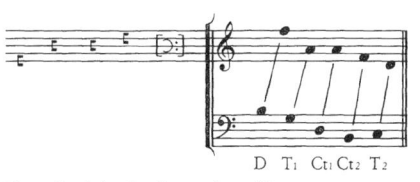

D T₁ Ct₁ Ct₂ T₂

Note· the clef in brackets is derived by canon

Tinctoris therefore contradicts the commonly held assumption that the only difference between tenor and contratenor lines in fifteenth-century polyphony was in their function. Evidently they were differently sung by different kinds of singers.

A similar conclusion comes from the Siena document of July 1481 discovered by Frank D'Accone.[13] The cathedral choir had three apparently adult *soprani* and two contratenors, but the single tenor had failed to return from a leave of absence. The document states that if the authorities had known that he would not return they would have fired the other singers because 'senza tenorista non si può cantare' – you cannot sing without a tenor. What is interesting about this comment is again that, while the tenor lines in the sacred repertoire of that time are basically simpler than the contratenor lines and lie in the same range, apparently neither of the resident contratenors could sing the tenor line.

Similarly, the payment lists for the singers at the Roman chapel of S. Pietro in Vaticano throughout the second half of the century often name the voice taken by a particular singer: 'tenorista', 'contratenorista' or 'suprano'.[14] Unfortunately the singers passed through this choir relatively quickly and it is difficult to use the information to draw inferences about their distribution. But the one clear conclusion is again that drawn from Tinctoris' statement and from the Siena document: that each voice was a specialist skill and a separate career.

Pending further study, it is also difficult to tell which of the many singers at S. Pietro called 'suprano' were grown men. I can only observe that Egidius Crispini who joined that choir as a 'suprano' in 1471 had been in the Duke of Savoy's choir ten years previously.[15] But there is little doubt that grown men were often called soprano. A document from Milan Cathedral dated as early as 1430 names a priest, Ambrosius de Machis, 'qui facit sopranum', as well as a *tenorista* and the composer Feragut 'facientem contratenorem'.[16] And it is in any case quite clear from the documentary information cited above that all the six *haultes voix* at the Burgundian court chapel were mature men.

But even if it is true that 'tenor', 'contratenor' and the rest were specialisations in the fifteenth century and that – contrary to most received opinion – the part-names in fact specified the singers who were to perform each line, this still

13　Frank A. D'Accone, 'The performance of sacred music in Italy during Josquin's time, c. 1475-1525', *Josquin des Prez: Proceedings of the International Josquin Festival-Conference, New York, 1971*, ed. Edward E. Lowinsky in collaboration with Bonnie J. Blackburn (London, 1976), p. 604.

14　Taken from the summarised information in Franz Xaver Haberl, 'Die römische "schola cantorum" und die päpstlichen Kapellsänger bis zur Mitte des 16. Jahrhunderts', *Vierteljahrsschrift für Musikwissenschaft*, iii (1887), pp. 236-8; also printed in Haberl, *Bausteine für Musikgeschichte*, iii (Leipzig, 1888, reprinted Hildesheim, 1971), pp. 48-50. Some of the more comprehensible details are incorporated into D'Accone, 'The performance of sacred music in Italy', p. 603. Fuller details can be found in Christopher A. Reynolds, 'The music chapel at San Pietro in Vaticano in the later fifteenth century' (Ph.D. dissertation, Princeton University, 1981).

15　Marie-Thérèse Bouquet, 'La cappella musicale dei duchi di Savoia dal 1450 al 1500', *Rivista italiana di musicologia*, iii (1968), p. 283; further on Crispini, see David Fallows, *Dufay* (London, 1982), p. 247.

16　Fabio Fano, *La cappella musicale del duomo di Milano*, i: *Le origini e il primo maestro di cappella: Matteo da Perugia*, Istituzioni e monumenti dell'arte musicale italiana, new ser., i (Milan, 1956), pp. 97-8.

tells us little about the pitch at which the choir sang. Given no boys, there are in general terms two alternatives: with or without falsettists.

If the *haultes voix* singing the top line were what we would today call tenors, the singing-range for all four voices would have an upper limit of around g' or a' at the top of the tenor register with (in the case of Example 1) a lower limit of F or E for the basses. This has the advantage that the two voices that are in the same range – the tenor and the contratenor – lie in the most common voice-range today, what one might call a high baritone. Logic might therefore support this low range, but the distribution suggests otherwise. The most surprising feature of the Burgundian court choir distribution of 1469 is that there should be as many as six singers on the top line. In such circumstances the balance at a low pitch would be extremely difficult to achieve: three basses on a line going down to F and E would stand little chance against six tenors at the top of their register. The consequence would surely be either a top-heavy balance or the need for everybody except the basses to sing as quietly as possible. Yet Nanie Bridgman has produced evidence to suggest that in Italy at this time church singing was in fact much louder than chamber singing.[17]

If falsettists were used on the top line the balance would be much easier to attain at a reasonably high dynamic level. Even here the falsettists, if such they were, would have needed to sing rather more quietly than is common for male altos today; but this higher range with the basses going no lower than A or B and the *soprani* going up to c'' or d'' seems much more feasible: all lower voices would be in a powerful range, sufficient to counterbalance the six men on the top line.

Nevertheless this is a purely subjective judgement. Given the present dispute about the early history of the falsetto voice, further evidence is needed. That evidence will emerge later in this discussion.

II. Dufay's Mass for St Anthony of Padua in 1474

It is over a century since Jules Houdoy first published Dufay's will, an amazing document with copious information on many important subjects. One item in it can now be interpreted in rather more detail than hitherto. Among the Masses to be sung in his memory, Dufay requests that on the day of St Anthony of Padua his own Mass for that saint should be sung by the master of the boys and some of the 'better singers':[18]

---

17 Nanie Bridgman, *La vie musicale au quattrocento et jusqu'à la naissance du madrigal (1400-1530)* (Paris, 1964), pp. 197-9. See also Zarlino's identical opinion mentioned in Robert Haas, *Aufführungspraxis der Musik*, Handbuch der Musikwissenschaft, viii (Potsdam, 1931), p. 110.

18 Jules Houdoy, *Histoire artistique de la cathédrale de Cambrai, ancienne église métropolitaine Notre-Dame* (Paris, 1880) [also published as Mémoires de la Société des sciences, de l'agriculture et des arts de Lille, 4th ser., vii (Lille, 1880)], pp. 409-14; this section is on p. 412.

118   David Fallows

> Item statuo in die sancti Anthonii de Padua in predicta capella perpetuo missam de
> eodem sancto . . . in qua assint magister puerorum et alii quicumque sufficientiores
> de choro, sive sint magni vicarii seu parvi, vel capellani, ad provisionem tamen
> dictorum magnorum vicariorum, qui missam per me compositam decantent, quibus
> assigno 30 solidos, inde quilibet 3 solidos 4 denarios.

> Item: I ordain that on the day of St Anthony of Padua in that chapel there should be a
> Mass for that saint . . . at which are present the master of the boys and several other of
> the better singers from the choir, whether they be *grands vicaires* or *petits vicaires* (or
> chaplains, in which case they should be paid for by the said *grands vicaires*), who
> should sing the Mass composed by me; and I assign for that 30s, from which each shall
> receive 3s 4d.

If each singer received 3s 4d, the sum of 30s was sufficient for nine singers.
And since the singers were to be chosen from among the *grands vicaires*, the
petits vicaires and the chaplains they were presumably all grown men.

Dufay's Mass for St Anthony of Padua can now be identified. The full argument has been published elsewhere,[19] but the conclusions can be summarised as
follows:

(*a*) from Dufay's will we know that he composed a Mass for St Anthony of
Padua and a Mass for St Anthony Abbot (*Sancti Antonii Viennensis*);

(*b*) the five three-part Ordinary movements published in the complete edition
as Dufay's Mass for St Anthony *Viennensis*[20] are quite certainly movements
from the Mass for St Anthony of Padua, as is particularly clear from Spataro's
Tractato di musica (1531) and his letter to Pietro Aron of 1532 (which means
that the Mass for St Anthony *Viennensis* is probably lost);

(*c*) the cycle also contained Proper movements, most probably including at
least some of those in the cycle of Propers for St Anthony of Padua in the manuscript *I-TRmn* 88, published by Laurence Feininger in 1947 with hypothetical
attributions to Dufay;[21]

(*d*) much of this music seems to have been composed in the 1440s.

This reconstructed plenary cycle for St Anthony of Padua is not without its
problems. The Ordinary movements as well as the Gradual and Alleluia seem
secure; the Introit contains no direct evidence that it is by Dufay but it is in a
style that leaves little doubt that it is his; on the other hand the Offertory and
Communion may well be liable to considerable doubt. They are at a lower pitch
– almost certainly because of the mode of the chants on which they are based.
And the Offertory is in four parts whereas the rest of the cycle is of three-part
music. So their position within the complete cycle is open to question, and for

19   Fallows, *Dufay*, pp. 182-92.
20   Heinrich Besseler, ed., *Guillelmi Dufay: Opera omnia*, Corpus mensurabilis musicae, i (Rome,
     1951-66), vol. 2, pp. 47-68. A more accurate transcription appears in Rudolf Bockholdt,
     Die frühen Messenkompositionen von Guillaume Dufay, Münchner Veröffentlichungen zur
     Musikgeschichte, v (Tutzing, 1960), vol. 2, pp. 68-86.
21   Laurence Feininger, ed., *Auctorum anonymorum missarum propria XVI, quorum XI Gulielmo
     Dufay auctori adscribenda sunt*, Monumenta polyphoniae liturgicae sanctae ecclesiae romanae,
     2nd ser., i (Rome, 1947), pp. 134-47.

the purposes of further examination they are best left aside (though it is easy to integrate them with the rest by transposing them up a fourth).

For the main body of the cycle, however, the ranges are as in Example 3. No movement has the full range in all three voices, but the unusually wide ranges here are not open to question: the second Agnus Dei, for instance, uses the entire fourteen-note range of the discantus, as does the Credo; and the Credo has the entire thirteen-note range of the contratenor.

Example 3. Ranges of Dufay, Mass for St Anthony of Padua

Note: clefs in parentheses denote changes between and within movements.

Once again, if all three voices were taken by men, probability favours the use of pitches that more or less correspond to modern pitch, in which case the singers on the top line must have used falsetto. But one could also accept the possibility of transposition downwards by a fourth. Here the top line would rise to a *c"* – which would still presumably require the singers to move into a head-voice for the highest notes.

How should the nine singers that Dufay required be divided among the three lines? Based on the singing of modern ensembles, 3/3/3 might seem the obvious answer; but the surviving information from the fifteenth century suggests something rather different. The Burgundian court choir's distribution 6/3/2/3 for four-part music gives the top line at least twice as many singers as any other line. And a similar conclusion arises from what it is possible to discern from the accounts of S. Pietro in Vaticano: the clearest information is for the year 1484 when there were five *suprani*, two tenors and two contratenors.[22] This is attractive since *bassi* are not mentioned in the accounts until 1490 and it seems likely that this choir concentrated on three-part music until then. For what it is worth, three-part polyphony takes up by far the greater proportion of the Vatican manuscript S. Pietro B 80 which seems to be for that choir in the late 1470s.[23] Yet the figures from S. Pietro in Vaticano need treating with considerable caution: as already noted, the singers came and went there so quickly that firm conclusions are dangerous; moreover, it is hardly likely that a choir with such a rapid turnover could represent the highest ideals

22   Haberl, 'Die römische "schola cantorum"', p. 238 (p. 50). The one singer whose voice is not specified there is Hieronymus Pazzillis, who is described as a contra in the next year.
23   Christopher Reynolds, 'The origins of San Pietro B 80 and the development of a Roman sacred repertory', *Early Music History*, i (1981), pp. 257-304.

120   David Fallows

in its performance standards.[24] But the Burgundian court information should be taken seriously and to some extent supports the findings at S. Pietro. Beyond that, we have already seen that the ordinances stipulated that there should never be fewer than two voices on the tenor or the contratenor and that this stipulation seemed to concern three-part music.

Would a 5/2/2 distribution work musically? At modern concert pitch and in the three-part sections there is little problem, even though the cycle shows considerable equality of contrapuntal importance in the lines. In the many duo sections, however, it seems more than likely that solo voices were used – not only because a distribution of 5/2 is more difficult to balance (nearly all the duos involve the discantus) but also because the entire cycle contains over an hour's worth of polyphony and there would otherwise be some danger of exhaustion, particularly for the singers on the top line. With that in mind, even remembering that the supporting information is extremely scanty, a 5/2/2 distribution seems an acceptable solution for Dufay's Mass for St Anthony of Padua.

At least, that is apparently how he wished it to be performed – or was prepared to pay for it to be performed – after his death in 1474. Dufay's will and probate, taken as a whole, suggest that although the composer was in his last years extremely stingy where others were concerned he was at least generous in providing for the salvation of his soul.[25]

What of the time when the work was composed, perhaps a quarter of a century earlier? There is further circumstantial evidence that he used the same ensemble. I have elsewhere argued that the cycle could have been composed, or at least completed, for the dedication of Donatello's high altar in the Basilica of S. Antonio at Padua on 13 June 1450.[26] The cornerstone of that argument was simply that, two weeks before the dedication, Dufay stopped a few nights in Turin, in transit from Cambrai to an unknown destination, and he had with him nine *religiosi* – precisely the number of singers named for that Mass in his will. There is a danger of circular arguments here; but if there should be any value in my hypothesis that he was on his way to Padua to perform his Mass for that saint, then it suggests in turn that the scoring he demanded in 1474 also applies to the time of the work's composition shortly before 1450.

III. Dufay's four-part antiphon 'Ave regina celorum' in 1474

A much more famous passage from Dufay's will tells us about the use of choirboys in polyphony. He directs that his own antiphon *Ave regina celorum*

24   Reynolds, 'The music chapel at San Pietro in Vaticano', pp. 195-200. The earliest mention of a bass (one year earlier than that registered by Haberl) is cited on pp. 187-8. I am grateful to Professor Reynolds for allowing me to see the relevant pages of his study before it became generally available.
25   Fallows, *Dufay*, pp. 80-2.
26   Fallows, *Dufay*, pp. 66-8.

should be sung at his deathbed – and surely this was the late four-part setting with its interpolated tropes in which Dufay prays for his soul. As performers he specifies 'pueri altaris, una cum magistro eorum et duobus ex sociis' – the altar boys with their master and two other men.[27] Given the voice-ranges of the piece, shown in Example 4, clearly one man sang each of the lower voices and from four to six choirboys sang the discantus. Presumably, too, the written pitches here more or less correspond to their modern equivalents.

Example 4. Ranges of Dufay, *Ave regina celorum* (4 voices)

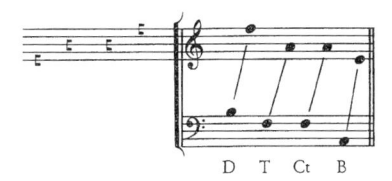

D   T   Ct   B

There is further documentation, also from Cambrai, for this different kind of ensemble, using boys but more lightly scored in the lower parts. In 1457 a Mass in memory of Jean d'Anchin required singing in polyphony by the choir-boys, their master and two contratenors[28] – though at that relatively early date there must be some doubt whether they really sang four-part polyphony.

Much more specific is the famous letter of Jachetto di Marvilla written from Rome in March 1469. Responding to Lorenzo de' Medici's apparently detailed requirements for a new choir at the Florence Baptistery, he offered to provide the following musicians: 'three very high treble singers with good, full and suave voices'; 'a good tenor who has a large voice, high and low, sweet and sufficient'; and a contratenor who was to be Jachetto himself and was therefore unfortunately not characterised. But we do know that this ensemble was speci-fically for three-part music, because Jachetto added that for four-part singing 'Bartholomeo could be the bass', pending the appointment of a more suitable singer from France.[29] Since no firmly Florentine musical manuscripts survive from this generation it is difficult to know what music Jachetto had in mind; moreover, his proposal was not accepted, and the ensemble never took up

---

27   Houdoy, *Histoire artistique*, p. 410; the work is printed in Besseler, *Dufay: Opera omnia*, v, pp. 124-30. Note that the information on the scoring of this antiphon cannot be transferred to Dufay's related Mass *Ave regina celorum* because the contra and bassus lines in the Mass both divide; moreover the discantus in the Mass goes down to low *g* in the second canonic part of the second Christe.

28   Craig Wright, 'Performance practices at the cathedral of Cambrai, 1475-1550', *The Musical Quarterly*, lxiv (1978), p. 301.

29   Frank A. D'Accone, 'The singers of San Giovanni in Florence during the 15th century', *Journal of the American Musicological Society*, xiv (1961), p. 324. It may be relevant to add that the proposed extra singer was to be one who could sing contratenor as well as bass. Reynolds, 'The music chapel at San Pietro in Vaticano', pp. 187-8, observes that the first bass at S. Pietro was a man who had previously appeared on the payment lists as a tenor.

122   David Fallows

residence in Florence. But such an ensemble does seem to have been fairly standard. There is also evidence of a slightly larger number of boys having been supported by what seems to have been double scoring on the men's voices: in 1478 Florence Cathedral had four boys plus their master, two *contras* and two tenors (figures which give rise to the pressing question of whether the master doubled one of the lower voices, doubled the boys or remained silent); and slightly later a conflation of information from 1479 and 1483, also at Florence Cathedral, gives eight boys, two *contra alti*, one tenor and two *contrabassi* plus the master of the boys (perhaps answering the previous question and suggesting in this case that the master doubled the single tenor).[30]

These details are surely less useful than the information in Dufay's will because they are not related to specific works, they are not coupled with assurances that everybody took part in polyphonic singing at the same time, and they are associated with an institution that, while it certainly had the right to expect the highest standards, did not have the distinguished and long tradition of Cambrai Cathedral. Nevertheless, the resulting information more or less fits in with what we would expect in a choir with boys on the top part: there are three or four times as many singers on the boys' line as on any of the others.

Craig Wright has recently provided considerable evidence to suggest that during the last quarter of the fifteenth century two distinct kinds of polyphonic choir performed at Cambrai Cathedral: one entirely of men and the other of boys with their master and possibly one or two other singers.[31] And it seems likely that this tradition went back some years. But the early history of choirboys singing polyphony is one of those tricky subjects fraught with the danger of misinterpreted or overinterpreted documents;[32] and sometimes in such situations the clearest answers come from the music.

There are in fact five works from the first half of the fifteenth century which seem to juxtapose the two kinds of choir that Wright identified, thereby not only adding confirmation to his suggestions and projecting them backwards in time, but also answering some of the unresolved questions of the present investigation.

(1) H. Battre's *Gaude virgo*[33] opens with a three-part section in which the upper part is marked 'mutate voces' – changed or broken voices. The next section is written on the facing page: here the clefs have changed and all three voices are marked 'pueri'. How the broken voices and the boys are distributed

---

30   D'Accone, 'The singers of San Giovanni', pp. 328-9.
31   Wright, 'Performance practices at the cathedral of Cambrai', pp. 305-6.
32   The best and most interesting study of the matter to date is by James T. Igoe, 'Performance practices in the polyphonic Mass of the early fifteenth century' (Ph.D. dissertation, University of North Carolina at Chapel Hill, 1971).
33   *I-TRmn* 87, ff. 262v-264v. It is edited by Rudolf von Ficker in *Geistliche und weltliche Kompositionen des XIV. und XV. Jhs.: Sieben Trienter Codices: VI. Auswahl*, Denkmäler der Tonkunst in Österreich, lxxvi, Jg. 40 (Vienna, 1933), pp. 90-1.

in the remainder of the piece is not always entirely clear.[34] But for the fully marked opening sections the ranges are as in Example 5a; and according to my reading of the work the total ranges are as in Example 5b. If the 'pueri' sang the line that goes down to tenor *a*, then it would surely be unrealistic to contemplate a singing pitch much below modern concert pitch. And in that case the 'mutate voces' would involve at least some degree of falsetto or head-voice – as indeed the very existence of the marking might imply.

Example 5. Ranges of Battre, *Gaude virgo*

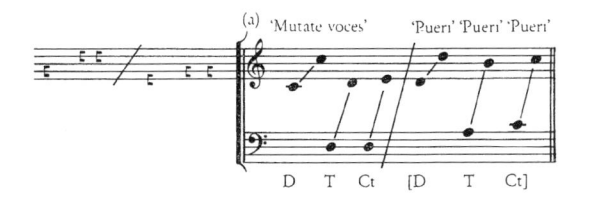 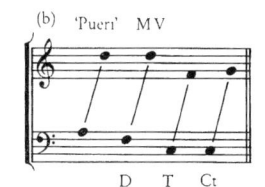

(2) A troped Gloria by Bourgois[35] contrasts sections marked 'chorus' with sections for a different ensemble in which the top line is marked 'pueri' and the two lower voices move into a slightly higher range. There are also four-part sections in which the two groups seem to combine; and, as in the Battre, there are several sections in which there is no clear information about the singers required, though the general pattern is that the 'pueri' are used for the trope sections. The tenor and contratenor for the 'chorus' have rests while the 'pueri' sing; and the tenor and contratenor for the sections with 'pueri' are notated separately. In the passages where the markings are unambiguous,[36] the ranges are as in Example 6a; according to my reading the total ranges are as in Example 6b.

Example 6. Ranges of Bourgois, Gloria

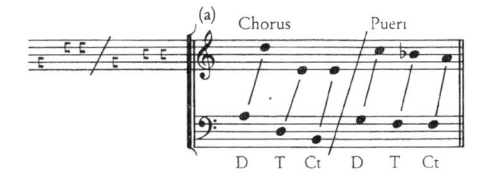 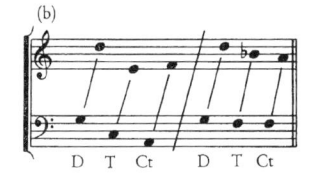

34 Ficker's edition is slightly misleading, particularly in not noting that the annotation 'Pueri' at bar 81 is editorial. At bar 73 the top part of the main choir rests while the two lower voices accompany the 'pueri' for the words 'ubi fructus ventris tui' to open the final three-line stanza of the poem. For the remainder of the piece there is only one top part. This has a C1 clef which is otherwise used only for the 'pueri', but the part was presumably also sung by the 'mutate voces' who otherwise have C2 clef (and C3 for one line on f. 263*v*).

35 *I-TRmn* 87, ff. 39*v*-43*r*. It is edited by Ficker in *Geistliche und weltliche Kompositionen des XV. Jhs.: Sieben Trienter Codices: V. Auswahl*, Denkmäler der Tonkunst in Österreich, lxi, Jg. 31 (Vienna, 1924), pp. 67-71. The work also appears anonymously in *I-TRmn* 88, ff. 323*v*-327*r*, but without the annotations for 'chorus' and 'pueri'.

36 Bars 82-136 and 197-238. The marking 'chorus' in the tenor at bar 19 remains unexplained in my reconstruction.

124   David Fallows

(3) Dufay's Sanctus 'Papale'[37] does not mention boys, but its layout suggests a plan similar to that in the Bourgois Gloria. Like the Bourgois work it is troped and evinces a slightly different kind of scoring for the trope sections. I have suggested elsewhere[38] that the work was, like the others, probably designed for performance by an adult choir for the words of the Sanctus itself and a contrasting choir of boys plus their master, with (in one passage) an additional contratenor, for the settings of the trope text *Ave verum corpus*; in addition it is possible that both groups took part at certain points, particularly the first 'Osanna' which in two sources has passages in six parts. The evidence of the ranges (Example 7) is in this case less impressive than the stylistic shift in the music and the abrupt clef-changes between sections in the manuscripts. The sceptical reader may well have to refer to the music and to my previous discussion of the work.

Example 7. Ranges of Dufay, Sanctus 'Papale'

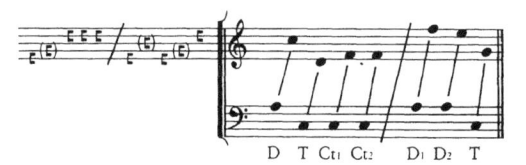

D   T   Ct₁ Ct₂   D₁ D₂   T

Note: clefs in parentheses denote changes within and between sections.

(4) and (5) A Gloria–Credo pair by Binchois[39] in which two opposing groups have the same range in the discantus but different ranges in the lower voices. In the manuscripts these two works are laid out as for four voices: [discantus], tenor, contratenor and 'subcontra'. None of the available editions presents them in quite that way, partly because all the manuscripts show evidence of confusion at some point or other. And indeed there are a few brief sections in four voices in both movements. But for the main body of both there seem to be two clearly defined groups: the first and almost certainly larger group is of the normal discantus, tenor and contratenor; while the second is of discantus, subcontra and tenor (which happens to have been copied into the contratenor line of the first group, though it unmistakably takes over the function of a tenor in these passages). The evidence of the works by Battre, Bourgois and Dufay mentioned above suggests that Binchois had in mind two opposing and contrasted choirs with different ranges in the lower voices, as in Example 8.

37   Edited in Besseler, *Dufay: Opera omnia*, iv, pp. 45-8. In that edition the second voice of section 'C' is written an octave too low; the second contratenor in sections 'D' and 'I' appears in only some of the sources.
38   Fallows, *Dufay*, pp. 179-81. The work is further discussed by Alejandro Planchart in the present volume, pp. 237ff.
39   Among various other sources, both movements appear together in *I-TRmn* 87, ff. 25v-29v, and *I-TRmn* 92, ff. 25v-30r. They are edited in Ficker, *Geistliche . . . V. Auswahl*, pp. 55-61.

Example 8. Ranges of Binchois, Gloria–Credo pair

D   T   Ct   D   'Ct'(T) 'Subcontra'

Note· the second voice of the second choir is labelled 'contra' but functions as a tenor.

In all these works it should be clear that the differences in range are not by themselves sufficient to demonstrate the truth of my analysis: the lower voices in Dufay's Mass for St Anthony of Padua (Example 3) each have a range quite as large as that obtained if we allot those in any of the above-mentioned works to a single group of singers. But the clear contrast between the sections in these works is entirely different from the more gradually evolving range of the Mass for St Anthony of Padua. Physical and technical considerations, then, make it possible to score the works for a single group of singers; but their layout, musical style and form suggest that in all five works the composers were working with an antiphonal scheme. And it is certainly true that the existence of two kinds of polyphonic ensemble, as proposed by Craig Wright for the later years of the century, would make these works relatively easy to perform impressively in any large choral institution. The Burgundian court, as an example, had a group of choirboys and their master. That group was normally kept separate from the main court chapel choir[40] but may have been required to perform with it for special occasions.

More important, however, if the foregoing analysis of these works is correct, it tells us something about the sounding pitch of the music. With boys taking part, these particular pieces can scarcely have been much lower than modern concert pitch. The crucial conclusion from this is that the men who sang lines marked 'tenor' and 'contratenor' – who, as we have seen, were specialists – apparently operated normally in a range from tenor c to g', which is to say that they correspond more or less to modern-day tenor range, not the lower range that has occasionally been proposed and was retained as a feasible hypothesis earlier in this enquiry. And, of course, if that higher range is correct for those singing the 'tenor' and 'contratenor' lines, then the grown men who sang the discantus – in the Burgundian court document mentioned in section I above

40 See Craig Wright, *Music at the court of Burgundy 1364-1419: a documentary history*, Musicological Studies, xxviii (Henryville, 1979), pp. 92-8; see also Marix, *Histoire de la musique*, pp. 135-8, 141, 143, 160-3. On this last page there is a document recording the foundation of Philip the Good's choir school at Dijon in 1425, where the choirboys were to celebrate each Saturday a Mass 'laquelle sera chantée . . . a note deschant et orgues, le plus solennlement que faire se pourra'. Both Philip and his son Duke Charles the Bold only rarely visited Dijon, preferring to remain in the north where their riches lay.

126   David Fallows

and in the directions for performing Dufay's Mass for St Anthony of Padua in section II – must have sung falsetto.

Indeed, it was again Craig Wright who first drew attention to another passage in Dufay's will which even without this information had seemed to specify falsetto singing. The will itself, which is in Latin, asks that eight adult singers at his deathbed should sing the hymn *Magno salutis gaudio* 'submissa voce'; and the executors' account of the will, which happens to be in French, quotes the same phrase with the words 'submissa voce' translated as 'en fausset'. Wright produces several further documents leading to the same conclusion.[41] His parallel suggestion that the falsettists were young men is well supported by the documents he presents there; but he also draws attention to some older men singing soprano in the sixteenth century, and the evidence on the ages of Burgundian court singers (cited above) shows clearly that falsettists were not necessarily so young. Given that mature men sang the discantus line, that boys sang in the same range, that tenors and contratenors were specialists singing lines that would normally occupy the range $c - g'$ if the discantus is adjusted to a range possible for boys, and given the information on ranges offered by Roger Bowers elsewhere in this volume, this surely more or less resolves the question of the normal performing pitch for fifteenth-century polyphony.

IV. The lower parts

At the same time it would be dangerous to regard these answers as relevant for all polyphonic singing in the fifteenth century. The answers are based on only a very small number of documents, selected because they are the only ones that seem sufficiently specific to serve as a basis for assertions about polyphonic performances but nonetheless so few in number that it would be absurd to assume that they represent the whole picture.

The information presented above makes no mention of instruments. There is of course some evidence, from as early as the beginning of the century, that the

---

41   Wright, 'Performance practices at the cathedral of Cambrai', pp. 308-13; see especially p. 309 where a document of 1536 again equates the two words – though it might just be wise to interject a note of caution by observing that the latter document describes choirboys as learning to sing *en fausset*. Wright interprets this as meaning that the boys were taught to sing falsetto in preparation for the day when their voice would break; but that explanation is slightly perplexing and the document could well be evidence that both 'submissa voce' and 'en fausset' meant something else entirely. Certainly, without the evidence of the actual pieces discussed above these documents would not be sufficient to demonstrate falsetto singing at that time. In general, the early history of falsetto singing is ripe for considerable further investigation – though an important contribution is Franz Müller-Heuser, *Vox humana: ein Beitrag zur Untersuchung der Stimm-ästhetik des Mittelalters* (Regensburg, 1963), especially pp. 124-32, 'Stimmregister'. Perhaps the most striking testimony to early falsetto singing is in Hermann Müller's magisterial study of Roger Bacon's comments on music, 'Zur Musikauffassung des 13. Jahrhunderts', *Archiv für Musikwissenschaft*, iv (1932), p. 410, where Müller shows that Bacon is almost certainly discussing falsetto singing as being part of the polyphonic tradition of his time.

organ and indeed other instruments occasionally took part in sacred poly-phony.[42] Particularly tantalising in this respect is Ulrich von Richental's famous eye-witness description of English musicians at the Council of Constance in 1416 who sang Vespers 'with organs and *prosunen* [slide-trumpets] above which were tenor, discant and medius'.[43] With that sort of information it is difficult to make much progress, except to say that it described a kind of ensemble rather different from the ones described in the more specific documents. In short, I am not excluding other kinds of ensemble but merely saying that the two possibilities that come down in the specific documentation happen to be for performance by singers alone. That to some extent endorses the conclusions reached by James McKinnon's survey of pictorial representations of the sung Mass through the middle ages: '*a cappella* ecclesiastical performance was the norm'.[44]

This raises the question of how the lower voices were texted, given that the surviving polyphonic sources from the fifteenth century tend to confine texting to the discantus line. Three particularly promising suggestions have been offered, and I believe that all three reflect practices that were current.

42 A few examples can be mentioned. In 1385 the Mass for a double princely wedding at St Aubert in Cambrai included 'molt brafs cantres et flusteurs musicals'. In 1389 Philippe de Mézières, in his *Le songe du vieil pelerin* (chapter 6), warns against excessive use of musicians; but of the 'grosses trompes sacrees' he says that at high feasts they should play softly at the Elevation of the Holy Sacrament. Jean Gerson, in his *De canticorum originali ratione* (before 1426), states that the organ is the only instrument that can play in church but that it is sometimes joined by trumpets, more rarely by *bombardes, chalemelies*, or large or small *cornemuses*. Giannozzo Manetti's description of the dedication of Florence Cathedral in 1436 mentions many instruments sounding together at the Elevation of the Host. In 1447 Guillaume Chartier is elected Bishop of Paris: an organ supports the singers in the Gloria and Te Deum. In 1480 a French calendar from Vienne distinguishes between feasts requiring only singers and those in which instruments (*banda*) are used as well. These are all well known and are summarised in studies such as André Pirro, 'Remarques sur l'exécution musicale de la fin du 14e au milieu du 15e siècle', *International Musicological Society Congress Report, Liège 1930* (Burnham, 1931), pp. 55-65 (this is perhaps the most notable of all studies of the subject), the first chapter of André Pirro, *Histoire de la musique de la fin du XIVe siècle à la fin du XVIe* (Paris, 1940), and Richard Rastall, 'Minstrelsy, church and clergy in medieval England', *Proceedings of the Royal Musical Association*, xcvii (1970-1), pp. 83-98; iconographic support for this view appears in Edmund A. Bowles, *Musikleben im 15. Jahrhundert*, Musikgeschichte in Bildern, 3rd ser., viii (Leipzig, 1977), Plates 1, 2, 5 and 7. In all these cases, where the information is specific it refers to instruments at the Elevation: and the opportunities for the use of instruments in church are sharply delineated in Frank Ll. Harrison, 'Tradition and innovation in instrumental usage 1100-1450', *Aspects of medieval and renaissance music: a birthday offering to Gustave Roosa*, ed. Jan LaRue (New York, 1966), p. 328. Yet the presence of instruments in church, often during the Mass, encourages the belief that they could sometimes have taken part in polyphony even if this was by no means the norm. The payment lists for the Savoy court chapel in the years 1450-5 include alongside the singers and the organist a single 'tromba', see Bouquet, 'La cappella musicale dei duchi di Savoia'.

43 Manfred Schuler, 'Die Musik in Konstanz während des Konzils 1414-1418', *Acta musicologica*, xxxviii (1966), p. 159.

44 James W. McKinnon, 'Representations of the Mass in medieval and renaissance art', *Journal of the American Musicological Society*, xxxi (1978), pp. 21-52. On a note of caution, and referring back to my opening paragraphs, it should be said that very few of the pictures discussed by McKinnon show any evidence that polyphony is being sung.

128   David Fallows

First, that rather more of the large Mass cycles were polytextual than we have perhaps assumed. Thus recent research is beginning to show, for instance, that in Dufay's Masses *Ecce ancilla Domini* and *Ave regina celorum* the text of the cantus firmus was probably added not only to the chant-based tenor but also to the lowest voice (which in some sources has the title 'secundus tenor').[45] Clearly, however, this is a solution applicable to only a limited number of works.

Second, that long notes and ligatures could be divided up by any intelligent singer so that the Mass text, for instance, could be sung to the long-note lines of the lower voices just as easily as to the more syllabic lines of the discantus.[46] There are in fact examples of works in which the long-note tenor of one source is divided up into shorter notes in another source.[47] An extempore solution of this kind almost certainly presupposes that there is only one singer on each of the lower voices, but that is a distribution implied in several of the documents cited above in passing. What is intriguing here is that the line that is always texted in the sources, the discantus, is the only line that almost invariably had several singers performing it. So it might conceivably be possible to argue that the text was underlaid to the discantus in order to coordinate the texting whereas it was not necessary on the lower voices which were taken by one singer each.

The third suggestion is that the lower voices were in fact vocalised without any text. And this leads to the only other surviving work by Dufay that contains any clear information about the ensemble used. His non-isorhythmic motet *Inclita stella maris*[48] is probably from the mid 1420s. It has two upper voices that take the same line in mensural canon: that is to say that they start in unison but move further and further apart until by the end there is a distance of twenty-one semibreves between them. Their texting is almost entirely syllabic except for the extended closing 'Amen' section. Below these are two lines, both called 'contratenor', in generally longer note-values, untexted and heavily ligatured. Perhaps the singers on the contratenor lines sang the text as best they

45   Alejandro Enrique Planchart, 'Guillaume Dufay's Masses: a view of the manuscript traditions', *Papers read at the Dufay Quincentenary Conference, Brooklyn, 1974*, ed. Allan W. Atlas (Brooklyn, 1976), pp. 43-9; Gareth R. K. Curtis, 'Brussels, Bibliothèque Royale MS. 5557, and the texting of Dufay's "Ecce ancilla Domini" and "Ave regina celorum" Masses', *Acta musicologica*, li (1979), pp. 73-86.

46   So far as I know, this was first fully argued in Gilbert Reaney, 'Text underlay in early fifteenth-century musical manuscripts', *Essays in musicology in honor of Dragan Plamenac on his 70th birthday*, ed. Gustave Reese and Robert J. Snow (Pittsburgh, 1969), pp. 245-51; it is further expanded in Gareth R. K. Curtis, 'The English Masses of Brussels, Bibliothèque royale, MS. 5557' (Ph.D. dissertation, University of Manchester, 1979), i, pp. 143-55.

47   Margaret Bent, 'New sacred polyphonic fragments of the early quattrocento', *Studi musicali*, ix (1980), pp. 174-5; Reaney, 'Text underlay', p. 247. For a later generation, see Wolfgang Osthoff, *Theatergesang und darstellende Musik in der italienischen Renaissance*, Münchner Veröffentlichungen zur Musikgeschichte, xiv (Tutzing, 1969), i, pp. 100-1.

48   Edited in Besseler, *Dufay: Opera omnia*, i, pp. 1-5, from its only source, Bologna, Civico Museo Bibliografico Musicale [*I-Bc*] Q 15.

could; but the phrase-structure suggests otherwise, and in any case it is difficult to know quite how the singers would judge when to change syllable since the two upper voices declaim their text at such different rates. In some works of this time with two equal upper voices and two equal lower voices it is possible to discern some kind of pairing, each upper voice having its complement in one of the lower voices. But although the structure of *Inclita stella maris* evinces such pairing, that could scarcely help the singer on a lower part to judge his text distribution, as is clear from the opening, given in Example 9.

Example 9. Dufay, *Inclita stella maris*

Far more likely is that they were indeed untexted, either played on instruments or vocalised. As it happens, the piece has an elaborate set of performance rubrics, allowing for the canon to be sung or not, for the lower voices to be added singly, and so on. Below the second contratenor is the following instruction:

> Secundus contratenor concordans cum omnibus: non potest cantari nisi pueri dicant fugam.

> Second contratenor concording with the rest: it cannot be sung unless the boys say the canon.

130   David Fallows

Two conclusions perhaps follow. First, the writer of the instruction (presumably the composer) envisaged the canon being sung by boys, not men. This conclusion rules out the possible interpretation that the second contratenor was to be sung only when the canon was sung by boys rather than by men; but for the present purposes this slight ambiguity in the Latin is irrelevant since it does at least make clear that boys on the upper parts were mandatory in the full four-voice version. And, if boys were singing, we must assume that transposition downwards in relation to modern concert pitch is out of the question, since the line goes down to *g*. That *g* appears only twice, but the *a* is often an extremely important note; perhaps the piece should actually be transposed upwards.

The second conclusion is that the writer of the instructions seems to have had in mind some distinction between the procedure of 'dicere', which the boys did on the top parts, and 'cantare', which happened to the lower voices. Certainly there is the possibility here that the writer was merely including the elegant variation that was a hallmark of enlightened Latin prose. But it seems likely that 'dicere' - in this particular case - means to sing with text whereas 'cantare' means to sing without text, to vocalise. Obviously, this is not a general linguistic observation. Any dictionary can give a whole range of meanings for both words. 'Dicere' can mean to say, to pray, to sing, to narrate and much else besides. 'Cantare' can be to sing, to shout, to perform on instruments – which could be relevant here – to do what birds do, and so on. We still talk of birds singing, violins singing, even, in certain circumstances, pianos singing.

But, in general, the idea that the bottom voices here were vocalised is surely the most likely. Whatever the cautions voiced earlier, instruments were clearly extremely rare in performances of sacred polyphony. An organ would have some difficulty in using the same copy used by the singers and would have even more difficulty in playing these two overlapping voices together from separately written parts. Vocalising may not always have been the performing medium used, but it was surely the most frequent. And it therefore seems likely that the writer's distinction between 'dicere' and 'cantare' was a specific rather than merely a literary one.[49]

---

49   Craig Wright, 'Voices and instruments in the art music of northern France during the 15th century: a conspectus', *International Musicological Society Congress Report, Berkeley, 1977*, ed. Daniel Heartz and Bonnie Wade (Kassel, 1981), p. 647 n. 25, draws attention to a use of the verb *dire* ('ne dit riens') in the tenor of Cambrai, Bibliothèque Municipale [*F-CA*] 11, f. 36r. This too could be an instruction to vocalise without adding text. After I had delivered the paper of which this is an extensively revised and expanded version, Professor James McKinnon mentioned to me that Craig Wright's paper had covered similar material; but the full extent of the overlap did not become clear until the published version became available to me in May 1982, through the kind offices of Clifford Bartlett. Whatever the embarrassment of the overlap, there is some comfort in knowing that Craig Wright and I, working independently and approaching the material quite differently, should have reached broadly similar conclusions on several matters. A further relevant detail which I had overlooked is mentioned below in note 88.

If so, it is possible to be fairly confident in predicting the correct performing forces. Since one of the top lines divides into two for the last note, at least two singers are required. Given that the normal group of boy trebles was four or six at this time, it seems clear enough that we are talking about two or three on each part. And given the disposition already discussed for Dufay's antiphon *Ave regina celorum* we can also say with some confidence that one man on each of the lower voices is the most likely allocation.

V. The song repertoire

Another work by Dufay from about the same date is syntactically similar to *Inclita stella maris*. This is the rondeau *Par droit je puis bien complaindre et gemir* (Example 10).[50] Here, the upper-voice canon is simple rather than mensural, the ranges are slightly different, and the different mensuration brings

Example 10. Dufay, *Par droit je puis*

---

50   Edited in Besseler, *Dufay: Opera omnia*, vi, p. 62; it appears in both Oxford, Bodleian Library [*GB-Ob*] Canonici misc. 213 and *I-Bc* Q 15.

with it differences in melodic line. Yet it is similar in several ways, particularly in contrapuntal syntax: in both, the canonic upper voices form between them the discantus–tenor pair which is more commonly formed by voices in different ranges; and the two lower voices are similarly labelled in the two pieces – both called 'contratenor' but the second called 'contratenor concordans cum omnibus'.

If we agree that vocalisation is appropriate for the two contratenors of *Inclita stella maris*, what are the reasons for believing that those of *Par droit je puis* cannot also be vocalised? The simple answer to that question is that repeated notes play an important role in the lower lines of the song whereas they are relatively rare in those of the motet. But it is also possible to say that there is no reason whatever why singers on the lower lines of the song could not articulate the repeated notes with simple consonants.

That may seem a wild suggestion; and I am the first to accept that it contradicts one's musical instincts about the piece. But, at the same time, there appears to be very little conclusive evidence for polyphonic songs having been sung as we would now expect – that is, with instruments on the untexted lower voices. There are of course several pictures of a singer with some instrumentalists, and there are descriptions of such groups performing;[51] but they are remarkably few in number, are mostly from very late in the fifteenth century, and in almost all cases leave no clear evidence – or even indication – that the musicians were performing a written polyphonic chanson.[52] To repeat: the central theme of this whole enquiry is the difficulty of knowing whether a particular item of evidence concerns monophonic music, perhaps with improvised accompaniment, or whether it concerns composed polyphony.

There is plenty of evidence that Italians sang to their own accompaniment on the lute or *viola* late in the century, though the accompaniments were ap-

51   The most recent summary of this evidence is Howard Mayer Brown, 'Instruments and voices in the fifteenth-century chanson', *Current thought in musicology*, ed. John W. Grubbs (Austin, Texas, 1976), pp. 89-137. Brown supports the voices-only approach as one possibility, pp. 93-5, following a lead from Besseler (though here too it is possible to interpret the evidence in a variety of ways). The lack of clear evidence for instrumental accompaniment is also raised in Howard Mayer Brown, *Music in the French secular theater, 1400-1550* (Cambridge, Mass., 1963), pp. 98-9.

52   For voices and instruments together in polyphony the strongest evidence is an illumination from a late fifteenth-century *Roman de la rose* (London, British Library [*GB-Lbm*] Harley 4425, f. 12v; reproduced in Robert Wangermée, *La musique flamande dans la société des XVe et VIe siècles*, Brussels, 1966, Plate 44), and one in the early sixteenth-century song partbook *B-Br* IV. 90, f. 11v (see Brown, 'Instruments and voices', Plate 9). An especially perplexing case is that of the famous tapestry of a lady playing a harp and apparently watching a scroll of music beneath which are the words 'De ce que fol pensé'. Although the music itself is unrecognisable here, it just happens that the harp has seven strings, the same as the number of notes in the unusual range of the tenor line of Pierre de Molins' chanson *De ce que fol pensé*. But whether this is evidence that she is actually playing the tenor of a polyphonic song, or that she was playing another setting entirely, or that the words were merely added as a motto for the picture, it seems impossible to say. This tapestry is discussed by Tilman Seebass in the present volume, and illustrated in his Plate 1.

parently largely improvised.[53] There is also evidence of instrumental ensembles and soloists performing polyphonically, even evidence that some of them based their work on extant polyphonic models.[54] But voice and instruments in the polyphonic song repertoire is without clear documentation. I do not wish to state that this never happened, merely that most of the evidence offered so far can be interpreted differently – as being concerned with monophonic and improvised repertoires.

In the meantime, the evidence known to me for the performance of written polyphonic secular song is as follows.

(1) In *Il Paradiso degli Alberti* by Giovanni Gherardi da Prato, written in the 1420s but recording fictional events supposed to have taken place in 1389, Landini's *ballata Orsù gentili spiriti* is sung by two girls and a man, Biagio di Sernello, who took the *bordone* – all this to the delight of everybody and particularly of the composer who was present: 'E prestamente con piacere di tutti, e singularmente di Francesco musico, due fanciullette cominciarono una ballata a cantare, tenendo loro bordone Biagio di Sernello'.[55] The full text of the poem follows, and it agrees with the one that survives in Landini's setting:[56] its ranges are as Example 11, clearly showing two higher lines in more or less the same range and a tenor in a range a fifth lower. Presumably in terms of modern concert pitch the piece would need to be transposed upwards by about a fourth. It is of course frustrating that this unique witness of performance practice for the trecento repertoire should fall just short of unambiguity where it describes the tenor line: 'tenendo loro bordone' could imply instrumental

53 See, for example, the opening chapter of Nino Pirrotta, *Li due Orfei* (Turin, 1969, and later edns; Eng. trans. 1982), and more recently Nino Pirrotta, 'Musiche intorno a Giorgione', *Giorgione: Atti del Convegno internazionale di studi, Castelfranco Veneto, 1978*, pp. 41-5. See also chapter 8 of Bridgman, *La vie musicale*.

54 Perhaps the earliest evidence is in letter 10 of Machaut's *Voir dit* in which he describes 'un chant . . . a la guise d'un Res d'Alemaigne', and adds: 'Si vous suppli que vous le daigniez oyr, et savoir la chose ainsi comme elle est faite, sans mettre ne oster . . . et qui la porroit mettre sus les orgues, sus cornemuses ou autres instrumens, c'est sa droite nature'; see *Guillaume de Machaut: Musikalische Werke*, ed. Friedrich Ludwig, ii (Leipzig, 1928, reprinted 1954), pp. 54-5*. On the playing of fifteenth-century lutanists, see David Fallows, '15th-century tablatures for plucked instruments: a summary, a revision and a suggestion', *The Lute Society Journal*, xix (1977), pp. 7-33.

55 *Giovanni Gherardi da Prato: Il Paradiso degli Alberti*, ed. Alberto Lanza, I novellieri italiani, x (Rome, 1975), pp. 176-7. Although the passage has often been mentioned in passing by historians of trecento music it seems not to have been examined for the clear, straightforward information it presents – possibly because that information failed to fit in with the received views on performing early music. Particularly since the days of Schering, scholars and performers have inclined to the view that the different nature of the different lines provides direct internal clues to vocal or instrumental performance. And although Schering's extreme views were rejected, most definitively in Lloyd Hibberd, 'On "instrumental style" in early melody', *The Musical Quarterly*, xxxii (1946), pp. 107-30, this 'internal' approach has survived – apparently contradicting the documentary information, as the following pages hope to suggest.

56 Ed. Leo Schrade, *The works of Francesco Landini*, Polyphonic Music of the Fourteenth Century, iv (Monaco, 1959), p. 184.

134   David Fallows

Example 11. Ranges of Landini, *Orsù gentili spiriti*

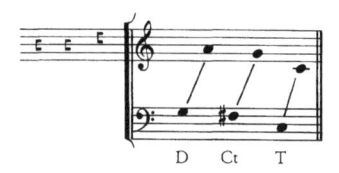

D   Ct   T

performance rather than singing. Yet other descriptions of instruments in *Il Paradiso*[57] suggest that if an instrument had been used here it would have been named. Moreover, it will soon become clear that this verb was commonly used to denote singing.

(2) A description of Philip the Good's visit to Cambrai in January 1449 tells how, because his departure was delayed, he was entertained by two of the choirboys (probably from the cathedral) singing a chanson, with one of the duke's gentlemen taking the tenor: 'Après fut grant tamps attendant apres ses gens . . . et vinrent devant luy II petits des enfans d'autel et canterent une canchonette de le quelle un de ses Gentils Hommes tint le tenure.'[58] Here again it is just possible the verb 'tenir' (in 'tint le tenure') could imply instrumental performance, though the context suggests otherwise. And in this case it is only the mention of a tenor line that indicates written polyphony. On the other hand, returning to the criteria with which this study began, Philip the Good's presence gives credibility to the manner of performance. So even the relative rarity of songs from that time with two equal high voices does little to detract from a useful piece of information.

(3) At Lille in February 1454 Philip the Good's *Banquet du voeu* gave rise to elaborate and detailed descriptions that have made the occasion a byword for late-mediaeval excess.[59] Among the welter of information, four details almost certainly concern polyphonic song, though only the last of them specifies a

57   Elsewhere in *Il Paradiso* the following instruments are named: 'arpa', 'lira', 'tamburi', 'organo', 'organetto', 'chitarra', 'leuto'. Moreover, there is a further passage in which songs of Bartolino da Padova are sung by musicians and girls, only after which there is singing and playing of instruments for a long time: 'E postasi a ssedere, parve al proposto che si dovesse qualque madriale cantare per li musichi e pelle donzelle che quivi si erano, e a loro dicendo che di quelli fatti a pPadova per frate Bartolino, sí famoso musico, cantare dovessono. E cosí fatto, fue cantato e sonato per grandissimo spazio' (Lanza edn, p. 272). Further references to music in this edition appear on pp. 75-6, 78, 83-4, 115-18, 125-6, 132, 134, 145, 154-5, 165-6, 170, 173-4, 176-7, 179, 185, 201-2, 208-9, 236-7 and 306; and on pp. 275-305 appears a story told by Francesco Landini. See also Howard Mayer Brown's paper in the present volume, pp. 57-60.

58   Dupont, *Histoire ecclésiastique et civile de la ville de Cambrai et du Cambrésis* (Cambrai, [*c.* 1759-67, issued in seven annual parts]), part 4 (vol. ii), p. xxi, copied from the eye-witness *Mémoriaux de Saint-Aubert* of Jehan le Robert.

59   Three synoptic accounts are collated in *Chronique de Mathieu d'Escouchy*, ed. Gaston du Fresne de Beaucourt (Paris, 1863-4), ii, pp. 116-237. A further narrative from the Phillipps collection was sold by Sotheby on 30 November 1976, lot 881. All the passages quoted below appear in Marix, *Histoire de la musique*, pp. 37-43, though I have standardised punctuation and diacritical marks in line with current practice.

Ensembles for composed polyphony, 1400-1474   135

known work. First: 'commencerent trois petis enfans d'eglise et ung teneur une tres doulce chansson: quelle elle fu, ne le saveroye dire'. Only the mention of a tenor here suggests polyphony, but since this was the first sophisticated musical contribution to the banquet it seems more than likely that the 'chansson' was polyphonic. Later another song was performed – with the word 'dire' perhaps used in the sense previously attributed to the Latin 'dicere': 'En l'eglise fut recommencié et dit une chanchon tres bien et tres douchement.' The context suggests that these were the same singers as before; and that is the only reason for assuming that the song was polyphonic. Later still a song was performed in the infamous pie containing twenty-eight musicians: 'et tantost apprez fut chanté, ou pasté, par trois douches voix, une chanchon tout du long, que se nommoit *La saulvegarde de ma vie*.' Nobody has managed to identify a polyphonic chanson with this title, though the 'three sweet voices' surely imply polyphony. There can be little doubt about the famous fourth item, however – the description of the twelve-year-old boy singing the discantus ('le dessus') of a song while the stag on which he sat sang the tenor:

> sy entra ung cherf merveilleusement grant et bel . . . Et par dessus icellui cherf estoit monté ung josne filz, de eage de XII ans . . . Et a l'entree de la salle commencha ledit enfant le dessus d'une chansson, moult hault et cler, et ledit cherf lui tenoit la teneur sans avoir autre personne, sy non l'enfant et l'artiffice du cherf, et nommoit-on la chanchon qu'ilz disoient: *Je ne vis onques la pareille.*

Where Mathieu d'Escouchy's version of the chronicle says that the stag 'lui tenoit la teneur', that of Olivier de la Marche has 'lui chanta le teneur' – possibly evidence that 'tenir' was indeed intended to mean 'to sing' in the two doubtful cases already mentioned, but quite certainly evidence that singing took place on this occasion. Also, in this context, 'dire' at the end clearly means 'to sing'. The rondeau *Je ne vis onques la pareille*, attributed variously to Binchois and Dufay,[60] is in three parts in all of its many surviving sources from the fifteenth century; and there seems at least the possibility that the self-consciously phrased 'artiffice du cherf' indicates that the stag contained two men – like the modern pantomime horse, and also explaining why it was 'merveilleusement grant' – of whom one sang the tenor and the other sang the contratenor. Certainly, it would be possible to omit the contratenor line which is technically dispensable in this and all fifteenth-century three-part chansons; but in spite of the words 'sans avoir autre personne' it is difficult to believe that on an occasion such as this the contratenor would really have been omitted. The ranges of the chanson are shown in Example 12: the importance of the low *g* in the discantus line suggests that if the boy was singing 'very loud and clear' it would need to have been performed at least a fourth higher than modern concert pitch. (That, in its turn, would compel the singer of the tenor line to

---

60 Ed. Besseler, *Dufay: Opera omnia*, vi, p. 109.

136   David Fallows

Example 12. Ranges of Dufay or Binchois, *Je ne vis onques la pareille*

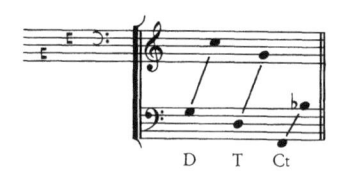

                                 D   T   Ct

employ some kind of falsetto voice, for he would then rise to *c″* and do so at a point where the discantus is an octave lower in the boy's weakest range.)[61]

(4) In his two separate narratives of Charles the Bold's wedding to Margaret of York in 1468, Olivier de la Marche describes performances of two named chansons that are undoubtedly polyphonic.[62] There is no trace of the music for either; but he presents the complete texts of both, and they are normal *rondeaux cinquains* with eight-syllable lines – the most common form for polyphonic chansons at that date. The first song was performed by two singers inside a lion; the two narratives read as follows:[63]

> (*a*) et quant ledit lyon entra parmy la salle, il commença a ouvrir la gorge et a la reclorre, par si bonne façon qu'il prononçoit ce que cy après est escript. Et commença ledit lyon a chanter une chanson faicte a ce propos, a teneur et dessus, qui disoit ainsi: *Bien viegne la belle bergiere* [etc.].

> (*b*) entra ung lion, dedans lequel estoient deux chantres chantans une chanson qui disoit: *Bien viengnant la doulce bergiere*.

Between the two narratives it is clear that there were two people in the lion, both singers, singing a *rondeau* in two voices, discantus and tenor. The second song was performed by four asses:[64]

> (*a*) et la s'apparurent quatre gros asnes moult bien faictz, lequelx dirent une chanson de musicque a quatre pars, faicte a ce propos, qui se disoit ainsi: *Faictes vous l'asne, ma maistresse* [etc.].

> (*b*) se monstroient, premierement, grans sengliers sonnans trompettes de guerre . . . [2nd] se monstrerent chievres jouans comme menestrelz tres melodieusement; tierchement, loups jouans de fleutes; et quartement, asnes qui chanterent une chanson tres plaisante.

Again, the two differently worded accounts help to clarify that it was a polyphonic chanson in four parts, all of which were sung.

---

61   Contrary to many modern descriptions of the banquet, it is certain that the famous lament for Constantinople delivered by Olivier de la Marche was spoken, not sung. See Fallows, *Dufay*, p. 287, n. 38. Two further items at the banquet which could concern polyphonic songs are discussed below.

62   *Mémoires d'Olivier de la Marche*, ed. Henri Beaune and Jean Jules Maulbon D'Arbaumont, 4 vols. (Paris, 1883-8), iii, pp. 101-201, and iv, pp. 95-144.

63   (*a*) *Ibid.*, iii, p. 136; (*b*) *Ibid.*, iv, p. 110.

64   (*a*) *Ibid.*, iii, p. 153; (*b*) *Ibid.*, iv, pp. 124-5.

A few more scattered references are rather less specific but point towards the same conclusion.

(5) In 1406 at the residence of Regnauld de Trie, Amiral de France, all kinds of French chanson seem to have been sung in several voices, beautifully harmonised: 'Alli oia ome cantar lais, é delais, é virolais, é chazas, é reondelas, é complaintas, é baladas, chanzones de toda el arte que trovan los Franceses, en voces diversas muy bien acordadas.'[65]

(6) At the end of the fourteenth century, according to Froissart, Gaston Fébus 'faisoit devant lui ses clercs volontiers chanter chançons, rondiaux et virelaiz'.[66]

(7) From as late as the 1490s is Gonzalo Fernández de Oviedo's description of the Aragonese crown prince, Don Juan: although he had a poor voice he took the tenor on many occasions when he performed songs with the composer Juan de Anchieta and four or five choirboys for two hours or more:[67]

> Era el prínçipe Don Johan, mi señor, naturalmente inclinado a la música, e entendiala muy bien, aun que su voz no era tal, como él era porfiado en cantar: e para eso, en las siestas, en espeçial en verano, yvan a palaçio Johanes de Ancheta, su maestro de capilla, e quatro o çinco muchachos, moços de capilla de lindas bozes, de los quales era uno Corral, lindo tiple, y el Principe cantava con ellos dos oras, o lo que le plazia, o les hazia thenor, e era bien diestro en el arte.

Presumably the repertoire they sang was more or less that of the *Cancionero de Palacio* or the *Cancionero de la Colombina* – mostly three-part songs, many of them in a style closely related to that of the Franco-Flemish chanson in the generation of Hayne van Ghizeghem and Busnois. Since Don Juan sang the tenor, Anchieta must have sung the contratenor and the boys the discantus line.

(8) The mid-fifteenth-century French prose romance *Cleriadus et Meliadice* contains several references to the singing of chansons by voices alone:[68] a seven-year-old girl and two young boys all sing together in a chanson, though it need not necessarily have been polyphonic; Cleriadus, the hero, sets a poem to music, using a harp to compose it and try it out but later singing it in court with the help of 'ung escuier de sa compaignie' who 'luy tenoit la teneur' – again raising the matter of the ambiguity of the word 'tenir' but from the context

---

65 *Cronica de Don Pedro Niño, conde de Buelna*, ed. Eugenio de Llaguno Amirola (Madrid, 1782), part 2, chapter 31 (p. 117). This is discussed in André Pirro, *La musique à Paris sous le règne de Charles VI (1380-1422)*, Sammlung musikwissenschaftlicher Abhandlungen, i (Strasbourg, 1930), p. 23.

66 Jean Froissart, *Voyage en Béarn*, ed. A. Diverres (Manchester, 1953), p. 68; cited in Nigel Wilkins, *Music in the age of Chaucer* (Cambridge, 1979), p. 25.

67 Gonçalo Fernandez de Ouiedo, *Libro de la cámara real del prínçipe Don Juan* (Madrid, 1870), pp. 182-3; a full translation of the passage is in Robert Stevenson, *Spanish music in the age of Columbus* (The Hague, 1960), p. 133. Tess Knighton kindly drew my attention to this passage.

68 *GB-Lbl* Royal 20 C.ii. All details here are cited from the article by Christopher Page, 'The performance of songs in late medieval France: a new source', *Early Music*, x (1982), pp. 441-50. I am most grateful to Dr Page for having allowed me to see his study in advance of publication.

138   David Fallows

implying vocal performance; and Cleriadus later performs another song with 'ung de ses escuiers pur tenir teneur a luy et a l'enfant [the page he had asked to sing with him]'. Possibly in this last case the squire sang the tenor, Cleriadus the contratenor and the boy the discantus. Here again we find the word 'dire' used to describe singing: 'la disoit bien Cleriadus et ceulx qui luy aidoient'.

(9) Finally, returning to the end of the fourteenth century, the passage that was discussed in detail by Christopher Page five years ago with the suggestion – apparently for the first time in modern writings – that it was clear evidence for all-vocal performance of the fourteenth-century chanson repertoire.[69] It comes in Eustache Deschamps' *L'art de dictier* and may therefore be appropriate with reference to the polyphonic chansons of Machaut. Concerning polyphonic song he explains that it can be performed without words, or with words alone, or with words and music. In certain circumstances, he says, it is better to perform the words only, as when in the presence of somebody who is sick. He continues:[70]

> et autres cas semblables ou le chant musicant n'aroit point lieu pour la haulteur d'icellui, et la triplicité des voix pour les teneurs et contreteneurs necessaires a ycellui chant proferer par deux ou trois personnes pour la perfection dudit chant.

> There are other similar cases where music would have no place because of its loudness, and because of the three voices for the tenors and contratenors that are necessary to perform the said music perfectly with two or three people.

This passage is by no means unambiguous. 'Voix' here could simply mean parts, polyphonic lines without any presupposition as to whether voices or instruments are to perform them. But Page, who is by profession a philologist, argues his case carefully. And in the context of all these other references it seems more than likely that singing voices were indeed what Deschamps meant.

Page's challenging interpretation made little impression and was all but ignored until three years later when he himself assembled a group of singers and directed some performances along those lines with voices alone. The results spoke for themselves. It was difficult to avoid concluding that the secular music of the French fourteenth-century composers comes across more clearly, more directly and more eloquently with voices alone than with the accompaniment of instruments.[71]

69 For such suggestions in fifteenth-century music, see above n. 51. By 'modern writings' I mean the secondary literature since about 1910. Before that it tended to be assumed that most mediaeval music was purely vocal. For a summary of the change of mind, see Haas, *Aufführungspraxis der Musik*, pp. 93-100.

70 Christopher Page, 'Machaut's "pupil" Deschamps on the performance of music: voices or instruments in the 14th-century chanson', *Early Music*, v (1977), p. 488; the English translation is also from Page, p. 489.

71 Whether the lower parts in such a performance should be texted or vocalised is a vexed question. In practical terms, today's singers tend to be happier with words; but that may simply be a matter of the techniques to which they are accustomed. It is easy enough to point to long

Moreover, if we accept Roger Bowers' demonstrations that there was no established pitch standard at the time, that singers simply placed the music in the range that was appropriate, then we must also accept the difficulty of combining voices with instruments that cannot transpose so easily and freely.

Nine scattered descriptions do not amount to proof, however: they span a whole century and originate in Spain, Italy, France and Flanders, all countries that could well have had entirely different traditions of musical performance; moreover, none of the descriptions quite fulfills the requirements outlined at the beginning of this paper. The performance of *Je ne vis onques la pareille* comes closest but still begs serious questions. And little has been said here about the many descriptions and pictures that might seem to be of voices and instruments performing together in the polyphonic repertoire: it could be argued that careful selection has made the case seem stronger than the situation merits. Certainly only a thorough examination of the entire evidence would make a watertight case. But it is unlikely that polyphonic songs were always performed in the same way: the conclusion I wish to offer is simply that all the descriptions I can find that certainly or almost certainly refer to performances of the polyphonic song repertoire apparently concern voices only.

To demonstrate the other aspect of this argument, here are three descriptions that could be construed as being of voices and instruments working together in a performance of polyphony but could also be interpreted otherwise.

(1) Again at the *Banquet du voeu*, the court's two famous blind vielle players performed together with a lute and a court lady: 'ou pasté, juèrrent les aveugles, de vielles, et aveuc eulx ung leu bien accordé; et chantoit aveuc eulx une damoiselle de l'ostel de ladicte duchesse nommée Pacquette, dont la chose ne valoit pas pis.'[72] This is d'Escouchy's reading, whereas Olivier de la Marche ends with the words 'et estoit grande et douce melodie a oir'. But even here there is no clear evidence that a composed polyphonic chanson was being performed: it could well have been a monophonic chanson with improvised or semi-improvised accompaniments. Earlier a lute played with two good voices: 'fut joué ou pasté d'un leux aveux deux bonnes voix'.[73] The same objection could be levelled here, although the presence of two voices does suggest that a balanced view would be that this may well have been a polyphonic chanson.

(2) When he entered Paris at his accession to the French throne in 1461,

melismatic sections in chant and in sacred polyphony which would support the idea of vocalisation in the polyphonic chanson. Closer analysis seems to suggest that different solutions are appropriate for particular repertoires and even for individual works. A preliminary study of this appears in my commentary to *Le chansonnier de Jean de Montchenu*, ed. Geneviève Thibault, Publications de la Société française de musicologie (Paris, forthcoming).

72   Marix, *Histoire de la musique*, p. 40.
73   Marix, *Histoire de la musique*, p. 39.

140   David Fallows

Louis XI was greeted near the Porte Saint-Denis by three sirens singing small 'motetz' and 'bergeretes', as well as some instrumentalists:[74]

> Et si y avoit encores trois bien belles filles, faisans personnages de seraines toutes nues, et leur veoit on le beau tetin droit, separé, rond et dur, qui estoit chose bien plaisant, et disoient de petiz motetz et bergeretes; et pres d'eulx jouoient plusieurs bas instruments qui rendoient de grandes melodies.

Here, as in many comparable descriptions or pictures, the two events are almost certainly independent: the three girls sang as one unit; the instrumentalists could have been taking part in the same works but probably were not. The girls, of course, were not necessarily singing polyphony: 'petiz motetz et bergeretes' in this description need not be scientifically specific.

(3) Simone Prudenzani's *Il Saporetto*,[75] written early in the fifteenth century, is often cited for its evidence of instruments performing in polyphonic songs; but here too an alternative explanation seems at least possible. In sonnets 25-35 there are many references to the performance of known polyphonic songs from the trecento repertoire; and instruments are mentioned – harp, 'sampognia', organ, monochord, lute, flute and so on.[76] But nowhere in this group of sonnets is there any reference to voice and instruments together. It is by no means stretching a point to suggest that the protagonist, Sollazzo, performed songs on an instrument without singing (just as Cleriadus seems to have used a harp to compose his song), perhaps in the case of non-chordal instruments simply performing the discantus line. Be that as it may, later in the book sonnets 47-8 specifically describe the polyphonic performance of known trecento songs with Sollazzo singing the discantus, brother Agustino singing the tenor and *maestro* Pier de Iovanale doing the contra:[77]

> Quella sera cantaro ei madriali,
> Cançon del Cieco a modo peruscino,
> Rondel franceschi de fra Bartolino,
> Strambotti de Cicilia a la reale.
>
> D'ogni cosa Solaço è principale,
> Comme quel que de musica era pino;
> El tenor gli tenea frate Agustino
> E'l contra mastro Pier de Iovanale.

A description of the performance follows, and the next sonnet names the works performed, among them the well-known polyphonic songs *Non al suo amante*, *A meço a sei pagoni* (*Nel mezzo a sei paon*) and *Donna s'i t'ò fallito*. In this latter sonnet, singing is repeatedly mentioned; 'Quive cantaro . . . cantâr con dolce canti . . . ancor cantaro avante' etc. And in the light of that it is difficult

74 *Journal de Jean le Roye connu sous le nom de Chronique scandaleuse*, ed. Bernard de Mandrot (Paris, 1894-6), i, pp. 27-8.
75 'Il "Sollazzo" e il "Saporetto" con altre rime di Simone Prudenzani d'Orvieto', ed. Santore Debenedetti, *Giornale storico della letteratura italiana*, supplement xv (1913).
76 *Ibid.*, pp. 104-10.
77 *Ibid.*, pp. 116-17.

to explain the complete absence of references to singing in the earlier sonnets[78] except as meaning that the works were performed there instrumentally.

This poem is yet another example of 'tenere' apparently meaning to sing. And it may be relevant to point to two further examples of the same word being used in that sense: in 1395 at the cathedral of Udine, Domenico da Buttrio was employed and instructed 'addiscere cantum ad tenendum tenorem' – to learn music in order to perform the tenor;[79] and in 1470 at the court of Savoy, Antonio Guinati was described as the man 'qui tient la teneur avecque lesdits innocens' – who performs the tenor with the choirboys.[80] Moreover, Ulland's extensive survey of words used to describe instrumental performance in the middle ages shows no use of 'tenere' or its cognates in any other European language.[81] Negative information though that may be, it becomes striking in the context of the eight references assembled here, all in passages where singing is implied and three in passages where there can be no possible doubt that singing is meant. And even if that information is to be tempered by the fact that in all cases 'tenir' or its cognates is associated with the tenor line,[82] that does little to diminish the circumstantial evidence that all are concerned with singing. Rather the reverse: it tends to endorse the theory that instruments were not normally used for the tenor line.

Yet anybody wishing to conclude that the secular song repertoire was never performed by voices and instruments together would need to explain each of the following: why instrumental soloists and ensembles clearly often did base their performances on composed polyphonic compositions, at least from the middle of the fourteenth century;[83] why there is evidence of instrumentalists who were musically literate and even composed from at least the last quarter of the fourteenth century;[84] and why a tradition of instruments and voices working together would have grown up quite suddenly in the first years of the sixteenth century. Without special pleading it is impossible to reconcile those facts with a theory that the polyphonic song repertoire was never performed by voices and instruments together.

---

78 A brief reference to singers and polyphony in sonnet 28 (*Ibid.*, p. 106) apparently concerns sacred music.

79 Giuseppe Vale, 'La cappella musicale del duomo di Udine', *Note d'archivio*, vii (1930), p. 89.

80 Bouquet, 'La cappella musicale dei duchi di Savoia', p. 257.

81 Wolfgang Ulland, *Jouer d'un instrument und die altfranzösischen Bezeichnungen des Instrumentenspiels*, Romanische Versuche und Vorarbeiten, xxxv (Bonn, 1970), pp. 170-3. For this and the previous two references I am indebted to Christopher Page.

82 In the passage from *Il Saporetto* the verb 'tenea' actually has two objects: *el tenor* and *'lcontra*.

83 See in particular the Machaut reference cited above, n. 54, and the Robertsbridge Codex from the mid fourteenth century which contains intabulations (perhaps, though not necessarily, for keyboard) of polyphonic works.

84 I refer in particular to the cases of Baude Cordier and Richard Loqueville; see my comments in *Journal of the American Musicological Society*, xxxiv (1981), pp. 550-2. It is worth noting, however, that all the early instrumentalists who can be documented as having been musically literate seem to have been harpists – information that may connect up with the story of Cleriadus mentioned above.

142   David Fallows

As a final detail along these lines, here is the earliest description I have encountered that is certainly of voices and instruments working together in what are clearly polyphonic chansons, albeit with sacred texts. It is in the mystery play *L'incarnation et nativité de nostre saulveur et redempteur Jesuchrist* apparently performed at Rouen in 1474 but possibly up to twenty years old at the time.[85] The printed edition (Paris, *c*. 1490) contains two highly unusual features. First, for the twelve songs it contains space is left for the music to be entered by hand – though it is not there in any copy known today – and the text, tenor incipits, contratenor incipits and later stanzas are laid out precisely as in the surviving chansonniers of the time, leaving no possible doubt that the music was like that of the chanson repertoire. The second feature is that several of the songs are preceded by detailed descriptions of their performance. That for the first song – a *rondeau cinquain* – reads as follows:[86]

> Adonc chantent [les anges] le premier vers de la chanson qui ensuit / et puis les joueurs d'instrumens derriere les anges repetent iceluy vers. Et tandis les anges qui tiennent les instrumens font maniere de jouer / Apres les anges chantent le second vers et puis les instrumens repetent trois lignes / Apres les anges chantent le tiers vers et puis les instrumens tout le premier / et puis la fin.

Even here there is no explicit statement that the voices and instruments perform simultaneously; but the exchange of vocal and instrumental performance at least assumes that the singers took their pitch from the instruments rather than from one another.

Nine angels were present, and apparently all took part in the singing of this three-part sacred chanson; so it is just possible that the ensemble and distribution were the same as for Dufay's Mass for St Anthony of Padua.

The other chansons have similar rubrics; but only the last indicates simultaneous performance by voices and an instrument, and even here only by implication. Five shepherds take part in the discussion preceding the chanson, and one of them refers to the tuning of his vielle: Handschin suggests that perhaps three shepherds sang this three-part chanson and two played instruments.[87]

There are undoubtedly many more references and documents that could contribute to this discussion of how to perform the secular songs of the time: my own search has been relatively informal and confined to secondary sources on

---

85   *Mystère de l'incarnation et nativité de notre sauveur et rédempteur Jésus-Christ représenté à Rouen en 1474*, ed. Pierre Le Verdier, Société des bibliophiles normands, xxviii (Rouen, 1885-6), Introduction and especially pp. xxiv-xxxi.

86   The comprehensive and characteristically thoughtful summary in Jacques Handschin, 'Das Weihnachts-Mysterium von Rouen als musikgeschichtliche Quelle', *Acta musicologica*, vii (1935), pp. 97-110, makes further details unnecessary. The texts are quoted from the unmodernised versions given there.

87   'Das Weihnachts-Mysterium von Rouen', pp. 103-4.

the performance of music.[88] But there is enough here to suggest that received views need substantial reconsideration.

In view of my suggestion that many of the pictures and descriptions of voices and instruments working together may in fact concern monophonic song, and given that there is considerable evidence for voices and instruments working together in the monophonic song repertoire,[89] the issue surely centres on important questions of historical interpretation which demand extremely careful answers. Namely: to what extent the fourteenth- and fifteenth-century polyphonic song traditions are an offshoot of the sacred polyphony, and vice versa; to what extent they owe something to the unwritten traditions of the time; and to what extent they are in a line of direct evolution from the thirteenth-century monophonic traditions (about which, in turn, the same questions can be asked, though answers have at least been attempted by several writers, notably Hendrik Vanderwerf). It is easy enough to see partial answers to these questions immediately: that the answer for Machaut's *rondeaux* is very different from that for Dufay's *rondeaux*; that the answer for Binchois' *rondeaux* is different again; certainly that the answer or answers are very different for some Italian polyphonic song (where again the questions have been tackled with some energy in recent years, largely by Nino Pirrotta). Until carefully focussed answers have been provided for all the main strands in the repertoire it will remain difficult to interpret descriptions and pictures as evidence for performance practice.

But for the rest it is perhaps better to return to my basic data: that in 1469 the Burgundian court chapel used the distribution 6/3/2/3 for four-voice music, presumably works such as the cycle of anonymous *L'homme armé* Masses now at Naples; that the six singers on the top line almost certainly sang falsetto and were mature men; that in 1474 and perhaps in 1450 Dufay's preferred performance medium for his Mass for St Anthony of Padua was nine men,

88 Wright, 'Voices and instruments', p. 648, gives a rather different list of references. Of those not mentioned here, most are either later or not necessarily concerned with written polyphony. But one is of particular interest and almost certainly describes the performance of a polyphonic song. When Duke Philip the Good of Burgundy entered Ghent on 23 April 1458 there was an elephant surmounted by a castle containing 'deux hommes et quatre enffans, qui chanterent une nouvelle et joyeuse chanson, dont les moz s'ensuivent'; and the following text is a complete *rondeau quatrain* beginning 'Vive Bourguongne est nostre cry'. Given the form of the poem, and given the documents discussed above, it is difficult to avoid concluding that this was a three-voice setting in which the two lower voices were taken by one man each and the top line was sung by four boys. See Jean Chartier, *Chronique de Charles VII*, ed. Vallet de Viriville (Paris, 1858), iii, pp. 86-7.

89 Ian Parker, 'The performance of troubadour and trouvère songs: some facts and conjectures', *Early Music*, v (1977), pp. 187-91 and 195, in fact draws attention to the singular shortage of clear evidence that the thirteenth-century monophonic repertoires in French and Provençal were performed with instrumental accompaniment. His findings would tend to suggest that even in the thirteenth and fourteenth centuries the 'high style' courtly song was normally performed without instruments and that it was closely related to the sacred repertoires: much of it was 'the music of a courtly liturgy', to use the happy phrase of John Stevens.

144   David Fallows

apparently in the distribution 5/2/2; that there are several pieces of evidence
suggesting that in the first three quarters of the fifteenth century when
choirboys sang the top line or lines of polyphony the lower lines were taken by
single voices, often vocalising; and that the evidence for all-vocal performance
of secular polyphonic songs in both the fourteenth and the fifteenth centuries is
far greater than has been supposed.

I also now think that much of the music sounds better that way.[90]

90 I cannot end without paying tribute to the Music Division of the British Broadcasting Corporation
which devoted considerable sums of money to testing the research offered here, providing the
first opportunities for Christopher Page to perform late fourteenth-century chansons with voices
only and for me to record Dufay's Mass for St Anthony of Padua in the distribution advocated
here.

145

Appendix: Passages in the Burgundian court ordinances of 1 January 1469 (new style) relevant to members of the court chapel and other musicians

The only known manuscript (*GB-Ob* Hatton 13; *Summary Catalogue*, no. 4097) is on thick parchment, *c*. 31 × 22 cm, in six eight-leaf gatherings with uniform handwriting and decoration; it is all probably the work of the copyist Jehan du Quesne, who was paid in March 1469 for preparing a manuscript whose description tallies exactly with this one.[1] The present binding is apparently from the seventeenth century.

Passages printed in capitals are in red ink in the manuscript. Punctuation, capitalisation and numerals have been modernised; i/j and u/v have been standardised; acute accents have been added where necessary to avoid ambiguity; abbreviations have been expanded silently. Words have been changed only when the manuscript form (footnoted) is likely to be confusing.[2]

[Introduction]

[f. 1*r*] CE SONT LES ORDONNANCES DE L'HOSTEL DE MONSEIGNEUR LE DUC DE BOURGOINE EN TOUS ESTAS. Comme il ait pleu a mon tresredoubté seigneur Monseigneur le duc de Bourgoine . . . mettre sus l'estat de son hostel, le quel pour la multitude des chevaliers, escuyers et autres serviteurs supostz d'ycelluy a besoing d'estre par grant activité et dilligence entretenu, adfin que les estatus et ordonnances d'icelluy ne soient en nulle maniere trespassees, enfraintes ne viollees, mais soient toutes choses faites et conduites reveramment, ordonnee-ment et rigleement a l'onneur de Dieu et de monditseigneur et de tous ceulx de

---

1   Brussels, Archives Générales du Royaume, Chambre des Comptes, 1924, f. 284*r*. The payment is printed, together with identification of the Hatton manuscript and an extended discussion, in Antoine de Schryver, 'Nicolas Spierinc calligraphe et enlumineur des ordonnances des états de l'hôtel de Charles le Téméraire', *Scriptorium*, xxiii (1969), pp. 434-58; see pp. 437-40, 451-2 and 455. The manuscript is further described at some length in Richard Vaughan, *Charles the Bold: the last Valois Duke of Burgundy* (London, 1973), pp. 193-6. A partial copy by the nineteenth-century archivist Alexandre Pinchart is now in *B-Br* II. 1200 coffret no. 9 and appears in Jeannine Douillez [Lambrechts-Douillez], 'De muziek aan het boorgondische-habsburgse hof in de tweede helft der XVde eeuw' (Ph.D. dissertation, University of Louvain, 1957), doc. 5.

2   Christine Hill of the Manchester University Department of French kindly gave me the benefit of her expertise in this. I am also grateful for further help from Dr Malcolm Currie and Dr Lily Segerman-Peck.

146   David Fallows

son dit hostel, la quelle chose pour la licence qui en tous estas a esté par long
temps nourrie en ceste maison n'est pas legiere a faire, se n'estoit que les
serviteurs d'icelle pour l'amour et desir qu'ilz en tous estas doibvent avoir de
complaire, honnourer et servir monditseigneur se voulsissent d'eulz meismes
rigler et mettre en ordre, la quelle chose tant par ygnorance comme autrement
ne seroit permanente ne durable . . .

[Section A: Enumeration of the household, ff. 2*r*-10*v*]
[f. 2*r*] CHAPELLE
Premierement mondit seigneur veult et ordonne que doresenavant sa chapelle
domestique soit entretenue et gouvernee en son hostel par le nombre de 25
personnes cy dessoubz desclarés: c'est ascavoir 13 chapelains, 6 clers, 5
sommeliers et 1 fourrier qui airont gaiges, lesquelz feront et continueront
journellement le divin service tant en meurs comme en maniere de honnestement vivre. . . [f. 8*r*] . . .
CONFESSEUR ET AUTRES CHAPELLAINS
Monditseigneur aura: ung confesseur servant sans ordonnance, present et
absent; ung aumosnier compté sans ordonnance, luy estant devers monditseigneur; [f. 8*v*] ung soubz aumosnier ausi compté sans ordonnance, luy estant
devers monditseigneur; ung chapellain des maistres d'ostel tousjours compté
comme dessus; ung varlet d'aumosne tousjours compté comme dessus; ung
porteur d'orgues servant sans ordonnance comme dessus. . . .
[f. 10*v*] TROMPETTES
Monditseigneur aura: cinq trompettes de guerre tousjours comptez, eulz estans
devers monditseigneur; six trompette de menestrelz comptés comme dessus;
troys joueurs de instrumens bas tousjours comptez comme dessus . . .

[Section B: Description of duties, ff. 10*v*-47*r*]
[f. 10*v*] ORDONNANCES TOUCHANT LA CHAPELLE
[1: priesthood irrelevant to status within the chapel]
Monditseigneur entent que ou nombre des douze chapellains denommés au
chapitre de la chapelle pourront estre auchuns non prestes qui neantmoins
auront gages entiers de chapelain; et ausi que au nombre des clercz et sommeliers pourront estre auchuns prestes qui neantmoins n'auront gages que de
clercz ou sommeliers; et selon les merites disponibles de voix et bons services [f.
11*r*] desdiz clercz et sommeliers ilz pourront monter[3] de degré en degré,
ascavoir sommelier en estat de clerc et clercz en chapelains quant l'oportunité y
sera et leurs merites le exigeront selon le bon plaisir de monditseigneur.

[2: members of the chapel to obey the first chaplain]
Monditseigneur veult et ordonne que tous les ditz douze chapelains, clercz,

    3   MS: moter.

sommeliers, et fourrier, soient obeisans au premier chapelain, luy portent honneur et reverence comme a leur chief, obtemperent a ces commandemens et ordonnances mesmement touchant le faict et estat de ladite chapelle; et ce auchuns sont rebelles et desobeisans ilz seront suspendus de leurs gaiges pour autant de jours qu'il semblera en bonne raison et justice que la rebellion et desobeisance exigera, pour lesquels jours lesditz rebelles et desobeissans perdront leurditz gaiges.

[3: Mass with polyphony celebrated daily according to the Use of Paris]
Item chascun jour de l'an a heure competente sera dite et celebree en la dite chapelle par iceulx chapelains, clercz et autres servans une haulte messe ordinaire a chant et deschant de tel saint ou sainte dont la feste escherra icelluy jour; et ce faiste n'y achet la dite messe sera du ferial selon l'office dominical de la sepmaine; et le tout en observant et gardant l'usage de l'eglise de Paris ainsi qu'il est acoustumé du temps des predicesseurs de monditseigneur.

[f. 11*v*]
[4: Vespers and Compline of the day or first Vespers of the following feast day]
Item semblablement a heure competente du vespre seront chantees vespres et complies de tel office que aura esté celluy de la messe, sinon que le lendemain soit feste double ou solempnelle ou quel cas les vespres seront de la solempnité sequente selon l'ordinaire observé par cy devant. Ausi veult monditseigneur que les secondes vespres de toutes festes soient aussi solempnelles que les premieres en cerimonies, paremens et toutes autres choses.

[5: Little Hours celebrated on certain feast days (named) and to follow immediately after Matins except on Christmas Day; Matins to be reinstated for the 'O antiphon' days]
Item aux festes et jours cy apres designez seront ditez et celebrees matines ensemble toutes les heures du jour jusques aux vespres exclusivement; lesquelles heures, a scavoir prime, tierce, midy et nonne, se diront incontinent apres matines sans faire auchune intermission depuis les dites matines jousques a nonne inclusivement, excepté au jour de Noel: apres les matines du quel jour, pour ce que l'office est long, y aura intervale competent jousques a prime a la discretion du chief de la dite chapelle; et au regard des vespres d'iceulx jours, elles seront dites a l'heure ordonnee cy dessus en l'article precedent. S'ensievent les festes et jours dessus mentionnés: premierement la Nativité Nostre Seigneur, la Circumcision, l'Apparicion, la Purificacion Nostre Dame, l'Annunciacion, la Visitacion, l'Assumption, la Nativité et la Conception d'ycelle, les festes de Pasques, de l'As[f. 12*r*]sention Nostre Seigneur, la veille et le jour de Penthecouste, la feste de la Trinité, celle du Saint Sacrement, la Nativité saint Jhan Baptiste, la feste de saint Pierre en juing, la feste de Toussains, la Commemoracion des Trespassés, les festes de sainte Katherine,

148   David Fallows

de saint Andrieu, et de saincte Barbe; item chascun jour de Karesme et de l'Avent. Et par ce sera abolie la coustume depuis aulcun temps introduite en la dite chapnele de non dire et chanter matines aux jours ou escheent les solempneles antyphones qu'on dist le 'O', lesquelz jours sont les plus prochains de la Nativité Nostre Seigneur, et doivent estre plus observés, pource veult et ordonne monditseigneur le divin service estre fait tout entier comme aux autres jours precedens.

[6: obits and obsequies to be observed as required by the duke]
Item toutes et quantes foiz que advendront cas de trespassement d'auchuns prince ou princesses du sang de monditseigneur, ou autrement quant bon luy semblera, les obitz et obseques d'iceulx princes ou princesses, ou d'autres qu'il luy plaira, seront faiz et celebrés des vigilles et haultes messes en la dite chapelle ou autre eglise ou lors sera monditseigneur.

[7: priests from the choir to take turns officiating at the altar for ferial Mass and reading the Gospel for double feasts]
Item ou nombre de ceulx de la ditte chapelle a la discretion du premier[4] chapelain, seront eslues quatre prestes propices pour officier a l'autel et desquelz on ce pourra le mieulz passer a la chanterie du livre, laquelle chan[f. 12v]terie sera prealablement formé de tel nombre de haultes voix, teneurs et contres que cy apres[5] est ordonné; lesquelz quatre prebstres seront deputés et auront la charge des messes ordinaires es jours non solempnelz pour icelles messes; et ausi les evvangilles aux festes doubles et solempneles estre celebrees et dites par sepmaines sans ce que ceulz qui seront deputez a la dicte chanterie du livre, ne autres fors seulement les quatre dessusditz, se doient ocuper desdites messes ordinaires, et ce adfin qu'il n'y ait faulte de voix au livre; et le tour de quatre sepmaines fait par lesditz quatre prebstres, les autres prenans gaiges de chapelain, et chascun de eulx, aussi non prebstres, seront tenus par tour de faire desservir les messes de la chinquiesme sepmaine par ung des ditz quatre deputés aux messes en luy baillant ung escu d'or pour la dicte sepmaine.

[8: Epistle at High Mass read by two *sommeliers*, alternating by the week, but by a *clerc* on a double feast or when a prelate officiates]
Item les epistres desdites haultes messes par tout le cours de l'an, a jours communs non doubles ne solempnelz, seront dites par les deux sommeliers servans en la dicte chapelle, c'est ascavoir par tour et par sepmaine qu'ilz feront l'ung apres l'autre; et au regard des epistres aux festes doubles ou quant prelat fera l'office, elles seront dittes par auchuns des clercz tel que le premier chapelain ordonnera, auquel a ce obeyront sur paine de perdre leurs gaiges pour ce jour.

---

4 MS: premie.
5 i.e., in paragraph 11, f. 13r.

[9: the chaplain on duty for the week to officiate at the Hours] [f. 13*r*]
Item le sepmainier de grant messe par tout le cours de sa sepmaine commencera les heures, dira les chapitres et collectes d'ycelles, ou en lieu de luy l'ung des autres deputés aux messes, et ce sur paine de deux solz parisis pour chascune fois qu'il sera deffaillant.

[10: defines when in the service the members of the chapel must enter]
Item lesditz chapelains, clercz et autres de la dicte chapelle feront entree aux matines dedens la fin du premier hynne, et aux messes dedens le Gloria Patri de l'introite, aux vespres dedens le Gloria du premier spaulme, et aux vigiles des mors dedens la fin du premier pseaulme, et ce sur paine de deux solz parisis pour chascune foiz que auchun des dessusditz feront faulte aux entrees dessusditez; lesquelles monditseigneur veult estre observvees indiferaument et sans distinctions de jours communs ou solempnelz, cecy adjoute que ceulx qui seront deffaillans en ce que dit est a jours sollempnez ou quant il y aura messe de prelat, obit de prince ou autre de par luy ordonné perdront leurs[6] gaiges dudit jour de leur deffaulte.

[11: for polyphony, minimum distribution 6/3/2/3]
Item pour le chant du livre y aura du moyns six haultes voix, troys teneurs, troys basses contres et deux moiens sans en ce comprendre les quatre chapelains des haultes messes ne les sommeliers lesquelz toutefoys s'ilz ne sont occupés a l'autel ou autrement raisonnablement seront tenus [f. 13*v*] de servir avec les dessus ditz.

[12: robing in the chapel]
Item tous les chapelains, ascavoir le premier et les autres douze, seront tenus d'estre et venir audit service en longues robes honnestes et ecclesiastiques vestus de sourplis et ayans leurs almuces grise en teste ou sur leurs bras, sans lesquelles ne devront estre audit service en quelque temps ou jour que ce soit; et pareillement les clercz et sommeliers qui ne porteront almuces seront en longues robes et sourplis durant ledit service, et ainsi sera observé chascun jour par tous les dessusditz, excepté aux jours que monditseigneur et son estat meismement sa ditte chapelle partira du lieu ou l'en aura sejourné ou qu'il seroit envoyé ou sur chemin sans deschargier leurs bagues ausquelz cas ilz seront excusés des habitz dessusditz et non autrement.

[13: clothing outside the chapel]
Item veult monditseigneur que lesditz de sa chapelle quant ilz yront par ville soient adez vestus de longues robes honnestes a haut collet tel qu'il puisse couvrir celuy du pourpoint sans en icelles avoir bord ne fourreures trop aparentes, ne manches froncees sur les espaules ne excessives en largeur, aussi

6   MS: lurs.

150   David Fallows

que en leurs pourpoins sur le hault des bras ne soit garniture[7] de bourre ou
cotton qu'on dist haulces, dont s'ensieut grant difformité soubz les chasubles,
chapes et autres [f. 14*r*] habilemens d'eglise; pareillement de non porter
chapeaulx en son hostel et quant ilz sont au service ne dagues de quelque
fachon que ce soit, dessus ne dessoubz leurs robes, anneaux en mains, patins en
piedz eulz officians a l'autel; et le tout sur la paine telle qui sera arbitree en
regard a la quantité du comptent apres la seconde reprehencion a luy faicte.

[14: chapel robing in livery for feast days or when a prelate says Mass]
Item a jours solempnelz et quant en la dicte chapelle aura messe de prelat ou
quant l'autel sera paree par son ordonnance, tous lesditz chapelains, clercz et
sommeliers seront tenus d'estre vestus pareil des robes de livree que derreniere-
ment ilz auront eu, et de chaperons de semblable couleur et deveront estre
barbiés de nouvel, et le tout sur paine de perdre les gaiges de la journee.

[15: further details of chapel services to be written down for all to see]
Item au regard de cerimonies que en faisant le service divin lesditz de la
chapelle deveront observer outre les choses contenues en ces presentes
ordonnances, monditseigneur veult que, par l'advis de son premier chapelain,
deux de ces conseillers que a ce deputera, et deux des plus anchiens de ladite
chapelle, soient icelles cerimonies redigees par l'escript et misses avec les
livres[8] de sa dicte chapelle adfin que chascun a qui appartient en puisse avoir
vision et lecture.

[16: code of behaviour] [f. 14*v*]
Item pource que monditseigneur de tout son ceur desire le divin service
dessusdit estre a Dieu agreable au salut des ames de ces predicesseurs et de luy,
et que de bouche de pecheur ne belle ne plaisant a Dieu la louenge, il en vertu
de sainte charité requiert et exorte ses ditz chapelains, clercz et autres de sa
dicte chapelle que, aians regard a sa bonne intencion, ilz se veueillent deter-
miner de si bien et honnestement vivre en bien observant leur saint et digne
estat que les sacrifices et louenges procedans de leurs bouches et voix soient
acceptables devant Dieu, et pourtant veueillent eviter toutes dissolutions de
habilemens de parolles et de fait, toutes compagnies de personnes diffamees ou
suspectes d'auchun maulvais vice, tous jeux de quartes, de dez, et autres
deffenduz par les saintz decretz,[9] aussi jeux de palmes, de barres, de luites et
traieries d'arcq a main et d'arbalestre en lieux publiques et communs, tavernes
publiques ce n'est en cas necessaire, tous bordeaulx indifferamment, aller de
nuyt faisant bruyt ou tumulte, chanter ou houver[10] par rues de nuyt ou de jour,

---

  7 MS: garnitu.
  8 MS: livre.
  9 MS: decrtz.
 10 The 'uv' element in this word is palaeographically ambiguous, comprising simply four minims.
      Its meaning is obvious enough, though none of the standard mediaeval dictionaries seems to
      give any appropriate word.

jurer desordonnement, comme par sang, par mort, par plaies ou par autre partie du precieux corps de Nostreseigneur, regnier ou despiter son saint nom qui sont sermens blasphematoires et parolles excecrables ou autres choses semblables et deffendues de droit a gens d'eglise; et s'ilz font au contraire ilz encourront la paine de perdition de gaiges pour autant de jours [f. 15r] que par le premier chapelain, eulx oys, sera arbitré et ordonné, en regard a la qualité et quantité du meffait.

[17: particular ruling on relations with women]
Item par expres ilz evitent tous concubinage et ne tiennent avec ou pres d'eulx ne mainent ne facent mener apres ne devant eux[11] femme suspecte; et s'ilz font du contraire apres la premiere monition dudit premier chapelain seront royés et suspendus de leurs gaiges; et ce ilz perseverent par ung moys apres la seconde monition dudit premier chapelain, ilz seront privés de l'abit et de l'entree de la dite chapelle.

[18: the Feast of Fools to be abolished]
Item et pource que les degrez, dignitez ou prelatures de nostre mere Sainte Eglise sont instituez pour representer la celeste gerarchye de paradis, et que user du nom d'icelles dignités et prelatures autrement que en ce a quoy elles sont institutees est grandement deroguier[12] a l'honneur de Dieu meismement quant soubz telz dignes noms sont faiz et excercez actes derisoires, illicites et non convenables a personnes ecclesiastiques, comme sont les choses qui communement sont faites et excercees soubz couleur d'une dissolue feste nommee vulgairement la feste aux folz, laquelle au temps passé a esté permise et tolleree chascun an estre faicte en ladite chapelle, en atribuant nom de abbé a auchun des supostz d'icelle, [f. 15v] soubz et avec lequel ainsi nommé les autres de la dicte chapelle se difforment et transforment de leur habit ecclesiastique en habitz seculiers et illicites a leur estat, font aussi plusieurs autres dissolutions en publique spectacle de leurs presonnes et autrement en exorbitant de bonnes meurs, toutes lesquelles chosses par les saintz decretz sont estroitement deffendus, monditseigneur, voulant ad ce pourveoier, et non tollerer ne permettre choses interdites ou auchunement derrogans a l'honneur divin et honnesteté ecclesiastique, ordonne et veult doresenavant et a tousjours la dicte feste cesser, et que nul de quelque estat qu'il soit en la dicte chapelle se evance de faire ou excercer auchunes des choses dessusditz; et ce sur peine d'estre privé a tousjours de la dicte chapelle.

[19: behaviour in chapel]
Item et adfin que chaschun soit ententif au service divin et que nul n'y soit empesché ou troblé durant iceluy, monditseigneur exorte ausditz chapelains, clercz et autres de sa dicte chapelle eviter tous langages, devises, collocutions,

---

11 MS: aux.
12 MS: deroguie.

152   David Fallows

mocqueries, signes, derrisions, jeux, riz immoderés et toutes autres choses vaines et legieres; aussi que nul d'eulx en delaissant la chanterie et service ne die ses heures particulierement ou ce occupe a autre chose que a la chanterie, ains entendent songneusement ou dit service[13] en telle gravité et sillence qu'il apartient, ou autrement encourront la paine de deux solz parisis [f. 16r] a exiger sur le delinquant toutes les foiz qu'il sera transgresseur ou contemptieur de ceste ordonnance.

[20: first chaplain to have authority over all secular servants of the duke when in chapel]
Item s'il y a auchun seculier serviteur de monditseigneur ou autre, de quelque estat ou preminence qu'ilz soient, qui par langages, devises, collocutions, jeux, ris ou autres choses semblables durant ledit service face empeschement ausditz chapelains ou audit service, sans dissimulation quelconcque, le premier chapelain le face taire et deporter en le faisant partir du parquet et soy eslongier d'illec ce besoing est; et ou cas que tel empescheur ou troubleur ne vouldra obtemperer, monditseigneur veult et ordonne que incontinent il luy soit denuncié par le dit premier chapelain pour y estre pourveu ainsi qu'il apartendra.

[21: first chaplain to ensure that chaplains treat one another peaceably]
Item et pour ce que nostre saulveur Jhesucrist, qui est aucteur et amateur de paix, veult et doit estre servy en paix et union, monditseigneur enhorte lesditz chapelains, clercz et sommeliers estre par bonne amour et concorde unis ensemble sans ce que entre eulx ait auchune rumeur, debat ou malvueillance; et ce entre auchuns d'eulx y a difference, discord ou question, soit apaisé par le premier chapelain leur chief, lequel sommierement les apointera, ce faire le peult, sinon sera referé en leur chapitre pour y estre apointé et ordonné comme il apartendra.

[22: more difficult disputes to be resolved by the entire college] [f. 16v]
Item pose ores que des discortz, debas, question ou hoyne par les parties ou auchuns d'icelles n'en soit faicte plainte ou raport au premier chapelain, il neaulmoins se informera de la verité et icelle sceue et congnue ou cas que au dit et ordonnance de luy ilz ne se volront appaser et acorder, il les convocquera en l'assemblee de tout le college et par fraternelle motion ne les peult ancores induire a eulx concorder et appaisier, lors par l'advis de tout ledit college les contraindra par tous bons moyens par luy et ledit college advisez adfin de entendre audit apaisement, et icelluy advis entretenir.

[23: first chaplain to ensure that debts are paid by members of the chapel]
Item ce auchunes personnes, comme hostes marchans ou autres, se plaindent et

---

13   MS: sevice.

font dolleances d'aulchun de la dite chapelle, ce c'est pour injure ycelle congnue par le dit premier chapelain, il la fera reparer par l'injuriant ainsi qu'il apartendra en competente moderation; et ce c'est pour debte constraindra le debteur luy ouy a celle debte a vray cogneue a contenter le complaignant, tant par la retention des gaiges dudit debteur jusque a fin de paye comme autrement par toute raison.

[24: organisational and disciplinary meeting of the chapel to take place weekly, normally on Monday morning]
Item chascun lundi de l'an du matin, ou autre jour en la sepmaine a la discretion dudit premier chapelain, seront tenus tous ceulx de la chapelle, chascun sur paine de deux solz parisis, de eulx assembler capitulairement au commandement du dit premier chapelain ou au lieu par [f. 17*r*] luy ordonné lequel presidera entreulx; et illec sera premierement ordonné du service des jours et festes qui escherront en la sepmaine ensieuvant et jusques au prochain chapitre avenir; puis sera ordonneement advisé se les ordonnances et cerimonies du service auront esté bien observés en la sepmaine precedente; s'il y a auchune chose a reformer et corriger sur les meurs de aucun ou auchuns d'iceulx de la chapelle, se les privees reprehentions et exortations ou correction dudit premier chapelain auront esté bien prinses et rechevez par les defaillans, et ce en auchune des choses dessusditez il treuve faulte, mesmement apres fraternelle[14] monition et reprehention, il declairera les faultes en la dite assemblee, en increpant les delinquans de leurs dictes faultes, et en icelle assemblee les reduira a humilité et obeissance, et si presistent en leurs dictes faultes ilz seront pugnis et corrigés selon l'exigence du cas, et seront les paignes exigees et levees sur leurs gaiges.

[25: the said meeting to include opportunities for more general discussion]
Item et apres les dessusditz ainsi assemblés traiteront des affaires communs de la dicte chapelle, et devra chascun d'eulx advertir leur president de toutes choses qu'il saura estre servans au bien commun d'ycelle, lesquelles choses seront misses en deliberation par le dit president qui demandera les opinions par ordre et conclura a la plus grande et saine partie desditz opinions; [f. 17*v*] et s'il y a auchun troublant l'assemblee ou l'ordre des deliberacions ou opinions le dit president luy imposera sillence, et s'il n'obeyst prendra[15] ces gaiges du jour.

[26: the meeting to end with an exhortation followed by prayers in the chapel]
Item en la fin de chascun chapitre ou assemblee, le dit premier chapelain leur fera tousjours aulcunes bonnes et salutaires exhortations pour adez les mouvoir a bien et honnestement vivre en[16] leur estat et eulx acquiter devant Dieu, aussi

---

14   MS: fraterle.
15   MS: predra.
16   MS: et.

154   David Fallows

a prier Dieu pour monditseigneur et son estat et qui luy doint grace de tellement regir et gouverner son peuple et pays selon sa sainte volunté. Apres ce
tous s'en yront par ordre en la chapelle, entreront en leur parquet, se mettront
tous a genoulz et en l'intention d'icelluyseigneur diront devotement le
psaulme, 'Exaudiat te Dominus in die tribulationis', &c. avec auchunes prieres,
maismement ceste oraison, 'Oremus pro principe nostro regem, Dominus con-
servet eum' &c., et en la fin de la colecte, 'Protege Domine ducem nostrum c.'
et autres telles qu'il plaira au president; et s'il y a auchun qui sans licence dudit
premier chapelain se departe de la dicte assamblee avant la fin de toutes les
choses dessusditez il perdra ces gaiges de celluy jour.[17]

[27: members of the chapel may absent themselves only with first chaplain's
permission]
Item ne devera ne pourra auchun de ceulx de la dicte chapelle soy absenter ne
aller dehors pour [f. 18r] quelque cause que ce soit sans la licence et congié
dudit premier chapelain; et s'il y a auchun qui sans congié ou licence de luy soy
absent, il sera royé pour tout le temps de son abcence et huit jours apres son
retour.

[28: permission for absence to be granted to only two at a time, and even then
ensuring that there are always two tenors and two contras]
Item adfin que le service ne soit diminué ou defectueux, le dit premier
chapelain, en donnant les ditz congié et licence de aller dehors, aura tel regard
que en ung meisme temps n'y ayt plus de deux absens, tellement que ung troi-
ziesme ne se peult absenter jousques au retour de l'ung des deux absens; ausi il
aura regard aux teneurs et contres tellement que le service soit tousjours fourny
de deux teneurs et de deux contres.

[29: if chapel members are ill they will be paid during their absence]
Item quant auchuns de la dicte chapelle seront vrayment malades, sans simula-
tion ou faintise, durant leur telle maladie ne seront tenus d'estre ne comparoir
au service et ne seront auchunement royez, ains gaigneront leurs gaiges comme
presens audit service.

[30: chapel members are financially responsible for providing their robes and
hoods in material designated by the first chaplain]
Item les deniers que lesditz de la chapelle recepvront pour leurs seront tenus
d'acheter draps de telle couleur et sorte que ordonnera et choisira le dit premier
chapelain et en feront robes longues, honnestes et [f. 18v] ecclesiastiques
comme cy dessus est escript; et seront ycelles robes fourrees de telles pannes et
fourrures que le dit premier chapelain ordonnera, a quoy chascun sera
optemperer et obeyr, et auront tous lesdessusditz chaperons a courte cornette
du meismes drap des dessusdites robes.

17   All of paragraph 26 is translated in Vaughan, *Charles the Bold*, p. 194.

[31: payment is quarterly from the hand of the first chaplain]
Item adfin que lesditz chapelains, clercz et sommeliers ne soient auchunement defaillans et destrais du divin service, ne occupés en difficilles poursieutes pour le paiement de leurs gaiges, et pour obvier aux grans fraiz, travail et despens qu'ilz aroient a la cause dessusdite s'il convenoit qu'ilz poursievissent leurdit paiement a grand longueur, monditseigneur veult, ordonne et luy plaist que tant pour les gaiges desditz de sa chapelle et leurs robes comme pour frais extraordinaires, qui sont achat de surplis, les gaiges d'ung jour en l'an de bisexte, fournir toutes autres chosses necessaires en sa chapelle, excepté livres nouveaulx, coffres, almuces, chosses d'or, d'argent, de fer et de cyre, la somme a quoy monteront yceulx gaiges, robes et fraiz extraordinaires, extimees a la somme de dix mil frans royaulx et au dessoubz, soit faicte et baillee asignation par descharge ou autrement, ainsi qu'il aparterdra audit premier chapelain, [f. 19*r*] pour chascun terme prendre et recepvoir la dicte somme par luy ledit terme escheu, sur le recepveur de la composicion ordinaire des aydes de la Conte d'Artois present et advenir a quatre termes, c'est ascavoir de troys moys en troys moys sans ce que pour quelconque cause la dicte assignation soit rompue, changié ou muee, et a chascun des ditz termes lesditz de la chapelle recepvront leurs gaiges par la main d'icelluy premier chapelain.

[32: members of the chapel to provide their own horses]
Item seront tenus lesditz chapelains d'avoir et tenir chevaulx honnestes, ascavoir le premier chapelain quatre chevaulx, chascun desditz chapelains deux chevaulx, clercz et sommeliers le deux troys chevaulx, et le fourrier ung cheval.

DE L'OFFICE DUDIT PREMIER CHAPELAIN
[1: duties and services]
Oultre les choses dessus ordonnees appartient il au dit premier chapelain servir monditseigneur de l'eaue benoiste devant la messe et pareillement aux [f. 19*v*] vespres et matines s'il n'y a prelat; item du livre de l'evvangille et de la paix se pareillement n'y a prelat ou dyacre; et ce dyacre y a tousjours portera l'evvangille et la paix, pose ores qu'il y ait prelat; et quant prelat y aura et non dyacre le dit premier chapelain luy baillera le livre de l'evvangille et aussi la paix, puys ce mettra devant et le conduira devers monditseigneur, et semblablement fera au service de l'eau benoite.

[2: to say all services in the absence of a prelate]
Item fera l'office de vespres, messes, matines et autres heures a jours solempnelz quant n'y aura prelat officiant, dira aussi la derreniere lichon a toutes matines et vigille de mors.

[3: perquisites to which he is entitled]
Item que pource que parcidevant le premier chapelain a voulu maintenir a droit, et tenir pour uzaige, que quant noepces et obseques se faisoient en la dicte

156   David Fallows

chapelle domestique de l'ostel de monditseigneur le drap de palle luy devoit appartenir, et semblablement les chierges beneys de Pasques et Penthecouste tantost qu'il avoient servy esditz jours, le blazon mis sur la representacion du corps dont ce faisoit l'obseque et ausi sa portion avec les autres chapelains et clercz des chierges et autres cyres qui avoient servi aux obseques faiz en ladicte chapelle, monditseigneur voulant a ce pourveoir a reservé et reserve a luy la determination et de[f. 20*r*]clation des chosses dessusdictez et chascune d'icelles pour auchunefoiz que le cas escherra.

[4: he must share offerings with the chaplains]
Item au regard des offrandes sera gardee l'usance et coustume anchienne sans derroguier ne auchunement prejudicier au droit parrochial et lesquelz offrendes seront parties entre lesditz chapelains egalement.

DES SOMMELIERS
[1: three of the five to attend on the duke in his oratory]
De cinq sommeliers monditseigneur en eslira troys telz qu'il luy plaira pour estre avec luy et le servir en son oratoire, dont le premier aura robe de chapelain comme dit est dessus et aydera monditseigneur a dire ses heures en l'absence de son confesseur, et les deux autres serviront a l'huys et aulx basses messes par tour.

[2: other two take turns serving at the altar]
Item les autres deulx sommeliers par tour de sepmaines serviront au grant autel pour les haultes messes, administreront au prestre, et diront les espistres; aussi serviront de livres au letery et de chapes a ceulx qui tendront ceur.

[3: the most junior of each group to sleep near the chapel to protect it]
Item sera tousjours delivree une chambrette et logiz competent pres de la chepelle pour deux desditz sommeliers, ascavoir ung de l'oratoire et ung de la chapelle, les plus jeunes et derreniers venuz en l'office, en la[f. 20*v*]quelle chambre aura ung lit pour lesdessus ditz et une couchette pour leur clercq, et seront tenuz les ditz sommeliers plus jeunes en l'office et ung leur clercq de y couchier pour garder tout ce qui sera en icelle chapelle et oratoire.

[4: these two to be in attendance early to help members of the household to celebrate Mass]
Item ceulx desditz sommeliers qui coucheront en la dicte chambrette seront tenus d'estre au matin de bonne heure en la chapelle pour[18] administrer aux chapelains de ceulx du sang, des chambellans, maistres d'ostel et autres serviteurs de monditseigneur qui en ladicte chapelle voulront avoir messe, aians regard a ce que les autelz ne soient occupés a l'heure que monditseigneur viendra a ses messes; et ne permetront auchuns prestres estrangiers, de

18 MS: pou.

quelque[19] estat ou profession qu'ilz soient, autres que les dessusditz celebrer en la dicte chapelle, ce n'est par le congié et licence des confesseur, premier chapelain ou aumosnier; et auront lesditz sommeliers chascun une quarte de vin de la bouche pour lesditz messes qui lendemain seront celebrees en la dicte chapelle laquelle quarte de vin ilz garderont bien honnestement.

[5: one of the oratory *sommeliers* to obtain times of Mass from the duke]
Item les sommeliers de l'oratoire seront ou sera l'ung d'eulx au lever de table auz graces devers monditseigneur, meismement au souper pour scavoir de quelle heure le lendemain il voulra avoir les ditz messes; et s'il [f. 21r] advient qu'il veueille avoir ses dictes messes de grant matin, il le fera scavoir au fourrier de la chapelle qui le fera ascavoir a tous les chapelains et aultres.

[6: the chapel *sommelier* who is serving at the altar responsible to see that all goes smoothly]
Item l'autre sommelier sepmainier servant au[x] basses messes soignera d'icelles messes devers lesditz confesseur et aulmosnier qui sont chargiez desdictz messes, adfin qu'il n'y ait auchune faulte.

[7: wood and candles to be supplied to the *sommeliers* who sleep near the chapel]
Item en yver sera delivré boys ausditz sommeliers couchans en la chambre pour fournir l'oratoire, et en auront en telle quantité qu'il souffira pour le dit oratoire et pour leur dicte chambrette, pareillement leur seront livrés filletz et chandeilles de sieuf a souffissance adfin qu'ilz ne usent des chierges et torches.

[8: and they must order more when necessary]
Item sont tenus les ditz sommeliers d'entendre et avoir soing sur le luminaire de la chapelle tellement que quant torches seront usees a moitié et chierges ung peu plus avant on les rendera au frutier qui en deliverra torches neufves et chierges neufz.

[9: and take responsibility for altar cloths and other appurtenances at major feasts]
Item troys jours devant chascune haulte feste ayant parement d'autel les som-meliers de la chapelle se trairont devers le premier chapelain pour scavoir de luy quel devera estre le parement d'autel, tant en [f. 21v] ymages et joyaulx comme en chierges, et que leur sera ordonné par ledit premier chapelain selon l'ordinaire de la chapelle le signifiront aux gardes des joyaulx et fruitier pour par eulx estre acompliz selon la charge et office de chascun d'eulx.

[10: responsibility for the jewels on the altar]
Item appartient aux deux sommeliers de la chapelle que du moins l'ung d'eulx soit present a porter les joyaulx sur l'autel et a les raporter; et ce faulte y a chascun desditz sommeliers perdra ces gaiges du jour.

19 MS: queque.

158   David Fallows

[11: to provide for a prelate giving Mass to the duke at a solemn feast]
Item aux festes solempneles, quant les messes doivent estre de prelat, le premier
chapelain a la solicitacion des sommeliers advisera de quel prelat bonnement et
sans son grief monditseigneur pourra estra servy, et luy sera escript de par luy
faire l'office devant luy au dit jour solempnel; et seront tenuz lesditz sommeliers d'avertir le dit prelat sur le faict de l'office tant de vespres que de messe,
en luy administrant livre, aornemens et aultres chosses servans a l'office et
aux cerimonies.

[12: *sommeliers* forbidden to ask for payment from such prelates]
Item pource que les ditz prelatz qui, pour decorer le service divin et l'estat de
monditseigneur, viennent officier devant luy en ce faisant soustiennent labeur
et fraiz, par quoy raison ne veult qu'ilz soient autrement chargiés envers lesditz
sommeliers et autres, mon avant [f. 22r] dit seigneur a deffendu et deffend aux
ditz sommeliers que d'iceulz prelatz qui doresenavant officieront devant luy,
soit pour la premiere foiz ou autrement, ilz ne exigent ne requierent auchune
somme de deniers en quelque[20] maniere que ce soit, se n'est que lesditz prelatz
de leur pure liberalité sans requeste ou impression leur vueillent faire auchune
courtoisie telle que bon leur semblera.

[13: arrangements for dining after Mass]
Item et pource que lesditz chapelains pourroient maintenir et tenir pour usaige
que a chascune foys que a jour sollempnel il y auroit prelat faisant ledit office ilz
deveroient disgner en sale et acompaigner ledit prelat, monditseigneur
ordonne, veult et declaire que lesditz de sa chapelle ne mengeront en son hostel
ne a sa charge, fors es quatre nataulz de l'an seulement, mais toutesfoys que en
aultres festes et solempnitez il y aura prelat ayant celebré devant luy, icelluy
prelat aura son plat de viande qui sera porté en son hostel.[21]

[14: the chapel *sommeliers* to use servants only to protect chapel jewels, etc.]
Item lesditz deux sommeliers ne prendront varletz ou serviteurs que ce ne soit
par le sceu et consentement dudit premier chapelain, et ce pour la sceureté de
joyaulx et autres choses de la chapelle.

---

20   MS: queque.
21   Later in the same document this information is repeated under 'Ordonnance touchant les offi-
     ciers particulliers': '[f. 31v] Et pour ce que les chapelains de la chapelle de monditseigneur
     [f. 32r] pourroient maintenir et tenir pour uzage que a chascune fois que a jour solempnel il y
     avoit prelat faisant l'office de la messe devant monditseigneur, ilz deveroient disgner en salle et
     acompaigner ledit prelat, monditseigneur ordonne, veult et declaire que lesditz de sa chapelle ne
     mengeront a son hostel ne a sa charge fos es quatre nataulz tantseulement, mais toutesfoiz que
     en autres festes et solempnitez il y aura prelat celebrant devant luy, icelluy prelat aura son plat de
     viande qui sera porté en son hostel, comme au chapitre des articles de la dicte chapelle cy devant
     mis et declairé.'

[15: oratory *sommeliers* in certain circumstances need not attend Matins or Hours wearing surplices]

Item les sommeliers de l'oratoire ne seront tenus d'estre aux matines et autres heures portans sourplis quant ilz seront occupés ou service du dit oratoire ou par l'or[f. 22*v*]donnance de monditseigneur et autrement deuement.

[16: perquisites of the five *sommeliers*]

Item quant aux drapz du siege de l'oratoire, courtines, coussins et couvertures des breviaires et heures de monditseigneur, lesquelz tantost qu'ilz sont renovelez lesdits troys sommeliers de l'oratoire dient qu'ilz leur doivent apartenir, et semblablement les treise chierges de tenebres, et les deux qui luisent en la custode ou repose le corps de nostreseigneur depuys le Grant Jeudi jusques au lendemain, les deux flambeaulz de la nuyt de Noel et les quatre bastons de quoy l'en porte le ciel a la feste du Sacrement, lesquelz lesditz chincq sommeliers ensemble dient a eulz devoir appartenir, monditseigneur veult et ordonne que tous yceulx sommeliers se riglent ou gouvernent entierement[22] de ces droitz et emolumens selon l'usance et la maniere que leurs predicesseurs en office en ont jouy et uzé par cy devant et jusques a present, et non autrement.

ORDONNANCE DU FOURRIER DE LA CHAPELLE

L'office du fourrier de la dicte chapelle est premierement de prendre quartier pour icelle en tous lieux ou monditseigneur yra, de distribuer les logis a chascun desditz de la chapelle selon son degré, d'estre ou divin service, et durant icelluy garder l'huis de la dicte chapelle, et avoir regard quelz gens il y devera [f. 23*r*] laisser entrer, de fournir may, et herbe verte en esté aux solempnités, et au Noel de l'estrain blancq ensemble du feu de la salle, de songnier des fons a Pasques et Penthecouste, du chandelier pour le chierge benoist, de celuy des treize chierges de tenebres, d'ung coullon blancq et autres oyseletz estoupés et nieulles a la messe du jour de Penthecouste, de fournir bancz et sieges pour les parquet et sieges desditz de la chapelle, de songner et ordonner les places desditz de la chapelle selon le degré de chascun d'eulx; quant monditseigneur mengera en sale a aulchune solempnité de soingnier des quatre chandeliers et d'estrain pour la representacion quant obseques se feront par l'ordonnance de monditseigneur, et de faire assembler lesditz de la chapelle quant par auchun sommelier ou autre[23] luy sera signifié de ce faire.

[colophon][f. 47*r*]

Donnons en mandement a nostre treschier et feal chevalier et chancellier le sieur de Goux et de Wedergrate . . . [f. 48*r*] 1 jenvier 1468 [= 1469 new style].

22 MS: etierement.
23 MS: autr.

Part II
Songs

[3]

Going beyond the limits: experiments with vocalization in the French chanson, 1340–1440

Christopher Page

To study the performance of medieval music is to approach the edge of a cliff. We can go so far and then the evidence abruptly comes to an end, leaving a sheer drop into a sea of troubles where performers must navigate as best they can. Two recent articles, by Dennis Slavin and Lawrence Earp,[1] provide a case in point. These two scholars agree that *a cappella* performance of the chanson repertory was common in the later Middle Ages; they are also united in their belief that the partial textings found in the sources of numerous pieces (predominantly of the 15th century) imply an *a cappella* scoring.[2] This is the path that leads them to the edge of the precipice, for in their discussion of how the textless lines in chansons should be sung Earp and Slavin (certain disagreements aside) both recommend vocalization. Slavin advocates 'wordless vocalization for untexted passages' in certain contexts, while Earp declares that 'performers must experiment with vocalization of textless passages'.[3] Both scholars halt at this point, but performers will wish to go beyond the limits of the evidence (as conventionally understood) by asking questions that musicologists are usually constrained to leave unanswered or even unasked. What is vocalization? How is it to be done? Can it be made to work today, and how are we to judge whether it is working or not?

The vocalization of textless parts in medieval polyphony has been advocated by various scholars for at least 25 years[4] so the time has come to explore this technique. In doing so here, I hope that this article may also explore the question of whether practical experiment by performers can ever be raised to the level of a research tool in the study of medieval music. An English broadcaster has recently remarked that, when hearing familiar voices on the radio, he does not form any coherent impression of what the speakers look like, and yet, when he discovers what they do look like, he is invariably both surprised and (in a strange way) disappointed. Many musicologists who study the Middle Ages may have a comparable conception of the music to which they devote their lives; they are both surprised and (often) disappointed when the music they know from manuscripts and editions shifts from that special state of poise, potential and perfection in which scholars hold the material they love and suddenly becomes contingent upon the tastes, abilities and prejudices of someone else. If there are some scholars who will always wish to resist any suggestion that practical experiment may have some legitimate research status it may partly be because of such a process as I have just described. More to the point, perhaps, is that a scholar's reluctance to accept the results of practical experiment will often rest upon the apparent impossibility of describing those results in an objective manner. In what follows I have accordingly tried to describe the results of experiments with vocalization conducted during the last five years[5] using the expertise of singers and acousticians to endow those descriptions with some degree of precision and impartiality. Unless fresh evidence comes to light (a description of vocalization in a medieval text, for example) it will never be possible to establish how singers vocalized in late medieval France; I wish to suggest, however, that it is possible to find a relatively objective way of describing certain phenomena in vocalization that were just as accessible to the ears of 14th-century singers as they are to ours and therefore just as likely to have influenced what was attempted.

Let us begin with evidence of a more familiar order, however, by succinctly placing the current debate about the *a cappella* performance of late medieval chansons in context. A summary of this kind is required since research in this area is now moving unexpectedly fast.

The debate has been inspired by several changes in current thinking. First, a body of literary evidence demonstrates that *a cappella* performance of chansons

1 Choirmaster and choristers. Illumination from *La Bible hystoriaux* (French, late 14th century)

was more common in the 14th and 15th centuries than was imagined as recently as the 1970s. This evidence is 'literary' rather than 'documentary' (a much abused word), in the sense that it is principally drawn from romances and chronicles, texts which are sometimes hard to distinguish from one another in terms of their diction and tone, even though the romances are nominally fiction, while the chronicles are supposedly constrained by fact. These materials are subject to certain limitations, not all of which may be completely understood at present, but taken together they possess an authority that seems not to have been recognized or acknowledged until recently.[6] There can be little doubt that more evidence of this kind is waiting to be discovered, and new research with literary sources hitherto unknown to the *a cappella* debate is already producing valuable results.[7]

Second, it is no longer possible to be confident that we understand the nature of instrumental traditions and repertories in the Middle Ages. This is a wider-ranging point whose significance is not always grasped in musicological research since it has been developed within the context of organology.[8] When did instrumentalists (other than keyboard players) begin to perform composed polyphony? Who were the musicians who first pushed instrumental technique in that direction? These questions—so easy to pose but so hard to answer— cannot be resolved at present. In more specific terms, little is known for certain about the playing techniques and capacities of most Gothic instruments, and the difficulty of defining the performing pitch of the chanson repertory only weakens still further our ability to assert with confidence that any given instrument was able to perform a line in a chanson at the appropriate pitch for singers and with the expected *musica ficta* adjustments.

Consider the late 15th-century instruments depicted (by a nice irony) on the cover of the number of *Early Music* which contains the articles by Earp and Slavin mentioned above (May 1991). Although several important instruments of the late 15th century are missing (the lute for example, and the harpsichord) this depiction of 'the men and women who compiled the Book of Psalms' shows real 15th-century instruments in their current state of technology. Real they may be, but it is none the less difficult to see how any of them could have been very useful in performing the textless parts of chansons. The fiddle (a proto viol) may be flat-bridged, in effect, since the strings appear to be secured on a stringholder like that of the modern guitar. The straight trumpet, restricted to the harmonic series, would have been a ceremo-

nial and signalling instrument, possibly of some use in simple kinds of dance music; something similar may probably be said of the frame drum. The portative organ might have doubled the cantus or an inner part at the octave, but contrary to what has often been suggested in the past, such portatives would have been of very limited use in the unsupported performance of textless parts because of their high tessitura.[9] The dulcimer has surprisingly few strings (in common with many other representations of this kind of instrument) and if a tolerably accurate assessment of its size may be made from the picture, it does not appear to be large enough for the strings to reach suitably low pitches, even if they were metallic, as seems likely.[10] The recorder, like the portative, might have doubled a part at the octave, but the inherent octave ambiguity of its sound might have made performers reluctant to entrust a tenor or contratenor part to it alone in company with singers. Of all the instruments depicted, only the harp seems a likely candidate for the performance of lines in chansons, but even there the problem of determining how 15th-century harpists produced chromatic adjustments causes a veil of uncertainty to descend.[11]

These are worrying doubts. What is certain is that the incursion of musical literacy into the realm of instrumental playing, formerly dominated by aural tradition and by heterophony,[12] was slow and uneven in the 14th century. Some time before 1325 the theorist Engelbert of Admont declared instrumentalists to be musicians working entirely *ex usu*, that is to say by manual dexterity and aural tradition alone,[13] while Jacques de Liège remarks, in characteristically emphatic terms, that voices are simply more musical than harps, lutes, fiddles and the rest.[14] Around 1400 Arnulf de Saint Ghislain speaks of instrumentalists (perhaps with some exaggeration) as being 'entirely lacking in musical art'.[15] In the light of testimony such as this, which has not received its due measure of attention, the role of instruments in performing chansons seems less clear than it did between 1965 and 1975, the Heroic Age of the medieval revival.[16]

Third—and this is a point whose importance cannot be overemphasized—the evidence of sacred polyphony suggests that vocalization was a standard resource of trained singers in the late Middle Ages. If we accept the prevailing view that musical instruments other than the organ were normally excluded from medieval liturgical celebrations,[17] then singers must have found *a cappella* solutions to textures of the kind shown in exx.1 and 2, the former in motet style and the latter in the manner of

Ex.1   Johannes Ciconia, Credo 4, opening (*The Works of Johannes Ciconia*, ed. M. Bent and A. Hallmark, Polyphonic Music of
the Fourteenth Century, xxiv (Monaco, 1985), p.18)

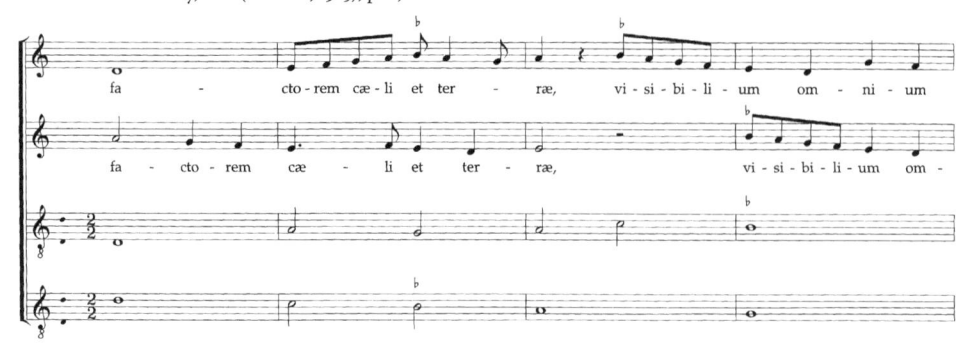

Ex.2   *O sacra virgo beata*, opening (*Fourteenth Century Mass Music in France*, ed. H. Stäblein-Harder, CMM, xix (American
Institute of Musicology, 1962), ii, p.17)

the contemporary chanson. In the absence of instruments, and with evidence of partial texting (or the use of
solmization syllables) surprisingly sparse, vocalization
seems a likely solution.[18]

Slavin and Earp have now added a fourth major consideration to these, for their articles bring the state of the
sources into sharper focus. It now appears to be an over-
simplification to declare that '15th-century scribes
almost never added texts to the lower voices' of polyphonic chansons.[19] Slavin's study shows how a scribe

texted all three voices of a Binchois chanson—thus
doing what some modern performers have been doing
for years—while both he and Earp emphasize the
importance of partial texting at points of imitation and
declamation as evidence for *a cappella* scorings.

It is worth dwelling upon the question of partial texting with 14th-century evidence not cited directly by
either Earp or Slavin. A search through French secular
songs from the 14th century reveals a number of pieces
where the presence of voices on a textless line is clearly

Ex.3 Jacob de Senleches, virelai *En ce gracieux tamps*, excerpt showing partial texting in the triplum (*French Secular Compositions of the Fourteenth Century*, ed. W. Apel, CMM, liii/l (American Institute of Musicology, 1970), i, p.175)

Ex.4 Matheus de Sancto Johanne, ballade *Science n'a nul annemi*, excerpt showing partial texting in the triplum and imitative passages, presumably for texting in tenor and contratenor (*French Secular Compositions*, ed. Apel, i, p.138)

implied. The 'presence of voices' is not the same as an *a cappella* scoring, of course, but it is none the less important to recognize that the vocal performance of entirely or predominantly textless lines is envisaged by the sources. A virelai by Jacob de Senleches, *En ce gracieux tamps*, appears in the Reina codex (F-Pn, n.a.f.6771, f.58v) with a texted cantus between a textless triplum and tenor, but in the B section the triplum suddenly acquires text as it imitates a repeated melodic phrase in the cantus carrying the word 'cocu' four times (ex.3). The triplum is not texted in *ModA* (I-MOe α.M.5.24, f.25v), providing a clear indication—if one were needed—that scribes were not always inclined to indicate a composer's intentions with regards to such instances of partial texting, and not always adept at discerning them. It is surely unlikely that the triplum of *En ce gracieux tamps* was designed for instrumentalists prepared to burst into song;[20] in all probability the predominantly textless triplum was intended for a singer.

A more concealed but equally revealing example is provided by the B section of a four-voice ballade by

Matheus de Sancto Johanne, a French composer who has recently been traced in England as a clerk in the household chapel of Queen Philippa in the year 1368.[21] *Science n'a nul annemi*, preserved only in the Chantilly codex, has a cantus part which includes the interjection 'Hay avant!' set to a rising 3rd. This motif is imitated in all the other parts and is anticipated in the triplum and tenor (ex.4). The scribe has texted the point of imitation in the triplum only, but it is probably safe to regard the textless tenor and contratenor parts as designed for vocal performance with the 'Hay avant!' motif texted. The words 'La mort Machaut' in F. Andrieu's well-known lament for Guillaume de Machaut (d 1377) would surely have been declaimed in all four parts, even though they are only underlaid to the two cantus parts in the Chantilly codex, the unique source for of the piece (ex.5). We may suspect something similar in the anonymous ballade *Marticius qui fu*, a three-part work whose musical idiom owes much to the mature style of Machaut; here the tenor suddenly imitates the cantus in one passage (ex.6), and the composer may have intended that the imitation in the tenor should follow the cantus and bear the text 'fu de Rome neis'. In this case the part must be performed by a singer who is presumably to vocalize his line throughout, except at this point. The case is slightly different, however, with a nearly identical passage in the B section of the same piece (ex.7); there the tenor can only be texted at the cost of breaking the text 'Toudis en loialté' into '-dis en loialté'. Would this have been acceptable practice? It is impossible to answer that question at present.

Taken together, the articles by Slavin and Earp begin to trace the outline of the vocalizing tradition. In the 14th century it would appear to have been a common technique, for Earp is surely right to maintain that the sources provide no warrant for texting the wordless tenors and contratenors of chansons by Machaut and his immediate successors. If these parts were sung at all, then they were vocalized, except when instances of partial texting like those described above (admittedly rare) indicated otherwise. With the songs of the early 15th century, however, the picture is somewhat different. A significant number of compositions, both sacred and

Ex.5   Andrieu, double ballade *Armes, amours/O flour des flours*, excerpt (*French Secular Compositions*, ed. Apel, i, p.3)

Ex.6   Ballade, *Marticius qui fu*, excerpt showing imitation between cantus and tenor (*French Secular Compositions*, ed. Apel, ii, p.77)

Ex.7   Ballade, *Marticius qui fu*, a second excerpt showing imitation between cantus and tenor (*French Secular Compositions*, ed. Apel, ii, p.78)

2   Singing angels. Detail of the altar-piece *The Mystic Lamb* in the Church of St Bavo, Ghent, painted by Jan van Eyck. (Another panel of the altar-piece is reproduced on p.464.)

secular, appear with at least one part either fully or partially texted in addition to the superius. Boldly interpreted, this evidence seems to indicate a recession of the vocalizing tradition in favour of a new, declamatory one. At the same time, instances of brief partial texting (generally at moments of imitation or declamation) increase dramatically in sources covering the early 15th century.

Whatever the force of this evidence, it may seem implausible to many performers—and to some scholars—that vocalization was a standard resource of late medieval singers. No contemporary theorist describes the technique, as far as I am aware, and no contemporary name for it is known; no rubric or canon in any medieval musical source can be confidently interpreted as a call for it,[22] and modern singers may be inclined to doubt that a technique which may well have locked the vocal organs into a single posture can ever have been systematically used by their counterparts in the Middle Ages.

These objections are not as weighty, nor perhaps as reasonable, as they may seem. Although no theorist describes vocalization, and no certain allusion to the technique has so far been recognized, it is equally true that no theorist describes or mentions instrumental participation in the polyphonic chanson, such practical matters are hardly ever broached by the theorists writing in pedagogical Latin. Vernacular authors are sometimes more flexible, and it has been observed that Eustache Deschamps may be referring to vocalization when he mentions singing in an artistic way without text.[23]

In the absence of any known contemporary term for the technique of vocalization a case might be made for three verbs. David Fallows has already suggested that several 15th-century sources may imply a distinction between *dicere/dire* and *cantare/chanter*, the former pair possibly meaning 'to sing with text' and the second meaning 'to vocalize'. In the full context of Fallows's argument this seems convincing.[24] A case might also be made for Middle French *bourdonner*, an imitative verb whose root meaning is 'to buzz'. There is a widely attested medieval tradition which employs the noun *bourdon* (in various spellings) to denote something relatively low in a musical texture—the drones of a harp or fiddle, for example—and the use of *bourdon* to name the lowest part in a polyphonic complex is attested in the Middle English part names, 'treble', 'mene' and 'bourdon'. A comparable usage of *bourdon*, with reference to what may be improvised polyphonic practice, can be traced in France as early as the 13th century.[25] A more

Ex.8   Guillaume le Grant, Credo, contratenor of the Amen (after Oxford, Bodleian MS Canonici misc. 213, f.107r). The complete composition is edited in *Polyphonia sacra*, ed. C. Van den Borren (London, 1931, rev. edn 1962), pp.127–33

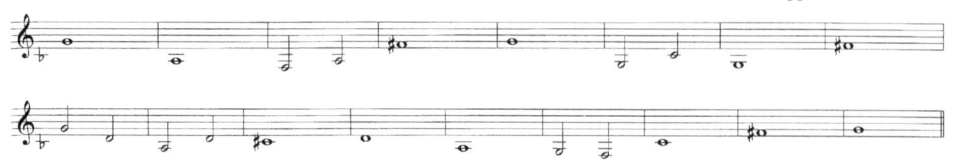

telling piece of evidence is that in the 1420s the idiom *tenendo bordone* is used by Giovanni Gherardi da Prato to denote the performance—probably vocalized—of the tenor part in a Landini ballata for three voices.[26] This confirms the evidence of the English sources that *bourdon* could readily wander away from the semantic field 'low drone' and come to rest denoting the lowest part (or in this case, with an idiomatic construction, the performance of the lowest, textless part) of a polyphonic composition. A similar development could have taken place in France, for one sense of the Middle French verb *bourdonner* in Guillaume de Machaut's lifetime was 'to sing a drone without words'. The evidence for that usage is provided by Evrard de Conty, whose translation of the *Problems* of Aristotle, together with the commentary of Petrus de Abano, tells how the human voice can 'bourdonner . . . tous dis d'une maniere . . . sans parler' (buzz . . . all in the same manner . . . without words'—the context shows the droning is implied).[27]

The early 15th-century Italian idiom *tenendo bordone* leads us to another Middle French term that may have been associated with the practice of vocalization—*tenir* (literally 'to hold'). It is well known that a description of Philip the Good's visit to Cambrai in 1449 tells how, when his departure was delayed, two of the choirboys (probably from the cathedral) sang a chanson with one of the duke's gentlemen who 'held' the tenor ('tint le tenure'). As Fallows remarks, it is just possible that this implies instrumental performance, but no instrument is mentioned and the context suggests otherwise.[28] We find the same idiom, 'tenir le teneur', in the mid-15th-century prose romance *Cleriadus et Meliadice*, each time in contexts where there is no reference to instruments and where the balance of probabilities favours *a cappella* performance.[29] Examples of this idiom might be multiplied. Although it is impossible to establish, in any of the cases in point, whether the tenor being 'held' is textless and therefore vocalized, it remains a possibility that Middle French *tenir* possessed this technical sense, at least in the 15th century. We may reject this evidence for being so

fragmentary, of course, but it should be emphasized that very little of the performance terminology which medieval singers employed has been preserved and in this respect our ignorance on the matter of vocalization terminology is no more than we would expect. (It is not known, for example, how Guillaume de Machaut would have referred to bad ensemble or to ungainly phrasing, a gap in our knowledge so large that, until it is filled, we cannot be sure those concepts existed for Machaut in the free-standing way that they do now.)

A more wide-ranging objection to the vocalization hypothesis would be to maintain, as many scholars have done, that the tenor and contratenor parts of many chansons are inherently 'unvocal' and are therefore unlikely to have been sung. The belief that some medieval music contains 'unvocal' material is so profoundly embedded in modern scholarship that I may perhaps be forgiven for returning to it. The weakness of the 'unvocal' argument is that late medieval polyphony contains many lines which a modern singer may instinctively deem 'unvocal' but which were almost certainly sung when they were first performed. Ex.8 shows the contratenor part from the Amen that closes a three-part Credo by Guillaume le Grant in the Oxford manuscript (GB-Ob 213). All the voices are texted at this point and we may therefore assume that the scribe believed them to be singable—the contratenor included. If such an angular part could be sung, then why not the equally challenging contratenor passages in secular compositions? Ex.9 shows a few bars from one of the finest ballades of the Ars Subtilior, *Amour m'a le cuer mis* by Anthonello de Caserta. The contratenor is angular, to say the least, and doubts must be entertained about the legitimacy of the *musica ficta* in the source at this point. However, modern experiment suggests that the leap of a 7th and the fall of an augmented 5th present no insuperable difficulty to a trained singer experienced in the performance of such a repertory. Such parts may have been sung with more pride than pleasure, and heard with more admiration than enjoyment, but we should be

Ex.9 Anthonello de Caserta, ballade *Amour m'a le cuer mis*, opening of second section (*French Secular Compositions*, ed. Apel, i, p.4)

reluctant to classify them as 'unvocal' with any finality.

The issue of vocal and unvocal writing in the chanson is more complex than this, however. As Lloyd Hibberd argued long ago,[30] the meaning of the terms 'vocal' and 'unvocal' is neither absolute nor unchanging. However, this is not to say that early 15th-century musicians might have regarded a passage like the one shown in ex.8 as 'vocal'; they would certainly not have done so. The theorists of the 14th and 15th centuries possess a clear concept of what constituted 'vocal' writing (called *dicibilis* or *cantabilis*)[31] based upon the idioms of plainchant.[32] That a melody should not generally exceed an octave, that it should leap no further than a 6th at once and should never leap a 7th—these and other characteristics which made a melody *cantabilis* and *dicibilis* were founded upon chant, and they absolutely exclude idioms like those shown in ex.8. Contratenor parts were often designed to challenge the singer in the 14th and earlier 15th centuries,[33] perhaps in accordance with a taste that was inclined to associate the *subtilior* with the *difficilior*.[34] We might almost venture to say that the more 'unvocal' a contratenor appeared to be, the more likely an experienced *contratenorista* would have taken a pride in singing it.

Here the usual kinds of musicological evidence give out and we go over the precipice. How did the singers of late medieval France vocalize their textless lines? There is no evidence to reveal whether they vocalized on a single vowel during a piece or upon several; nor can it be established whether all the vocalizing singers in a single performance generally agreed to use the same vowel(s) or not. Let us begin, therefore, with some frankly impressionistic observations. Experiment suggests that the variables just mentioned have a significant effect upon the sound produced. Singers who agree on one vowel, for example, and who then simultaneously change it,

can colour a particular moment or passage in a striking way, for while the effect of such a synchronized vowel change is far less abrupt in performance than might be imagined by those who have never heard it, the change none the less suddenly encloses the texted voice(s) in a new envelope of harmonics.

This is the point where we naturally seek a technical and objective way to describe the results of experiments with vocalization. Before doing so, let us clear one misapprehension from our path. It is axiomatic that a successful vocalizing technique will be one which allows the texted voice or voices to be clearly heard, and this obviously requires that the vocalized parts should not appear to be too loud. In the performance of a four-part chanson such as *Joieux de cuer* (ex.10), by the late 14th-century composer Solage, there will be three singers vocalizing and only one declaiming the text; the danger of overwhelming the texted part with the tenor, contratenor and triplum always threatens, especially in such a densely textured work as this. There is more to good balance in the performance of a piece like *Joieux de cuer*, however, than careful control of the volume of sound; the quality of the vowel chosen is of cardinal importance in establishing a perspective that places the texted line forward and the textless ones further back. Here it will be helpful to define a viable vocalizing method in precise terms: a successful vocalizing technique may be defined as one in which the unchanging harmonic spectrum of the vocalizing voices (if they are all singing one vowel) does not obscure the changing harmonic spectrum of the texted voice(s), singing many vowels. We may add that the vowels chosen for vocalization should not exhaust or otherwise disturb the singers during as much as seven minutes of performance (which is required when some 14th-century ballades are sung with all three stanzas).

The vocal tract, extending from the vocal folds to the lips, possesses its own resonance frequencies; when singers move the tongue, the jaw, the lips and so on to shape a particular vowel sound they modify the internal constitution of the vocal tract and thereby adjust the relative position of these resonance frequencies. Three principal frequencies, known as the formants,[35] are of crucial importance in establishing the individual quality of each vowel. Illus.3 shows the average frequencies of the first three formants (F_1, F_2 and F_3) for four tenor voices singing the vowel sounds [i], [e], [a], [o] and [u]. This table provides an objective means of judging the impression, shared by many English-speaking singers, that the vowel [a], close to the sound in the stem syllable of Received Pronunciation English 'father', is ideal for vocalizing since it feels 'open'. Experiment shows that if a piece such as *Joieux de cuer* is performed with three parts vocalizing on [a], then, while the counterpoint is often admirably clear, the vocalizing sometimes drowns the texted voice, whatever adjustments of volume are made. (Such adjustments of volume can only be made within certain limits, of course, for there is a level of sound beneath which a singer cannot comfortably fall,

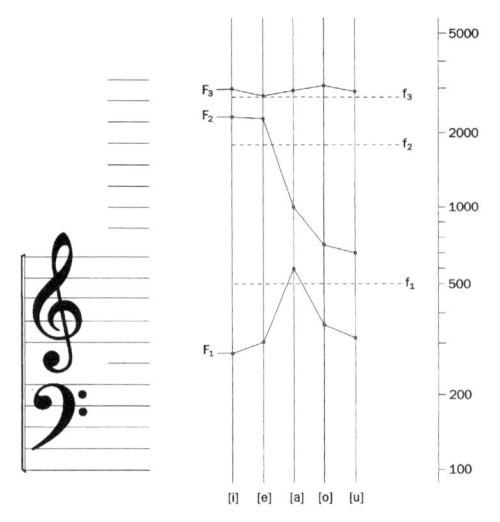

3   Average frequencies for the first three formants (F_1, F_2 and F_3) for four tenor voices singing the vowels [i], [e], [a], [o] and [u]. The pitches of the first three resonances of the cylindrical tube model of the vocal tract (f_1, f_2 and f_3) are shown for comparison. (After M. Campbell and C. Greated, *The Musician's Guide to Acoustics* (London, 1987), p.482)

Ex.10   Solage, virelai *Joieux de cuer*, opening (adapted from *French Secular Compositions*, ed. Apel, i, p.196)

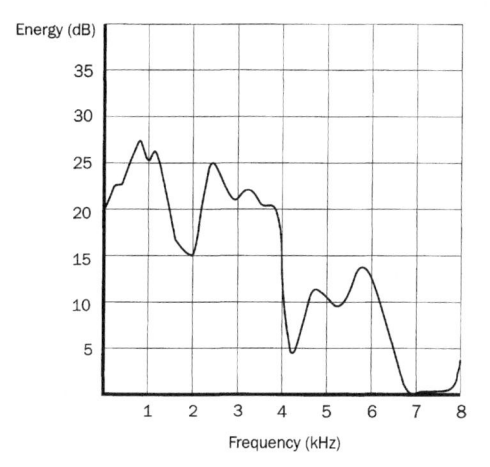

4 Spectrographic section of [a] sung by a tenor voice

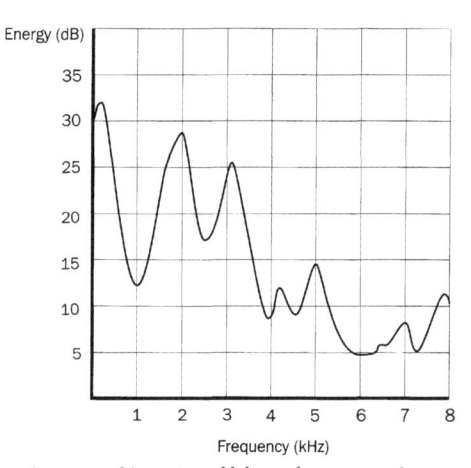

5 Spectrographic section of [y] sung by a tenor voice

although that level will vary according to the timbre and degree of projection that the singer is attempting to achieve.) To express the same point in the technical terms that were broached above: the unchanging harmonic spectrum of the vowel [a] tends to obscure the changing harmonic spectrum of the varied vowels in the texted voice. We might also add that the long [a] formed on the soft palate, which comes so easily to British English speakers, did not exist in Middle French.[36]

Individual performances will inevitably vary, but some of the unchanging reasons for the sheer size of [a]

in a vocalized performance are revealed by illus.1. The first and second formants of [a] are bunched, making it an inherently loud vowel (a phenomenon observed in a music treatise of *c*.1200);[37] in addition, this bunching occurs at a relatively low frequency and therefore [a] is inherently dark. This contributes to the effect known to psychoacousticians as 'low masks high', the process whereby lower harmonics obscure higher ones.[38] In this way [a] fails to meet the definition of a successful vocalizing vowel offered above: it tends to obscure some of the changing harmonics in the texted voice. This bunching of formants can be clearly seen in illus.4, a spectrographic section of [a] sung by a tenor voice, made with a spectrograph KAY 5501–1. The vertical axis measures energy and the horizontal axis measures frequency in a unitary scale of kilohertz. (The spectrograph takes an average of the energy and frequency of the sound source during approximately one-third of a second.) The first and second formants can be seen amalgamated together in the first dual peak.

Illus.3 shows that the bunching of formants 1 and 2 is also a distinguishing quality of the back vowels [o] and [u]. The front vowels [i] and [e], on the other hand, show a wide separation of the first and second formants, and this is the principal explanation for their efficiency as vocalizing vowels. They are neither inherently loud nor inherently dark, and they do not produce the effect of 'low masks high'.

The front vowel which is missing from illus.3, and which was a prominent feature of Middle French (as it is of modern French), is [y], heard in Modern French *tu*. Illus.5 shows a spectrographic section of [y] sung by a tenor voice, and the clear separation of all three formants is evident. The vowel [y] is strong in high harmonics (as illus.5 reveals, and as every singer knows), and it can produce a colourful, sharply focused and buzzing sound (just such a noise, indeed, as medieval French musicians might have wished to denote by the verb *bourdonner*, 'to buzz'). At first this may seem an unwelcome choice to English-speaking singers, for the English language does not employ [y] and makes hardly any use of the lip-rounding which is necessary to produce that vowel and which is so characteristic of French. English singers asked to vocalize on [y] for extended periods, therefore, will sometimes gradually relax and unround the lips, drawing the sound away from [y] and carrying it towards [i]; they may even respond to a call for [y] with [i] from the very beginning. Both vowel sounds work very well and can be blended, leaving (in a careful performance) the changing harmonics of the

6   Cristoforo de' Predis (or school of),
Garden of Delights (before 1470) (Modena, Biblioteca Estense MS 209)

texted voice perfectly conspicuous, even in a crowded
and sonorous texture like that of *Joieux de cuer*.

It would be idle to suggest that the singers of late
medieval France always vocalized with the same sound;
modern performers will find that each piece may require
its own solution. However, it is possible to claim that
certain types of vowel sound—principally those in the
region of the high front vowels—are particularly useful
for vocalization because they possess appropriate acoustic properties; these properties can be measured today
and were available for medieval French singers to discover within the vowel sounds of their vernacular.

The primary vocalizing sound advocated in this
article, [y], requires some definition in vocal rather than
merely phonological terms. As a technical postscript, I
would report the judgement of professional singers who
have worked extensively with this sound as follows. Let
the lips be rounded and the soft palate be raised. The
high soft palate creates a chamber in which the sound
can resonate; lowering the soft palate adds a quality of
nasality to the sound. Let the larynx be lowered and the
tongue relaxed. There is no need for any more than
slight tension in the cheeks. This position can be held by
trained singers, without discomfort, for the duration of
any piece of 14th- or 15th-century polyphony.

*An earlier version of this article was read at the Eighteenth
Conference on Medieval and Renaissance Music in the
University of London in 1990. I am most grateful to Mar-
garet Philpot, David Howard, David Fallows, Daniel
Leech-Wilkinson, Ann Lewis, John Milsom and Anita*

Crowe for their comments.

*The vocalization technique described here may be heard
on the following recordings by Gothic Voices:* The Medieval Romantics *(Hyperion, CDA66463), tracks 1, 3*
(Joieux de cuer), *5, 7, 9, 10, 12* (En ce gracieux tamps), *14,
16, 17;* Lancaster and Valois *(Hyperion, CDA66588), tracks
1, 3, 4, 8, 10, 14, 15, 16, 17.*

*Christopher Page is director of the ensemble Gothic Voices.
He has written extensively on aspects of medieval music
and performance practice. His books include* Voices and
Instruments of the Middle Ages *(1987),* The Owl and the
Nightingale *(1989),* A Thirteenth Century Manual for
Singers: the Summa Musica *(1991) and* Discarding
Images: Reflections on Music and Culture in Medieval
France *(forthcoming). He is currently University Lecturer
in Middle English Literature in the University of
Cambridge.*

[1]D. Slavin, 'In Support of "Heresy": Manuscript Evidence for the *a
cappella* Performance of Early 15th-Century Songs', *EM*, xix (1991),
pp.178–90; L. Earp, 'Texting in 15th-Century French Chansons: a Look
Ahead from the 14th Century', *EM*, xix (1991), pp.194–210

[2]Slavin, 'In Support of "Heresy" ', p.189; Earp, 'Texting', p.207

[3]Slavin, 'In Support of "Heresy" ', p.189, is cautious; Earp, 'Texting',
p.207, is more bold. On texting see especially G. Reaney, 'Text Underlay
in Early Fifteenth-Century Musical Manuscripts', *Essays in Honor of
Dragan Plamenac*, ed. G. Reese and R. J. Snow (Pittsburgh, 1969/
R1977), pp.245–51; *The Works of Johannes Ciconia*, ed. M. Bent and A.
Hallmark, Polyphonic Music of the Fourteenth Century, xiv (Monaco,
1985), p.xviii; M. Bent, 'New Sacred Polyphonic Fragments of the Early
Quattrocento', *Studi musicali*, ix (1980), pp.171–89. For the complex
issue of texting in Guillaume de Machaut's *Messe de Nostre Dame*, see
the recent discussion in D. Leech-Wilkinson, *Machaut's Mass: an
Introduction* (Oxford, 1990), pp.106–10. For a bold and innovative
approach to the editing of early 15th-century music with full texting see

A. Lewis, *Johannes de Lymburgia: Four Motets* (Newton Abbot, 1985). The matter of texted tenors and contratenors in the secular repertories has been less well studied (a failing which the articles of Earp and Slavin have done much to remedy) and there is no doubt that modern editors have sometimes done a disservice by generally choosing to print tenors and contratenors which are partially texted in the sources without text, consigning the information about the partial texting to the critical commentaries where there is a great danger of error and where few performers seek out the information.

⁴See, for example, F. Harrison, 'Tradition and Innovation in Instrumental Usage, 1100–1450', *Aspects of Medieval and Renaissance Music*, ed. J. la Rue (New York, 1966), p.328; M. Bent, musical supplement to 'The Old Hall Manuscript', *EM*, ii (1974), pp.2–14 (an edition of a piece by Power that has since been recorded with vocalization of the textless parts on the Hilliard Ensemble's recording from 1981, *Leonel Power* (IC 069-46 202)); D. Fallows, 'Specific Information on the Ensembles for Composed Polyphony, 1400–1474', *Studies in the Performance of Late Mediaeval Music*, ed. S. Boorman (Cambridge, 1983), pp.109–59; W. Kemp, *Burgundian Court Song in the Time of Binchois* (Oxford, 1990), p.49.

⁵I am grateful to the following singers for their time and expertise: Margaret Philpot, Rogers Covey-Crump, Charles Daniels, Andrew Tusa, Leigh Nixon, Stephen Charlesworth and Donald Greig.

⁶For the use of literary evidence see D. Fallows, 'Specific Information', pp.132–44; C. Page, 'The Performance of Songs in Late Medieval France', *EM*, x (1982), pp.441–50; C. Page, 'Machaut's "Pupil" Deschamps on the Performance of Music', *EM*, v (1977), pp.484–91; C. Wright, 'Voices and Instruments in the Art Music of Northern France during the 15th Century: a Conspectus', *Report of the Twelfth Congress [of the International Musicological Society] Berkeley, 1977*, ed. D. Heartz and B. Wade (Kassel, 1981), pp.643–9.

⁷I am most grateful to Dr Tess Knighton for showing me her paper on late 15th-century Spanish sources presented to the Eighteenth Annual Conference on Medieval and Renaissance Music at the University of London, 1990, a version of which will appear in the November issue of *EM*.

⁸See D. Fallows, 'Secular Polyphony in the Fifteenth Century', *Performance Practice, i: Music before 1600*, ed. H. M. Brown and S. Sadie (London, 1989), pp.201–21, esp. p.207, nn.19–21; C. Page, 'Polyphony before 1400', *ibid*, pp.98–9

⁹Compare K. von Fischer, 'Suggestions for Performance', *Francesco Landini: Complete Works*, ed. L. Schrade reprinted from *Polyphonic Music of the Fourteenth Century* (Monaco, 1982), p.iv.

¹⁰For the string materials of instruments of this family in the Middle Ages see C. Page, *Voices and Instruments of the Middle Ages* (London, 1987), pp.210–42.

¹¹See Page, *Voices and Instruments*, pp.111–25, and H. M. Brown, 'The Trecento Harp', *Studies in the Performance of Late Mediaeval Music*, ed. Boorman, pp.35–73.

¹²Page, *Voices and Instruments*, pp.111–38; C. Page, 'In the Direction of the Beginning', *The Historical Harpsichord*, i, ed. H. Schott (1984), pp.109–25

¹³*De musica*, in Gerbert, *Scriptores*, ii, p.289

¹⁴*Jacobi Leodiensis: Speculum musicae*, ed. R. Bragard, Corpus Scriptorum de Musica, iii (American Institute of Musicology, 1955–73), i, p.54

¹⁵The Latin text is edited, with translation, commentary and discussion, in C. Page, 'A Treatise on Musicians from ?c.1400: the *Tractatulus de differentiis et gradibus cantorum* by Arnulf de Saint Ghislain', *JRMA*, cxvii (1992), pp.1–21. The full passage runs: 'Secunda vero differentia patet in illis laycalibus qui, licet sunt totius artis musicalis experte, zelo tamen ducti dulcedinis delicatas aures suas ad quevis musicalia prebent, attentius adamantes et associantes muslcos . . .' ('The second category [of musician] is manifest in those lay persons who, even if they are entirely lacking in musical art, are none the less drawn by a zeal for sweetness and so lend their pleasure-loving ears to

any music, attentively cherishing trained musicians and associating with them . . .'). It remains a delicate and unresolved question how often medieval theorists of mensural music have instruments in mind when they generalize. Occasionally a theorist will broaden the scope of a very general remark to encompass instruments, usually with the implicit recognition that some instruments have certain capacities (such as extended range) that exceed the power of voices. See, for example, *Ars (Musicae) Johannis Boen*, ed. F. A. Gallo, Corpus Scriptorum de Musica, xix (American Institute of Musicology, 1972), p.26. Generally, however, theorists of mensural music are either rigorously abstract, or, if they do hint at the musical milieu to which they believe their work pertains, they speak of liturgical music, both monophonic and polyphonic, and therefore relate what they say to the human voice, the *organum . . . vocis*. Compare the remarks of Johannes Vetulus de Anagnia in *Iohannis Vetuli: De anagnia liber de musica*, ed. F. Hammond, Corpus Scriptorum de Musica, xvii (American Institute of Musicology, 1977), p.64. The central problem in assessing the evidence of the theorists on this point is therefore that their writings generally reflect the *a cappella* sound-world of liturgical music, both plainchant and polyphony. It is perhaps in this light that we should judge the comment of the theorist Petrus frater dictus de palma ociosa (*fl.*1336) who gives a definition of simple discantus—the basic material of 14th century measured music—which seems designed to eliminate instruments from consideration: 'simplex discantus . . . nihil aliud est quam punctus contra punctum, sive notula, naturalibus instrumentis formata, contra aliam notulam . . .' ('plain discantus . . . is nothing other than one notational figure, or one note, against another, formed with the human voice'). Text in J. Wolf, 'Ein Beitrag zur Diskantlehre des 14. Jahrhunderts', *Sammelbände der Internationalen Musik-Gesellschaft*, xv (1913–14), p.506

¹⁶For a thorough statement of the position which was advocated in many recordings and performances of the period see G. Reaney, 'Voices and Instruments in the Music of Guillaume de Machaut', *Revue belge de musicologie*, x (1956), pp.3–17, 93–104, and D. Munrow, 'The Art of Courtly Love', *EM*, i (1973), pp.195–9. The extent to which performances of medieval music in the 1960s and 1970s relied upon Renaissance instruments was sometimes noted with anxiety during the period. See F. Harrison, 'Tradition and Innovation in Instrumental Usage, 1100–1450', and (from a decade later) J. Montagu, 'The "Authentic" Sound of Early Music', *EM*, iii (1975), pp.242–3.

¹⁷This question has given rise to a large literature, most of which is listed in Fallows, 'Specific Information', p.127, nn.42–4. Recent contributions have tended to concentrate upon the later 15th century and are not directly relevant here. Much of this scholarly literature is based upon iconographical sources, so it is important to remember two absolutely explicit literary references upon which the *a cappella* hypothesis of sacred polyphonic performance can be based, at least for the 13th and 14th centuries. First, there is the comment by the English Franciscan Bartholomaeus in his *De proprietatibus rerum* (composed, or a revised version edited, c.1250); the comment is repeated verbatim in the *Ars musica* of Aegidius of Zamora, where it may be read in a modern edition: 'Et hoc [sc. the organ] solo musico instrumento utitur ecclesia in diversis cantibus et in prosis, in sequentiis et in hymnis, propter abusum histrionum eiectis aliis communiter instrumentis' ('the Church uses only this instrument [i.e. the organ] in various chants and proses, in sequences and in hymns, having rejected, as a whole, all other instruments on account of the abuses of minstrels'). The crucial words 'as a whole' (*communiter*) deserve attention, since an alternative translation would be 'generally' which somewhat changes the sense. See *Johannes Aegidius de Zamora: Ars musica*, ed. M. Robert-Tissot, Corpus Scriptorum de Musica, xx (American Institute of Musicology, 1974), p.108. Second, there is the remark by Petrus frater dictus de palma ociosa (*fl.* c.1336) that the liturgy is performed 'dimissis instrumentis quibuscumque manufactis' ('with all instruments made by the human hand having been put aside') and that divine praise is only given 'ex instrumentis naturalibus' ('with the natural instruments

7   Luca della Robbia (1400–1482), marble relief of a group of singers (Florence, Museo di S. Maria del Fiore)

[i.e. with the organs of the human voice]'). See Wolf, 'Ein Beitrag', p.506

[18]The question of whether the textless lines in chansons may sometimes have been solmized is a significan tone that cannot be entered into here.

[19]Slavin, 'In Support of "Heresy"', p.179

[20]We may surely agree with Earp ('Texting', p.207) that 'Nobody puts down an instrument to sing occasional words . . .'

[21]A. Wathey, 'The Peace of 1360–69 and Anglo-French Musical Relations', *Early Music History*, ix (1989), pp.144–51

[22]See Fallows, 'Specific Information', pp. 130, 135

[23]Page, 'Machaut's "Pupil" Deschamps', p.498: 'et se puet l'une [musique artificiele] chanter par voix et par art, sanz parole'. Bearing in mind that Deschamps distinguishes 'artificial' music (i.e. music in our sense of the term) from 'natural' music (i.e. poetry and rhetoric), this passage may be translated thus: 'and so one kind [of music, that is to say music in our sense of the term] can sing with the voice in an artistic way without text'. Deschamps's point is that the arts of music and poetry, though married in the polyphonic chanson, also have an independent existence.

[24]Fallows, 'Specific Information', pp.130, 135

[25]For the instrumental terminology see Page, *Voices and Instruments*, pp.118–19; for the Middle English part names, see B. Trowell, 'Faburden—New Sources, New Evidence: A Preliminary Survey', *Modern Musical Scholarship*, ed. E. Olleson (Stocksfield, 1980), pp.28–78. The French 13th-century reference is quoted and translated in C. Page, 'Music and Chivalric Fiction in France, 1150–1300', *PRMA*, cxi (1984–5), pp.17, 26. The passage in question is taken from *Les quatre fils Aymon*, a *chanson de geste* of c.1200.

[26]Fallows, 'Specific Information', p.133. The reference is taken from *Il Paradiso degli Alberti*, written in the 1420s but recording fictional events supposed to have taken place in 1389.

[27]Paris, Bibliothèque Nationale, fonds français 210, f.229r

[28]Discussed in Fallows, 'Specific Information', p.134

[29]For full text, translation and discussion of the relevant extracts see Page, 'The Performance of Songs', *passim*.

[30]'On "Instrumental Style" in Early Melody', *MQ*, xxxii (1946), pp.107–30, opposing the views of Arnold Schering, *Aufführungspraxis alter Musik* (Leipzig, 1931). As Fallows ('Specific Information', p.133, n.550) comments: 'Particularly since the days of Schering, scholars and

performers have inclined to the view that the different nature of the different lines provides direct internal clues to vocal or instrumental performance . . . this "internal" approach has survived—apparently contradicting the documentary information . . .'

[31]For the terms *dicibilis* and *cantabilis*, used by Jacques de Liège, see *Jacobi Leodiensis: Speculum Musicae*, iv, p.106

[32]See, for example, Engelbert of Admont, *De musica*, in Gerbert, *Scriptores*, ii, p.322

[33]Compare the pertinent remarks in D. Fallows, *Galfridus and Robertus de Anglia: Four Italian Songs* (Newton Abbot, 1977), note on performance: 'The ungainly intervals in the two contratenor parts should perhaps be seen less as instrumental than as part of the nature of the contratenor in 15th-century polyphony . . .'

[34]See the comments of Jacques de Liège in *Jacobi Leodiensis: Speculum Musicae*, vii, pp.12–14. Jacques regarded it as essential for good pieces of music to be pleasing and simple to sing ('ad cantandum faciles sint').

[35]For accounts of the formants see B. M. Doscher, *The Functional Unity of the Singing Voice* (London, 1988), *passim*; J. Sundberg, 'The Voice as a Sound Generator', *Research Aspects of Singing* (Stockholm, 1981), pp.56–64, and M. Campbell and C. Greated, *The Musician's Guide to Acoustics* (London, 1987), pp.471–83

[36]For an excellent and compact account of Middle French phonology see J. Alton and B. Jeffery, *Bele buche a bele parleure* (London, 1976).

[37]See the remarks in the *Summa musice* of c.1200, in C. Page, *The Summa Musice: a Thirteenth Century Manual for Singers* (Cambridge, 1991), Latin text, lines 630–31.

[38]On this effect see B. C. J. Moore, *An Introduction to the Psychology of Hearing* (London, 1982), *passim*.

[4]

Performance practices in the frottola

An introduction to the repertory of early 16th-century Italian solo secular song with suggestions for the use of instruments on the other lines

WILLIAM F.
PRIZER

The *frottola*, the secular song of early 16th-century Italy, flourished from around 1490 to 1530. The centres of its cultivation were chiefly the smaller courts in the north-east of the peninsula—Ferrara, Urbino, Padua, and, above all, Mantua. Left to the modern-day performer is a large corpus of elegant works, much of which is available in modern edition,[1] by a wide variety of composers. The most important of these were Marchetto Cara (*c.*1470-1525), Bartolomeo Tromboncino (*c.*1470-after 1535), Michele Pesenti (*c.*1470-after 1524), and Filippo de Lurano (*c.*1475-after 1520).

Before he starts performing these works, the modern musician must make several crucial decisions; among those most important are the relationship of rhythm to metre, the medium of performance, the technique of ornamentation, the problem of text underlay, and the interpretation of the Italian poetic forms.[2]

Frottole are generally short compositions whose texts, written in the Italian *formes fixes*, are most often courtly in tone and amorous in language. The length of the musical phrases is dependent upon that of the poetic lines, since most *frottole* employ a text setting that is more or less syllabic. Written for four voices, the *frottola* has a vocal *cantus* part that is rather conjunct and lies within the range of an octave. Below this are the *altus* and *tenor*, which either are rhythmically active and produce thereby a texture of non-imitative polyphony (much like the 15th-century chanson), or else move in the same note values as the *cantus*, producing a homorhythmic texture. Finally, a 'functional' *bassus* rounds out the structure; it too alternates in style between rapid passages and slow-moving sections, the latter in fourths, fifths, and seconds. The harmonies are generally full, most often including both the third and fifth.[3]

The rhythmic nature of the *frottola* strongly affects the performance, both within the *cantus* and in the lower voices as well. Most of the works are written in duple time, the mensuration being either ¢ or C; many compositions, however, have a rhythmic logic that is opposed to the metre. Phrases tend to begin in duple time, to move to a triple, hemiola-like rhythm for the middle of the phrase, and then back to two for the typical feminine cadence (Ex. 1: ᴵ = the rhythmic stress):

Io non com - pro più spe - ran - za, Che gli è ca - - - ra mer - can - ti - a

Ex. 1. Marchetto Cara: 'Io non compro più speranza'
(*Frottole, libro primo*. Venice: Petrucci, 1504)[4]

Others, however, are completely in duple time; the combination of word-stress and the logical rhythmic grouping of the melodic line usually makes clear the rhythmic nature of the work.

The *frottola* appears to have been solo song, that is, only the *cantus* was sung. This is apparent both from the layout of the original sources, in which only the top voice contains the entire text, and from the nature of the lower voices, to which the text can be added only with difficulty. The *bassus* often contains too few notes to accommodate the verses, whereas the *altus* and *tenor* contain too many. In addition, the middle voices tend to elide interior cadences and to span a rather wide range. Documentary evidence from Mantua, the centre of *frottola* production, tends to confirm a solo practice, rarely mentioning more than one singer

Textual and musical form in the Frottola

Text Form	Published Appearance	Manner of Performance

1. *Barzelletta* with 2-line *volta*, only *ripresa* and refrain set

Published Appearance: 1 2:‖:3 4 | 1 2'

Manner of Performance:

Ripresa				*Refrain*		*Piedi*		*Volta*		*Refrain*	
1	2	3	4	1	2'	‖:1	2:‖	3	4	1	2'
a	b	b	a	a	b	c	d	d	a	a	b
						c	d				

2. *Barzelletta* with 4-line *volta*, only *ripresa* and refrain set

Published Appearance: 1 2:‖:3 | 4:‖:1:‖:2'

Manner of Performance:

1	2	3	4	1	2'	‖:1	2:‖	3 ‖:4:‖:1	:‖2
a	b	b	a	a	b	c	d	d e a	b
						c	d	e a	

3. *Barzelletta* with 2-line *volta*, both *ripresa* and stanza set

Published Appearance: 1 2 3 4 | 5 6:‖:7 8 | 1 2'

Manner of Performance:

1	2	3	4	——	‖:5	6:‖	7	8	1	2'
a	b	b	a		c	d	d	a	a	b
					c	d				

4. *Barzelletta* with 4-line *volta*, both *ripresa* and stanza set

Published Appearance: 1 2 3 4 | 5 6:‖:7 | 8:‖:9 | 1 2'

Manner of Performance:

1	2	3	4	——	‖:5	6:‖	7 ‖:8:‖ 9	1	2'
a	b	b	a		c	d	d e a	a	b
					c	d	e		

5. *Strambotto*, only 1st couplet set

Published Appearance: 1 2

```
‖:1  2:‖
  A  B
  A  B
  A  B
  C  C
```

6. *Strambotto*, 1st and last couplets set

Published Appearance: 1 2:‖:3 4

```
‖:1  2:‖ 3  4
  A  B   C  C
  A  B
  A  B
```

7. *Strambotto*, entire strophe set

Published Appearance: 1 2 3 4 5 6 7 8

```
1  2  3  4  5  6  7  8
A  B  A  B  A  B  C  C
```

8. Sonnet, 1st quattrain set

Published Appearance: 1 | 2:‖:3

```
1 ‖:2:‖ 3 ‖:1  2  3:‖
A  B  A  C  D  C
   B     C  D  C
A  B  A
   B
      Da
      Capo
```

9. Sonnet, 1st quattrain and 1st tercet set

Published Appearance: 1 2 3 4 | 5 6 7

```
‖:1  2  3  4:‖:5  6  7:‖
  A  B  B  A  C  D  C
  A  B  B  A  C  D  C
```

10. *Capitolo*

Published Appearance: 1 2 3 | 4

```
‖:1  2  3:‖ 4
  A  B  A
  B  C  B
  C  D  C
  . . .
  Y  Z  Y  Z
```

11. *Oda*

Published Appearance: 1 2 3 4

```
1  2  3  4
a  b  b  c
c  d  d  e
etc.
```

Key

numerals = musical phrases

2' = extension of 2nd phrase of music

letters = poetic lines and rhyme scheme (capital letters = lines of 11 syllables; lower case letters = lines of less than 11 syllables).

228

Title page of Andrea Antico's Canzoni nove, *Rome, 1510.*

at each performance. It is also clear from Mantuan documents that women as well as men might have sung the works. For example, Marchetto Cara's first wife, Giovanna Moreschi of Novara, was a professional singer employed in Mantua during the early 16th century.

It should not be supposed, however, that all-vocal performance of *frottole* did not take place. The title page of Andrea Antico's *Canzoni nove* (Rome, 1510) shows four singers reading off the typical small, oblong choirbook of the *frottola* prints (I), and a small number of *frottole* have texts printed in the lower voices. Thus, in Pesenti's *barzellette*[5] 'Questa è mia l'ho fatta mi' and 'S'io son stato a ritornare', the refrain is texted in all parts. Cara's 'Forsi che sì' has a dialogue between the *cantus* and the inner parts (Ex. 2), and Sambonetti's *Canzoni, sonetti, et frottole, libro primo* (Siena, 1515) contains no less than thirteen works in which at least one of the lower voices is texted.

Ex. 2. Marchetto Cara: 'Forsi che sì, forsi che no'
(*Frottole, libro terzo.* Venice: Petrucci, 1505)[6]

Finally, virtually all of the *villotte*, frottola-like settings based on popular melodies, were apparently intended for an all-vocal performance. The popular tune lies generally in the *tenor*, and the *cantus* often does not include the entire text. Others feature dialogues between upper and lower voices.[7] These works must be regarded as representative of a small

2

Shawms, sackbuts, and trumpets in outdoor
festivities; detail from Gentile Bellini's
Procession in Piazza S. Marco *(1496).*

group of exceptions, however; even those more homorhythmic compositions to which texts may be fitted in all parts were more likely intended
for solo voice and lira da braccio in the style of the 15th-century
improvisators.

Granted that the *cantus* was in general the only vocal part, what sort
of instruments should be used for the other lines? The following are
several suggestions for performance: (1) the top voice may be sung and
the lower voices played on a consort of like instruments; (2) the top voice
may be sung and the lower voices played on a consort of mixed instruments; (3) the top voice may be sung and the lower voices played on a
plucked chordal instrument; (4) the top voice may be sung while all voices
are played on a keyboard instrument; (5) all voices may be played on
soft or loud instruments; (6) all voices may be played on a chordal
instrument; (7) one instrument may play the *cantus* while a chordal
instrument plays the lower voices.

In general, louder instruments such as shawm and rauschpfeife should
be reserved for *villotte*, carnival songs, and those *frottole* with more
boisterous, popular texts. (See illustration 2 for shawms, sackbuts, and
trumpets in outdoor festivities.) Almost all contemporary accounts of
the performance of *frottole* refer to their delicate nature, often indicating
also that they were sung in small rooms (*camerini*).

Whether full or mixed consort should be used in the *frottola* is problematic. Howard Brown has shown that the 16th century (and particularly the first half of the century) might be called the 'consort period' and that the most popular combinations were full consorts doubling voices.[8] However, the roots of the *frottola* are in the late 15th century, and, although simpler, the genre is similar to the Burgundian chanson in texture, for which Brown suggests that mixed consorts be used.[9]

In general, mixed consorts are to be preferred in those works which feature a high degree of non-imitative polyphony so that the individual lines are more clearly differentiated. Mixed consorts that are particularly apt for the performance of *frottole* include ensembles of viols and flutes or recorders, or consorts made up of louder instruments such as crumhorn and cornett. Capped double reeds (crumhorn, cornamuse, etc.) often are not suitable for the inner parts, as the range exceeds their modest ninth, and indeed sometimes exceeds the range of an eleventh that modern-day extensions give the instruments. Double-channelled capped reeds, such as the kortholt, do have the requisite range and may be considered, although there is no documentation that they were used in the performance of *frottole*.

Another viable possibility is the mixed consort of cornetti and sackbuts that had moved indoors by the 16th century.[10] In most *frottole*, however, the *altus* must be played by either a tenor cornett or sackbut, as the range of this part is generally too low for the cornett in a.

For those *frottole* that contain a large amount of note-against-note writing and perhaps also for later *frottole*, full consorts should be considered. These consorts could include flutes, recorders, or viols. Viols seem particularly appropriate for the performance of *frottole*, as Isabella d'Este at Mantua owned a consort of the instruments by 1495.

Whatever ensemble is chosen, care should be taken that both *tenor* and *bassus* sound in the same octave, for voice-crossings are frequent in the *frottola*, particularly at cadence points where the typical 'octave-leap' cadences are often found. Here, the *bassus* leaps an octave while the tenor descends a step and forms the root of the final sonority (Ex. 3). If the two parts were not in the same octave, a second-inversion triad would result:

Ex. 3. Bartolomeo Tromboncino: Final cadence of 'Dolermi sempre voglio' (*Frottole, libro nono*. Venice: Petrucci, 1509)

Chordal instruments were also used in the performance of *frottole*. Lute was used both with voice (in which case the lute would omit the *altus* and play only the *tenor* and *bassus*) and in solo instrumental performance.[11] Documents also suggest that two lutes might have been used. In this case, it is probable that one lute would concentrate on the embellishment of the *cantus* while the other would play the lower parts.

3

Harp, spinettino, and lute from intarsia door in Isabella d'Este's grotta nuova, *Palazzo Ducale, Mantua.*

Another chordal instrument that probably saw use was the harp. When included, it must have functioned much like the lute, omitting the *altus*. A small harp is included in an *intarsia* on the door of a cabinet in Isabella d'Este's private apartments in the Ducal Palace at Mantua (3).

Finally, both chamber organ and harpsichord were used. Andrea Antico published *Frottole intabulate da sonare organi, libro primo* (Rome, 1517), containing *frottole* intended for keyboard performance. Although organ is specifically referred to in the title, the woodcut on the title page shows a typical Italian single-manual harpsichord (4). (According to Plamenac and Radole, the harpsichordist represents Antico himself, whereas the displeased lady and monkey-lutenist represent the performers of the rival Petrucci's lute intabulations.[12]) Antico's intabulations are for keyboard instrument alone; if used with a singer, it is probable that the organ or harpsichord should still double the *cantus*.

Ornamentation was apparently used often in *frottole*. This tendency is generally seen in instrumental versions, although some works also show vocal embellishments.[13] The Capirola lute manuscript shows a great deal of ornamentation of the *cantus*, and Antico's organ print, referred to above, demonstrates a high degree of decoration both in the *cantus* and in the lower parts. Many of these ornaments are suitable for voice as well as instruments. The following are some suggestions for ornaments taken from the Antico print:[14]

Ex. 4. Typical cadential ornaments (*Frottole intabulate da sonare organi, libro primo* (Rome: Antico, 1517)

Ex. 5. Typical ornaments within phrases (*Ibid.*)

232

Title page of Andrea Antico's Frottole intabulate da sonare organi, libro primo, *Rome, 1517*

4

Cantus and tenor of Marchetto Cara's 'To non compro più speranza', Frottole, libro primo. Venice, Petrucci, 1504.

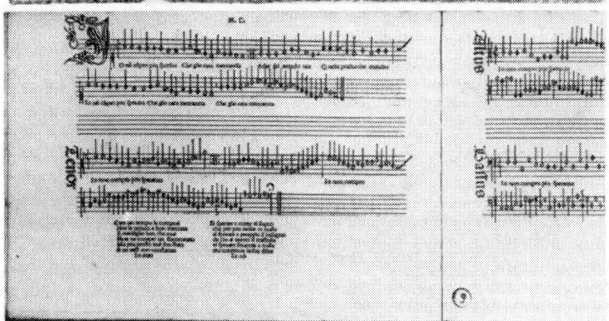

5

There remain two concerns in performing *frottole* that are less usually associated with the concept of 'performance practices' than those discussed above, but which are crucial to authentic performance. These are the areas of text underlay and the relation of the *formes fixes* to the musical form of the compositions.

Text underlay is a particular problem in the *frottola*, not only because Italian poetry tends to elide vowels whenever practical, but also because much of the poetry of the genre is strophic. Even in poems of a single strophe, both original sources and modern editions generally do not underlay the entire text and thus the performer is forced to share the editorial duties with the transcriber of the work. While a complete explanation of text underlay is outside the scope of this study, a few indications may be given to aid the singer:[15]

1 The second of two repeated pitches should almost always be texted. In the frottolesque 'feminine' cadence, both of the final two notes should be texted (Ex. 6, bars 3 and 6).

2 Given a choice, the singer should add text to white notes in the original values rather than to black notes. Many editions of *frottole* reduce the

values of notes either by two or by four; in the former case, crochets are the smallest value that should generally bear a syllable of text, in the latter case, quavers.

3 Within a poetic line, adjacent vowels are generally elided. (the letter 'h' is silent and may also be elided when it begins a word.) Thus, 'Se m'è grato il tuo tornare, Io el so ben che giaccio in foco' becomes the following when placed under the music:

Se m'è gra-to il _____ tuo   tor - na - re,   Io el so ben che _____ giac - cio in   fo - co;

Ex. 6. Filippo de Lurano: 'Se m'è grato il tuo tornare'
(*Tenori e contrabassi intabulati . . . libro primo*. Venice: Petrucci, 1509)

4 Adjacent vowels at the end of a poetic line are generally not elided, as a two-syllable ending is necessary to make a true rhyme in Italian (see ex. 1, bar 6, above).

Finally, the performer must have a knowledge of the Italian *formes fixes* and their relation to the musical structure as published in the original prints and in modern editions. While somewhat technical, at least a passing acquaintance with the poetic forms is necessary for correct performance. Since these forms are considerably less well known than their French counterparts (*rondeau, virelai,* etc.), some explanation is necessary. In this brief summary, strictly literary and historical considerations are omitted.

By far the most popular text form of the *frottola* was the *barzelletta,* a variant of the *ballata* in which all lines were octosyllabic. Like the *ballata,* it is made up of three parts: a four-line *ripresa,* a six- or eight-line stanza, and a refrain which may be either all or part of the *ripresa* and is sung at the conclusion of each stanza. The stanza itself is divided into two parts— the *piedi* (also called the *mutazione*) and the *volta,* the latter linking the stanza with the refrain through a return to the original rhyme. The *volta* may consist of two or, occasionally, four lines. The rhyme scheme of a typical *barzelletta* is therefore as follows: abba (*ripresa*), cdcd (*piedi*), da or deea (*volta*), and ab, ba, or abba (refrain).

The composer treated this poetic structure in one of two ways: (1) he might provide music for only the *ripresa* and refrain; (2) less often, he might provide music for the whole poem, frequently allowing the entire *ripresa* to act as a refrain. Only the first of these choices provides problems for the performer, as both early printers and modern editors tend to conserve space by writing out the music only once. Since there are more lines in the stanza than in the *ripresa,* some sort of system of repetition was necessary. The table presents a list of the text forms of the *frottola,* together with their published appearance and the manner of performance. (Certain variations on the patterns listed occur, particularly through the repetition of a line of text and music. These are not taken into account in the table; however, even these variations maintain the general outlines listed.) It should be noted that, both in the original source and in many modern editions, the beginning of a repeated section is marked only with a heavy vertical line through the staff and that the repetition signs themselves have dots on both sides (:ll:), even though they indicate a repetition only of the section immediately preceding them.

A *barzelletta* with a *volta* of two lines (no. 1 on table) includes, in the

[1] Modern editions of the *frottola* include R. Schwartz, *Ottaviano Petrucci: Frottole Buch I und IV,* Publikationen älterer Musik, vol. 8 (Leipzig, 1935); G. Cesari, R. Monterosso, and B. Disertori, *Le frottole nell'edizione principe de Ottaviano Petrucci* (Cremona, 1954); B. Disertori, *Le frottole per canto e liuto intabulate da Franciscus Bossinensis* (Milan, 1964); A. Einstein, *Canzoni sonetti strambotti et frottole, libro tertio (Andrea Antico, 1517),* Smith College Music Archives, vol. 4 (Northampton, Mass., 1941); and W. Prizer, *Canzoni, frottole, et capitoli da diversi eccellentissimi musici . . . libro primo de la croce* (Rome: Pasoti and Dorico, 1526), Yale University Collegium Musicum Series (New Haven, Conn., forthcoming).

[2] Other areas of performance practices such as tempo and *musica ficta* are the same for *frottole* as they are for other contemporary genres and are not treated here. On *ficta,* see Howard M. Brown, 'On the Performance of fifteenth-century Chansons', *Early Music,* vol. 1, no. 1 (1973), pp. 4-5.

[3] For more detailed consideration of the musical nature of the *frottola,* see W. Rubsamen, 'From Frottola to Madrigal: The Changing Pattern of Secular Italian Vocal Music', *Chanson and Madrigal, 1480-1530,* ed. by J. Haar (Cambridge, Mass., 1964), pp. 51-87; and W. Prizer, 'Marchetto Cara and the North Italian Frottola', Ph.D. dissertation, 2 vols. (University of North Carolina at Chapel Hill, 1974).

[4] Modern edition in Schwartz, *Ottaviano Petrucci,* pp. 6-7; Cesari, *Le edizione principe,* p. 8; and Disertori, *Le frottole per canto e liuto,* pp. 390-91.

[5] The term *frottola* was used in two senses in the early 16th century, one meaning the genre of secular music in vogue, and the other, the particular text form also known as

the *barzelletta*. For the sake of clarity, the term *frottola* is used only in the more general sense in this study, *barzelletta* being substituted for its specific meaning. Both of Pesenti's *barzellette* are available in modern edition in Schwartz, *Ottaviano Petrucci*, pp. 28-29 and 31. They are also published in Cesari, *Le frottole nell'edizione principe*, pp. 30 and 33.

[6] Modern edition in Cesari, *Le frottole nell'edizione principe*, pp. 118-19.

[7] For modern editions of *villotte*, see F. Torrefranca, *Il Segreto del Quattrocento* (Milan, 1939; reprint: Bologna, 1972) and Prizer, *Canzoni, frottole, et capitoli*

[8] H. M. Brown, *Sixteenth-Century Instrumentation: The Florentine Intermedii*, American Institute of Musicology, Musicological Studies and Documents, vol. 30 (n.p., 1973), p. 78.

[9] Brown, 'On the performance of fifteenth-century chansons', p. 5.

[10] Brown, *Sixteenth-Century Instrumentation*, pp. 60-61.

[11] For modern editions of lute intabulations of *frottole*, see Disertori, *Le frottole per canto e liuto*; O Gombosi, *Composizione di Messer Vincenzo Capirola, Lute-Buch (um 1517)* (Neuilly-sur Seine, 1955); and H. Mönkmeyer, *Joan Ambrosio Dalza, Intabulatura de Lauto (Petrucci, 1508)*, Die Tabulatur, vols 6-8 (Hofheim, 1967). The latter two editions are for lute alone.

[12] D. Plamenac, 'The Recently Discovered Complete Copy of A. Antico's *Frottole intabulate* (1517)', *Aspects of Medieval and Renaissance Music: A Birthday Offering to Gustave Reese*, ed J. LaRue (New York, 1966), p. 686; and G. Radole, introduction to the facsimile reprint of *Frottole intabulate* (Bologna, 1972), pp. [vii-viii].

[13] Vocal embellishment in *frottole* is discussed in W. Rubsamen, 'The *Justiniane* or *Viniziane* of the 15th Century', *Acta Musicologica*, vol. 29 (1957), pp. 172-84. The works in question are published in their ornamented version in Disertori, *Le frottole per canto e liuto*, pp 248-63.

[14] For further on ornamental patterns in Antico's *Frottole intabulate*, see K. Jeppesen, *Die italienische Orgelmusik am Amfang des Cinquecento* (Copenhagen, 1943; rev. ed., 1960), vol. 1, pp. 58-67. For editions of *frottole* from the print, see *ibid* , pp. 3°-25°; Disertori, *Le frottole per canto e liuto*, pp. 271-301, and Plamenac, 'The Recently Discovered Complete Copy', pp. 688-92.

[15] For further on text underlay, see E. Lowinsky, *The Medici Codex of 1518*, Monuments of Renaissance Music, vol. 3 (Chicago, 1968), pp. 90-107; D. Harrán, 'New Light on the Question of Text Underlay Prior to Zarlino', *Acta Musicologica*, vol. 45 (1973), pp. 24-56; and *ibid.*, 'Vicentino and His Rules of Text Underlay', *Musical Quarterly*, vol. 59 (1973), pp. 620-32.

William F. Prizer is a Professor in the School of Music, College of Arts and Sciences, at the University of Kentucky, Lexington, USA

musical setting, a repetition sign after the first two phrases of music. This repetition sign is intended only for the *piedi* and must be disregarded in the performance of the *ripresa*. Thus the first time through, the musician should sing the *ripresa* and refrain without the repeat and use the repeated section for the four lines of the *piedi* (cd/cd). The manner of performance of such a work is illustrated in the right-hand column of the table. (See also 5.) In all types of *barzellette*, the entire *ripresa* should not be repeated at the end of each stanza unless the composer did not provide separate music for the refrain.

Barzellette with a *volta* of four lines (no. 2) are much the same, in that the repetition signs must be disregarded for the performance of the *ripresa* and the refrain. They differ in that additional repetition signs are necessary for the *volta* and refrain.

Barzellette with separate music for the stanza (nos. 3 and 4) are much less problematic since each part has its own music. Whether the *volta* is of two or four lines, the repetitions are to be observed wherever present.

The remaining frottolesque forms, without refrain, are considerably simpler. The most popular of these, particularly in the earlier *frottola*, was the *strambotto* (nos. 5-7), a lyric *ottava rima* generally of a single strophe and consisting of eight lines of eleven syllables each, rhyming ABABABCC. The composer set this structure in three ways: (1) he might write music only for the first couplet, the setting thereby requiring four statements (no. 5); (2) he might write music for the first and last couplets, so that the first two phrases must be stated three times and the last two, once (no. 6); (3) he might write music for the entire *strambotto*, creating a through-composed form (no. 7).

The sonnet (nos. 8 and 9), made up of fourteen lines of eleven syllables each divided into two quattrains and two tercets, was set with increasing frequency throughout the period of the *frottola*. The composer generally treated the poem in one of two ways: (1) he might write only three phrases, indicating that the second was to be repeated, in which instance the music would be stated four times, twice with repeats for the quattrains and twice without for the tercets (no. 8); (2) he might compose music for the first quattrain and for the first tercet, in which instance the first section of music is repeated for the second quattrain, and the second is repeated for the concluding tercet (no. 9).

Also set occasionally was the *capitolo* (no. 10), a species of *terza rima* made up of eleven-syllable lines rhyming ABA, BCB, CDC, etc. The *capitolo*, of numerous strophes, often concludes with a quattrain of alternating rhyme. In this case, the first three phrases should be repeated for all tercets, the last phrase of music being sung only for the concluding line of the quattrain.

Last, composers often set poems in the form of *ode* (singular, *oda*). These were typically long strophic poems of four-line strophes, the first three lines having seven or eight syllables and the last, four or five syllables. Here the music should simply be repeated for each strophe (no. 11).

It is not surprising that until recently problems such as text underlay and the relationship between textual and musical form have tended to discourage performance of *frottole* by those interested in early music. Admittedly, preparing a performing edition of such works requires more effort than some other genres, but once these efforts have been made, musicians will have at their disposal a large and significant repertory.

[5]

The *a cappella* heresy in Spain: an inquisition into the performance of the *cancionero* repertory

Tess Knighton

The performance of the French chanson in the 14th and 15th centuries has been illuminated by the study of contemporary literary sources; the same is true of the Italian trecento madrigal.[1] An examination of Iberian literature of the later Middle Ages also yields useful information. The literary sources of a given period and geographical area—ranging from poetry and romances to correspondence and chronicles—can provide clues not only to the mode of performance (what kinds of vocal and/or instrumental forces might have been used), but also to the contexts in which musical settings of lyric verse were conceived, performed, and heard. However, the interpretation of this evidence is subject to limitations similar to those that apply to pictorial sources. These limitations have been outlined by James McKinnon: 'pictures cannot always be taken at face value. They must be interpreted with due regard to the evidentiary inadequacies of art works, stylistic limitations, for example, or the constraints of iconographic convention.'[2] When examining literature it is essential to identify literary convention and to determine the extent to which aspects of performance may be reflected in a work of fiction (or the embellished or idealized reality found in the chronicles of the period).

Most of the sources considered here relate approximately to the lifetimes of the Catholic Monarchs Ferdinand and Isabella, that is to say from the mid-15th century to the first decades of the 16th, the period of the first flowering of Spanish song. They are all essentially fictional; even the chronicles commissioned by nobles and princes for the glory of their own houses conform to conventional models that barely differ from the romances narrating the lives of fictitious heroes. The distinction between fact and fiction is gossamer fine: in many ways the writing of the Spanish lyric poets and romancers of the later Middle Ages conforms more to established literary convention than to any attempt to portray 'real life'. Yet many writers had an eye for realistic detail which created 'a mode of authenticating realism'

in which readers could recognize features of their own lives the better to absorb the moral of the tale.[3]

At times the desire to authenticate the story is so strong that the actual song that was sung at a particular moment in the story or poem is cited: the music of several songs quoted in this way survives, while references to others that no longer exist point to a lost repertory.[4] Most sources are less specific, but taken together they can reveal much about the underlying assumptions of a writer whose aim was to enable the reader to identify with the world, ostensibly fictional or otherwise, he represented. Usually the writer was not primarily concerned with how to perform a polyphonic song (for the most part, he would assume such knowledge on the part of his reader), but rather with the provision of realistic detail that made his narrative the more convincing. However, for all that such detail may in itself be subject to literary conventions of one kind or another, it can yet reveal something about how to perform a specific repertory.

The repertory under consideration here is that of the Spanish polyphonic songbooks of the late 15th century and the early 16th, including the vast compilation of more than 450 extant songs known as the Palace Songbook (*CMP*), as well as the smaller but still important Colombina (*CMC*) and Elvas collections and those songs contained in mixed manuscripts preserved in Segovia and Barcelona.[5] Although these songs have mostly been available in modern editions for many years, they have been relatively little studied and their performance context still less so. Interpretations have tended to be colourful in terms of instrumentation (the recordings of Hespèrion XX and the New London Consort are representative of this tradition), often with the use of percussion which seems to work well with the lively rhythms and simple textures of the songs.[6] Rarely are the complete texts of the songs performed or recorded (the recent recording from Margaret Philpot, Shirley Rumsey and Christopher Wilson is an admirable

1 The story of Dives and Lazarus, Breviary of Isabella (Flanders, *c*.1497) (London, British Library, MS Add. 18851), f.252. See cover for detail.

exception in this respect), giving a false impression of their overall length and sometimes of their basic structure. It is as if modern performers fight shy of the repetitive strophic forms in which most songs of the period are conceived and prune and orchestrate in a search for variety that is surely a response to a late 20th-century aesthetic. The evidence culled from diverse literary sources and presented here may well frustrate those usually instrument-based groups keen to exploit the different timbres of the huge variety of instruments portrayed in iconographical and literary forms from at least the 13th century; but the illuminations of the *Cantigas de Santa María* and the marvellous, almost fantastical list of instruments in the Archpriest of Hita's *Libro de buen amor* are not reliable testimonies (indeed, the latter is a classic example of the literary convention of enumeration).[7]

Yet, within a much more limited sound spectrum, the sources do point to a variety of ways in which polyphonic songs were performed in the Spanish kingdoms at the time of the reign of the Catholic Monarchs, usually according to the context for which they were originally intended. The three basic modes of performance for the *cancionero* repertory that emerge from the evidence of the literary sources are: all-vocal; all-instrumental; and vocal soloist accompanied by a plucked instrument such as lute, vihuela or harp.

All-vocal performance of the *cancionero* repertory

The Iberian sources have their own contribution to make to the so-called '*a cappella* heresy' in that they clearly point to a tradition of performing polyphonic songs with unaccompanied voices, usually but not exclusively with one voice to a part.[8] A passage from *Tirant lo Blanc,* the most famous of Catalan chivalric novels of the 15th century, and one praised and discussed for its 'realism', illustrates the point that the functions of voices and instruments tended, at this period, to be rather different.[9] *Tirant lo Blanc* is thought to have been compiled largely by the Valencian nobleman Joannot Martorell between 1460 and his death in 1468, and it does indeed abound in the sort of realistic detail found in other romances such as *Cleriadus et Meliadice.* The hero, Tirant, takes up arms not only in response to the demands of chivalry, but also in real battle against the Infidel—much of the book is in fact set in the Levant—a theme of special relevance to Moorish-occupied Spain. In effect *Tirant* is a subtle mixture of fiction and reality, of literary convention and verisimilitude: Tirant's journeys, whether to England or Greece, are accurately

charted (the author certainly visited England and his precise description of the Order of the Garter is held up as an example of his first-hand knowledge of matters English); while real names are mingled with invented or mythological ones (King Arthur makes an appearance). The following description of Tirant's qualities as captain and of the life in his army camps during the war effort against the Turks may well reflect reality even though it clearly also belongs to the literary convention of extolling the hero in every aspect of his character:

E és molt alegre ab sos amics donant-los delits: ab menistres dansen e ballen entre dones; és molt afable a totes gents e de cor molt fort, que no té temor de res. En les sues tendes, los uns lluiten, los altres salten, e juguen los uns a taules, los altres a escacs; los uns se fan folls, los altres assenats; los uns parlen de guerra, los altres d'amor; los uns sonen llaüt, los altres arpa, uns mija viola, altres flautes e cantar a tres veus per art de musica. No és negú qui en plaer puga pensar, que allí no el trobe ab lo nostre Capità.

(*Tirant lo Blanc*, pp.520–21)

He [Tirant] is very cheerful with his friends, providing entertainments for them: they dance to the sound of minstrels and with women. He is also very friendly towards other people and is very courageous, for he is not afraid of anything. In his tents, some wrestle and others exercise; some play cards and others chess; some play the fool, others become very wise; some talk of war, others of love; some play the lute, others the harp or vihuela, others recorders and [some] sing in three voices in the art of music. No one could dream up a pleasurable pastime that was not already to be found there courtesy of our Captain.

In this brief passage are found various aspects of contemporary performance practice that differ little from the patterns established for the rest of Europe from other sources, including that of the iconographical tradition of the 'Garden of Delights': the minstrels (probably *ministriles altos*) accompany the dancing, and soft or 'bas' instruments are played as pleasurable pastimes, which also include wrestling, conversation or playing games of various kinds. Illus.2 is not set in a garden, but conforms to the tradition in its depiction of assorted pastimes—chess, conversation, the singing of songs (apparently with four singers) and the playing of 'bas' instruments. There is no reason to suppose that here, any more than in Martorell's description, the vocal and instrumental ensembles played together. Whether the instruments in the army camps under Tirant were played in ensembles or by individuals is not clear— Martorell seems here to slip momentarily into the 'list' convention—but they are clearly separated from the singing in three-voice counterpoint, for that is how the reference to 'a tres veus per art de musica' must surely be interpreted. Even though instruments are mentioned in

2 The Emperor Maximilian and Empress Marie of Burgundy, tapestry (Flanders, *c*.1480) (Riggisberg, Abegg-Stiftung Bern Austellung)

the same sentence, this is nevertheless clearly a reference to the *a cappella* performance of three-voice polyphonic songs, the three-voice texture being by far the most common in songs of the earliest generation of composers represented in the songbooks.[10] The context evoked by the passage is also realistic, with songs and instrumental music serving as pastimes in the army camp much as they would have done at court in peacetime: the importance of the role of music in a parallel 'real-life' situation is made clear by the chroniclers of Ferdinand and Isabella in their accounts of the campaigns against the Moors in Granada (see below under 'Solo song with instrumental accompaniment').

Martorell's description does not make it clear exactly who was doing the singing, whether Tirant's camp followers themselves or professional singers in their employ (though the qualification 'per art de musica' implies sufficient skill to sing polyphony), nor does it specify what they were singing, though polyphonic

songs would perhaps have been more likely in a non-liturgical context such as this. Martorell was probably less knowledgeable about musical matters than he was about travel and warfare. There is, however, another literary source from much the same period as *Tirant* that is much more explicit on both counts. This is an anonymous poem included in the so-called Chansonnier d'Herberay, a collection of verse in Castilian compiled at the court of Navarre probably between 1461 and 1464.[11] David Fallows has already drawn attention to the importance of the poem *En Ávila por la A* for its references to the song repertory of this early part of the period, much of which, though not quite all, has been lost.[12] It conforms to the 'list' convention (as well as that—widespread in Iberian verse of the period—of quoting poems), being an ABC of a royal itinerary (from Ávila to Zara) in which the recurring descriptive elements—the names of the town and hosts visited, the food provided, the type of wood burnt and the songs sung during the evening's entertainment—share the same initial letter. Of the 23 songs cited (i/j and u/v were considered the same in the alphabet of the period), only two of those with Castilian texts have survived in polyphonic settings: Juan de Cornago's *Señora qual soy venido* (*CMC*, 22; *CMP*, 52) (ex.1) and the anonymous *La gracia de vos donzella*.[13] Both are three-voice songs and can probably be dated from the 1450s or early 1460s, and the poem itself makes clear reference to the performance of songs in three parts with voices alone. In lines 34–6 the poet refers to the 'B' song *Buena pascua y ventura* (now lost) as being performed in three parts ('a tres vozes cantaran/por quitarle de tristura' ['they will sing in three voices/to alleviate his sadness']). Here he does not indicate who will sing, but elsewhere he is more specific: in lines 94–6 he mentions the song *En esto siento per dios* (also lost) which 'el obispo y otros dos/le canten quando comiere' ('the bishop and two others/sing for him while he eats').

In other instances, two-voice polyphony is implied:

> *Canten delante su alteza*
> *Iohan de la Carra y su hermano*
> *Dama de gran gentileza.*

They sing for his highness/Juan de la Carra and his brother/ *Dama de gran gentileza.*

In yet others, only one singer is mentioned, possibly implying a monodic performance, though not necessarily: compare lines 54–5:

> *Con qualquier pena que siento*
> *le cante Iohan de la Fuente*

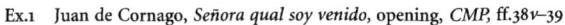

Ex.1 Juan de Cornago, *Señora qual soy venido*, opening, *CMP*, ff.38v–39

Juan de la Fuente sings for him *Con qualquier pena que siento* with lines 354–7:

> *Porque tiene buen sentido*
> *mossen Iohan de Villalpando*
> *Señora qual soy venido*
> *entrara contrapuntando*

Because it makes sense/mossen Juan de Villalpando/will enter with a contrapuntal version of (?)/*Señora qual soy venido.*

The exact meaning of 'entrara contrapuntando' is obscure: in order to 'make counterpoint' (the verbal form used) Villalpando would have to be assisted by others, unless he were to accompany himself on an instrument, of which there is no mention. Indeed, only one reference to an instrument occurs in the whole poem and then as a humorous allusion rather than as a manner of performance. In the last verse, the poet is clearly stuck for song titles beginning with z, so he avoids the issue (lines 454–6):

> *Por cançion mossen d'Anbrun*
> *como çinfonia de çiego*
> *fara zun zun y zun.*

For his song mossen d'Anbrun/like a blindman's organistrum/will go zun, zun, zun.

The songs are invariably sung at dinner; the question as to what the 'bas' instrumentalists in illus.1 might be supposed to be playing will be discussed below.

The basic assumption throughout this poem, highly unusual for its reference to named performers, is that songs are sung by one or more voices: instruments are not even considered. Furthermore, even in less specific contexts, the writers of the period seem to assume an underlying distinction between the function of voices and instruments. This commonly arises in chivalric romances like *Tirant lo Blanc* in accounts of fictionalized festivities, descriptions that often correspond very closely to contemporary chronicles of such events. Thus, in Tirant's description of an English pageant (the detail of which is suggestive of an eye-witness account), such a distinction is clearly made:

> . . . *sobtosament ab un gran tro s'obri la porta de la roca. E lo rei e la Reina ab tots los estats a peu entran dins un gran pati, tot entorn emparamentat de draps de ras, llovorats d'or e de seda e de fil d'argent, de diverses històries, les imatges fetes per art de subtil artifici. Lo cel era tot cobert de draps de brocat blau, e alt, sobre los draps de ras, havia entorn naies on se mostraven àngels tots vestits de blanc, ab ses diademes d'or al cap, sonant diverses maneres d'esturments, e altres cantant per art de singular musica, que les oints estaven quasi alienats d'oir semblant melodia.*
>
> (*Tirant lo Blanc*, p.201)

. . . suddenly, with a great clap of thunder, the door of the rock opened. And the King and Queen and all the other estates walked into a large room, all of which was adorned with silk cloth, embroidered with gold and silk and silver-thread, with various illustrations, depicted with subtle skill. The sky was covered in blue brocade, and high up, above the silk, were various galleries in which there were angels dressed in white, and wearing golden crowns on their heads, playing different kinds of instruments, and others singing with such special skill that the listeners were almost taken out of their senses by hearing such music.

The phrase 'per art de musica' (a possible reference to polyphony) recurs here, but the problem, as in the case of the pictorial evidence, is whether the voices and instruments performed together. Angel musicians were clearly as important a part of fictional and real-life pageants as they were in contemporary iconographical traditions of portraying choirs of angels; illus.3 depicts two groups of angel musicians—three singers reading from a music book, and an instrumental trio of two lutes and recorder—suggestive of this separateness, but whether the singers are performing three-voice counterpoint cannot necessarily be assumed. However, angel musicians and the all-vocal performance of polyphony come together in a relatively rarely found literary convention in fray Iñigo de Mendoza's *Coplas de vita Christi*, a work thought to have been written in 1467–8 and almost certainly known by the young princess Isabella.[14] Mendoza draws on the imagery of polyphony to describe the joy and harmony of the birth of Christ:

> *Do fueron los conbidados*
> *a cantar, que no a yantar,*
> *los nueve coros sagrados*
> *de angeles confirmados*
> *en ya no poder pecar,*
> *los quales con alegria*
> *lleuauan de lo cantado*
> *la boz y la melodia,*
> *y los tenores Maria,*
> *las contras su desposado.*   (*Coplas*, p.145)

There the guests went to sing, rather than to feast, the nine sacred choirs of angels, who are without sin, who happily sang the top part and melody of what was sung, while Mary [sang] the tenor parts, and her husband [Joseph] the contra parts.

There are several other examples of the individual voice parts being used in this way as a poetic conceit of harmony, suggesting that the concept of all-vocal performance of, in this instance, three-voice polyphony was sufficiently familiar to make such an image meaningful. The question is whether there is another underlying assumption of performance practice to Mendoza's poetic conceit: that of several voices to the top line ('la boz y la melodia'), with only one on each of the lower voices. It is not clear whether this reflected a tradition of nativity plays in which Mary (perhaps played by a young man), Joseph and some angelic choirboys actually performed three-voice polyphony in this way, although there is evidence to suggest that polyphonic songs were a part of shepherd plays performed on Christmas matins in the Aragonese royal chapel from at least the time of the reign of Ferdinand's father Juan II (1458–79).[15]

It might seem a little excessive to have the nine choirs of angels to one vocal line, but it is clear that at least on some occasions more than one singer sang the top line of a polyphonic song while the two lower lines were taken by one singer each, so that Mendoza's image is based on reality if exaggerated in its poetic context. The proof for this comes from a chronicle, a detailed account by the royal chronicler Gonzalo Fernández de Oviedo of the life of prince Juan, only son and heir to the Catholic Monarchs who died young in 1497.[16] Fernández de Oviedo served at court for most of his life, and can be taken as an eye-witness, although even his description of the prince's musical abilities seems to verge on convention in the enumeration of the instruments that the prince had in his chambers, all of which he was supposedly able to play. But the still more precise account of how the prince was wont to spend his afternoons while the rest of the court enjoyed a siesta can be verified from other sources. The panegyrical tone also slips a little when Fernández de Oviedo describes the prince's voice, perhaps a more reliable indicator that he may here be telling the truth.

> *Era el prinçipe don Johan, mi señor, naturalmente inclinado a la musica, e entendiala muy bien, avn que su voz no era tal, como el era porfiado en cantar; pero en compañia de otras bozes passaua adelante: e para eso, en las siestas, en espeçial en verano, yuan a palaçio Johanes de Ancheta, su maestro de capilla, e quatro o çinco muchachos, moços de capilla de lindas bozes, de los quales era vno corral que despues fue muy eçelente cantor y tiple, y el Prinçipe cantaua con ellos dos oras, o lo que le plazia, e les hazia thenor, e era bien diestro en el arte.*
>   (*Libro de la camara*, pp.182–3)

My Lord Prince Juan was naturally disposed to music and he understood it very well, although his voice was not as good as he was persistent in singing; but it would pass with other voices. And for this purpose, during siesta time, especially in summer, Juan de Anchieta, his chapel master, and four or five boys, chapel boys with fine voices (among whom was Corral who later became an excellent singer and *tiple*), went to the palace and the prince sang with them for two hours, or however long he pleased to, and he took the tenor, and was very skilful in the art.

The accuracy of Fernández de Oviedo's account, as in the case of the alphabet poem *En Ávila por la A*, would seem to be borne out by his mention of 'real' people: the singer-composer Juan de Anchieta was indeed *maestro de capilla* of the Castilian chapel, serving during his life-

3 Anonymous, *Virgin and child* (15th century) (Barcelona, Museo Diocesano)

time not only Juan, but also Isabella, Ferdinand and their daughter Juana 'la loca' between 1489 and his death in 1523.[17] The 'Corral' to whom the passage refers was almost undoubtedly Antonio de Corral, who also served in the royal chapels for a considerable length of time as a singer. After being a chapel boy in the Castilian royal chapel, he was appointed an adult singer in January 1499, serving Isabella until her death in 1504 and subsequently transferring to the Aragonese chapel where he stayed until Ferdinand's death in 1516.[18] The term 'tiple' would indicate that Corral in his adult years remained a singer of the top line, possibly as a falsettist.[19] There is no reason to doubt, therefore, the veracity of Fernández de Oviedo's description, and this clearly represents one way in which three-voice polyphony was performed at the Castilian court as, apparently, it was elsewhere in Europe:[20] with a handful of boys on the top line, and one adult voice on each of the lower parts (the prince singing the tenor, Anchieta the contra). No mention is made of any instrument participating in this context, even though the prince's chambers were so full of musical instruments and the prince apparently knew how to play them.

Nor is any reference made to the kind of polyphony that was sung during those long summer afternoons, but, given the setting, songs or even devotional motets are perhaps more likely than liturgical polyphony. It is possible that almost any of the three-voice songs in the Palace Songbook dating from before 1497 were performed in this way. One that would appear to have been tailor-made for the delectation of an heir to the throne is Juan del Encina's *El que rige y el regido* (ex.2). This is in three parts, with a tenor line that is remarkably straightforward in both rhythm and underlay. The strongly didactic tone of the text follows closely in the tradition of Rodrigo Sánchez de Arévalo's *Vergel de los príncipes*, which was dedicated some decades earlier to Juan's uncle Enrique IV and which propounds the virtues of music in the education of the heir to the throne.[21]

Fernández de Oviedo's chronicle is perhaps unique—and certainly untypical—in its description of the *a cappella* performance of polyphony by a combination of amateur and professional singers. Fictional romances of the period generally portray the hero as noble amateur, with musical talent being one of the qualities of the perfect courtier. Tirant lo Blanc is himself untypical in this regard, as he is nowhere described as participating in the

Ex.2   Juan del Encina, *El que rige y el regido, CMP,* ff.197v–198

music-making that goes on around him. Not so in the case of the hero of another mid-15th-century Catalan chivalric novel, *Curial e Güelfa*.[22] This extraordinary precursor to *Tirant* (it was probably written between 1440 and 1460) displays a similar degree of licence with fantasy and reality. It makes reference to the reign of Pere the Great (1276–89), but is a more accurate mirror of its own time. The anonymous author describes Curial—who, as his name would suggest, is the personification of courtliness—at the start of his career in terms of the accomplishments he acquires through noble protection:

E no obstant que ell fos molt ben acostumat, de continent ques viu crexer destat, cresque axi mateix en virtut, e lexada a un depart la altra manera que tenia solia, si be se era bona, torna molt prudent e abte, car tantost fonch molt bel cantador e apres sonar esturments, de que deuench molt famos; axi mateix caualcar, trouar, dançar, junyir e totes altres abteses que a noble joue e valeros se pertanyia.

(Curial e Güelfa, p.10)

Although he was already very cultivated, as soon as he began to rise in the world he grew also in virtue; and having left behind his old way of life (though that was in any case good), he became very wise and skilful, for he soon became a very fine singer and he learnt to play instruments for which he earned great renown, and to ride, to write poetry, to dance, to joust and all the other accomplishments a young and valiant nobleman must possess.

In the course of the novel, Curial sings with and without instrumental accompaniment. While he is held captive by a Moorish nobleman outside Tunis, going under the name of John, he entertains his master's daughter, Camar, who, impressed by his vocal prowess (among other things), falls in love with him. 'John' teaches Camar some of the songs he knows, and sings with her in two-part harmony:

Cantaua molt be Cammar, e Johan mostrali moltes cantiques, e ab acorts cantaua ab ella, e tant frequenta la tendra donzella aquest fet, ques pres esment de la bellesa del cors de Curial e de la resplandor dels seus ulls . . .

(Curial e Güelfa, pp.409–10)

Camar sang very well, and John taught her many songs, and sang with her in harmony, and so often did the young girl do this that she became aware of the beauty of Curial's body and of his sparkling eyes . . .

From the context, the phrase 'ab acorts cantaua ab ella' suggests that Curial either improvised a second part to the melody he had taught Camar, or that they sang pieces in two composed parts. Later in *Curial e Güelfa* the author interestingly alludes to a *cartella*;[23] when Curial has escaped from slavery, he has a dream, full of

musical allusions, in which the nine Muses appear to him to make sure that he does not stray from the way of the true courtier:

Tantost prop daquesta staua una altra Reyna, de varies colors vestida, empero molt ricament abillada, e staua tan alegre cantant que aço era una gran merauella. E tenia en la ma un cartell scrit e notat a nota de cant, en lo qual miraua continuament e ab una ploma esmenaua, . . .

(Curial e Güelfa, p.459)

Next to that was another Queen, dressed in many colours and very richly, and she was so happily engaged in singing that it was a marvel to see. And in her hand she had a *cartella* notated with music, at which she looked continuously and which she corrected with a pen, . . .

This must surely reflect contemporary practice and presumes on the technical knowledge of the author, which, in the light of the musical references in *Curial e Güelfa* as a whole, was considerable.

The evidence so far accumulated shows that it was not unusual for polyphonic (and monodic) songs to be performed unaccompanied in the Iberian peninsula during the 15th century. That this was often done throughout this period with one voice to a part would seem to be confirmed by the plays dating from the 1490s of Juan del Encina (1468–1529/30).[24] Performed at the court of the Duke of Alba, Encina's Eclogues invariably ended with a song (usually polyphonic, for polyphonic settings of several of these songs have been preserved in the Palace Songbook). Encina himself took part in the performance of the plays; in the eighth Eclogue, in the guise of the shepherd Mingo, he presents his published collection of 1496 to the Duke. He was joined by the three other characters in the play (his shepherdess wife Menga, and the courtier Gil with his country-girl wife Pascuala) to sing two villancicos, *Gasajémonos de huzía* (*CMP*, 165) and *Ninguno cierre las puertas* (*CMP*, 167), both of which have survived in four-voice versions in the Palace Songbook. Each song is introduced rather deliberately in the preceding dialogue as, for example, in the case of *Ninguno cierre las puertas*, where the shepherd couple Mingo (Encina) and Menga agree to try out courtly life:

Assí que todos cuatros juntos, muy bien ataviados, dieron fin a la representación cantando el villancico del cabo.

MINGO: *Daca Gil, por buena entrada*
           de la vida del palacio,
           cantemos de gran espacio
           alguna linda sonada,
           y, luego, sin tardar nada.
GIL: *Que digo que soy contento.*
MINGO: *Tú, Pascuala?*

Ex.3   Juan del Encina, *Ninguno cierre las puertas*, opening, *CMP*, ff.102v–103

PASCUALA: *Que consiento.*
GIL: *Y tu, Menga?*
MENGA: *Que me agrada.*
Villancico: Ninguno cierre las puertas.

(*Églogas*, pp.191, 222)

So that all four together, dressed in finery, end the play by sing-ing the final villancico.

MINGO: Come on Gil, for such an initiation
          into the courtly way of existence,
          let's sing with great persistence
          some pretty composition,
          and that without further consultation.
GIL: I think that's just the thing to do.
MINGO: And you Pascuala?
PASCUALA: I agree with you.
GIL: What about you, Menga?
MENGA: Without hesitation.

The four characters then sing, presumably in four-part polyphony, with one voice to a part, and without instru-ments, the song *Ninguno cierre las puertas* (ex.3). The narrow vocal ranges and the extreme simplicity of the musical style (basically homophonic and presenting no problem for the underlay of the text of the six verses of the song) could well have meant that not all the actor-singers were, like Encina, professional musicians. This simple homophonic style, so characteristic of Encina's songs of the 1490s, and so typical of the second gener-ation of court composers represented in the Palace Songbook, also served admirably to allow the words to be heard in the context of a play.

Occasionally in Encina's plays an extra character has to be brought on for the final song, as in the fifth Eclogue, where the three main characters call on a fourth for that very purpose.[25] Another example occurs in a Christmas play by Lucas Fernández (1474–1524), in which one of the four shepherds refuses to sing because he is so full of garlic he is afraid he will choke on it: so they call on an extra, Mingo Pascual, who, as the synopsis given at the beginning suggests, 'helps them to sing'.[26]

Ex.4   Lucas Fernández [?], *Dí, por qué mueres en cruz, CMP,* f.278v

Y en la vltima copla llaman otro pastor que se llama Mingo pascual que los ayude a cantar . . . y el Juan los lieua a bethlen a ado-
rar al señor cantando y vaylando el villancico en fin escripto en
canto de organo.

(*Farsas,* p.189)

And in the last verse they call on another shepherd called
Mingo Pascual who helps them to sing . . . and Juan leads them
to Bethlehem to adore the Lord singing and dancing the villancico written at the end in polyphony.

The song, *Gran deporte y gran conorte,* has not survived
in a musical setting, but there can be no doubt from this
that it was sung in polyphony with one voice to a part.
That it must have been in four parts is clear from the
need to replace one of the actors who was not able to sing
with someone who could. This rubric also raises another
aspect of the performance of songs from the *cancionero*
repertory: some at least were danced to.

Fernández was trained as a singer at Salamanca
Cathedral and spent most of his life there until 1522
when he became Professor of Music at Salamanca University. He was paid by the Cathedral for Christmas and
Easter plays, and it is likely that he, like Encina, took one

of the roles himself. He was probably the shepherd called
Pascual in the fourth play of his 1514 collection to whom
the other characters (another shepherd, a shepherdess
and a soldier) turn for the choice of the final song on the
basis that he is familiar with the *cancionero* repertory
(*Farsas,* p.162). No setting of the song he 'chooses'—
Quien sirve al amor—survives. However, one of the two
villancicos sung at the end of his *Auto de la Pasión* is preserved in an anonymous three-voice setting in the Palace
Songbook (ex.4). The setting of *Dí, por qué mueres en
cruz* (*CMP,* 417) is simply but dramatically conceived
and, according to the rubric, would have been performed with the actor-singers kneeling in front of the
Holy Week monument ('Aqui se ha de hincar de rodillas
los recitadores delante del monumento cantando esta
cancion y villancico en canto de organo', *Farsas,* p.235).
The cast comprises seven players—saints Peter, Mat-
thew, Jerome and Dionysius and the three Marys, who
have already sung in three-voice polyphony earlier in the
play in two brief laments (settings of which do not
appear to survive). Given that it was customary for the
cast to join in the singing of the concluding villancico,

and if it was indeed this three-voice setting of *Dí por qué mueres en cruz* that was sung, this may have been an instance where there was more than one singer to a part: possibly the three Marys were played by choirboys from Salamanca Cathedral who would have taken the top line while the four men doubled on the two lower parts.

Nowhere in the plays of Encina and Fernández is there any suggestion of instrumental participation in the performance of these songs; a close study of the *autos* of the Portuguese playwright Gil Vicente (*c*.1465–1536/7) may well reveal a shift in favour of instrumental participation by the second decade of the 16th century; at one point in *Dom Duardos* there even appears to have been a moment of 'melodrama', with the instruments accompanying a brief spoken exchange before the song.[27]

Instrumental performance of the *cancionero* repertory

The fact that in most literary sources from the 15th century voices and instruments seem to fall into different performance groupings would seem to be confirmed by an extract from the chronicle of the Constable of Castile, a rich source of information for performance practice in the 1460s and 70s.[28] The celebrations held in 1470 on the eve of the wedding of Fernán Lucas, the court treasurer, included a banquet followed by music and dancing:

Sonando a tienpos vnas veces las chirimias, otras el claueçinbalo, otras veces muy buenos cantores que alli estauan, pasando muy gentiles canciones e desechas.

(*Hechos del Condestable*, p.437)

At intervals there was music, the shawms playing at times, the harpsichord at others, and at others there were some very good singers there, performing sweet songs and *deshechas*.

The shawms were almost certainly providing dance music; the singers sang songs; but what was played on the harpsichord? Instruments of all kinds are constantly referred to in poems and romances, but the sort of music that was played on them is almost always left undefined, although it is probable that even if voices and instruments tended not to perform together they did share some of the same repertory.

So far only one instance of instruments being associated with the polyphonic repertory of the *cancioneros* has come to light, but it is all the more valuable for that. A poem by Costana in the *Cancionero general* (1511), the largest printed anthology of lyric verse from the time of the Catholic Monarchs, suggests that the concept of all-instrumental performance of a song was a perfectly acceptable one.[29] Entitled 'How Love and Hope appeared one night as minstrels to ask for gifts' ('Como el afiçion y el esperança le vinieron a pedir estrenas en forma de menestriles'), the poem describes a dream in

5 Anonymous, *Vive leda, si podrás*, opening, *CMC*, ff.41v–42

Vi - ve le - da,_____ si po - drás y non pe - nes,

Vi - ve le - da, si po - drás [y non pe - nes,

Vi - ve le - da, si po - drás [y non pe - nes,

a - ten - dien - do que se - gún,

a - ten - dien - do___ que se - gún,]

a - ten - dien - do___ que se - gún,]

Ex.6   Anonymous, *De la vida deste mundo*, opening, *CMP*, ff.72v–73

which three minstrels appear to the poet as he lies on his bed unable to sleep for his passion:

> ni durmiendo ni despierto
> ni bien biuo ni bien muerto
> . . .
> sin saber como venian
> oy que dulce tañian
> tres muy dulces tañedores

not sleeping nor awake/neither dead nor alive/. . ./not knowing how they came/I heard the gentle playing/of three of the sweetest instrumentalists.

The poet bids the three players enter: Love carries a harp, Desire a bowed vihuela and Hope a lute. His amatory torment is then relieved by their music; having played some dance music, an 'alta' and then a 'baxa', the trio of allegorical minstrels go on to play three songs suited to the mood of the tormented poet—*Vive leda, si podrás, De la vida deste mundo* and *Amor, temor y cuidado.* Anonymous settings of two of these survive in the songbooks: a three-voice version of *Vive leda si podrás* (*CMC,*

25) survives in the Colombina Songbook, and a four-voice setting of *De la vida deste mundo* (*CMP,* 121) can be found in the Palace Songbook (exx.5, 6). The style of these two settings is quite different: the Colombina song belongs to the more complex, though essentially non-imitative idiom of the earlier generation of court composers; the song preserved in the Palace Songbook is in the homophonic style cultivated by Encina and his contemporaries. In each case, however, a performance on lute, harp and bowed vihuela would be perfectly feasible; such a combination is commonly found among pictorial representations of angel consorts (illus.4). Possibly there were other settings, and possibly the minstrels improvised around the melodies associated with these songs, perhaps each taking one song, but Costana's poem provides at least some evidence for the interpretation of the *cancionero* repertory on 'bas' instruments. It is noteworthy that there is no mention of singing in this context: the verb consistently used is 'tañer' ('to play [an instrument]'), although *De la vida deste mundo* is

4   Anonymous, Retable of St Nicholas (detail) (15th century) (Barcelona, Instituto Amatller)

referred to as a 'sad song' ('canto doloroso'). Interest-ingly, too, there are indications as to the manner of the performance—'muy sin compas' ('very free' [literally, 'very without a beat']) and 'con gran reposo' ('very relaxed'); clearly the minstrels were in tune with the poet's melancholy mood.

Solo song with instrumental accompaniment

It is perhaps not impossible, however, that the 'tañe-dores' in Costana's dream accompanied themselves on their instruments. There is at least one example of a court 'tañedor' who was also a singer: Rodrigo Donaire was paid as a 'tañedor de vihuela' in the Castilian royal household from as early as 1489 until at least 1500, serv-ing both Isabella and the royal children, first prince Juan, and, after the prince's death in 1497, Princess Maria, who married Manoel I of Portugal in 1500.[30] A letter from the Monarchs' ambassador at the Portuguese court describes the Christmas festivities there that same year:[31]

En acabando de comer vino el señor rey [Manoel] a la camara de la señora reyna [Maria], e yendose la infanta, mando despejar la camara, y despues estovieron el rey e la reyna solos oyendo musica de Rodrigo Donayre y sus compañeros.

And after eating, the king came to the queen's chambers and

the Infanta [Manoel's daughter by his first marriage to Maria's sister Isabel], leaving, ordered the room to be cleared, and then the king and queen were alone together listening to the music of Rodrigo Donaire and his companions.

It is not known who Donaire's companions in Portugal were, though a rebec player ('tañedor de rabel') called Diego de Madrid may well have been one of them.[32] Nor is it known what the king and queen were listening to, though it is clear from the correspondence of the Count of Tendilla,[33] one of Donaire's later employers, that he was a singer as well as a vihuelist and that, like Antonio Corral, he was a *tiple*, a singer of the top or melody line. On 11 April 1513 the Count wrote to don Iñigo de Mendoza:

Truxe a Rodrigo Donaire, como vuestra merced concerto y agora para sobrehusa de Galiano he tomado otro tañedor y tanbien es criado de Diego Hernandes; si un triple oviese, tengo otros tres singulares para canciones y para mas. Qualquier cosa de musica que por alla atrevesara venga aca que esta es agora la tema.

(*Correspondencia*, p.230)

I brought Rodrigo Donaire, as your honour agreed, and now, because of Galiano's refusal I have taken on another instru-mentalist who is also a servant of Diego Hernandez; if he has one *tiple* I have three others exceptional for songs and more. Anything to do with music you might come across there, let it come here, for this is all the rage now.

In another letter dated only 12 days later the Count informs the Count of Palermo that:

Ya se me fue Rodrigo Donaire; creo que va a cantar donde crean que cantava bien, que yo cada ora le dezia que callase.

(*Correspondencia*, p.266)

Rodrigo Donaire has already left me. I think he is going to sing where they think he used to sing well, for I was always telling him to be quiet.

Whether the Count's judgement on Donaire's singing can be taken seriously or not, it is clear from these letters that he was both singer and vihuelist. There is documentary evidence to suggest that songs were performed to the accompaniment of plucked instruments from at least the 14th century (see Maricarmen Gómez's article elsewhere in this issue). From the literary sources it is clear that there were two contexts usually associated with the performance of songs in this way—for the private consolation of the tormented lover and in the more public tradition of singing ballads.

Curial e Güelfa provides a typical example of the love-sick knight singing to the accompaniment of a plucked instrument. Early in the romance Curial, sick with love for the unforgiving Güelfa, performs for some Catalan knights he has met as a knight errant and with whom he is to fight in a tourney:

. . . trames per los seus cathalans, e poetant ab lo gest, mostra alegria finguint, si be sen havia poca. Los quals venguts Curial los conuida, els feu gran festa e pres una arpa e sona marauellosament axi com aquell quin ere gran mestre, e canta tant dolçament que no semblaua sino veu angelical e dolçor de parays. Los cathalans hagueren plaer com lo veren alegrar e fonch los dit ques metessen a la taula car lo dinar era prest . . .

(*Curial e Güelfa*, p.105)

He sent for his Catalan companions, and dissimulating his demeanour, pretended to be cheerful, though he felt very little like it. When they arrived, Curial invited them in and made much of them, and took up his harp and played wonderfully, as would a great master of the instrument, and sang so sweetly that his voice seemed that of an angel with the beauty of paradise. The Catalans were delighted to see him so cheerful, and they sat at table and ate, for supper was ready . . .

It is probably not by chance that Curial accompanied himself on the harp. Although it is possible that the harp was still used in this way in the 15th century, it is also likely that the anonymous author was once again making a deliberate reference to an instrument associated with the chivalric romance tradition of the past. This passage is also unusual in that Curial tries to hide his torment with a cheerful song. The image of the courtier assuaging his passion through playing or listening to songs is common in the literature of the period—Costana's poem is merely a variation on a theme—one of the most famous examples being found in Fernando de Rojas's *La Celestina*.[34] *La Celestina* is, among other things, a parody of the estate of the courtly lover, and it opens with the courtier Calisto pining for his beloved Melibea. He calls on his servant Sempronio to bring his lute and then to sing and play the saddest song he knows:

CALIXTO: *Sempronio!*
SEMPRONIO: *Señor!*
CALIXTO: *Dáme acá el laúd.*
SEMPRONIO: *Señor, vesle aquí.*
CALIXTO: *¿Cuál dolor puede ser tal*
que se iguale con mi mal?
SEMPRONIO: *Destemplado está ese laúd.*
CALIXTO: *¿Como templará el destemplado? ¿Como*
sentirá el armonía aquel que consigo está
tan discorde? . . . Pero tañe y canta la más
triste canción que sepas.
SEMPRONIO: *Mira Nero de Tarpeya*
a Roma como se ardía:
gritos dan niños y viejos
y él de nada se dolía.

(*La Celestina*, pp.48–9)

C: Sempronio! S: Sir! C: Bring me the lute. S: Sir, here it is. C: What pain could ever equal mine? S: This lute's out of tune. C: How can the out-of-tune be tuned? How can he who is so discordant in himself appreciate harmony? . . . But play and sing the saddest song you know. S: Nero looked from Tarpeya/at how Rome was burning:/young and old were screaming/but he cared nothing.

So Sempronio, the servant, sings, to the accompaniment of an out-of-tune lute, a song that is hardly likely to bring consolation to his lovesick master. A version of *Mira Nero de Tarpeya* for voice and vihuela has survived in Juan Bermudo's *Declaración de instrumentos* of 1555 (illus.5). It may well represent a later arrangement of the song, and not the one that Sempronio would have known at the end of the 15th century if, that is, a song was actually sung at this point in the story when *La Celestina* was originally performed. Would those who read it after its publication in 1499 have known the song and heard it in their heads or hummed the melody to themselves? Would a servant have been able to play even the simple accompaniment found in Bermudo or did this add to the humour, the courtier not even having that accomplishment? The choice of song, so out of tune with Calisto's mood, may also be significant in that it is a *romance* or ballad, the type of song most frequently associated with this mode of performance.

Four settings of ballads for voice and vihuela are preserved in the earliest published vihuela collection, Luis Milán's *El maestro* (Valencia, 1536); two of these are also found in four-voice polyphonic versions in the Palace Songbook.[35] However, as Howard Mayer Brown points

5 An anonymous setting of *Mira Nero de Tarpeya*, from Juan Bermudo, *Declaración de Instrumentos* (1555)

out, it is possible that, although the ballads included in the Songbook are notated according to the convention of three or four separate vocal parts, the music itself might be 'strictly speaking neither vocal nor instrumental, but more or less artistically refined blueprints of the essential features of a process to be realized in sound'. Brown goes on to isolate two of the Palace Songbook *romances*—*Durandarte* (*CMP*, 445) and *Los braços trayo cansados* (*CMP*, 446), both by Francisco Millán—as 'instrumental arrangements simply because their texture is so very different from almost every other piece in the anthology' (illus.6). Further non-musical evidence for the performance of *romances* as solo songs with lute or vihuela accompaniment—a long-standing tradition that received a new impetus in the reign of the Catholic Monarchs when the ballad was used for the purposes of royal propaganda during the Reconquest of Granada—is available from a variety of literary sources. A summary of the situation, though perhaps a rather idealized one, is found in Diego Rodríguez de Almela's *Compendio historial*,[36] written in 1479, but not formally presented to Isabella until 1491:

Aquellos reyes e principes antiguos, considerando el muy gran resplandor de los fechos e actos de guerra, manda[va]n que les leyesen las coronicas de los fechos famosos de cavalleria que sus antepasados fizieron; y por estar mas desocupados quando comian e cenavan y quando se acostar querian, mandavan otrosi que los menestrilles e juglares viniesen con sus laudes y vihuelas y otros ynstrumentos para que con ellos les tañessen e cantasen los romançes que heran ynventados de los fechos famosos de caval-

6 Settings by Francisco Millán of *Durandarte* and *Los braços trayo, CMP*, ff.290v–291

leria; todo esto mandaban para atraer e reduzirles a memoria aquellos buenos fechos e de los contrarios apartarse.

(Menéndez Pidal, pp.376–7)

Those kings and princes of old, bearing in mind the great splendour of the deeds and acts of war, ordered that the chronicles of the celebrated chivalric deeds of their forebears be read to them; and in order to be more at their leisure when they lunched and dined, and when they wanted to go to bed, they also commanded that the minstrels and singers came with their lutes and vihuelas and other instruments so that they might play and sing the ballads that were devised to tell of the celebrated knightly deeds; all this they commanded to preserve and commit to memory those good deeds and to forestall inaccuracies.

Although 'other instruments' are allowed for, it is significant that in this context the author itemizes 'lutes and vihuelas' even when referring to times past. Unlike the author of *Curial e Güelfa*, who had his chivalric hero accompany himself on the harp, Almela makes reference to contemporary performance practice. The revival of interest in the *romance* as a song of royal propaganda may well date from before the final phase of the Reconquest of Granada begun by Ferdinand in the early 1480s. According to Menéndez Pidal, in 1462 Isabella's brother Enrique IV (1454–74) commissioned a ballad to be written for an unspecified Granadine campaign and then ordered his chapel singers to set it to music.[37]

Further light on the situation during the reign of the Catholic Monarchs is shed by the employment in the Aragonese household of the *trobador* Hernando de Ribera, who was paid from 1 August 1483 (almost the start of the campaign) until at least August 1501 (well after it ended in 1492).[38] His duties included recording in verse events in the Kingdom of Granada, as is clear from a historiographical study by the 16th-century royal chronicler Galíndez Carvajal,[39] who, in a discussion of chroniclers of the reign of Ferdinand and Isabella, places Ribera fourth:

El cuarto fue Hernando de Ribera, vecino de Baza, que escribio la guerra del reino de Granada en metro; y en la verdad, segun muchas veces yo oi al Rey Catolico, aquello decia el, que era lo cierto; porque en pasando algun hecho o acto digno de escrebir lo ponia en coplas y se leia a la mesa de su Alteza, donde estaban los que en lo hacer se habian hallado, e lo aprobaban o corregian, segun en la verdad habia pasado.

(*Anales*, p.243)

The fourth was Hernando de Ribera, a native of Baza, who wrote about the Granadine wars in verse; [he also wrote] the truth, as I often heard the Catholic King say, so it must be true, for when an event or something worthy of note happened, he put it into rhyming verse and read it at his highness's table, where all those who were involved in the deed approved or corrected it, according to what had really occurred.

Galíndez Carvajal goes on to say that the truth was not always what everyone wanted to hear: he describes how Don Enrique Enríquez, the king's uncle, was not satisfied with Ribera's account of his part in a particular campaign; when the *trobador* refused to alter it the furious noble took hold of the manuscript of the versified chronicle and tore out the offending pages.[40] Perhaps this is one reason why Ribera's account of the Reconquest has failed to survive—unless fragments are extant in some of the polyphonic ballad-settings in the Palace Songbook. *Pascua d'Espíritu Sancto* (*CMP*, 136) composed for, or in memory of, the celebrations held on the feast of Corpus Christi, the day after the surrender of Ronda on 1 June 1485, might well be an example. One of four ballads attributed to Francisco de la Torre, singer-composer in the Aragonese royal chapel from 1 July 1483 until at least 1503 (and thus a curiously exact contemporary of Ribera's), its text might well represent the sort of versified homage to the exploits of a latter-day crusader-king expected of his *trobador*. La Torre's musical setting (ex.7) is typical of the Palace Songbooks ballads; its four musical phrases, in a simple homophonic style, are repeated as many times as required to accommodate the text. This could indeed be seen as a melodic-harmonic blueprint, notated according to vocal conventions, possibly because tablature had not yet been developed or become widely used. (See Antonio Corona-Alcalde's article elsewhere in this issue.)

Voices and instruments

One manner of performing ballads, and probably other songs, during the reign of the Catholic Monarchs was with solo voice accompanied by lute and vihuela. References that clearly demonstrate that other instruments were used in an accompanying role are rare indeed. An example is found in the musical dream sequence in *Curial e Güelfa*, which would seem to imply polyphony accompanied by organ:

ia pur prop de Baço, havia una altra Reyna e sonaua uns orguens e cantaua ab tanta dolçor de melodia, que yo no crech que millor so ne millor cant fos james, ne sia ara ne pusca esser daci auant. Stauan li dauant tres donzelles les quals ab diverses veus cantant se concordauan ab ella, e certes si los angels cantauan deuant lo Saluador maior dolçor no porien mostrar.

(*Curial e Güelfa*, p.459)

still nearer Bacchus was another Queen and she played the organ and sang with such sweetness of melody that I do not believe there has been or could ever be a lovelier sound or better singing. In front of her were three maidens who sang in different voices in harmony with her, and certainly if the angels were singing before the Saviour they could produce no greater sweetness.

Ex.7   Francisco de la Torre, *Pascua d'Espiritu Sancto, CMP,* f.80

Even if this can be taken as a rare reference to accompanied polyphony, it is not clear what type of piece was being sung; the angel simile might suggest sacred music, but then again it might once again reflect the iconographical conventions of those heavenly choirs (see illus.5 in Kimberly Marshall's article elsewhere in this issue). One piece of iconographical evidence from a rather different and, no doubt significantly, a slightly later source might just reflect actual performance practice rather than a pictorial ideal. In the frontispiece to the 1527 edition of the *Cancionero general*, that mighty collection of lyric version first published in 1511, two groups of musicians are portrayed in balconies adorned by the sun and the moon (illus.7a). In the moon balcony there are two lutenists, two recorder players, and at least four others, at least some of whom seem to be singing

(illus.7b). In the sun balcony there is only one lutenist and a single recorder-player who are again set amid a number of others who, though it is still less clear, may well be singing (illus.7c). Although a few cherubs are involved, not all the musicians have wings; some seem to be dressed and some of the singers on the moon side appear to be tonsured. It was the singers of the royal chapels (most of whom were at least in minor orders) who composed and undoubtedly performed the repertory of the musical *cancioneros.*

The question of voices and instruments in the early *cancionero* repertory must remain open, but the literary sources nowhere suggest that voices were doubled by a wide variety of instruments in the time of the Catholic Monarchs. On the contrary, the evidence seems rather to confirm that singers and instrumentalists had separate

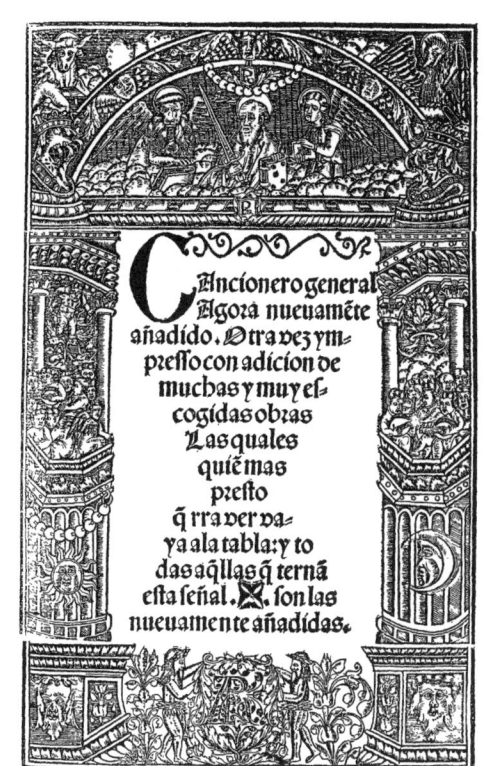

7 (a) Frontispiece from Hernando del Castillo, *Cancionero general* (1527)

(b) The moon balcony

(c) The sun balcony

functions, though their repertory may well have over-lapped. On the other hand, a tradition for solo song with instrumental accompaniment (usually lute or vihuela) was well established. The situation may well have changed by the 1520s, with the combination of voices and instruments becoming much more common.

A version of this article was read as a paper at the Twentieth Annual Conference of Medieval and Renaissance Music at Royal Holloway College, London, July 1990.

[1]See C. Page, 'Machaut's "Pupil" Deschamps on the Performance of Music: Voices or Instruments in the 14th-century chanson?', *EM*, v (1977), pp.484–91; C. Page, 'The Performance of Songs in Late Medieval France: a New Source', *EM*, x (1982), pp.441–51; H. M. Brown, 'The Trecento Harp', *Studies in the Performance of Late Medieval Music*, ed. S. Boorman (Cambridge, 1983), pp.35–74, esp. pp.55–61.

[2]J. W. McKinnon, 'Fifteenth-century Northern Book Painting and the *a cappella* Question: an Essay in Iconographic Method', *Studies in the Performance of Late Medieval Music*, ed. Boorman, p.1. A fas-

cinating corollary to this study is that so much of the musical imagery in literary and pictorial sources of the period seems to have been shared.

[3]Page, 'The Performance of Songs . . . ', p.448.

[4]D. Fallows, 'A Glimpse of the Lost Years: Spanish Polyphonic Song, 1450–70', *New Perspectives in Music: Essays in Honour of Eileen Southern*, ed. J. Wright, with S. A. Floyd, Jr, Detroit Monographs in Musicology (Warren, Mich., 1992), pp.19–36.

[5]Only the Palace, Colombina and Elvas Songbooks are currently available in modern editions. Palace Songbook: *La música en la corte de los Reyes Católicos*, ii–iii: *Cancionero Musical de Palacio*, ed. H. Anglès, Monumentos de la Música Española [MME], v, x (Barcelona, 1947–51). Colombina Songbook: *Die weltliche Vokalmusik in Spanien um 1500*, ed. G. Haberkamp (Tutzing, 1968); *Cancionero Musical de la Colombina (siglo XV)*, ed. M. Querol Gavaldá, MME, xxxiii (Barcelona, 1971). Elvas Songbook: *O cancioneiro musical e poetico da Biblioteca Publia Horténsia*, ed. M. Joaquim (Coimbra, 1940); also available in a facsimile edn with an introductory study by M. P. Ferreira, *Lusitana musica*, i: *Opera musica selecta*, iii (Lisbon, 1989).

[6]Recent recordings include: (*a cappella*) The Hilliard Ensemble, *Spanish and Mexican Renaissance Vocal Music* (EMI Reflexe CDS 7 54341 2); (solo voice/vihuela accompaniment) Margaret Philpot/Christopher Wilson/Shirley Rumsey, *From a Spanish Palace Songbook* (Hyperion, CDA66454); (voice and instruments) Circa 1500/Gerard Lesne, *O Lusitano* (Virgin Veritas VC 7 91500–2); New London Consort, *Music from the Time of Christopher Columbus* (Linn Records CKH007); Hesperion XX, *Juan del Encina romances & villancicos* (Astrée/Auvidis E8707); *El Cancionero de Palacio* (Astrée/Auvidis E8762) and *El Cancionero de la Colombina* (Astrée/Auvidis E8763). See also the reviews in this issue by Owen Rees and Ivan Moody.

[7]See K. Marshall, 'The Organ in 14th-century Spain', elsewhere in this issue. Other musical 'lists' from 15th-century poems are reproduced in E. M. Ripin, 'Towards an Identification of the Chekker', *GSJ*, xxviii (1975), pp.11–25.

[8]C. Page, 'The English *a cappella* Heresy', *Companion to Medieval and Renaissance Music*, ed. T. Knighton and D. Fallows (London, 1992), pp.23–9.

[9]J. Martorell, *Tirant lo Blanch*, ed. M. de Riquer (Barcelona, 1979; Eng. trans. D. H. Rosenthal (London, 1984). For a discussion of the question of verisimilitude in *Tirant*, see A. Torres, *El realismo del 'Tirant lo Blanch' y su influencia en el 'Quijote'* (Barcelona, 1979).

[10]For the interpretation of a similarly ambiguous passage concerning three-voice polyphony see Page, 'Machaut's "Pupil" Deschamps . . . ', pp.485–6.

[11]*GB-Lbl* MS Add.33382, ff.195v–206; *Le chansonnier espagnol d'Herberay des Essarts (XVe siècle)*, ed. C. V. Aubrun, Bibliothèque de l'École des Hautes Études Hispaniques, xxv (Bordeaux, 1951), pp.188–96.

[12]Fallows, 'A Glimpse of the Lost Years', pp.23–5.

[13]Fallows, 'A Glimpse of the Lost Years', pp.20–5, discusses *La gracia de vos*, preserved in the *Chansonnier de Jean de Montchenu*, ed. G. Thibault and D. Fallows, Société Française de Musicologie (Paris, 1991).

[14]Fray Iñigo de Mendoza, *Coplas de vita Christi*, ed. M. Massoli (Florence, 1977).

[15]T. Knighton, *Music and Musicians at the Court of Fernando of Aragon, 1474–1516* (PhD diss., Cambridge U., 1983), i, p.169; T. Knighton, 'Sacred Song in the Royal Chapels of Ferdinand and Isabella', *Journal of the Plainsong and Medieval Music Society* (forthcoming).

[16]G. Fernández de Oviedo, *Libro de la Camara real del Principe don Juan*, Sociedad de Bibliófilos Españoles (Madrid, 1870), pp.182–3; reproduced in D. Fallows, 'Ensembles for Composed Polyphony, 1400–1474', *Studies in the Performance of Late Medieval Music*, ed. Boorman, p.137.

[17]See 'Juan de Anchieta' in Knighton, *Music and Musicians . . .* , i, pp.251–3.

[18]Knighton, *Music and Musicians . . .* , i, pp.72–5, 94

[19]On the falsettist in Spain, see J. M. Gregori i Cifré, 'El *tenorista*, un antecesor del falsetista del siglo XVI y el problema de su técnica vocal: el único registro', *Nassarre*, iv/1–2 (1988), pp.119–26.

[20]On the participation of choirboys in the singing of polyphonic songs, see Fallows, 'Ensembles for Composed Polyphony . . .', pp.134–7.

[21]R. Sánchez de Arévalo, *Vergel de los principes*, ed. D. M. Penna, Biblioteca de Autores Españoles, cxvi (Madrid, 1959).

[22]Anonymous, *Curial e Guelfa*, ed. A. Rubió y Lluch (Barcelona, 1901); Eng. trans. P. Waley, *Curial and Guelfa* (London, 1982)

[23]On the *cartella*, see *A Correspondence of Renaissance Musicians*, ed. B. J. Blackburn, E. E. Lowinsky and C. A. Miller (Oxford, 1992), chap.5.

[24]J. del Encina, *Obras dramáticas, I (Cancionero de 1496)*, ed. R. Gimeno (Madrid, 1975) [*Églogas*]

[25]Encina, *Églogas*, p.147.

[26]L. Fernández, *Farsas y Églogas* (1514/*R* Madrid, 1929); modern edn, Mª. J. Canalleda, Clásicos Castalia, lxxii (Madrid, 1976) [*Farsas*]

[27]G. Vicente, *Dom Duardos*, in *Obras dramáticas Castellanas*, Clásicos Castellanos, clvi (Madrid, 1962), p.200. The references to music, song and dance in Vicente's works are gathered together in A. Braamcamp Freire, *Vida e obras de Gil Vicente* (rev. edn Oporto, 1944), pp.500–16, and considered in A. E. Beau, 'A musica na obra de Gil Vicente', *Estudios*, i (Coimbra, 1959), pp.219–49. A further study is currently being undertaken by Manuel Morais.

[28]Anonymous, *Hechos del Condestable Don Miquel Lucas de Iranzo*, ed. J. de Mata Carriazo y Arroquia (Madrid, 1940), p.437 [*Hechos del Condestable*]. Other passages from this chronicle are reproduced in La *música en la corte de los Reyes Católicos*, i: *Polifonía religiosa*, ed. H. Anglès, MME, i (2/Barcelona, 1960), pp.30–36, and the musical life at the Constable's court has been considered by Maricarmen Gómez in a paper entitled 'La música laica en el reino de Castilla en tiempos del Condestable don Miguel Lucas de Iranzo (1458–73)' given at the Simposio Musical 'El Cancionero de Palacio: cien años de la edición de Barbieri', Palacio Real, Madrid, 14–16 December 1990.

[29]H. del Castillo, *Cancionero general* (1511); facsimile edn, A. Rodriguez-Moñino (Madrid, 1958–9)

[30]Knighton, *Music and Musicians . . .* , i, pp.213–14, 216

[31]*Documentos referentes a las relaciones con Portugal de los Reyes Católicos*, iii, ed. A. de la Torre and L. Suarez Fernández (Valladolid, 1963), p.7 (doc.497).

[32]Diego de Madrid is listed as 'minstrel of the Queen of Portugal' in various pay documents of the Castilian household: see T. Knighton, 'Queens and Infantas: their Contribution to Musical Developments in Late Medieval and Renaissance Spain', *Rediscovering the Music: Women's Musical Traditions*, ed. K. Marshall (Northeastern University Press, forthcoming).

[33]*Correspondencia del Conde de Tendilla*, ii, ed. E. Meneses García, Archivo Documental Español, xxxii (Madrid, 1974) [*Correspondencia*]

[34]Fernando de Rojas, *La Celestina*, ed. D. L. Severin (Madrid, 1983) [*La Celestina*]. On this and other settings of *Mira Nero de Tarpeya*, see R. Stevenson, *Juan Bermudo* (The Hague, 1960), p.57; for a transcription, see F. Pedrell, *Cancionero musical popular español* (Valls, 1922), iii, pp.135–6.

[35]H. M. Brown, 'Reflections of an Oral Tradition in 15th-century Spain: the *romances* in the *Cancionero Musical de Palacio*', paper given at the Simposio Musical 'El Cancionero de Palacio . . .', Madrid, 1990

[36]D. Rodríguez de Almela, *Compendio historial*, cited in R. Menéndez Pidal, *Poesía juglaresca y juglares* (Madrid, 1924), pp.376–7, Eng. trans. in G. Chase, *The Music of Spain* (2/New York, 1959), p.35

[37]R. Menéndez Pidal, *Flor nueva de romances viejos*, (Madrid, 1933), p.16

[38]Knighton, *Music and Musicians . . .* , i, p.221

[39]L. Galíndez Carvajal, *Anales breves del reinado de los Reyes Católicos*, ed. in *Colección de Documentos Inéditos para la Historia de España*, xviii [*Anales*].

[40]Galíndez Carvajal, *Anales*, pp.243–4

[6]

Tenorlied, Discantlied, polyphonic lied: voices and instruments in German secular polyphony of the Renaissance

Stephen Keyl

1 The fools' musical offering, woodcut attributed to Albrecht Dürer printed in Sebastian Brant, *Narrenschiff* (Strasbourg, 1494)

One of the most fruitful periods for German music before the Baroque era was the beginning of the 16th century, when lieder by such composers as Heinrich Isaac, Paul Hofhaimer and Ludwig Senfl were written and soon reached a wide audience through the printing press. Building on 15th-century precedents that were deeply indebted to the French chanson of Binchois's generation, this repertory is characterized by a melodious tenor within a four-part texture; the tenor's contrapuntal primacy is tempered by the increasing use of imitation and affective homorhythm. At its best, the polyphonic lied was a highly expressive and remarkably flexible genre, capable of giving voice to amorous sentiments (of both the tender and the ribald variety), high-spirited merriment, introspection and melancholy, and even religious devotion. The early 16th-century lied found its crowning achievements in the work of Ludwig Senfl; the genre also had an important descendant in the Lutheran chorale.

A central question for the performance of the polyphonic lied, as of other genres of Renaissance music, is the relationship between voices and instruments. For nearly 80 years widespread opinion has held that German secular polyphony of the 15th and 16th centuries was written for a solo voice—the tenor—accompanied by instruments.[1] Although this view has occasionally been challenged, it still remains prevalent; the idea is implicit in the name by which the repertory is often designated, *Tenorlied*.[2]

The term *Tenorlied* is a modern coinage; during the Renaissance such compositions were called simply *Lieder* or, in the diminutive, *Liedlein*. I suggest that the preference for performing this repertory with a tenor and accompanying instruments may in some measure likewise be modern in origin. The *Tenorlied* theory was based, as we shall see, on the manner in which the sources are texted and on stylistic criteria. In the light of recent scholarship in other repertories, these lines of argument may reasonably be questioned. Musical style has been found to be an uncertain indicator of vocal or instrumental intent, and in recent years it has been widely argued that the absence of text in a part does not in itself prove that the part was instrumental.[3] In the case of these lieder, there is also substantial evidence for modes of performance that did not treat the tenor as a solo line, but lent equal weight to all four voices or even emphasized the discantus. This suggests that the role of the tenor within the composition may need to be re-evaluated.

The archival evidence currently available does little to illuminate the problem. Indeed, until recently, comparatively little information specifically relating to performing ensembles in 15th- and early 16th-century Germany had been published.[4] Lately, however, a great deal of material on this subject has been brought to light by Keith Polk.[5] Polk has established that ensembles of winds, of strings (including bowed as well as plucked strings), and of singers were all widespread at German courts and towns in the 15th and early 16th centuries, and that when instruments collaborated with solo voices the instruments were likely to be strings.[6] There are some references to solo male singers performing alone or with lutes or other stringed instruments; although we cannot say with any certainty what sort of music these musicians were performing or, assuming that it was polyphony, what part the singers were executing (could some have been falsettists?), these documents do lend some support to the *Tenorlied* theory.[7] More surprising are frequent references in the documents to female or boy singers performing together with lutes or other stringed instruments, which, at least in the admittedly selective data published by Polk, outnumber the references to adult male singers with instruments.[8] Although (again) we cannot tell what these high voices were singing or what their instrumental colleagues were playing, it is entirely possible that at least some of these ensembles were performing polyphonic lieder. If they were, then their singing of non-tenor parts would tend to undermine the *Tenorlied* theory. The ambiguity of the archival evidence makes a re-examination of the sources all the more urgent.

The case for the *Tenorlied*—that is for the performance of polyphonic lieder of the 15th and 16th centuries by a solo tenor voice accompanied by instruments—was first made on stylistic grounds. In a once-influential

book entitled *Die niederländische Orgelmesse im Zeitalter des Josquin,*[9] Arnold Schering argued that only the slow-moving, predominantly conjunct cantus firmi of 15th- and early 16th-century Masses were intended to be sung, and that the remaining parts, quicker and more disjunct, were intended for performance on the organ or other instruments. Schering and other scholars, most notably Hans Joachim Moser, subsequently applied this idea to polyphonic lieder, whose tenors are generally slower and more even in rhythm, smoother and more regularly contoured in melody than the other parts.[10] Further support for this view was sought, as will be seen, in the disposition of text in the sources.

Schering's stylistic arguments now seem untenable: the presence of disjunct, rhythmically active lines does not in itself militate against vocal performance and may in fact point to vocal virtuosity rather than to instrumental conception.[11] It is almost universally accepted that the repertory upon which Schering first based his ideas, the Masses of the 15th and early 16th centuries, was normally performed by singers without instruments.

Moreover, the contrast in melodic and rhythmic character between the tenor and the remaining voices of polyphonic lieder is by no means always so great as proponents of the *Tenorlied* theory would have it. It is true that in many lieder the discantus, altus and bassus parts are both quicker and more disjunct than the tenor. An extreme example is Senfl's four-part setting of *Ich weiss nit, was er ihr verhiess,*[12] which in all parts but the tenor abounds with sequences, wild leaps and exuberant scalic passages—the sort of writing which scholars have often characterized as particularly apt for instruments (whether or not it was demonstrably intended for them) and which probably few singers would care to attempt.

2   Discantus from *Hertzliebste fraw,* Peter Schöffer's second book of lieder, *c.*1515 (Munich, Bayerische Staatsbibliothek)

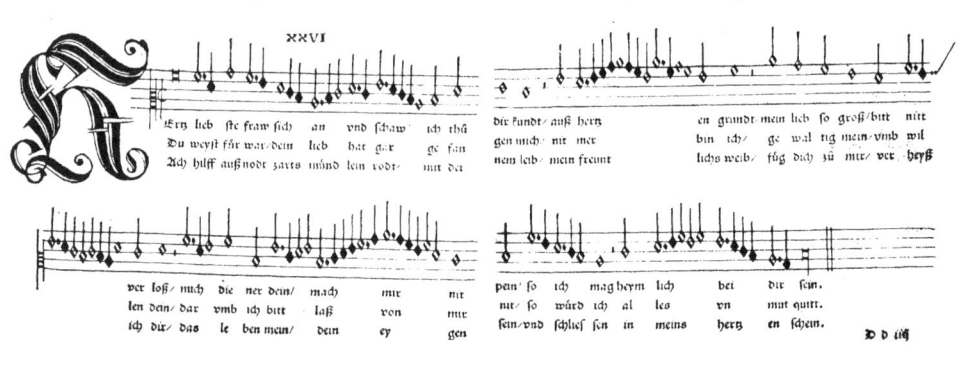

One can scarcely imagine that the piece would have been performed by four singers; such a song makes little sense except as a *Tenorlied*. Nevertheless, it is not difficult to find lieder, particularly among the many that use imitation or homorhythmic passages, in which all the parts are comparable both in rhythmic activity and in melodic outline. Indeed, in compositions employing imitation, the melodic style of the voices is by definition similar at least part of the time. An example of such a piece is *Ade mit leid*, composed probably by Paul Hofhaimer and published in Erhard Öglin's collection of 1512 (ex.1). The tenor of this lied moves as quickly as any other voice; in the ratio of conjunct to disjunct motion employed it is comparable to the discantus. The altus is somewhat more disjunct than the tenor or discantus, the bassus considerably more so; but the greater frequency of leaps in these voices should probably be attributed to the contrapuntal role they play rather than to any instrumental thinking on the part of the composer: if one examines a Mass by Obrecht, Josquin or any of their contemporaries, the altus and bassus parts are usually more disjunct than the tenor and discantus, and such Masses are now thought to have been conceived as purely vocal music.

Yet a glance at almost any early 16th-century lied source does suggest that the tenor had a privileged position with respect to the other voices. In his first anthology, published in 1513 (RISM 1513²), the printer Peter Schöffer of Mainz placed his name, together with the date and the city, only at the end of the tenor partbook, leaving the other parts without a colophon. Erhard Öglin did the same in his first publication, printed in Augsburg in 1512 (RISM 1512¹). In Schöffer's discantus, altus and bassus partbooks, the first letter of the text incipit at the beginning of each composition is a plain Roman capital, while in the tenor book it is a more ornate black-letter capital. Moreover, in most of the surviving early sources (with one major exception to be discussed below) only the tenor part is provided with text: the words for each lied are given following the music, usually on the facing page. The other parts generally have no more than a brief text incipit. Further, when one attempts to underlay the text to the four voices, it almost always fits the tenor more readily than the others. This suggests that the projection of the text was a more important issue in the composition of tenors than of other voices.

In the mid-1530s German printers began to underlay the text in all four partbooks. The anthologies compiled by Christian Egenolff, published beginning in 1535, and the first collection of Georg Forster, published in 1539,

were largely retrospective—they included much of the repertory printed during the 1510s by Schöffer, Öglin and Arnt von Aich, adding some newer compositions—but they provided words under the notes rather than after them, as had been the rule in the earlier prints, and printed them in all four partbooks.[13] This procedure would obviously not have prevented instrumentalists from playing some or all of the parts, but would have made it much simpler for all of the parts to be sung. For us, it raises the question whether the performance of polyphonic lieder by voices without instruments was an innovation of the 1530s—a 'subsequent acappellization', as one scholar put it, of a repertory originally intended for a tenor soloist accompanied by instruments[14]—or whether the singing of all parts was also an option in the 1500s and 1510s, when the songs were new.

A neglected early source points to the conclusion that all parts could indeed be sung: Schöffer's second anthology, printed between 1513 and 1518 and surviving in a single copy of the discantus partbook in the Bayerische Staatsbibliothek in Munich (RISM [*c*.1515]³). In this partbook Schöffer underlaid each composition with all stanzas of the text.[15] Although we cannot know whether the lost altus, tenor and bassus partbooks were similarly underlaid, it does not seem implausible that they were. If Schöffer did provide text for all four voices, it would be a strong indication that performance without instruments was contemplated in the second decade of the 1500s, when the repertory was relatively new. Even if it could be shown that Schöffer texted only the discantus part (or the discantus and tenor), the texted discantus partbook in the Bayerische Staatsbibliothek would still be a damaging blow to the hypothesis that only the tenor was intended to be sung. And if non-tenor parts were sung—even if only the discantus or discantus and tenor were sung—this would draw attention away from the tenor line, the supposed 'melody' of the lied.

Though no other source of lieder dating from before *c*.1535 is as uniformly texted as Schöffer's second anthology, one print and a number of manuscripts do contain a handful of pieces texted in all parts among a majority of pieces texted only in the tenor.[16] Further, some lieder present the cantus firmus (and the text associated with it) in some other voice such as the discantus or bassus, the most famous instance being Isaac's *Isbruck, ich muss dich lassen*. While German songs were undoubtedly sometimes performed as *Tenorlieder*, it would be wrong to exclude other options. Printers and scribes occasionally took the trouble to underlay text in parts other than the tenor, and it is reasonable to think that

Ex.1   Paul Hofhaimer, *Ade mit leid,* bars 1–12 (after H. J. Moser, *Paul Hofhaimer,* Anhang, pp.30–31)

German sopranos, altos and basses sang more than the few parts that were texted for them. Clearly the non-tenor parts of polyphonic lieder were sung at least some of the time, despite the lack of text in most of the sources.

How could the singers have managed without words? One solution was proposed by Arnold Geering: 15th- and 16th-century singers may have rehearsed by singing neutral syllables, adding the words only when they had mastered their parts. In Geering's view, this procedure would remove the necessity of placing the words and music on the same page. To support his hypothesis Geering cited the preface to Georg Forster's second anthology (RISM 1540[21])—Forster wrote that the text should be 'diligently sung into' the music[17]—and the use of the same rehearsal technique in Geering's day in many places in the Romance-language-speaking countries.[18] This can scarcely be considered ironclad proof, and one may well choose to disbelieve Geering's hypothesis, but a close examination of the texting of the early sources shows that whether through this practice or something similar, singers were sometimes required to cope with the placement of music and text some distance apart.

I have already mentioned that in the tenor partbooks of early lied prints and manuscripts (with the exception of Schöffer's second volume), the text is not underlaid but appears after the music, usually on the facing page. This in itself places the words at some small remove from the music and calls for a bit of mental and ocular dexterity to co-ordinate the two.[19] The demands on the tenor are magnified in a few longer compositions in which part of the text appears only after a page turn.[20] If the singers of the tenor part wished to sing the latter verses of these songs, then they must have memorized either the text or the music. And if the tenors could do so, precisely in the longest pieces when memorization would have been most difficult, why could not the singers of the other parts? Geering suggested that singers may have memorized the music, or learned it so well that they could easily add the words; while this is possible (and although any such hypothesis is difficult to prove or disprove), singers may equally well have begun with the text. The texts of lieder, direct in expression and strongly metrical, are generally not difficult to memorize; in an age when the written word was less ubiquitous than today, and when human memory may have been correspondingly more retentive, singers might have found little difficulty in memorizing the text of a lied—perhaps learning it initially by singing it to the tenor melody?—and then applying it to the contrapuntal parts.

Another alternative to the instrumental performance of untexted discantus, altus and bassus parts is singing without words. This option has been suggested by several writers over the past decade for untexted parts in French chansons of the 14th and 15th centuries; the practice may have been widespread throughout Europe.[21] Against its application to the lied speaks the texted discantus partbook of Schöffer's second print, which suggests that vocal performances of lieder preferably used words: if wordless vocalization had been acceptable to Schöffer, he would have had little reason to go to the trouble of underlaying the text. Still, the preponderance of sources untexted except in the tenor is reason enough to think that wordless vocal performance of the discantus, altus and bassus parts should not be excluded.

It seems, then, that the presence of text in only the tenor part in most early sources should not preclude the singing of the other parts. In this connection it is worth noting the title page of Arnt von Aich's collection (Cologne, *c*.1519, RISM [1519][5]): 'In this book one finds 75 pretty lieder, jolly to sing with discantus, altus, bassus and tenor, also several suitable for use on flutes, pipes [*Schwegel*], and other musical instruments.'[22] Hans Joachim Moser interpreted this title to mean that Arnt intended only the tenor to be sung.[23] In my opinion, this is a misreading. Arnt employs the word 'etlich' ('some', 'several') in a parallel construction with 'lieder'; when he writes that 'several' of something are suited to instrumental use, he refers to entire compositions, not to individual parts. Thus, according to the publisher, instrumental performance is appropriate only for some of the pieces in the collection. Moreover, Arnt lists this option only in the second place; he gives priority to all-vocal performance. Regrettably, Arnt did not specify the lieder he considered suited to instruments; however, his wording seems to indicate that all 75 are appropriate for voices. Thus Arnt did not expect his texting practice to deter the purchasers of his book from singing all four parts: whether they sang words or vocalized, the publisher expected that they would sing. Contrary to Moser's belief, Arnt did not even mention the possibility of singing the tenor while playing the other voices on instruments.

Close attention to the preface of Georg Forster's second collection points to a similar interpretation of Forster's often-quoted remarks on vocal and instrumental performance of lieder. Forster wrote:

In the past year I had a selection (containing only those German songs which are suitable for use on all sorts of instruments) published through the press. But since not all songs, as is also true of other compositions, are suitable for instruments, I have not wanted to mix among them the present songs (which are most suited to be sung, and most jolly for merrymaking), but rather to let them remain separate. Since, then, they are, as mentioned, the best for singing, the text should be most diligently sung into them; therefore it has also been somewhat more diligently set and applied under them than perhaps was done in the previous ones.[24]

The contents of Forster's first two books differ markedly in style: the first book is devoted largely to the more serious repertory first published in the 1510s, while the second volume for the most part contains simple, highly homophonic compositions, including many drinking songs, explicitly targeting the student market. The preface quoted above makes it clear that by 1540 Forster considered the polyphonic lied of the early part of the century to be suited to instruments. But Forster said nothing about how voices and instruments might be combined—he certainly did not distinguish between a sung tenor part and an instrumental accompaniment—and in both collections he facilitated all-vocal performance by underlaying the text in all four voices. In addition, Forster included charming ditties in the partbooks of his 1539 collection describing the character of the four parts: the discantus is said to be suited to the voices of young boys or girls,[25] the altus to lively young fellows who constantly run up and down, the tenor, a part of moderate range compared to the others, is most suited to men, and the bass to men of ripe years who growl like bears.[26] Despite Forster's suggestion in his 1540 book that the pieces in his earlier collection had been suited to instruments, these characterizations can refer only to vocal types and ranges. Thus, when Forster wrote that the songs in his first book were suited to instruments, he does not seem to have meant that they were unsuited to voices.

Thus the prefaces of Forster's publications do not support the theory that the polyphonic lied was intended for performance by a tenor accompanied by instruments; on the contrary, Forster seems to have thought of the genre as being performed by like forces—all voices or all instruments. Arnold Geering suggested 50 years ago that Forster distinguished between vocally and instrumentally appropriate lieder because his publications were aimed at amateur performers, who are likely to have found the quicker, more disjunct lines of the earlier repertory easier to execute on instruments than to sing. For the skilled singers at the courts for which the lieder were originally composed, Geering wrote, these lines would have posed little problem.[27] I find Geering's suggestion extremely persuasive; so far as I know, it has not been answered.[28]

If lieder were performed by voices alone or by groups of like instruments, then all four voices would receive roughly equal prominence in performance—if any one voice stood out, it would presumably be the discantus by virtue of its higher range.[29] Evidence that the discantus part could indeed be prominent in performances of lieder is found in instrumental practices of the 15th and early 16th centuries that magnify the role of the highest part. The clearest instance of such a procedure is found in Arnolt Schlick's *Tabulaturen Etlicher lobgesang vnd lidlein* (RISM 1512²).[30] Although Schlick's book is best known for the organ compositions that fill about three-quarters of its pages, it also contains 15 intabulations of

polyphonic lieder. Three intabulations are for lute alone; the remaining 12 are for lute and voice. In these arrangements the tenor and bassus are assigned to the lute; the part given to the voice is not the tenor, but the discantus; the altus is omitted.

Schlick provided the discantus in mensural notation directly above the intabulated tenor and bassus parts. He gave no text. This omission has prompted one commentator to conclude that Schlick intended the highest part to be played on a solo instrument.[31] I have argued elsewhere that Schlick intended the discantus parts to be sung; he used the word 'singen' in reference to them, and although in 16th-century German this word could be applied to instrumental performance, the context in which Schlick used it makes this meaning unlikely.[32] As to the words of the lieder, a singer could probably have obtained them from other sources—most of the pieces Schlick intabulated circulated fairly widely[33]—or could have sung without words. But even if the discantus parts of Schlick's arrangements are played on a solo instrument, they are still much more prominent—they sound much more like the melody—than the tenors.

Closely related to Schlick's practice of intabulating the tenor and bassus parts while assigning the discantus to a singer is a prescription of the Viennese lutenist Hans Judenkünig in one of his lute primers.[34] Judenkünig published many intabulations of polyphonic lieder;[35] several of the simpler ones intabulate only two parts—the tenor and bassus. But in his instructions to beginning lutenists, Judenkünig hinted at how such intabulations could be fleshed out:

> But if in the bass a few notes would go too low or deep, then begin in all voices a 4th higher on one lute; and especially if you want to set the tenor and bass, then always begin a 4th higher than the song is pitched, because the discant lute should always be tuned a 4th higher than the larger lute when two wish to play together, etc.[36]

As Kurt Dorfmüller has pointed out, Judenkünig refers to a tradition of playing intabulations of lieder and other compositions on two lutes: a tenor lute (the standard size) performed the tenor and bass, and a discant lute took the highest part, the discant player perhaps embellishing the part with divisions according to his ability.[37] Although the practice of playing such lute duets is amply documented in Germany, Italy and elsewhere in the late 15th and early 16th centuries,[38] and although examples of similar arrangements have been speculatively identified among the pieces in the Buxheim Organ Book (which dates from about 1460) and elsewhere,[39] to my knowledge no examples of two-lute intabulations of

Ex.2 Hofhaimer, *Mein einigs A.*, bars 1–10, keyboard intabulation by Johannes Kotter and the original (text omitted) (after *Tabulaturen des XVI. Jahrhunderts, Teil 1*, ed. H. J. Marx, Schweizerische Musikdenkmäler, vi, p.11, and H. J. Moser, *Paul Hofhaimer*, Anhang, p.66)

polyphonic lieder from the 16th century have survived. Judenkünig himself came closer than anyone else to providing such examples in arranging the tenor and bass parts of a few lieder for a tenor lute.

Although Judenkünig referred to the collaboration of a discant lute with a tenor lute, he did not print a part for the higher instrument. The reasons for this omission are unknown; I offer the following as speculation. Judenkünig's books, like most German lute books of the 16th century, were intended for amateurs. Discant lute playing, as the fabled exploits of Paumann and Pietrobono suggest, seems to have been more of an expert skill.[40] Perhaps discant lutenists could improvise divisions directly from the partbook or from their memory of the part, or could even improvise a new discantus above a given tenor–bass pair. If this were the case, discant lutenists would not have required a separate part.

In any event, it is clear that both Schlick and Judenkünig treated the tenors of the pieces they arranged not as solo voices, but as part of the foundation for more prominent discantus parts. This realization casts new light on the earliest surviving source of German lute music, the Königstein Liederbuch, which dates from the early 1470s.[41] For most of the many poems it contains, the manuscript transmits only the texts, but for four of them, it also gives a single line of German lute tablature without rhythmic signs.[42] The presence of this instrumental notation in a book of poetry has so far not been satisfactorily explained. David Fallows has suggested that the lute tablature may not have been intended for any instrument, but used rather as a shorthand vocal notation—an attempt to achieve the same ends as staff notation, as Fallows put it, but with a little less fuss.[43]

While German lute tablature might create a minimum of fuss on the written page, it is difficult to view it as a ready substitute for staff notation. The number of singers who could read a melody from lute tablature must have been small at any time, but especially so in the

1470s, when tablature notation was (presumably) relatively new.[44] It may make more sense to consider the four melodies written in lute tablature in the Königstein Liederbuch as further examples of tenors played by a lutenist while another musician, in this case a singer, performed (possibly improvised) a discantus against them.

One finds the highest part emphasized through ornamentation in any number of intabulations and instrumental settings of lieder from the 15th and 16th centuries. Though in most such arrangements each voice receives some embellishment, generally it is the discantus that is most highly decorated, while the tenor, especially in 15th-century intabulations, recedes into the background. Examples could be multiplied from the Buxheimer and Lochamer Liederbücher or from the 16th-century keyboard books of Hans Kotter and Leonhard Kleber as well as numerous 16th-century lute manuscripts and prints. Ex.2 is an excerpt from a keyboard arrangement of Hofhaimer's *Mein einigs A.* from Kotter's book (Basel, Universitätsbibliothek, Ms. F.IX.22); the model is also given for comparison.

It may be objected that instrumentalists had different aims than did the original composers: virtuoso lutenists and keyboard players were apt to transform the pieces they intabulated into vehicles for their technique, which generally meant a lot of fast playing in the upper register of the instrument. Can we really accept these musicians as reliable witnesses concerning the nature of the polyphonic lied? I think that we can. If the tenor part had been considered the principal melody, it would not have been difficult for an intabulator to have inverted the discantus and tenor parts so as to place the tenor in the most prominent place and to make it the melody underlying the divisions. Even without recourse to inversion, Schlick and Judenkünig had the option of giving prominence to the tenor rather than to the discantus; they could easily have intabulated the bassus and discantus, giving soloistic treatment to the tenor. That they did not do so suggests that they saw the tenor as a framework for elaboration rather than as a prominent solo line.

It may be useful to think of this function—a framework for polyphonic elaboration—as the most important function of the tenor in German secular polyphony of the early 16th century, and perhaps of the 15th and 16th centuries generally, not only in intabulations, but in the lied overall as a polyphonic genre. As in much polyphony of that era, the tenor was the starting point. It was probably composed with the text in mind, as indicated by the ease of text underlay with this voice; this would

explain why the text is associated particularly with the tenor partbooks in the early sources, and this may also be why the printer Peter Schöffer, in his first lied publication, gave greater visual decoration to the tenor books.

But its status as the part particularly associated with the text does not necessarily mean that the tenor was the only vocal part. We have seen that the discantus part was also texted in one of the earliest prints, and that the lack of text in non-tenor parts does not in itself make them instrumental. In the sacred repertory of the same era, many sources contain untexted or inadequately texted parts which singers, it is now generally agreed, nonetheless found ways to sing.

Nor does the tenor's position as the starting point of a polyphonic composition necessarily imply that it was either the most aurally prominent or the most conceptually important part in the finished piece. I do not dispute that lieder may often have been performed by a tenor accompanied by instruments, though the evidence presently available for this practice is more stylistic than documentary. Nevertheless, many intabulations, most notably Schlick's, single out the discantus for special emphasis, not the tenor, and their testimony should be taken seriously. When lieder were performed by like forces, as Öglin's and Forster's prints suggest they often were, then all four voices would have had roughly equal weight. Again there is an obvious analogy with the sacred repertory: in a cantus firmus Mass or motet, the cantus firmus is the starting point, and its disposition manifests, in some measure, the artistry of the composer. But to a much greater degree, the skill of a polyphonic composer is embodied in the contrapuntal elaboration of the cantus firmus. So it is, I believe, with the polyphonic lied. A tenor melody might have been beloved as a popular folksong, or it might have been prized as the invention of a first-rate composer; but when a melody was set polyphonically, the polyphony was also prized.[45] It follows that the polyphonic aspects of the repertory are as interesting and deserving of study as are the melodic features of the tenors.[46]

As yet far too little is known about the circumstances in which polyphonic lieder were written and performed. Future documentary studies, particularly of the courtly and urban environments where lieder were composed and sung, may clarify these issues and refine our understanding of the performance practice of the genre. In the meantime, I offer the following suggestions by way of conclusion.

1. Judging from the title page of Arnt von Aich's col-

lection, from the texted discantus part of Schöffer's second anthology (RISM [*c*.1515][3]), and from a balanced consideration of Forster's somewhat contradictory statements, the vocal performance of all parts was possible and may have been usual. Schöffer's book provides a model for texting non-tenor parts; singers may also choose to sing non-tenor parts without words.

2. There is ample evidence in Arnt, in Forster and in Polk's documents for the performance of polyphonic lieder by instruments without voices. Arnt suggests flutes or recorders; Polk's research has shown that strings were also in wide use.

3. Polk's documents offer some evidence for the performance of lieder by a tenor soloist with instruments, at least during the 15th century; to judge from the documents strings were apparently preferred to winds. The large number of sources texted only in the tenor lends some weight to this option, though arguments from the texting of the sources should not be overvalued.

4. Polk's documents also offer evidence for the use of soprano soloists with strings (whether plucked or bowed) during the 15th century; 16th-century intabulations, especially Schlick's, encourage this concept. As in the all-vocal performance of lieder, singers may take Schöffer's second anthology as a model for the placement of the words or may choose to sing without text.

Stephen Keyl is on the editorial staff of the Journal of Medieval and Renaissance Studies; *he has taught at Duke University and St Augustine's College. He is preparing an edition of the two* Liederbücher *of Peter Schöffer (RISM 1513² and [c.1515]³) and a monograph on the organist Arnolt Schlick.*

[1]A. Schering, *Deutsche Haus- und Kirchenmusik im 16. Jahrhundert* (Langensalza, 1912); H. J. Moser, *Paul Hofhaimer: ein Lied- und Orgelmeister des deutschen Humanismus* (Stuttgart, 1929/*R* Hildesheim, 1966), p.119; Moser, Foreword to *Das Liederbuch des Arnt von Aich* (Kassel, 1930), p.viii; Schering, *Aufführungspraxis alter Musik* (Leipzig, 1931), pp.86–92; H. Osthoff, *Die Niederländer und das deutsche Lied (1400–1600)* (Berlin, 1938/*R* Tutzing, 1967), pp.55–9

[2]The most direct challenge to the *Tenorlied* theory came from A. Geering, 'Texturierung und Besetzung in Ludwig Senfls Liedern', *Archiv für Musikforschung*, iv (1939), pp.1–11, an excellent essay that has been all but ignored by subsequent writers. Two studies share Geering's viewpoint but treat the subject more tangentially (and without reference to Geering's work): K. Dorfmüller, *Studien zur Lautenmusik in der ersten Hälfte des 16. Jahrhunderts*, Münchner Veröffentlichungen zur Musikgeschichte, xi (Tutzing, 1967), pp.109–13; and W. Seidel, 'Ein- und Mehrstimmigkeit im deutschen Liedsatz der Renaissance', *Musica antiqua: acta scientifica*, v (1978), pp.383–91. For the persistence of the *Tenorlied* theory, see H. Besseler, 'Renaissance-Elemente im deutschen Lied, 1450–1500', *Studia musicologica Academiae scientiarum hungaricae*, xi (1969), p.63; K. Gudewill, ed., Foreword to *Der Ander Theyl kurtzweiliger guter frischer teutscher Liedlein*, Das Erbe deutscher

Musik, lx, p.vi; T. J. McGee, *Medieval and Renaissance Music: a Performer's Guide* (Toronto, 1985), p.219. A narrower definition of the term *Tenorlied* is offered by W. Suppan, *Deutsches Liedleben zwischen Renaissance und Barock* (Tutzing, 1973), p.83; for Suppan the key element is the presence of a cantus firmus, no matter in which voice it occurs. Suppan does not address the issue of vocal or instrumental performance.

[3]See for example *A Florentine Chansonnier from the Time of Lorenzo the Magnificent: Florence, Biblioteca Nazionale Centrale, Banco rari 229*, ed. H. M. Brown, Monuments of Renaissance Music, vi (Chicago, 1983), text volume, pp.68, 179.

[4]Some material was gathered by Moser, *Paul Hofhaimer*, pp.71–3, 119, 197–8; other information is available in local studies such as C. Valentin, *Geschichte der Musik in Frankfurt am Main* (Frankfurt am Main, 1906/*R*1972).

[5]K. Polk, 'Vedel and Geige—Fiddle and Viol: German String Traditions in the Fifteenth Century', *JAMS*, xlii (1989), pp.504–46; Polk, 'Voices and Instruments: Soloists and Ensembles in the 15th Century', *EM*, xviii (1990), pp.179–98

[6]Polk, 'Voices and Instruments', pp.183, 195

[7]Polk, 'Voices and Instruments', pp.193, 195. Polk (p.184) has suggested that these singers may be associated with a tradition of *Sprecher*, or reciters of narrative poetry in courtly entertainments, and that this tradition as well the ensembles he describes may be connected with the *Tenorlied*.

[8]Polk, 'Voices and Instruments', pp.193–4

[9]Leipzig, 1912

[10]For studies presenting this argument see n.1 above. Earlier writers on the lied such as Robert Eitner do not seem to have explicitly addressed the issue of performing forces, although their editions of 16th-century lieder usually texted all parts. See *Erhart Oeglin's Liederbuch zu vier Stimmen*, ed. R. Eitner and J. J. Meier, Publikationen älterer praktischer und theoretischer Musikwerke, ix (Berlin, 1880); Heinrich Isaac, *Weltliche Werke*, ed. J. Wolf, DTÖ, xxviii (Vienna, 1907); *Das deutsche Gesellschaftslied in Österreich von 1480–1550*, ed. L. Nowak, DTÖ, lxxii (Vienna, 1930).

[11]Geering, 'Texturierung und Besetzung', p.11; L. Hibberd, 'On "Instrumental Style" in Early Melody', *MQ*, xxxii (1946), pp.107–30

[12]See Ludwig Senfl, *Sämtliche Werke*, ed. A. Geering and W. Altwegg, iv (Wolfenbüttel and Zurich, 1940/*R*1962), pp.36–7.

[13]To be precise, Egenolff began underlaying text in all partbooks with the second printing, in one volume, of his *Gassenhawer und Reutterliedlin* (RISM [*c*.1535][13]); the first printings, in separate volumes (RISM 1535[10] and 1535[11]) had adhered to the older practice of placing the text after the tenor part of each song. See H. J. Moser, Foreword to *Gassenhawerlin und Reutterliedlin* (Augsburg and Cologne, 1927/*R* Hildesheim, 1970), p.9. Moser assumes, probably erroneously, that [*c*.1535][13] was printed after Forster's first book (1539[27]) and that Egenolff followed Forster's lead in underlaying text.

[14]Moser, Foreword to *Das Liederbuch des Arnt von Aich*, p.viii; his phrase is 'eine nachträgliche Acappellisierung'.

[15]The texting of this print has generally been overlooked in discussions of polyphonic lieder, though it was pointed out by J. J. Maier in *MfM*, xii (1880), p.7 and again by Geering, 'Texturierung und Besetzung', p.4. Two fragments of the tenor partbook of this print have recently been found in the binding of a book owned by the Landesbibliothek Coburg; an article by Robert Münster, forthcoming in *Musik in Bayern*, will give further details. I am grateful to Dr Münster for informing me of this discovery.

[16]The print is Schöffer's first collection (Mainz, 1513; RISM 1513²), in which Jörg Schonfelder's 'Ich weis ein hubschen pawren knecht' is underlaid with text in all parts. Among the manuscripts containing a few pieces underlaid in all parts (or all surviving parts) are Basel, Universitätsbibliothek, Mss. F.IX.32–5, F.IX.59–62, F.X.1–4, F.X.5–9 and F.X.25–6; also Munich, Bayerische Staatsbibliothek, Ms. mus. 4483. The Basel manuscripts are described in J. Kmetz, *Die Handschriften der*

Universitätsbibliothek Basel: Musikhandschriften des *16. Jahrhunderts* (Basel, 1988); for the Munich manuscript see M. L. Göllner, *Bayerische Staatsbibliothek: Katalog der Musikhandschriften: Tabulaturen und Stimmbücher bis zur Mitte des 17. Jahrhunderts*, Kataloge Bayerischer Musiksammlungen (Munich, 1979), v/2, p.180. There are also a few manuscripts in which nearly all lieder are underlaid with text in all voices, such as Ulm, Von Schermar'sche Familienstiftung, Mss.235, 236, but these are too late to provide convincing evidence of early 16th-century practice.

[17]'Sol der Text auffs fleissigest darein gesungen werden'; G. Forster, prefatory letter to *Der Ander Theyl kurtzweiliger guter frischer teutscher Liedlein* (Nuremberg: Johannes Petreius, 1540); ed. K. Gudewill, *Das Erbe deutscher Musik*, lx, p.xiv.

[18]Geering, 'Textierung und Besetzung', p.2

[19]It might be felt that the same dexterity is required of present-day churchgoers in singing verses of hymns that are not underlaid. To this I would reply that in general hymn singers (1) do not have to count rests; (2) are concerned with a relatively small array of note values; (3) do not need to co-ordinate their part with contrapuntal voices having contrasting rhythms; and (4) are accompanied by an organ.

[20]See *Ach hülff mich leidt* in Schöffer's first volume (RISM 1513²), ff.A3v–A4v; also *Zucht er vnd lob* in Öglin's first book (RISM 1512¹), ff. G2v–G4r.

[21]A cogent summary of the arguments on this subject is D. Fallows, 'Secular Polyphony in the 15th Century', *Performance Practice: Music before 1600*, ed. H. M. Brown and S. Sadie (New York, 1990), pp.203–12. For the opposing viewpoint, see H. M. Brown's comments in the same volume, pp.152–4.

[22]'In dissem buechlyn fynt man Lxxv hubscher lieder myt Discant. Alt. Bas. vnd Tenor. lustick zů syngen. Auch etlich zů fleiten/schwegeln/vnd anderen Musicalisch Instrumenten artlichen zů gebrauchen.'

[23]Moser, Foreword to *Das Liederbuch des Arnt von Aich*, p.viii

[24]'Ich hab im verschienen jar ein außzug (im welchem allein die Teutsche liedlein/so auff allerley Instrumenten zu brauchen vast dienstlich) durch den Truck lassen außgehen/Weyl aber nit alle liedlein/wie auch anderer gesang/auff die Instrument tüglich/hab ich gegenwertige Teutsche liedlein/als die zum singen zum füglichsten/vnnd zur kurtzweyl am frölichsten/nicht wöllen darunter mischen/sonder die selben allein bleiben lassen. Dieweyl sie denn/wie gemelt/zum singen am besten/sol der Text auffs fleissigest darein gesungen werden/Darumb er denn auch etwas fleissiger/denn villeicht in den vorigen beschehen/darunter gesetzt vnd applicirt ist werden [sic].' Forster, prefatory letter to *Der Ander Theyl*, p.xiv.

[25]For references to women singers in 15th- and 16th-century Germany, see Moser, *Paul Hofhaimer*, pp.72–3; also Polk, 'Voices and Instruments', pp.184, 193. As far as I know, this subject has not received detailed scholarly treatment.

[26]The four poems are as follows:

Discantus
Jr Kneblin vnd ir Meidlein rein
Ewer stimlein schallen also fein
Den Discant lernent vnbeschwert
Kein ander stimm euch zu gehört.

Altus
Der Alt gehört Jung gsellen zu
Die lauffen auff vnd ab on rhw
Also ist auch des Altes weiß
Drumb lerne mich mit allem fleiß.

Tenor
Mein art vnd weiß in mittel maß
Gen andern stimmen ist mein straß
Die habent acht auff meine stimm
Den Mennern ich für andern zimm.

Bassus
Mein ampte ist im nidern stat
Drumb wer ein bstanden alter hat
Vnd brommet wie ein rauher Ber
Der komm zu meiner stimme her.

The same poems or similar verses in German or Latin are occasionally found in manuscripts of polyphonic lieder. An example is Basel, Universitätsbibliothek, F.IX.32–5; see Kmetz, *Handschriften*, p.109.

[27]Geering, 'Textierung und Besetzung', p.6

[28]It was ignored by the otherwise exemplary editor of Forster's five volumes, Kurt Gudewill; cf. the Foreword to *Der Ander Theyl*, p.vi.

[29]This tendency could of course have been overcome by such means as a greater number of singers on the tenor part, or by the use of a loud instrument on that part, but I know of no evidence for such practices.

[30]Mainz: Peter Schöffer, 1512

[31]H. Mönkemeyer, Foreword to Arnolt Schlick, *Tabulaturen Etlicher lobgesang*, Die Tabulatur, iii (Hofhaim am Taunus, 1965), p.2

[32]S. Keyl, *Arnolt Schlick and Instrumental Music circa 1500* (PhD diss. Duke U., 1989), pp.271–3

[33]Keyl, *Schlick and Instrumental Music*, pp.239–47

[34]Judenkünig published two volumes of lute music with elementary instructions for playing the instrument and making intabulations; the second is an expanded German translation of the first, Latin book. They are *Utilis et compendiaria introductio* (Vienna: [Hans Singriener, c.1517]) and *Ain schone kunstliche vnderweisung* (Vienna: Hans Singreiner, 1523).

[35]For the contents of both volumes, see H. M. Brown, *Instrumental Music Printed Before 1600* (Cambridge, Mass., 1965), pp.23–6.

[36]'Wann aber ym bas ettliche noten zu nider oder tyeff gieng/so fach in allen stymen/ain quart höher an/auff ainer Lautten/vnnd sonderlich/wann du Tenor vnd baß setzen wildt/so fach alltzeyt ain quart höher an/dann der gesang clauiert ist/dan die discant Lautten sol alleezeit ayn quart höher gezogen sein dann die grosser Lautten/wann zwen zusamen schlahen wellen &c.' *Ain schone kunstliche vnderweisung*, f. k iiij. The passage does not appear in Judenkünig's earlier, Latin book.

[37]Dorfmüller, *Studien zur Lautenmusik*, pp.105–9; cf. D. Stevens, 'German Lute-Songs of the Early Sixteenth Century', *Festschrift Heinrich Besseler zum sechzigsten Geburtstag* (Leipzig, 1961), pp.253–7

[38]Two of the outstanding virtuosi associated with this tradition were Conrad Paumann and Pietrobono di Burzellis. See P. Canal, 'Della musica in Mantova', *Memorie del R. Istituto di Scienze, Lettere ed Arti*, xxi (1881), pp.659–60 (*R* Geneva, 1978); N. Pirotta, 'Music and Cultural Tendencies in 15th-century Italy', *JAMS*, xix (1966), pp.140–41; L. Lockwood, 'Pietrobono and the Instrumental Tradition at Ferrara in the Fifteenth Century', *Rivista italiana di musicologia*, x (1975), pp.115–33.

[39]D. Fallows, '15th-Century Tablatures for Plucked Instruments: a Summary, a Revision, and a Suggestion', *LSJ*, xix (1977), pp.30–33; M. Morrow, 'Fifteenth-Century Lute Music: Some Possible Sources', *Le luth et sa musique*, ii, ed. J.-M. Vaccaro (Paris, 1984), pp.31–3; V. Ivanoff, 'Das Lautenduo im 15. Jahrhundert', *Basler Jahrbuch für historische Musikpraxis*, viii (1984), pp.157–62

[40]See n.38 above; cf. Ivanoff, 'Das Lautenduo', p.148.

[41]Berlin, Staatsbibliothek Preußischer Kulturbesitz, Ms. germ. qu. 719. The manuscript has been edited by P. Sappler, *Das Königsteiner Liederbuch*, Münchner Texte und Untersuchungen zur deutschen Literatur des Mittelalters, xxix (Munich, 1970).

[42]Sappler published the melodies, relying on transcriptions made for him by Kurt Dorfmüller, in his edition of the volume, pp.327–8, 375–80. They were not noticed in the musicological literature until Hans Tischler re-edited and discussed them in 'The Earliest Lute Tablature?', *JAMS*, xxvii (1974), pp.100–103.

[43]Fallows, '15th-Century Tablatures for Plucked Instruments', pp.9–10

[44]Sebastian Virdung, writing in 1511, credited the invention of

German lute tablature to Conrad Paumann (*c.*1410–73); see *Musica getutscht* (Basel: Michel Furter, 1511), f. K iiiv; facsimiles of Virdung's book were published by R. Eitner, Publikationen älterer praktischer und theoretischer Musikwerke, xi (1882); L. Schrade (Kassel, 1931); and W. Niemöller (Kassel, 1970). While modern writers have been cautious about accepting Virdung's attribution of German lute tablature to Paumann, they have generally agreed that the notation originated during Paumann's lifetime. For a suggestion that something resembling French lute tablature was in use as much as a century earlier, see C. Page, 'French Lute Tablature in the 14th Century?', *EM*, viii (1980), pp.488–92.

[45]Seidel, 'Ein- und Mehrstimmigkeit', makes a similar argument based primarily on a reading of lied texts from a sociological point of view.

[46]Among other topics, the use of polyphonic techniques to project the meaning of the text or to highlight significant words promises interesting results; for some preliminary work in this area see Keyl, *Schlick and Instrumental Music*, pp.78, 89, 91–2. I am planning a more detailed study of the subject.

[7]

Performance practice in the *seconda prattica* madrigal

Rinaldo Alessandrini

Seconda prattica, de la quale è statto il primo rinovatore ne nostri caratteri il Divino Cipriano Rore ... seguitata, & ampliata ... dal Ingegneri, dal Marenzio, da Giaches Wert, dal Luzzasco, & parimente da Giacoppo Peri, da Giulio Caccini, & finalmente da li spiriti più elevati & intendenti de la vera arte, intende che sia quella che versa intorno alla perfetione de la melodia, cioè che considera l'armonia comandata, & non comandante, & per signora del armonia pone l'oratione.[1]

By Second Practice, which was first renewed in our notation by Cipriano de Rore ... was followed and amplified ... by Ingegneri, Marenzio, Giaches de Wert, Luzzasco, likewise by Jacopo Peri, Giulio Caccini, and finally by loftier spirits with a better understanding of true art, he understands the one that turns on the perfection of the melody, that is, the one that considers harmony not commanding, but commanded, and makes the words the mistress of the harmony.

M ONTEVERDI'S inclusion of Marenzio in his list of composers of the *seconda prattica* is recognition of his place among those who initiated a radical reform of musical language at the end of the 16th century and the beginning of the 17th. The *seconda prattica* expounded by Monteverdi (or, at least, his brother) favoured the primacy of *orazione* over *armonia*, reversing what he perceived as being the priorities of the *prima prattica*. The new claims of rhetoric and the importance granted to the poetic text not only transformed the madrigal but also had an impact on the younger generation of poets— Guarini, Chiabrera, Marino—who, resolving to meet the aspirations of these new aesthetic trends, set out to enchant and astonish the public with their virtuoso technique and use of surprise (*meraviglia*), audacious similes and paradox.

The changes in musical direction were accompanied by exploration of the emotional power of disso-

nance (Monteverdi, Marenzio), chromaticism and contrapuntal daring (Gesualdo), and the use of *basso continuo* and *obbligato* instruments (Monteverdi again). But these changes were not easily achieved. The Bolognese theorist Giovanni Maria Artusi castigated these novelties as offences against nature and reason.[2] And although Artusi ended up as an admirer of Monteverdi (if we are to believe the claim Monteverdi made in his letter of 22 October 1633 to Giovanni Battista Doni),[3] the Artusi–Monteverdi controversy epitomized the same conflict between authority and empiricism as the period's most famous literary quarrel, the controversy regarding the stylistic propriety of Guarini's pastoral tragicomedy *Il pastor fido*.[4]

This was the period when composers and performers took upon themselves the responsibility of continually renewing the rules and of creating a new and comprehensive artistic expression encompassing meaning, word and music. One of the most important changes was in fact the emergence of two distinct (though not necessarily opposed) spheres of competence, those of the composer and the performer, the first required to translate into music the contents of the poetic text, the second to translate that synthesis of text and music into sound and emotion. Nicola Vicentino emphasizes that the music should correspond to the mood and affects of the words: thus rapid note-values are equated with cheerfulness, while a slow pace, soft progressions (*gradi molli*) and minor 3rds and 6ths are associated with melancholy, and he complains that composers often introduce devices contrary to the meaning of the words.[5] Luzzaschi (or rather Alessandro

Rinaldo Alessandrini is the director of the ensemble Concerto Italiano, which has a particularly high reputation for its interpretations of Monteverdi. He also follows an international career as a conductor of opera.

Guarini, ghost-writing for the composer) spells out in considerable detail the primacy of words over music in the dedication to his *Sesto libro de' madrigali a cinque voci* (Ferrara, 1596):

> ... *se il Poeta inalza lo stile, solleva eziandio il Musico il tuono. Piagne, se il verso piagne, ride, se ride, se corre, se resta, se priega, se niega, se grida, se tace, se vive, se muore, tutti questi affetti, & effetti cosi vivamente da lui vengon espressi, che quella par quasi emulazione, che propriamente rasomiglianza dè dirsi. Quinci veggiamo la Musica de nostri tempi alquanto diversa da quella, che già fu ne' passati, percioche dalle passate, le Poesie moderni sono altresi diverse.*

> ... if the poet raises his style, the musician also raises his tone. He cries if the verse cries, laughs if it laughs; if it runs, stops, implores, denies, screams, falls silent, lives, dies, all these affects and effects are so vividly expressed by music that what should properly be called resemblance seems almost competition. Therefore we see in our times a music somewhat different from that of the past, for modern poetic forms are similarly different from those of the past.[6]

As for the performer, it was no longer enough simply to convey, as pure sound, the melodic lines of a madrigal; there was also an obligation to demonstrate, if not display, technical and artistic expertise. Thus for Giovanni Maria Trabaci a performance of either vocal or instrumental music cannot succeed 'unless there is a very graceful hand, a mature and detailed study, and those touches of elegance and those *accenti* which this music requires'.[7] And a much earlier source for the new style of singing, a passage from Nicola Vicentino's *L'antica musica ridotta alla moderna prattica* (Rome, 1555), is worth quoting at length:

> ... *& s'avvertirà che nel concertare le cose volgari a voler fare che gl'oditori restino satisfatti, si dè cantare le parole conformi all'oppinione del Compositore; & con la voce esprimere, quelle intonationi accompagnate dalle parole, con quelle passioni. Hora allegre, hora meste, & quando soavi, & quando crudeli & con gli accenti adherire alla pronuntia delle parole & delle note, & qualche volta si usa un certo ordine di procedere, nelle compositioni, che non si può scrivere. [sic] come sono il dir piano, & forte, & il dir presto, & tardo, & secondo le parole, muovere la Misura, per dimostrare gli effetti delle passioni delle parole, & dell'armonia, & la esperienza, dell'Oratore l'insegna, che si vede il modo che tiene nell'Oratione, che hora dice forte, & hora piano, & più tardo, & più presto, & con questo muove assai gl'oditori, & questo modo di muovere la misura, fà effetto assai nell'animo, & per tal ragione si canterà la Musica alla mente per imitar gli accenti, & effetti delle parti dell'oratione ...*

He is also advised that in coordinating vernacular works, he

should sing the words in keeping with the composer's intention, so as to leave the audience satisfied. He should express the melodic lines, matching the words to their passions—now joyful, now sad, now gentle, and now cruel—and adhere to the accents and pronunciation of the words and notes. Sometimes a composition is performed according to a certain method that cannot be written down, such as uttering softly and loudly or fast and slow, or changing the measure in keeping with the words, so as to show the effects of the passions and the harmony. The experience of the orator can be instructive, if you observe the technique he follows in his oration. For he speaks now loud and now soft, now slow and now fast, thus greatly moving his listeners. This technique of changing the measure has a powerful effect on the soul. For this reason music is sung from memory, so as to imitate the accents and effects of the parts of an oration.[8]

The early madrigal presented very few technical difficulties from the standpoint of performance. Rather, the focus was on the composer's subtle handling of counterpoint and texture, and performance seems to have had little or no bearing on how the work as such was assessed. Thus in 1592 Lodovico Zacconi contrasts the 'antichi' (Josquin, Gombert), who obtained their effects from 'points of imitation and other observations [of the rules]' ('fughe, & altre osservationi') with the 'new and graceful effects' ('nuovi, & vaghi effetti') of Willaert and Rore; likewise he observes that the singers of old 'sang their parts as they were written in the books, without adding a single *accento* or giving them any touch of grace, since they were intent only on pure and simple *modulatione*'.[9]

However, things were changing around 1600. The madrigal was the polyphonic vocal genre *par excellence* in this period. The market conditions for the genre were favourable, given that it could cater for all tastes and situations. Another important factor was the influence of singers on composers. With their expanded range of technical possibilities, singers were able to offer a wider range of vocal and expressive effects. At the beginning of the 17th century the level of expertise was continually rising: vocal ranges widened, especially those of sopranos, who gained at least a 4th in their upper register. In addition virtuoso techniques such as rapid and extended coloratura were developed, requiring a more economic use of breathing. These and other issues have a significant bearing on performance in the *seconda prattica*.

Vibrato

Christoph Bernhard was given the task of bringing from Italy to Germany singers for the *cappella* of the Elector of Dresden. Describing the various types of ornamentation in fashion in Rome at the beginning of the 17th century he says:

> … *fermo*, or the maintenance of a steady sound, is required on all the notes except where a *trillo* or *ardire* is performed. This is to be considered a decoration [*Zierde*] of the *fermo*, because the *tremulo* is a vice (except on the organ, where all the voices can vibrate [*tremuliren*] at the same time and sound well together because of the [uniformity in the] change [of pitch]). It is used by older singers, but not as an artistic device; rather, they use it inadvertently, because they can no longer hold the note. If one were to seek further confirmation about the undesirability of *tremulo*, one should listen to an old person singing alone. Then he would understand why the most elegant singers do not use *tremulum* except when performing an *ardire* … However, basses may use it from time to time, as long as it is not too frequent, and only on short notes.[10]

Italian organs were in fact equipped with a register at first known as a *fiffaro*, then, starting at the beginning of the 17th century, as a *voce humana*. It was a series of Principal-scaled reed pipes tuned slightly higher than the Principal 8'. Coupled with the Principal itself, the tuning discrepancy produces a regular beat the speed of which is proportional to the degree of discrepancy. The effect resembles an unobtrusive vibrato, and is especially atmospheric when the pulsation is slow and gentle. The fact that this register is called *vox humana* is obviously a reference to the vibrato characteristic of the human voice. In registration tables it is designated for use only with the Principal rather than, for example, the louder Ripieno registers,[11] being reserved for slow, particularly expressive pieces, mainly the *toccate per l'Elevatione* or, by extension, the slow, sustained pieces designated *Durezze e ligature*. These indications tend to limit the use of vibrato to special expressive situations and demonstrate that it had an expressive function.

Acoustically speaking, vibrato may be defined as an oscillation in pitch (of which a violinist's oscillating finger on the string of his instrument is the visible counterpart). It is therefore easy to imagine that the overall purity of an ensemble's intonation is undermined if vibrato is used by four or more voices at the same time. This is an important consideration bearing in mind the tuning systems current in Italy during this period (and still used for organs until the beginning of the 19th century). The mean-tone system, commonly used in this period as a standard tuning system for polyphonic instruments and decisively preferred to the equal-tempered system (which was nevertheless known in theory), was characterized by the use of absolutely pure major 3rds. This greatly restricted the tonal space that it was possible to use, but it was a price composers were willing to pay, given that they were rewarded by the beauty and sweetness of chords with pure major 3rds and, in the case of *a cappella* vocal performances, with absolutely pure 5ths. So, as with the *vox humana* on the purest Principal of an Italian organ, with vocal ensembles it is better to keep the vibrato to a minimum in order not to impair the intonation. And it would be interesting for singers and teachers, once they had refined their ability to produce a sound without vibrato, to explore ways of using the device to expressive ends. This could lead them to reflect on the occasional need for a particular kind of vibrato (which seems in any case to have been somewhat different to the modern variety, to judge from the examples given in contemporary treatises), on the specific occasions where it might be used, and on how to control it, avoiding its indiscriminate or unconscious use.[12]

Pitch, range, vocal technique

Italian organs from the end of the 16th century and during the next two centuries give fairly clear indications of the pitches used. It is a safe generalization to say that in northern Italy a high pitch was used (about a semitone above modern pitch), and in southern Italy a low one (a semitone or a tone below modern pitch).[13] Obviously, when the organ was used, these pitches were compulsory (unless the organist transposed), but with *a cappella* singing, whether in sacred or secular music, there was complete freedom of choice to choose a pitch which allowed the greatest convenience during performance. But the tessituras found in pieces requiring instrumental accompaniment suggest that it was the middle of the vocal range that was considered the most convenient and suitable for sound production. Moreover, common sense would suggest that pieces notated in normal clefs and those written in *chiavette* would not have been placed side by side in the same prints if their ranges were so divergent. The written pitch of pieces in *chiavette* is very high (a 4th or 5th above the norm) and is totally ill-suited to the fluid expressive means of the madrigal. Confirmation of this practice comes indirectly from the rubric which Monteverdi places at the beginning of his *madrigale Dolcissimo uscignolo* (in his eighth book of madrigals of 1638):[14] the first soprano is notated in the G2 (not C1) clef, whereas the other parts are all in *chiavi naturali*. Monteverdi therefore adds the instruction 'Canto in tuono' ('at pitch') in order to prevent the downward transposition by a 4th or 5th that the high clef would normally prescribe. Further, more incontrovertible confirmation comes from the organ bass part of the 1608 edition of Palestrina's *Motettorum quinque vocibus liber quartus* (first printed in 1583)— published in Venice by Alessandro Raverii as *Motectorum … addita parte infima pro pulsatoris organis comoditate*—where the organ part of the pieces notated in *chiavette* is transposed by a 4th when there is a signature of one flat or a 5th when there is no signature.

Nowadays, female voices seem the best possible choice for the soprano parts. To a greater degree than a falsettist, the female voice brings variety of timbre to the ensemble and provides a natural balance to the sound of the male voices. This voice can be soprano, or mezzo-soprano in cases where the range does not exceed *e″*. Often one finds genuine mezzo-soprano ranges in a second soprano part in which the ambitus is exactly a 3rd below that of the first soprano (as in Monteverdi's fourth and sixth books of madrigals). The use of a falsetto for the parts in the medium range is always possible, if only for practical reasons, but it is interesting to note that Adriano Banchieri, in his *Festino nella sera del giovedì grasso* (1608), includes a *Vinata di brindesi, e ragioni* which prescribes the use of a 'falsetto' to sing the part of the second soprano (both soprano parts are notated in the C1 clef) and not that of the alto.[15] Usually the alto part is better suited to a male singer capable of reviving the old technique of the head-voice or the falsetto for notes above the 'break'.

These alto parts normally extend down to *g* or *f* and upwards as far as (but never beyond) *bb′*. In Monteverdi it is not rare to find *d* as the lowest note, which suggests a need to use a tenor rather than a female contralto or a falsettist who would too frequently be obliged to use the chest voice.

A relatively low register (or the use of low pitch in general) makes it easier for the voices to produce sounds in a range close to that used in speech.[16] A vocal technique which allows for a delivery midway between speaking and singing (Peri's *cosa mezzana* or 'intermediate style')[17] or at any rate an articulation of the text and a way of enunciating the consonants that is close to spoken language—so long as it is sustained by a correct use of breath to guarantee stability of intonation—could contribute to the cultivation of a vocal sound more in keeping with the madrigal. The case for an excessively wide dynamic range is not supported by documentary evidence. Quite the contrary; as Zarlino observes, 'one way of singing is used in churches and public chapels, and another way in private chambers: because in the first one sings with a full voice … and in chambers one sings with a more subdued and soft voice, without making any loud sound'.[18] In other words, secular music is sung in a fairly moderate dynamic range, where the sound can grow or diminish in accordance with the musical effect and the accentuation of the words.

The extreme flexibility and malleability of the resulting sound seems the perfect vehicle for the aesthetic ideas of the late Cinquecento. According to Vincenzo Giustiniani (*c.*1628), the famous female singers of Mantua and Ferrara

… facevano a gara non solo quanto al metallo et alla disposizione delle voci, ma nell'ornamento di esquisiti passaggi tirati in opportuna congiuntura e non soverchi … e di più col moderare e crescere la voce forte o piano, assottigliandola o ingrossandola, che secondo che veniva a' tagli, ora con strascinarla, ora smezzarla, con l'accompagnamento d'un soave interrotto sospiro, ora tirando passaggi lunghi, seguiti bene, spiccati, ora gruppi, ora a salti, ora con trilli lunghi, ora con brevi, et or con passaggi soavi e cantati piano …[19]

… vied with each other not only in regard to the timbre and disposition of their voices but also in the ornamentation of exquisite *passaggi* delivered at opportune moments, but not in excess … Furthermore, they moderated or increased their voices, loud or soft, heavy or light, according to the demands of the piece; now dragging, now breaking off with a gentle, interrupted sigh, now singing long *passaggi* legato or detached, now *gruppi*, now leaps, now with long *trilli*, now with short, and again with sweet *passaggi* sung softly ...

Likewise, Francesco Patrizi, in his description of the voice of Tarquinia Molza, gives a clear idea of the level of agility, elasticity and subtle flexibility which was considered the ideal:

La voce adunque sua è un soprano non fosco, non soppresso, non sforzato, ma chiarissimo, aperto, delicatissimo, piano, eguale, soavissimo; in somma se ei si potesse dire senza peccato, più che angelico; et quello che i musici sogliono appellare rotondo, che tanto vale di sotto, quanto di mezzo, e di sopra.

So her voice is a soprano not dark, not suppressed, not forced, but very clear, open, very delicate, soft, even, very sweet; in sum, if one may say it without sinning, more than angelic; and what musicians usually call round, of the same worth in the lower registers, as in the middle, and in the top, which is something very rarely found.[20]

Powerful dynamic and extremes of pitch were not sought after. A modern technique, based on a kind of sound production needed to fill a modern 2,000-seat hall or theatre cannot be considered suitable for the delicacy and sense of detail required in the madrigal. The different relationship that existed between wind pressure and the passive contraction of the vocal chords is highlighted by the technique of throat articulation for rapid and light notes generally known as *gorgia*, which according to Camillo Maffei required a 'soft, flexible throat'.[21] As Zacconi points out in his *Prattica di musica* (1592, f.58v), *petto* ('chest', i.e. powerful breath) and *gola* (i.e. a flexible, agile and relaxed 'throat') and *fianco* (i.e. strong 'hips', or diaphragm support) are the basis of good singing, without which *gorgia* would not be recognizable as such:

Due cose si ricercano à chi vuol far questa professione: petto, & gola; petto per poter una simil quantità, & un tanto numero di figure à giusto termine condurre; gola poi per poterle agevolmente sumministrare: perche molti non avendo ne petto ne fianco, in quattro over sei figure convengano i suoi disegni interrompere ... & altri per difetto di gola non spiccano si forte le figure, cioè non le pronuntiano si bene che per gorgia conosciuta sia.

Two things are required by whoever wishes to follow this profession: breath, and the throat: a breath powerful enough to sing such a quantity of notes right through to the end; and the throat to accomplish this in a comfortable way: because many, having neither breath or diaphragm support, have to interrupt their phrases after four or six notes ... while others with a deficient throat do not sound the notes distinctly, that is, do not articulate them to the point where they can be distinguished as *gorgie*.

Tactus

Leaving aside the issue of the metrical or proportional relationship between the notes and the time signature, the most important evidence concerning tempo seems to indicate an extreme liberty in the treatment of rhythm, relating to the expressive essence of the text. Rhythmic flexibility became an element of virtuoso ensemble performance to the point where increased refinement made it necessary for someone to keep time in 'modern madrigals' by giving a beat, as Frescobaldi observes.[22] The role of director need not to be external to the group of singers but can be assumed by one of the singers themselves. However, the need for such a director seems to increase in proportion to the degree of subtlety aimed at in the performance.

Pronunciation

The vast majority of original madrigal prints reveals a notational procedure which suggests that the singer should make an obvious elision between words ending and beginning with a vowel—thus 'dolc'aure', not 'dolci aure'; a modern tendency towards presumed consistencies of pronunciation has misled singers into opting for the latter. The same tendency has also led them to neglect the practice—present in many dialects, including Tuscan, and useful for preventing semantic misunderstanding—of doubling the consonants at the beginnings of words. For example, the correct pronunciation of 'e se voi non havete' is 'e sse vvoi non havete'. However, this is not nearly so bad as the barbarisms of singers whose mother tongue is not Italian, who are often deluded into thinking that an indiscriminate doubling of consonants (especially the 'r' and the 'l') can re-create the sound of the Italian language. To my astonishment, I have often heard the word 'dolore' changed to 'dol-lore', also with both 'o' sounds open to the point of sounding ridiculous. (Both the 'o's in 'dolore' are dark, the second a shade more than the first.)

Ornamentation

Light ornamentation, which takes into consideration the use of a *ribattuta* (*trillo*) at cadences, or greater use of the rhetorical flourish usually known as *accento*,[23] changes significantly the conception and colour of a madrigal. A less appropriate form of ornamentation would seem to be the use of diminutions and long, rapid ornaments which detract from the clarity and transparency of the polyphonic web, as occur for instance in Luzzaschi's *Madrigali ... a uno, e doi, e tre soprani* (1601). Describing the Roman style, Bernhard refers to a repertory of small, rapid ornaments, often light *portamenti*, anticipations and delays of notes which, used in phrases where the melody unfolds in a narrow range, give the expression a sense of lively mobility and delicate casualness.[24]

Unfortunately, except in rare cases such as Caccini's *Le nuove musiche* (1601/2), we have few precise details of the smaller ornaments, and it is generally supposed that it is the large diminutions that provide the basis for ornamentation. In reality, especially in vocal music, ornamentation is inextricably bound up with minute alterations in sound, ranging from tiny, rapid *accenti* through brief *passaggi* to *trilli* and *groppi* of a certain length. We can also think of ornamentation as the *sprezzatura* described by Caccini in his *Nuove musiche e nuova maniera di scriverle* (1614):

La sprezzatura è quella leggiadria la quale si dà al canto co'l trascorso di più crome, e simicrome sopra diverse corde co'l quale fatto à tempo, togliendosi al canto una certa terminata angustia, e secchezza, si rende piacevole, licenzioso, e arioso, si come nel parlar comune la eloquenza, e la fecondia rende agevoli, e dolci le cose di cui si favella.

Sprezzatura is that charm lent to a song by a few 'faulty' eighths and sixteenths [quavers and semiquavers] on various tones, together with those [similar 'faults'] made in the tempo. These relieve the song of a certain restricted narrowness and dryness and make it pleasant, free, and airy, just as in common speech eloquence and variety make pleasant and sweet the matters being spoken of.[25]

The art of madrigal performance is a difficult combination of technical precision (intonation, minute dynamic shadings, timbre) and expressive mobility. The difficulty derives from this combination of technical and expressive elements, often in opposition to one another. The fact that madrigals were in essence destined to be sung in small chambers is a good indication of how subtle, and also how indispensable, was the expressive dimension of the madrigal. A complete understanding of the text and a flawless intonation are not in themselves sufficient to give justice to these compositions: only a total, artistic immersion in the emotional content of the poetry and words, combined with an extreme vocal fluidity, are capable of restoring that atmosphere of timelessness characteristic of *a cappella* vocal performance.

1 From Giulio Cesare Monteverdi's 'Dichiarazione' glossing his brother Claudio's postface to his *Quinto libro de' madrigali a cinque voci* (1605)— and responding to criticisms of Monteverdi's style by Giovanni Maria Artusi—published in Claudio Monteverdi's *Scherzi musicali* (Venice, 1607); see *Claudio Monteverdi: Tutte le opere*, ed. G. F. Malipiero (2/Viennā, 1954– 68), x, pp.69–72, at p.70. The translation is taken from *Source readings in music history: from Classical Antiquity through the Romantic era*, ed. O. Strunk (New York, 1950), pp.408–9.

2 In *L'Artusi, overo Delle imperfettioni della moderna musica* (Venice, 1600) and *Seconda parte dell'Artusi overo*

Delle imperfettioni della moderna musica (Venice, 1603). For the former, see also the partial translation in *Source readings*, ed. Strunk, pp.393–404.

3 *Claudio Monteverdi: Lettere*, ed. E. Lax (Florence, 1994), pp.200–202, at p.201; *The letters of Claudio Monteverdi*, trans. D. Stevens (Oxford, 2/1995), pp.416–22, at p.421.

4 See G. Tomlinson, *Monteverdi and the end of the Renaissance* (Oxford, 1987), pp.3–30, esp. pp.17–21.

5 Nicola Vicentino, *L'antica musica ridotta alla moderna prattica* (Rome, 1555; R/ Kassel, 1959), ff.81r–81v; trans. as *Ancient music adapted to modern practice*, trans. M. R. Maniates (New Haven, CT, 1996), p.254.

6 For Alessandro Guarini's authorship of this dedication, see *Luzzasco Luzzaschi: Madrigali per cantare e sonare a uno, due e tre soprani* (1601), ed. A. Cavicchi (Brescia and Kassel, 1965), pp.12–13, which also includes a partial transcription (with some errors). The text given here is taken from the original, and the translation from T. Carter, *Music in late Renaissance and early Baroque Italy* (London, 1992), p.17.

7 G. M. Trabaci, *Il secondo libro de ricercate & altri varii capricci* (Naples, 1615; R/ Florence, 1984), preface: 'se non vi è una leggiadrissima mano, & un studio maturo, & particolare, & che si diano quei garbi, & quelli accenti che detta Musica ricerca'.

8 Vicentino, *L'antica musica ridotta alla moderna prattica*, ff.94r–94v; *Ancient music adapted to modern practice*, trans. Maniates, p.301.

9 Lodovico Zacconi, *Prattica di musica* (Venice, 1592; *R/* Bologna, 1967), f.7v: 'cantavano le cantilene come le stavano scritte sopra de libri, senza porgerli poi un minimo accento, ò darli qualche poco di vaghezza: perche non erano intenti ad altro…che alla pura, & semplice modulatione'.

10 Translated from Christoph Bernhard, *Von der Singe-Kunst oder Manier* (1649), transcribed in *Die Kompositionslehre Heinrich Schützens in der Fassung seines Schülers Christoph Bernhard*, ed. J. M. Müller-Blattau (Kassel, 1926, 2/1963), pp.31–9, at pp.31–2.

11 See, for example, the registration tables in *Costanzo Antegnati: L'arte organica (1608)*, ed. R. Lunelli (Mainz, 1938), p.72; Girolamo Diruta, 'Discorso sopra il concertar li registri dell'organo', *Seconda parte del Transilvano: dialogo diviso in quattro libri* (Venice, 1622; *R/*Bologna, 1978), pp.22–3.

12 Compare Mozart's complaints about Joseph Nikolaus Meissner's excessive vibrato in a letter to his father dated 12 June 1778; *The letters of Mozart and his family*, trans. E. Anderson (3/London, 1985), pp.551–3.

13 See Giovan Battista Doni's findings reported in J. J. K. Rhodes and W. R. Thomas, 'Pitch', *New Grove*, xiv, p.783.

14 *Monteverdi: Tutte le opere*, ed. Malipiero, viii, pp.271–9.

15 *Adriano Banchieri: Festino nella sera del giovedì grasso avanti cena a 5 voci miste (1608)*, ed. B. Somma, Capolavori Polifonici del Secolo XVI, i (Rome, 1948), pp.68–70

16 See *Delle lettere del Signor Gio. Camillo Maffei da Solofra* (Naples, 1562): 'La settima [regola] è che tenga la bocca aperta, e giusta, non più di quello che si tiene quando si ragiona con gli amici'. Quoted in N. Bridgman, 'Giovanni Camillo Maffei et sa lettre sur le chant', *Revue de musicologie*, xxxviii (1956), pp.3–34, at p.20.

17 In his preface to *Euridice* (Florence, 1600), ed. H. M. Brown, Recent

Researches in the Music of the Baroque Era, xxxvi–xxxvii (Madison, 1981), pp.xli–xlii.

18 Gioseffo Zarlino, *Le istitutioni armoniche* (Venice, 2/1573), p.240: 'ad altro modo si canta nelle Chiese & nelle Capelle publiche, & ad altro modo nelle private Camere: imperoche ivi si canta a piena voce … e nelle camere si canta con voce più sommessa & soave, senza far alcun strepito'.

19 Vincenzo Giustiniani, *Discorso sopra la musica* (c.1628), in A. Solerti, *L'origini del melodramma* (Turin, 1903; *R/*Hildesheim, 1969), p.108.

20 F. Patrizi, *Amorosa filosofia* (1577), ed. J. C. Nelson (Florence, 1963), p.39; trans. in L. Stras, 'Recording Tarquinia: imitation, parody and reportage in Ingegneri's "Hor che 'l ciel e la terra e 'l vento tace"', *Early music*, xxvii (1999), pp.358–77, at p.362.

21 See *Delle lettere del Signor Gio. Camillo Maffei* (1562), given in Bridgman, 'Giovanni Camillo Maffei et sa lettre sur le chant', p.18: According to Maffei, the 'voce passeggiata' 'non è altro ch'un suono caggionato dalla minuta, et ordinata ripercussione dell'aere nella gola' ('is none other than a sound produced by the minute and ordered repercussion of the air in the throat') and cannot be produced without 'l'istromento pieghevole e molle' (i.e. a soft, flexible throat).

22 In the preface to his *Il primo libro di toccate d'intavolatura di cembalo e organo* (Rome, 1616), ed. E. Darbellay, Monumenti Musicali Italiani, iv (Milan, 1977), p.xxvii (rule 1). Compare the preface to *Paolo Quagliati: Il primo libro de' madrigali a quattro voci (1608)*, ed. J. Cohen, Recent Researches in the Music of the Baroque Era, lxxix (Madison, WI, 1996), pp.lxxviii–lxxix, and Aquilino Coppini's letter to Hendrik van der Putten concerning madrigals from Monteverdi's third, fourth and fifth books, given in P. Fabbri, *Monteverdi*, trans. T. Carter (Cambridge, 1994), p.105: 'Those [madrigals] by Monteverdi require, during their performance, more flexible rests [*respiri*] and bars that are not strictly regular, now pressing forward or abandoning themselves to slowings down, now also hurrying. You yourself will

fix the tempo. In them there is a truly wondrous capacity for moving the affections.'

23 For descriptions and musical examples see Michael Praetorius, *Syntagma musicum*, iii (Wolfenbuttel, 2/1619; *R/*Kassel, 1958), p.233. See also the details of ornaments in the preface to Giulio Caccini, *Le nuove musiche* (Florence, 1601 [= 1602]; *R/* Florence 1983).

24 Bernhard, *Von der Singe-Kunst oder Manier*; see *Die Kompositionslehre Heinrich Schützens*, ed. Müller-Blattau, pp.31–9.

25 For the original and translation, see *Giulio Caccini: Nuove musiche e nuova maniera di scriverle (1614)*, ed. H. W. Hitchcock, Recent Researches in the Music of the Baroque Era, xxviii (Madison, 1978), pp.xxxii–xxxiii.

Part III
Sacred Music

[8]

THE PERFORMING ENSEMBLES IN JOSQUIN'S SACRED MUSIC

Paper: David Fallows (Manchester)

The published proceedings of the 1971 Josquin Festival-Conference at New York devoted over one hundred pages to matters of performance practice,[1] more perhaps than any other composer before Bach has yet received. They are now a fascinating historical document, for they came at a delicate time in the history of changing ideas. In 1971 most performances of Josquin's sacred music included instruments. The papers and discussions in the Festival proceedings show an uneasy tact and avoidance of confrontation between those who assumed instrumental participation and those who rejected it. Since then, particularly with the writings of Frank D'Accone, James McKinnon and Craig Wright,[2] most people have come to agree that instruments had no place in church polyphony around 1500 and that Josquin's sacred music is better without them. In universities throughout the world, those crumhorns, shawms and even renaissance recorders so eagerly purchased during the 1960s are now gathering dust, virtually relegated to the limbo of a musicological past.

But I do believe that this is limbo rather than inferno. Like all sudden changes of attitude, this one has perhaps gone a little too far and fails to take account of a fair number of qualifying documents and considerations. So my first task is to attempt a refinement of the now current view that instruments have no place in Josquin's sacred music.

Instrumental participation

A few simple points are necessary as a backdrop to any discussion of instruments in sacred music. First, the performance of sacred polyphony was by no means confined to the church. We have plenty of descriptions of such music performed out of doors, in noble households, in bourgeois homes and even, if the illustrations in several books of hours are to be taken at all literally, in boats. Recent writings have stressed the difficulty of reconciling much of the surviving motet repertory with any kind of liturgy.[3] Anthony Cummings has also drawn attention to the number of references to motets being performed after dinner in the papal household. It would be easy enough to add similar references from other households, ranging from that of Margaret of Austria to that of Martin Luther.[4] In fact there may well be more evidence for what one might call the secular performance of sacred motets than there is for liturgical performance.

The second point is related. In the 15th century it seems clear enough that much of the surviving polyphony was composed for special occasions and not really intended to be part of the day-to-day services in even the richest chapels.[5] Clearly the years around 1500 represent something of a change in that respect, with a massively growing polyphonic repertory and increasing evidence of polyphony being sung most days in certain establishments.[6] But it is surely dangerous to discuss this matter in terms of what 'normally' happened. Composed polyphony was itself only just beginning to become a normal phenomenon in the second half of the 15th century. And even then, monophonic chant remained more 'normal' in church than other kinds of music. Polyphony in Josquin's day therefore had a history of being exceptional and being associated with exceptional occasions.

Third, and growing out of that, the unquestionable truth that instruments were not normally allowed in church, and particularly not during Mass, must be qualified by the equally unquestionable evidence that on many occasions instruments were used in church, specifically during Mass. Among the clearest cases are the dedication by the pope of Florence Cathedral in 1436,[7] the wedding Mass of Costanzo Sforza and Camilla of Aragon at Pesaro in 1475,[8] that of Roberto Malatesta and Isabetta Aldrovandino at Rimini in the same year,[9] that of Maximilian I and Bianca Maria Sforza at Milan in 1493,[10] that of John the Steadfast and Sofie von Mecklenburg at Torgau in 1500[11] and the Mass at Rome hosted by Louis XII in the presence of the pope and many cardinals in 1501.[12] And indeed many 15th-century and early 16th-century pictures show trumpets present specifically at wedding and coronation Masses.[13] These combine to suggest that on certain kinds of occasion instruments in church were almost *de rigueur*. In these particular cases there is no clear information about what the instruments may have performed, but they were certainly present in church and playing during Mass.

Fourth, one important development in the last quarter of the 15th century was the emergence of instrumental ensembles capable of playing a wide range of composed polyphony. These are the years that see the arrival of bowed string instruments with a curved bridge;[14] that see the first appearance of crumhorns;[15] that see the first clear evidence of sackbuts;[16] that see the earliest examples of lute tablature, something that becomes necessary as more lutenists wish to perform sophisticated polyphony.[17] These years also show the earliest substantial repertory of polyphony that was plainly composed independently of text – in the chansonniers I-Rc 2856 and I-Fn Banco Rari 229.[18] Even for those who look with suspicion on earlier indications that instrumental ensembles were performing composed polyphony – I am thinking of the description of English slide-trumpet players at the Council of Constance in 1416,[19] of matched sets of wind instruments purchased by the Burgundian court in 1423, 1426 and 1439,[20] of the evidence of the manuscript owned by Zorzi Trombetta in the 1440s as recently analysed by Daniel Leech-Wilkinson,[21] and many other scattered details – it seems impossible to avoid the conclusion that instruments of all kinds were capable of playing composed polyphony during the last quarter of the 15th century.

Fifth, one characteristic of all the evidence for instruments in church mentioned under point three was that it comes from eye-witness descriptions and pictures, not from payment records. The explanation is obvious. At court households the instrumentalists were on salary, often as part of the *écurie*.[22] A good example here is the case of Augustin Sobinger at the courts of Burgundy and France. The chronicler Antoine de Lalaing tells us that when the Burgundian court chapel visited Toledo in May 1502 Augustin played the cornett with them; a year later at Bourg-en-Bresse he did the same; and in 1520, as a member of the French royal *écurie*, he appears to have led the French instrumentalists who played with the singers during the Credo at the Field of the Cloth of Gold.[23] All this information, too, comes from eye-witness descriptions. Sobinger never appears in chapel accounts; no special accounting process was required for him and other instrumentalists to play with the chapel or in church. Such players were members of the household not only in secular courts but also in those of many church potentates, among them several popes. The absence of instrumentalists in chapel accounts therefore has virtually no bearing on whether they took part in church polyphony. Clearly this is in some ways a dangerous line of argument. But it is less dangerous than to assume that the absence of payments means that they cannot have performed in church.

My argument, then, is that on certain kinds of special occasion instruments were quite often present in church and performing during Mass. They were perfectly capable of taking part with the singers in composed polyphony, and in the case of Augustin Sobinger clearly did so. In an age when courtly culture placed considerable emphasis on magnificence as evidence of political power, it would in any case be extremely surprising if instrumentalists were not used to contribute to the glory of the occasion.[24]

The earliest unambiguous evidence of instrumentalists on a cathedral staff – excluding, that is, the slightly perplexing appearance of a *tromba* in the court chapel of Savoy in 1449-55[25] – is at Toledo in 1531, when three minstrels were hired on a twenty-year contract.[26] So far as I know, the matter of minstrels in Spanish churches has not yet received the comprehensive investigation it clearly requires, though scattered references in the writings of Anglés and Stevenson suggest that they are found playing with the singers from the 1470s and become extremely common after about 1530.[27] To some extent Spain was a separate culture – as it still is – but throughout Josquin's lifetime the musical interchange between Spain and the Low Countries is so extensive that it would be dangerous to dismiss the Spanish evidence as eccentric.

In 1520 Cardinal Wolsey was informed that the French king François I had heard high Mass at the church of the Jacobins at which shawms and sackbuts had played together with the singers.[28] Two years earlier Erasmus had inveighed against the current use of instruments in the divine service: "we have introduced a kind of artificial and theatrical music into churches. . . Everything resounds with trumpets, cornetts, shawms and sackbuts, and the human voices must compete with them";[29] a few years later he wrote that "today things have come to the point where churches reverberate with cornetts, shawms and trumpets and sometimes even bombardes, and scarcely anything is audible but the babbling of disparate voices, and a kind of artificial and lascivious music such as the pagan theatres never knew."[30]

These last three citations clarify a point that is surely true of all the other evidence mentioned earlier: that the surviving information on instruments in church during Josquin's lifetime all concerns what are classified as 'loud' instruments – sackbuts, cornetts and shawms. Lutes are occasionally recorded in church, but not alongside singers; and I have not encountered bowed instruments. This fits well with the view that the instrumentalists were there primarily to add to the glory of the occasion.

The aesthetic issues

The evidence that instrumentalists sometimes took part in sacred polyphonic performance in Josquin's time is likely to be unpopular within the present climate of opinion;[31] and to be perfectly honest I rather dislike the idea myself. But it would be dishonest to ignore that evidence, for it seems overwhelming. Moreover the nature of the events mentioned above is important: they are all great state occasions, precisely the occasions on which musicians would have wished – and been expected – to perform the most magnificent works of the era. Needless to say, those works inevitably include the most famous compositions of Josquin.

With that said, it is necessary to turn to Josquin's music and ask whether there are any works there that could conceivably benefit from instrumental participation. Clearly it is difficult to offer answers that are independent of prejudice or preference: in the absence of unambiguous documentation we all inevitably react as children of our time. Within the last fifteen years musicologists of the utmost seriousness and probity have continued to support the now almost unacceptable notion that the majority of sacred polyphony from the 14th and 15th centuries firmly required instrumental participation. Looking further into the past, the extreme case of Arnold Schering's work shows how an apparently objective and sensitive scrutiny of the facts can lead to conclusions which we would now regard as untenable nonsense.[32] The entire subject needs approaching with caution and humility; and I do not believe that we yet know enough of the various possibilities to countenance rigid-minded answers. So with those thoughts in mind I would like to consider a few specific pieces.

The first is the five-voice motet *Illibata dei virgo* (9/27).[33] Its Tenor line in long notes with the solmization syllables *la mi la* is entirely unrelated to the other voices with their famous acrostic text; and it to some extent clarifies the structure of the work. In my view the performance on Wednesday evening by the King's College

Choir suffered in that the Tenor was virtually inaudible, as can so easily happen if the work is performed by a choir assembled primarily for the needs of music in four evenly-distributed parts. Ex. 1 shows the voice-ranges of *Illibata dei virgo*: in a choir such as King's, the boys will take the top line, the countertenors will be to some extent superfluous, and there are three lines suitable for the tenors. No wonder that the balance was unconvincing.

Example 1
Josquin: *Illibata* (9/27)

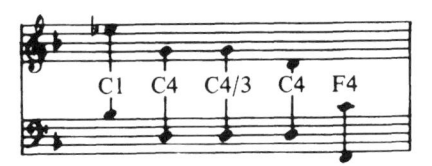

Yet to perform just the Tenor line on a sackbut, for instance, would create more problems than it solved. There are 52 *breves* of polyphony before the Tenor enters; and unless at least one other voice was doubled by an instrument it would be extremely difficult for the pitch to remain sufficiently stable for the instrument on the Tenor line to enter with confidence. Certainly, the singers of Dialogo Musicale achieved such a feat in their concert on Thursday night, and I am told that none of them has perfect pitch; but this would surely be considerably more difficult in an era of floating pitch standards.

For what it is worth, pitch stability could be maintained throughout the piece by doubling just the contratenor primus with an instrument, since this is a line with enough continuity and flexibility to control the intonation of the entire ensemble. But that is surely worth little, because by doubling just one of the other voices you obscure the structural point intended by having a sackbut on the Tenor. The case of *Illibata dei virgo* is therefore precisely the same as with many isorhythmic motets of the 14th and 15th centuries: if you wish to play the Tenor on an instrument, prudence dictates that you double the other lines as well.

After the presentation of this paper it was pointed out[34] that the discussion here should have mentioned the Mass *Hercules dux Ferrarie* (17/7) which uses its Tenor in a similar manner. Yet this work is less problematic for two reasons. First, the long-note tenor is motivically more fully integrated into the polyphonic texture than is that of *Illibata dei virgo*. Second, the work is in four voices, thus creating less difficulty of balance or texture; and when it moves into six voices for the final Agnus dei it is the Discantus and Bassus that divide, thereby giving more prominence to the Tenor (see ex. 9). It seems to me therefore – to put a firmly subjective viewpoint – that the cycle works better with voices alone.

But the case of *Illibata dei virgo* is just one of several which suggest that what one might call analytical scoring is misguided. To take the parallel example of the 15th-century chanson repertory, we have only recently learned that views on its scoring were confused by the temptation to say that, for instance, the Tenor is melodic and should therefore have a sustaining instrument whereas the Contratenor is jumpy and would be well served by a plucked instrument.[35] In that particular case it now seems more sensible to say that the lines are in themselves sufficiently differentiated and they need no extra help from 20th-century notions to sharpen the edges. I suspect that the same is the case with the sacred music of Josquin's time. It is difficult to know whether Schering was right in saying that skilled organists of Josquin's time were expected to be able to play the full texture of a piece of polyphony with only the parts before them: the earliest statement of that is in Bermudo's book of 1555, by which time polyphonic notation had become simpler, the music itself was more predictable, and it was easier to supply an extra copy of the choirbook for the organist's use.[36] But there does seem a strong case for suggesting that in general if one voice was doubled all voices were doubled and therefore that to ask, as I did, whether any of Josquin's works would benefit from instrumental participation is to ask the question in the wrong way.[37] An analytical orchestration of early 16th-century polyphony is probably no more historical than is Webern's orchestration of the Bach six-voice Ricercar. Instruments were there to add richness to the sound, glory to the occasion.

There are two more motets in which the case for analytical orchestration might just be pursued. One is the five-voice *Salve regina* (35/48). Here the cantus firmus, with its four-note repeated motif, enters almost immediately (b.4) thereby creating no real intonation problems if this line is performed instrumentally. And it continues its ostinato of three-bars-off, four-bars-on, throughout the piece. The fascinating phrase-structure created by that seven-bar framework surely represents one of the most attractive features of the work. Subjectively speaking, I find that a solo sackbut on that line alone works extremely well; but on the other hand it should not be difficult to achieve the same end by a careful balance of the voices. (On the evening of the day when this paper was presented, the singers of Chanticleer did precisely that.) Texting is no real problem: Smijers was surely right in giving each statement of the Tenor just the one word "Salve".[38]

Texting does present a problem, however, in the other work, the five-voice *Stabat mater* (21/36) with its Tenor in augmented values taken from the chanson *Comme femme desconfortee* perhaps by Binchois. Unlike the cantus firmus of the *Salve regina*, this Tenor remains entirely independent of the close imitative patterns in the other four voices. Moreover no form of texting seems convincing: Smijers adds six lines of the *Stabat mater* text to the Tenor, a procedure which surely becomes meaningless after the opening bars; some might prefer to add the French text of the chanson, which may be a logical solution and in many ways fits the mood of the motet but seems unsatisfactory not only because in this particular chanson the French text happens not to fit the Tenor at all well,[39] but also because of the extremely long notes of the line. Clearly instrumental performance would solve those problems; but equally clearly there is nothing against simple vocalisation of the line. Seeing the work in a broader historical context reaching back to the beginning of the 15th century, that is in many ways the most likely solution.

The same may also apply to the somewhat similar five-voice *Missus est angelus Gabriel* (24/40) which is obviously modelled on *Stabat mater* and takes its Tenor from the chanson *A une dame* by Busnois. Because of the nature of that Tenor it fits the French chanson text well; Busnois' Tenor is itself generally in shorter note-values than that of *Comme femme*, so French texting would in this case be considerably less absurd; and sections of the motet text can relatively easily be added to the Tenor (indeed it was the presence of some of that text in certain sources that was used by Lowinsky in his otherwise convincing argument that the motet is by Mouton, not Josquin[40]). But in this particular case the chanson text, which begins appropriately for the motet text, continues by including a specific reference to the d'Haqueville family; so the case for bitextual performance here is almost certainly to be excluded.[41]

All of these works present problems for the editor; but those problems are perhaps best resolved by remembering that there must have been a considerable tradition of vocalisation. The chant repertory – which, to repeat, was still in Josquin's time the most common kind of church music – contains many enormous melismas; and the sacred music of the early 15th century includes lower voices which by their style and ligaturing virtually exclude the possibility of coherent texting. To propose instrumental allocation of a line merely because it cannot easily be texted is to ignore the historical context. Hypotheses related to analytical scoring, that is, scoring that attempts to separate one voice from the texture, are surely misguided.

What evidence there is would seem to suggest that instrumental participation, favoured for certain magnificent purposes, took the form of doubling and had no more sophisticated musical intent. And while the *ex vacuo* argument is always dangerous, it does seem likely that if particular lines had actually been conceived for instruments there would be some clear indication of that somewhere in the surviving sources.

Singing ensembles

The preceding pages are offered partly as a corrective to some disturbingly rigid views in recent literature. But if it is accepted that the position of instruments in church polyphony around 1500 was simply to double the lines and add to the magnificence of the occasion, it follows that the vocal ensemble not only remains more or less unaffected by the presence or absence of instruments but is the fundamental group for which the music would have been conceived in the first place. The 'normal' ensemble of singers which is basic to many recent discussions of what has been called the 'modified a cappella hypothesis' may have been the preferred ensemble rather less often than has been suggested; but it must nevertheless be considered to some extent paradigmatic. So it is to the singing ensembles that we must now turn.

In the proceedings of the 1971 conference Frank D'Accone published an extremely full summary of the available information on Italian choral institutions during Josquin's lifetime.[42] For French and Franco-Flemish institutions it is not yet possible to provide anything so extensive.[43] At New York in 1961 and again in 1969 François Lesure issued a call for more archival research on the choirs of French cathedrals;[44] his plea has in general still not been answered. But the information assembled in table 1 provides some clues.

First, the indication from the French royal chapel, the Burgundian chapel and the choirs of Cambrai and Antwerp is that the standard body of vicars choral consisted of twelve men throughout the last quarter of the 15th century. D'Accone's information from Italy suggests that Italian choirs during those same years were generally smaller but that they grew to that size during the first years of the 16th century; they were more and more attempting to emulate the choirs of the Low Countries. Italian choirs were largely run and staffed by Franco-Flemish musicians; the famous choirs of Cambrai, Condé, Antwerp, Bruges and elsewhere were the model and the touchstone as concerned repertory, distribution of voices and presumably vocal style.

Second, French and Franco-Flemish choirs grew larger in the first quarter of the 16th century: the sixteen vicars choral at Cambrai in 1516 and at Condé in 1523 seem to be characteristic for their time; and D'Accone's compilation suggests that the Italian choirs followed suit just slightly later. Methodologically speaking, there is no evidence of danger in using the information on Italian choirs to fill out what little we know about those which they emulated in the Low Countries, though it is my impresssion that the northern choirs were by then more consistent than those in war-torn Italy.

Third, however, there is a serious methodological problem in accepting that twelve was the standard number of singers in a polyphonic choir in the 15th century. We know that twelve was the number of vicars choral in many foundations from at least the beginning of the 15th century and in many cases considerably earlier; and quite often that number is specified in foundation documents. A glance at the rosters of Cambrai Cathedral and the Burgundian court chapel in the course of the 15th century shows relative stability in numbers, see table 2. Now it is surely agreed that one of the most significant changes in music during the course of the 15th century is the move from soloist polyphony to choral polyphony. So far as we can tell, at the beginning of the century most vicars choral sang monophonic chant only, with figured polyphony entrusted to soloists.[45] Yet the available documentation betrays not the slightest hint of that change. I would interpret that paradox as being similar to the case of wind players taking part in church performances as witnessed by reports but not the accounts. The singers were there, being paid to

39

TABLE I

Choirs in France and the Low Countries

1. Collegiates

Cambrai, Notre-Dame[a]	1474: 12 vicars; 1486: 15; 1495: 13; 1506: 19; 1516: 16; 1527: 21; 1536: 20; 1547: 21. In addition, consistently 4-6 boys and 9 grands-vicaires
Condé, Notre-Dame[b]	1523: 16 vicars, 6 choirboys
Antwerp, Onze-Lieve-Vrouw[c]	15th-century: up to 12 vicars and 8 choirboys
Bruges, St-Jacques[d]	?: 10-12 men, 4 boys

2. Private chapels

Savoy[e]	1455-6: 11 cantori, 2 tenori, 1 'cappellanus, recevitore e cantore', 1 organist
	1460: 15 cantori, 4 tenori, 1 'cappellanus, recevitore e cantore', 2 organists
	1500: 15 cantori, 3 cappellani, 1 maestro boys: 7 or 8 in 1476, 6 in 1478
France[f]	1462: Ockeghem plus 11 men
	1474-5: Ockeghem plus 14 men
	1482: Ockeghem plus 12 men
	1515: 23 men
Burgundy	1469: 12 chaplains, 4 clercs, 6 sommeliers (including 6 dessus, 3 tenor, 2 haute-contre, 3 basse-contre)[g]
	1477: 12 chaplains, 4 clercs or sommeliers, 1 organist[h]
	1492-6: 16 men, including at least 4 tenors and 1 haute-contre; 1 organist
	1497: 12 chaplains, 1 organist (counted as chaplain), 2 clercs, 2 sommeliers (including at least 3 tenors)
	1500: 13 chaplains, 1 organist (counted as chaplain), 1 clerc, 3 sommeliers (including at least 5 tenors and one haute-contre)
	1506: Marbriano de Orto plus 20 chaplains, (including an organist, 2 tenors and 3 basses-contres), 1 clerc, 2 sommeliers[i]

Notes and sources

a. C. Wright, *Musiciens à la cathédrale de Cambrai 1475-1550*, in RdM 62 (1976), pp. 204-28.
b. Unpublished communication from Herbert Kellman.
c. J. van den Nieuwenhuizen, *De koralen, de zangers en de zangmeesters van de Antwerpse O.-L. Vrouwekerk tijdens de 15e eeuw*, in Antwerpens Kathedraalkoor (Antwerp 1978), pp. 29-72.

d.   A. Basso, ed., *Dizionario enciclopedico universale della musica e dei musicisti*, vol. I (Turin 1983), p. 404.

e.   M.-Th. Bouquet, *La cappella musicale dei duchi di Savoia dal 1450 al 1500*, in RIM 3 (1968), pp. 233-85.

f.   L. L. Perkins, *Musical Patronage at the Royal Court of France under Charles VII & Louis XI (1422-83)*, in JAMS 37 (1984), pp. 507-66.

g.   D. Fallows, *Specific Information on the Ensembles for Composed Polyphony, 1400-1474*, in Studies in the Performance of Late Mediaeval Music, ed. S. Boorman (Cambridge 1983), pp. 109-59.

h.   This and the following based on G. van Doorslaer, *La chapelle musicale de Philippe le Beau*, in Revue belge d'archéologie et d'histoire de l'art 4 (1934), pp. 21-57 and 139-65. But the information is refined by comparative analysis of the various lists and their apparent meaning. The numbers of singers on any particular voice are assembled from any document designating them as such.

i.   This is the special choir that Philip the Fair took to Spain.

TABLE 2

1. Burgundian court choir

year	chapelains	clercs	sommeliers	total	source★
1395	18	4	2	24	W p. 221
1404	21	3	4	28	W p. 230
1419	15	3	4	22	W p. 234
1436	17	3	3	23	M p. 242
1452	14	6	5	25	M p. 251-2
1468	14	4	6	24	M p. 260

★   W = C. Wright, *Music at the Court of Burgundy 1364-1419: a Documentary History* (Henryville-Ottawa-Binningen 1979); M = J. Marix, *Histoire de la musique et des musiciens de la cour de Bourgogne sous le règne de Philippe le Bon* (Strasbourg 1939).

2. Cambrai cathedral

year	petits vicaires	source★
1409-10	10-13	4G 6789/1
1453-4	11-13	4G 6789/3
1462-3	15	4G 6789/6
1468-9	15	4G 6789/10

★   Lille, Archives départementales du Nord.

sing, and as the century progressed they were increasingly expected to take part in polyphony. It may therefore be permissible to make a simple but important historical point about the development of 15th-century polyphony: namely that the music was mostly intended for a group of singers established by ordinances whose original purpose was virtually forgotten; the composers and choirmasters were simply redeploying a traditional ensemble.

Inasmuch as the northern choirs show no evidence of a significant change in size until after about 1500, it is perhaps only then that the number of singers being paid can be considered any clear guide to the number who took part in polyphonic music. From that point of view, therefore, the information on Italian choirs is probably much more useful as a guide to the distribution for 15th-century polyphony. Many of these ensembles were newly established and used largely French or Franco-Flemish personnel as well as Franco-Flemish repertory when they sang polyphony. The very evanescence of the Italian choirs makes their evidence all the more useful. After all, when Jachetto di Marvilla sent Lorenzo de' Medici a blueprint for a new polyphonic choir for the Florence Baptistery in 1469,[46] he is unlikely to have insulted Lorenzo by proposing anything cheap, but he offered only five singers. A particularly useful detail in Jachetto's letter is that he stated precisely what each singer was to do; and we therefore know that he was concerned with three-voice polyphony, adding the possibility of later including a further singer to cope with the small but growing trend for four-voice polyphony.

On the other hand, there is one piece of clear northern evidence for a larger polyphonic ensemble which happens to come from the very same year: that in the new Burgundian court ordinances promulgated by Duke Charles the Bold. In an earlier paper I discussed this information in some detail, in particular the evidence that the minimum preferred distribution of singers in four-voice polyphony was three on the Bassus, three on the Tenor, two on the Contra and six men on top.[47] I also demonstrated (a) that we know their names and enough about their ages to say confidently that everybody in the 3/3/2/6 distribution was an adult man; (b) that the six men on top were certainly falsettists (a word I use to cover the various disputed means and results when adult men sing in the treble register); and (c) that the wording of the document as well as its context were such as to argue that this was an optimum based on a full understanding of the repertory and its requirements.

Given the contrast between these fourteen singers and the mere five proposed to Lorenzo de' Medici in the same year, there might be some cause to suspect Charles the Bold of seeking mere exhibition and glory. One could conclude the same from the figures in table 1 showing that the normal French or Franco-Flemish choir size at the time was only twelve. But on the other hand there is copious evidence to suggest that Charles was not merely a composer and a performer himself but musically more interested and better educated than any other patron of his time.[48]

More than that, it is at least possible that Charles proposed his apparently new and grander disposition on the advice of Busnois, a rising star and one of the few musicians we know to have been part of his personal household before he became Duke in 1468. Certainly a document that assumes four-voice polyphony in 1469 is forward-looking; it seems to be setting a new standard for what we now inevitably call the Josquin era. It should therefore be no surprise to find similar distributions in early 16th-century Italy from D'Accone's lists: Florence Cathedral in 1512 had two basses, three tenors, two contras and on the top line one adult soprano plus four to six boys; in 1510 the Florence Baptistery had grown to precisely the same size; Treviso Cathedral in 1527-8 had two basses, two tenors, three contras and four boys who appear to have been doubled by the two maestri; and several other documents show the same.

Yet it must always be borne in mind that none of these documents specifically states that everybody took part in every, or indeed any, polyphonic performance. Such information must be treated cautiously with the single exception of the Burgundian court ordinances from 1469. In fact I have not encountered any such clear statement of distribution until the inscription on the sole source of Brumel's twelve-voice Mass *Et ecce terrae motus* naming the singers who apparently took part in a performance under Lasso in 1568-70.[49] For the three Discantus lines no name is given, presumably because they were sung by boys (Boetticher reckons a dozen); for each of the three Contra lines four names appear; for each of the three Tenors, three names; and for each of the three Basses, four names. But even this is not as satisfactory as it may seem since we know that Lasso's Kapelle normally had instruments doubling the lines.[50]

Boys

In my earlier study I suggested that in the 1470s when three or four boys alone were on the top line then the lower lines would have only one singer each; my evidence was primarily the information in Dufay's will and certain documents from Cambrai presented by Craig Wright. On reconsideration, I see that this smaller grouping (a) also occurs with falsettists on the top line, namely at the choir of S Pietro in Vaticano at Rome during the 1480s,[51] and (b) more or less mirrors the distribution of the larger Burgundian ensemble. Moreover, several of D'Accone's Italian ensembles, in particular those from Florence and Treviso mentioned earlier, suggest that the proportions remained more or less the same irrespective of whether the top line was sung by falsettists or boys or a combination of the two. The conclusion would therefore be that boys and falsettists were not only comparable in volume but may well have had a similar tone colour; the differences were merely that boys were in some ways less reliable and needed more intensive training but that they were to be encouraged as being cheaper and as representing an excellent training-ground for future churchmen – this latter being almost certainly the main reason why Pope Eugenius IV in the 1430s set up so many new choirschools in various parts of

Europe at a time when he was clearly becoming disillusioned with elaborate polyphony.[52]

All of the French and Franco-Flemish institutions on which there is any published information had boys, normally between four and eight in number; and in fact there are many such establishments for which the published literature discusses only the boys.[53] But again these groups of boys remain virtually unchanged from the beginning of the 15th century; their presence tells us almost nothing about whether or when they took part in polyphony. During Josquin's lifetime the papal chapel appears to have had no boys,[54] and there is no evidence that their repertory was thereby limited.[55] Moreover documents from Cambrai presented by Craig Wright make it easy to conclude that from the middle of the 15th century when boys performed polyphony they normally did so separately from the main body of choirmen.[56]

From the years before Josquin, so far as I can see, there are just three works that specify the participation of boys; and in two of them the boys are designated for lines that are in every way identical to other lines equally specifically designated as for mature men. These I discussed in my earlier paper, slightly expanding the subject to include three further similar works.[57]

From Josquin's lifetime there are a few scattered cases of choirbooks containing a vocal line designated 'secundus puer'. The choirbooks of the time characteristically have no voice designation for the top line, which is copied on the top left-hand side of the opening; and the appearances of 'secundus puer' are in works with two more or less equal voices in the top register. A simple case is in the five-voice isorhythmic motet *Celsi tonantis/Abrahae fit promissio* by Johannes Regis surviving only in the Chigi Codex.[58] The ranges, in ex. 2a, perhaps conceal the fact that the two upper voices for the most part overlap and imitate at the unison. Another motet of Regis, *O admirabile commercium/Verbum caro*, has the same designation in a much later manuscript, NL-L 1439 copied in 1559,[59] though here it is for the voice which the Chigi Codex presents as the top line: ex. 2b shows why the Leiden choirbook exchanged the two top lines:

Example 2
(a) Regis: *Celsi tonantis*   (b) Regis: *O admirabile commercium*

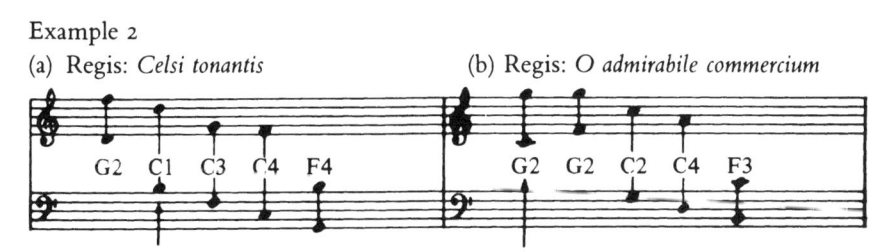

Those two sources may seem to present a simple case for the use of boys on the upper lines of sacred music from the Josquin era. But three further cases suggest that the evidence should be approached circumspectly. One is in the Kyrie of Isaac's six-voice Mass *Paschale* as presented in the Alamire manuscript I-Rvat Cappella Sistina 160,[60] see ex. 2c: the manuscript was prepared for the papal chapel which, according to all available information, had no boys at the time;[61] and the other two sources for the Mass designate that voice with the much more common rubric 'secundus discantus'. Obrecht's six-voice *Salve regina* has the rubric 'secundus puer' for both its second and third voices in D-Mbs Mus. Ms. 34;[62] the ranges are in ex. 2d, and while it is clearly both possible and convenient to perform the work with boys on the three top lines at a pitch standard approximating to A = 440 cycles,[63] material to be presented in the next section of this article will suggest that this is by no means the only solution.

Example 2
(c) Isaac: *Missa Paschale* Kyrie   (d) Obrecht: *Salve regina*

Finally, the marking 'secundus puer' appears for the second line of the Credo of Ockeghem's Mass *Fors seulement* in its unique source, the Chigi Codex.[64] This case is especially tricky. The Credo is in general approximately a fifth higher than the other two movements in its written pitches, see ex. 3:

Example 3
Ockeghem: *Missa Fors seulement*
Kyrie & Gloria   Credo

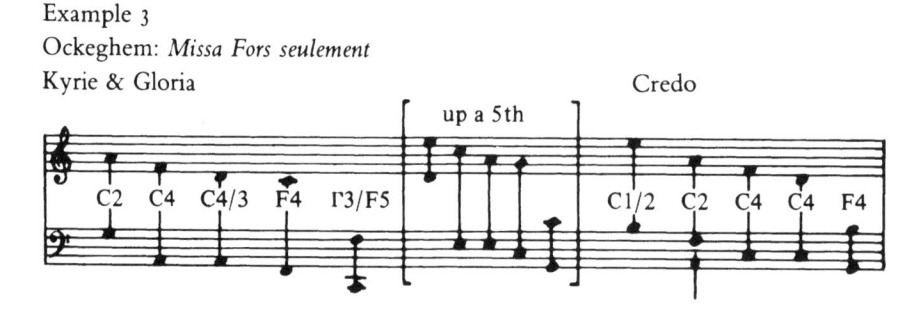

There would be a temptation to suggest that some kind of chiavette transposition was involved here – that is, that the movements of the cycle should be read against different pitch-standards so that they become comparable in their ranges – but there are two apparently strong arguments against that: first, that the chanson Tenor on which the cycle is based seems to be basically at the same pitch throughout; and second, that the designation 'secundus puer' appears only in the higher movement.[65]

These five appearances of the rubric 'secundus puer' are almost certainly not the only ones among the surviving sources; and clearly there is a need for a more complete survey, one that puts these designations into the context of all part-names from the era. My earlier essay on performance ensembles up to 1474 gave strong grounds for believing that part-names were specific indications as to who should perform a line,[66] whereas it is clear that for the Josquin generation the very range of conflicting and even of bizarre part-names shows a move away from the earlier fixity. Within that context it does not yet seem possible to draw rigid conclusions about the participation of boys purely on the basis of that rubric.

Using a different kind of evidence Craig Wright recently identified a piece as having been intended almost certainly for boys alone, Brumel's three-voice *Ave Maria* which he convincingly associated with documents stipulating performance by the choirboys of Notre-Dame de Paris around 1501.[67] Though this tells us nothing about the main question – polyphonic performance by men and boys together – it is at least a relatively clear case and could lead to identifying further pieces for boys alone. Its high clefs (C1 C2 C2) and eleven-note range (ex. 4a) make it comparable with, for instance, the Josquinian Offertory *Recordare, virgo mater* (Supp. 8) in four voices with similar clefs and a twelve-note range (ex. 4b):[68]

Example 4
(a) Brumel: *Ave Maria*   (b) Josquin?: *Recordare* (Supp. 8)

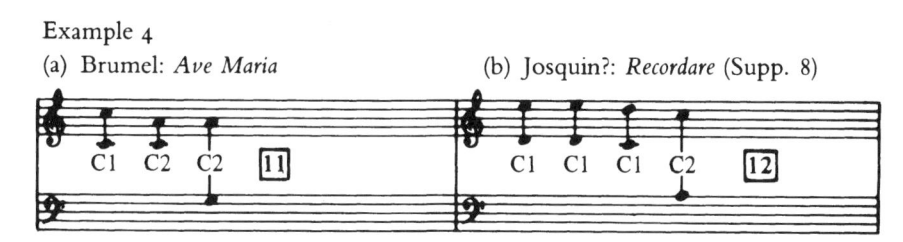

Two more pieces in the *Werken* have a similarly restricted range: *Alma Redemptoris mater* (21/38) with a range of fourteen notes, and *Domine ne in furore* (21/39), with fifteen notes (ex. 5):

Example 5
(a) Josquin: *Alma redemptoris* (21/38)   (b) Josquin: *Domine ne in furore* (21/39)

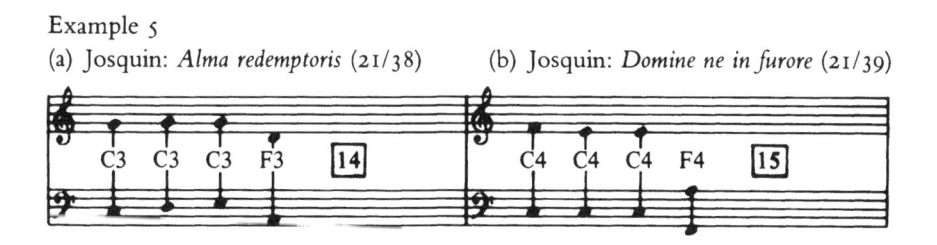

Both have clefs as though for men's voices; and while it may seem naive to assume that this means they are for men, I hope that considerations to follow will make that assumption seem at least viable. For that it is necessary to turn to the treacherous matter of pitch-standard and the associated matter of voice-ranges.

46

Pitch

It now seems agreed that at least in the early 15th century there was virtually no pitch-standard. The written note middle C was understood not as a pitch in any modern sense but as a relationship within a hexachordal framework.[69] That situation is modified for 16th-century music by two considerations: the increasing use of organ and other instruments along with the voices; and the documented codes of chiavette transposition which clearly imply a pitch-standard, however approximate (for without a pitch-standard there can be no such thing as transposition). In the mid-15th century the total range of four-voice polyphony was normally around eighteen or nineteen diatonic steps – that is, two and a half octaves – and within that the lines usually divide into three ranges: one high, two roughly equal ones in the middle, and one low.[70] The question at issue was simply whether that two and a half octave range was to be considered as being at a low pitch that did not require falsettists – so, in terms of modern concert pitch, perhaps from low D up to A above middle C – or whether the pitches were about a fourth higher, clarifying the lowest notes by bringing them into a more manageable range and requiring some kind of head technique for the singers on the highest line. I believe that in my earlier paper I resolved that problem for most mid-15th-century music definitively in favour of the higher pitch.[71]

As the century progresses, however, the range expands, so that four of Josquin's Masses, for example, have a total range of twenty-two notes, three octaves, as in ex. 6.[72] (And that figure excludes the complicated cases of the Masses *Fortuna desperata* (13/4) and *De beata virgine* (30-31/16) where one could argue that certain movements use a pitch-standard different from the rest.)

Example 6
Josquin: Masses

| *La sol fa* | *Gaudeamus* | *Malheur* | *D'ung aultre* |
| (11/2) | (12/3) | (19/8) | (23/11) |

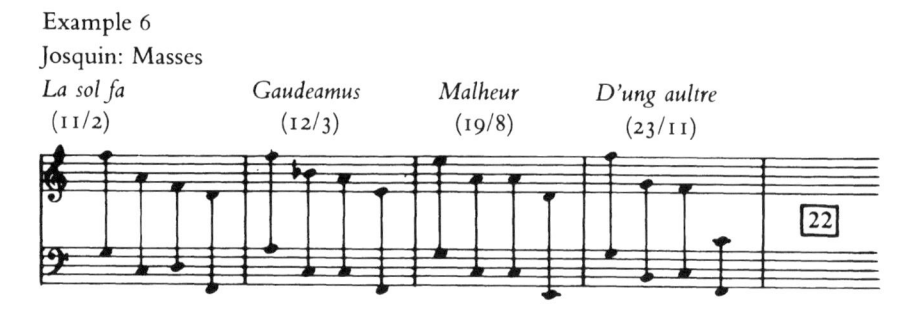

Such ranges inevitably change the focus somewhat and raise the possibility that they require the participation of boys. But this seems not to be the case, for two reasons: first, in Josquin's Mass cycles and in the vast majority of his motets the voices are still laid out unambiguously in three 'layers', thus individually offering just an expansion of the mid-15th-century pattern; and second, it is clear that adult singers in Josquin's time had learned to master considerably wider ranges than before. In the last Agnus of the Mass *Mater Patris* (26/12) the Bass has a range of sixteen notes, two octaves and a tone; in the four-voice *Laudate pueri* (42/68) the Contratenor has its full fourteen-note range within five bars (bars 135-9); and near the beginning of the Gloria of the Mass *D'ung aultre amer* (23/11) the Discantus covers a fourteen-note range within twelve bars (bars 20-31). An early example of a fourteen-note range is in the second Agnus of Dufay's Mass for St Anthony of Padua, perhaps from the 1440s;[73] but that is presumably a solo section, whereas the Josquin examples are taken from passages that are scarcely likely to be for less than the full ensemble. In general Dufay's Mass, through in only three voices, is a remarkable harbinger of the wide ranges found in polyphony nearer the end of the century.

The case for believing that continental falsettists were perfectly capable of covering the highest range in Josquin's music receives some support from a comparison with the English Eton choirbook, containing a repertory of motets more or less contemporary with Josquin's output.[74] Over the past twenty years students of the Eton choirbook and subsequent English music have devoted much energy to determining the sounding pitch and voice-distribution of the repertory; and one matter on which most of the occasionally strident disputants happen to agree concerns the use of a special 'high' treble voice apparently unique to the English choirs.[75]

At first glance, a simple comparison of ranges, in table 3, appears to suggest that there is very little that is special about the Eton choirbook music. Over one-third of its 93 pieces have a range of twenty-two notes, just like those four Josquin Masses; and a further dozen have a range one note wider, which does not appear in Josquin.[76] Thirty-two sacred pieces in the *Werken* have a range of twenty-one notes or more. Wherein, then, lies the difference between a line entrusted to boys and one performable by men?

There are two considerations that clarify the difference between the two repertories and support my earlier contention. First, whereas the individual lines in Josquin works fall into three ranges, those of the Eton choirbook fall equally clearly into four ranges. Second, in Eton the individual lines normally have a ten-note or

TABLE 3

Ranges in diatonic steps

	12	13	14	15	16	17	18	19	20	21	22	23
Eton Choirbook	–	1	12	6	–	1	2	2	1	17	39	12
Josquin Missen & Motetten*	(1)	–	1	1	1	3(2)	4(1)	19(8)	28(10)	16(6)	6(3)	(1)

*   Excluding the Masses *De beata virgine* and *Fortuna desperata*; numbers in parentheses are pieces in the *Werken* but of questioned authorship (see n. 78)

48

TABLE 4

Individual wide voice ranges

	pieces	parts	12-note	13-note	14-note	15-note	16-note
Eton Choirbook	53	288	15 (5%)	2 (0.7%)	–	–	–
Josquin: unchallenged motets	63	274	53 (19%)	17 (6%)	5	1	–
Josquin: 16 Masses	16	64	11 (17%)	22 (34%)	7 (11%)	–	1

eleven-note range. As table 4 shows, among the fifty-three more or less complete works surviving in Eton there are 288 separate voices, of which only seventeen exceed eleven notes – specifically, fifteen with twelve notes and just two with thirteen notes.[77] Among the sixty-three Josquin motets that have so far escaped the stigma of being thought spurious or dubious,[78] there are 275 separate voices: twelve-note range appears in fifty-three of them, thirteen-note range in seventeen, a massive fourteen-note range appears in five lines, and one has a fifteen-note range.[79] For the sixteen unproblematic Josquin Mass cycles the figures are even more startling.

The simple explanation of those figures would be that English adult singers never bothered or needed to cultivate the considerable range needed for the polyphony of Josquin, Ockeghem and other continental composers, whereas continental boys did not cultivate the high range used in English music.[80] Moreover, among the unquestioned Josquin works, the Discantus line has a fourteen-note range in two motets and one Mass; and it has a thirteen-note range in five motets and two Mass cycles. These ranges seem to add to the unlikelihood that the works were conceived with boys in mind, though they by no means exclude the possibility that boys were often used and that certain works with a more limited range might have been composed for boys.

Looking again at table 3, one can see that the Eton pieces bunch in two groups: nineteen pieces have a range of around two octaves, all of them in relatively low clefs as though composed for tenors and basses alone, whereas the remainder almost all have a range of around three octaves. For Josquin the picture is rather different, with the main bunching around the twenty-note range. None of the figures offered here takes account of tessitura, of course: some lines make fuller use of one or other extreme of the range. But the difficulty involved in quantifying that information with anything approaching objectivity means that it is better to keep to the actual ranges and simply to avoid conclusions that reach beyond the capabilities of that information. Yet, with that taken into account, there is no apparent danger in concluding that many of Josquin's sacred works require for all voices men with a range capability unknown to English music of the time.

If it is therefore accepted that none of Josquin's music requires boys, I believe it becomes possible to propose a quite sturdy solution to the question of sounding pitch. With a maximum required range of three octaves for Josquin's music – and I have encountered no wider range in continental music of Josquin's day or earlier, apart from the anomalous and difficult case of Ockeghem's Mass *Fors seulement* (ex. 3) which if read all at a single pitch-standard would have a range of twenty-four notes – the room for manoeuvre is small. Today's falsettists can mostly sing up to f² but are more comfortable if the line goes no higher than d². Basses can sing down to low F with relative security but below that tend to lose control of tone colour, dynamics and precision of pitch.[81] Add, for what it is worth, that today's tenors are at their best in the range of a twelfth between d and a¹; then we have a formula that leaves little scope for disagreement. The appropriate singing range will be in the three octaves from about F, as in ex. 7:

Example 7

Obviously those pitch suggestions need the added caution that Josquin's singers may have been different, both physically and in their training; and the most slippery component in my own calculations concerns the range preference of present-day tenors. Such matters are likely to be influenced both by training and by ideals of voice quality. Moreover the experience of the concerts and workshops at the Cologne conference showed that the singers of the American ensemble Chanticleer – who were chosen primarily for their flexibility of voice, according to their director – have less difficulty with the high notes than do the singers in the European ensembles. At the workshop after this paper it became clear that a 'comfortable' pitch for the Americans was rather higher than for the Europeans.

Nevertheless, *mutatis mutandis*, the proposed ranges work surprisingly well when applied to Josquin's Mass cycles and motets. Of the sixteen Mass cycles that I have been considering, all but four fit beautifully at modern concert pitch. Of the others, *L'homme armé sexti toni* (14/5) needs transposing up a third, *Di dadi* (29/15) and *L'homme armé super voces musicales* (10/1) need transposing up a tone, and *Ave maris stella* (15/6) needs transposing down a tone.

Similarly with the 63 unchallenged motets. Twenty-seven work at modern pitch. Nineteen need transposing up a tone, and eight need transposing down a tone. That accounts for all but nine motets. Three of these transpose up a third, like the Mass *L'homme armé sexti toni*: *Liber generationis* (6/15), *Missus est Gabriel* (6/17) and *Qui habitat in adiutorio* (37/52). Three more transpose down a third: *Mittit ad virginem* (2/3), *In principio* (38/56) and the canonic four-voice *Salve regina* (52/95). Two more motets initially seemed confusing but work untransposed if it is simply assumed that there are two voices in the top range but only one in the middle range: *Gaude virgo* (7/23) and *Memor esto* (16/31).[82]

Within that pattern there are certain obvious qualifications, many of which can be worked out for individual pieces by the individual reader or performer. But the main qualification is that the pattern is based on the four-voice music which comprises over three-quarters of the Josquin sacred repertory. For his motets in five voices the extra voice is always in the middle range (see ex. 1). Two of the most famous six-voice motets have four voices in that middle range, *O virgo prudentissima* (35/45) and *Pater noster* (36/50); the remainder have three voices in the middle range and two in the lowest range, see ex. 8:

Example 8
Josquin: six-voice motets   *Huc me sydereo* (16/32)

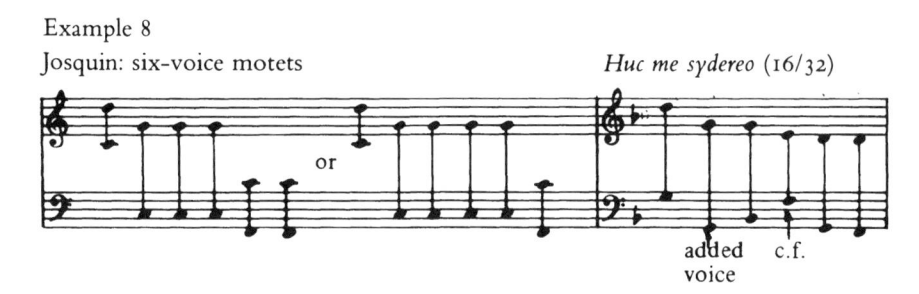

With the single exception of *Huc me sydereo* (16/32) – which in its six-voice version yet again becomes a thorn in the flesh of any discussion of Josquin's ensembles – the six-voice motets have a top voice with an unusually restricted range. This might conceivably imply that it was sung only by boys and that any men who normally sang with them simply transferred to one of the middle lines. Another qualification is that in those Mass cycles that move from four voices to six for the final Agnus Dei the pattern is by no means so simple; see ex. 9:

Example 9
Josquin: Mass cycles with six-voice Agnus III
L'homme armé sexti toni (14/5)   *Hercules dux Ferrarie* (17/7)

Malheur me bat (19/8)   c.f.

But the explanation of this surely lies in the difference between a work conceived *ab initio* in six voices and a work in which the six voices represent a simple subdivision of four-voice texture.

Three pieces mentioned earlier can now be reconsidered. Obrecht's *Salve regina* (ex. 2d) seems to fit this pattern best if it is transposed down a tone: that conclusion may seem simplistic and literal-minded, but it is worth bearing in mind as a further indication that the rubric 'secundus puer' may, at the end of the day, not necessarily specify boys so much as men singing in a 'boyish' range. The two Josquin works in ex. 5, with their three lines in the middle range, clearly fit the pattern if left at a low pitch and performed without altos.

I am painfully aware that at first glance this attempt to quantify and pigeon-hole the entire range of Josquin's sacred music may seem unduly glib. It is not intended as providing a 'code' for the pitch of Josquin's works. But it does, I think, show that if certain positions are accepted – that his singers were happy with the wide ranges of a thirteenth and a fourteenth that turn up relatively often; that the singers were basically adult males with voices in the three registers we call alto, tenor and bass; and that pitch standards at the time were flexible – then one conclusion follows: that a performing ensemble with the layout of ex. 7 is capable of singing all Josquin's sacred polyphony.

In those pieces for which I propose transposition, it seems unlikely that any clef-code was used: the clefs of his works too often vary between sources and even within pieces. Nor are the proposals rigid: they are relative, and in several cases they are open to modification, particularly taking account of tessitura. But they do work equally well for all three voice-ranges; and the simplicity with which everything fits is, to say the least, extremely comforting.

It seemed wise to delay until this point discussion of one final motet: *Absalon, fili mi* (Supp. 5). As is well known, it occurs in two forms: with astonishingly low ranges in the Alamire manuscript GB-Lbm Royal 8 G.vii; and with extremely high ranges, a ninth higher, in two later German prints, RISM 1540[7] and 1559[2], see ex. 10:

Example 10

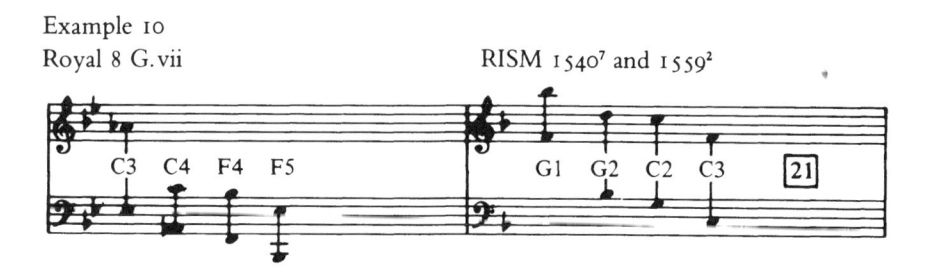

In the present context one must inevitably point out that exactly half way between those two sets of written pitches the motet fits precisely to the pattern of Josquin's other sacred music, as in ex. 11:

Example 11

Put another way: if Josquin had really intended *Absalon, fili mi* to sound as much below the other works as the written notes in the Alamire manuscript appear to suggest, then it is difficult to see why he should have persisted with the same layout as his remaining four-voice motets, namely one high, two in the middle range and one low, distributed in fifths. The layout would suggest either that Josquin knew of no other way of composing four-voice polyphony or that he intended the motet to sound at approximately the same pitch as his other sacred works. It is hard to resist the latter conclusion.

Balance

From there I wish to return to the matter of the Burgundian court chapel distribution of 1469 with six falsettists on the top line against two, three and three on the lower lines, because it remains the only clear and unchallengeable information available on distribution and balance. The question whether such a distribution continued to be favoured in the subsequent years is to some extent imponderable, but there are two relevant considerations: first, as mentioned earlier, the available documentary information shows little evidence of change before the second decade of the 16th century, and at the beginning of the century the Italian choirs appear to be approaching that same distribution; and second, the differences between the four-voice Mass repertory of the 1460s and the works of Josquin and Obrecht are differences of detail and scope, not of substance.

What seems difficult about the Burgundian distribution is obviously the balance, with so many singers on the top line. One could argue that this would be most suitable for homophonic music with a melody on top, as in much of the apparently Milanese repertory of the time. But there is no evidence that such music was known at the Burgundian court of Charles the Bold. We do know that they had the Mass cycles.[83] In these, a movement almost invariably begins with a duet between Discantus and Contratenor, that is to say – if everybody is singing – with six voices balanced against two. Clearly there is the possibility that such opening sections, and all duos, were sung by soloists (as has been suggested for much of Bach's choral music), but the increasingly complex imitative techniques in Dufay's late music and other Mass cycles of the time suggest that this is no panacea.

In fact the situation becomes less problematic when seen in a broader musical perspective. Perhaps one could explain the top-heavy distribution of the normal baroque string section by saying that the tune was on the top line; but the controlling essence of the music was surely in the Bass, performed often by a pathetically small number of musicians.[84] It is not difficult to balance a violin concerto so that the solo violin can be heard clearly above a substantial string section, nor is it difficult to balance a solo voice against a chorus. Normally in such cases the soloist would have a richer tone, would be prominently placed and would have a musical line designed to stand out. But the main reason why a soloist is easily heard is a matter of simple acoustics: each extra performer on a particular line adds only a small amount to the volume – in the region of 3 decibels. To take another case: the balance of Schubert's Octet may be slightly different from that of his symphonies; but the main difference is not so much in balance as in sound quality.

So also with 15th-century polyphony. As far as I know, acousticians have not yet devised ways of evaluating acceptable balance (though Rudolf Rasch's recent work has made important steps in that direction[85]), and they have some difficulty in describing the kind of sound-quality change I am discussing; but it should be clear that the issue here is balance not of dynamics but of tone colour.

In that context, three matters are perhaps relevant. First, documents from slightly later in the 16th century clearly state that church music was sung at a considerably higher dynamic level than court music.[86] Second, precisely the same is suggested by the material I presented at the beginning of this paper showing that when instruments were used to support church polyphony they were sackbuts, shawms and cornetts, not lutes and viols. Third, the falsettists whose sound ought to be virtually interchangeable with that of choirboys should perhaps bear in mind that the distinction between the role of choirboys in the Eton choirbook and in continental polyphony would suggest that continental choirboys used something more of a chest register as against the head tone of English choirboys. In general, of course, this distinction obtains even today; and many writers have suggested over the years that it has causes connected with language and race rather than simply tradition and training.[87] Any attempt to reproduce the sound implied by the Burgundian ordinances of 1469 should bear those considerations in mind.

I believe that the first such attempt in modern times was at the Cologne conference, to which the *Westdeutscher Rundfunk* invited the ensemble Chanticleer from San Francisco with the stipulation that they should sing with that distribution. Their performances were to my ear overwhelmingly convincing; but it was difficult to be certain precisely why they sounded so different from, for example, the Hilliard Ensemble balanced along more conventional lines. The Americans had in any case a different approach to Josquin's musical gestures, and their voices were of a kind unlike those of the English cathedral tradition. Briefly, nothing in their singing argued conclusively in favour of an ensemble with so many altos on the top line. On the other hand, it was abundantly clear that singers accustomed to a more equal distribution did not easily adapt to the Burgundian balance. At the workshop after this paper the distribution was attempted with a group made up of all the available non-Chanticleer singers plus two members of Chanticleer to make up the numbers. The results never settled down in the time available. Subsequent discussions with Chanticleer's director, Louis Botto, revealed that it took them some two months of rehearsals before this rather different approach to Renaissance polyphony began to feel comfortable.

Moreover, even if this should turn out to be the best solution for the four-voice music, it is hardly likely that Josquin's motets in five or six voices were composed with that 6/2/3/3 distribution in mind: for these, either he expected an ensemble with more voices in the middle register, or instruments were used to moderate the balance. In fact, whatever conclusions can be drawn from the preceding pages need qualifying by the observation that the motets in more than four voices have their own separate problems.

And that may be a good way to end. In some matters this paper has offered answers that differ from current opinion; in others it has reaffirmed accepted views, though approaching them from a different angle; but much remains inconclusive pending considerable further research on the musicians and the musical institutions of Josquin's time.

1. Josquin des Prez: Proceedings of the International Josquin Festival-Conference, ed. E. E. Lowinsky with B. J. Blackburn (London 1976), pp. 601-719.

2. F. A. D'Accone, *The Performance of Sacred Music in Italy during Josquin's Time, c. 1475-1525*, in Josquin des Prez (see n. 1), pp. 601-18; J. W. McKinnon, *Representations of the Mass in Medieval and Renaissance Art*, in JAMS 31 (1978), pp. 21-52; C. M. Wright, *Performance Practices at the Cathedral of Cambrai 1475-1550*, in MQ 64 (1978), pp. 295-328.

3. E. Nowacki, *The Latin Psalm Motet 1500-1535*, in Renaissance-Studien: Helmuth Osthoff zum 80. Geburtstag, ed. Ludwig Finscher (Tutzing 1979), pp. 159-84; A. M. Cummings, *Toward an Interpretation of the Sixteenth-Century Motet*, in JAMS 34 (1981), pp. 43-59; see also Nowacki's *Communication*, in JAMS 35 (1982), pp. 200-201, and Jeremy Noble's discussion printed above, pp. 9-22.

4. Cummings, *Toward an Interpretation* (see no. 3), pp. 45-6; H. Osthoff, *Josquin Desprez*, vol. II (Tutzing 1965), pp. 4-5; D. Fallows, *Dufay* (London 1982), pp. 61-2; D. van de Casteele, *Maîtres de chant et organistes de St-Donatien et de St-Sauveur à Bruges* (Bruges 1870), pp. 23-4.

5. D. Fallows, *Specific Information on the Ensembles for Composed Polyphony, 1400-1474*, in Studies in the Performance of Late Mediaeval Music, ed. Stanley Boorman (Cambridge 1983) pp. 109-59, passim; N. Pirrotta, *Music and Cultural Tendencies in 15th-Century Italy*, in JAMS 19 (1966), pp. 127-61, esp. pp. 128-39.

6. Even in the papal chapel after 1500 polyphony appears not to have been performed more than about once a week; see the balanced consideration in R. J. Sherr, *The Papal Chapel ca. 1492-1513 and its Polyphonic Sources* (diss., Princeton University 1975), pp. 86-109.

7. "Interea tantis tamque variis canoris vocibus quandoque concinebatur, tantis etiam symphoniis ad celum usque elatis interdum cantabatur. . . In sanctissimi corporis elevacione tantis armoniarum symphoniis, tantis insuper diversorum instrumentorum

consonationibus omnia basilice loca resonabant." Giannozzo Manetti, *Oratio de secularibus et pontificalibus pompis*; fully edited in Eugenio Battisti, *Il mondo visuale delle fiabe*, in Archivio di filosofia, 1960, ii/iii: Umanesimo e esoterismo (Padua 1960), pp. 291-320, on pp. 310-20; a full account of the manuscript sources is in H. W. Wittschier, *Giannozzo Manetti: das Corpus der Orationes* (Cologne and Graz 1968), pp. 52-8.

8. "Fu trionfante la Messa di organi, pifari, e trombetti e d'infiniti tamburini eziando di due capelle e di molti cantori, li quali cantavano mò l'uno, mò l'altro, et erano circa 16 cantori per capella." *Ordine delle nozze dell'Illustrissimo Signor Missier Constantio Sforza* (Vicenza 1475; copy in I-Vnm); see O. Kinkeldey, *Orgel und Klavier in der Musik des 16. Jahrhunderts* (Leipzig 1910), pp. 165-6, with reference to modern editions and one further source.

9. "Si condusse alla cattedrale. . . e poco dopo giunserò Roberto, Federigo, molti prelati, e l'ambasciarie tutte, ove subito si cantò da Bartolomeo vescovo Messa solenne, con una piena e sonora musica di diversi concerti d'istromenti, e di voci; & il levarsi del Santissimo Sacramento fu accompagnato da cento piferi, e da cinquanta trombetti, mandati da diverse potenze al servigio di queste nozze." Cesare Clementini, *Raccolto istorico della fondatione di Rimino* (Rimini 1617-27), vol. II, p. 528.

10. "Ne li dui extremi canti del coro erano facti doi lochi eminenti, l'uno per li cantori, l'altro per li trombetti. . . El reverendissimo arcivescovo de Mediolano. . . comenzò a celebrare la Missa cum grandissime solemnitate de soni de trombe, pifferi et organi et canti de la capella, li quali nel celebrare de la Missa se accomodavano al tempo suo." Letter of Beatrice d'Este to her sister Isabella, dated 29 December 1493: Mantua, Archivio Gonzaga, Busta 1612; see W. F. Prizer, *Bernardino Piffaro e i pifferi e tromboni di Mantova: strumenti a fiato in una corte italiana*, in RIM 16 (1981), pp. 151-84, on p. 175.

11. "Dinstag nach 'esto mihi' hat der Brewtigam und die Brawt sampt andern Fürsten und Fürstinnen in der Capeln auf dem Slosse Messe gehoret, haben die genannten Synger meiner gnedigsten und gnedigen Hern zwue Messen gesungen mit Hulf der Orgall, dreyer Posaun und eins Zincken, desgleichen vier Cromhorner zum Positief fast lustig zu horen." See B. Boydell, *The Crumhorn and other Renaissance Windcap Instruments* (Buren 1982), p. 16, and various other sources back to A. Aber, *Die Pflege der Musik unter den Wettinern und wettinischen Ernestinern* (Bückeburg 1921), p. 82, citing Weimar, Ernstinisches Gesamtarchiv, D.46.

12. "E in Roma una chiesecta di questo Santo [i.e. St Louis], ignobile, et che mai non vede 50 persone insieme; et questo anno, per havere facto la invitata lo Re di Francia a tutti li cardinali, oratori, prelati et baroni di Roma, stamattina vi è stato ogniuno, videlicet 16 cardinali, tutti l'ambasciatori si truovono in Roma, tutti li baroni et altri signori, e tutti stati a la Messa, che durò 3 hore di lungo. Fuvi la capella del Papa, che è cosa mirabile; li sua [i.e. the Pope's] pifferi che ad ogni cardinale arrivando li faceano lor dovere; tutti li trombecti; altri delicatissimi instrumenti, id est l'armonia papale che è cosa dulcisona et quasi divina; non sò per hora nominare nissuno de' sei instrumenti per nome, di che non credo Boetio facci mentione, quia ex Hispania." Letter from Agostino Vespucci da Terranova (the Florentine ambassador to Rome) to Machiavelli, dated 25 August 1501. fully edited in P. Villari, *Niccolò Machiavelli e i suoi tempi* (Florence 1877-82), vol. I, p. 561, citing Carte del Machiavelli, cassetta III, n. 39. The letter is discussed in Sherr, *The Papal Chapel* (see n. 6), pp. 114-5. These examples are by no means a comprehensive listing of the evidence, but they do attempt to include the most watertight examples from various parts of Europe. More are cited in W. Salmen, *Zur Geschichte der Ministriles im Dienste*

geistlicher Herren des Mittelalters, in Miscelánea en homenaje a Monseñor Higinio Anglés, ed. Miguel Querol (Barcelona 1958-61), pp. 811-19, on pp. 814-5, including the Breslau regulation of 1487 requiring the minstrels to play during Mass in the St Jakobskirche once a year on the Thursday before Shrove Tuesday. For pointing me to many such items I am most grateful to Hugh Robertson of North Carolina State University at Raleigh. In this context I should mention one incorrect reference which found its way into the spoken version of this paper. Art. *Te Deum,* in The New Grove 18, p. 643, asserts that at the coronation of Pope Pius III in 1503 "tibia una et tribus tubis contortis quos trombones vulgo appelant" responded to the intonations of the Te Deum; but the source cited – Curzio Mazzi, *La congrega dei Rozzi di Siena nel secolo XVI* (Florence 1882), vol. I, p. 46, transcribed from I-Fn Magl. XXVII, 18. 8, a report by (probably Simone) Borghesi – makes it clear that this is a description not of the coronation itself but of a spectacle mounted at Siena to celebrate the event.

13. See, for example, E. A. Bowles, *Musikleben im 15. Jahrhundert,* Musikgeschichte in Bildern, ed. W. Bachmann, III/8 (Leipzig 1977), plates 1-4, and additional pictures listed, *op. cit.,* p. 175.

14. I owe this observation to Peter Holman who has yet to publish his findings; similar conclusions can be drawn from discussions of the evolution of the viol in the last years of the 15th century in I. Woodfield, *The Early History of the Viol* (Cambridge 1984).

15. Boydell, *op. cit.,* pp. 14-20, 198-203 and passim; K. T. Meyer, *The Crumhorn: its History, Design, Repertory, and Technique* (Ann Arbor 1983), pp. 151-60 and passim.

16. J. Höfler, *Der 'trompette de menestrels' und sein Instrument,* in TVNM 29 (1979), pp. 92-132, esp. pp. 96f and 104f; A. C. Baines, art. *Trombone,* in The New Grove 19, p. 166.

17. D. Fallows, *15th-Century Tablatures for Plucked instruments: a Summary, a Revision and a Suggestion,* in The Lute Society Journal 19 (1977), pp. 7-33.

18. W. Edwards, *Songs without Words by Josquin and his Contemporaries,* in Music in Medieval and Early Modern Europe: Patronage, Sources and Texts, ed. I. Fenlon (Cambridge 1981), pp. 79-92; L. Litterick, *On Italian Instrumental Ensemble Music in the Late Fifteenth Century,* in Loc. cit., pp. 117-30; H. M. Brown, *A Florentine Chansonnier from the Time of Lorenzo the Magnificent: Florence, Biblioteca Nazionale Centrale MS Banco Rari 229,* Monuments of Renaissance Music, vol. VII (Chicago 1983), passim.

19. M. Schuler, *Die Musik in Konstanz während des Konzils 1414-1418,* in AcM 38 (1966), pp. 150-68, on. pp. 159 and 165.

20. J. Marix, *Histoire de la musique et des musiciens de la cour de Bourgogne sous le règne de Philippe le Bon (1420-1467)* (Strasbourg 1939), pp. 102-3.

21. D. Leech-Wilkinson, *Il libro di appunti di un suonatore di tromba del quindicesimo secolo,* in RIM 16 (1981), pp. 16-39.

22. St. Bonime, *The Musicians of the Royal Stable under Charles VIII and Louis XII (1484-1514),* in Current Musicology 25 (1978), pp. 7-21; see also H. Anglés, *La música en la Corte de los Reyes Católicos,* vol. I (MME I, Barcelona 1960), p. 51.

23. M. Brenet, *Notes sur l'introduction des instruments dans les églises de France,* in Riemann-Festschrift (Leipzig 1909), pp. 277-86, on pp. 280-2; see also M. Picker, *The Chanson Albums of Marguerite of Austria* (Berkeley and Los Angeles 1965), pp. 24-5.

24. On the use of music to glorify state occasions and demonstrate political power, see J. Stevens, *Music & Poetry in the Early Tudor Court* (London 1961), pp. 233-64, and R. F. Green, *Poets and Princepleasers: Literature and the English Court in the Late Middle Ages* (Toronto 1980), esp. pp. 17-8.

25. For the fullest account, see A. E. Planchart, *Parts with Words and without Words: the Evidence for Multiple Texts in Fifteenth-century Masses*, in Studies in the Performance of Late Mediaeval Music, ed. Stanley Boorman (Cambridge 1983), pp. 227-51, on pp. 229-30. The credit for first presenting this extraordinarily interesting body of information goes to M. Th. Bouquet, *La cappella musicale dei duchi di Savoia dal 1450 al 1500*, in RIM 3 (1968), pp. 233-85.

26. R. Stevenson, *Spanish Cathedral Music in the Golden Age* (Berkeley and Los Angeles 1961), p. 121, n. 170. F. W. Galpin, *Old English Instruments of Music* (rev. 4th edn., London 1965), p. 142, states that in 1532 Canterbury Cathedral had on its staff "duo Sambuciarii (vulgo Sackbutteers) et duo Cornutarii (vulgo Cornetteers)" (precise phrasing from Galpin, *The Sackbut, its Evolution and History*, in Proceedings of the Musical Association 33 (1906-7), pp. 1-25, on p. 15), but Dr Roger Bowers kindly assures me that this document in fact dates from 1632.

27. Stevenson, *op. cit.*, passim; Higinio Anglés, *La música en la Corte de los Reyes Católicos* (see n. 22) pp. 31 (Jaén Cathedral 1461), 32 (1468, 1470), 33-5 (1464, 1465), 48 (Seville Cathedral 1475), 49 (1478).

28. "Your grace shall also knowe, that the kynge was thys daye at Masse, at the Jacobyns, wher the hye Masse was songe by the bisshop of Amyens, and at the kynges offeryng, the chappel and the haultboys with sacbuttes sange and playde toghydder whych was as melodious a noyse as ever was harde; and at the retorne of hym fro the saide Masse, he callyd me unto hym and showyd me of his newes." Letter of Sir Richard Wingfield to Wolsey, London, Public Record Office, SP 1/20, pieces 91-2, summarized in J. S. Brewer, ed., *Calendar of Letters and Papers of the Reign of King Henry VIII*, vol. III, pt. 1 (London 1867), no. 843.

29. "Operosam quadam ac theatricam musicam in sacras aedes induximus. . . Omnia tubis, lituis, fistulis, ac sambucis perstrepunt, cumque his certant hominum voces." From his commentary on I Corinthians 14, 26 in *Novum testamentum*, ed. in *Desiderii Erasmi Roterdami opera omnia emendatiora et auctiora* (Leiden 1703-6), vol. VI, col. 731f. In this and the following passage I have without clear authority translated 'tuba', 'lituus' and 'fistula' as trumpet, cornett and shawm respectively; it is difficult to think that they can mean anything else, though very different translations appear in J.-C. Margolin, *Érasme et la musique* (Paris 1965), p. 49.

30. "Nunc res eo devenit, ut Templa lituis, fistulis ac tubis, atque adeo bombardis personent, vixque aliud audiatur quam varius vocum garritus, ac musices genus tam operosum atque lascivum, ut simile numquam habuerint Ethnicorum Theatra." From *Ecclesiastes, sive Concionator evangelicus*, ed. in *Desiderii Erasmi Roterdami opera* (see n. 29), vol. V, col. 942b; it is translated in Margolin, *op. cit.*, p. 64.

31. A similar point was made more briefly in H. M. Brown, *Choral Music in the Renaissance*, in Early Music 6 (1978), pp. 164-9, esp. pp. 167f.

32. See especially A. Schering, *Die niederländische Orgelmesse im Zeitalter des Josquin* (Leipzig 1912), and *Studien zur Musikgeschichte der Frührenaissance* (Leipzig 1914). The major statements against Schering's view appear in H. Leichtentritt, *Einige Bemerkungen über Verwendung der Instrumente im Zeitalter Josquin's*, in ZIMG 14 (1912-13), pp. 359-65, R. Haas, *Aufführungspraxis der Musik* (Potsdam 1931), pp. 98-100 and 135-7, and L. Hibberd, *On 'Instrumental Style' in Early Melody*, in MQ 32 (1946), pp. 107-30.

33. Here and in all later references to pieces in the Josquin *Werken* I have designated the work by two numbers: first, the *aflevering* number, for the benefit of those using sets bound in order of publication; second, the sequential number given to the actual piece, irrespective of whether it is among the *Motetten* or *Missen* unless there should be any reason for possible confusion (i.e. the presence of Latin works among the *Wereldlijke werken* or of a motet among the *Missen*).

34. By Dr John Milsom.

35. Fallows, *Specific Information* (see n. 5), pp. 131-43.

36. Kinkeldey, *Orgel und Klavier* (see n. 8), pp. 187-90. I might add here that the whole topic of organs taking part with the singers in polyphonic performance is among the slipperiest of all, though there is of course ample documentation for alternatim performance.

37. A. E. Planchart, *Fifteenth-century Masses: Notes on Performance and Chronology*, in Studi Musicali 10 (1981), pp. 3-29, offers a highly ingenious and important argument which may eventually provide the main exceptions that test my rule. He demonstrates beyond any question (pp. 13-15) that Obrecht's Mass *Caput* is misleadingly presented in its single surviving source: there are three voices with more or less consistent range throughout the cycle, whereas the voice carrying the *Caput* melody has a range of three octaves and is presented in the manuscript as, in the respective movements, Tenor, Discantus, Tenor, Contratenor and Bassus. It is difficult to resist his conclusion that the line is for performance on an organ; and that conclusion is obviously an important qualification of what I propose. He may well also be right in drawing the same conclusion for Ockeghem's Mass *L'homme armé*, though here the 'Tenor' presents few problems that are not also found in the Bassus (and the Mass *Prolationum* includes similar problems).

38. The work is texted in precisely this way in D-Mbs Mus. Ms. 34, but the word "Salve" is always written in red. Elsewhere in that manuscript (as in several others, especially from the same Alamire workshop) it seems clear enough that red ink is used for words that are not to be sung: ascriptions; "verte" at the end of the page; and the names of tunes on which a particular work is based. Yet Josquin's *Salve regina* opens the manuscript and is in some ways more elaborately done, with pictorial initials; it is also possible that the pattern of the remainder of the manuscript was not yet established when this piece was entered.

39. Among the many sources for the chanson there are two that do in fact apply text to the tenor line: the Chansonnier Cordiforme (F-Pn Rothschild 2973) and D-Mbs Mus. Ms. 9659. For considerations against taking such information literally, see my discussion of texting in G. Thibault and D. Fallows, eds., *Le Chansonnier de Jean de Montchenu* (Paris forthcoming).

40. E. E. Lowinsky, *The Medici Codex of* 1518 (Chicago 1968), commentary to no. 48 (pp. 223-4).

41. There is one circumstance in which bitextual performance might be acceptable for this piece. Notre-Dame de Paris had in 1500 a canon named Nicolas de Haqueville; see C. Wright, *Antoine Brumel and Patronage at Paris*, in Music in Medieval and Early Modern Europe: Patronage, Sources and Texts, ed. I. Fenlon (Cambridge 1981), pp. 37-60, on pp. 54f. Mouton appears to have been frequently in Paris as a result of his association with the French royal family, perhaps from as early as 1499 but certainly from 1502, see H. M. Brown, art. *Mouton*, in The New Grove 12, pp. 656-60. Josquin's association with the court remains difficult to document but must have been in the years around 1500.

Thus either of the possible composers of the work could well have known Canon Nicolas de Haqueville, who made a special accommodation on account of the composer Brumel and whose family had evidently been patrons of Busnois some years earlier. The possibility that *Missus est angelus Gabriel* was a special commission from Nicolas de Haqueville cannot therefore be ruled out; and in such circumstances it must be considered conceivable that the Tenor was indeed to be sung to the d'Haqueville text of Busnois. On the other hand, W. Elders, *Zur Aufführungspraxis der altniederländischen Musik*, in Renaissance-Muziek: donum natalicium René Bernard Lenaerts, ed. J. Robijns (Leuven 1969), pp. 89-104, on pp. 98-102, offers compelling source-based arguments in favour of instrumental performance for the Tenor of both *Stabat mater* and *Missus est angelus Gabriel*.

42. D'Accone, *The Performance of Sacred Music in Italy* (see n. 2), pp. 603-9.

43. F. Ll. Harrison has done this for England, see *The Social Position of Church Musicians in England, 1450-1550*, in Report of the Eighth Congress [of the International Musicological Society] New York 1961, ed. J. LaRue (Kassel 1961-2), vol. I, pp. 346-55.

44. F. Lesure, *Pour une sociologie historique des faits musicaux*, in Report of the Eighth Congress [of the International Musicological Society] New York 1961, ed. J. LaRue (Kassel 1961-2), Vol. I, pp. 333-46, on pp. 337-8; Lesure, *Archival Research: Necessity and Opportunity*, in Perspectives in Musicology, ed. B. S. Brook, E. O. D. Downes and S. van Solkema (New York 1972), pp. 56-71, on. pp. 63 and 70.

45. The fundamental statement on this remains M. F. Bukofzer's 'The Beginnings of Choral Polyphony' in his *Studies in Medieval and Renaissance Music* (New York 1950), pp. 176-89.

46. F. A. D'Accone, *The Singers of San Giovanni in Florence during the 15th Century*, in JAMS 14 (1961), pp. 307-58, on p. 324.

47. Fallows, *Specific Information* (see n. 5), on pp. 110-7 and 122-6.

48. D. Fallows, *Robert Morton's Songs: a Study of Styles in the Mid-fifteenth Century* (diss., U. of California at Berkeley, 1979), pp. 303-24.

49. W. Boetticher, *Orlando di Lasso und seine Zeit, 1532-1594* (Kassel 1958), pp. 858-60, including the statement that the names are in Lasso's own hand. Also in the same hand, it seems to me, are numbers above any ligature more complex than the usual *cum opposita proprietate*, which would imply that Lasso's use in 1568-70 of a manuscript copied well before 1530 was exceptional. The Mass is published in *Antoine Brumel: opera omnia* (CMM V), ed. B. Hudson, vol. III (1970), though it might be noted that since the final verso of the manuscript is blank one should look with suspicion on the editor's view that an extra Agnus Dei (in only six voices) can be added from elsewhere.

50. W. Boetticher, *Aus Orlando di Lassos Wirkungskreis: neue archivalische Studien zur Münchener Musikgeschichte* (Kassel 1963), pp. 56-7, gives the full chapel list for 1568-9; see also A. Sandberger, *Beiträge zur Geschichte der bayerischen Hofkapelle unter Orlando di Lasso*, vol. III (Leipzig 1895), pp. 35-6. The manuscript itself (D-Mbs Mus. Ms. 1) is easily read from seven metres' distance, which might imply that Brumel originally envisaged a comparably large ensemble for the work.

51. Fallows, *Specific Information* (see n. 5), pp. 119-20, and F. X. Haberl, *Bausteine für Musikgeschichte*, vol. III (Leipzig 1888), pp. 48-52.

52. G. Cattin, *Church Patronage of Music in Fifteenth-century Italy*, in Music in Medieval and Early Modern Europe: Patronage, Sources and Texts, ed. Iain Fenlon (Cambridge 1981), pp. 21-36, on pp. 22-4.

53. The fullest assembly of references is in O. F. Becker, *The Maîtrise in Northern France and Burgundy during the Fifteenth Century* (diss., George Peabody College for Teachers, 1967).

54. Sherr, *The Papal Chapel* (see n. 6), p. 79. However, given the extraordinary difficulty of being confident about such *ex vacuo* generalisations, it might be worth mentioning two details that could be construed as suggesting that boys occasionally took part but must almost certainly be construed otherwise. Both are in manuscripts that were prepared for the papal chapel. First, F. X. Haberl, *Bausteine für Musikgeschichte*, vol. II (Leipzig 1888), p. 14, mentions decorative initials at the beginning of a four-voice work in I-Rvat Cappella Sistina 35, f. 22, depicting four boys and five men; and he concludes: "diese vierstimmigen Sätze scheinen also mit einer Besetzung von 9 Sängern ausgeführt zu sein." In fact these drawings would be better described as adult faces and baby faces; their distribution shows no logic except pictorial convenience; the faces are entirely schematic, scarcely portraits, and they show no signs even of representing singers; moreover they continue in varying numbers for many folios thereafter, stretching into at least two further works (f. 23v-24, for example, has thirteen faces: one for the Discantus, four (including a baby) for the Contra, three for the Tenor and five for the Bassus). These drawings contain no possible information about performing ensembles. The second detail is more difficult: I-Rvat Cappella Sistina 160 designates the second line of Isaac's Mass *Paschale*, on f. 91, 'secundus puer'; but on that topic see the considerations to be raised in the remainder of this paper.

55. Sherr, *The Papal Chapel* (see n. 6), pp. 66-7, gives a full list of Josquin works in the Cappella Sistina manuscripts; it includes fourteen of the Masses, omitting only the Masses *Di dadi, Mater Patris, Sine nomine* and *Una musque de Biscaya*, which happen simply to be the four Masses with the smallest number of sources.

56. C. Wright, *Performance Practices* (see n. 2), on pp. 305-6.

57. Fallows, *Specific Information* (see n. 5), pp. 122-5.

58. I-Rvat Chigiana, C. VIII. 234, f. 262; see *Johannis Regis: opera omnia* (CMM IX), ed. C. W. H. Lindenburg, vol. II (1956), pp. 5-13.

59. F. 168; see *Johannis Regis: omnia opera*, vol. II, pp. 49-60, and commentary on p. 5.

60. *Heinrich Isaac: opera omnia* (CMM LXV), ed. E. R. Lerner, vol. I (1974), pp. 1-10.

61. See n. 54.

62. F. 43v-44; these designations do not appear elsewhere in the piece, nor indeed anywhere else in this manuscript, a large collection of 29 *Salve regina* settings from the Alamire workshop. The motet is published in *Werken van Jacob Obrecht*, ed. J. Wolf, vol. VI (afl. 2), pp. 1-14.

63. The same conclusion is reached by R. Bowers in his review of a recording of the motet, in Early Music 8 (1980), p. 257.

64. F. 48. The Mass is published in *Johannes Ockeghem, Collected Works*, ed. D. Plamenac, vol. II (rev. 2/1966), pp. 65-76.

65. See also *Johannes Ockeghem* (see n. 64), p. XXXIII.

66. Fallows, *Specific Information* (see n. 5), pp. 114-6.

67. Wright, *Antoine Brumel and Patronage at Paris* (see n. 41), pp. 51-2. The motet is published in *Antoine Brumel: opera omnia* (CMM V) ed. B. Hudson, vol. V (1972), pp. 6-7.

68. Josquin's authorship for this motet has been doubted by both Osthoff, *Josquin Desprez*, vol. II (Tutzing 1965), p. 80, and J. Noble in the worklist to art. *Josquin Desprez*, in The

New Grove 9, pp. 728-36, on p. 735. Its repetitive form, repeated D cadences and somewhat aimless partwriting would endorse their doubts.

69. R. Bowers, *The Performing Pitch of English 15th-Century Church Polyphony*, in Early Music 8 (1980), pp. 21-8; Bowers, *Further Thoughts on Early Tudor Pitch*, in *ibid.*, pp. 368-75; and Bowers, *The Performing Ensemble for English Church Polyphony, c. 1320- c. 1390*, in Studies in the Performance of Late Mediaeval Music, ed. S. Boorman (Cambridge 1983), pp. 161-92.

70. Fallows, *Specific Information* (see n. 5), pp. 111-2.

71. *Op. cit.*, pp. 122-6.

72. A. Mendel, *Towards Objective Criteria for Establishing Chronology and Authenticity: What Help can the Computer Give?*, in Josquin des Prez (see n. 1), pp. 297-308, presents, p. 301, a list of ranges for Josquin's Masses as calculated by a computer, including the information that two of the Masses have a total range of twenty-three notes. These figures appear to be incorrect, as do some of the other ranges presented there; and presumably they go back to faulty insertion of the data. My own information on ranges here and in the subsequent paragraphs is based on calculations made by hand and eye. It would be idle to insist that they are absolutely correct, but the crucial ones have been carefully checked, and the remainder are, I hope, sufficiently accurate for the present purposes.

73. The passage is published in *Guillaume Dufay: opera omnia* (CMM I), ed. H. Besseler, vol. II (Rome 1960), p. 67. On the identification of this work, published by Besseler and others as the Mass *Sancti Antonii Viennensis*, see D. Fallows, *Dufay* (London 1982), pp. 182-5.

74. GB-WRec 178: complete edition in *The Eton Choirbook*, ed. F. Ll. Harrison, Musica Britannica X-XII (²1967-73). This edition most usefully indicates the precise range of each voice (a feature astonishingly absent from most scholarly editions until comparatively recently); and the manuscript itself contains an original index that gives the total range of each work (see XII, pp. 180-82; but note that the range of Richard Davy's *Virgo templum trinitatis* is twenty-three notes, not twenty-two as given in the index). These ranges, with considerable further information on the manuscript, appear also in F. Ll. Harrison, *The Eton Choirbook: its Background and Contents*, in AnnM I (1953), pp. 151-75.

75. D. Wulstan, *The Problem of Pitch in Sixteenth-century English Vocal Music*, in PRMA 93 (1966-7), pp. 97-112; H. Benham, *Latin Church Music in England c. 1460-1575* (London 1977), pp. 30-5; P. Le Huray, *Music and the Reformation in England 1549-1660* (Cambridge ²1978), pp. 119-24; D. S. Josephson, *John Taverner Tudor Composer* (Ann Arbor 1979), pp. 127-8; Roger Bowers, *opp. cit.* (see n. 69); R. Bray, *More Light on Early Tudor Pitch*, in Early Music 8 (1980), pp. 35-42; Chr. Page, A. Parrott and R. Bowers, *False Voices*, in Early Music 9 (1981), pp. 71-5; and, at the greatest length, David Wulstan, *Vocal Colour in English sixteenth-century Polyphony*, in Journal of the Plainsong & Mediaeval Music Society 2 (1979), pp. 19-60. P. Phillips, *Performance Practice in 16th-century English Choral Music*, in Early Music 6 (1978), pp. 195-9, on p. 198 mentions that "many foreigners remarked on the extraordinary phenomenon of the high *trebles. . .* in 16th-century English choirs", but he gives no documentation. Strangely enough the only relevant report I can find suggests the opposite. It is in a letter from Nicolò Sagudino to Alvise Foscari, dated 3 May 1515, with the comment: "Ditta messa fu cantata per la capella de questa Maestà [Henry VIII], qual veramente à più presto divina che humana; non

cantavano ma jubilavano, et maxime de contrabassi, che non credo al mondo sieno li pari", see *I diarii di Marino Sanuto*, ed. F. Stefani, vol. XX (Venice 1887), col. 266.

76. The one 'doubtful' work with that range is the twelve-voice *Inviolata, integra et casta es* (Supp. 10), ascribed only in a later source of notable untrustworthiness, presumably through confusion with Josquin's famous five-voice motet of the same title (25/42).

77. There is no apparent chronological sense to the pattern of these ranges: thirteen-note range appears in pieces by one early composer, Hugo Kellyk (his five-voice *Magnificat*, no. 45), and one of the youngest, William Cornysh (his five-voice *Stabat mater*, no. 30); twelve-note range is spread evenly across the years covered by Eton.

78. I have included all complete motets in the *Werken* whose position in the Josquin canon has never been questioned – but excluding *Magnificat* and hymn settings. The most up-to-date summary is in J. Noble's excellent worklist for art. *Josquin Desprez*, in The New Grove 9, pp. 729-31. Among the four-voice motets, I have retained *Planxit autem David* (6/20) and *Virgo prudentissima* (9/25), for nobody seriously doubts their authorship, despite contrary ascriptions. The cycle of five Circumcision motets, *O admirabile commercium* (2/5-9), has been counted as one piece; similarly, *Christum ducem* (2/4) has been considered only as part of the cycle *Qui velatus facie* (4/11). That leaves 46 four-part motets. (There are works even here in which the stylistic and documentary evidence for Josquin's authorship is decidedly slim, but this is not the place to be entering into disputes about the authenticity of Josquin works, merely one to establish a rational way of discussing the voice-ranges that he used.) The undisputed five-voice motets are nine in number (that is, excluding *Huc me sydereo* (16/32) as being in six voices, despite Jeremy Noble's obviously correct observation, *loc. cit.*, p. 722, that it was originally conceived in five voices). Among the six-voice motets, seven works remain. Noble's doubts about *Sic Deus dilexit mundum* (51/86) and *Christus mortuus est* (51/87) are refined at length by J. Milsom, *Circumdederunt: 'a favourite Cantus Firmus of Josquin's'?*, in Soundings 9 (1982), pp. 2-10. This approach, leaving Josquin with a mere sixty-three motets, may seem drastic; but to consider, for example, all the motets published in the *Werken* would be to include too much that cannot be by Josquin.

79. This is the added voice of *Huc me sydereo* (16/32) mentioned in the preceding note.

80. It seems clear enough that this extraordinary range was not favoured for very long or very widely. Among the thirty-two four-voice motets in the Medici Codex of 1518, the 128 voices include only twelve with twelve-note range. Moreover, Nicola Vicentino, *L'antica musica ridotta alla moderna pratica* (Rome 1555), Bk 4, ch 17, required that music in up to seven voices have a range of no more than nineteen notes plus a semitone, but permitted a range of up to twenty-two notes when in eight or more voices "per commodità delle parti". He added that "per commodità de i cantanti, & acciò che ogni voce commune possi cantare la sua parte commoditamente. . . mai si dè aggiognere righa alcuna, alle cinque righe, ne di sotto, ne di sopra, in nissuna parte ne manco mutar chiavi." The same is said more obliquely in Gioseffo Zarlino, *Le istitutioni harmoniche* (Venice 1558) Bk 3, ch 47: "Ne debbe comportare, che le estremità delle parti trappassino nel grave, o nell'acuto fuora de i loro termini, contra la loro natura, & contra la natura del modo, sopra il quale è fondata la cantilena; cioè non debbe fare, che il soprano pigli il luogo del tenore, ne questo il luogo del soprano: ma fare, che ciascuna parte stia nelli suoi termini."

81. Ganassi reports Gombert's view that in cases of extreme range one should "pitch the

piece so that the lowest notes of the bass are just audible"; see H. M. Brown, *Notes (and Transposing Notes) on the Viols in the Early Sixteenth Century*, in Music in Medieval and Early Modern Europe: Patronage, Sources and Texts, ed. I. Fenlon (Cambridge 1981), pp. 61-78, on p. 78.

82. All of these figures cast a flexibly blind eye on the two exceptionally wide ranges in Josquin's sacred music: that of the added bass in the third Agnus of the Mass *Mater Patris* (26/12) and that of the added sixth voice in *Huc me sydereo* (16/32). It is perhaps worth mentioning that I can find no apparent chronological pattern to the various details of range distribution and pitch-standard in Josquin's sacred music, though it remains perfectly possible that such considerations may eventually help to refine the chronology.

83. Fallows, *Specific Information* (see n. 5), pp. 111-5.

84. See art. *Orchestra*, in The New Grove 13, pp. 679-91, esp. p. 690, including Handel's 1728 distribution at the King's Theatre: 28 violins, 2 violas, 3 cellos, 2 basses.

85. R. Rasch, *Aspects of the Perception and Performance of Polyphonic Music* (Utrecht 1981).

86. This information is normally quoted from N. Bridgman's absorbing *La vie musicale au quattrocento* (Paris 1964), p. 197, where there is no documentation; and its context might seem to imply that it concerns 15th-century music. I am most grateful to Laura Macy for locating the reference and assembling the relevant contextual information. The letter to Ottavio Farnese from Carlo Durante concerning a new contralto dates from 11 January 1568 and reads as follows: "è sicurissimo nel cantare, compone e ha bonissimo contraponto; però mi dice che si crede che per voce da camera hora non lo servirà, perchè quasi sempre canta o in capella overo in casa perchè fa scuola; et come la voce sara riposata si crede gli servirà per camera", see N. Pelicelli, *Musicisti in Parma nei secoli XV-XVI: la capella alla Corte Farnese*, in Note d'archivio 9 (1932), pp. 41-9, on p. 45, citing a letter in Parma, Archivio di stato, Mazzo I, Teatri, 1545-1697. The earliest clear reference to the difference in volume between church and chamber singing is in Nicola Vicentino, *L'antica musica* (see n. 80), Bk 4, ch 29: "nelle chiese. . . si canterà con le voci piene, & con moltitudine de cantanti. . . ma nella musica da camera, cioe quando si cantera piano. . ." Zarlino says the same in *Le istitutioni harmoniche* (Venice 1558), Bk 3 ch 45: "Ad altro modo si canta nelle chiese & nelle capelle publiche, & ad altro modo nelle private camere: imperoche ivi si canta a piena voce. . . & nelle camere si canta con voce piu sommessa & soave, senza fare alcun strepito." Similarly Lodovico Zacconi, *Prattica di musica* (Venice 1592), Bk 1, ch 40, writes: "chi dice che col gridar forte le voci si fanno s'inganna doppiamente, prima perche molti imparano di cantare per cantar piano & nelle cammere, ove s'abborisce il gridar forte, & non sono dalla necessità astretti a cantar nelle chiese, ò nelle capelle ove cantano i cantori stipendiati." Concerning these matters see also M. Uberti, *Vocal Techniques in Italy in the Second Half of the 16th Century*, in Early Music 9 (1981), pp. 486-95. While this essay was in proof William Prizer kindly supplied the wording of a document which almost certainly implies this camera/chiesa distinction as early as the 15th century. On 24 October 1491, Francesco Bagnacavallo wrote to Isabella d'Este reporting her brother's views on a new Hungarian soprano: "dice che non ha grande vocce da capella, ma che da camera è suficienti et dice che canta bene in uno liuto, una violla, in tali istromenti sa cantare bene." Mantua, Archivio Gonzaga, Busta 1232, f. 97, mentioned in passing in W. F. Prizer, *Courtly Pastimes: the Frottole of Marchetto Cara* (Ann Arbor 1980), pp. 7 and 12.

87. Wulstan, *Vocal Colour* (see n. 75), pp. 20-9.

[9]

Performance practice in the Papal Chapel during the 16th century

Richard Sherr

The suggestion was recently made in this journal by Jean Lionnet that polyphony in the Papal Chapel was normally performed by soloists during the 17th century.[1] My purpose in this article is to consider similar questions of performance practice for the 16th century, by examining documents from that period (often unspecific and ambiguous) in conjunction with some from the 18th century (generally specific and unambiguous).

A 16th-century memorandum preserved in the archives of the Cappella Sistina in the Vatican Library appears to contain notes taken by Antonio Calasanz, one of those who attended a meeting of the papal singers on 24 July 1564. The purpose of the meeting, which was called by the *maestro di cappella*, was to reinstitute certain practices that had been usual in the papal choir but had fallen into disuse (hence, practices that could have been followed in the early 16th century). One of these concerned the way the singers grouped themselves around the music lectern:

Antiquitatus ad decantandam musicam cantores prout D. Decanus petulit costruebant [ante legium seu facistorium hoc videlicet modo: − in the margin] suprani ad sinistram et contralti ad dexteram prope legium seu facistorium, et tenores ad sinistram retro suprani et bassi ad dexteram retro contralti.[2]

Formerly, when music was sung, the singers, as the dean requested, stood in front of the lectern in this way: sopranos on the left and contraltos on the right of the lectern, and tenors on the left at the back of the sopranos and basses on the right at the back of the contraltos.

This is, of course, precisely the grouping that would be expected, for it exactly mirrors the layout of the parts in the manuscripts. As well as providing documentary confirmation, even of the obvious, it also explains various references in the *Diarii Sistini*[3] to the fining of contraltos for not turning the page in time.[4] But the contraltos seem to have had several specific functions, for Calasanz went on to discuss another practice whose neglect was causing difficulties:

Officium contraltorum erat in servire pro ebdomad[ari]us et querere divina officia dei [illegible word] tam in cantu plano quam figurato.

The office of the contraltos was to act as the hebdomadarius, and to find out the [pieces to be sung during] Divine Office of the day, whether in chant or in polyphony.

He added that because the contraltos had not been carrying out this duty there were daily errors and incidents in the chapel.[5] Chapter XV of the 1545 Constitution of the Chapel also refers to the contraltus hebdomadarius, stating specifically that he was responsible for indicating which books were to be put on the lectern.[6] The *Diarii Sistini* testify further to the special function of the contraltos by recording times when they failed in their duties.[7] The hebdomadarius was normally the person chosen on a weekly basis to celebrate the liturgy; in the case of singers, the term appears to refer to the person who chose the polyphony and made sure that the correct order of pieces was followed. Why this person had to be a contralto, however, is not clear.

The instruction 'Let this custom be observed by the most senior and expert [singers]' was added in the margin beside another of Calasanz's comments:

Antiquitatus in decantanda musica, vox que primo incipiebat [cuiuslibet vocis—in margin] videlicet supranus, tenor, altus, vel bassus intonabat ad libitum suum.[8]

Formerly when singing music, the voice which began first whatever it is—that is, soprano, tenor, alto or bass—intoned as he wished.

Though it is not at first clear what is meant by 'intoning', it is most likely that Calasanz is talking about setting the pitch level (the main function of an intonation) both in chant and in polyphony (hence, his use of the general term 'musica', instead of 'cantus planus' or 'cantus figuratus'). When they performed in the Sistine Chapel, the papal choir sang without the accompaniment of instruments. There was thus no

1   The canonization of Carlo Borromeo, 1610: interior of St Peter's, Rome. Engraving by G. Maggi (Biblioteca Angelica, Rome)

way of giving the pitch to the choir (through an instrumental toccata, for instance), and the solution seems to have been to allow whoever began to choose the pitch level. This is implied also by a decision recorded after an apostolic visitation of the choir in 1630:

Quando si ha da cominciare a cantare, ciascuno lasci cominciare il più vecchio, quale se non intonarà bene, doverà essere punctato con rigore.[9]

When the singing begins, everyone will allow the oldest singer [of his voice part] to begin, and if he does not intone well, he should be severely fined.

18th-century documents clarify the meaning of 'intoning', and demonstrate that the pitch level was determined by the first singer, who began without any reference to an absolute pitch. The problems that could arise concerning pitch level were addressed by Matteo Fornari, who in the midst of a general discussion about castrati in the Papal Chapel attempted to explain why there were no contralto castrati in the choir.[10] The reason he gave was that their level tessitura was not low enough, so that:

Nelle cantilene dove i contralti danno il primo regolamento della voce al rimanente del coro, si prendesse il tuono dai contralti non naturale, questo riuscirebbe alto in forma si disadatta alle altre parti che renderebbe, anziché armonia, una notabile confusione, et così derogherebbesi affatto a quella gravità ecclesiastica con cui si è sempre conservato il canto della pontificia cappella.[11]

In the music where the contraltos give the first indication of the pitch to the rest of the choir, if one were to take the pitch from the unnatural contraltos [castrati], this would turn out to be so high in such bad relation to the other parts that it would cause notable confusion instead of harmony, and would thus detract from the ecclesiastical gravity which the music of the pontifical chapel has always maintained.

Another treatise, the *Istruzione per gl'officiali della cappella pontificia*, contains a passage that must refer to the same problem; that of the singers starting at an inappropriate pitch level:

Alli 28 di Gennaro 1718 fu stabilito che in qualsivoglia cantilena o di canto figurato o di canto fermo, quando si prendesse la voce troppo alta o troppa bassa, e conoscendo non poterla seguitare, sia obligato l'anziano che prende la voce a calare o crescere, ma prima deve avvisare il coro. Quando poi entrassero tutte le parti assieme, o fosse nel canto fermo, sia obligato l'anziano de' bassi sempre dando prima l'avviso al coro, e non facendolo sia sotto posto al punto.[12]

On 28 January 1718, it was decided that in whatever music whether in chant or polyphony, when the pitch chosen is too high or too low, and realizing that he cannot continue, the

senior singer who chose the pitch is obliged to lower or raise [it], but first he must advise the choir. When all the parts enter together [that is, at the same time], or in chant, the senior bass is obliged, always first advising the choir, and if he does not do this let him be fined.

References in the *Diarii Sistini* of the early 18th century (including Diary 147 of 1728 compiled by Fornari himself) also show that the word 'intonare' is to be read in its usual sense. All pieces, whether chant or polyphony, apparently began with an intonation; that is, the senior bass intoned the beginning of the chant[13] and the senior singer of whichever part began the polyphony sang the first few notes as a means of giving the pitch (rather than humming or singing a single note as might be done today); this was followed by a new start from the beginning either by the whole choir for chant or by all the singers of the appropriate part for polyphony.[14] This seems to be the only explanation for problems such as that recorded in the *Diarii* for 2 November 1700:

L'Antiano, nel principiare la Gloria, non tenne la prima nota, la quale valeva due battute, benché da suoi compagni fosse stata tenuta giusta, onde rese qualche sconcerto, & perciò – si punta solo il Signor Gagliardi.[15]

The senior singer, when beginning the Gloria, did not hold the first note which was worth two beats [long enough], although it was held correctly by his companions; this caused some confusion and therefore only Signore Gagliardi [the senior contralto] was fined.

The reference to 'battute' suggests that this was 'measured music' or polyphony, and the senior contralto must have begun by singing the actual music; furthermore, there would have been no way of knowing if he had held the first note for a different length of time than the others if he had not sung it first and they followed. Another reference is even clearer:

Nel principiar la Messa, cioè il primo Chirie, toccava a principiare alli signori tenori. Il signor Mezzoni, toccando a lui a pigliare come primo anziano, invece di principiar Chirie disse A quasi volesse dire Amen o Alleluia, per tale inavertenza si punta il signor Mazzoni 05.[16]

At the beginning of the Mass, that is, the first Kyrie, the tenors were to begin. It fell to Signor Mazzoni to choose [the pitch], as he was the senior singer, [but] instead of beginning with 'Kyrie', he sang 'A', almost as if he wanted to sing 'Amen' or 'Alleluia'. For such negligence, Signor Mazzoni is fined 5 [baiocchi].

Similarly, on 8 September 1728, four sopranos were fined:

Per aver alterato il tuono della voce presa dall'anziano al mottetto, che cagionò molto stonamento.[17]

For having altered the pitch taken from the senior singer in the motet, which caused much disharmony.

Altering a pitch given as a single note would hardly cause 'disharmony', but repeating at a different pitch the opening of the piece would surely be noticed. And it would be easier to alter the pitch if a piece was actually begun anew, rather than for the alteration to occur as other singers joined a piece that had already begun.

There was sometimes confusion when singers forgot who was to perform the intonation.

Avendo presa al motetto O magnum il Sig. Baldini anziano la voce, la presse nell'istesso tempo ancora il Sig. Resi sottoanziano un tuono più basso, di modo che obligò l'anziano a cedere, con qualche sconcerto; ondo è puntato il Sig. Resi b. 20.[18]

The senior singer Signor Baldini, having begun to give the pitch [that is, begun singing] for the motet O magnum, the vice-senior Signor Resi began singing at the same time a whole step lower and forced the senior singer to stop singing, which caused certain confusion; for which Signor Resi is fined 20 baiocchi.

Nell'agnus dei della messa a 4 voce del Pelestrina, dovendo il Sig. Bastianelli anziano de'contralti pigliar la prima voce al cenno del sig. maestro, e avendo negligente tardato, pigliò il Sig. Mattia la voce col quale si seguitò la cantilena, ma per avere il Sig. Bastianelli sopragiunta la voce dissonante, si punta il medemo S. Bastianelli bai. 20.[19]

In the Agnus Dei of the 4-voice Mass by Palestrina, Signor Bastianelli, senior contralto, was supposed to give the pitch at the cue of the maestro, but as he waited negligently, Signor Mattia gave this pitch with which the singing continued. But because Signor Bastianelli added a dissonant pitch, he is fined 20 baiocchi.

A reference for 6 April [Good Friday] 1703 concerns the occasion mentioned by Fornari when all the parts entered together and the responsibility for intoning fell on the senior bass. The piece being performed was the *falsobordone* setting of the *Improprerii* by Palestrina.

Incominciato l'Improprii, cioè Popule meus a due chori a 8. finito che hebbe il primo choro il primo verso, attacò il secundo choro l'altro verso Quia eduscit te, pigliando la medesima voce che lasciò il primo choro, dove dovevano pigliare nel lasciar che fece il primo choro una quarta sopra. Ma l'errore lo fece il basso che si pigliò male l'intonatione, dunque per tale errore vien puntato solo il signor Spinacciati 20.[20]

We began the Improprerii, that is 'Popule meus' *a* 8 for two choirs. The first choir had sung the first verse, the second choir began the next verse 'Quia eduscit te', taking the same pitch on which the first choir ended, instead of beginning a 4th higher than the ending pitch of the first choir. The error

2 Detail from illus.1, showing the five singers

was made by the bass who sang the intonation incorrectly, therefore for that error only Signor Spinacciati will be fined 20 [baiocchi].

An incident that occured on 1 March 1700 points again to the duties of the senior singer of each voice, and also to those of the contraltus hebdomadarius, with regard to repertory.

Questa mattina per esser giornata feriale, è solito cantarsi, solamente il Sanctus e l'Agnus Dei. Il contralto edomadario inavertentemente prende la messa a quatro intitolata Missa paris vocibus di Vincenzo Pellegrini, con un mezzo soprano, due tenori, et un basso. Terminato il Prefatio, toccava a principiare il Sanctus alla parte del tenore, la quale era situata nel luogo del contralto, e per esser la chiave in terza riga, il suddetto, susponendo che fosse la sua parte, la principiò come anziano in voce di contralto, dal che ne nacque grandissimo sconcento, onde per tale inavertanza non essendo mai solito cantarsi niuna Messa senza contralto, e per essere l'errore molto sensibile, il puntatore in vigore del capitolo 3. a delli novi regolamenti, punta il Signor Gagliardi 20.[21]

This morning, since it was ferial feast day, it is the custom to sing only the Sanctus and Agnus Dei. The contraltus hebdomadarius, without thinking, chose the Mass for four voices entitled 'Missa paris vocibus' by Vincenzo Pellegrini, with a mezzo-soprano, two tenors and one bass. After the Preface, the tenor part was supposed to begin the Sanctus, which was placed [in the choirbook] in the position of the altus,[22] but because the clef was on the third line, the above mentioned [contralto], thinking that it was his part began it, as [he was] the senior contralto. Great disharmony came from this mistake, it never having occurred that a Mass was sung without the contralto part, and because the error was very obvious, the punctator, according to Chapter 3 of the new regulations, fined Signor Gagliardi 20 [baiocchi].

What this seems to mean is that Signor Gagliardi had momentarily forgotten that he had chosen a Mass *a voci pari*, in which the contralto part appeared on the upper left of the choirbook in the space usually reserved for the soprano. Instead, following the tradition whereby the senior singer of the part that began the piece 'intoned' the beginning, he started to read from the normal place for the contralto part (upper right), which in this case was occupied by one of the tenor lines. But the real problem here (that the Sanctus was sung without the contralto part) is best explained by assuming it was being performed with one singer on a part, so that when the one contralto began singing the tenor part, there was no other contralto to sing the correct part.

The question of solo performance is, of course, the crux of the matter. The use of the word 'intonare' implies continuation by a choir, and the fact that countless fines are recorded in the 18th-century *Diarii* to groups of singers on the same part for making mistakes in the performance of polyphony suggests strongly that choral performance was by then the rule.[23] Occasionally, however, the pattern of fines suggests performance by soloists: this tends to relate to *terzi e quarti* (trio and quartet sections).[24] As Lionnet has pointed out, the *Diarii Sistini* and other documents from the 17th century are full of references to *terzi e quarti*, phrased in such a way as to indicate that they were sung by soloists. Mention is made of fines for singers who refused to sing them, and exhortations that the Master of the Chapel be very careful in choosing the right singers.[25] Corroboration that this continued in the 18th century comes from Matteo Fornari who described the process of auditioning for a bass for the Sistine Chapel in 1737:

Invocato dal signor maestro lo spirito santo, si chiamono uno per volta dal custode li concorrenti videlicet per la voce di basso, e fatto salire sul coro dove si ritrovano alcuno signori cantori, stando gli altri a sedere al bancone dell'emminentissimi cardinali. Si trova un terzo col basso, e gli si fa cantare in concerto.[26]

The Custode calls the applicants for the position of bass one by one, and has them ascend to the singers' box where a few other singers are, the rest of the singers sit on the benches reserved for the cardinals. A trio is found to sing with the bass, and they sing in concert.

Since the point of the audition was to judge the applicant's voice, the *terzo* must have consisted of soloists: presumably it allowed the singers to hear how well the applicant blended with others.[27]

But can this have any relevance for the 16th century? Although we must proceed cautiously in attempting to extrapolate backwards from a period of the papal choir's decadence (the 18th century) to the period of its greatest glory, Calasanz's 1564 statements concerning the contraltus hebdomadarius and the intonations are a direct link between those two centuries, and imply that those practical matters of performance had not changed. On the question of solo performance in the 16th century, however, there is evidence both to support and to contradict the hypothesis defended by Lionnet. First of all, Calasanz's use of 'intonare' implies that some sort of choral performance was contemplated.[28] On the other hand, there is evidence that the use of solo singers was also an option.

For instance, one document shows that in music for double and triple choir in Rome in the late 16th century, at least one of the choirs was made up of soloists (as in Venice).[29] This is demonstrated through a dispute the Master of the Chapel had with one of the singers, Giovanni Santos, about a botched performance of the motet during the Mass of the Feast of St James on 24 July 1594, when the singers went, as they did every year, to sing at San Giacomo degli Spagnoli. Santos took charge of distributing the parts for the motet without consulting the Master, and since the Master (who had to conduct the performance) thought the motet was for two choirs when in fact it was for three, 'notable confusion' arose. The Master accused Santos of usurping his authority to control the music and demanded that he be fined. Santos claimed that the Master knew about the motet since he had already sent

quattro cantori all'organo per cantar il motetto.[30]

four singers to the organ to sing the motet.

As the Master thought the motet was for double choir, it follows that one of those choirs had to be made up of soloists. And as only 23 singers were present, there cannot have been more than two on a part in the other two of the three choirs, once the problem had been

3 Coronation of Charlemagne (Vatican Palace, Stanza dell'Incendio, fresco by Raphael, Penni and others (Monumenti, Musei e Gallerie Pontificie)

resolved.[31] Similarly, in his autograph of a setting of the *Improprerii* to be used in the Cappella Giulia in the 1570s, Palestrina carefully indicated the names of the eight singers who were to make up the two 'choruses'.[32]

It also appears that soloists were used in the performance of the *terzi* and *quarti* included within the music for five and more parts that was usual in the late 16th century. On 31 May 1583, the punctator of the College of Singers noted the following incident:

Ad Benedictus D. Cesar Bellucius incepit canere, quia D. Marinus Luppus ei precipit. D. Johannes Baptista Martinus eciam ipse cantavit, quia D. Paulus de Magistris cani ei dixit, adeo quod ambo derelinguere nec cedere alter alteri voluerunt. D. Cesar Bellucius ordinem capelle nesiebat, sed D. [Marinus Luppus – crossed out] Johannes Baptista Martinus dolose egit, ut D. Marinus retullit, quia multocies precipit ut canaret et nunquam canere voluit, hodie quia D. Marinus dixit D. Cesari cani, ipse cantare voluit; unde post Benedictus multa verba inter eos habuerunt propter hoc.[33]

At the Benedictus, Cesare Bellucius [a bass] began to sing

because Marinus Lupi [another bass] told him to. Johannes Baptista Martini [a bass] also sang because Paulus de Magistris [a bass] told him to sing, such that neither one of them wanted to stop or make way for the other. Cesare Bellucius did not know the rules of the chapel, but Johannes Baptista acted badly, as Martinus reported, because he was often told to sing and never wanted to, but today because Marinus told Cesare to sing, he [Martini] wanted to sing; thus, after the Benedictus they had much discussion about this.

A Benedictus in 1583 was likely to be a *terzo* or *quarto*, and the problem was clearly caused when two and not one of the basses began to sing.[34]

But what about music that was not *terzi* or *quarti* (or music that was entirely *terzi* and *quarti*, as was most of the music of the early 16th century)? Again, an entry from the *Diarii Sistini* suggests soloistic performance. On 1 November 1583, the same Cesare Bellucius was fined

Quia D. Cesar Bellucius in Gloria in excelsis que cantare oportebat non cantabat, et propter disonantiam causa magne subversionis fuit.[35]

Because Cesare Bellucius in the Gloria in excelsis which he was supposed to sing, did not sing, and because of the dissonance was the cause of great subversion.

Now, the absence of one voice from a choir might be noticed, the absence of a soloist singing an intonation or chant would of course be noticed, but only the absence of the bass voice from a polyphonic work sung by soloists could cause 'dissonance'. The Gloria was not normally a *terzo* or *quarto*, so this entry seems to suggest that all polyphony was sung soloistically. Similarly, on 25 May 1577, Francesco Druda was fined because he refused to sing the motet and the Agnus Dei, surely a greater offence if these were to be performed by single voices and another singer was forced to take his place.[36]

There is also contradictory evidence. Following a very old tradition, on special feast days a motet was sung for the pope as he was dining; the descriptions of this event in the *Diarii Sistini* are always phrased 'we sang the motet', implying that all the singers took part. On the other hand, on 18 August 1585, the *Diarii* specify that eight singers were sent to sing a motet for the pope (two on a part for a four-part piece, but it was almost certainly a piece in more than four parts).[37] And on 4 February 1596, mention is made of four singers who went to sing a motet at the pope's private Mass: here, certainly one on a part.[38]

Even more conflicting evidence exists. It can be demonstrated, for instance, that in the 1530s and 1540s the chapel employed a more or less equal number of sopranos, altos, tenors and basses, all of them men, the soprano part being taken by falsettists.[39] In February 1544, the breakdown was 7 sopranos, 14 contralto/tenors and 8 basses.[40]

The *Diarii Sistini* also indicate that between one and three to a part was considered an acceptable ensemble. On 5 August 1546, four singers (S, 2C/T, B) were given permission to perform at Santa Maria Maggiore, and on 10 February 1544, eight (2S, 4C/T, 2B) were given permission to sing Mass at a convent to celebrate the admission of the daughter of the singer Blasio Nunez. On a similar occasion on 11 June 1546, the eight singers were disposed 2S, 4C/T, 2B, and earlier that year, 21 January, six singers (2S, 2C/T, 2B) were sent to the Council of Trent, then meeting in Bologna. When Paul III made a pilgrimage to Loreto, he took twelve singers (3S, 6C/T, 3B).[41]

Another entry in the Diary for 1545 shows what was unacceptable. On 30 August 1545 (13th Sunday after Pentecost), Mass was not sung, but was read, 'because of the scarcity of singers, mostly sopranos, caused by the rain'. It was decided that all those absent would be fined, and nine singers are listed. This is approximately a third of the choir, and includes only two sopranos, but considering that three other sopranos were sick, one was away, and another had been banned from the chapel, this left only one soprano, and he clearly was not judged to be enough.[42]

But what does all this mean? If these numbers indicate a desire for an equal number of singers on each part, this would run counter to the idea that more soprano falsettists were needed in order to balance the lower parts in choral music.[43] On the other hand, if solo performance was the norm, the concern would only be that enough singers be available to share the load by taking turns, and that it was considered unacceptable for one singer to shoulder the entire burden (hence the problem on 30 August 1545). The documents do not give a clear answer. In 1630, it was agreed by the singers that the absolute minimum needed was three to a part. Does this say something specific about performance practice, or were they merely trying to provide enough singers if two- and three-part choral music was to be performed, and otherwise sang with one to a part?[44] Does the great concern for choosing the right singers to perform *terzi* and *quarti*, a concern not expressed for other parts of Masses and motets, indicate that only those sections were sung by soloists?[45] Or does it simply mean that trios and quartets naturally appear more exposed in music for five to eight voices sung one on a part?

But even if performances were generally given with more than one singer on a part, there is evidence to indicate that the massed singing of the entire choir in the 16th century was extremely unusual. Take, for instance, a remark made by Paris de Grassis, papal master of ceremonies during the reigns of Julius II and Leo X, concerning the Credo of the Mass on the Saturday after Easter (Sabbato in Albis), 10 April 1507: a Mass celebrated by Francesco Guastaferro, Bishop of Sessa Aurunca and Master of the Papal Chapel:

Credo cantatum fuit hodie nescio qualiter per cantores ut dixerunt per xvi voces quia celebrans est magister capellae ideo voluerunt eum hoc novo modo honorare.[46]

The Credo, I don't know which one, was sung today by the singers, which they sang in sixteen voices because the

4 The canonization of Diego d'Alcala, 1588 (Vatican Library, fresco by Nebbia and Guerra) (Monumenti, Musei e Gallerie Pontificie)

celebrant was the Master of the Chapel; therefore, they wanted to honour him in this new manner.

Either de Grassis is referring here to a genuine 16-part Credo (practically, if not totally, unheard of in 1507) or he is referring to the 'new manner' of having 16 people singing at once (four to a part in a four-part piece). I would opt for the latter interpretation; what was new, what honoured the Bishop of Sessa Aurunca, was the massed sound of all or almost all the singers present (the choir at the time numbered about twenty) in a period when it was usual for only a few of them to sing at any given time (and de Grassis never mentions this 'new manner' again).

Also suggestive is some evidence from the reign of Leo X. When Leo made his first and only state visit to Florence in November 1515, on his way to Bologna to meet François I, the whole papal court went with him, including, naturally, the choir (which then numbered about 30). In Florence, he chose not to stay at Santa Maria Novella, the usual residence of visiting pontiffs, but instead resided in the family palace, now the Palazzo Medici-Riccardi. After he had ordered that the family parish church of San Lorenzo should serve as the papal chapel, his sister-in-law Alfonsina Orsini ordered building work in the church: the enlargement of the choir, the construction of a platform for the papal throne, benches for the cardinals, and so on. The payments for this work are quite detailed and show the setting up of two bronze pulpits (which must be those made by Donatello). One of these was without question used as a singers' box. The payments for erecting it refer to the work of putting it on its stand, attaching it to the pilasters, and also to five planks of beechwood purchased

per fare le spalliere et agiunta a dicto pergamo in modo fusse capace de' cantori.[47]

to make the railing and addition to the said pulpit so that it could hold the singers.

5 The canonization of Francesca Romana, 1608, showing five singers (Vatican Library, fresco by G. B. Ricci) (Monumenti, Musei e Pontificie)

It seems to me that an addition to either of the Donatello pulpits to make it large enough to hold over 30 grown men at one time would require more than five planks of wood, even long ones;[48] furthermore, it would be expected that some mention of it would be found in the accounts, as with the other works carried out in the church.[49] This suggests that the 'bellissima messa di figurato' sung every morning by the papal singers in San Lorenzo was performed by a small group, possibly only one to a part.[50] It may be, then, that Raphael's depiction of singers at a papal ceremony in his *Coronation of Charlemagne* in the Vatican Stanze is truer to life than might appear at first glance, considering the awkwardness of their positions and placement (see illus.3).[51] Performance of polyphony in the chapel of Leo X (musically the most brilliant in Italy, if not Europe) may then have consisted of only a few singers on a part, with soloists certainly performing duet and trio sections and perhaps all the polyphony

as well, in spite of the large number of singers (at one point over 35) that belonged to the choir.

Some tentative conclusions may be drawn from this evidence:

It does not seem to me that knowing either the size of the papal choir or the number of singers on each part can be used as evidence of the numbers who sang at any given time.

Nor can the word 'coro' be taken to mean more than one singer on a part; in the 16th century it merely designated more than one person singing at the same time (for example, four soloists singing four-part polyphony formed a 'coro').

It is almost certain that duet, trio and quartet sections of Masses were sung by soloists.

The evidence for the use of soloists in other parts of Masses and motets is ambiguous; nevertheless, it suggests that only rarely if ever did all the singers perform together, and that the use of soloists was always an acceptable possibility.

But if performances did involve more than one on a part, polyphony in the Sistine Chapel from the 16th to the 18th centuries (and probably also in the 15th) would still have begun with a solo intonation. Solo singing in that sense would have then formed a constant part of what the 'period ear' (to borrow a term from Michael Baxandall) heard during papel ceremonies in the Renaissance.

Richard Sherr received his Ph.D from Princeton University and is currently Professor and Chair of the Department of Music at Smith College. He is working on a major study of music and musicians in Rome in the early 16th century.

[1] J. Lionnet, 'Performance practice in the Papal Chapel during the 17th century', *EM*, xv/1 (Feb. 1987), pp.4–15

[2] The MS is part of the *fondo Cappella Sistina, I-Rvat* S [hereafter VatS] 680, f.98r.

[3] On the *Diarii*, see Lionnet, 'Performance practice', *op cit.*

[4] For instance:
D. Johannes Lucas Confortus [a contralto] propter folium quos tempore non vertit mulctatus est' (*Diarii* 12, f.12v: 6 April 1583
'D. Thomas Benignus [a contralto] ex quo dum sacrum celebraretur coram S.mo ni volvendo folium cantus firmi decepit aperiendo unum pro alio non sine magna omnium pertubatione, ideo fuit acetu omnium absque alia dissentione mulctatus in julios quinque' (*Diarii* 14, f.7r. 10 March 1585)
That the singers still used this configuration in the 18th century is implied by Matteo Fornari, a papal singer and author of several manuscript treatises concerning practices there, when he writes in VatS 606 that 'Un contralto nelle cappelle papali se non volta in tempo la carta si punta era costitutione ducati 20'.

[5] VatS 680, f.98r.

[6] 'Ad ultimum cantorem pertinet amovere libros et ad penultimam cantorem ipsos situare in legio seu facistorio, juxta ordinationem cantorum, videlicet contralti hebdomadarii seu decani dictae capellae.' The Constitution is published in F. X. Haberl, *Die römischer 'schola cantorum' und die päpstliche Kapellsänger bis zur Mitte des 16 Jahrhunderts*, Bausteine für Musikgeschichte, iii (Leipzig, 1888).

[7] For instance:
'Dedit corectionem D. Agostino [Martini, a contralto] quia in matitutinis Natalis Domini non providit himnum, et in contrapunctum fuit cantatum.' (*Diarii* 11, f.12v: 12 February 1577
D. Augustinus [Martini] hodie ad missam cum esset ebdomadarius fecit cantare un introitum pro alio.' (*Diarii* 11, f.41v: 1 October 1577)
'Austino [Martini] fece levare il libro dal ligio quale ci era cantato li Kirie et la Gloria et era a preposito, et ne fece mettere un altro di nota piccola che per rispetto del tempo non era a preposito: il decano gli disse che ne mitesse un altro, non la volse mai mettere in questo contrasto; venne l'ora da cantare il Sanctus non era trovato niente, et ci fu fatto gran dissordine.' (*Diarii* 11, f.92v: 9 March 1579
That all these references concern the same person may not be coincidental.

[8] VatS 680, f.98r

[9] Another reference reads: 'Nel cominciare a cantare ciascuno lasci nella sua parte cominciare al più vecchio.' See S. M. Pagano. 'Una visita apostolica alla Cappella dei cantori pontifici al tempo di Urbano VIII (1630)', *Nuova rivista musicale italiana [NRMI]*, xvi (1982), pp.40–72, esp. pp.69 and 52.

[10] VATS 606. See discussion in Helmut Hucke, 'Die Beseztung von Sopran und Alt in der Sixtinischen Kapelle', *Miscelanea en Homanaje a*

Monsenor Higinio Angles (Barcelona, 1958–61), i, pp.379–406.

[11] VatS 606, pp.33–4. Whether Fornari gives the real reason that alto castrati were not admitted to the chapel is not at issue here.

[12] VatS 639, p.22

[13] It was sometimes specified that the chant be intoned by sopranos or contraltos, however.

[14] The senior singers would be experienced enough to know what a comfortable pitch level was, although, as Fornari's statement, and many entries in the *Diarii Sistini* show, sometimes they erred and chose a pitch level that was not practicable. At that point, I assume that they were supposed to stop, tell the choir they were beginning the intonation again, and start again on a different pitch.

[15] *Diarii* 119, f.112r–112v

[16] *Diarii* 122, pp.108–9: 13 May 1703

[17] *Diarii* 147, f. 35r

[18] *Diarii* 147, f.9v: 1 January 1728

[19] *Diarii* 145, f.11r. 2 February 1726

[20] *Diarii* 122, pp.45–46. In the *Improprerii* preserved in VatS 205–206, the first verse ends on *C* and the second verse begins on *f*.

[21] *Diarii* 119, f.34r–34v

[22] That is, at the top of the right hand side of the opening, as in the printed choirbook of Pellegrini's Masses that the chapel owned and must have used on this occasion. See VatS 79, V. Pellegrini, *Missarum Liber Primus* (Coenobio, 1604).

[23] One example of many: 'All mottetto del'Offertorio li secondi signori soprani entrorno mezza battuta dopo che non dovevano, per non esser stati attenti vengono puntati, e sono li signori Adami, Monaci, Marchitelli, e Pippe'. *Diarii* 122, p.63: 18 March 1703 (Fourth Sunday of Quadragesima, celebrated in the Sistine Chapel).

[24] For example: 'Al Domine Jesu Christe, cioè l'offertorio, vi fu un quarto. Per esser uscito di tuono due volte che fu rimesso dall signor Adami come antiano, si punta in baiocchi cinque per volta il signor Francesco Besci'. *Diarii* 122, p.7 (7 January 1703, special funeral services in the Chiesa Nuova).
'Al terzo dell'Benedictus, per non haver contato le battute giuste che cantava una battuta indietro, si punta il signor Petrucci 05.' *Diarii* 122, p.148 (2 July 1703: Visitation of the Blessed Virgin).

[25] See Lionnet, 'Performance practice', *op cit.*

[26] VatS 639, p.201

[27] It is also highly likely that the *Improprerii* and *Lamentations* were sung by soloists in the 18th century as they were in the 17th. See Lionnet, *op cit.*

[28] Unless, of course, he used the term only in the sense of beginning a piece.

[29] See J. H. Moore, 'The *Vespero delli Cinque Laudate* and the Role of *Salmi Spezzati* at St Mark's', *JAMS* xxxiv (1981), pp.249–78, and D. Bryant. 'The *cori spezzati* of St Mark's: Myth and Reality', *Early Music History*, i (1981), pp.165–86.

[30] VatS 678, f.112r–112v

[31] See H. W. Frey, 'Das Diarium der Sixtinischen Sängerkapelle in Rom. für das Jahr 1598', *Analecta Musicologica*, xiv (1974), p.479.

[32] See R. Casimiri, *Il 'codice 59' dell'Archivio musicale lateranense autografo di Giovanni Pierluigi da Palestrina* (Rome, 1919), pp.17–19.

[33] *Diarii* 12, f.19r

[34] For another incident suggesting that *terzi* and *quarti* were sung by soloists, see Lionnet, *op cit*, p.7.

[35] *Diarii* 12, f.35v

[36] 'D. Druda non cantavit motetum neque agnus absque ulla cause vel necessitate sed qui aspiciebat D N. et colegium ill.orum punctatur in uno julio.' *Diarii* 11, f.26r

[37] 'Eodem die DD. cantoribus congregatis ordinarunt octo cantores eorum coram pontifice inter sciiphos mottecta canere, quorum nomina sunt videlicet:
D. Honofrius
D. Jacobus Gallus
D. Horatius
D. Tomas Benignus

D. Ippolitus

D. Vincentius Musactus

D. Vincentius Zambonus

D. Decanus [Petrus Bartholomuccius]

D. Johannes Maria Nanino si placet sibi ipsi tamen ad libitum' [Nanino was probably the composer.] *Diarii* 14, f.19*v*

[38]'M. Leonardo [Crescenzio], Messer Antonio [Manni]. [Pietro] Montoya, et M. Hercole [Ferrucci] sono andati a cantare il motetto alla Messa di N. Sig. mentre faceva communione alla famiglia et sono tornati in Cappella mentre si diceva prima.' H.-W. Frey, 'Das Diarium der Sixtinischen Sängerkapelle in Rom für das Jahr 1596 (Nr.21)'. *Analecta Musicologica*, xxiii (1985), p.145

[39]The first castrato apparently entered the chapel in 1558.

[40]These figures result from a comparison of the chapel list of February 1544 in RAS, Camerale I 878 with the voice designations of the individual singers as determined by Josef Llorens. (See 'Cristobal de Morales, cantor en la Capilla Pontificia de Paulo III (1535–1545)', *Anuario Musical*, viii (1953), pp.39–69, esp. p.46.) The ingenious way Llorens arrived at his voice designations should not go unremarked. While it is true that only a few of the singers are specifically designated as 'soprano', 'tenore', etc. in the documents, Llorens noticed through a careful reading of the *Diarii Sistini* that singers often deputized for colleagues (each singer was allowed one day a week off excluding Sundays and certain feasts, and sometimes a singer would work on his day off in place of a colleague). The *Diarii Sistini* are full of references to this, and by comparing the substitutions with what we know about voice designations, it can be seen that singers only substituted for colleagues of the same voice. By extension, then, it was possible to learn the voice parts of almost all the singers in the chapel. Llorens considered contraltos and tenors as one part, and I have followed this in my estimations.

[41]The sources for this are the *Diarii Sistini* as published by Casimiri in *Note d'Archivio*, where the names of the singers are given, and Llorens, who gives the voice designations. See *Note d'Archivio*, xi (1934), p.77; x (1933), p.149, 342, 335; iii (1926), p.259.

[42]'Propter inopiam cantorum maxime supranorum ob pluviam non fuit cantata missa sed plane celebrata, ideo ordinatum fuit ut quia non compuerunt punctarentur.

(Antonius) Calasans (B)

Genesius (Bultheti T)

(Antonius) Loyalis (B)

Jo. Abbat (T)

Matheus Floranus (B)

Paulus Bursanus (S)

Virgilius Amanditis (T)

(Petrus) Ordognez (B)

Octavianus (Gemelli S)

Federicus Algisius (T)

Of the other sopranos, Simon Perusinus had received permission to absent himself from Rome; Johannes Le Conte, Blasius Nunez and Virgilius Fortin were sick; and Bernardo Pisano had been banned from the chapel by the Master. This left only Stephanus de Thoro to sing on that day. Details are in the Diary for August 1545; see *Note d'Archivio*, x (1933), pp.263, 275–76.

[43]As argued by D. Fallows, 'Specific information on the ensembles for composed polyphony 1400–1474', in *Studies in the Performances of Late Mediaeval Music*, ed. S. Boorman (Cambridge, 1983), pp.109–60.

[44]See Pagano, 'Una visita apostolica alla Cappella dei cantori pontifici al tempo di Urbano VIII (1630)', *op. cit*

[45]Many singers consulted as part of the Apostolic Visitation of the chapel in 1630 declared that the Master of the Chapel should exercise great care in choosing singers to sing *terzi e quarti*; see Pagano, 'Una visita apostolica', *op cit*. On 20 November 1584, the Master of the Chapel reported complaints he had received 'de aliquibus nostris senibus qui in tertiis et quartis malum agunt effectum. Itaque ut magis S.mo D.no N. et III.mi Cardinalibus placere ut ipsi senes in tertiis et quartis taceant'. *Diarii* 13, f.33*r*

[46]See VatL 12413. f.156*v*. Mentioned in R. Sherr, 'The singers of the Papal Chapel and liturgical ceremonies in the early sixteenth century: some documentary evidence', in *Rome in the Renaissance: the City and the Myth*, ed. P. A. Ramsey (Binghamton, 1982), pp.249–64.

[47]*I-FR* Archivio di San Lorenzo [AL] 2471, f.306*r*

[48]The entry refers to the planks being '11 b', which may mean 11 *braccia* or about 20 feet. But these were certainly cut up in order to make the railing and the addition.

[49]See *I-FR* AL 2471, f.305*r*. The pulpits are 280cm (9.33 feet) and 292cm (9.73 feet) wide; in order to accommodate 30 singers standing around a lectern, they would have had to be made wider, thus separating the sculpted panels. This does not seem likely.

[50]See F. A. D'Accone, 'Heinrich Isaac in Florence: New and Unpublished Documents', *MQ*, xlix (1963), p.482.

[51]The fresco shows three singers singing in a pulpit at the far left overlooking the scene (which presumably is taking place in St Peter's rather than in the Papal Chapel), but the arch of the top of the fresco itself makes it impossible for the artist to have included many more singers. A recent article by Neils Rasmussen provides further pictorial evidence. Rasmussen presents a number of late 16th- and early 17th-century frescos and engravings showing in accurate details various ceremonies of canonization. Three of his illustrations also show singers (always standing in pulpits), and in each case they are few in number. Considering the general attention to the detail of the rest of the ceremony being depicted, we could perhaps conclude that the representation of the number of singers also reflects reality. See Neils Krogh Rasmussen, O.P., 'Iconography and Liturgy at the Canonization of Carlo Borromeo', *Analecta Romana Instituti Danici* 15 (1986), pp.119–50: fig.2 (canonization of Diego d'Alcala, 1588, showing 3–5 singers), fig.4 (canonization of Francesca Romana, 1608, showing 5 singers), fig.9 (canonization of Carlo Borromeo, 1610, showing 5 singers; see illus.1 and 2 of my article). All of these ceremonies took place in St. Peter's, but the singers must have been members of the papal choir. Furthermore, Rasmussen's fig.2 takes place in a portion of the church that has the aspect of the Sistine Chapel (see illus.4).

[10]

The performance of Palestrina

Some questions, but fewer answers

Graham Dixon

Anyone who examines documents relating to the performance of Palestrina's music and that of his circle will soon conclude that many ambiguities remain. It would be unrealistic to imagine that a single article can resolve all, or, indeed, any of the problems; rather, my intention is to indicate where the difficulties lie, and so to encourage an imaginative approach to the performance of Palestrina's sacred music. The basic problem for both scholars and performers arises because archives tend to note deviations from standard practice: everyday aspects of performance were so obvious to everyone involved that it was superfluous to write them down.

Palestrina worked successively on a full-time basis in many of the major basilicas of the city. Although it is impossible to establish exact repertories in any single church, there is considerable justification for drawing on a variety of archives throughout the city to examine performing conditions, since Palestrina was from an early date considered core repertory, as the number of prints and documentary references testify. This article might seem to embrace the approach of looking down the wrong end of the telescope, and trying to see the music of Palestrina through Baroque eyes. But the idea of a self-contained Baroque period beginning in 1600 has been conclusively dismissed by scholars, and a far more fluid view encouraged. If we can identify the general musical ambience in Rome during the last decades of Palestrina's life, we can also begin to identify a sense of direction in his compositional achievement: clearly the *Missa Ecce sacerdos* inhabits a totally different world from the *Missa Assumpta est Maria*. Put simply, the former is polytextual and modal, whereas in the latter the words are more distinct, and the tonality more tonal. Clearly these demand different approaches, and the performance styles advocated here may well apply to the latter, but not to the former. Any such realization is helpful in dispensing with the monolithic view of Palestrina, in which he is represented as a composer

Graham Dixon is Editor, Early Music for BBC Radio 3, and musicological advisor to the York Early Music Festival. The ideas presented in this article were worked out in a series of Palestrina reconstructions broadcast on Radio 3 and internationally during 1994.

without change, development, and devoid of new ideas, since he had (from the start) effortlessly attained perfection.

One of the most controversial issues in contemporary musicology concerns how the music of Palestrina and his contemporaries was performed by the choir of the papal or Sistine Chapel. Even though instruments were forbidden for use by the papal choir in liturgical performance, the question remains extremely complex. Palestrina was employed by this institution for only a matter of months; nonetheless, the archives of the Cappella Sistina are dominated by his music, showing that there was a strong performing tradition even after he left. The recent conference in Heidelberg, which met solely to discuss this choir, deliberately avoided the question of performance because of its complexity, and the informal discussions showed a great diversity of approach. It is also probable that avoiding the issue helped avoid an international incident—feelings run high in this field. The question centres around the practice of one-voice-to-a-part performance. Obviously the important *cappelle* of Rome had a number of voices available in each tessitura, but were the members rostered in such a way that they sang together only infrequently?

Institutions with power and wealth, such as the Sistina, present us with atypical case studies, since they were in a distinct minority. It is far easier to begin by drawing some conclusions about how music must have sounded in more modest institutions during Palestrina's own lifetime. I propose therefore to begin with a discussion of what may have been the 'normal' performance in a church of average stature, and then to deal with the exceptional cases of large institutions which boasted abundant resources. The small church can establish the norm for us, though almost certainly not representing the ideal. While taking this as our starting point, we should not forget that most of Palestrina's own career was spent in the most magnificent of ecclesiastical surroundings where singers were available in considerable numbers.

Writing in 1602 about the situation in Rome that

he observed at the time of Palestrina's death—the mid 1590s—Ludovico Grossi da Viadana explains that conditions for the performance of polyphonic music in many churches had led to his invention of a new musical style:[1]

There have been many reasons (courteous readers) which have induced me to compose concertos of this kind, among which the following is one of the most important: I saw that singers wishing to sing to the organ, either with three voices, or two, or to a single voice by itself, were sometimes forced by the lack of compositions suitable to their purpose to take one, two, or three parts from motets in five, six, seven, or even eight ...

Clearly no present-day performer would seriously seek to emulate such unfortunate conditions, except out of pure curiosity to discover how strange it must have sounded. It would be 'authentic' to perform an eight-voice motet using three voices and an organ, but it is hardly ideal. What this does demonstrate is that some choirs were being forced by the lack of music in an appropriate style to perform works which were beyond them in terms of the number of voices required. And if the lack of singers was so acute in some churches which actually attempted to perform composed music, then a bare minimum of one singer to a part must have been the norm for polyphony, and anything extra must have counted as luxury. Clearly, outside the major basilicas, there was a shortage of skilled singers. No wonder Viadana's motets caught on so quickly, even in pirated editions.

Little documentary evidence about the smaller churches in Rome has yet come to light for the period up to the death of Palestrina. But an interesting list, dating from 1694, gives the size of the *cappella* in many Roman churches exactly one hundred years later. It is interesting to notice that the statistics available for 1694 do not differ markedly from the position which my own researches in Rome have uncovered for the years immediately after the turn of the century.[2] If anything, one would have expected choirs to increase in size during the Baroque period, since the early 17th century, in particular, emerges as a period of considerable expansion: new *cappelle* were formed; constitutions were redrafted; and there was a general consolidation.[3] While the *cappelle* remained the same size, more churches were able to afford singers as time progressed. Both the Cappella Giulia and the Cappella Sistina remained constant in size, with about 18 and 30 singers respectively. The worthy second-rank institutions (S. Maria in Trastevere; S. Lorenzo in Damaso; S. Spirito in Sassia) also seem to have remained constant in membership throughout the century, maintaining the norm of eight voices, with a choir such as the cappella for singing the *Salve regina* at S. Maria Maggiore only slightly better provided.[4] The eight-voice scoring, often found in second-rank institutions, enabled the performance of SATB music with consistent doubling of parts, while double-choir music of the Roman school could be managed without difficulty using one voice to a part. But the ensemble for five-part music must have been either an unbalanced tutti, or sung with a single voice to a part, with three singers simply waiting their turn rather than performing.

The remarkable vogue of writing motets for one to four voices in the early years of the century followed Viadana's concern to provide music for those institutions which already existed, though with a repertory that they could often perform only inadequately. Evidently, the standard Roman *cappella* of the 1590s was stretched by even the most basic Palestrina works, and we must assume that when they were adequately performed there were no spare voices for doubling, even if this was thought desirable. Indeed, choirs seem to have been smaller in Palestrina's time than those of a century later (or even just a few years later), pointing us increasingly in the direction of single-voice performance.

My research in the early 17th century has already shown that, when extra singers were employed in Rome, it was in order to form supplementary choirs for polychoral music.[5] Noel O'Regan has recently traced this practice back to the period of Palestrina, and has shown that an institution generally employed extra freelance singers in connection with certain feast-days when polychoral music was

required, not simply to provide a fuller texture for few-voiced music.[6]

Indeed, Maugars implies 'single-voice' performance in his comments about a service with lavish music which he attended in the church of S. Maria sopra Minerva.[7] He found it remarkable how one voice from one choir could remain in time with another voice from a different choir in polychoral performance. And this is supported by the evidence of a large number of pay-lists for singers on specific days. When these archives are so arranged as to indicate division into various choirs, it clearly emerges that, in festal music, extra voices were employed to form independent vocal groupings, rather than simply bolstering the choir which already existed.

I shall concentrate for a little on the German College, since it was a flourishing institution, not hidebound by the age-long traditions of the major basilicas. Moreover, despite its name, it was thoroughly Italian in its music. Its archives—some of the most detailed in Rome—contain an intriguing reference to the men singing in three voices a motet written by Palestrina for four: this underlines the fact that singers were each treated as soloists even in single-choir music. *Nos autem* (*a 4*) with a part missing cannot have created a particularly edifying sound, yet it shows us that even in a leading establishment extra singers were not a regular part of the ensemble.[8] Other documents bear this out: Matthias Schrick, writing on Michael Lauretano's period as rector of the college between 1573 and 1578, is a reliable source since he was a student there from 1583 until 1589. Schrick mentions that:[9]

It was, however, by no means contrary to this his instruction, if, now and then, either one voice alone, or several more supple voices, took, together with the organ, some particular verse, either from the psalms or the sacred hymns, or sang in between (in [its] entirety), some skilfully elaborated song (proper to the time), [which] they commonly call motets.

A specific instance is cited in the college archives when, on 9 June 1583, the Benedicamus at Vespers was replaced by 'a short motet for two voices sung to the organ'.[10] And in the same year, motets and the Lamentations were sung 'to the organ with two or three soloists', causing great devotion among the hearers.[11] By 1589 a singer from the papal chapel was living in college, and on occasions when his commitments prevented him from singing in college, he sent a trombone player as a replacement.[12] Not only does this demonstrate that occasional instrumental substitution was unexceptional, but it also shows that his voice would certainly have been missed in polyphonic music—it is difficult to imagine that a trombone would have doubled in chant. In March 1589 it seems that the professional musical establishment of the college comprised three boy sopranos, two altos and one bass. Singing was encouraged as part of the seminarians' studies, and evidence survives that students (20 or so at a time) formed a choir. Some of them certainly formed a choir *di musica* (for composed music), but it seems that most attention at the college was directed towards the pastorally applicable activity of singing chant. I would hesitate before identifying the choir of 20 students referred to in various documents with anything other than a plainsong *schola*, and I certainly cannot see a proud member of the papal chapel being willing to sing alongside students: if this was all he did, why send a replacement trombone? Whatever the repertory of the choir of 20, it seems most reasonable to regard it as completely distinct from the professional musical establishment of the college. Perhaps the clearest surviving image of college music emerges from an account of the Corpus Christi procession in 1583, when a chant choir of 25 voices was answered by a *falsobordone* body of three in the festal hymns.[13]

But our problems regarding the performance of Palestrina are far from resolved, even if we can decide on the number of singers. Various other possibilities still present themselves. Only in the performances of the Cappella Sistina was the organ actually outlawed, though even that conservative institution relaxed its general regulations when the *vespri segreti* were performed in the presence of the

pope on four occasions each year.[14] Organs were used with greater regularity in most other institutions, however, and while one might have thought that their role was to provide 'incidental' music for the liturgy, various references even suggest that they were used with the voices in polyphony at quite an early date. Apart from Viadana's reference to the organ helping an insufficient number of singers to stumble through a polyphonic motet in the mid-1590s (clearly no isolated incident), there seem to be two further uses of the organ—namely, in accompanying polyphonic singing and supporting a solo performance. Apart from a performance of Palestrina's eight-part motet *Surge illuminare* to the organ which took place on the feast of the Epiphany in 1585,[15] the German College archives refer to music for few voices to the organ—as we have already seen. Indeed, the use of the organ as an accompaniment instrument for voices must have been established for some time before the turn of the century, for in explaining the merits of the basso continuo in his *Del sonare sopra'l basso* of 1607, Agostino Agazzari does not so much point to the introduction of a new style, as indicate that much labour will be saved in copying out the vocal lines into a score or tablature. Musicians had been doing this for some time in order to provide accompaniments, but now they were released both from this chore and from the need to build new shelving for an ever increasing quantity of paper. But performing a motet to the organ itself was not a novelty in 1607, rather it was a well established tradition.

The participation of other instruments—not simply trombones as vocal replacements—cannot be ruled out in performances of polyphony: within ten years of Palestrina's death, Agazzari published a volume of motets in a safe Palestrina-like *prima prattica* idiom, in which the possibility of instruments doubling or replacing the voices is clearly indicated; his *Sacrae laudes de Iesu … cum basso ad organum, & musica instrumenta, liber secundus* appeared in Rome in 1603, and its contents were soon reprinted in Venice and Frankfurt. At the time of its publication Agazzari was *maestro* at the German College, and if we look back into the archives we can see that he was not actually innovatory as far as instruments are concerned. In the 1580s mention is made of 'soft instruments of musicians', though their exact role is not clear.[16] They could have been required to provide sinfonias, or alternatively to play with the voices: the former practice is referred to in an unusual rubric in Agazzari's *Psalmi sex ... opus duodecimum* of 1609, where an instrumental sinfonia is prescribed before the psalm *Laudate Dominum*. On 4 April 1593 the Offertory motet was sung with organ and cornett, and the Communion motet by the voices.[17] From 1573 references to a harp appear; perhaps we can see here the influence of Victoria, in adopting what was standard Spanish practice.[18]

Moving away from the German College, a document dating from 1595 shows that instruments were more widely used as an integral part of festal polychoral music; this quotation applies to the situation in the city as a whole:[19]

On a feast, when a *maestro* brings together musicians for two Vespers and a Mass, he will invite members of the papal chapel, and instruments such as cornett, trombones, violins and lutes.

Lists of payments from the period bear this out, though once again no specific roles or pieces of music are mentioned: we know who was present, but not what they did.

Performance to the organ seems to have been more common than performance with the participation of other instruments. The use of the organ that we see established in archives in the closing years of the 16th century seems to provide the background to a tradition that only becomes evident in published form during the early years of the 17th century. Indeed, it is important at this stage to explain my application of early 17th-century material to a consideration of the style of a composer who died in 1594. Perhaps more than in any other period, the way in which music was presented on paper—as distinct from its style—underwent a con-

siderable change in the years around 1600. In the case of Caccini's songs, exemplifying the use of the monodic style in general, publishing showed itself to be almost 20 years behind practical music-making, and archival evidence suggests the same length of time, if not longer, elapsed between practice and print in the case of organ parts in church music.

Palestrina arrived in Rome to take up his first adult appointment in 1551, and his career there spanned 40 years; therefore the scant archival evidence on organs and instruments available applies to the entire second half of his activity in the city. The delay between practice and print is exemplified by the fact that only much later, in 1614, did Giovanni Francesco Anerio publish a set of original *prima prattica* Masses with 'Bassus ad organum' parts. Some motets were still written in a *prima prattica* style during the new century, and these were sometimes published with organ parts; in addition to Anerio himself, the composers responsible were Curzio Mancini and Abundio Antonelli. And just as organ accompaniments to sacred polyphony were found in practical music-making before 1600, so music specifically intended for unaccompanied voices persisted in the traditional choirbook format after that date. That publishers continued for many years to produce Masses by Soriano (1609), Crivelli (1614) and even Landi (1639) in this archaic form, even after the partbook and continuo revolution of the first years of the century, is impressive testimony that the musical traditions, both new and old, represented by their different formats, coexisted for many years. The new style appeared in print for the first time only reticently, while the old lingered on for many decades.

As well as publishing some original *prima prattica* music, Anerio arranged Masses by Palestrina for performance 'to the organ' in his *Messe a quattro voci ...* This 1619 publication has already been regarded as an updating of Palestrina to make his music acceptable in another era, but the print surely also represents an accepted way of performing the music in Palestrina's own lifetime. In addition to such continuo reworkings, another type of rearrangement appeared during the 17th century, reflecting the rising popularity of polychoral music. Some of Palestrina's Masses were rewritten for two, or even for three choirs, and on occasion published. The best known example of this is Soriano's version for eight voices of the *Missa Papae Marcelli*, which we know to have been performed in St Peter's in September 1618,[20] though it had been published some nine years earlier. Such arrangements also exist in manuscript, including an eight-part setting by Ruggiero Giovannelli of *Missa Vestiva i colli*, based on Palestrina's own version. The 12-part *Missa Tu es Petrus*, long regarded as Palestrina's own, must surely fall into the same category. Rewriting a work to make it more up-to-date was considered a compliment to the composer, rather than an insult to his original composition.

But even if one can decide who is to perform, there remains the problem of how Palestrina's contemporaries actually executed the individual lines. The many books of instruction on ornamentation demonstrate that we are dealing here with an art largely concerned with soloists: improvisation with more than a single singer to a part could never have produced edifying results. Bovicelli published his arrangement of Palestrina's *Benedicta sit sancta Trinitas* in Venice in 1594, the year of Palestrina's death, in his *Regole, passaggi di musica, madrigali e motetti passeggiati*. It shows that singers would have added extremely lavish formulas to a relatively plain vocal line.

In case this predilection for the florid is dismissed as a North Italian extravagance, it should be borne in mind that one of the leading exponents of the art was Giovanni Luca Conforti, a member of the papal chapel, who published a handbook on the practice, probably in 1593, *Breve et facile maniera d'essercitarsi ad ogni scolaro … a far passaggi*. The Roman diarist and writer on music, Pietro della Valle, recalls having heard Conforti perform embellishments: 'I remember Giovanni Luca, the falsettist, the singer of *gorgie* and *passaggi*, who went right up to the stars.' As a Roman commentator, della Valle would most likely have heard Con-

forti singing with the musicians of the Cappella Sistina of which he was himself an important member.[21] It would be curious for an institution to employ a singer, and then to forbid him from exercising the skill for which he was famed.

Indeed, the chapel was famed for its improvisation: on major feasts its members created spontaneous counterpoint to the Offertory chants, and to the Magnificat antiphon. It seems highly unlikely that they restrained themselves in composed music, especially with one of the leading practitioners of the art of embellishment in their midst.

Those Roman churches which had a music tradition, but which were not among the major basilicas, show a great diversity of styles: they were using instruments and the organ occasionally, and one-to-a-part performance must have been the norm, if for no other reason than the size of their resources. As noted above, it was this lack of resources which prompted Viadana, at the time of Palestrina's death, to invent a new small-scale polyphonic style (distinct from Florentine monody), in which the organ was the basis of harmonic support.

Other types of diversity also existed in the major churches of Rome: in the Cappella Sistina one would hear castratos on the top line, whereas in the Cappella Giulia (at St Peter's), at S. Maria Maggiore and S. Giovanni in Laterano boys performed this role.[22] And the Cappella Sistina was distinct from the others in its rejection of instrumental accompaniment except on the rarest occasions.

The Sistina is perhaps the most interesting of these institutions, and also the one which poses the most vexed questions. The focus of these discussions is an article by Jean Lionnet, published in 1987.[23] His thorough examination of the archival documents led him to the conclusion that, on all but the most exceptional occasions, the papal singers performed polyphony with one voice to a part. True, there were in the region of 30 singers on the payroll, but on weekdays only half the *cappella* attended, and only 24 were active, since six were in receipt of pensions. Therefore the normal number of singers one would expect to find would have been in the order of 12. Lionnet argues that the singers took turns (determined by seniority) to perform the music assigned to their particular voice part, citing, in defence of this position, documents which show that heated debates took place regarding which singer should perform, and that on occasion the carelessness of a single singer substantially upset the performance. Lists of singers with their specific parts are available for Holy Week, and frequently a new singer was auditioned by singing as a member of the choir: clearly it would have been difficult to assess one potential new singer if he was pitted against over two dozen others. Indication of Palestrina's involvement in a similar practice (outside the Sistina) survives, since in the 1570s he noted which of the Cappella Giulia singers should perform the Improperii on Good Friday.[24]

Lionnet's work has given rise to much discussion, since the examples he uses seem to rely heavily on certain sections of the liturgy, such as the 'Crucifixus', which were frequently set for fewer voices, and because of the large number of his documents which refer to Holy Week, when a particular austerity might have been thought desirable. Nonetheless, it would generally be accepted that reduced sections and Holy Week music should be performed by single voices, but the remainder of the repertory is still contentious.

In the course of a short account, I am reluctant to deal too closely with Lionnet's conclusions and arguments, since they relate primarily to the early 17th century. Richard Sherr has already been stimulated by Lionnet's article into tackling the same problem for the 16th century, and he is prepared to admit the ambiguities of the situation.[25] Though Sherr draws interesting parallels with 18th-century practice in the chapel, it is appropriate in this context to review his Renaissance material. An incident on 31 May 1583 confirms the use of soloists in reduced sections: two singers began at the Benedictus; neither would give way, and their behaviour was called into question. Another entry from the same year suggests that single-voice performance was more widespread: Cesare Bellucio was fined for refusing to sing in the Gloria, and for creating thereby a dissonant effect. If other basses had been singing there would have been no question of dissonance, whereas only the complete absence of the line would have created the offensive dissonances. And in 1596 four singers performed a motet at the papal Mass—clearly one to a part. Other documents cited by Sherr do not definitively solve the problem: just because Paul III took 12 singers to Loreto on pilgrimage, it does not mean to say that they all sang at once in composed music, though in chant they probably would have done so. Another type of reference which lends support to the notion of single-voice performance is that small group of documents which refers to a motet being sung by everyone, often in non-liturgical contexts. Regularly this occurred while the pope was dining, and the same practice is mentioned during a banquet given by Urban VIII for the emperor in 1638.[26] Nonetheless, as early as 1507, an archival reference records a completely new experience, a Credo sung by 16 voices: it is difficult to imagine 16 real parts in this period, so it would seem that it was simply the fact that so many people sang at once made an impression on the papal master of ceremonies, who recorded the event.[27]

But even if the voices sing in appropriate numbers, with some ornamentation, and keeping open the possibility of instrumental participation, the battle to salvage Palestrina's music from the world of the large, unaccompanied choir, simply singing the notes, has not yet been won. Andrew Parrott has conclusively argued that certain combinations of clefs indicate that the notes as written should be transposed down a 4th; I refer readers to this article rather than repeat the complex reasoning here.[28] On the basis of his article, we should consider pitch before beginning the first read-through, or even booking singers. Indeed, we should no more think of ignoring these findings in performance than we should consider deliberately transposing a Mozart symphony up a 4th because we prefer it that way. The results in both cases would be equally shocking to Palestrina and Mozart respectively.

In case one might be concerned that pieces which are familiar at a high pitch sound oppressively dark when transposed down, it is worth mentioning that the Italian Renaissance seemed to have a predilection for a considerably lower sonority that we might nowadays seek to create in contemporary works for a modern orchestra. Coryat's famous description of the feast of San Rocco mentions a ensemble which contemporary taste would probably consider to be strongly biased towards low instruments: ten sackbuts, four cornetts, two viole da gamba 'of an extraordinary greatness', and two theorbes.[29] The same conclusions may be drawn from the popular addition of extra low strings to the basic lute, the encouragement of a large continuo group in Agazzari's 1607 treatise,[30] and many surviving scorings, such as those for the Florentine weddings of 1539 and 1565.[31] Ignoring this practice, as do surprisingly many present-day ensembles, is substantially to change the original character of the music.

In conclusion, one might urge upon today's performers the same diversity of expression that the archives and documents indicate. We cannot categorically state that single-voice performance would have been practised everywhere, though it certainly seems to have been the norm. Whether the norm was also the ideal is a question which we cannot at this stage answer with confidence. Instruments must have been used at services at which Palestrina's works were performed, but they seem to have been employed most frequently in connection with polychoral music. Perhaps we should begin to experiment with their use, replacing parts, and also doubling them. As for the organ, most churches which employed a choir also employed an organist, and therefore we can be quite generous in our use of the organ, remembering that archival evidence points to the use of the instrument in conjunction with singers. The arrangements of Palestrina, sensitively done by his pupils, are worthy of rediscovery: one cannot imagine a pupil doing violence to the spirit of the work of an admired master, and such works probably show the direction in which

Palestrina's music would have developed had the composer himself lived on.

All the above suggestions are relatively easy to carry out, and make little essential difference to the way in which we perceive Palestrina's flowing vocal lines. But the 400th anniversary of his death gives us the chance to reflect on the real way in which such long-admired and elegantly constructed lines should flow. We must consider whether performing the notes is sufficient, or whether we cannot more deeply reawaken the sound of Palestrina's music by exploring the lost tradition of improvised embellishment. To do this, most present-day singers must return to the lessons that they would have learned if they had been fortunate enough to have attended a Renaissance choir school: embellishment formulas have to be memorized, rehearsed and then applied in performance with flexibility, spontaneity and subtlety. An ensemble which tackles this time-consuming challenge successfully would have the satisfaction of reviving the lost singing tradition of the Roman basilicas, and afford the public an essentially new conception of Renaissance music, in which the fluid lines are enhanced by the judicious use of ornamentation. When the performance of Palestrina has advanced beyond what is written on the page, we should be able to understand how prized virtuosity was in that period, and how the skilled singer was not excluded from exercising his abilities in music written by the leading figure of the age. In scholarly terms, we shall have established a bridge between the vocal lines of Palestrina and the more floridly notated vocal parts of the early Baroque.

1 O. Strunk, *Source readings in musical history* (London, 1952), p.421.

2 O. Mischiati, 'Una statistica della musica a Roma nel 1694', *Note d'archivio* (new series), i (1983), p.209.

3 G. Dixon, 'The cappella of S. Maria in Trastevere: an archival study', *Music and letters*, lxii (1981), pp.30–32.

4 J. Lionnet, 'La "Salve" de Sainte Maria Majeure: la musique de la Chapelle Borghese au 17me siecle', *Studi musicali*, xxii (1983), p.97.

5 G. Dixon, 'The origins of the Roman "Colossal Baroque"', *Proceedings of the Royal Musical Association*, cvi (1979–80), p.115.

6 N. O'Regan, *Sacred polychoral music in Rome, 1575–1621* (diss., U. of Oxford, 1988), pp.59–75.

7 André Maugars, *Response faite a un curieux sur le sentiment de la musique d'Italie ...*, ed. in E. Thoinan, *Maugars, célèbre joueur de viole ... sa biographie suivie de sa response* (Paris, 1865/R1965).

8 T. D. Culley, *A study of the musicians connected with the German College during the 17th century and of their activities in Northern Europe, Jesuits and music*, i (Rome–St Louis, 1970), p.84.

9 Culley, *A study of the musicians ...*, p.78.

10 Culley, *A study of the musicians ...*, p.81.

11 Culley, *A study of the musicians ...*, p.84.

12 Culley, *A study of the musicians ...*, p.87.

13 Culley, *A study of the musicians ...*, p.83.

[11]

The performance of Palestrina: some further observations
Noel O'Regan

Noel O'Regan is a lecturer in music at the University of Edinburgh. His research centres on Roman sacred music in the late 16th and early 17th centuries, particularly on the musical patronage of the city's confraternities.

Two articles in the November 1994 issue of *Early music* raised questions of performance practice in 16th-century Rome, giving evidence which, on the face of it, seemed irreconcilable.[1] Richard Sherr quoted Johannes Burkhard, the papal master of ceremonies in the 1480s, as complaining of the result when more than 12 papal singers sang together—implying that such a manner of singing was common. Graham Dixon, relying mainly on 17th-century sources, spoke of one-per-part performance as the norm for Palestrina. In this he was following the position taken in earlier articles in this journal by Sherr and Jean Lionnet;[2] both used evidence from the *libri dei punti* of the Cappella Pontificia to support single-voice performance of virtually all polyphony in the papal chapel in the 16th and 17th centuries. In this short response to those articles I would like to re-examine three areas in particular: one-per-part performance; solo singing with the organ; and the question of whether or not the students at the German College sang polyphony; in the process it may be possible to answer some of the questions posed by Dixon as well as finding a way out of the conundrum posed by Sherr.

In his November 1994 article Graham Dixon spoke of a recent Heidelberg conference on the Cappella Pontificia as having ducked the issue of performance in the interests of international harmony. In fact there have been two such conferences: the first, held in 1989, to which Dixon refers, did indeed hardly touch on the issue (and feelings ran high when it came up briefly in discussion); by the second, in 1993, things had settled somewhat and my own paper presenting evidence for more than one-per-part performance of Mass Ordinaries was received in an atmosphere of calm. Some of what follows was included in that paper, publication of which is promised in the conference proceedings.[3]

Two entries from the diaries of the *puntatori* of the Cappella Pontificia in 1560–62 deal directly with the question of specially highlighted sections of Mass Ordinaries.[4] In 1560 Cardinal Carafa, newly appointed Protector of the Cappella, 'charged the master of the chapel [who at this period was not a singer] that he should be present with the singers in the choir at papal Masses in order to enforce the order of keeping silent and singing duos, trios and other [such sections]' ('comisit magistro capelle ut in missis papalibus esset in choro cum cantoribus, ut servaretur ordo silentii et cantandi duo et tria et alia'). This system clearly did not work, and on 2 January 1562 it was decreed that 'in papal Masses and Vespers, no singer should sing alone in duos or trios unless nominated or required to do so, and to this effect they elected four of the most senior singers, one from each voice-type, [Antonio Calasans, Virgilius de Amanditis, Nicolaus Clinca and Federicus Lazisus]' ('fuit decretum, in missis et vesperis papalibus, non debeant aliqui cantores singulariter decantare duos vel tertios, nisi fuerint nominatus vel requisitus, et ad efectum huiusmodi elegerunt quatuor antiquiores cantores unum vz. ex qualibet pretense voce …').

It was clearly a problem area. The duos and trios can refer only to those sections of the Mass Ordinary and of the hymn and Magnificat at Vespers, which, since the mid-15th century, had been highlighted by reducing the number of voices. The 'alia' in 1560 must refer to 'quarti', similar sections for four voices which became more common as duos were phased out in the later 16th century and Mass Ordinaries were more commonly written for five and six parts. The clear implication of these entries is that only these sections were being sung by solo singers: otherwise they would not have needed to be singled out in this way (a more general reference could have been made to the organization of singers for all the Mass Ordinary and Vespers polyphony). This is confirmed by a rubric on papal singer Archangelo Crivelli's four-voice *Missa Credo maius* in Fondo Cappella Sistina 25, copied in 1617 by Domenico Brancadori. The Benedictus is set for four voices (i.e. the same number as the rest of the Mass); the scribe has written 'cum quatuor tantum si placet' ('for four voices only if desired') on the altus part and 'cum quatuor si placet' on cantus, tenor and bassus parts. The important point here is that there was no reduction in the number of parts and so the rubric was considered necessary in this case to suggest solo singing of the Benedictus. The appending of the words 'si placet' by Crivelli (or his scribe Brancadori) indicates flexibility as well as a desire for contrast between group and solo performance. In reduced-voice sections in the same manuscript, no such rubric is given since it was customary for these to be sung by soloists. An intriguing question is whether the 'si placet' written here applied at times to other special sections as well.

Similar rubrics are found on two Masses in the 1567 print of Giovanni Animuccia's *Missarum liber primus*, found as Cappella Sistina 177, but written for use in the first instance by the Cappella Giulia at St Peter's, and so closer to the normal milieu in which Palestrina worked after 1571. The *Missa Ad coenam agni* is scored for SATB. The 'Christe eleison' is for SAT only and the rubric 'bassus tacet' is given, as was commonly the case. For the 'Domine Deus' section of the Gloria the same four SATB parts are used but the rubric '4 tantum vocibus' appears on the tenor and bassus parts. Similarly, at the Benedictus the rubric 'cum quatuor vocibus' is found on the cantus part. At the 'Crucifixus' section of the Credo, on the other hand, there is no rubric, despite its being for an SATT combination; in fact, there is no room on the page here for a 'bassus tacet' rubric. Where the rubric was essential was for movements which did not reduce or change the vocal scoring and where the singers needed to be reminded to leave it to soloists. However, the same composer's five-voice *Missa Christe Redemptor* has the rubric 'quinque tantum vocibus' on the 'Crucifixus' section of the Credo, despite its changed vocal scoring from the overall SATTB to SAATB. Reduced-voice sections in this Mass are all marked 'cantus tacet' or 'bassus tacet' as appropriate. Here as elsewhere there is no instruction telling the singers to resume tutti singing; they clearly knew from experience when this was appropriate.

Solo singing, then, could apply to the special sections of the Mass Ordinary ('Crucifixus', 'Benedictus' etc.) even if the number of voice parts was not reduced. It could also apply to the beginning of the second half of the Gloria; this might have been the case more often than printed or manuscript sources make clear. This could explain the fine imposed on the papal bass Cesare Bellucio in 1583 for not singing in the Gloria when he was supposed to, resulting in dissonance and great disruption ('in Gloria in excelsis que cantare oportebat non cantabat et propter disonantiam cause magne subversionis fuit'). This is the only such case involving the Mass Ordinary among those quoted by Sherr and Lionnet which seemed not to refer to a special section, and so it was used by Sherr to imply solo singing throughout the Ordinary.[5]

The evidence of the 1560–62 *Diarii* and of the Crivelli and Animuccia Masses given above, however, clearly suggests that the bulk of the Ordinary was sung by whatever singers were available (presumably with some allowance for balance). I would contend that this remained the case for Mass Ordinaries, which for the most part continued to be written in the *stile antico*, well into the 17th century—just as it must have been in Johannes Burkhard's time in the late 15th. The same applied also to Office hymns, where the older settings continued to be used (forcing an adaptation in the papal chapel of Palestrina's and Victoria's settings to accommodate Urban VIII's revised texts of 1631), and to *stile antico* Magnificats, though the Magnificat was also increasingly set in the concertato or polychoral idioms by the early 17th century. Within each voice-part the papal singers present used seniority as the normal means of deciding the order in which they sang solo in special sections. That problems continued is clear from the number of fines handed out to papal singers in this connection.

The discussion so far has centred on the Ordinary of the Mass. We know that the Tenebrae Lamentations were sung by single singers on each part. What about motets? Here there seems to have been considerable flexibility. There are examples from the archives of the Cappella Pontificia of motets being sung by solo singers.[6] At the same time there are some references to more than one singer on each part. In the 1622 *Diario Sistino* there is a reference to a Low Mass at which a five-voice motet was sung by all the singers as the pope vested and one for eight voices by soloists at the elevation. It has been argued that the former was an exception, but if this were the case, are we similarly to regard the performance of the double-choir piece as exceptional, even though in this idiom solo singing seems to have been the norm?[7] The two types of performance mentioned here are mirrored in the description of the classes given to the more experienced (in singing) students at the German College, written in 1611 but describing practices in use since the college's foundation:

every workday … after the second table is finished, for at least a half hour in the *sala* … the more experienced in singing repair. There the *maestro di cappella* trains them in various types of singing—now all together, now divided in two or three choirs, now having sung a *terzetto* of a hymn or of another thing.[8]

This seems to me a succinct summary of the three ways of singing non-concertato sacred music in late 16th- and early 17th-century Rome: more than one to a part for four- to six-voice Mass Ordinaries and some motets; divided into choirs of mainly solo singers for polychoral music; one-per-part singing for *terzetti* and *quarti* sections of Mass Ordinaries, hymns and Magnificats.

This brings us to the question of the regular participation of the students at the German College in polyphony, upon which Graham Dixon cast doubt in his article. His statement that the clearest surviving image of the College's music is found in the account of the Corpus Christi procession in 1583 'when a chant choir of 25 voices was answered by a *falsobordone* body of three in the festal hymns' is misleading. The full description of that procession makes it quite clear that there were three separate groups of singers separated by other students saying the rosary: about 25 singing *Pange lingua* in plainchant; three singing *Sacris solemnis* in *falsobordone*; and finally the singers of polyphony (what they sang is not recorded). That all three bodies were made up of students is clear from the description of the extended rehearsal of the whole procession which took place the previous evening.[9]

Certainly the singing of chant was stressed at the College, but it was precisely the amount of time devoted to polyphony by the students which brought forth the periodic criticisms of the College's curriculum described in Thomas Culley's study of the institution. The documents make a clear distinction between the *cantori di musica* (about 20 of the most musical students) and the *choristi* who sang plainchant. In 1592 there is a breakdown of student voices in the former group into four altos, eight tenors and five basses. The choir was stiffened by some priests and noble seminarians (who could presumably read music). There were also some outside singers, but these remained few until the 1590s (there were seven by 1592). During the rectorship of Michele

Lauretano (1573–87) the outsiders were mainly boy sopranos, since there were none among the students. It was for the same reason that a bass from the papal chapel was offered free board and lodging after Lauretano's death: finding a real bass among the students was rare. (Significantly, it was a trombonist who was engaged to cover for the papal bass and support the students, when he was employed at the chapel.) In the 1580s the papal singers had not yet settled into the arrogance which was to characterize them in the 17th century and I do not see a problem about the papal singer joining with the students: the confraternities of S. Rocco and SS. Trinità dei Pellegrini both employed two papal singers on a part-time basis to sing polyphony together with much less competent singers in the 1580s and 1590s respectively.[10] In the case of the German College, the papal bass might of course have confined himself to singing occasional motets with the organ (see below). Certainly, by the 1610s the singing of festal polyphony at the German College's church of S. Apollinare was largely in the hands of professionals (though, as we saw above, the students continued to be taught figured music); this was not, however, the case during the 16th century. A description of a procession to S. Giovanni dei Fiorentini on 21 June 1592 with the relics of SS. Protus and Hyacinth in which the College took part reports that 'there were up to 40 singers, all from the College without even one outsider, and they sang such beautiful and lively polyphony that all marvelled and it was reported also to the pope that the polyphonic singing of the German College was the best that could be' ('erano da 40 cantori tutti del Collegio che non si prese pure un forastiero, e feceno cosi bella e gagliarda musica, che tutti si maravigliavano, e fu referito anco al Papa, che la musica del Collegio Germanico e stata la migliore che ci fosse').[11]

During the 1580s the most characteristic image of the College is provided by the numerous descriptions of double-choir performances of motets, psalms and litanies in polyphony by the students, sometimes by choirs of single singers and other times by the whole group; frequently the polyphony alternated with plainchant so as to involve the maximum number. For example, on Easter Tuesday 1583 two choirs, each of four voices, sang a double-choir refrain alternatim with verses of Psalm 43 sung in plainchant.[12]

The German College was at the forefront in pioneering solo singing by one or more singers with organ.[13] While this may have been done at times by professionals, the better students were also trained in it. The singing of motets 'to the organ' was much favoured in Rome and the practice may go back a long way; Ignatius Loyola wrote in 1556 of his Jesuit community in Rome that 'here there is a mixture of figured singing and that with organ', and a few days later that 'here we have both types of singing'.[14] Usually, one or more parts were abstracted from polyphonic music written in the normal way, with the organ making up for the missing voices. There is no evidence that the Romans found this unsatisfactory or that they did it because of a lack of available singers; it was clearly a practice that appealed to them. Important evidence here is provided by Asprilio Pacelli's *Chorici psalmi et motecta* of 1599, published while he was *maestro di cappella* at the German College. Although not having a *bassus ad organum* part, this is the first known Roman publication in the new style and pre-dates Ludovico da Viadana's *Cento concerti ecclesiastici* by three years; indeed, it is clearly one of the rival publications referred to in the introduction to Viadana's publication.[15] Pacelli's foreword is worth quoting in part since it has hitherto been overlooked:

I have thus resolved to discharge my obligation to many close friends. ... by publishing this book of psalms and motets, composed more as *concerti* with organ, such as is nowadays the custom in Rome, and for spiritual delight ... than as ordinary church music [*musica ordinaria di cappella*] ... And since not everyone will have voices appropriate for singing these works, the skilled organist should bear in mind that, according to the voices which are available, almost all of these compositions can be easily transposed downwards, or upwards in various modes as is judged convenient ... And if they are written for four [voices], some of them will make a better effect if sung by three, e.g. two sopranos and a bass. Note, however, that if the transposition is very low, the same bass part can be sung an octave higher by the bass or by another voice ...

In fact, leaving out one part from some of these Pacelli pieces and supporting the remainder with the organ yields results very similar to Viadana. Pacelli also included a Magnificat setting for three voices in the new style, but none for fewer than this.

Apart from the lack of solos and duets there is no appreciable musical difference between what Pacelli and Viadana produced. Pacelli advocates maximum flexibility, making a clear distinction between the older 'musica ordinaria da cappella' and the new popular '*concerti* with organ'. Although he does not say so explicitly, the implication is that different performance practices were associated with the two idioms.

Pacelli was clearly continuing an established German College (and Roman) tradition and it may well be that Viadana learned from the Romans rather than the other way around, in spite of his assertions to the contrary. The traditional reading of his foreword is followed by Dixon, who speaks of the organ helping singers to stumble along; this must undoubtedly have sometimes been the case, and Viadana may have found some of the music used to have been inappropriate, but this must be seen in the context of his desire to claim priority for himself in writing small-scale motets. Nor should present-day performers be discouraged from taking one, two or three parts from motets in five, six or eight parts

because of Viadana's propaganda; it was clearly a popular Roman practice in the late 16th century. While recommending ornamentation of vocal lines, Dixon fails to make the clear connection between this practice and its obvious context in the Romans' picking out one or more parts for singing by soloists—exactly what is illustrated by arrangements such as Bassano's of Palestrina's *Benedicta sit sancta Trinitas* or those by Bovicelli. Another example is the version of the same composer's *Dum complerentur* with *basso seguente*: this is missing its first tenor part, discussed by Patrizio Barbieri in the November 1994 issue of *Early music*.[16]

Let us return to the question of one- versus many-per-part performance. There can be no doubt, from the size of most choirs, that one-per-part performance was common in Palestrina's Rome. Apart from the three major institutions the standard choir consisted of six adults (two per part on ATB) and four boy sopranos. We know enough about 16th-century Roman churches to realize that this was the number aimed at, as it was in the late 17th century, even if not always achieved. Poorer establishments like SS. Trinità, S. Rocco, or S. Maria di Monserrato tried but failed to support this level; they often fell back on three or four less experienced singers (who frequently doubled as chaplains) and a couple of boys. Even the richer churches like S. Luigi dei Francesi, S. Maria Maggiore, S. Giovanni in Laterano and S. Lorenzo in Damaso had trouble keeping their numbers up, because of sickness, absence or the mobility of singers which followed the increase in opportunities in the wake of the Council of Trent. Having two singers per part on one's list was more an insurance of having one in attendance at any one time than necessarily wanting to have two singing each part. This is confirmed by the archives of S. Rocco, where a second soprano was hired to join a small one-per-part choir, since the single soprano was 'often missing at the offices and other services, leaving the oratory without a soprano … especially in processions and other important occasions … with an extra soprano, if one is missing the other can supply'.[17] Much of the regular polyphony (such as it was) at these establishments (including Mass Ordinaries) was sung by one singer on each part. When large-scale polychoral music was to be performed extra singers were hired, usually with one to a part in each extra choir.

All this, however, did not necessarily apply to the Cappella Pontificia, the German College or the Cappella Giulia. Richard Sherr has shown us that little more than half the papal singers had useful voices for church singing at times, but this still left about 15 singers, the equivalent of Palestrina's Cappella Giulia.[18] It is important to stress that this was the choir that was the composer's workshop, with four adults on ATB and six boys (though it too was not always up to strength); it was this, rather than the Cappella Pontificia, that called forth the bulk of his music and first tried it out. The availability of the *Diarii Sistini* and the German College diaries can distort our view of Palestrina's norm. Unfortunately, we have virtually no information on performance practice from the surviving records of the Cappella Giulia during Palestrina's tenure, while that available for the succeeding period must be treated with caution because of the dramatic change to the basilica's shape after the composer's death. We do know that the choir, like the Cappella Pontificia, was split for weekday

ferial singing, but in both cases this is less relevant to the performance of polyphony, which was mainly done on Sundays and feast-days when the whole choir was present. We know too that only four singers went on occasion to the smaller churches which were dependent on St Peter's for their clergy and liturgy, but again this tells us nothing about the basilica itself. In the absence of any evidence it is dangerous to draw firm conclusions one way or the other about the performance of normal-scale music there. It does, however, seem safe to assume that the practice represented by Animuccia's Masses of 1567 would have continued to apply, i.e. more than one singer per part for Mass Ordinaries, with reduction to solo voices for the specially highlighted sections. For polychoral settings, of which Palestrina composed a large number, we know that there can only have been one or two on each part since no outside singers were hired to supplement the basilica's own forces before 1597. Evidence from other establishments suggests that in fact it was sung by solo voices. In 1576 Palestrina took eight singers (and an organist) to provide Lenten music at the oratory of SS. Trinità dei Pellegrini, where music for two choirs was undoubtedly performed.[19] Single voices would have been adequate for a relatively small oratory, as they would have been for the truncated nave and Cappella del Coro of the old St Peter's. By the early 1600s, on the other hand, with the huge dome area and its surrounding chapels opened up for liturgical use (and the nave after 1615), large numbers of extra singers were employed by St Peter's on its two major patronal feast-days (SS. Peter and Paul on 29 June and the anniversary of the basilica's dedication on 18 November), which meant that there was considerable reinforcing of voices in some choirs in order to cope with the huge acoustic space.[20]

In conclusion, the conundrum posed by Sherr can be reconciled in only two ways: either performance practice changed between the late 15th and late 16th centuries, or singing by single and multiple singers on each part coexisted throughout the period. It would seem that both were the case: there was certainly an increase in one-per-part singing as the 16th century progressed, by one or more singers accompanied by the organ; this accelerated from the 1570s onwards. At the same time, particular sections of the

Mass and Office were always sung (often unaccompanied) by single singers, while more than one per part could sing the bulk of the more traditional genres if available. Of course, there were never more than four on the adult parts, and usually fewer, so there was no question of large choral performance. Finally, I would like to endorse Graham Dixon's call for more imaginative experimentation in the performance of late 16th-century music. We are still left with many unanswered questions. With Crivelli's 'si placet' in mind let us not be too dogmatic, but try various ways of singing and playing this music, within the boundaries of what we know to have been possible at the time.[21]

1 R. Sherr, 'Competence and incompetence in the papal choir in the age of Palestrina', *Early music*, xxii (1994), pp.606–29; G. Dixon 'The performance of Palestrina: some questions, but fewer answers', *ibid.*, pp.666–75.

2 R. Sherr, 'Performance practice in the papal chapel during the 16th century', *Early music*, xv (1987), pp.453–62; J. Lionnet, 'Performance practice in the papal chapel during the 17th century', *Early music*, xv (1987), pp.4–15.

3 All the topics addressed here will be dealt with in more detail in my forthcoming book, *Roman sacred music in the age of Palestrina*.

4 The *diarii* for these years (including 1562) were published in H. W. Frey, *Die Diarien der sixtinischen Kapelle in Rome der Jahre 1560 und 1561* (Düsseldorf, 1959).

5 Sherr, 'Performance practice in the papal chapel during the 16th century'.

6 See Sherr, 'Performance practice in the papal chapel during the 16th century' and Lionnet, 'Performance practice in the papal chapel during the 17th century'.

7 See N. O'Regan, *Sacred polychoral music in Rome, 1575–1621* (Diss., U. of Oxford, 1988) and my article 'The performance of Roman sacred polychoral music in the late 16th and early 17th centuries: evidence from archival sources', *Performance practice review* (forthcoming).

8 Quoted in T. D. Culley, *A study of the musicians connected with the German College during the 17th century and of their activities in Northern Europe, Jesuits and music*, i (Rome–St Louis, 1970), p.72.

9 Archive of the German College in Rome, M. Lauretano, *Diario dall' Ottobre 1582–1583*, p.94.

10 See N. O'Regan, 'Musical ambassadors in Rome and Loreto: papal singers at the confraternities of SS. Trinità dei Pellegrini and S. Rocco in the late 16th and early 17th centuries', *Cappellae apostolicae sixtinaeque collectanea acta monumenta*, iii (Rome, 1994), pp.75–95.

11 Archive of the German College, *Diario 1591*, p.37. In this context the word *musica* always refers to polyphony.

12 Archive of the German College, Lauretano, *Diario*, pp.81–2.

13 Some of the archival references are given in Dixon, 'The performance of Palestrina'; others can be found in Culley, *A study of the musicians connected with the German College*.

14 T. D. Culley, 'Musical activity in some 16th century Jesuit colleges, with special reference to the Venerable English College in Rome from 1579 to 1589', *Analecta musicologica*, xix (1979), p 11.

15 For Viadana's preface see O. Strunk, *Source readings in music history*, iii: *The Baroque era* (London, 1981), pp.59–63.

16 P. Barbieri, 'On a continuo organ part attributed to Palestrina', *Early music*, xxii (1994), pp.587–605.

17 See N. O'Regan, 'Music at the Roman Archconfraternity of San Rocco in the late sixteenth century', *La musica a Roma attraverso le fonti d'archivio, Atti del convegno internazionale, Roma 4–7 Giugno 1992* (Lucca, 1994), pp.521–52.

18 R. Sherr, 'Competence and incompetence in the papal choir'.

19 N. O'Regan, 'Palestrina and the oratory of SS. Trinità dei Pellegrini', *Atti del secondo convegno internazionale di studi palestriniani* (Palestrina, 1991), pp.95–121.

20 See O'Regan, *Sacred polychoral music in Rome* and 'The performance of Roman sacred polychoral music'.

21 Two recent recordings by French groups do this very successfully: on the Accord CD 210662 the Ensemble Sagittarius, directed by Michel Laplenie, convincingly performs Palestrina's *Missa Ecce ego Johannes* with a choir exactly the size of the Cappella Giulia, cutting down to solo voices for the reduced-voice sections only. On the Pierre Verany CD PV795092 the Akademia Ensemble, directed by Françoise Laserre, uses a variety of vocal/instrumental combinations with ornamentation for the same composer's Song of Songs cycle.

[12]

What Can the Organ *Partitura* to Tomás Luis de Victoria's *Missae, Magnificat, motecta, psalmi et alia quam plurima* of 1600 Tell Us about Performance Practice?[1]

Noel O'Regan

Tomás Luis de Victoria's *Missae, Magnificat, motecta, psalmi et alia quam plurima, 3, 4, 8, 9, 12vv* of 1600 was a landmark publication, bringing together in a single print all of his polychoral music, much of it already published in Venice and Rome. It introduced Victoria's version of the Roman polychoral idiom to the Iberian peninsula, where it was to have great influence, spreading from there into the new world.[2] It was clearly intended as a major publication project and was dedicated to the new Spanish King Philip III whose aunt, the dowager Empress Maria of Austria, Victoria was serving; it also provided the Madrid royal printer Ioannes Flandrus with the opportunity to show his skill in printing music for multiple parts.[3] Most significantly it included, for the first time with a vocal print, an organ *partitura* in four-voice open score. This, for the most part, reproduces the music of the first choir only (even in triple-choir pieces), with rests when that choir is not singing. On first glance it appears to follow the vocal lines of Choir I exactly but, on closer examination, there are considerable modifications that throw some light on its function and have implications for contemporary performance practice in Madrid and in Rome.[4]

---

[1] I would like to dedicate this paper to Prof. Robert Stevenson in admiration of his lifetime's outstanding work on Hispanic music.

[2] Noel O'Regan, "From Rome to Madrid: the polychoral music of Tomás Luis de Victoria," *Atti del Convegno internazionale: La tradizione policorale in italia, nella penisola Iberica e nel Nuovo Mondo, 27-29 Ottobre 2006* (Venezia: Fondazione Levi, in press).

[3] Robert Stevenson, "Tomás Luis de Victoria: unique Spanish genius," *Inter-American Music Review* 12 (1991), 1-100; idem., "Tomás Luis de Victoria," *New Grove Dictionary of Music and Musicians*, ed. Stanley Sadie (London: Macmillan, 2001).

[4] The copy of the *partitura* in Munich, Bayerische Staatsbibliothek, has been consulted, as have the part-books in the Biblioteca Nazionale in Florence and in the library of Valladolid Cathedral. I am grateful to Clara Mateo Sabadell for consulting the Valladolid part-books on my behalf.

Victoria himself was conscious that having the *partitura* printed was something new. In a letter sent to Jaén Cathedral Chapter in February 1601, accompanying a copy of the print, he said:

> "I have had this book of Masses, Magnificats, Psalms, Salves and other things printed for two and three choirs together with this particular book for the organ, the like of which, glory to God Our Lord, has not previously been issued in Spain or Italy. This is produced for organists in the case where there are not four voices present or just one who sings with the organ – similarly the [triple-choir] Mass and Magnificat [can be sung] with voices, organ and instrumentalists."[5]

This tells us that Victoria envisaged his *partitura*, not as providing a fully-realised organ part to accompany Choir I, which is how it has sometimes been regarded, particularly by some groups recording this repertoire,[6] but either to substitute for Choir I entirely or to accompany a soloist singing just one of its parts. His reference to singing with the organ could refer in particular to his nine-voice *Missa pro Victoria* where Choir I has five vocal parts, including two soprano lines, the upper of which is not included in the organ *partitura*. This top line could have been sung, with the organ playing the other four Choir I parts, and all the second choir parts being sung by voices. It is significant that, even where the texture of Choir I thins out and the first soprano part of this Mass could have been included in the *partitura*, it is not.

There are four sections in two of the double-choir Masses in this print, which are set for five voices only. Two are in the *Missa Alma Redemptoris Mater*: the *Christe eleison* and the *Benedictus*, where the four voices from Choir II are joined by the tenor from Choir I. Victoria includes both sections in his *partitura*, despite their being sung mainly by Choir II, and leaves out the Tenor I part, presumably intending it to be sung, with the organ supplying the other four parts where there were not enough singers available. The same two movements of the *Missa Ave Regina* are also set for five voices: in this case it is the alto from Choir I that is added to Choir II. The *partitura* leaves out this Altus I part in the *Benedictus*, but, in the *Christe eleison*, it excludes the Altus II part instead. Again Victoria must have intended both to be sung. His suggestion to have just one singer from Choir I, with the other parts played on the organ, presumably can apply to the bulk of the print's contents as well. As for two of the three triple-choir items – the *Missa Laetatus sum* and the *Magnificat Sexti toni* – Victoria seems to be suggesting in his letter that the organ could play the Choir I parts, with voices and instruments each performing the parts of one

---

[5] *Yo he hecho ymprimir esos libros de misas magnificats Salmos salves y otras cossas a dos y a tres choros para con el organo dequesto libro particular que a gloria de dios nostro señor no a salido en españa ni en ytalia libro particular. Como esto para los organistas porque con el donde no hubiere aparejo de quatro voces una sola que cante con el organo ara coro de por ssi – tambien la misa y magnifica para voces organo y ministriles.* The letter was first published in Samuel Rubio, "Dos interessantes cartas autógrafas de T. L. de Victoria," *Revista di Musicología* 4 (1981), 333-341 and subsequently republished in Stevenson, "Tomás Luis de Victoria: unique Spanish genius," 30.

[6] For example, in the recording *Tomás Luis de Victoria, Volume 1: Devotion to our Lady* by The Sixteen, directed by Harry Christophers, Collins 15012/Coro COR16035.

3

of the other choirs. The separation in his wording implies that voices take one choir and instruments the other. He does not include the third triple-choir setting in the publication – the psalm *Laetatus sum* on which the Mass is based – but there are no significant disparities in this setting that would suggest treating it differently.

What Victoria is essentially doing here is providing for church choirs that did not have eight or twelve singers available, but that might still wish to sing (and buy) his music. We know from the preface to Viadana's *Cento Concerti Ecclesiastici* of 1602, for instance, that this sort of situation was common around 1600, with choirs taking certain parts from compositions to suit the available singers, often without sufficient awareness that leaving out some parts might make musical nonsense of the result; this was Viadana's stated reason for providing these small-scale concertato motets.[7] In 1599, Asprilio Pacelli had done something similar, writing in the introduction to his *Chorici Psalmi et Motecta* (Rome: Nicolò Muti) that, although he was having his music printed in four vocal part-books (without a *Bassus ad organum* in his case), the music would sound just as well, or even better, if one of the vocal parts – the altus - were left out and the organ used to fill up the harmony.[8]

The organ was being increasingly used both for accompaniment and to substitute for voices at this period, especially in devotional contexts and in oratories such as those of confraternities. In the same introduction, Pacelli stated that his four-voice alternatim psalms and motets were "composed more as *concerti* with organ, such as is nowadays the custom in Rome for spiritual delight, so that they can entertain piously, than as ordinary church music."[9] Gabriele Fattorini in the preface to his *I Sacri Concerti a due voci* of 1600 said the same thing: "Although [...] it cannot de denied that music with many instruments gives great pleasure on days of high solemnity, and, indeed is then most fitting, experience teaches over and over again that with one, or at the most two, voices, which now and then nicely and skilfully sing with an organ, the weary souls of sinners can be refreshed and the pious minds of listeners charmed and captivated by divine love."[10] In fact, both Pacelli and Fattorini included extra *ripieno* parts for a second choir

---

[7] See the translation of Viadana's preface in Oliver Strunk, *Source Readings in Music History* 3, The Baroque Era (London and Boston: Faber, 1952, 1981), 60-63.

[8] Noel O'Regan, "Asprilio Pacelli, Ludovico da Viadana and the Origins of the Roman *Concerto Ecclesiastico*," *Journal of Seventeenth-Century Music*, 6 (2000), http://www.sscm-jscm.org/v6/no1/oregan.html.

[9] *Mi sono risoluto dunque per sodisfattion di molti dar alla stampa il presente Libro di Salmi et Mottetti fatti più per concerti con organo, quali hoggidi si usano in Roma, diletto spirituale, per potersi trattenere piamente, che per musica ordinaria di cappella.* See O'Regan, "Asprilio Pacelli."

[10] *Quamquam [...] harmonicos, et graves multifariis symphoniis concentus in magnis sollenibus maximopere oblectare, ac optime convenire, inficias iri minime possit: una tamen, aut altera summum voce cum organo aliquando perite, et suaviter divinas laudes canente, tum defessos cantorum spiritus recreari, tum pias auditorum mentes mulceri, supernoque amore captari, identidem perdocet experientia.* Gabriele Fattorini, *I sacri concerti a*

in order to increase the flexibility of their publications, essentially turning it into polychoral music.[11] Victoria was working in the convent of the *Descalzas Reales* in Madrid where both music of high solemnity and for devotional contexts would have been called for; similarly, in Rome, where he worked for a number of confraternities as well as for the *Collegio Germanico*, his music could have been heard in a variety of large- and small-scale contexts.[12]

Flexibility was the key, especially in adapting published music. Pacelli's preface reminds us that, just because it was standard and convenient for sacred music to be printed in part-book format with all parts texted, this was not necessarily the only way of performing it. There are, for instance, examples of Victoria's sacred music arranged for lute with one or two solo voices singing the upper part(s).[13] Victoria was taking a risk in publishing so much music for eight and twelve voices in his 1600 print with just eight short three- and four-voice works added as an appendix. Hitherto he had always added his polychoral music to prints that mainly contained music for fewer voices. People might well have been put off buying the 1600 print if they thought they had to have eight or twelve singers to perform it, and so he is providing an alternative for churches that had fewer singers, but at least employed an organist.[14] Rather than expect that organist to use a *Bassus ad organum* part to improvise from, he provides a *partitura*

---

due voci, Murray C. Bradshaw (Neuheusen-Stuttgart: AIM, Hänssler-Verlag, 1986). This translation is by Murray Bradshaw.

[11] Pacelli included an extra part-book in a 1601 reprint containing Choir 2 parts for optional double-choir settings of the doxologies to his psalms and Magnificats. He further promised in his preface to issue a second volume, which would contain *risposti*, presumably settings for Choir 2 of the alternate verses to the *alternatim* psalms. See O'Regan, "*Asprilio Pacelli*."

[12] Noel O'Regan, "Tomás Luis de Victoria's Roman churches revisited," *Early Music*, 28 (2000), 403-418.

[13] For example, there are eight pieces by Victoria arranged for lute in the manuscript Tenbury 340 from c. 1615 now in the Bodleian Library, Oxford, one of a series of manuscripts associated with the recusant English Catholic Edward Paston. The vocal part-books do not survive, but the Cantus parts are not included in the lute tablature, implying that they were intended to be sung. See James L. Mitchell, *An Examination of Manuscript Tenbury 340 and a Critical Edition of Six Works from its Repertory* (Unpublished M.Mus dissertation, University of Edinburgh, 1998).

[14] This may have been one of the reasons why the chapter of Avila Cathedral decided that this print was not appropriate for their church and authorised its return to Victoria with some polite words. They felt this particularly about the *Missa pro Victoria*. See Samuel Rubio, "La misa *Pro victoria* de Tomás Luis de Victoria," *Ritmo* 52 (1982), [not paginated]. Quoted in Eugene Casjen Cramer, *Tomás Luis de Victoria: A Guide to Research* (Garland Publishing, New York and London, 1998), 164.

5

with four of the voice parts included. Victoria was nothing if not a good marketer of his publications.[15]

Looking more closely at Victoria's organ score we find that, for about half of the twenty-four pieces, the organ reproduces the vocal parts of Choir I exactly. However, for thirteen of these works it does not just follow Choir I, but makes various changes and additions that fall into a number of categories. The most common change is to substitute the Bassus II part for Bassus I, in order to avoid the fifth – or more rarely the third - of the harmony when it falls in Bassus I.[16] There are also places where the Bassus I part has dropped out, leaving Tenor I with the fifth of the harmony; in these cases the Bassus II part is again added to complete the harmony.[17] Other changes involve adding one or more voices from Choir II, where there are only one or two parts singing in Choir I, in order to fill up the harmony.[18] There is one place where the organ adopts the Cantus II part rather than Cantus I, where the former is higher in pitch than the latter.[19] Another type of change is to simplify the bass part—and occasionally one or more of the others—by eliminating ornamental figures such as scalic runs, keeping the organ part on a held breve.[20]

What is most significant about these changes (apart from the last) is that almost all occur in those pieces that Victoria had first published in or before 1581, i.e. in his earliest essays in the polychoral idiom. The pieces with the most changes are those first published in 1572 (*Ave Maria*) and 1576 (*Nisi Dominus, Regina Coeli, Salve Regina, Super flumina Babylonis*). There are fewer changes in those from 1581 (*Alma Redemptoris Mater, Ave Regina, Dixit Dominus, Laudate Dominum, Laudate Pueri*) and virtually none in any of the pieces published subsequently in 1583 (*Laetatus sum, Litaniae Beatae Maria Virginis*), 1585 (*Lauda Sion*), 1592 (*Missa Salve Regina*) and those newly composed for the 1600 print (see Table 1 below). There is an easy explanation for this: in his early polychoral pieces Victoria did not write for split choirs singing at a distance from each other and so did not necessarily make his two choirs harmonically independent of each other. Groupings of voices could be taken across both choirs and one of the bass parts (usually Bassus I) could have the fifth of the harmony. As long as the

---

[15] There are various examples of Victoria, as in the case of Jaén Cathedral, sending copies of his prints to princes and institutions and asking for money in return. See Stevenson, *op. cit.*, 28-29.

[16] E.g. in the final nine bars of *Nisi Dominus*.

[17] E.g. in bars 34-35 of *Alma Redemptoris mater*.

[18] E.g. in bars 10, 27-29 of *Ave Regina*.

[19] Bars 63-66 of *Dixit Dominus*.

[20] E.g. in the last eight bars of *Salve Regina*. Some of these changes have also been described in Daniele V. Filippi, *Tomás Luis de Victoria* (Palermo: L'Epos, 2008), 92.

two choirs were adjacent to each other this was not a problem but, by the early 1580s in Rome, choirs were being physically separated, and composers began to write for harmonically independent choirs, avoiding the fifth in either bass part and keeping the two choirs distinct rather than mixing voices across them.[21] Clef combinations were rationalized, with the same combinations—and voice-types—in both choirs. This made it easier to have both bass parts doubling the root of the harmony, at the same pitch or an octave apart. The third above the root was used occasionally in triple-choir music but not commonly. After 1581 Victoria and his Roman contemporaries generally used contrary motion between the bass parts, or rests when writing for three choirs, to avoid parallel octaves.

Evidence for the change in approach in Rome comes from a number of rewritings of double-choir pieces found in a series of related Roman manuscripts from the early 1580s. Music by Giovanni Animuccia, Orlando di Lasso, Luca Marenzio, and Giovanni P. da Palestrina was altered, to allow performance by spatially-separated choirs, by rewriting bass parts to eliminate fifths and tidying up overlaps between voices across the choirs into a cleaner takeover from one choir to the next.[22] It clearly became important for Rome-based composers to adapt this new idiom and, while there is no evidence for the rewriting of Victoria's earlier pieces to make them singable by real *cori spezzati*, he too adapted the new procedures after 1581. In that context, it is odd that, in republishing his early pieces in 1600, Victoria chose not to rewrite the vocal parts, but he did adapt the organ *partitura* so that it reflects the split-choir ideal. Victoria did revise his work in other contexts, and one might well have expected him to do so here, particularly as he was producing an organ *partitura* with revisions.[23] The fact that he did not implies that, when all parts were sung by voices, he still assumed that in these early pieces the two choirs would be adjacent to each other. Otherwise listeners who were positioned closer to Choir I would hear second inversion harmony, which by then, in Rome at least, was not acceptable. That this was also the case in Madrid is shown by the fact that in all of the pieces first published in 1600 (and presumably composed after Victoria returned to Madrid in about 1587) there are no instances of second inversion harmony in one of the choirs, even in pieces for three choirs where its avoidance is more challenging for the composer.

The provision of the revised versions in the organ *partitura*, on the other hand, suggests that when the organ was used to substitute for (or perhaps accompany) Choir I, then such separation was expected. It was common, at least in Rome, for the singers in Choir I to serve as

---

[21] Noel O'Regan, "Sacred Polychoral Music in Rome 1575-1620," (Ph.D. diss., University of Oxford, 1988). Idem., "The Performance of Roman Sacred Polychoral Music in the late 16th and early 17th Centuries: Evidence from Archival Sources," *Performance Practice Review,* 8 (1995), 107-146.

[22] Noel O'Regan, "The Early Polychoral Music of Orlando di Lasso: New Light from Roman Sources," *Acta Musicologica,* 56 (1984), 234-251.

[23] It is particularly odd that, in *Super flumina Babylonis*, Victoria returned to the original version of 1576 rather than incorporate the revisions of 1585, which had been in line with more recent Roman practice.

soloists and be positioned at the main organ with the *maestro di cappella* while other *ripieni* choirs sang from platforms some distance away, often with their own conductor and portative organ. An interesting consequence of Victoria's rewriting of the organ part is that it introduces parallel octaves between the organ part and the bass of Choir II, something he otherwise studiously avoids. Even here he does try to avoid them by using contrary motion, but cannot do so all the time. Other composers of the period were not fussy about parallels between bass and other lines: Ludovico da Viadana in the preface to his *Salmi a quattro chori* of 1612 makes no apology for doubling up bass and other lines: "Because they stand apart from one another the listener cannot distinguish whether they are singing in octaves or in unison [...] For if one wishes to follow the rules strictly in the *ripieni*, one must introduce whole rests and half rests, dotted notes and syncopations; as a result the music becomes distorted, clumsy, and unyielding, and the singing reckless and less attractive." He finishes by saying: "But when all is said and done I have done things in my own way."[24]

Another important area in which Victoria's organ *partitura* gives information is the practice of transposition. The organ parts for two of the Masses have the rubric "Ad quartam inferiorem" at the beginning of the Kyrie: the *Missa Alma Redemptoris Mater* and the *Missa Salve Regina*. Both use the *chiavette* or high-clef combination and both have a B♭ in the key signature. They are not the only pieces in the collection to use the *chiavette* but the others, which include the antiphons *Alma Redemptoris Mater* and *Salve Regina* on which the two Masses are based, as well as *Dic nobis Maria* (*Victimae paschali*), *Dixit Dominus*, and the *Magnificat primi toni*, do not have the same rubric on the organ *partitura*. This can probably be explained by the fact that the two Masses are the first two pieces in the *partitura* to use the *chiavette*; they are the first and third items respectively in the publication, separated by the *Missa Ave Regina* that is in standard clefs or *chiavi naturali*. The two Masses in *chiavette* each end on one of the only two final notes used in this publication, the *Missa Alma Redemptoris* on F and the *Missa Salve Regina* on G. There are no pieces here notated in *chiavette* and with no flat in the key signature, which generally led to transposition down a fifth. So it is reasonable to assume that Victoria, or his printer, having included the transposition rubric on the first two relevant items in the publication, did not see the need to keep reminding the organist to transpose. Of course, one could argue that the omission of the rubric on the antiphons and other pieces in *chiavette* meant that Victoria did not intend them to be transposed, but only the two Mass settings. Let us therefore examine the clefs and ranges used by Victoria in this print in some more detail.

---

[24] Lodovico Grossi da Viadana, *Salmi a quattro chori*, ed. Gerhard Wielakker (Madison: A-R Editions, 1998), 2-3.

TABLE 1. CLEF COMBINATIONS,[25] KEY SIGNATURES AND FINALS OF PIECES IN VICTORIA'S *MISSAE, MAGNIFICAT, MOTECTA, PSALMI ET ALIA QUAM PLURIMA* OF 1600.

(Dates of original publication are given in brackets. The pieces are grouped according to clef combination, key signature and final, and are in alphabetical order within each grouping.)

Standard clefs, F final:

Ave Regina (1581)	$2 \times C_1C_3C_4F_4$	♭	F
Ecce nunc (1600)	$2 \times C_1C_3C_4F_4$	♭	F
Missa Ave Regina (1600)	$2 \times C_1C_3C_4F_4$	♭	F
Missa pro Victoria (1600)	$C_1C_1C_3C_4F_4 \quad C_1C_3C_4F_4$	♭	F

Standard clefs, F final, Choir I *a voci pari*

Laudate Pueri (1581)	$C_1C_1C_3C_4 \quad C_1C_3C_4F_4$	♭	F
Nisi Dominus (1576)	$C_1C_1C_3F_3 \quad C_1C_3C_4F_4$	♭	F
Regina Coeli (1576)	$C_1C_1C_3F_3 \quad C_1C_3C_4F_4$	♭	F
Super flumina (1576)	$C_1C_1C_3F_3 \quad C_2C_3C_4F_4$	♭	F

Triple-choir pieces, F final: Standard clefs for Choirs I & III, Choir II *a voci pari*

Laetatus sum (1583)	$2 \times C_1C_3C_4F_4 \quad C_1C_1C_3F_3$	♭	F
Magnificat sexti toni (1600)	$2 \times C_1C_3C_4F_4 \quad C_1C_1C_3F_3$	♭	F
Missa Laetatus sum (1600)	$2 \times C_1C_3C_4F_4 \quad C_1C_1C_3F_3$	♭	F

Standard clefs, G final

Litaniae BVM (1583)	$2 \times C_1C_3C_4F_4$	♮	G
Lauda Sion (1585)	$2 \times C_1C_3C_4F_4$	♮	G
Ave Maria (1572)	$2 \times C_1C_3C_4F_4$	♭	G

---

[25] In describing clefs, the usual system is employed where the letters C, F, and G describe the type of clef and the subscript number is the line on which it is placed, counting from the bottom of the staff upwards.

9

Laudate Dominum (1581)	2 x $C_1C_3C_4F_4$	♭	G
Veni Sancte Spiritus (1600)	2 x $C_1C_3C_4F_4$	♭	G

Chiavette, F final

Alma Redemptoris (1581)	2 x $G_2C_2C_3F_3$	♭	F
Missa Alma Redemptoris (1600)	2 x $G_2C_2C_3F_3$	♭	F

Chiavette, G final, Choir I *a voci pari*

Magnificat primi toni (1600)	$G_2G_2C_2C_3$	$G_2C_2C_3F_3$	♭	G
Dic nobis Maria (1600) (Victimae paschali)	$G_2G_2C_1C_3$	$G_2C_2C_3C_4$	♭	G

Chiavette, G final (some variation in Choir I or Choir II)

Dixit Dominus (1581)	$G_2C_2C_3C_4$	$G_2C_2C_3F_3$	♭	G
O Ildephonse (1600)	$G_2G_2C_2C_4$	$G_2C_2C_3F_3$	♭	G
Salve Regina (1576)	$G_2G_2C_2C_4$	$C_1C_2C_3F_3$	♭	G
Missa Salve Regina (1592)	$G_2G_2C_2C_4$	$G_2C_2C_3F_3$	♭	G

Table 1 gives details of clefs, key signatures, and finals for each of the twenty-four polychoral pieces in the 1600 print. At first glance the range of clef combinations seems considerable – there are thirteen different combinations – but they can be rationalized into seven groups as in the table. Taking into account the use of *voci pari* combinations, where one choir has two sopranos, alto, tenor and no bass, and seeing the triple-choir pieces as an extension of the double-choir standard clef ones, the number of different combination can be further reduced to four: standard and *chiavette* combinations with either F or G as final. Using the signifiers that make up the tonal-type method of analysis, in which only the soprano clef, key signature, and final are delineated, we have five tonal types: C_1 ♭ F, G_2 ♭ F, C_1 ♮ G, C_1 ♭ G and G_2 ♭ G. Of the twenty-four pieces only seven use the *chiavette*; F and G finals are almost evenly balanced, with thirteen of the former and eleven of the latter.

The use of *voci pari* combinations in one of the choirs, something of which Victoria was fond, does not affect the overall clef combination, which can be established from the clefs of the outer soprano and bass parts. Similarly the variations in clef (and hence in voice type) within

Choir I in *Dixit Dominus*, *O Ildefonse*, and the *Missa Salve Regina* do not affect the intended overall clef combination. Interchanging C_4 and F_3 clefs for the bass in *chiavette* was common practice, and the use of C_2 rather than C_3 for the third part down simply indicates an alto rather than a tenor range. There are two pieces where Victoria unusually uses the C_1 clef within the *chiavette*, *Salve Regina*, and *Dic nobis, Maria*; in both cases this is to cover a mezzo-soprano range and does not alter the overall function of the clef code. His analogous use of the C_2 clef for the top part of Choir II in the standard-cleffed *Super flumina Babylonis* also indicates a mezzo-soprano voice and again does not affect the clef code.

It is important to note here the unreliability of the Pedrell complete edition of Victoria's works in regard to the clefs of two of the works in *chiavette*: the *Salve Regina* and the *Missa Alma Redemptoris Mater*.[26] The first two editions of the *Salve Regina*, in 1576 and 1581, started with the normal *chiavette* clefs, but for the fourth verse "Eia ergo," and subsequent verses, the Bassus II part changed from F_3 to F_4, in order to accommodate some low Gs without using ledger lines. The 1576 print did the same thing in the case of the final *Agnus Dei* sections of the *Missa Simile est Regnum* and the *Missa Beatae Mariae*. This does not affect the transposition code since that would have been indicated to the singers by the clefs at the start of these works. In 1600, Victoria or his publisher used the F_3 clef for Bassus II throughout. Pedrell used F_4 for Bassus II but did not indicate by a prefatory clef the original use of F_3 at the start of the piece, or its use throughout in 1600. For the *Missa Alma Redemptoris Mater*, Pedrell also used F_4 for Bassus II without a prefatory indication that the original 1600 print used F_3. In the 1600 print, Victoria/Flandrus was happy to use ledger lines below the Bassus II staff to accommodate low notes. These normally come at the ends of sections, and they might be compared to the low strings of the theorbo, then becoming popular as an accompanying instrument. Downward transposition does bring these notes even lower but, since this is the case in the two Masses for which Victoria provides the instruction to transpose, it cannot have posed a problem. In Madrid, we know that from at least 1601 onwards, the singers in the *Descalzas Reales* were supported by a *bajon* (bassoon) that would have ensured that these low notes would have been heard.[27] In answer to the question posed above then, it would seem logical to apply the transposition instructions to all of the pieces using *chiavette* in the 1600 print.

Victoria's publication seems to have been the earliest to include a rubric indicating downward transposition of a fourth on an organ part.[28] This was to become relatively common

---

[26] *Thomae Ludovici Victoria Abulensis Opera omnia*, ed. Felipe Pedrell (Leipzig: Breitkopf und Härtel, 1902-13). Pedrell is also unreliable in the case of the original clefs of *Dic nobis, Maria (Victimae Paschali)*, where he does not indicate that the original clef of the Altus II part was C_2 rather than C_1.

[27] Stevenson, "Tomás Luis de Victoria: Unique Spanish Genius," 23.

[28] Lute intabulations transposed down a fourth or fifth appear earlier, for example the large collection published by Jacob Paix in Lauingen in 1583. See Ala Botti Caselli, "Musiche di Giovanni Pierluigi da Palestrina nelle partiture e nelle intavolature organistiche tra Cinque e Seicento," *Bolletino della Deputazione di Storia Patria per L'Umbria*,

11

practice in the early seventeenth century, and theorists such as Adriano Banchieri in 1601 wrote of transposing pieces in *chiavette* down by a fourth when there was a flat in the key signature and by a fifth when there was none.[29] The increasing use of organ for accompaniment or substitution from the 1590s meant that transposition needed to be codified more clearly. It must also have applied to unaccompanied pieces in *chiavette*, but there was not the same need to coordinate voices and organ in that case. Andrew Parrott has summarized the evidence, though he overlooked this Victoria print, saying that the earliest example was to be found in Viadana's *Cento Concerti* of 1602.[30] Victoria's primacy was not helped by the fact that, in the Pedrell edition, the rubric was omitted from the *Missa Alma Redemptoris*, though he did print it for the *Missa Salve Regina*.

Victoria's 1600 organ score was a novelty that did not catch on, at least as a means of providing organ parts for sacred music. Publishing books for organ was certainly in the air around 1600. In 1599, the Venetian printer Giacomo Vincenti published an anthology of double-choir music by mainly Rome-based composers "con le parte dei bassi per poter sonarli nell'organo."[31] This was a *basso seguente*, conflating the two vocal bass parts without any figures or accidentals. The composers included five of Victoria's Roman contemporaries: Felice Anerio, Ruggiero Giovanelli, Luca Marenzio, Giovanni M. Nanino, and Giovanni P. da Palestrina. Fattorini's *I Sacri Concerti a due voci* of 1600 was published in Venice by Ricciardo Amadino with a "basso generale per maggior commodità degli'organisti."[32] The organ part of *Laetamini in Domino* is notated a fourth lower than the rest. Murray Bradshaw mistook this for an error but, since the piece is the only one in the collection to use the *chiavette* and has a flat in the key signature, the print is clearly providing the necessary transposition ready-made for the

---

105 (2008), 217-251). Simone Verovio's *Diletto spirituale* published in Rome in 1586 has redactions for both organ tablature (on two staves) and lute as well as three/four vocal parts. All those with vocal parts in *chiavette* are transposed down a fourth or fifth. The same applies, with some exceptions to Verovio's later publications. See Patrizio Barbieri, "«Chiavette» and Modal Transposition in Italian Practice (c. 1500-1837)," *Recercare*, 3 (1991), 5-79.

[29] Adriano Banchieri, *Cartella, overo Regole utilissime à quelli che desiderano imparare il canto figurato* (Venice, 1601). The lute parts in the publications mentioned in the previous footnote are transposed in accordance with Banchieri's writings. See also Patrizio Barbieri, "Chiavette," *New Grove Dictionary of Music and Musicians*, ed. Stanley Sadie (London: Macmillan, 2001).

[30] Andrew Parrott, "Transposition in Monteverdi's Vespers of 1610. An 'Aberration' Defended," *Early Music*, 12 (1984), 490-516.

[31] The pieces by Rome-based composers had been published in 1592 in Rome by Francesco Coattino, but without an organ part; they had been collected and edited by Giovanni Luca Conforti.

[32] Fattorini, *op. cit.*

organist.[33] In the same year, Nicolò Muti in Rome published Emilio de'Cavalieri's *Rappresentatione di Anima, et di Corpo*, which, for the first time, added figures and accidentals to an organ bass.[34] In 1601, Muti published the first volume of the Roman singer Giovanni Luca Conforti's *Salmi passaggiati...con il basso sotto per sonare, et cantare con organo, con altri stromenti* with an organ bass,[35] and in 1602, Lodovico da Viadana's influential *Cento Concerti Ecclesiastici*, published by Vincenti in Venice, also included a figured organ bass.[36]

The *basso seguento* or *basso continuo* was easier to print and easier for the organist to work from. Lodovico da Viadana confirms this in the preface to his *Cento Concerti Ecclesiastici*:

> "No tablature has been made for these concertos, not in order to escape the trouble, but to make them easier for the organist to play, since, as a matter of fact, not every one would play from a tablature at sight, and the majority would play from the *partitura* as being less trouble; I hope that the organists will be able to make the said tablature at their own convenience which, to tell the truth, is much better."[37]

Viadana uses both the words "intavolatura" (translated here as "tablature") and "partitura." Since the latter is what he provides, it must mean the basso continuo, with the former indicating either an open score or a version in keyboard tablature. While praising the former he recognises that the latter is becoming the preferred medium for organists. Victoria's score would indeed have been difficult to play from at sight: the parts are not lined up against each other, and so the organist would have had to read the four parts individually, a skill which, of course, organists did possess prior to the introduction of keyboard tablature.[38] It is printed in three consecutive staves,

---

[33] Ibid., xix.

[34] Warren Kirkendale, *Emilio de'Cavalieri "Gentilhuomo Romano." His Life and Letters, His Role as Superintendent of all the Arts at the Medici Court, and His Musical Compositions* (Florence: Olschki, 2001), Chapter 9.

[35] See the edition by Murray C. Bradshaw (Neuheusen-Stuttgart: American Institute of Musicology, Hänssler-Verlag, 1985).

[36] Lodovico da Viadana, *Cento Concerti Ecclesiastici*, ed. Claudio Gallico (Kassel: Bärenreiter, 1964).

[37] *Che non si è fatta la intavolatura à questi concerti, per fuggir la fatica, ma per rendere più facile il suonargli à gli'organisti, stando che non tutti suonarebbero all'improviso la intavolatura, e la maggior parte suonaranno la partitura, per essere più spedita: però potranno gl'organisti à sua posta farsi detta intavolatura, che a dirne il vero parla molto meglio.* Lodovico Viadana, *Cento Concerti*, 122. The English translation is taken from Strunk, *Source Readings*, 62.

[38] There are earlier examples of open-score *partiture*: In 1577 Angelo Gardano issued two publications, *Musica di diversi autori* and *Tutti i madrigali di Cipriano di Rore a quattro voci* in four-stave open score, but these were intended as much for private study as for keyboard performance. Keyboard *partiture* also appeared in some

13

continuing from left to right across the two pages of each opening. There are bar lines, which do help, generally placed after every eight minims, but often after six, ten or more, in the manner of contemporary lute tablature.

The big difference between Victoria's *partitura* and these other *bassi seguenti* is, of course, that Victoria mostly only intabulated the music of Choir I. We have seen his explanation for this in the letter to Jaén. Does this rule out the use of organ to accompany both choirs, deriving a *basso seguente* from the two bass parts or using two organs, one with each choir? Presumably not, since this was also such a common practice at the time, certainly in Rome, where each choir often had its own small organ to accompany it.[39] The two sets of part-books with double- and triple-choir music copied for Duke Giovanni Angelo Altaemps in Rome, while not containing any works by Victoria, both have single organ books to accompany polychoral music by Palestrina, Felice Anerio, and others of his Roman contemporaries.[40] If the organ is to be used as an accompanying instrument for Victoria's large-scale music it would seem more sensible to use it for both choirs, rather than just the one. We can be similarly flexible in using instruments to substitute for, or to accompany, some of the vocal parts.

The fact that Victoria chose not to go down the route of the *basso seguente* but sought to reproduce only the vocal parts of Choir I, and those not exclusively, means that his score provides us with some useful information about performance practice, as well as about transposition. Taken together with the composer's letter to the chapter of Jaén Cathedral, it reminds us that we needn't take sets of printed part-books published around 1600 at face value, but should rather be prepared to adapt and experiment, especially in substituting voices with organ. As Asprilio Pacelli, who had followed Victoria as *moderator musicae* at the Collegio Germanico in Rome, said at the end of the preface to his 1599 *Chorici Psalmi*: "All of this can be left to the judgement of the experienced and perceptive *maestro di cappella*, or the capable and sensible organist; with their knowledge and understanding, further advice and examples are unnecessary."[41] While we still know little about performance practice in 1600 Madrid, viewing Victoria's publication of that year in the context of contemporary Italian developments can give us a broader view of the composer's intentions. His polychoral music can be equally apt for

---

theoretical works in the late sixteenth century, for example in Juan Bermudo, *El Libro llamado Declaración de instrumentos musicales* (Osuna: Juan de Leon, 1555).

[39] See Noel O'Regan, "The performance."

[40] See Luciano Luciani, "Le composizioni di Ruggero Giovnnelli contenute nei due codici manoscritti ex Biblioteca Althaempsiana, detti «Collectio major» e «collectio minor»," *Ruggero Giovannelli «musica eccellentissimo e forse il primo del suo tempo». Atti del Congegno Internazionale di Studi (Palestrina e Velletri, 12-14 giugno 1992)*, eds. Carmela Bongiovanni and Giancarlo Rostirolla (Palestrina: Fondazione Giovanni Pierluigi da Palestrina, 1998), 281-318.

[41] *Il che tutto si lascia in arbitrio del dotto svegliato mastro di capella, dal valente, et giuditioso organista: alla cui dottrina, valore: non fa di mestieri usare simili essemplificationi, et avvertimenti.* See O'Regan, "Asprilio Pacelli."

14

making a big show on days of high solemnity and for captivating pious souls in more intimate contexts, as envisaged by Gabriele Fattorini.

[13]

Minstrels in Spanish churches, 1400–1600
Kenneth Kreitner

The use of instruments in the sacred polphony of the Middle Ages and Renaissance has long been a matter of active and sometimes bitter debate. In recent years the trend, among scholars and performers alike, has been toward what James McKinnon has called a 'modified *a cappella* hypothesis'—the idea that long into the 16th century, European church music, including polyphony, was usually performed by voices alone (or in alternatim with organ), and that instrumental accompaniment in our usual sense was rare.[1]

But even some of the most persuasive advocates of *a cappella* performance have been careful to observe one important potential exception—Spain. Both McKinnon and David Fallows, noting several fragments of evidence from 15th- and 16th-century Spain, have speculated that Spanish churches may have anticipated the rest of Europe in allowing instrumentalists inside, and that instrumental accompaniment of sacred music may in fact have been fairly common south of the Pyrenees as early as the lifetime of Dufay.[2]

The suggestion needs to be explored in detail, not only as a matter of historical interest, but because the sacred music of Renaissance Spain seems to be on the verge of widespread rediscovery, and this great music deserves to be done right. A good deal of relevant information has already been collected, especially in Spanish periodicals, local cathedral histories and the like; in this article I propose to assemble the information that has been available to me and to try to develop a coherent image of the place of the minstrel (a word I shall use, as a translation of the Castilian *ministril* or the Catalan *ministrer*, to mean the player of any instrument besides the organ) in Spanish churches during the late Middle Ages and Renaissance.

Three questions, in approximately chronological order, will add structure to this investigation. When and where and what did instruments play in Spanish churches before 1500 or so? When and how did they manage, beginning in the 1520s, to become a regular part of the musical staff in many cathedrals? And what did they do when they got there?

Unambiguous evidence of instrumentalists in Spanish churches before 1500 is relatively rare—partly because fewer and sketchier cathedral records survive from the 15th century than from the 16th, but also, one senses, because such performances were themselves relatively rare. Yet a small steady trickle of information suggests that the use of minstrels to adorn the music of church services was by no means unheard of in the 15th century.

Instrumentalists did, of course, play in outdoor religious processions in Spain throughout the Middle Ages. The annual Corpus Christi procession, which became increasingly elaborate in many Spanish cities during the 14th and 15th centuries, was universally accompanied by instrumental music: in Barcelona the Corpus parade included, in addition to a number of choirs, a band of ten trumpeters and an ensemble of ten soft instrumentalists dressed as angels.[3] And other religious processions, though perhaps smaller, used instruments too. To choose three other examples from Barcelona, all from the mid-15th century: a procession in April 1455 to celebrate the election of the Catalan Pope Calixtus III featured two trumpets and a drum, paid from the cathedral accounts; a second parade the following February to honour the canonization of St Vincent Ferrer included six trumpets and a drum; and in November 1459, when a newly acquired finger of St Candida was presented to the municipal hospital, the parade included not only a large loud ensemble of 13 trumpeters and three drummers, but a soft band of six string players.[4]

Many of these processions went into or through churches along the way; the question is whether the minstrels followed the rest of the parade inside and played while they were there. Very few of the contemporary accounts specify this, but the problem may lie more in the nature of the documentation (which tends to list the forces rather than describe their duties) than in the events themselves. Another example from Barcelona in the 1450s does, in any case, show the instrumentalists inside quite clearly. On 7 August 1457 the city put on a large ceremony to mark the departure of its fleet; the procession went into the cathedral with 'eight pairs of trumpets playing' and 'three minstrels [shawms?] playing'; after Mass and the blessing of the banners they went out:

1 Anonymous (Aragonese school), Virgin and child (15th century) (Barcelona, Museu d'Art de Catalunya)

E passant per lo mig del dit cor, precehint les dites trompes, e suc-
cehint los dits II. homens qui portaven les dites banderes, . . . ven-
ien mediate los minstrés, tots sonants, davant los dits honourable
capitá e a ell acompanyants.[5]

and passing through the middle of the choir, the trumpets pro-
ceeded, and the two men who carried the banners . . . followed
them, and then went the minstrels, all playing, before the
honourable captain [of the fleet] and those accompanying
him.

Just as clearly, however, the instrumentalists sometimes stayed outside. A good example is given by the
Hechos del Condestable don Miguel Lucas de Iranzo; this
Castilian chronicle of the 1460s and 70s, whose remarkable supply of musical details has been often quoted,
describes a wedding in Jaén in 1461, where the procession
to the church was accompanied by

tan gran moltitud & ruydo de atabales, tronpetas bastardas &
ytalianas, chirimías, tanborinos, panderos & locos[6]

a great multitude and noise of drums, bastard and Italian
trumpets, shawms, tambourines and people rejoicing

as well as a band of three dolzainas,[7] and that they were
accompanied back home by

tantas tronpetas y atabales, & los otros estormentos, que no par-
esçía sinó que se vinie el mundo abaxo.[8]

so many trumpets and drums, and the other instruments, as
had never appeared in the world below.

The wedding Mass itself, however, was celebrated only
with 'muy solepnes cantores & órganos' ('very solemn
singers and organ').[9]

None of this is surprising. Instrumentalists are known
to have marched in religious processions all over 15th-
century Europe, and their playing in churches as part of
these processions is at least sporadically documented in
a number of cities.[10] Where Spain seems to have differed
from the rest of the continent, however, is in the use of
minstrels as part of the regular church service. And
again, the best evidence comes not from the ecclesiastical records, but from the *Hechos del Condestable,*
which gives a long account of how its hero, the constable
Miguel Lucas, spent all the religious holidays of a typical
church year (1463–4) in his home town of Jaén; it provides meticulous musical details for various parts of each
day and descriptions of the church services,[11] and most
significantly, two clear references to instrumentalists
playing in church. At Mass on Christmas morning, the
constable and his household marched to church with
'many trumpets and shawms', and, while they were
there,

Los quales tronpetas & cherimías tocauan a tienpos, así al tienpo

que andaua la procesión como al alçar del Cuerpo de nuestro
señor Dios; e avn así mesmo quando el preste salía a decir la
misa.[12]

These trumpets and shawms played at various times, both
when the procession was moving and at the raising of the body
of our Lord God; and also when the priest went out from saying Mass.

On the morning of Epiphany, they marched once again
to the church,

con los dichos tronpetas & cherimías, los quales tocauan en la
eglesia, a la proçesión, & quando sacauan la Verónica, & quando
la adorauan, segúnd & en la manera quel día de pascua.[13]

with those trumpets and shawms, which played in the church,
at the procession, and when they brought out the Verónica and
adored it, in the same way as they did at Christmas.

These two passages are in the chronicler's only explicit
descriptions of instruments in church; with unspecific
phrases and references to aforementioned feasts he
seems to suggest that they may also have played on Circumcision, Easter, Pentecost, Assumption and St
Luke's,[14] and indeed his wording makes it hard to rule
them out for a number of lesser feasts. In general, however, the richness of his musical and liturgical detail
would appear to imply that when instruments were not
mentioned, they were not present, and thus that these
minstrels (probably from the constable's own household, hired or lent for the occasion) took part in
religious services only, on average, every couple of
months at the most, and possibly only twice a year.

Throughout the 15th century, the monarchies of Aragon, Castile and Navarre maintained not only substantial chapel choirs but corps of loud and soft minstrels as
well. Most of the Spanish musicians whose polyphonic
compositions survive can be traced to one or another of
these royal courts.[15] Evidence that singers and instrumentalists performed together in the royal chapels
remains, however, extremely sparse and equivocal. In
1396 Carlos III of Navarre 'paga a los juglares de voz e de
instrumentos de la nuestra capiella 60 florines' ('paid 60
florins to the vocal and instrumental juglars of our
chapel'), but this may be no more than a stereotyped
official wording.[16] In 1420 Alfonso V of Aragon ordered
for his chapel 'orguens petits que sien intonats ab los
ministres, ab cinch tirants' ('a small organ tuned to the
minstrels'), but whether this means that the royal instrumentalists played in the chapel or that the organ was also
used for secular music-making (or both) is not quite
clear.[17] And in 1478, when Prince Juan, son of Ferdinand
and Isabella, was baptized in the cathedral of Seville, the
royal chronicler Andrés Bernáldez reported that

2 Shawms and sackbuts.
Bronze medallion by Juan
Marín and Bautista Vázquez,
cast by Bartolomé Morel
(1564) (Seville Cathedral)

Fué traido el Príncipe á la iglesia, con una gran procesion . . . con infinitos instrumentos de músicas de diversas maneras de trompetas, é chirimias, é sacabuches.[18]

The prince was brought to the church in a great procession . . . with infinite musical instruments of various types—trumpets, shawms and trombones.

However, Bernáldez stopped just short of specifying whether they went into the church and played.

Although these scattered 15th-century references do not provide anything like a complete and authoritative picture of the performance practices throughout the whole peninsula during the course of the century, they do suggest a few generalizations. Above all, the documents seem to show that while the appearance of minstrels may have been a widespread and well established tradition in 15th-century Spanish churches, such performances were nowhere a matter of frequent routine. Instrumentalists were reserved for the most special occasions, particularly for the celebrations that also included a parade, and for the most solemn feast days of the

church year. Second, the instruments used in church were invariably those of the loud band—brass and shawms. And third, there is no evidence at all that these instruments were used to accompany singers; the *Hechos del Condestable* is quite specific in describing them only as providing background or acclamatory music during wordless parts of the Mass—the procession, the raising of the host, the adoration of a relic, the exit of the priest.

At the end of the 15th century, then, the appearance of instrumentalists in Spanish churches was perhaps conspicuous, but still very intermittent. By the end of the 16th, minstrels would be playing in most of the larger churches regularly, and in many they would be employed full-time. The mechanism and chronology of this change varied widely in different places, but a survey of the cathedrals of Seville, Palencia and Barcelona will serve to illustrate some of the general trends.

We have already seen 'trumpets, shawms and trombones' marching in a religious procession to the cathedral of Seville in 1478. This practice surely persisted through the 15th and early 16th centuries, the musicians in these processions being not members of the cathedral staff, but secular minstrels from the community or court: in August 1507, for example, the cathedral paid a band of ducal minstrels to play in a parade for the Assumption of the Virgin.[19] How often such performances took place is difficult to say from the available documentation;[20] however, by the mid-1510s the cathedral chapter was beginning to hire minstrels with some regularity. In 1518 it paid instrumentalists for Easter, Corpus Christi, Sts Peter and Paul, and the Assumption,[21] and on at least two of these occasions (possibly Easter and Corpus Christi) the instruments are specifically referred to as appearing within the church.[22]

Such sporadic hiring of minstrels continued at Seville during the early 1520s,[23] until 1526, when the chapter voted for a more permanent arrangement:

> . . . *como sera muy honrroso en esta santa iglesia y en alavança del culto divino tener salariados e por suyos algunos menestriles altos sacabuches e chirimias para que tengan en algunas fiestas principales e procesiones que faze esta santa iglesia . . . determinaron e mandaron que se resciban çinco menestriles altos en esta santa iglesia tres chirmias que sean tiple e tenor e contra e dos sacabuches personas habiles en su arte para que sirvan en esta santa iglesia . . .*[24]

. . . it would be very honourable in this holy church and in the praise of the divine worship to have on salary, for their own use, some loud minstrels, trombones and shawms, to use in various of the most important feasts and the processions that the church makes . . . they determine and order that five loud minstrels be received into this church: three shawms (treble, tenor and contra) and two trombones, persons skilled in their art, to serve in this church . . .

The ensemble thus created would later suffer some vicissitudes before being rebuilt by the composer and chapelmaster Francisco Guerrero in 1553;[25] but it remains the earliest known cathedral band in Spain—possibly in all Europe.

The admission of instrumentalists into the cathedral establishment of Palencia took place later and by rather different means. Although secular minstrels must have taken part in processions and other religious festivals in Palencia in the 15th and early 16th centuries just as everywhere else, no mention of them is made in the cathedral documents from 1428 to 1552 recently published by José López-Calo;[26] the earliest reference to any instrument besides the organ is from 1553, when the chapter decided to hire 'para el servicio de la música un bajón contrabajo' ('for the service of the music a *bajón contrabajo*')[27]—literally a contrabass bassoon, but presumably a bass dulcian or, especially this early in the century, a bass shawm.[28]

The *bajón* (I shall use the Castilian term to preserve the possible ambiguity) seems to have remained in service as the only minstrel in the church for some years; López-Calo provides a number of references to it from the early 1560s.[29]

In early November 1564 an attempt was made to hire unos ministriles para el servicio desta santa iglesia' ('some minstrels for the service of this holy church');[30] the effort was apparently repelled within a few weeks as being contrary to the cathedral statutes.[31] A little over three years later, however, the rules were relaxed, and amid some controversy, the band of instrumentalists was founded in December of 1567 'en aumento del culto divino y decor [*sic*] del servicio desta santa iglesia' ('to augment the divine worship and honour of the service of this holy church')[32]—note the similarity to the wording of the Seville document above.

The size and instrumentation of this ensemble are not made explicit in the cathedral records, but it was almost certainly a loud band of four or five: only shawms, trombones and *bajón* are mentioned in the documents, and at one point in 1592 when the band was down to two players, the chapter resolved to look for two or three more, 'o por lo menos dos, para que la capilla estuviese cumplida' ('or at least two, so that the chapel would be complete').[33] By the 1580s the cathedral minstrels were playing in all the cathedral's outdoor processions, for the visits of important guests, and at several services a day on all the major feasts of the church year.[34]

Significantly, well into the 17th century the *bajón* continued to be employed at Palencia separately from the other minstrels, with separate duties, accompanying singers on his own.[35] Musicians who could serve double duty were valuable: in 1592 an applicant for a position was accepted

> por la necesidad que hay de su persona, principalmente para que sirva de bajón en los cantos de órgano y taña tambien los tiples en la capilla de los ministriles, pues todo lo hace muy bien.[36]

because of the need for him, principally because he serves as *bajón* in polyphony and also plays the treble shawms in the chapel of the minstrels, and does both well.

The third important pattern, which consists essentially of no pattern at all, can be identified at the cathedral of Barcelona: neither Àngel Fàbrega nor Josep Maria Gregori, in either of their meticulous examinations of the cathedral archives, has found any evidence of a regular staff of instruments there in the 16th century at all.[37] Yet the cathedral chapter undoubtedly continued to employ local minstrels on a freelance basis throughout the century. Much of the evidence is dispersed throughout the municipal records, which naturally tend to favour the most spectacular civic events; but there is plenty of reason to believe that the minstrels appeared on more ordinary occasions as well.

First of all, it is clear that the use of instruments in religious processions, demonstrably well established in the 15th century, continued during the 16th. For example: a dancing-master and his musicians were hired by the chapter for a procession on the feast of the martyrdom of St Eulalia (the cathedral's patron) in 1524;[38] a royal chronicler reported the participation of 'todos los ministriles de la sancta yglesia e çibdad' ('all the minstrels of the holy church and city') at the formal entry of Charles V in 1533;[39] and the chapter hired minstrels to accompany a papal legate to Mass in 1566.[40]

A related practice was to station instrumentalists just outside or inside the church door to greet an important procession as it arrived: this is documented in March 1519, when the knights of the Order of the Golden Fleece, meeting in Barcelona for its only time on the Iberian peninsula, entered the cathedral through the main door and 'comensaren a sonar los menestrils y sacabutxos, los Clarins y Trompetas' ('the minstrels and trombones, the clarions and trumpets, began to sound');[41] in October 1598, when the city councillors attended the Mass of St Luke at the 'studi' (presumably at a chapel at the university) and the trumpets and minstrels, because of mourning for Philip II, did *not* play upon their arrival (suggesting that usually they did);[42] and the following July, when the Cortes were being held at the local Franciscan monastery and the king was opening the ceremonies at the church of Sant Francesc, drums, shawms, trumpets and other minstrels were there to greet him.[43]

But instruments also appeared in the cathedral on more purely local occasions and as part of the normal services; in 1593, for example, when the cathedral moved the relics of a local saint, St Matrona, to a new casket, 'en dit offici y ague ministrils y molta musicha' ('in the service there were minstrels and much music').[44] Over the course of the century, instrumentalists came to take a bigger and bigger part in the annual Corpus Christi celebration: the archivist and historian Pere Joan Comes, describing the festivities of his time (around 1582), mentioned them in a number of roles not specified by 15th-century sources, including at least one service in the cathedral,[45] and in 1555, when the city was in mourning for Juana the Mad the councillors made their usual procession from city hall to cathedral for the morning service without trumpets, the latter being stationed in the choir of the cathedral to play for the entry of the councillors instead.[46]

Perhaps even more significant are two items from November 1589, noting that the *Te Deum*, which in Barcelona as elsewhere in the 15th century had usually been sung with alternating versets of organ and chant,[47] was now performed with loud and soft (!) instruments instead.[48] If these represent more or less typical performances of the *Te Deum* in the late 16th century,[49] there may have been a great many minstrels in and around the cathedral, for the hymn was sung often, not only in the regular liturgy but also in special ceremonies of celebration or supplication. Exactly how much instrumental music is represented by these documents is hard to judge; but it is worth pointing out that the musicians themselves appear to have regarded playing in church as a significant part of their professional lives. When the local minstrels chartered the confraternity of Sts Gregory and Cecilia in 1599, they described themselves as those who were paid 'per sonar en professons esglesias dançes balls y altrament en qualsevol llochs publichs y privats' ('to play in processions, churches, dances, balls and otherwise in any public or private places').[50] But despite the amount of this kind of work that there was to do, the cathedral and other churches of Barcelona seem throughout the century—and, indeed, in the following one as well—to have engaged minstrels *ad hoc* from this local community of freelance musicians, rather than employing a regular band as at Seville and Palencia.[51]

I have chosen the cathedrals of Seville, Palencia and Barcelona for the purposes of this investigation because their documents are readily available; for other churches, it is necessary to rely on secondary literature that varies a good deal in age and purpose, often making

Table 1   Chronological list of Spanish cathedral bands

city	bajón established	band established
Seville	–	1526
Pamplona	by 1530	?
Toledo	–	1531
Granada	–	1561–2
Jaén	–	by 1540
León	–	1544
Palencia	1553	1567
Sigüenza		1554
Córdoba	–	1556
Ávila	–	by 1557
Valencia	–	1560
Salamanca	–	by 1570
Lleida	by 1576	?
Huesca	1577	1578
Valdemoro (parish church)	–	by 1582
Seu d'Urgell	1582	c. 1612
Badajoz	by 1598	–

precise comparisons impossible. But even a preliminary survey, subject to much change as further evidence comes to light, shows that these basic patterns were well represented throughout the peninsula; the results of this are summarized in table 1.

Something like the sequence of events at Palencia, with minstrels first in church on an irregular basis, then the hiring of a staff *bajón* player, and finally a regular band of cathedral minstrels, can be traced in at least five other cathedrals.[52] The cathedral of Pamplona paid a man to repair one or more *bajones* as early as 1530, suggesting that the instrument was already in regular use well before that time.[53] At the Seu d'Urgell, the composer Joan Brudieu, then serving as chapelmaster, brought some wooden instruments (shawms? recorders?) back from France in 1550;[54] these were apparently played by freelance musicians, for the first known reference to a full-time cathedral instrumentalist is the hiring of Agustí Serra, a 'musich de baixó i corneta', in 1582.[55] Serra remained in this position for a time, and then after a documentary hiatus, the payrolls for 1601 and 1611 regularly refer to *bajones*, while cornetts and trombones, along with unspecified minstrels, begin to show up more and more after 1612.[56] At Huesca, Antonio Durán has found evidence of an *ad hoc* band in 1570;[57] of the hiring of a minstrel in 1577 'to play the *bajón* in the chapel of singers' and to teach the boys and others of the church without payment;[58] and of the formation of a trio of 'músicos de baxón, menestriles y flautas' the following year, an ensemble to which trombone and cornett were added in the 1580s.[59] At the cathedral of Lleida, only one document for the whole century describing a church minstrel has come to my attention; the reference, from 1576, is to a 'pulsatorem del baixó'.[60] And finally, from rather later: in his studies of the cathedral at Badajoz, Santiago Kastner's earliest reference concerns payment to a freelance band in 1596;[61] two years later the chapter was apparently hiring a *bajón* (as a replacement, implying an older practice);[62] but Kastner finds no evidence of a regular ensemble of minstrels at Badajoz cathedral in the 16th century.

The Seville pattern is harder to identify securely in the secondary literature: lack of reference to a *bajonista* may really mean no *bajonista*, or it may just reflect a gap in the evidence. But at least two cases do seem to fit. In Toledo, where instruments were recorded in processions and church services as early as 1212,[63] the cathedral gave 20-year contracts to a trio of treble shawm, alto shawm and trombone, each of whom was to choose an assistant (apparently playing the same instrument), in 1531.[64] And

in Granada, López-Calo has traced the use of instruments in religious processions back to the cathedral's founding in 1492, including appearances within the church as early as 1518;[65] unsuccessful attempts were made to hire a regular cathedral band in 1543 and 1557; and the ensemble was eventually established in the early 1560s.[66]

For a number of other churches, the evidence is suggestive but more equivocal. Jaén cathedral had official minstrels by 1540, and had enough of them by 1545 to require the construction of a new loft;[67] León founded a 'capilla de ministriles' in 1544;[68] Sigüenza admitted a quartet in 1554;[69] Córdoba had four or five minstrels by 1556;[70] Ávila had instrumentalists as early as 1557;[71] Valencia's quartet of 'shawms, sackbut, flutes, cornetts, crumhorns (?) and trombone' was created in 1560;[72] Salamanca had minstrels on the payroll by 1570;[73] perhaps most remarkable of all, and suggesting that this movement was not restricted to the major cathedrals, even the parish church at Valdemoro had minstrels, or at any rate owned a dozen instruments (shawms, flutes, trombone, *bajón*), by 1582.[74]

Other churches, like the cathedral of Barcelona, must have resisted this trend: at Santa María in Cáceres, for example, the first known band, a trio, seems to have been hired in 1595.[75] Churches like this (and especially smaller parish churches in general) have been less enthusiastically studied, and their musical traditions are much less clear. But there can be little doubt that, whether for reasons of local taste or sensibility or economy, the use of instrumentalists was by no means universal in the churches of Spain even in 1600. In most cities, minstrels seem to have been a luxury employed by only the main church or cathedral; and the evidence from Barcelona shows that even some of the largest metropolitan cathedrals continued to rely on freelance bands to the end of the 16th century.

The acceptance of instrumentalists into the cathedral hierarchies of 16th-century Spain took place in very different ways, and under very different schedules, in different parts of the country; it is not one story but dozens. At the moment the state of the evidence allows only the most tentative speculations on these questions of chronology and geography. (Is it significant or illusory, for example, that the custom of engaging a *bajón* player first and a full band later is best documented in northern cities, and that the early hiring of the full band seems to have originated in the south, where the influence of the rest of Europe was fainter?) But with this caution in

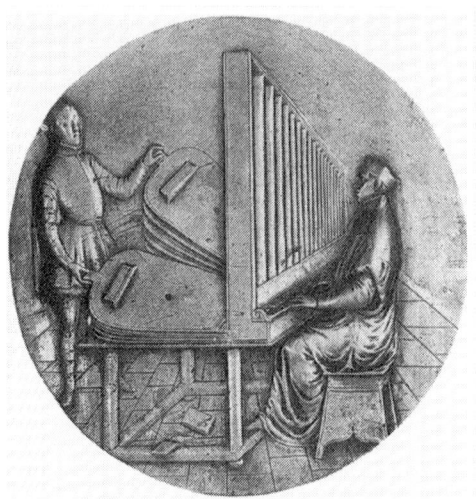

3   Positive organ. Bronze medallion by Juan Marín and Bautista Vázquez, cast by Bartolomé Morel (1564) (Seville Cathedral)

mind, it is worth approaching the matter from a different angle, and asking, in the most general terms, who these cathedral minstrels were and what they did.

All these ensembles seem to have been loud bands; their members are universally described as playing the trombone (called *sacabuche* or the like), shawm (called either the generic *chirimía* or a word indicating a particular size of shawm, such as *tiple* [treble], *contralto*, *tenor*, or *bajón*) or occasionally cornett (*corneta*). Exact forces are often harder to determine, but two examples have already been cited: at its founding in 1526, the cathedral band of Seville was a quintet of treble, contralto, tenor shawms and two trombones, and five years later, when Toledo formed its ensemble, the six members consisted of two trebles, two contraltos and two trombones. And the story of the Seville band shows that there could be a good deal of variation even within the same ensemble: by 1571 the band had grown to a brass-heavy sextet of two trebles, tenor and three trombones,[76] and by 1586 it had two trebles (doubling on cornett and probably flute), a contralto, at least two trombones, and a tenor player doubling on *bajón*.[77]

Doubling of this sort, particularly by shawmists playing not only different sizes of their own instrument but also cornetts and *flautas* (probably recorders, but possibly transverse flutes as well), became increasingly common in the latter part of the century and must have given

these bands considerable musical versatility;[78] as will be demonstrated shortly, it was not unusual for musicians to play several different instruments during the course of a piece.

For churches that had a regular band, four or five players seems to have been regarded as a practical minimum;[79] the largest such ensemble known to me is the octet of unspecified instrumentation maintained by the cathedral of Valencia from 1580 onwards.[80]

After a certain cathedral establishment had taken in an official loud band, other ensembles and other instrumentations tended to be heard there less often. The noise and symbolic pomp of trumpets and drums continued to be exploited in religious processions and festivals,[81] but I know of no record of their appearance inside church. In Palencia, at least during the late 1560s, there was a custom of presenting music for harp and voices in the main chapel of the cathedral on the octave of Corpus Christi.[82] And the use of bowed viols in church, while rare, was not unknown; when Philip II entered the cathedral of Seville in 1570, he was greeted by six loud minstrels on one side and seven viols on the other.[83]

There were, however, limits on this liberality. After Christmas 1597, when some guitars had been played in the cathedral of Palencia, the chapter debated whether to forbid the practice because the guitar was 'el instrumento el más común y con que más se cantan y tañen cosas deshonestas y lascivas' ('the most vulgar instrument and the one most used for singing and playing dishonest and lascivious things').[84] Indeed, the guitar and its relatives seem to have been singled out for censure: Jaime Moll, in his review of musical information in various cathedral constitutions of the Spanish Renaissance, cites a number of documents listing the vihuela as an instrument especially associated with dancing and other unholy activities.[85]

All known church minstrels were men, and most seem to have attained their post not by rising through the musical establishment of the cathedral, but by proven excellence in the local community of secular minstrels. Many had wives[86] or concubines;[87] one in Seville was accused of murder.[88] A few minstrels may, however, have had musical training within the cathedral system: Juan Vásquez of Palencia, for example, began his career as a choirboy at the cathedral, was an acolyte in his youth, and spent his adulthood as a minstrel in the cathedral band.[89] One Seville minstrel also served as a singer in the polyphonic choir,[90] which suggests that his original training too may have been vocal rather than instrumental. And indeed, Guerrero himself was said to have learned the seven-course vihuela, the harp and the cornett along with his singing lessons;[91] so perhaps some instrumental instruction was in fact a routine part of musical education in 16th-century Spain.

After they became established, the church minstrels may have had a hand in training their successors: at Ávila, Huesca and Palencia at least, and probably elsewhere too, cathedral minstrels were contracted not only to practice their art but to teach it to members of the congregation.[92] And at the parish church of Valdemoro, a group of acolytes were taught to play the shawms as a band in church festivals.[93]

Mention of the education of these minstrels, and particularly of the possibility that some of them may have been trained in the cathedral music schools, naturally brings up the question of their musical literacy. It is not always an easy question, for it was unlikely to be mentioned in the capitular acts unless, for example, a cathedral band bought music for its own use rather than using the choir's music. But a few bits of evidence, beginning in the 1560s, seem suggestive: López-Calo cites two references, from 1569 and 1585, to 'libros de los ministriles' at the cathedral of Granada,[94] for example, and Stevenson has uncovered a payment to a cathedral instrumentalist at Toledo for music copying (both for the choir and the cathedral band) in 1590.[95] But the most abundant evidence, as usual, is from Seville, where the chapter bought 'a certain book of music for the shawms' in 1560; where in 1572 the minstrels requested 'a book of Masses by maestro Guerrero' (probably the *Liber primus missarum*, published at Paris in 1566)[96] and also had 'a book of Venites for Matins' repaired; where another book for the minstrels was requested in 1580; and where a book of Victoria motets bought in 1587 was specifically ordered to be given to the singers and not the minstrels—implying that as a general rule, newly purchased music went directly to the shawms and trombones.[97] Evidently, then, musical literacy was expected as a matter of course for minstrels in at least a few cathedrals, and by the end of the century, instrumentalists may have been reading music (including, if the evidence from Seville is any indication, some of the great sacred music of the age) in churches all over Spain.

The purchase of this book of Guerrero Masses is especially intriguing, for it seems to signal an important change in the role of minstrels in the service—that somewhere along the line the instrumentalists had stopped just playing during wordless parts of the Mass and had begun to accompany the singers in the Ordi-

nary. This again is difficult to prove beyond doubt (conceivably, for example, the Seville minstrels played Mass movements as instrumental pieces outside the liturgy, or used the book to construct improvised background music or alternatim settings to use with a Mass otherwise sung); but a few scattered documents appear to support the possibility of instrumental accompaniment further. In 1551 the cathedral chapter at Málaga paid a mixed ensemble of travelling loud minstrels and singers for participating in a church festival;[98] in 1557 the cathedral of Granada attempted to hire instrumentalists 'por los pocos cantores que hay en la capilla' ('because there are so few singers in the chapel'),[99] which suggests that it was permissible, at least as a practical compromise, for minstrels to substitute for singers; and by the first decades of the 17th century, it was possible for composers to write music with vocal and instrumental parts specified: the Valencian composer Juan Bautista Comes, for example, wrote a vernacular song dedicated to St Michael with a texted voice labelled 'Tiple' and three untexted voices labelled 'Bajoncillo', 'Sacabuche' and 'Bajón grande'.[100] An intimate look at the kind of playing these minstrels did is provided in an extraordinary document uncovered by Robert Stevenson: a set of guidelines issued to the cathedral band of Seville by their chapelmaster, none other than Francisco Guerrero, in July 1586.

primeramente que Rojas y lopes tañan siempre los tiples de las chirimias y que guarden con mucho cuydado horden en el glosar en sus lugares y tiempos de manera que cuando el uno glosare el otro vaya con llaneza aguardandose el uno al otro porque glosando juntos se haçen disparates para tapar los oydos.

Ytem que los mismos Rojas y lopez quando vuiere cosa de cornetas las tañan ellos Guardando el mesmo horden cada uno de moderarse en las glosas esperandose el uno al otro porque como ya es dicho glosar juntos es disonançia ynsufrible. Que juan de Medina taña de hordinario el contralto y de lugar a los tiples no turbandolos con exceder de la glosa que debe a contralto y que quando el dicho Juan de medina tañere solo el contralto por tiple con los sacabuches se le dexa el campo abierto para hacer las galas y glosas que quisiere que en este ynstrumento las sabe bien hacer. que Aluanches taña tenores y el baxon.

Que en las fiestas del choro aya siempere un berso de flautas. que en las salues los tres versos que tañen el uno sea con chirimias y el otro con cornetas y el otro con flautas porque siempre vn instrumento enfada y ansi lo proveyeron.[101]

First, that Rojas and Lopez should always play the treble shawms, and that they should take great care in the order of the time and place of their glossing, so that when one is glossing, the other plays the music unadorned, each being careful of the other because when they gloss together it makes such absurdities as would stop up the ears.

Item: that the same Rojas and Lopez, when they play something on cornetts, should play them taking the same care to moderate the glosses, each waiting for the other because, as has already been said, to gloss together is an insufferable dissonance. And that Juan de Medina should ordinarily play the contralto shawm, and should give way to the trebles, not bothering them by exceeding the sort of gloss that is given to the contralto; and that when the same Juan de Medina plays the contralto alone as a treble with the trombones, the field is open to him to make whatever decorations and glosses he wants and can play well on his instrument. And that Alvanches should play tenor shawms and *bajón*.

That in the feasts with the choir, there should always be one verse on flutes.

That in the Salves, the three verses that they play, one should be with shawms, another with cornetts, and the other with flutes, for having them always on the same instrument is annoying, and they should provide for this.

There is a good deal of information here. First, Guerrero makes clear what is elsewhere undocumented but might have been surmised, that Spanish cathedral instrumentalists were expected not just to play the music, but to improvise ornaments around it; indeed, he seems to have had to restrain them from improvising too much. Second, he shows that variety of instrumentation was considered essential, and that this variety was achieved not only, as we have seen, by having the woodwind players double (treble shawmists on cornett and probably flute, tenor shawmist on *bajón*), but by actually creating a sort of second band with a deeper sonority—contralto shawm on top and trombones below.

And third, the reference to the *Salve regina* is especially tantalizing: Guerrero wrote two polyphonic settings of the antiphon,[102] and thus this would appear to be that rarest of Renaissance commodities—instructions from a composer on how some of his music should be performed. Unfortunately, however, some pieces of the puzzle are there, but not quite all.

In saying that the minstrels are to play for three verses, Guerrero clearly implies some sort of alternatim performance, and alternatim performances of the *Salve regina*, typically singing the even verses polyphonically and filling in the odd verses with chant or organ, were common throughout Europe.[103] Of Guerrero's own versions, one sets the whole text continuously, thus ruling out alternatim performance, but the other divides it into eight rather than the usual nine verses and sets only the even ones.[104] But two important questions remain unanswered. Most obviously, if division into eight verses, or anything besides six, represents the usual Sevillian practice, then why were the minstrels playing on only

4   Choristers. Bronze medallion by Juan Marín and Bautista Vázquez, cast by Bartolomé Morel (1564) (Seville Cathedral)

three? And second, even if that can be hypothetically solved (say, by giving the missing verse to the organ), we are still left with too many possibilities. Perhaps the minstrels were doing what organists traditionally did, improvising on the odd verses while the polyphonic choir took the even; perhaps they were accompanying the choir on the even while the odd were being played by the organ or sung in plainsong; or perhaps the instruments were in fact alternating with chant—in which case the document has no relevance for Guerrero's composition after all.

The schedule of the church minstrels—what days in the year, what services in the day, what part of the service they accompanied—must have varied a good deal from church to church, and for most it remains impossible to reconstruct. There are, however, a few striking exceptions; calendars of the feasts of the church year, with the duties of the various musicians, survive for a number of cathedrals from the mid-16th to the mid-17th century, and these provide some invaluable musical details.[105] The earliest, which governed the musicians of the León cathedral around 1550,[106] is also one of the best and will serve as a representative example.

For 18 of the most solemn feasts of the church year (Circumcision, Epiphany, Purification, Annunciation, Holy Saturday, Easter, Ascension, Pentecost, Trinity, Corpus Christi and its octave, Transfiguration, Assumption, Nativity of the Virgin, the feast of the cathedral's patron St Froilán, All Saints, Immaculate Conception and Christmas), the minstrels of León had, with a few specified exceptions, the following duties:

En las fiestas susodichas antes de que se empiecen las primeras vísperas han de tañer un motete; después alternar con el órgano y cantores en el primero y postrer salmo; item tañerán el primer verso y postrero del hymno y lo mismo del magnificat y el Deo gratias. En la procesión han de tañer a la salido del coro, en los tres ángulos de la claustra y delante de Nuestra Señora del Dado; así mismo al entrar la procesión en el coro. Y en la misa tañerán el primer y postrer kyrie, a la ofrenda, al alcen y a la Deo gratias. En las segundas vísperas se tenga la orden que en las primeras, salvo el alternar de los salmos.[107]

In these feasts, before first Vespers begins, they must play a motet; afterwards they alternate with the organ and singers in the first and last psalm; also they play the first and last verse of the hymn and the same of the Magnificat and the *Deo gratias*. In the procession, they must play at the exit to the choir, in the three angles of the cloister and in front of Nuestra Señora del Dado; and the same as the procession enters the choir. And in the Mass they play the first and last Kyrie, at the Offertory, at the raising of the host, and at the *Deo gratias*. In the second Vespers, the same order is followed as in the first, except the alternation of the psalms.

On lesser feasts (the document lists about 35 of these), more modest versions of this basic pattern were observed. All in all, then, the cathedral minstrels of León were required to perform on average for about one holiday a week, and each holiday involved several services.

In a famous sentence from his *Ars musica*, probably written around 1270, Egidius of Zamora wrote of the organ: 'This instrument alone is used by the church in various chants, in proses, in sequences and in hymns, for other instruments have generally been thrown out on account of abuse by minstrels.'[108] Less well known, however, is the very next paragraph, in which Egidius listed 'stirring people to the praise of God' among the uses of the trumpet.[109] And in the disparity between the two passages lies the heart of an ambivalence that would persist in Spain for centuries to come.

The forces that kept instrumentalists out of churches all over Medieval and Renaissance Europe, whether for considerations of propriety (musical, liturgical or moral) or, as McKinnon has argued, as a more practical matter of training and literacy,[110] were at work in Spain as well. Spain, like the rest of the continent, had its share of conservative voices lambasting the corruption of the liturgy with noisy instruments and gaudy embellishments.[111] But for one reason or another, these forces were overcome in Spanish churches with increasing frequency over the course of the 15th and 16th centuries.

The earliest stages of this process are hard to document, but it does seem to have happened as a series of gradual steps, from the marching of loud bands in outdoor secular parades, to their appearance in church as part of religious processions, to their use in the regular service on special occasions during wordless parts of the Mass and Office, and finally to their acceptance as part of the regular musical establishment of the cathedral, accompanying singers, substituting for missing singers, improvising around them. In 1526, a year before the cathedral of Cambrai, in a famous document, was prohibiting 'tamburini aut joculatores' inside its walls,[112] the cathedral of Seville was actually putting a loud band on its payroll.

The temptation would seem to be strong, then, to conclude that here is one repertory where we should bring back the instruments in force. But two cautions are essential. First, the use of instruments to accompany singers or to play written polyphony is not at all well documented before 1550 or so. It would certainly be wrong to use them in the sacred music of 15th-century composers like Cornago and Urreda, and risky in the music of Josquin-era composers like Peñalosa and Escobar—even, indeed, in that of Morales, who after all died in 1553.

And second, for all their apparent liberality in allowing the minstrels inside, Spanish churches were careful to restrict the amount of their playing, even to the end of the Renaissance. If the León document and others like it are representative, minstrels probably participated in less than half the music of the most elaborate Vespers, and a much smaller fraction of the Mass (indeed, of the Ordinary, only the Kyrie I and II). And beyond this, there must have been plenty of churches that, like the cathedral of Barcelona, continued to sing all their music unaccompanied up to the end of the century. Monophony and *a cappella* polyphony were still the dominant forms of music heard in Spanish churches.

And so it goes: the scholarship of Renaissance performance practice has always seemed to give the musician more prohibitions than proposals. But still, there are a number of places where the documents and the repertory come together in ways that suggest, if not widely applicable performing rules, at least a few musical experiments that might be worth a cautious try: the reconstruction of a festal Mass or Vespers—chant, polyphony, instruments and everything—in the manner of León cathedral; a performance of Guerrero's *Salve regina* using some interpretation of his instructions to the band at Seville; an experiment with the substitution of instruments to cover an insufficiency of singers, as at Granada; the accompaniment of some Spanish sacred polyphony in the Palencia style, with a single bass shawm or dulcian.[113] None of these, of course, is an explicit and self-sufficient recipe. In each case, critical pieces of information are missing and vital performing decisions will have to be made on very uncertain grounds. We may never know exactly how this accompaniment was done or exactly what the glosses of the shawm players, whether tasteful or a 'disonancia ynsufrible', sounded like; but it is worth making at least a tentative guess.

A number of questions and mysteries remain, and some of them may one day be answered as Spain, Spanish musicology and foreign interest in Hispanic culture continue to reawaken. But one point is quite clear: the sacred music of the Spanish Renaissance is worth singing again, and worth singing in a manner sympathetic to the musical tastes and thinking of its time. And that may mean opening up the old collegium closet again and blowing the dust off the shawms and sackbuts.

Portions of this article were read at the annual meeting of the American Musicological Society, Southern Chapter, Hattiesburg, February 1991, and at the 19th Annual Conference on Medieval and Renaissance Music, Oxford, July 1991.

Kenneth Kreitner took his PhD from Duke University with a dissertation on ceremonial music in late medieval Barcelona. He is assistant professor of music at Memphis State University.

[1] The phrase 'modified *a cappella* hypothesis' is from J. W. McKinnon, 'Representations of the Mass in Medieval and Renaissance Art', *JAMS*, xxxi (1978), pp.21–52; see also McKinnon, '15th-Century Northern Book Painting and the *a cappella* Question: an Essay in Iconographical Method', *Studies in the Performance of Late Medieval Music*, ed. S. Boorman (Cambridge, 1983), pp.1–17, and McKinnon, 'A cappella Doctrine versus a cappella Practice: a Necessary Distinction', *La musique et le rite sacré et profane (Actes du XIII' Congrès de la Société Internationale de Musicologie)*, ed. M. Honegger and C. Meyer (Strasbourg, 1986), i, pp.238–42. For a recent dissenting view, see also L. Korrick, 'Instrumental Music in the Early 16th-Century Mass', *EM*, xvii (1990), pp.359–70.

[2] McKinnon, 'Representations of the Mass', pp.50–52; D. Fallows, 'The Performing Ensembles of Josquin's Sacred Music', *Tijdschrift van de Vereniging voor Nederlandse muziekgeschiedenis*, xxxv (1985), pp.32–64, esp. p.34.

[3] K. R. Kreitner, *Music and Civic Ceremony in Late-15th-century Barcelona* (diss., Duke U., 1990), pp.291–333. Most of the information on this ceremony is taken from a document dated 1424, which was apparently used as a guide (and was gradually updated) for some decades, even centuries, thereafter.

[4] Kreitner, *Music and Civic Ceremony*, pp.502–11. The ensembles are referred to in the documents as (1455) '.ii.trompetas & tanborino'; (1456) 'sis trompedors o trompadors trompants e un tabaler'; and (1459)

'.XIIJ trompetes IIJ tabalers . . . anant sonant ab llurs trompes e fluviols [literally flutes, but possibly implying that the ensemble was really a loud band including shawms], e VJ sonadors de corde qui sonaven devant la custodia de la reliquia . . .'

[5] Kreitner, *Music and Civic Ceremony*, p.444. See pp.442–7 for fuller quotation and discussion of this passage. 'Choir' is of course used here in the architectural and not the musical sense.

[6] *Hechos del Condestable don Miguel Lucas de Iranzo: Crónica del siglo XV*, ed. J. de Mata Carriazo (Madrid, 1940), p.43. *Bastard* and *Italian* seem to refer to two different sizes of trumpet; see P. Downey, *The Trumpet and Its Role in Music of the Renaissance and Early Baroque* (diss., Queen's U. of Belfast, 1983), i, p.39, and Kreitner, *Music and Civic Ceremony*, p.52. The word *locos* here is more puzzling; literally, of course, it means 'madmen', but I am taking it as a more positive metaphor. It may mean dignitaries or some such, or conceivably it was a local word for some musical instrument.

[7] *Hechos del Condestable*, p.44: 'vna copla de tres ministreles de duçaynas, que muy dulçe & acordadamente sonauan'

[8] *Hechos del Condestable*, p.45

[9] *Hechos del Condestable*, p.45

[10] On Flemish traditions of this time, see, for example, K. Polk, 'Ensemble Instrumental Music in Flanders—1450–1550', *Journal of Band Research*, xi/2 (Spring 1975), pp.12–27, esp. pp.20–21, and K. K. Forney, 'Music, Ritual and Patronage at the Church of Our Lady, Antwerp', *Early Music History*, vii (1987), pp.1–57, esp. pp.27–8.

[11] *Hechos del Condestable*, pp.152–83

[12] *Hechos del Condestable*, pp.154–5

[13] *Hechos del Condestable*, p.160. The Verónica, or scarf of Veronica, is the most sacred relic of the cathedral of Jaén: see the photograph and explanation facing p.272

[14] *Hechos del Condestable*, pp.156, 165, 167, 177, 178

[15] See, for example, H. Anglès, *La música en la corte de los Reyes Católicos*, i: *Polifonía religiosa*, Monumentos de la Música Española, i (Madrid, 1941); Anglès, *Historia de la música medieval en Navarra* (Pamplona, 1970); Anglès, various shorter works in *Scripta musicologica*, ed. J. López-Calo (Rome, 1975–6); M.C. Gómez Muntané, *La música en la casa real catalano-aragonesa durante los años 1336-1432* (Barcelona, 1977); T. W. Knighton, *Music and Musicians at the Court of Fernando of Aragon, 1474-1516* (diss., Cambridge U., 1983); and A. W. Atlas, *Music at the Aragonese Court of Naples* (Cambridge, 1985).

[16] L. Hernández Asunce, 'Música y músicos de la Catedral de Pamplona', *Anuario musical*, xxii (1967), pp.209–46, quotation p.211.

[17] Anglès, *La música en la corte de los Reyes Católicos*, i, p.19

[18] A. Bernáldez, *Historia de los Reyes Católicos D. Fernando y Doña Isabel*, ed. F. de Gabriel y Ruiz de Apocaca (Seville, 1870), i, p.95. This procession was made on 9 July 1478; see also p.97 for a second procession one month later, also in Seville, to offer the prince to God in the cathedral: 'íbanles festivando muchos instrumentos de trompetas é chirimías, é otras muchas cosas, é muy acordadas músicas que iban delante de ellos.'

[19] R. Stevenson, *La música en la Catedral de Sevilla, 1478-1606: Documentos para su estudio* (Madrid, 1985), p.21, doc. 85 (16 August 1507): 'a los ministriles del duque mill maravedíes por el travajo que tomaron el dya de santa maria en yr en la prosecyon tañendo'.

For convenience, I shall cite only this collection of documents (abbreviated as *Sevilla*) whenever possible; many of its items, especially from later in the century, are translated or summarized in R. Stevenson, *Spanish Cathedral Music in the Golden Age* (Berkeley, 1961), and some also appear, sometimes with different dates and details of transcription, in H. Anglès, 'Cristóbal de Morales y Francisco Guerrero: su obra musical', *Anuario musical*, ix (1954), pp.56–79, and J. M. Llorens Cisteró, *Francisco Guerrero: Opera omnia*, iii: *Motetes I–XXII*, Monumentos de la Música Española, xxxvi (Barcelona, 1978), pp.44–51.

[20] See Anglès, 'Morales y Guerrero', p.71 (doc. of April 1509), which does not appear in Stevenson; and Stevenson, *Sevilla*, pp.22–3, doc. 99 (24 April 1514), doc. 107 (1 June 1517), doc. 108 (26 June 1517), doc. 109

(13 November 1517)

[20]Stevenson, *Sevilla*, pp.24–5, doc. 113 (29 March), doc. 114 (9 April), doc. 117 (2 June), doc. 119 (16 June), doc. 121 (30 June), doc. 122 (2 July), doc. 125 (11 August), doc. 129 (20 August).

[21]Stevenson, *Sevilla*, p.24, doc. 119 (16 June 1518): 'a los menestriles altos por las dos vezes que vinieron a seruir en esta dicha santa iglesia . . . [y] a los tronpetas e atabales e por las vezes que vinieron a seruir.'

[22]Stevenson, *Sevilla*, p.25, doc. 132 (18 August 1522), doc. 135 (11 May 1524)

[24]Stevenson, *Sevilla*, p.27, doc. 149 (9 July 1526)

[25]See Stevenson, *Sevilla*, pp.39–40, doc. 274 (26 July 1553), and Stevenson, *Spanish Cathedral Music*, p.144

[26]J. López-Calo, *La música en la Catedral de Palencia*, (Palencia, 1980–81) [hereafter *Palencia*], i, pp.449–68

[27]López-Calo, *Palencia*, i, p.468, doc. 209 (27 September 1553)

[28]On the history of the Spanish *bajón*, which surely meant a dulcian in the 17th century (and thus, potentially, in many of the documents here), see B. Kenyon de Pascual, 'A Brief Survey of the Late Spanish Bajón', *GSJ*, xxxvii (1984), pp.72–9, and Kenyon de Pascual, 'El bajón español y los tres ejemplares de la catedral de Jaca', *Nassarre*, ii/2 (1986), pp.109–33.

[29]López-Calo, *Palencia*, i, pp.471–4 (docs. 252, 253, 265, 276)

[30]López-Calo, *Palencia*, i, p.476, doc. 296 (4 November 1564). In the quotations from this collection, Spanish words in brackets are from López-Calo, not from the original.

[31]López-Calo, *Palencia*, i, p.476, doc. 298 (22 November 1564): 'Mandaron que de aquí adelante inviolablemente no se trate cosa en cabildo que vaya contra el estatuto de las gracias, especialmente en tomar menestriles ayudando la mesa para parte dellos.'

[32]López-Calo, *Palencia*, i, p.478, doc. 321 (9 December 1567), doc. 322 (15 December); quotation from doc. 323 (16 December). The [*sic*] is López-Calo's.

[33]López-Calo, *Palencia*, i, p.533, doc. 813 (14 March 1592). For more on this search, see pp.535–6, docs. 831–7.

[34]See the 'Constituciones del Obispo Axpe y Sierra', transcribed in López-Calo, *Palencia*, ii, pp.680–700; the passage about the minstrels appears on pp.686–90. The document is dated 11 May 1584, but parts of it may be older or newer.

[35]See the 'Instrucción de Apundadores' of 1643 in López-Calo, *Palencia*, ii, pp.637–67, esp. pp.658–66 for the band of minstrels and pp.666–7 for the *bajón*.

[36]López-Calo, *Palencia*, i, p.536, doc. 841 (22 August 1592); see also docs. 840, 842.

[37]À. Fàbrega i Grau, *La vida quotidiana a la Catedral de Barcelona en declinar el Renaixement: any 1580* (Barcelona, 1978), and J. M. Gregori i Cifré, *La música del Renaixement a la Catedral de Barcelona, 1450–1580* (diss., Universitat Autònoma de Barcelona, 1986), esp. i, pp.221–3.

[38]Gregori, 'Música del Renaixement', i, p.223 (February 1524), a payment 'al senyer n·Astiader mestre de dansar per el e per sos companyons per la música que feren a la prosesó, lo dia del martiri de Santa Eulàlia per ordinalið novament feta en Capitol . . .'

[39]H. Anglès, *La música en la corte de Carlos V*, Monumentos de la Música Española, ii (Barcelona, 1944), p.41 (6 May 1533)

[40]Gregori, 'Música del Renaixement', i, p.223 (22 April 1566): 'donasen als ministrils que sonaren quant vingué lo legat del Papa a oyr missa a la Seu . . .'

[41]Barcelona, Institut Municipal d'Història, MS. B.157, p.4. The manuscript is a copy of a contemporary record of this meeting, written by an anonymous scribe in both French and a kind of Castilianized Catalan; the quotation is taken from the account of 6 March 1519, the second day of the meeting.

[42]*Dietari del Antich Consell Barceloní*, ed. F. Carreras y Candi and F. Schwartz y Luna (later volumes by other editors) (Barcelona, 1892–1975), vii, p.153 (25 October 1598): 'En aquest dia anaren los S.ors consellers al studi a ohir lo offici per fer se la festa de S.t Luc, hi noy sonaren los trompetas ni tampoc los ministrils quant arribaren dits

S.ors consellers per causa del dol de sa mag.tat, mes lo offici se feu ab dits menestrils.' Note especially that the instrumentalists did perform during the service; apparently only the musical greeting was considered to violate the proprieties of mourning.

[43]*Dietari del Antich Consell*, vii, pp.225–6 (7 July 1599): 'y encontinent sonaren los tabals pifanos trompetes y menestrils de sa ma.' . . .' Then, after a description of the ceremonies, 'E acabada la dita ceremonia tornaren ha sonar los matexos musichs de sa ma.t qui havien sonat quant ere entrat en dita sglesia . . .'

[44]*Dietari del Antich Consell*, vi, pp.465–8 (16 September 1593), quotation p.468

[45]P. J. Comes, *Libre de algunes coses asanyalades succehides en Barcelona y en altres parts*, ed. J. Puiggarí (Barcelona, 1878), pp.630–39, esp. pp.631–2, where Comes shows that on the day before Corpus Christi, a wide variety of instruments, 'los dits tabales y trompetes los sacabutxos y los musichs de corda de viola', would meet the councillors at city hall and at least the trumpets and drums would accompany them to the cathedral for vespers; upon entering the cathedral through the main door, 'restant los tabals de fora y entrant las trompetes' ('the drums stay out and the trumpets come in').

[46]*Dietari del Antich Consell*, iv, p.290 (13 June 1555): 'les trompetes estigueren a la trona entrant per lo cor per sonar com entraren y com sen anaren'.

[47]See Kreitner, *Music and Civic Ceremony*, pp.478–80.

[48]*Dietari del Antich Consell*, vi, p.154 (6 November 1589): 'En aquest dia de VJ de nohembre fonch fet *tadeum laudamus* ques lo die de S.t Sever, per dins la seu ab tabals y trompes y girbaus [shawms, according to the editors' footnote]'; *ibid*, p.157 (21 November): 'En aquest die de XXJ fonch feta la festa dels quinse grahons de la purificatio de nostra senyora y fonch fet segon *tedeum laudamus* per fora la yglesia major sens portar sivera ni talem, y aguey tabals trompetas y menestris y musica sorda ab molta solempnitat . . .'

[49]For other 16th-century Spanish performances of the *Te Deum* using minstrels, see López-Calo, *Palencia*, i, p.532, doc. 862 (10 April 1593) and López-Calo, *La música en la catedral de Granada en el siglo XVI* (Granada, 1963), i, p.230 (4 February 1566) and pp.242–3 (mid-16th century?)

[50]From the charter of the Confraternity of Sts Gregory and Cecilia, dated 13 July 1599, in *Gremios y cofradías de la antigua corona de Aragón*, v.2, ed. F. de Bofarull y Sans, Colección de documentos inéditos del Archivo General de la Corona de Aragón 41 (Barcelona, 1910), pp.373–95, quotation p.388.

[51]On instrumentalists in Barcelona Cathedral in the 17th century, see J. Pavia i Simó, *La música a la catedral de Barcelona durant el segle XVII* (Barcelona, 1986), esp. pp.295–307. Two items of especial interest: first, Pavia identifies a staff *bajonista* at the cathedral at least by 1625 and possibly as early as 1614 (pp.301–2); second, he reports on an abortive attempt to form a cathedral band in 1648 (p.297), but finds no evidence that such an ensemble was established at any time before 1700.

[52]Two additional examples that do not quite fit the requirements here are worth noting: first, on the cathedral *bajonista* of Barcelona, see n.51 above; second, in 1562 the royal chapel of Philip II (which at that point in the century I am reluctant to call a Spanish church) included two organists (Juan and Antonio Cabezón) and a certain Melchor de Canzer, who 'sirve con el baxón'—see A. M. Virgili Blanquet, 'La capilla musical de Felipe II en 1562', *Nassarre*, iv (1988), pp.271–80, esp. p.279.

[53]Hernández, 'Música . . . de la Catedral de Pamplona', p.215 (23 November 1530): a payment 'A Juan de la Rosa por compostura de bajones, 2 ducados'

[54]F. Pedrell and H. Anglès, *Els madrigals i la missa de difunts d'en Brudieu* (Barcelona, 1921), p.156 (16 June 1550): 'dona a mossèn Joan Brudieu, mestre de cant de la present seu, y son per paguar los instruments al boixs pera sonar que li portat de Fransa . . .'

[55]Pedrell and Anglès, *Els madrigals . . .*, pp.48, 138 (10 May 1582). The reference to the cornett here is puzzling, for as will be shown, Anglès

has found no other documents mentioning cornetts until the second decade of the 17th century. Probably, then, Serra was put on the payroll to play the *bajón*, but his additional expertise on the cornett was used to the cathedral's advantage on those special occasions when a freelance cornettist would ordinarily have been hired.

[56] Pedrell and Anglès, *Els madrigals . . .* , pp.138–51

[57] A. Durán Gudiol, 'La capilla de música de la Catedral de Huesca', *Anuario musical*, xix (1964), pp.29–55, quotation p.40 (2 January 1570): 'los menestriles que han hecho música en la iglesia . . . al tiempo de los officios . . .'

[58] Durán Gudiol, 'La capilla de música . . ', p.40 (6 June 1577): Melchor del Rey hired 'para tanyer el baxón en la capilla de cantores de la Seo de Huesca . . .' and 'sea obligado a ensenyar a tanyer a los escolares, infantes y otros de dicha iglesia sin pagar cosa alguna por ello . . .'

[59] Durán Gudiol, 'La capilla de música . . .', pp.40–42 (from 10 November 1578, 7 January 1584, 20 September 1586). Curiously, in 1605 this cathedral ensemble would apparently be shared with the city; Durán (pp.43–4) transcribes a table showing when they were to play in the chapel and when they would be needed to serve in municipal celebrations.

[60] H. Anglès, *Mateo Flecha: las ensaladas* (Barcelona, 1954), p.25 (19 July 1576)

[61] S. Kastner, 'La música en la Catedral de Badajoz (años 1520–1603)', *Anuario musical*, xii (1957), pp.123–46, quotation p.143: the payment is to 'Músicos de chirimías, vecinos de Villa Viçosa'.

[62] Kastner, 'La música en la Catedral de Badajoz', p.143 (11 December 1598): 'del remedio que se a de tener para suplir la falta que haze el bajón para navidad a causa de su enfermedad, y si fuere menester se hable a João Gomes portugués contrabajo q[ue] al presente está en esta ciudad para q[ue] cante en su lugar . . .' Kastner points out that there is an ambiguity here, which he resolves by concluding that the verb 'cantar' is being used here to mean 'tañer'. The possibility remains, however, that 'bajón' is a mistake for 'bajo' and the sick man is in fact a singer.

[63] Rodericus Toletanus, *De rebus Hispaniae*, quoted in H. Anglès, *El còdex musical de Las Huelgas* (Barcelona, 1931), i, p.48; the reference is to the return of Alfonso VIII of Castile from a military victory: 'cum pontificibus et clero et universo populo in ecclesiam Beate Marie Virginis processionaliter est receptus, multis Deum laudantibus et in musicis instrumentis acclamantibus . . .' This may, of course, refer to an organ rather than to minstrels; still, the wording is significant.

[64] Stevenson, *Spanish Cathedral Music*, pp.32, 121–2, 144 (28 June 1531). The instrument names are given as 'tiple', 'contralto' and 'sacabuche'.

[65] López-Calo, *La música en la catedral de Granada*, i, pp.213–16

[66] López-Calo, *La música en la catedral de Granada*, i, pp.216–20

[67] Stevenson, *Sevilla*, p.89, doc. 799 (17 September 1540), a reference to a 'francisco de flandes ministril' in the cathedral archives, and doc. 804 (14 January 1545) (see Stevenson, *Spanish Cathedral Music*, p.139)

[68] J. M. Álvarez Pérez, 'La polifonía sagrada y sus maestros en la catedral de León (siglos XV y XVI)', *Anuario musical*, xiv (1959), pp.39–62, esp. pp.44–5, 50

[69] L. Jambou, 'La capilla de música de la catedral de Sigüenza en el siglo XVI. Ordenación del tiempo musical liturgico: del renacimiento al barroco', *Revista de musicologia*, vi (1983), pp.271–98, esp. pp.281–2, 297 (29 January–2 February 1554)

[70] Stevenson, *Spanish Cathedral Music*, p.305

[71] Stevenson, *Spanish Cathedral Music*, p.469

[72] J. Climent, 'La capilla de música de la catedral de Valencia', *Anuario musical*, xxxvii (1982), pp.55–69, esp. pp.64–5 (17 December 1560): 'chirimies, sacabuig, flautes, cornetes, orlos e trompon'.
Two matters of terminology are not quite clear here. First, the apparent duplication of 'sacabuig' and 'trompon' may reflect ignorance on the part of the author of the document, or possibly a distinction between different types of brass instrument (trombone and trumpet? slide trumpet and trombone?). And second, the *orlo*, though

mentioned fairly frequently in the documents of the time, remains something of a mystery; Sebastián de Covarrubias, in his Castilian dictionary of 1611, defines it vaguely as a curved instrument, and Anglès, in *La música en la corte de Carlos V*, p.12, cites a document showing that 11 'orlos de Alemania, hechos a manera de cornetas', were owned by the Spanish royal court in 1559. These descriptions, combined with the instrument's use in the loud band here, would seem to make the crumhorn, whose popularity in Germany is clear, a logical choice. See J. Corominas and J. A. Pascual, *Diccionario crítico etimológico castellano e hispanico* (Madrid, 1984–6), iv, pp.301–2.

[73] Stevenson, *Spanish Cathedral Music*, p.245

[74] A. Gallego, 'Un siglo de música en Valdemoro (1582–1692)', *Revista de musicologia*, i (1978), pp.243–53, esp. p.246 for an inventory of church possessions in 1582 including:
'—Un bajón grande con su funda de baqueta.
—Dos tiples de chirimías con sus cajas.
—Dos tenores gastados con sus cajas.
—Un sacabuche.
—Una caja pequeña de cuatro flautas.
—Otra caja grande con dos flautas bajos.'

[75] P. Barrios Manzano, 'La música en Cáceres: datos para su historia (1590–1750)', *Revista de musicologia*, viii (1985), pp.139–44, esp. pp.142–4 (2 June 1595). The reference is to three 'ministriles de chirimias, vezinos de la villa de Villaviciosa, en el reyno de Portugal'—curiously, the same description given to some minstrels hired by the cathedral of Badajoz in 1596 (see n.61 above). Perhaps they were the same players?

[76] Stevenson, *Sevilla*, p.60, doc. 477 (26 January 1571), which describes an ensemble (probably the full cathedral band, but conceivably a delegation) returning from a long official tour; see Stevenson, *Spanish Cathedral Music*, pp.157–8.

[77] Stevenson, *Sevilla*, p.72, doc. 616 (11 July 1586); see Stevenson, *Spanish Cathedral Music*, pp.166–7.

[78] Cf. the inventory of instruments at the church of Valdemoro in 1582, quoted in n.74 above, which includes not only shawms and trombone, but four 'flautas' and two 'flautas bajos', probably bass recorders.

[79] Cf. the case of Palencia cathedral in 1595.

[80] Climent, 'Capilla de . . . Valencia', p.65

[81] Stevenson, *Sevilla*, p.39, doc. 266 (26 June 1551): 'Este dicho dia los dichos señores mandaron dar quatro ducados a los chirimias y sacabuches y que vengan tropetas y atabales para tañer la noche de san pedro en la torre.'

[82] López-Calo, *Palencia*, i, p.478, doc. 329 (4 June 1568): 'Votóse secreto si esta octava de Corpus Xpi habría en la capilla mayor música de arpa y voces como el año pasado o no; salió por mayor parte se esté como el año pasado.'

[83] Stevenson, *Spanish Cathedral Music*, p.157

[84] López-Calo, *Palencia*, i, p.555, doc.987 (7 January 1598). López-Calo does not give the original text in full, but does include the phrase quoted here. His summary goes on to show that during the debate much was said on both sides, the pro-guitar side pointing out that 'no era indecencia' and that the same practice was observed at many other cathedrals in the Christmas season. (Perhaps the guitars were being used to accompany villancicos or liturgical dramas?) In the end, the decision seems to have been to allow the guitars, but to monitor what was sung—so perhaps it was the singers who were going outside the bounds of customary propriety.

[85] J. Moll, 'Música y representaciones en las constituciones sinodales de los Reinos de Castilla del siglo XVI', *Anuario musical*, xxx (1975), pp.209–43, esp. pp.216–17, 239–42. None of these documents specifically refers to the use of instruments in the church service, but they do go far toward showing the general associations these instruments had. An example from the cathedral of Astorga in 1553 (p.240): 'Porque muchas vezes acontesce los tales acogidos o retraydos ponerse a las puertas de las yglesias y ciminterios a dar bozes, burlando ellos entre sí o con otros algunos que pasan por la calle, al tiempo que los sacerdotes

están diziendo missa o vísperas o administrando algún otro sacramento o haziendo algunas otras obras tocantes al culto divino, tañiendo vihuela, guitarra o vandurria, cantando vanos y deshonestos cantares, chistes o chançonetas, que provocan e incitan a los que los oyen a lascivia y deshonestidad . . . Por ende . . . Sancta Synodo aprovante, estatuymos y ordenamos que . . . ni se pongan a las puertas de las yglesias, ni en los cimunterios a burlar, ni a tañer vihuelas, ni con otros géneros de instrumentos . . .'

[86]See Stevenson, *Sevilla*, docs. 402, 641 and López-Calo, *Palencia*, doc. 554.

[87]Stevenson, *Sevilla*, doc. 668

[88]Stevenson, *Sevilla*, doc. 425

[89]López-Calo, *Palencia*, docs. 353, 361, 395, 563, 668 etc. Coincidentally, Vásquez is also the minstrel cited in n.87 above. He was not, however, the composer of the same name, who died around 1560; the first reference to the minstrel Vásquez (doc. 353) dates from 1569.

[90]Stevenson, *Sevilla*, p.75, doc. 637 (26 November 1586); 'el señor chantre de boto que sirua de menestril, y todos los dias que obiere canto de organo sirua en el choro con los cantores . . .'

[91]F. Pacheco, *Libro de descripcion de verdaderos Retratos de Illustres y Memorables varones* . . . (Seville, 1599), quoted in Stevenson, *Spanish Cathedral Music*, pp.138, 226

[92]On Ávila, see Stevenson, *Spanish Cathedral Music*, p.469 (9 July 1568); on Huesca, see n.57 above; on Palencia, see López-Calo, *Palencia*, ii, p.686 (11 May 1584)

[93]Gallego, 'Siglo de música en Valdemoro', p.249 (1588): a payment 'porque los acólitos aprendan a tañer las chirimías y tocarlas en fiestas de la iglesia, por auto de los visitadores.'

[94]López-Calo, *La música en la Catedral de Granada*, i, p.230 (29 August 1569, 31 December 1585)

[95]Stevenson, *Spanish Cathedral Music*, p.302 (24 September 1590)

[96]Guerrero's second book of Masses was not published till 1585; conceivably the chapter was purchasing a manuscript or ordering one to be made, but the casual wording of the document would seem to imply a print.

[97]Stevenson, *Sevilla*, p.46, doc. 343 (15 May 1560): 'que çierto libro de canto para las cheremias que este dia se traxo a cabildo los señores contadores lo manden conprar sy fuere menester'; p.61, doc. 487 (16 April 1572): 'que siendo necesario para los menestriles vn libro de misas del maestro guerrero lo compre y se lo de y asimesmo haga adereçar el libro de venites de maytines'; p.67, doc. 548 (12 September 1580): '[el] señor mayordomo de fabrica compre el libro que propuso para los menestriles por el menosprecio que pudiere'; p.76, doc. 652 (18 September 1587); 'Que se compre el libro de los motetes de victoria y se comete al chantre que le concierte en lo que tiene referido y le haga pagar y enquadernar en tabla y le haga poner entre los libros de la musica i no se entregue a los menestriles.' See also Stevenson, *Spanish Cathedral Music*, pp.149, 158, 162, 169; Stevenson believes the Victoria print in question was *Motecta festorum totius anni* (Rome, 1585)

[98]Anglès, 'Morales y Guerrero', p.66 (doc. of 16 April 1551): 'Y los dichos Señores mandaron dar a los chirimyas que vinieron a este cibdad y a cantores con ellos para servicio deste yglesia tres mill mrs. para ayudo a su camino y por un servido estos días.'

[99]López-Calo, *Música en la Catedral de Granada*, i, p.217 (doc. of 28 July 1557). A similar request was made in 1563; see *ibid*, i, p.88 (7 September 1563).

[100]The piece, entitled 'Quién será aquel caballero', is edited by J. Climent in *Juan Bautista Comes (1582?-1643): Obras en lengua romance, v.4* (Valencia, 1979), pp.13-14; on the labelling of the parts, see p.9.

[101]Stevenson, *Sevilla*, p.72 (docs. 616-617, 11 July 1586). See also Stevenson, *Spanish Cathedral Music*, pp.166-7, for a commentary and perhaps more elegant translation.

[102]Edited by Llorens in Monumentos de la Música Española, xxxvi, music pp.56-65, 65-71

[103]On the various divisions of the *Salve* text and their implications for alternatim performance, see S. S. Ingram, 'The Polyphonic *Salve*

regina, 1425-1550' (diss., U. of North Carolina at Chapel Hill, 1973), esp. pp.91-7.

[104]The polyphony and chant are both edited in A. T. Davison and W. Apel, *Historical Anthology of Music* (Cambridge, Mass., 1959), pp.150-51. The texts set polyphonically are (2) 'Vita, dulcedo, et spes nostra, salve; Ad te clamamus'; (4) 'Ad te suspiramus gementes et flentes in hac lacrimarum valle'; (6) 'Et Jesum benedictum fructum ventris tui'; and (8) 'O clemens, o pia, o dulcis virgo Maria'.

[105]There are a number of these calendars, of greater or lesser completeness and musical detail, in the books and articles cited here; some are very rudimentary, but the following are among the best: León *c.*1550, Álvarez, 'Polifonía sagrada . . . en la catedral de León', pp.58-61; Valencia 1560, Climent, 'Capilla de . . . Valencia', pp.64-5; Palencia 1584, López-Calo, *Palencia*, ii, pp.686-90; Cáceres 1595, Barrios, 'Música en Cáceres', p.143; Pamplona 1598-9, Hernández, 'Música . . . de la catedral de Pamplona', pp.220-21; Huesca 1605, see n.57 above; Palencia 1643, López-Calo, *Palencia*, ii, pp.658-67; León 1663, Álvarez, 'La polifonía sagrada y sus maestros en la catedral de León durante el siglo XVII', *Anuario musical*, xv (1960), pp.141-63, esp. pp.156-61.

[106]The document does not specify a date, nor does Álvarez provide one; my estimate of 1550 is based on the numeration of its volume in the cathedral archives and the dates given in other documents transcribed by Álvarez.

[107]Álvarez, 'Polifonía sagrada . . . en la Catedral de León', p.60. The exceptions are listed with the dates on pp.59-60; these generally involve additions of a service, a procession, or a dawn concert in the cathedral tower.

[108]Johannes Aegidius de Zamora, *Ars musica*, ed. M. Robert-Tissot, Corpus Scriptorum de Musica, xx (n.p., 1974), p.108: 'Et hoc solo musico instrumento utitur ecclesia in diuersis cantibus et in prosis, in sequentiis et in hymnis, propter abusum histrionum eiectis aliis communiter instrumentis.'

[109]Aegidius de Zamora, *Ars musica*, p.110: 'Item utebantur tubis in festis et in conuiuiis, propter populi conuocationem, propter excitationem ad Dei laudem, et propter laetitiae et gaudii praeconizationem et inuitationem.'

[110]McKinnon, 'A cappella Doctrine'

[111]See, for example, Stevenson, *Spanish Cathedral Music*, pp.333-4.

[112]C. Wright, 'Performance Practices at the Cathedral of Cambrai, 1475-1550', *MQ*, lxiv (1978), pp.295-328, esp. p.322. The Latin here is from the typescript of original documents offered by Prof. Wright at the end.

[113]This last experiment has in fact been undertaken, convincingly to my ear, by Mark Brown and Pro Cantione Antiqua in 1981 on their recording *Voces Angelicae: Portugiesische Kirchenmusik der Renaissance* (Telefunken 6.35582 GK).

'Some [choir directors], who forget that they are in the presence of God, beat with a stick on the book so that the noise can be heard throughout the church. I can hardly bring myself to mention others who clap their hands to keep time. He who is beating time need do no more than raise his hand two or three times if he wants the tempo to go faster or slower than that at which the singing began.'

Juan Bermudo, *Declaración de instrumentos* (1555), book 1, chap. 19, f.xviii, col.2 ('On directing the choir')

Part IV
Instrumental Music

[14]

Voices and instruments: soloists and ensembles in the 15th century

Keith Polk

1 Lute and voice: Master of the Garden of Love (c.1460), from M. Lehrs, Late Gothic Engravings of Germany and the Netherlands (New York, 1969)

Doubt still clouds the understanding of some important aspects of 15th-century performance practice. Nonetheless, a great deal of information about ensemble practices of that time has been established through the work of scholars in various fields, with most of the more recent research being based on iconographical and literary sources, and on the very few musical ones that specifically refer to performance. But there is one further body of archival documents containing a large quantity of untapped information that can be brought to bear on this subject: financial records from German cities, especially those that detail payments to 'visiting' players (*varenden leutten*, or similar). These visitors' records are unique to German accounting procedures; they survive in large numbers in German cities (notably Augsburg, Nuremberg, Regensburg, Nördlingen and Basel), but rarely elsewhere (neither in Flanders nor

Italy, for example). These sources, brought to our attention by Walter Salmen and Gerhard Pietzsch, add a great deal to our knowledge of the conditions of 15th-century music making.[1]

What follows is a discussion of musical practices as disclosed by the traffic of instrumentalists and singers within a network of German cities. The narrative forms a commentary, while details of payments are given in the Table. Its sources are primarily German (entries in Roman type), with a few relevant documents from other countries (entries in Italic). It should be noted that while the sources are German, the leading instrumentalists of the time emanated from German cities and courts. This was especially true of lutenists, keyboard players, viol players and trombonists, whose influence was felt particularly in Italy (especially in Florence, Milan and Ferrara) and in Flanders. In short, it can be assumed that the practices revealed in German accounts would have had wide currency in the musical life elsewhere in Europe too.[2]

The most subtle problems are those posed by conditions relating to *bas* (or soft) instruments, especially in ensembles; these provide the focus for this article. It should be added, however, that loud (*haut*) ensembles are encountered in the accounts far more often than soft ones. Certainly the trumpet bands and shawm ensembles, according to the tastes of the time, were considered most appropriate to the image of dignity and magnificence so valued by both court and city. Still, loud ensembles were much more rigid in constitution, and posed few problems from the standpoint of ensemble alternatives.[3] As will be shown, only when players of loud instruments began to perform regularly on soft instruments, in combination with other *bas* performers, did the situation become more complex.

The primary *bas* instruments were the lute, viol (and other bowed string instruments), organ, harp and, perhaps, 'flute'. The lute was by far the most common instrument to appear in German accounts, and a highly selective list of solo lutenists (which gives an idea of their geographical and chronological distribution) is provided in section I.1 of the Table. By 1400, lutenists appeared regularly in city accounts, and after about 1430 performances were so recurrent that individual enumeration would be pointless.

More complete, though still selective, are the listings for two lutes. In the early 15th century the lute duo was one of several favoured ensembles. This pairing probably consisted most often of the small lute

2   Two lutes and harp: The Bride's fainting spell, from Buch der Kunst (Augsburg, 1477), f.82v

(the quintern in Germany) and the lute proper (see I.2, 1401), a combination that had also been fashionable in the 14th century.[4] By 1450, however, the lute duo was no longer simply one of several popular ensembles, but assumed the position as the premier ensemble for cultivated 'chamber' music. The patronage was largely courtly, and the setting for this refined combination was the intimate entertainment of courtly ladies and gentlemen (I.2a: the dates given are for only the earliest date known for a duo associated with a particular court). Note, by the way, the frequent identification of the lute pair with women patrons. The term 'tenorist' that was applied to the second player in Ferrara (I.2, 1459, when the 'soprano' performer was Pietrobono) does not appear in German accounts, even though the phenomenon must have been the same. An ensemble of two lutes was evidently a standard practice amongst German musicians, probably with one playing and elaborating the discant, while the other, the 'tenorist', performed the tenor and provided supporting voices below. That is, the skill of the 'tenorist' included not just playing the tenor melody, but also in providing some version of a tenor/contratenor complex. Early in the 15th century the lute was played with a plectrum, and was a monophonic instrument. A very different technique (one which involved plucking with the fingers) was discussed by Tinctoris in about 1487; he described lutenists who were capable of playing 'not only in two parts, but even in three or four . . . the German [Conrad Paumann] was supereminent in playing this way'.[5]

3 Lute and fiddle: Tafelmusik, tapestry, Nuremberg c.1460 (Nuremberg, Germanisches Nationalmuseum, Gew 672)

Given that Paumann began his professional career by c.1440, this kind of polyphonic 'tenorist' support was probably generally known in Germany by about 1450—about the same time as the rise to preeminence of the lute duo.

The combination of three and more lutes was less common, but consistent, mostly as an ensemble. This must be the meaning of the indication that the players together 'performed in the procession before the holy sacrament' (I.3, 1418 and 1468; see also I.4, 1418). More problematic are payments to five lutes; in both examples the language suggests collective payments to individual players (see I.5).

The lute was also the most common participant in ensembles of mixed instruments. The most usual of such groups in German cities consisted of lute and *geige* (or *vedel*), generally in an ensemble of two players (see I.6). The popularity of German players abroad, especially in Italy, provides further evidence of the strength of the German tradition of both lute and bowed stringed instruments (see I.6, 1460 and 1475; also B.3, 1469 and 1482). A note of caution should be

sounded regarding the scribal language which is less than ideally precise in indicating mixed combinations. For example, in Basel 1455 (I.6), payment is recorded to two 'gigern und lutenschlachern', that is, two players each of whom played *both* lute and viol. A number of other entries in section I.6 are ambiguous in this way.

The teaming of the lute with organ was probably more common than the few entries suggest (I.7), and appears to have experienced a surge of popularity between about 1420 and 1450. The 'organ' of this pairing would have been the portable version, the portative. The kinds of occasions funded by cities included entries, processions, banquets and dancing, i.e. those for which the fixed larger organ and even the movable, but cumbersome positive organ were not appropriate. Both of these larger instruments were central to German musical life, but were not commonly ensemble instruments through most of the 15th century. The 'portatifer' in the Nuremberg duo (I.7, 1425) from 1447 to 1450 was Conrad Paumann. His career reveals a characteristic trait of Germany *bas* minstrels, however, for while he was primarily an organist, he appeared in the accounts of both Augsburg and Regensburg specifically mentioned as a lutenist, not a keyboard player (I.1, 1457; I.3, 1455 and 1459). Terms applied to the duo of *bas* players of the court of Brandenburg, 'lauttenschlagern und portatifern' (I.7, 1449), imply the same model, for the terms are plural, indicating again that both players played both instruments, and, in fact, the Brandenburg ensemble of soft musicians was on occasion described as lutenists ('lauttenschlagern') as in Windsheim in 1441.[6] This characteristic doubling by soft minstrels will be taken up below. After 1450 the portative appeared less often, a development evidently tied to the rising preeminence of the lute duo after 1450.

The scarcity of ensembles consisting of lute and harp is surprising because these are often encountered in iconographical sources. They were, however, extremely rare in German accounts of the 15th century. (I.9). Very curious is the combination documented in Frankfurt (I.10, 1467) of lute and muted trombone.

Bowed stringed instruments were referred to as *vedel* or *geige*. The meanings of these terms remain vague, but perhaps what was intended was to distinguish between the medieval fiddle (*vedel*), and, especially in the second half of the 15th century, the viol (*geige*). The term *geige* at any rate was more widely used after about 1440.

The individual string players listed in section II.1 were evidently soloists, and there is no evidence that they either provided an accompaniment for poetry sung by others, or that they would have been poets themselves (none of the players in section II.1 are ever referred to as poets, i.e. as 'sprechers', 'dichters', or as singers). Bowed string instruments combined with both organ (II.7) and lute, but the most common ensembles in the 15th century were those of two or three bowed string instruments.

Groups of two and three *geigen* (not *vedels*) became increasingly common after about 1440 (II.2 and II.3). These probably reflect the tradition described by Virdung in 1511, with two instruments, one small (an unfretted rebec, the *kleine Geigen*) and the other large (a fretted viol-like instrument, the *grosse Geigen*).[7] The Renaissance viol, according to Ian Woodfield, appears to have developed in Italy, just before 1500, with strong influence from Spain.[8] A 'German' viol may have developed at about the same time, given the clear evidence of string playing in Germany throughout the

15th century, and the emphasis there on ensembles which would have needed a large instrument to provide low countertenor parts. In other words, the stimulus which produced the viol in Italy was also at work in German territories, and may also have engendered an indigenous instrument, a 'German' viol. Still, the players around 1440 seem to have been versatile in the usual fashion of contemporary soft minstrels. The Brandenburg 'geigern' of 1442 (III.3) were almost certainly the same players as the Brandenburg 'lutenists' of 1441 (I.3). The German viol tradition of the 16th century, on the other hand, does appear to have been of a different nature, one which involved specialists: the players in the ensembles of Maximilian I, once they were identified in the capacity of violists, do not appear to have performed on other instruments. Also, the records provide little evidence in the crucial years, between 1470 and 1500. Woodfield's thesis concerning Spanish/Italian development of the viol north of the Alps should be adjusted to include recognition of the fact that a continuous pattern of string playing in Germany can be traced throughout the 15th century. At some point the Renaissance viol (i.e. the Spanish/Italian viol) became widely accepted in Germany. Whether it was a new phenomenon, or supplanted a native instrument remains a speculative question.

Organists appear with some frequency in the accounts; the listing given in section III.1 of the Table is highly selective. Particularly interesting is the item from Nördlingen in 1468, in which the town provided a small subsidy for Sebald, the city organist, to travel to Munich to study with Conrad Paumann. In Nuremberg, a player of the portative organ and a lutenist (two performers) were subsidized regularly from 1425 to the end of the 15th century; otherwise references to the combination of organ (portative) and lute are not frequent (discussed above, see I.7). The rarity of *vedel* or *geige* with organ is unexpected, however, and again markedly at odds with iconographical evidence.

Even more out of step with pictorial evidence is the scarcity of references to the harp (IV), especially early in the century. The instrument was very common in French and Flemish sources, but does not begin to appear in visitors' accounts until after 1440. Harpists were evidently active in German cities (IV.1, 1420, Nördlingen), but for some reason were not engaged for the kind of performances supported by visitors' accounts.

Rare as the harp may have been, recorders are

4 Lute and harp: Musicians playing at a well, late 15th century. Israhel van Meckenem (1450–1503) (Washington, National Gallery of Art)

mentioned even less frequently. No examples of musical ensembles including 'flutes' have been found ('Swiss pairs' excepted). What is odd is that Flemish civic musicians not only performed on recorder, but they did so within recorder ensembles. The Flemish players characteristically purchased such instruments in matched sets, using the term 'coker' (see V.6, 1481 and 1501).

From a pragmatic point of view the voice may be considered a *bas* instrument, to be combined freely with lute, viol or organ.[9] Vocalists were not involved in performances with loud instruments until almost 1500, although, as discussed below, the date may be earlier than previously thought.

German practices relating to singers seem to have been quite varied. Often payments were made to soloists, performing with no apparent ensemble, either vocal or instrumental (see VI.1). Perhaps they were accompanied (by a lute, for example), but any such presence is characteristically not mentioned.

German accounts establish the consistent activity of professional women singers throughout the 15th century (see VI.2). In an attempt to convey an ample picture of the activities of performances of women of professional calibre, both solo and chamber choir appearances are included in this Table.

The *sprecher* was a popular figure in German courts and cities; section VI.3 gives a sampling of references. *Sprechers* appear to have functioned in several distinct ways: some were primarily narrative poets, whose musical skills may have been secondary (see VI.3a, where Michel Behaim is named as an example), while others seem to have combined the skills of singing and poetry (see VI.3b, where Jorig Sailer may be an example). Yet others seem to have acted as entertainers, poets, singers and instrumentalists (VI.3c, where Hans Teufel is mentioned). Music historians have largely ignored this category of gifted and versatile entertainers. The popularity of the Tenor Lied as a characteristically German phenomenon certainly seems more comprehensible within the context of a very strong tradition of solo singers.

The participation of boy singers in the 15th century has been discussed by Craig Wright, who believes that boys were used either as the soprano section of a choir with adult male voices, or as a separate entity in a boys' choir. To this can be added the fact that a boy soloist is known occasionally to have performed with lute (see VI.4, 1464, 1488).

The next two categories may seem arbitrary in that they make a distinction between a small vocal ensemble (2–4 singers) and a 'choir' (5 or more). This is suggested firstly by the inclusion of women in some smaller groups (VI.5, 1404, 1490), and secondly because the larger groups seem to have been more often involved in the performance of sacred repertory. Finally, singers at this time often improvised, a relatively straightforward procedure for two, three or four, but impractical when five or more were involved. 'Large' ensembles were hardly that: even Maximilian I, who normally employed a choir numbering between 12 and 16, could call on a 'travelling' group of 8 singers (VI.6, 1491). Regardless of any fine differentiation that might be made between small and 'large' vocal ensembles, the scribal language itself verifies the distinct identity of such ensembles. They are always mentioned as separate units and only at the end of the 15th century are indications found of instruments being incorporated into choral performances. While the repertory is almost never specified, visitors' accounts support the view that not only was sacred music normally performed *a cappella*, but for secular music, too, this was a favoured medium. This is consistent with comments on performance practice recently put forward by Fallows and Page.[10]

However, voices and instruments are known to have combined, especially in secular music (see VI.7). Many of the *sprechers* (particularly those listed in VI.3c) performed their narrative poetry with instrumental accompaniment. The description of the woman who sang for Maximilian I in 1486 (VI.7) is significant in that she sang both chansons and motets with a variety of instruments. David Fallows recently proposed the idea that 'composed' chansons were performed by preference and perhaps exclusively *a cappella*; an exclusively vocal medium certainly appealed to German patrons and musicians.[11] Yet it seems highly unlikely that a *bas musique* performer as gifted as this young woman, or one of the stature of Conrad Paumann, would not have known many works of the standard repertory. Paumann and his students played such pieces as *Je loe amours* and *Se la face ay pale* in versions which, while they are elaborated, establish that the framework of the 'composed piece' was the starting point of such repertory.[12] Finally, a document from Nuremberg in 1442 concerning performances during Corpus Christi celebrations is significant: musicians were to be drawn from young citizens (burghers) and artisans of the town, and the forces included a lutenist (who might well have learnt his skills from Hermann Kirschbaum), an organist (a player of the portative like Paumann), a quinternist, with (if possible) a harpist, and one musician to sing with these instruments.[13]

The ability of the talented woman who sang for Maximilian to play a variety of instruments prompts another observation that follows from the documentation relating to *bas* instrument performers: that these musicians were characteristically competent on a variety of instruments. Conrad Paumann was a famous organist, but he was also a fine lutenist (as has been shown above). Herman Kirschbaum, civic lutenist in Nuremberg, was also mentioned as the 'city fiddler' (I.6, 1431). The versatility of German soft minstrels has tended to blur the issue of patronage. The three players of 'geigen' associated with the Margrave of Brandenburg in 1442 or those with the Duke of Bavaria in 1447 (II.3) appear only then—but these were not 'free-lance' fiddle players hired for a series of engagements in those years. The Brandenburg performers

5 Lute, portative and harp: the Madonna with eight saints in a garden, Master of the Berlin Passion (late 15th century)

were the same three who were described as lutenists in 1441 and as 'players' ('spielleuten') in 1444 (I.3). Similarly, the Bavarian fiddlers were the same as those described as lutenists in 1455 and 1459 (I.3). Both courts, in other words, were consistently, year after year, supporting a stable of three soft minstrels who would play whatever instrument was required for a particular performance.[14]

Versatility acted within the medieval conventions of *haut* and *bas*. Until 1450 loud performers seem not to have played *bas* instruments (as discussed below) and *vice versa*. Furthermore, specialities within the two categories may have involved quite different dimensions. Soft players, for example, were more often expected to appear as solo players (particularly lutenists and organists), and were more likely to have been musically literate.

Of fundamental importance is the fact that until about 1450 the general distinction of *haut* and *bas* continued to operate. Sometime after then, however, new ideas swept through the world of instrumental music. A crucial development seems to have been brought about by soft minstrels after about 1470 with specialization becoming more the order of the day. Until about 1450, lutenists were often noted as playing other instruments; after this time it becomes remarkably less often the case as the lute duo began to predominate. Paumann (trained *c*.1440), the most extraordinary keyboard talent of his day, was the quintessential doubler, and dazzled his audience with the range of his competence. Hofhaimer, the outstanding organist of the next generation, is almost never indicated as performing on an instrument other than the organ. The more exclusive focus allowed greater concentration of effort in terms of learning technique, and it is toward the end of the 15th century that we begin to hear more often of virtuoso performances.

The recasting of basic notions of music-making involved both new instruments and new instrumental combinations, as well as new contexts for instrumental performance (as is shown in the last four catagories, VI.8 and B1–3). The zinck appeared on the scene by about 1450, and the popularity of the instrument increased rapidly from about 1475. From its inception the zinck seems to have been linked to performances with trombones, and, more significantly, with choirs (i.e. not just solo singers, but with vocal ensembles). The most renowned zinck player was Augustein Schubinger. He began his professional

life as a trombonist in the city ensemble in Augsburg, then served the city of Florence (1489–93) and the Hapsburg court (1494–1532) as a trombone specialist. His performance speciality began to change in about 1490 as the zinck became his main instrument.[15] It seems most likely, however, that he learned to play the zinck in his apprentice years, around 1470: talented young wind players in German cities were thus probably learning this instrument regularly from about 1470.

The range of doublings included the crumhorn (B.2) and, more significantly in terms of changes in attitudes to performance practice, strings (B.3). As the range of instrumental doubling widened, the foundations of the *haut* and *bas* tradition crumbled. The circumstances under which lute, viol and zinck players worked would have involved them with singers, and even with sacred music in a liturgical context (see Augustein Schubinger, B.1, 1502; also Hans Nagel, VI.8, 1507), where reading music must have been a normal requisite.

The evidence now available suggests that this was true earlier than previously thought. As Lewis Lockwood has established, the Casanatense MS was compiled in about 1480 for use by the pifferi of Ferrara.[16] The most prominent player there was, significantly, Michel Schubinger, locally known as Michele Tedesco. The collection incorporates many pieces, i.e. chansons, from the international repertory. It therefore follows that Michel Schubinger would have had access to the manuscript, and would have read and performed 'composed' chansons, just as his brother Augustein (and Hans Nagel) would have read and performed Masses and motets.[17]

Much of this information has been noted before, but what has not been emphasized is the implication of the players' identity. Augustein Schubinger was playing on the zinck in *c*.1500, but began his career *c*.1479, the same year of the first notice of Hans Nagel. Michel Schubinger first appears in 1469.[18] Thus the training years, when they would have all learned their basic performance skills were between *c*.1460 and 1475—and both the Schubingers and Nagel were probably trained by their fathers. The evidence suggests that new trends had arrived on the scene by *c*.1490, but looking at the careers of the players involved, it would appear that these trends had been set in motion significantly earlier, perhaps as early as 1460.

Page after page of urban ledgers reveal a remarkably

composite picture of patronage. Nothing is more dramatic in these documents than their confirmation of the establishments supported by noble houses, courts for which there was previously only very fragmentary evidence. In about 1450 the Margrave of Brandenburg maintained an ensemble of three soft players, as well as his five-part shawm band and his troupe of some six trumpets. Duke Albrecht of Bavaria had almost identical forces, three soft players, four shawms and four or five trumpets. These totals are strikingly similar to those of the brilliant musical retinue of the court of Burgundy (in 1450, two soft players, a five-part shawm band, and four trumpets).[19] Duke Philip the Good was clearly a more discerning patron as regards vocal music and composers, but in instrumental music, given the presence of Paumann in Munich and the preeminence of German wind players, he was clearly rivalled by his cousin Albrecht.[20]

The city accounts allow the modern viewer to build up what has been a very incomplete image of patronage at the courts of Bavaria and Brandenburg. With Maximilian I, the effect is the opposite: the cutting down to size of a deliberate, albeit glorious forgery, the *Triumph of Maximilian I* of c.1518. This explicitly deceptive series of engravings was concocted as an 'enhanced' image of imperial music, one which illustrates a total of some 84 instrumentalists. Weighed against this fantastic self-image, is the evidence of the day-to-day payment records which reveal the forces Maximilian was actually able or willing to support: six or seven soft minstrels [an organist (Hofhaimer), two to three lutes, and four viols] and three distinct units within the loud category [a six-part shawm band (including Augustein Schubinger and Hans Neuschel), 12 trumpets (with tympany) and a small three-part fife and drum corps].[21] This represents a largish number (about 30), including some brilliant talent, but far less than the vision of Maximilian and his artists.

The cities and courts of Germany proved lavish patrons. The music they supported was of astonishing quantity as well as quality, and their patronage was a significant element in stimulating change in instrumental practices. The importance of this cannot be underestimated, for German musicians were active not only within their own territory, but enjoyed a wide reputation and were influential throughout Europe in the late Middle Ages. Any composite picture of 15th-century musical culture which fails to take into account their brilliant contributions is incomplete.

TABLE

Entries in Roman type are German in origin, entries in Italics show related sources, abbreviations are listed at the end

A   BAS INSTRUMENTS

I   LUTE

I.1   Lute solo (highly selective)

1410	Regensburg, Sterl, p.256	'dez pischofs von wirczburg lautenslacher'
1423	Augsburg, BB, f.88	'der von Abensperg luttenschlaher'
1429	Augsburg, BB, f.54	'ainem luttenschlaher'
1431	Augsburg, BB, f.79	'ainem Spilman mit ainem Lutlin'
1433	Nördlingen, KR, f.42	'des margrafen lutenslager'
1436	Augsburg, BB, f.49	'hertzog Ernstz luttenschlaher'
1445	Freiburg, Fellerer, p.70	'ein Lautenspieler aus Basel'
1457	Augsburg, BB, f.45	'maister Cunraten blinden lutenslaher'
1461	Innsbruck, Moser, 1929, p.72	'eine lautenslaherin aus munchen'
1471	Regensburg, Sterl, p.284	'margraf albrechts lawttenslaher'
1487	Basel, Ernst, p.222	'des römischen kunigs luttenschlacher';
1487	Innsbruck, Senn, p.10	'Clara mit der Lauten'
1498	Basel, Ernst, p.233	'des ro. ko lutenschlaher'

I.2   Two lutes (selective)

1404	Cologne, PietzschK, p.52	'des kunigs quinterner und lutenslegern'
1429	Augsburg, BB, f.54	'zwayn luttenschlahern'
1431	Augsburg, BB, f.79ᵛ	'zwain luttenschlahern'
1432	Nordlingen, KR, f.43	'zwey lutenslagern'
1434	Nördlingen, KR, f.41	'[zwain] lutenslaher'
1436	Freiburg, Fellerer, p 55	'zwei Lautenspieler'
1437	Augsburg, BB, f.77ᵛ	'[zwain] luttenschlahern'
1440	Freiburg, Fellerer, p.68	'zwei Lautenspieler'
1447	Augsburg, BB, f.46	'der grafen von helffenstain und der von Rechperg luttenschlaher'
1454	Bavaria, expenses for journey of Duke Philip the Good of Burgundy, Marix, p.71, two lutenists in Regensburg, p.73, two lutenists in Basel	
1459	*Ferrara, Lockwood, p 317*	*Pietrobono, with his 'tenorist'*
1460	Nuremberg, SR, f.102	'zweyen lautenslahern des Bisschofs und der stat Eystett'
1464	Augsburg, BB, f.53	'dem Tüfel und seinem gesellen . . lutenslaher'; Teufel was paid as an instrumentalist in Nördlingen in 1456 (KR, f.25, 'dem

Teufel von Nuremberg spilman'),
as a sprecher in Nuremberg in
1472 (SR, f.220), and again as a
'spilman' in Nuremberg in 1475
(Sch. f.219).

1464   Nördlingen, KR, f.32   'zwaien lutenslagern von Augs-
                                     burg'

1467   Nördlingen, KR, f.31   'zway lautensl' who played 'in der
                                     Mess' [i.e. the annual trade fair]

1.2a   **Lute Pairs patronized by noble houses:**

Maximilian I (1486, Augsburg, BB, f.16); Duke of Austria
(1454, Marix, p.70); Duke of Bavaria/Landshut (1490,
Augsburg, BB, f.17ᵛ); Duke of Bavaria/Munich (1454, Regens-
berg, Sterl, p.275); Margrave of Brandenburg (1443, Nuremberg, GR [Rep. 54/180], f.159ᵛ); Duke of Brunswick (1466,
Nördlingen, KR, f.32); Duke of Cleve (1461, Essen, SR, f.7),
Count of Henneberg (1493, Nördlingen, KR, f 38ᵛ); Landgrave
of Hessen (1471, Nuremberg, Sch. f.235); Duke of Jülich
(1458, PietzschA, p 43); Court of Pappenheim (1443, Windsheim, ZB, unfoliated); Duke of Saxony (1458, Nuremberg, SR,
f 92); Count of Weinsberg (1476, Windsheim, ZB, unfoliated);
Count of Württemberg (1484, Augsburg, BB, f 15ᵛ)

Duchesses of· Berg [= Cleve] (1446, Wesel, PietzschA, p.43);
Brunswick (1479, Würzburg, PNL II, 767); Jülich (1461,
PietzschA, p.40); Saxony (1444, Nuremberg, Sch f.30);
Countess of Henneberg (1499, Konigshöfen im Grabfeld, SA,
SR, p.27) and of Weinsberg (1482, Nuremberg, SR, f 218ᵛ)

Bishops of Cologne (1444, Nuremberg, Sch., f.37), Eichstätt
(1486, Nördlingen, KR, f.33), Mainz (1481, Nuremberg, Sch.,
f.102ᵛ); Würzburg (1440, Windsheim, ZB, f.70ᵛ)

1.3.   **Three lutes**

1418   *Ypres, Brussels ARA*   'dnen ghesellen die met haren luuten
       38643, f 60ᵛ   ende ghisternen speelden voor 't
                                     sacrament'

1421   Augsburg, BB, f.84   three 'luttenschlahern'

1422   Windsheim, ZB, unfoliated 'dreyen gesellen zu luten'

1438   Freiburg, Fellerer, p.68   three lutenists of Duke Ludwig of
                                     Bavaria (Landshut)

1441   Windsheim, ZB, f.66ᵛ   '3lb. marckgraff Albrechts lutten-
                                     schlagern'

1454   Bavaria, Marix, p.71   among the expenses for Philip the
                                     Good's visit to Bavaria, 'a trois
                                     guiterneux, jouans de lutz'

1457   Augsburg, BB, f.45   'maister Cunrat (und) zwain andern
                                     hertzog Albrechts [Duke of Bav-
                                     aria/Munich] lutenslahern'

1459   Regensburg, Sterl, 278   'dem plinnten und andern ij herc-
                                     zog Albrechts von Pairn lawten-
                                     slahern'

1468   Nördlingen, KR, f.39   'iii lautenslachern . . . die vor dem
                                     sacrament lautenslagen, vi lb'

1470   Augsburg, BB, f 49ᵛ   'dreyen luttenschlaher'

1471   Trier, Baser, 1976, p.24   banquet performance, after listing

of other musicians who had
played, 'darnach 3 mit luten'

1472   Nördlingen, KR, f.33   'marggrauff albrechts 3 lauttens-
                                     laher'

1475   Nördlingen, KR, f.36ᵛ   a 'luttenslaher und ii sein gesel-
                                     en' of Brandenburg

1475   Nördlingen, KR, f.36ᵛ   'marggrauff albrechts 3 lauttens-
                                     laher'

1478   Nördlingen, KR, f.35   'des vom Eybergs iii luttensla-
                                     hern'

1496   Augsburg, BB, f.17ᵛ   'Kunigs dreyen luttenschlagern'

1498   Königshöfen im Grabfeld,
       SA, SR, p.29,   drey lautenschlager der von Henn-
                                     berg'

1.4   **Four lutes**

1418   *Ypres, Brussels ARA, 38643,* 'viere ghisteners   van dat zij
       f 60ᵛ   voor de Reliquienen speelden'

1466   Nördlingen, KR, f.32   'des von Wurtemberg iiii lauten-
                                     slaher'

1489   Nördlingen, KR, f 42ᵛ   'iiii luttenschlagern' of the 'Rom-
                                     isch Kunig'

1.5   **Five lutes (ensembles?)**

1442   Nuremberg, Sch., f.34ᵛ   'lawtenschlahern zu samen der
                                     waren fünff'

1458   Nuremberg, SR, f.96   combined payment to five 'lau-
                                     tenslahern'

1.6   **Lute and bowed stringed instrument (Geige or Vedel)**

1403   Den Haag, PietzschA, 25   'twee speellunden mit eenre luten
                                     ende vedel toebehorende den
                                     heren van Ravensberch'

1418   Desden, PNL I, p.164   'der hertzogin von Beyern luten-
                                     sloer und fedelern'

1427   Nuremberg, KR, f.76   salary to Hansen Kratzer, lutenist,
                                     and Hermann [Kirschbaum], 'socio
                                     suo'—see entry for 1430

1430   Nuremberg, KR, f.59   special payment to 'Hansen Krat-
                                     zer und seinem gesellen Herman
                                     der stat vidler'

1437   Freiburg, Fellerer, p.68   'Zwei Frauen, die Geige und Laute
                                     spielten'

1442/ Essen, SA, SR, f.13ᵛ   'den lutensleger ind [und] fede-
1443   ler'

1444   Nuremberg, Sch., f.37   'herzog Albrechts fidler und lau-
                                     tenslaher'

1449   Mainz, PNL 4, pp.140ff.   'm.h. von Meintz lutensleger und
                                     giger'

1451	Frankfurt, PNL 2, p 238	the 'lutensleger und fiddeler' of the Bishop of Mainz
1455	Basel, Ernst, p.224	'gigern und lutenschlachern'
1458	Augsburg, BB, f 52^V	'ainem lutenslaher und ainem Gyger des jungen herrn von Sachsen pfyfern'
1459	Augsburg, BB, f.30^V	'herczog Albrechtz lutenslaher und gijger'
1460	Innsbruck, Senn, p 9	a 'Lautenslager und Fiedler, so van Munichen, die gen wellischen Landen zogen'
1469	Nordlingen, KR, f.38^V	'Lautslah. und geyger—ir zwayen'
1470	Nördlingen, KR, f.37^V	'Lauttensl und aym geyger—ir zwaijen'
1471	Wesel, SR, f.20 (PNL II, p.738)	'den speelluden myyten luten ind vedelen'
1475	*Milan, E Motto, (R/Geneva 1977), Musica alla corte degli Sforza, pp 53-7*	*Johannes, 'todesco', performed with 'suo compagno che sona de viola' —this companion was probably Stegano de Alemania, 'pifero et sonatore de la viola'*
1476	Nördlingen, KR, f.36	'der von Eyberg luttenslaher und eym Geijger'
1484	Nördlingen, KR, f 30	'August Geiger und henslin Sweitz [lutenist]'
1485	Nördlingen, KR, f.30	'Henslin Sweitz und sein gesellen' [see previous entry]
1486	Cologne, PietzschK, p.92	'geyger und lutensleger'
1487	Solothurn, PNL III, p.1181	'einem luttenschlacher und einem giger'
1497	Solothurn, PNL III, p.1184	'einem giger und sinem luttenschlacher' [also] 'einem luttenschlacher und einem giger'

1.7 Lute with organ

1404	(Den Haag) PietzschQ, p 698	'ii gesellen toebehoorende dem nyen keyser spelende op een orgel ende op een quinterne'
1425	Nuremberg, P Sander, *Die Reichsstadtische Haushaltungs Nurnbergs* (Leipzig, 1902), I, pp.127–129	Lute and portatif this year and regularly thereafter for the remainder of the 15th century
1446	Nordlingen, KR, f 33^V	'portatifern und lutenslaher'
1447	Nördlingen, KR, f.33^V–34	'portatifer' and lute
1447	Windsheim, SA, ZB unfoliated	'margrave albrechts lawtenslaher und portatifer'
1449	Windsheim, ZB, f 44	'4 gr marggraf Alb. lautenschlagern und portatifern' (same entry in 1450, ZB, unfoliated)
1470	Nuremberg, SR, f.125	Medallion payments for the 'portativer und lautenslahern'

1482	's-Hertogenbosch, Smijers, p.173	den spoeluyden die voer onse lieve Vrouwe spoelden te weeten 2 luyten unde een cleyn orgele'

1 8 Lute and zinck

1485	Augsburg, BB, f.14	'bayder herren von Wirttemberg luttenschlager und zinckenplasern'

1.9 Lute and harp

1409	*Ypres, Brussels, ARA 38638, f 51*	*3 'speelieden metten lute ende metten aerpe'*
1444	Nuremberg, Sch., f 37	'des kunigs harppfer und hertzog Albrechts lautenslaher'
1450	*Leuven, vdSt, 4, p 239*	*'Gheram met synder herpen en Wouter Loeten met synder luyten'*
1454	Ulm, Marix, p.69	'deux joueurs de harpes et de lus'
1487	Nuremberg, SR., f.219^V	'Marggraf Fridrichs' harper and lutenist
1498	Nördlingen, KR, f.50	'marggraf Fridrichs harpfen und Lauttenschlagern philyp und utzen'

1.10 Lute and muted trombone (with voices)

1467	Frankfurt, from Bernhard Rorbachs *Liber gestorum*, 'in feste b. Marie Magdalene trugen in solenni procesione; so giengen vor dem sacrament der statt drompten Peter mit einer gedempten drompten und sin son Hensle mit einer luten zu discantiren und unser dri mit einer luten zu tenoristen mit namen Peter Marpurg, Henn Cammerer und ich Bernhard Rorbach' R Froning, *Frankfurter Chroniken* (Frankfurt a.M., 1884), p 216
1468	Frankfurt, same group, see previous entry, Froning, p 218

1.11. Lute, Vedel and Organ

1410	*Ypres, Brussels ARA 38639, f 62^V*	*3 'spiellieden metten orghele, vedele ende lute'*
1492	Strasbourg, Moser (1929), p.11	report of three brothers who performed on lute, vedel and organ

[Lute and voice—see VI.7]

II   BOWED STRINGS (Vedel and Geige)

II.1   Vedel or geige solo

1404   Hamburg, PNL I, 298   payment to 'Clawes veddeler'

1416   Regensburg, Sterl, p.258   'dem Chuntzen herczog Albrechtz
                                     fidlär von Osterreich'

1427   Windsheim, ZB, unfoliated 'des marschalks geyger oder eine
                                     pfeifer des von pappenheim'

1429   Augsburg, BB, f.54   'dem Bützzlin geijger'; also in 1431
                                     (BB, f.79), 1432 (BB, f.62) and 1437
                                     (BB, f.77ᵛ)

1429   Windsheim, ZB, unfoliated 'des marschalks geiger von pap-
                                     penheim'

1433   Nördlingen, KR, f.42   'Heintz gygere'

1436   Augsburg, BB, f.77   'hertzog Ernstz geijger'

1440   Augsburg, BB, f.70   'dem Schur geijger'

1455   Augsburg, BB, f.39   'dez bischoffs von Mainz viden-
                                     ler'

1465   Augsburg, BB, f 41ᵛ   'dem Fröschlin gyger'; also in 1469
                                     (BB, f.20ᵛ), 1470 (BB, f.50ᵛ), 1473
                                     (BB, f.25ᵛ) and 1477 (BB, f.40ᵛ)

*1470   Ferrara, Lockwood, p 97   payment to Berniero da Sala, of
                                     Naples, viola*

1485   Augsburg, BB, f 14   'Ulrich . . des Bischofs von Cos-
                                     tantz geiger'

1486   Wertheim, PNL II, p 724   'Geschkenkt Jacob dem Fidel-
                                     lern'

*ca   The string instruments of choice for Tinctoris (for his own
1488   performing?) were the viola and rebec, H M Brown, 'Instruments
         and Voices in the 15th-century chanson', Current Thought in
         Musicology, ed J Grubbs (Austin, 1976), p 117*

1494   Augsburg, BB, f.17   'Ulrich am Stain des Bishofs von
                                     Costennz luttenschlager') See en-
                                     try for 1485

II.2   Two bowed stringed instruments

1404   [Den Haag], PietzschQ,   'des Keysers .   ij vedelairs'
        p.698

1410   Zwolle, GA, SR, f.77   'tween seydenspeelres des biss-
                                     cops van Colen'

1416   Augsburg, BB, f.49ᵛ   '2 guldin dez herczogen von Öster-
                                     rich fidellern'

(1423   Augsburg, BB, f.88   'zwayn spilluten Graf Rudolfs von
                                     Montfort'—see entry for 1425)

1424   Erfurt, SR, f.361 (PNL I),   'des herzogen von Beyern fede-
        p.213   lern', also 'herzogen Wilhelms von
                                     Boerge fedelern'

1425   Freiburg, Fellerer, p 65   'zwei Geigern des Grafen Wilhelm
                                     von Montfort'

1427   Windsheim, ZB, unfoliated 'zwaien . . . geigern'

1429   Windsheim, ZB, unfoliated 'zweien geyger von bebenberg'

1431   Nördlingen, KR, f.48ᵛ   2 'gygern' of Duke Henry of
                                     Bavaria (Landshut)

1432   Freiburg, Fellerer, p.67   'zwei Geiger aus Konstanz'

*1433–1456 Strohm, p 88   two players of vielle on the salary
                                     rolls of the Court of Burgundy*

1434   Freiburg, Fellerer, p.67   'Zwei Frauen, die sangen und sich
                                     auf der Geige begleiteten'

1435   Deventer, De Meyer, VI,   'ons   heren   speellude   van
        p.64   Utrecht van den zeiden spele,
                                     12 d.'

1437   Deventer, De Meyer, VI,   'ons heren van Utrecht Camer
        p 167   speellude myd den zeiden spele,
                                     12 d '

1439   Deventer, De Meyer, VI,   'ons heren van Utrecht zeiden-
        p.262   speellude twe, 12 d.'

1440   Deventer, De Meyer, VI,   '2 ons heren speellude myd den
        p.365   zeiden spoele, 12 d.'

1440   Wesel, PNL II, 733   'kamerspeleluden des bisscops
                                     van Utrecht'

1441   Freiburg, Fellerer, p.69   'zwei Geigerinnen'

1442   Windsheim, ZB, unfoliated 'margr alprechts [von Branden-
                                     burg 2] geigern'

1455   Basel, Ernst, p.114   '2 gulden des fürsten von Oester-
                                     rich gigern und lutenschlach-
                                     ern'—that is, this payment is for
                                     two players, who appeared both as
                                     'giger' and as players of lute.

1466–1500 Lockwood, p 97   two 'violas' on the salary rolls

1471   Wesel, SA, SR, f.20 (PNL   '2 speelluden myt vedelen'
        II p.738)

*1488   Strohm, pp 88–9   description by Tinctoris of two virtu-
                                     oso players of 'vielle'*

ca.   German players parodied in Florentine carnival songs, but
1490   they were noted as masters ('bon maestri') of both 'ribechine'
        and 'gran ribechaze'; that is, they played on at least two sizes
        of bowed stringed instruments, see T. McGee and S. Mittler,
        'Information on instruments . . .', EM 10 (1982), p 458

1496   Augsburg, BB, f.17ᵛ   4 fl. to 'hertzog Philips Geygern
                                     und Singern'—four musicians,
                                     perhaps two string players and
                                     two singers

1497   Freiburg, Fellerer, p.75   'zwei fremden Geigern'

1499   Freiburg, Fellerer, p 75   'zwei Geigern aus Luzern'

1500   Freiburg, Fellerer, p.75   'zwei Geiger mit einer Sängerin'

1500   Freiburg, Fellerer, p.75   'zwei Geiger aus Solothurn, von
                                     denen einer blind war'

1508   Nuremberg, GR, Rep 54/   'zwayen des konigs von Polen
        181, f.446   geygern'

II.3   Three bowed stringed instruments

1440   [Den Haag], PietzschW,   '3 Fiedler [of the Duke of Bavaria/
        p.126   Munich]'

1418   Freiburg, Fellerer, p.54   'drei Freiburgische Spielleute, Gei-
                                     ger' performed during visit of the
                                     Pope to Freiburg

6 Lute and harp: young man and woman playing a lute and a harp, Israhel van Meckenem (1450–1503)
(Washington National Gallery of Art)

1432	Freiburg, Fellerer, p.67	'drei Geiger aus Schwyz'
1447	Augsburg, BB, f.46	'iii guldin hertzog Albrechts Gaijger', 1 e. 3 players
1451	Augsburg, BB, f.46	'iii guldin hertzoginn [Bavaria/Munich] spilluten'—the same players as those of 1447?
1460	Milan, G Barblan, 'Vita musicale alla corte sforzesca'. Storia de Milano IX (1961), p 804	'tre todeschi sonaton de leyuto et de viola'
1471	Trier, Baser, 1976, p.24 p.24	banquet performance, musicians with lutes played, and then 'darnach 3 mit gygen'
1478	Nördlingen, KR, f.35ᵛ	'der . . von autrich und wirttemberg . . Geijgern' [probably 3 players, although no figures are given]
1482	Halle, W. Salmen, *Der fahrende Musiker im europaischen Mittelalter* (Kassel, 1960), p 89	three 'saitenspieler' on the city payroll
1501	Cologne, PietzschK, p.93	3 'gigern' of the Bishop of Cologne
1515	Augsburg, BB, f.28	three 'geigern' of Maximilian I, the players named were Casper and Gregorien Egkern and Jorigen Berner

1516/ 1517	Nuremberg, GR, Rep. 54/ 181, f.617	'dreyen pfaltzischen geigern'

II.4   Four bowed stringed instruments

1502	Leipzig, G. Wustmann, *Aus Leipzigs Vergangenheit* (Leipzig, 1909), III, p.72	payment to four players who had performed for the city council 'dem Rath zu Ehren gefiehatte'
1506	Hapsburg Court, H. Anglés, *La Música en la Corte de Carlos V* (Barcelona, 1965), p.3	ensemble of Philip the Fair, four players of stringed instruments ('cuatro violines'),
1508	Augsburg, BB, f.24	'iiii guldin des konigs von Bolland geyger' (i.e. four players)
1516	Augsburg, BB, f.28	four 'geygern' of Maximilian I, the players named were Caspar and Gregorien Berner and Heronimus Hagen
1517	Augsburg, BB, f.30	four 'geigern' (the same as in the previous year) of Maximilian I
1518	Augsburg, BB, f 30ᵛ–31	four 'geigern' of Maximilian; also four 'geigern' of the Duke of Bavaria

II.5   Vedel or geige and lute (see under Lute, I.6)

II.6   Geige and harp

1449	Augsburg, f.46	'hertzog Albrechttz harpffer und gijger'—the payment was of 3 guldin, which indicates three players, probably 2 geigen and 1 harp [this was probably the same ensemble that was 3 'geigern' in 1447, and 3 'lutes' in 1455]

II.7   Geige and organ

1425–1431	Nuremberg, GR, 1425, f.228ᵛ; 1430, f 489	Hansen Kratzer, 'orgelist', was also termed a lutenist; Kratzer performed with Hermann, 'der stat vidler' see I.6, 1430

III   ORGAN

III.1   Organ solo (highly selective)

1406	's-Hertogenbosch, Smijers, p.32	'brueder Jan van Rijswijc gegeven van spele op die orghele ende dat hi me coemt singhen als men wil ende van den gheselle te leren singhen ende spelen die leren willen'
1410	Nördlingen, KR, f.44	'dem orgelmaister'
1430	Nördlingen, KR, f.41ᵛ	'dem orgelmaister'
1441	Nuremberg, SR, f.81	'margraff Albrechts portatifer'
1451	Augsburg, BB, f.46ᵛ	'dem blinden von Nuremberg'
1466	Nördlingen, KR, f.32	'maister Conrat blinden geschenkt von der newen orgel wegen'
1467	Nördlingen, KR, f.31	'des Babst port[at]ifer'
1468	Nördlingen, KR, f.38ᵛ	'geschenkt her Sebolt unsern organisten das der zu maister Conrat plinden ziehen wolt und bass von Im lernen uff der orgelen ze schlahen'
1472	Nördlingen, KR, f.33	'des von Salzburgs pfeiffern und organisten', almost certainly solo organist separate from a group of shawmists
1472	Nördlingen, KR, f 31	'fur maister Conrat plinden . . was er ains tags und nacht leng hije'

[Organ with lute, see I.7; with Bowed string, see II.7]

IV   HARP

IV.1   Solo harp

(1420	Nördlingen, KR, f.15ᵛ	'Hans herpfer' on the roll of new citizens)
1422	*Ferrara, Lockwood, p 315*	*salary to Rodolfo dall'Arpa*
1442	Nuremberg, Sch, f.34	'des kunigs harpffer'
1442	Regensburg, Sterl, p.273	'ainem härpfenslaher'
1444	Nuremberg, Sch, f.37	'des kunigs harpffer'
1445	Duke of Austria accounts, Tiroler Landesarchiv Innsbruck, Ms.203, II, f.5ᵛ	'Harfensloher' in Salzburg
1450	*Ferrara, Lockwood, p 317*	*salary to Giovanni dall'arpa Inglese*
1473	Regensburg, Sterl, p.285	'einem des Kunigs von Hungern härpfer'
1487	Augsburg, BB, f.16ᵛ	'Marggraf Friderichs harpffer'; also in Nördlingen, KR, f.37
1489	Augsburg, BB, f.16ᵛ	'marggraf Friderichs harpffenschlager'; also in 1495 (BB, f.17ᵛ) and 1498 (BB, f.21ᵛ)
1493	Württemberg, Sittard, p.3	the musical forces at the court included a harpist

IV.2   Two harps

1440	*Bruges, Strohm, p 81*	
1446	Essen, SR, f.5ᵛ	'eynem manne ind [und] eynem wive metten harpen'

[See also Lute and harp, and Bowed string with harp]

V.1   'Flutes'—no examples in visitors' accounts

1468	*Bruges, Marix, p 106*	*quartet of flutes at the wedding of Margaret of York and Charles the Bold*
(1474	Regensburg, Sterl, p.285	'herczog Albrechts pfewffern mit den klein pfewfflein', flutes?)
1481	*Bruges, Polk, Ensemble, p 18*	*purchase of a set (a 'coker') of flutes for the civic wind players*
1492	*Ghent, Polk, Ensemble, p 18*	*contract between city player and an apprentice, among the instruments to be taught was the 'fleute'*
1500	Augsburg, accounts of Maximilian I, Wesseley, p.130	'vier knaben . . . auff den fleyten gepiffen haben'

VI	BAS INSTRUMENTS: voice and combinations of instruments with voice

VI.1 Solo singer (probably male)

1417	Regensburg, Sterl, p.259	payment to the 'singer' of the Count Palatine
1429	Regensburg, Sterl, p.266	'dem Nachtigal, herczog Ludweig [Bavaria/Ingolstadt] singer'
1437	Nördlingen, KR, f.33ᵛ	'dem Cantor geschenkt als er ... die heilige zeit zu weinachte de Schul und Chor verwesen hat'
1448	Nördlingen, KR, f.35	'margraf Albrechts Singer'
1454	Augsburg, BB, f.54	'hertzog Albrechtz singer Michel'
1472	Nördlingen, KR, f.31ᵛ	'aym fromden pfaffen der sich nempt das keysers capplan'
1477	Augsburg, BB, f.40ᵛ	'hertzog Sigmunds von Osterreich Singer Wilhalmen'
1482	Augsburg, BB, f.20ᵛ	'Jörigen Sayler . . . der frauwen von Osterrich singer' (1490, BB, f.17, Sailer a sprecher)
1485	Augsburg, BB, f.14	'Andre Eyttelman, marggraf Hannsen Singer'
1486	Augsburg, BB, f.16	Andre Eyttelman
1487	Augsburg, BB, f.16	Jorig Sailer 'von wirttembergs singer'
1489	Augsburg, BB, f.16	the 'Romischen Kunigs singer', also the 'Marggraf von Brandenburgs singer'
(1498	Augsburg, BB, f.21ᵛ	the 'Kunigs zangmaister')

VI.2 'Solo' voice—female (see also voice with instruments, VI.5)

1403	Savoy, Dufour & Rabut, p.20	'la ménéstrière Marie de Roddes' (a singer?)
1410	French court, I. Cazeaux, *French Music in the Fifteenth and Sixteenth Centuries* (New York, 1975) p.11	Gracieuse Alegre, menestrelle, with musicians of Isabeau of Bavaria
1422/ 23	Luzern, SR, f.14ᵛ (PNL III, p.1175)	'der singerin'
1424/ 25	Luzern, SR, f.13ᵛ (PNL III, p.1175)	'der singerin'
1429	Regensburg, Sterl, p.266	'des von Maincz singerinn'
1430	Mainz, Pietzsch¹, p.84	a female singer [singerin] of the Bishop of Mainz
1434	Freiburg	'zwei Frauen', see VI.7
1442	Freiburg, Fellerer, p.69	'eine Sängerin mit ihrem Bruder'
1442	Solothurn, PNL III, p. 1181	'einem lutenschlacher und einer sängerin'

1444	Duke of Austria accounts: 'zwain singerin' in Constance, Tiroler Landesarchiv Innsbruch, ms.158, f.82ᵛ; in Ulm, 'ainer Singerin', f.39ᵛ
1455	Innsbruck, Senn, pp.8–9 'der Singerin von München'
1460	Innsbruck, Senn, p.9 — a 'Lautenslaher misambt einer singerin'
1464	Nördlingen, KR, f.32 — 'des herzogin singerin'
1471	Regensburg, Sterl, p.284 — 'two women singers (?)', 'Marggraf Albrechts zwain gmayn frawen'
1471	*Naples, A Atlas, Music at the Aragonese Court of Naples (Cambridge, 1985), p 105* — *Madama Anna*
1486	Frankfurt — woman singer with Maximilian I, see VI.7
1490	Augsburg, BB, f.17ᵛ — 'des Romischen Kunigs Singerin'
1490	Nördlingen, KR, ff.40ᵛ–41 — 'des Kunigs Singerin'
1491	Nuremberg, PNL IV, p.568 — Anna Nuserin, of Nuremberg, the 'konigs singerin', died in 1491
1496	Augsburg, BB, f.16ᵛ — 'der k. mt. singerin von Ulm'
1500	Augsburg, Wesseley,. p.130 — 'Dreyen Jungkfrawen, so vor d[er] ku[niglichen] M[ajestät] gesungen habn'

VI.3 Solo voice – Sprecher, Dichter, etc. (highly selective)

a Sprecher—as narrative poet:

1455 Augsburg, BB, f.39 'Kunig Lasslaws sprecher Micheln Behem'; in Nuremberg in 1467 (Sch., f.114ᵛ) he was termed the 'Keysers Tichter'; he may also have been the 'Michel, Singer' mentioned in Augsburg in 1451 (BB, f.46ᵛ) and 1454 (BB, f.54), see VI.1

b Sprecher—as singer and perhaps narrative poet:

1482 Augsburg, BB, f.20ᵛ Jorig Sailer termed a singer, also in 1487 (BB, f.16), 1491 (BB, f.19), 1494 (BB, f.17), and 1499 (BB, f.22ᵛ); in 1490 (BB, f.17) he was termed a 'sprecher'

1458 Augsburg, BB, f.52 Hans Wernlin was paid as a 'maistersinger', in 1459 and 1465 he performed as a 'sprecher' (BB, 1459, f.30; 1465, f.41), and in 1464 as a 'fürtretter' (BB, f.53ᵛ)

c Sprecher—as poet, entertainer and instrumentalist:

1460 Nuremberg, SR, f.104 a musician, Kilian, was termed a 'sprecher'; Kilian was paid as a 'spilman' in Regensburg in 1454 (Regensburg, Sterl, p.275) and in 1462 (Regensburg, Sterl, p.279). He had been termed a knight, 'Ritter Kilian' in 1470 Nördlingen, KR, f.37ᵛ—and was also termed a 'Swatzer' in 1469 (Nuremberg, SR, f.214ᵛ). He was termed a 'jester' ('narren') in Basel (Ernst, p.223).

1463 Nördlingen, KR, f.32ᵛ payment to 'Wilhelm und dem drachsel von ir narischen wise wegen'; Drechsel was also paid in 1466 (KR, f.32, 'dem Trechsel von bobbfing und sein gesellen') and in 1467 (KR, f.31). In 1475, the participation of the lute is explicit, 'eym luttenslaher der mit dem drechsel hije waz' (KR, f.30ᵛ).

VI.4 Children (boys and choirboys)—appearance of boys as singers was infrequent in visitors' accounts, see Wright V&I, pp.644 & 648 for discussion of boys voices alone and in choral ensembles in 1449, 1454, 1458 and 1467. See also VI.5, VI.6 and VI.7

1439/ 40	Essen, SR, f.10	'den sengern der sengery, dey sungen . . . waner daer en weren gene scholere' [i.e. the children were usually present]
1464	Nördlingen	1 lutenist with 2 'knaben', see VI.7
1470	Ambach, Ruhnke, p.271	'chorus' of 3 chaplains and 3 choirboys
1487	Augsburg	two singers with knaben, see VI.5
1487	Württemberg	see VI.6, 1487
1488	Nuremberg	lutenist and 'einen knaben', see VI.7
1492	Sterzing, Moser, 1929, p.14	vocal forces of 'acht Sänger, fünf junge und drei Meister'
1492	Innsbruck, Moser, 1929, p.12	'zwei Musikmeister mit fünf Jungen, die verschiedene Gesänge vortrugen . . . mit trompeten klang . . . ohne irgend ein Buch zu sehen'
1494	Augsburg	choir of male singers and choirboys, see VI.6
1498	Habsburg Hofkapelle	6 boys and 2 basses, see VI.6
1499	Torgau, VI.6	choir of Friedrich the Wise, singers and choirboys,

1480	Frankfurt a/M, PNL I, p.246	'4 englisch cantoribus zu Bonomese zu singen'
1482	Nördlingen, KR, f.31	'marg. Hansen . . . iii singern'
1483	Nördlingen, KR, f.31	'mrg. Hensen . . . iiii singern'
1483	Würzburg, SR, f.84	'marggraff Hansen in der Marck singern, der vir gewest sind'
1484	Hamburg, K. Koppmann, *Kammerrechnungen der Stadt Hamburg 1350–1562* (Hamburg, 1869–1864) IV, p.79	'cantoribus domini marchionis'
1484	Regensburg, Sterl, p.290	'marggraf Hansen aus der Margk singern', probably 2–4 musicians
1487	Augsburg, BB, f.16	'marggraf Hannsen (von) der Mark Singer Andre Eyttelman mit 3 knaben von Basel'
1490	Nördlingen, KR, f.40^v–41	'des romischen Kunigs iii Singer, Utz, Adam und Margreth Haydelin'
1491	Mühldorf a/I, SR PNL 451	'des kunigs singern 1 gulden', probably 2 singers
1492	Deventer, SR, f.12^v	'2 Sanger sRoemischen kunynx'
1492	Nördlingen, KR, f.41	the 'Kunigs Singern, iii Jung, i alt'; same entry, 1494, KR, f.39^v
1494	Augsburg, BB, f.17^v	'vier singer' of Herzog Albrecht 'von Saxen'
1498	Konigsberg, Ruhnke, p.139	4 singers of Friedrich von Sachsen

---

VI.5 'Solo' voices in small vocal ensembles—i.e. 1–4 singers, includes female performers

1401	*PietzschR, pp 80–81*	*singers of the Count of Holland*
1417	Regensburg, Sterl, p.259	'des von Weinsperg singern j rh. gulden', probably 2–4 singers
1444	Duke of Austria accounts; ms.158, f.33^v Tiroler Landesarchiv Innsbruck	'hertzog Ludwigs signern'; f.35^v 'des von Salczburg singern'
1450	Freiburg, Fellerer, p.56	payment to four singers of the Duke of Austria
1455	Xanten, PietzschA, p.115	'vier Sänger des Herzogs von Cleve'
1459	Nördlingen, KR, f.27	'herzog Ludwigs singern 4 lb', probably 2, perhaps 4, musicians
1467	Regensburg, Sterl, p.281	'Graf Ludwigs von Hessen zwain Singern'
1469	Basel, Ernst, p.222	payment of one gulden to the 'Keisers und pfaltzgrafen sengern', probably a small group (see, however, VI.6 1467)
1473	Deventer, SR, f.9	'zangers [van] myner vrouwen van Elten' (?)

VI.6 'Choir' i.e. 5 or more singers

1401	(Den Haag) PietzschK, p.35	expenses 'for the mass, the king's singers who sang the high mass' ('van der missen . . . des konigs senger songen de homisse')
1442	PietzschK, pp.59–60	the singers of Friedrich III ('des konigs senger'); also, 'item de cantores'
1465	Innsbruck, Senn, p.9	'den sechs Singern . . . von Mailand'
1467	Wiener Neustadt, Moser, 1929, p.170	the emperor's choir consisted of nine singers, (see also VI.5, 1469)
1470	Ambach, Ruhnke, p.271	choir of 3 chaplains and 3 choirboys, see above, VI.4
1474	Court of the Count Palatine, PietschH, p.31	'Es sang (in the mass) die pfalzgräfliche Kantorei'
1479	Innsbruck, Senn, p.9	'Bartholomeus Franck, Kantor, und seine fünf Gesellen'
1481	Regensburg, Sterl, p.288	'des Kunigs von Behaym singern lxxxiiii dn.', probably eight singers, see amount in entry 1490, Regensburg, below

1481 Regensburg, Sterl, p.288 'den purgundischen syngern lxxxiiii dn.', probably eight singers

1486 Cologne, PietzschA, p.47 Vespers sung by the singers ('chantées par les chantres') of Archduke Maximilian

1486 Württemberg, Sittard, p.3 the choral forces of the court consisted of '5 Singern' and '6 Knaben'

1487 Augsburg two singers with children see VI.4

1489 Nördlingen, KR, f.42^v 'dem Romischen Kunigs viii singer'

1489 Regensburg, Sterl, p.291 'des Romischen Königs singern'

1489 Utrecht, PietzschK, p.97 the 'sex cantoribus' of the Count Palantine' sang the mass 'in discantu'

1490 Basel, Ernst, p.222 'den ro. kg. sengern geschenkt'

1490 Regensburg, Sterl, p.292 'des Römischen Konigs singern, ir achten, lxxxiiii d. rheinisch'

1491 Augsburg, BB, f.19 'acht singern des Ro. kunigs', Maximilian's choral forces at this time normally consisted of at least 12 singers, Cuyler, p.56

1491 Marburg, PNL II, p.432 'des koniges von Ungern sengern'

1493 Basel, Ernst, p.222 'des romischen konigs sengern'

1494 Augsburg, Cuyler, p.51 the choir of Maximilian I consisted of the chapel master 'mitsamb 12 Knaben und Gesellen', i.e. about 8 adults and 4 choirboys

1498 Vienna, Cuyler, p.56 the 'Hofmusikkapelle' included a 'children's choir' which consisted of 6 choirboys and 2 basses

1499 Torgau, Ruhnke, p.271 chapel of Frederick the Wise, with 5 chaplains, 7 singers, and 12 choirboys

---

VI.7 'Solo' voice or voices with instruments

1428 Freiburg, Fellerer, p.65 a 'maistre qui tragitave sus la corde'

1428/ Brussels ARA 1794, f 77 court, Duke of Brabant, woman
29 singer with two instruments, 'tween speeluyden ende eene vrouwen die speelden ende songen"

1434 Freiburg, Fellerer, p.67 'zwei Frauen, die sangen und sich auf der Geige begleiteten'

1442 Nuremberg singer with lute, organ, quintern, and (when possible) harp, see note 13 below

1442 Solothurn lute with female voice, see VI.3

1443 Freiburg, Fellerer, p.69 a performer 'celluy qui ha tragitey sus la corda'

1444 Duke of Austria accounts 'ainen lautenslaher mit dem klain Tiroler Landesarchiv knaben'
Innsbruck ms.158, f.33^v

1446 Ghent, SA, SR, f 340^v payment to the 'dichtere sanghere ende anderen ghesellen van consten die dichten, songhen ende speelden (see also 1449, Ghent, SA, SR, f 60)

1454 Bavaria, Marix, p.73 'ung homme jouant d'un luz et une fame chantant avec lui'

1460 Nuremberg, H. Riedel, a 'knecht . . . met de harfe . . . *Die Darstellung von* sang he met liblicher stimme' (see *Musik und Musiklebnis* VI.3.c. Kilian) *in der erzählenden* (Bonn, 1961), p.320

1463 Nördlingen see VI.3.c. (Drechsel, sprecher, performing with a lutenist)

1464 Nördlingen, KR, f.32 2 'knaben' with two lutes

1464 Augsburg see I.2

1467 Frankfurt performance by a lute and 3 singers, see I.10

1468 Munich, Moser, 1929, 'ain lautenslaher mit ainem p.72 weib, die wol singen kund'

1471 Solothurn, PNL III, p.182 'Meister Hans von Züchten dem senger und harpfenschlacher'

1474 Bavaria, PietzschH, p.31 two boys ('Knaben'), 'einer sang der ander schlug di lauten'

1486 Frankfurt, Cuyler, p.35 a woman singer 'the best singer and instrumental performer . . . anyone had yet heard . . . she performed alone chansons and motets, singing and playing on the lute, harp, rebec, and claviecembalo'

1488 Nuremberg, Sch., f.179 'marggraf Fridrichs von Brandenburg lautenslaher . . . und einem knaben seinem gesellen'

1490 Solothurn, PNL III, p 182 'einem luttenschlacher und einem knaben'

1492 Solothurn, PNL III, p.182 'einer frouwen mit einer gigen, die minen herrn sang'

1496 Augsburg, BB, f.17^v 4 fl. to 'hertzog philips geygern und Singern', 4 musicians, probably 2 string players and 2 singers

1500 Freiburg, Fellerer, p.75 'zwei Geiger mit einer Sàngerin'

VI.8 Choir with instruments

1500 Bergen op Zoom, performance of motets with Polk, Ensemble, p.21 choral singers, organist and the city wind players

c 1500 Torgau, G. Reese, Adam von Fulda directed a mass *Music in the Renaissance* performance which was accom-(New York, 1959), p.655 panied by 'organ, three trom-a zink and four cromhorns',

1502	Toledo, vdSt 7, p.154	the singers of Philip the Fair sang 'une partie de la messe', and with them 'jouait du cornet maistre Augustin' [Augustein Schubinger]
1503	Innsbruck, Cuyler, p.67	a polyphonic sung mass was heard, in which 'les saqueboutes du roy . . . began the Gradual and played for the Deo Gratias and Ite misa est'
1507	Hapsburg Court, Brussels, vdSt 3, p.269	'Hans Naghele et Jehan van Vincle, joueurs d'instruments . . . pour . . . avoir servy continuellement . . . en chantant et jouant journellement en discant les heures et service divin'

B   BAS INSTRUMENTS NORMALLY PLAYED BY PERFORMERS OF LOUD INSTRUMENTS

B.1   Zinck (cornetto)

1454	*Lille, Marix, p 39*	*payment to a player 'joué d'un cornet d'Allemaigne, moult estrangement'*
1476	PietzschQ, p.729	Hans Schwartz 'zinckenplaser' of the Count Palantine
1483	Innsbruck, Senn, p.16	a 'Zinckenplaser von Bayern'
1487	Nuremberg, SR, f.219ᵛ	'zwayen Zinckenplasern marggraf Fridrichen und dem hertzogen zu Meykelburg'
1495/ 1496	Basel, Ernst, p.222	'des romischen konigs zinken bloser'
1496	Bavaria, PietzschH, p.34	Duke Friedrich's 'Zcyngkenblaser'
1498	Innsbruck, Wesseley, p.129	'Hannsl Zincken plaser des pfallunczgrafen'
1500	Innsbruck, Wesseley, p.115	'Augustin schubinnger zinngkennplaser'; p.132, 'Hennslin des phaltzgraven Zingenplaser'
1500	Torgau	see VI.8

B.2   Crumhorns (?doucaine?)

1409	*Ypres, Brussels ARA 38638, f 51*	*4 'speellieden met 2 aerpen ende 2 doucheinen', and also 3 'andere speelieden met doucheinen'*
1418	Regensburg, R. Sterl, 'Materialien zum Spielmann und Stadtpfeifer im spätmittelalterlichen Regensburg', *Die Oberpfalz* 56 (1968), p.78	delivery to the city of a crumhorn; a lute maker 'liefert dem Rat 1418 . . . ein Krummhorn'
1419	*Ypres, Brussels ARA 38644, f 52ᵛ*	'den 6 ghesellen spelende . . luuten, ghisternen ende doucheinen'
1428	Nördlingen, KR, f.39	'des Wuerttemberg pfeiff. mit der krume pfeiffn'

1440	*Bruges, Strohm, pp 81–82*	*'dulcian', with harp and lute*
1454	Ulm, Marix, p.60	performance by a player of 'doulcenne'
1461	Regensburg, Sterl, p.279	a pfeifer with a 'krumpen horn'
1465	Regensburg, Sterl, p.281	'zwain pfewffern mit dem krumpen Horn', same duo in 1466 (p.281) and 1468 (p.282)
1469	Regensburg, Sterl, p.282	'pfewffern . . . mit dem krumppen horn, ir dreyen'
1482	Augsburg, BB, f.20ᵛ	'ainem pfeyffer mit dem kromenhorn'
1486	Brandenburg, K.T. Meyer, *The Crumhorn* (Ann Arbor, 1983), p.158	notation of 'krumpfeiffen' played by the Margrave of Brandenburg's musicians
1500	Dresden, Meyer, *Crumhorn*, p.162	performance of 4 crumhorns

B.3   Stringed instruments players by players of loud instruments

1427	Windsheim	see II. 1 ('geiger . . . oder pfeifer')
1437	Nördlingen, KR, f.33ᵛ	'der von Segkendorff pfeyffern oder luttenslahern' (also hired in the civic ensemble of the city this year, KR, f.84ᵛ was hennslin egkin (Egkern) as a shawmist, see entry for 1515, below)
1458	Augsburg, BB, f.52ᵛ	payment to 'ainem lutenslaher und ainem Gyger, der jungen Herrn von Sachsen pfyffer'
1469	Augsburg, BB, f.79ᵛ–80	Michel Schubinger (Michele Tedesco) began his career in Augsburg, first, apparently as a bombard player (see also 1473, BB, f.65ᵛ); in 1499, in Ferrara he was noted also as a player of viol, see Prizer, Bernardino, p.163.
1475	Milan, Prizer, Bernardino, p.163.	Stefano, a German wind player (piffero), was also a player of the viol
1477	Augsburg, BB, f.92ᵛ	Augustein Schubinger began his career as a trombonist (see also 1481, BB. f 64ᵛ). In 1500 and 1505, while he was in the service of Philip the Fair, he was designated as a lutenist, vdSt, 7, pp.170 –172.
1482	Augsburg, BB, f.62ᵛ	Ulrich Schubinger, Jr., began his career in as a trombonist. In 1522 he was described as a player of 'Geigen, pusaunen, lawten, und andern instrumenten', see Polk, Vedel, Table C.
1486	Nördlingen, KR, f.33	Hans Schnitzer paid as a lutenist, paid there previously as a trombonist (1484, KR, f.30, 'trummeter' with Count of Montfort), in Augs-

	berg in 1488, BB, f.16ᵛ, he was termed a 'pfeiffer'.	der Musik am kurpfälzischer Hof zu Heidelberg bis 1622', *Akademie der Wissenschaft und Literatur, Abhandlung der Geistes- und Sozialwissenschaftlichen Klasse*, 6 (1963), pp.583–763

1493 Nördlingen, KR, f.38ᵛ '2 lautenschlager und pfeyffer', the forms are evidently plural, thus both players played both instruments (see also 1493, KR, f.39ᵛ).

1515 Augsburg, Polk, Vedel, Caspar Egkern was paid as a
       Table A.4 member of the string band of Maximilian I. In 1509 he had been paid as a trombonist, in 1510 as a wind player (pfeifer)

Abbreviations used in the Tables

Augsburg BB: Augsburg, Stadtarchiv, Baumeisterbücher, the term used in Augsburg for yearly financial account books.

Basel, Ernst: F. Ernst, 'Die Spielleute im Dienste der Stadt Basel im ausgehenden Mittelalter (bis 1550)', *Basler Zeitschrift für Geschichte und Altertumskunde*, 44 (1945), pp 79–237

Baser, F., *Musik am Hof von Baden* (Baden-Baden, 1976)

Brussels ARA: Brussel, Algemeen Rijksarchief/the Belgian National Archive, Brussels

Cuyler: L. Cuyler, *The Emperor Maximilian I and Music* (London, 1973)

De Meyer: G. De Meyer, *De Stadsrekeningen van Deventer, Rijksuniversiteit Utrecht Teksten en Documenten*, uitgegeven door het Instituut voor Middeleeuwse Geschiedenis, ed. W Jappe Alberts (Groningen, 1968–84), 6 vols.

Dufour & Rabut: A. Dufour and F. Rabut, *Les musiciens, la musique et les instruments de musique en Savoie du XIIIe au XIXe siècle* (Chambery, 1878)

Ernst: see Basel

Freiburg, Fellerer: F. G. Fellerer, *Mittelalterliches Musikleben der Stadt Freiburg im Uechtland* (Regensburg, 1935)

GA: Gemeentearchief/Municipal Archive

Lockwood: Lewis Lockwood, *Music in Renaissance Ferrara 1400–1505* (Cambridge, Mass., 1984)

Marix: J. Marix, *Histoire de la Musique et des Musiciens de la Cour de Bourgogne sous la règne de Philippe le Bon (1420–1467)* (Strasbourg, 1939)

Moser: H J. Moser, *Paul Hofhaimer* (Stuttgart, 1929)

Nördlingen, KR: Nördlingen, Stadtarchiv, Kammerrechnungen [SR]

Nuremberg, SR: Nuremberg, Bayerisches. Staatsarchiv, Stadtrechnungen (Kleine Register, Rep. 54 1/26)

Nuremberg, GR: Nuremberg, Bayerisches Staatsarchiv, Grosse Stadtrechnung, Rep. 54/179 (1419–1431)

Nuremberg, Sch · Nuremberg, Bayerisches Staatsarchiv, Schenkbücher (1400–1451, Rep. 52b, no.314; 1466–88, Rep. 60b., Ratsbuch 1 a)

PietzschA: G. Pietzsch, *Archivalische Forschungen zur Geschichte der Musik an den Höfen der Grafen und Herzöge von Kleve-Julich-Berg (Ravensberg) bis zum Erlöschen der Linie Jülich-Kleve im Jahre 1609* (Cologne, 1971)

PietzschH: G. Pietzsch, 'Die Beschreibungen deutscher Fürstenhochzeiten von der Mitte des 15. bis zum Beginn des 17. Jahrhunderts als musikgeschichtliche Quellen', *Anuario Musical* 15 (1961), pp.21–62

PietzschK: G. Pietzsch, *Fürsten und fürstlichen Musiker im mittelalterlichen Koln* (Cologne, 1966)

PNL: Pietzsch Nachlass: The collected papers of Gerhard Pietzsch, now housed in the Library of the Institute for Musicology of the University of Cologne. Roman numerals refer to typed volumes, arabic numerals to manuscript folders.

PietzschQ: G. Pietzsch, 'Quellen und Forschungen zur Geschichte

PietzschR: G. Pietzsch, 'Musik in Reichstadt und Residenz am Ausgang des Mittelalter', *Jahrbuch für Geschichte der oberdeutschen Reichstädte, Esslingen Studien*, Band 12/13 (1966/67), pp.73–79

PietzschW: G. Pietzsch, 'Die Hofmusikkollegien wittelsbachischer Fürsten bis zur Ende des 16. Jahrhunderts', *Musik in Bayern* 13 (1976), pp.24–8

Polk, Civic Patronage: K. Polk, 'Civic Patronage and Instrumental Ensembles in Renaissance Florence', *Augsburger Jahrbuch für Musikwissenschaft* (ed. Franz Krautwurst), III (1986), pp.51–68

Polk, Ensemble: K Polk, 'Ensemble Instrumental Music in Flanders', *Journal of Band Research*, 11 (1975), pp.12–27

Polk, Vedel: K Polk, 'Vedel and Geige—Fiddle and Viol, German String Traditions in the 15th Century', *Journal of the American Musicological Society* 42 (1989), pp.484–526

Prizer, Bernardino: W. F. Prizer, 'Bernardino Piffaro e i pifferi e tromboni di Mantova', *RIM* XVI (1981), pp.151–184

RB: Ratsbuch

Regensburg, Sterl: R. Sterl, 'Die Regensburger Stadtrechnungen des 15. Jahrhunderts als Quellen für fahrende und hofische Spielleute', *Regensburger Beiträge zur Musikwissenschaft* (ed. H. Beck), Band 6 (Regensburg, 1979), pp.249–312

Ruhnke: M. Ruhnke, *Beiträge zu einer Geschichte der deutschen Hofmusikkollegien im 16. Jahrhundert* (Berlin, 1963)

SA. City Archive (Stadsarchief in Flemish and Dutch, Stadtarchiv in German)

Senn: W Senn, *Musik und Theater am Hof zu Innsbruck* (Innsbruck, 1954)

Sittard: J. Sittard, *Zur Geschichte der Musik des Theaters am Württembergischen Hofe*, I, 1458–1733, (Stuttgart, 1890)

Smijers: A. Smijers, *De Illustre Lieve Vrouwe Broederschap te 's-Hertogenbosch* (Amsterdam, 1932)

SR: City Account Book (Stadsrekeningen, Dutch, and Stadtrechnungen, German)

Strohm: R. Strohm, *Music in Late Medieval Bruges* (Oxford, 1985)

vdSt: E. van der Straeten, *La musique aux Pays-Bas avant le XIXe siècle* (Brussels, 1867–88), 8 vols.

Wesseley: O. Wesseley, *Archivalischen Beiträge zur Musikgeschichte des Maximilianschen Hofes Studien zur Musikwissinschaft*, ed. E Schenk, 23 (1956), pp.79–134

Windsheim, ZB: [Bad] Windsheim, SA, Zinsbücher [=SR]

Wright, V&I: C. Wright, 'Voices and Instruments in the Art Music of Northern France during the Fifteenth Century; a conspectus', *Report of the Twelfth Congress of the International Musicological Society, Berkeley, 1977* (Kassel, 1981), pp.643–9

Keith Polk is Professor of Music at the University of New Hampshire. He is both a scholar and a professional performer (of natural and valved horn). His book on German instrumental music of the late Middle Ages is soon to be published by Cambridge University Press.

[1]The contributions of Howard Brown, David Fallows and Christopher Page are well known to readers of this journal. The German musicologists Gerhard Pietzsch, Walter Salmen and Raimund Sterl have investigated the visitors' accounts. Salmen's *Der Spielmann im Mittelalter* (Innsbruck, 1983) offers a recent survey. For the works of Pietzsch and Sterl see the bibliographic entries at the end of the Tables.

[2]I might add that the scribal tradition is such that the groupings of musicians together usually implies an ensemble. This is perhaps most clear in the groupings of two and three lutes (see Tables A I.2 and I.3). Also, very seldom do lower class or 'rustic' performers

appear. Consistently named are musicians such as Conrad Paumann, Augustein Schubinger and Hans Nagel.

³K. Polk, 'Ensemble Performance Practice in Dufay's Time', ed. A.
Atlas, *Dufay Quincentenary Conference* (Brooklyn, 1975), pp.62–3.
German society reveled in ceremonial groups, and this reflected an
attitude widespread throughout European society in general;
trumpet bands were especially characteristic. As J. Huizinga
remarked, the 'culture of the expiring Middle Ages tends to oust
beauty by magnificence', *The Waning of the Middle Ages* (New York,
1954), p.248.

⁴On the quintern and lute in the 14th century, see H.M. Brown, 'St
Augustine, Lady Music and the Gittern, *MD*, 38 (1984), pp.25–65.
The instrumentation of quintern and large lute continued to be a
standard German duo into the 16th century—for these were still the
instruments described by Sebastian Virdung in his *Musica getuscht*
(Basel, 1511).

⁵*De inventione et usu musicae*, quoted here from W. Prizer, 'The
Frottola and the Unwritten Tradition', *Studi Musicali*, XV (1986), p.12,
who discusses the polyphonic tradition in Italy (which he suggests
had been introduced into Italy through the influence of Paumann in
1470). That Paumann began his career in Nuremberg about 1440
would indicate that the German polyphonic tradition was significantly earlier than that of Italy. For a discussion of the performance
practice of the 'tenorist' see: D. Fallows, '15th-Century Tablatures for
Plucked Instruments: a summary, a revision and a suggestion', *Lute
Society Journal*, 19 (1977), pp.28–32

⁶Windsheim [now Bad Windsheim], SA, ZB, 1441, unfoliated

⁷S. Virdung, *Musica getutscht*, f.Bii and Biii; for a recent study of
string playing in Germany see Polk, 'Vedel'

⁸I. Woodfield, *The Early History of the Viol* (Cambridge, 1984), see
especially Chapters 4 and 5.

⁹Polk, 'Ensemble Performance', pp.62–3

¹⁰D Fallows, 'Specific information on the ensembles for
composed polyphony, 1400–1474', ed. S. Boorman, *Studies in the
Performance of late Medieval Music* (Cambridge, 1983), pp. 109-59; C.
Page, 'The performance of songs in late Medieval France', *EM*, x,
(1982), pp.441–50. Note that even when instruments are present, in
most cases only a 'solo' voice is involved. The 'chorus' was clearly *a
cappella* until the end of the century.

¹¹Fallows, 'Specific information', p.139

¹²For German organ settings of *Je loe amours* and *Se la Face ay pale*
see *Das Buxheimer Orgelbuch*, ed. B. Wallner, *Das Erbe Deutsche Musik*,
xxxvii (Kassel, 1937), vol.ii, pp.222–3, 263, and vol.iii, p.155. The
'Maastricht town band manuscript', evidently an instrumental
source, contains a selection of well-known chanson melodies from
just after the mid-century, indicating that such chansons as *De tous
biens plaine* formed the basis of an instrumental repertory in the
Cologne area and in Flanders; see J. Smits van Waesberghe, 'Een 15e
eeuws muziekboek van de stadsminstrelen van Maastricht?',
Renaissance Muziek 1400–1600, fs. R. Lenaerts, ed. J. Robijns
(Leuven, 1969), pp.247–73.

¹³The document is fascinating in that it assumes a reasonably
high level of competence amongst amateur players, and implies a
broad base of music making within this urban society. It reads: 'Item
so muss ein Pfleger alle Jahr bestellen zu unsers Herrn Leichnams
Tage Hofirer, die vor dem Sacrment hofiren, von etlichen jungen
Burger und von Handwerkleuten, die das kuennen, zu der Vesper
und Messen an dem Abend und an dem Tage zu der Prozessen des
Morgens, und zu der Tagmess und zu der Non und zu der andern
Vesper, und auch desselben gleichen am achten Tage zu der Vesper
und Messen des Abends und des Morgens zu der Processen und
Tagmesse. Auch muss ein Pfleger denselben Hofirern ein Zech
halten am Sunntage vor unsers Herren Leichnams Tag, das sie sich
mit dem Saitenspiel gleich zusammen richten. Und was dieselbig
Zech kost, das bezahlt der Pfleger von des Gotthaus Geld. Und
derselbigen Hofirer sullen sein; einer auf der Lauten, einer mit dem
Portativ und einer mit der Quintern. Und mag man einen au der

Harpfench gehaben, den nimmt man auch darzu, und einen, der in
das Saitenspiel singet . . '

¹⁴The fact that the Bavarian fiddle players were not specialists
must also affect any proposed German string 'tradition', a fact not
adequately taken into account in my own recent discussion of the
subject; see Polk, 'Vedel', pp.498–509.

¹⁵On Augustein Schubinger, see K. Polk, 'Instrumental music in
the urban centres of Renaissance Germany', *Early Music History* VII
(1987), p.182.

¹⁶L. Lockwood, *Music of Renaissance Ferrara 1400–1505* (Cam-
bridge, Mass., 1984), pp.224–5. The MS is *I–Rc* 2856. On Michele, see
W. Prizer, 'Bernardino Piffaro e i pifferi e tromboni de Mantova',
RIM, XVI (1981), pp.161–3.

¹⁷The inclusion of sacred texts in such sources as the Maastricht
and the Casanatense manuscripts serves as a reminder that sacred
repertory appears to have been common fare for 'secular' musicians
during the late Middle Ages. The city band in Bruges, for example,
routinely performed motets from about 1480 onwards in the special
Marian services sponsored by the city fathers; see Strohm,
p.144.

¹⁸On Nagel and the Schubingers see Polk, 'Instrumental music',
pp.181–2.

¹⁹For the shawms and the trumpets of Brandenburg, see Augsburg,
BB, 1459, f.30, and Sterl, p.274; for those of Bavaria see Sterl, pp.275
and 278; for their soft ensembles, see Tables I.3 and II.3. The figures
for Burgundy are in Marix, p.271.

²⁰There are striking similarities between the structures of the
instrumental forces of the courts of southern Germany and
Burgundy.

²¹For Maximilian's soft ensembles see the Tables I.2, II.3 and II.4;
his shawm band was recorded in Augsburg, BB, 1496, ff.17–17ᵛ; his
trumpets in Nuremberg, Sch. (Rep. 54/182), f.42ᵛ; and the fife and
drum unit in Augsburg, BB, 1506, f.24ᵛ.

[15]

A COOK'S TOUR OF FERRARA IN 1529

Howard Mayer Brown

We know remarkably little about the occasions when music was performed during the Renaissance. It is clear, of course, that polyphonic Masses and motets were intended for the liturgy, but we cannot always say with certainty for which service a particular composition was intended; we are apt to underestimate, I suspect, the extent to which plainsong remained the normal musical fare in churches and cathedrals; we are largely ignorant of the extent and scope of instrumental participation in the performance of sacred music during the fifteenth and sixteenth centuries; and we cannot explain satisfactorily why arrangements of Masses and motets were prepared for solo lute and vihuela. Moreover we have scarcely any idea of the variety of occasions when secular compositions – Italian madrigals, French chansons and German lieder – were played and sung at princely courts and in the homes of the bourgeoisie.

For several reasons it is useful, and even necessary to our understanding of the music, to find out where, when, why and how it was performed. Without this information we cannot understand the place of music in the life of the times nor re-create imaginatively both the everyday and the extraordinary events of the past. Most important, without knowing the circumstances of performance, we cannot reconstruct this music, to hear it again in versions close to those enjoyed by its original audiences, nor can we ever hope to understand the nature of the written sources that have come down to us. One of the central tasks of the philologist, I take it, is to establish a good text, one that reflects the best intentions of its author. Musical philologists have a more difficult task than that faced by their colleagues in other disciplines, for they not only need to determine the best version of an individual composition by time-honored means – by collating variant readings, for example, by distinguishing good from corrupt manuscripts, and so on – they must also decide what the written notes represented to the musicians of the fifteenth and sixteenth centuries. Performers in earlier times regarded printed or manuscript parts not as sets of inviolable instructions from which they dared not depart without offending the canons of good taste, but as outlines to be filled in; and composers left many decisions that later came to be a part of the compositional process itself to the imagination and skill of the singers and players, such as the precise way the syllables of texts fitted the musical notes in vocal music, which accidentals to add in performance and whether or not to embellish the melodic lines, how a composition was to be scored, and so on. The performing musicians felt free to adapt the music to changing circumstances: the number of people available, the size and layout of the hall, and even the nature of the occasion that required music.

Documents like the cook book, *Banchetti, composizioni di vivande e apparecchio generale* (Ferrara: Giovanni de Buglhat and Antonio Hucher 1549), written by a steward for the Este family in Ferrara, Cristoforo da Messisbugo, are, therefore, of primary importance for the social history of music during the Renaissance, as well as for the study of performing practice.[1] Messisbugo gives a vast and mouthwatering array of recipes in the book. Equally important for the social historian, he introduces the recipes by a short preface listing all of the things necessary to assemble when a visiting prince comes to stay, when the court goes on a journey, or whenever a banquet or wedding is planned. His lists seem to be comprehensive; they include furniture, kitchen utensils, food, things with which to entertain the courtiers, and the kinds of servants they will expect to wait on them. He also describes in some detail various festivities that he himself organized during his career: ten banquets, three lunches and an evening party (a « festino»). This preliminary matter is fascinating

---

[1] Messisbugo's book is available in a modern edition made by Fernando Bandini (Venice, Neri Pozza, 1960). The musical information appears there, pp. 31-56. Lord WESTBURY, *Handlist of Italian Cookery Books* (Florence, Olschki 1963) lists fifteen editions of the cookbook between 1549 and 1626. Messisbugo's descriptions of the music at the banquets has also been reproduced and partially discussed in José LLORENS, *Estudio de los instrumentos musicales que aparecen descritos en la relación de dos festines celebrados el año 1529 en la corte de Ferrara*, in « Anuario Musical », XXV (1970), pp. 3-26.

HOWARD MAYER BROWN

for the tangible picture it gives us of the hedonism of Italian aristocrats during the Renaissance – the richness and variety of their diet, the elegance of their surroundings, and the care and good taste lavished on them both in the manner and the matter of their entertainment. Messisbugo's descriptions of particular events are most fascinating to musicians for the details he gives about the music performed during each course at three of the banquets, information summarized in Appendices I-III. Messisbugo tells us more than we know from any other writer about one significant type of occasion in sixteenth-century Italy at which musical performances were appropriate and customary.[2]

The book is especially informative in that its author includes summaries of particular occasions not merely to commemorate great moments in his own life but to provide patterns for others who wish to arrange successful entertainments, very much like the model menus that appear in present-day cook books. In other words he supplies a context from which to judge his intentions and we can, therefore, form some general picture of music at sixteenth-century Italian banquets from this one document; it represents at least one man's opinion of the prerequisites for a good party. Music was clearly not absolutely necessary for the success of a banquet. Six of the ten he describes seem to have done without, and at several of the parties he arranged, music played only a small role. Thus at the evening party he gave at his own house for the Duke of Ferrara, Girolamo Parabosco's play, *La notte*, was given before the guests ate, with its appropriate music and intermedii (« con le sue musiche e intermezzi »), but no music accompanied the meal, although the guests afterwards danced until dawn. One of his lunches ended with « una musica di voce e stromenti »; and a banquet with a « farsetta » followed by a Moresca, after which the guests danced. But the two most elegant,

---

[2] For an equally detailed description of banquets and other entertainments at the court of Duke Wilhelm V of Bavaria in 1568, see *Dialoghi di Massimo Troiano: ne' quali si narrano le cose più notabili fatte nelle nozze dello Illustriss. & Eccell. Prencipe Guglielmo V. Conte Palatino del Reno, e Duca di Baviera; e dell'Illustriss. & Eccell. Madama Renata di Loreno* (Venice, Bolognino Zaltieri 1569). Troiano's report is briefly summarized in WOLFANG BOETTICHER, *Orlando di Lasso und seine Zeit, 1532-1594* (Kassel and Basel, Bärenreiter 1958), pp. 331-43. On music at medieval banquets, see EDMUND A. BOWLES, *Musical Instruments at the Medieval Banquet*, in « Revue belge de musicologie », XII (1958), pp. 41-51.

elaborate and formal banquets he described, that given by Ippolito d'Este, then Archbishop of Milan, for his brother Ercole, later Duke of Ferrara (see Appendix I), and another given by Ercole for his father the Duke and his aunt, Isabella d'Este, Marchioness of Mantua (see Appendix II), were accompanied by music from beginning to end; and at a third formal dinner – much less large – to which only gentlemen were invited, when Duke Alfonso entertained the ambassadors of the Holy Roman Emperor (see Appendix III), singers and instrumentalists also performed for the guests during almost every course.

Ippolito's party was given at Belfiore, one of the smaller but very elegant palaces of the Estes. It was used as a hunting lodge, though it came to be included within the city walls during the sixteenth century.[3] Since the banquet took place during the spring, it could be held out of doors, in Belfiore's superb gardens. On one side of the garden a bower had been constructed for the musicians, to hide them from the guests. During some of the courses, music sounded from within the bower; during others, groups of players, singers, dancers, or buffoons made their entrances from it and performed around the banqueting table; and as a grand finale, twenty-four musicians, presumably all or almost all the performers who had taken part in the preceding festivities, appeared from the bower, dressed alike and each holding a blazing torch; they danced a Moresca to signal the end of the evening.

Messisbugo does not make clear where Ercole had held his banquet several months previously, nor where the performers were stationed. Belriguardo, one of the other grand country palaces of the Este family, had a musicians' gallery in the great hall for such

---

[3] On Belfiore and some other Este palaces, see *Art and Life at the Court of Ercole I d'Este: The 'De triumphis religionis' of Giovanni Sabadino degli Arienti*, ed. WERNER L. GUNDERSHEIMER (Geneva, Droz 1972). The loggia opposite the main entrance of Belfiore enclosed a cycle of frescoes celebrating Alberto I d'Este, including a panel showing young people beside a fountain, dancing « al suono de cythare e tibie et al suono de una arpa sonata da una dama » (GUNDERSHEIMER, p. 68). In another room of Belfiore, a cycle of frescoes depicted the life of Duchess Eleonora, including scenes of courtiers dancing « al suono de tympano e zuffuli » and also dancing at Eleonora's wedding feast (GUNDERSHEIMER, p. 71. A full quotation of this passage is given by A. Cavicchi in this volume, pp. 65-69).

Sabadino describes one of the Este gardens as a place where the Duchess used to sit with her companions and at times « lì sonavono lieti instrumenti e l'aere s'empiva de amorosi canti » (GUNDERSHEIMER, p. 55).

occasions.[4] Doubtless the principal reception rooms in the main Este palaces, the Castel Vecchio and the Castel Nuovo in the center of Ferrara, also had special places for musicians. Or, the performers at Ercole's banquet may have stood at one corner of the hall to play or wait their turn, perhaps around a table on which their instruments rested, as pictures show was sometimes the case at banquets during the Renaissance.[5]

Except for the beginning of the first banquet – when several broken consorts played one after the other – the musical portions of each evening were arranged to give the guests the greatest possible contrast and variety of sound from course to course. Groups of loud instruments alternated with soft; unaccompanied madrigal singing gave way to colorful combinations of voices with instruments; instrumental and vocal solos interrupted the ensembles from time to time; and during one course at each banquet the music stopped altogether to allow the guests to enjoy feats of acrobatic skill or slapstick routines by acrobats and buffoons, or else (at the third course of the third banquet) to give them a complete respite from entertainment. But detailed conclusions about the character and conventions of music at sixteenth-century Italian banquets ought not to be made from Messisbugo's descriptions, since the specific arrangements for the three Ferrarese banquets are all quite different. At the first event, for example, over half the music was played by instruments alone and there was only one grand concerto of the sort that made the Ferrarese court so famous in the second half of the century; while at the second there were four concerti, three purely instrumental consorts and no soloists at all. On the other hand, some elements did recur each time: the trombone-cornett band, for example, the group of shawms (the « pifferi »), unmixed consorts of voices or instruments, and, of course, the troupe of non-musical buffoons.

At least twenty-four and more probably thirty musicians took

---

[4] See GUNDERSHEIMER, p. 65.

[5] See, for example, the etching of Nikolaus Solis showing the musicians of Duke Wilhelm V of Bavaria standing around a table to play at the Duke's wedding banquet in 1568, reproduced, among other places, in *Die Musik in Geschichte und Gegenwart*, vol. I, cols. 1435-36; and the woodcut by Hans Burgkmair showing the musicians of Emperor Maximilian I playing for a masked dance at a banquet, reproduced in GEORGE KINSKY, *Album musical* (Paris, Delagrave 1930), pl. 75,3, and in PAUL COLLAER and ALBERT VANDER LINDEN, *Atlas historique de la musique* (Paris 1960), no. 208.

part in the first banquet; twenty-two performed in the final concerto, and twenty-four danced the last Moresca to the sound of shawms. The largest ensemble at the second banquet involved twenty singers and instrumentalists. Who were these musicians? It seems likely that all or almost all of the musical establishment at the Ferrarese court participated in entertaining the guests on those two evenings, and presumably on other equally formal occasions. Not the least interesting aspect of Messisbugo's account is the glimpse it affords us of the court in action, allowing us to fill out a bit the outline drawn from the ducal financial records.[6] The chapel singers, of course, took pride of place at every court. They were mainly responsible for performing at Mass and Office hours. Messisbugo's cook book is a rare record – especially so early in the century – that they also took so active a part in the court's secular entertainments. Evidently, though, the whole choir did not perform at banquets; four, five or six singers from the larger group – doubtless one to a part – made up a standard and sufficient ensemble for madrigals and concerti. Those of the Duke's singers actually named by Messisbugo as taking part in the first banquet (Appendix I, 6) – M. Giovan Michele, M. Gravio and M. Giannes del Falcone – are all recorded as salaried members of the chapel during the 1530's.[7] The four French boys who sang towards the end of the evening (Appendix I, 16) presumably formed a part of the treble section of the Duke's choir. They were probably among the half dozen or more choirboys usually attached to chapel or cathedral choirs and put in the charge of one of the adult members of the group, who was responsible for their musical and general education. That the Ferrarese choirboys were French is hardly surprising; it is one more indication of the high regard Europeans of the time had for the musical abilities of the Franco-Netherlanders.

---

[6] See especially WALTER WEYLER, *Documenten betreffende de Muziekkappel aan het Hof van Ferrara*, in « Vlaamsch Jaarboek voor Muziekgeschiedenis », I (1939), pp. 81-113.

[7] WEYLER, pp. 86 ff. Sabadino (GUNDERSHEIMER, p. 89) reports that Duke Ercole I had forty-eight singers, twenty-four youngsters and an equal number of adults, who sang Mass every day, adding organ on feast days: « Facesti duo chori in la musica de periti cantori: uno de vintequatro adoloscentuli e l'altro de magiori, de tanto numero, peritissimi, che insignavano ali minori. Et cosi ogni giorno dove la sua ducal Alteza si trovava, audivi in optimo canto messa celebrare et li festivi giorni quella con l'organo se cantava ». On music at Ercole's court, see LEWIS LOCKWOOD, *Music at Ferrara in the Period of Ercole I d'Este*, in « Studi musicali », I (1972), pp. 101-31.

The trumpeters who announced the beginning and end of dinner at Ercole II's party for his father and aunt (Appendix II, A and 9) are likely to have played simple fanfares in fulfilling their purely ceremonial duties. If they were the Duke's own trumpeters – and possibly the prerogative of his rank – there may have been no more than two, the number listed among the members of his chapel in 1533.[8] Aside from the trumpeters, though, whose duties would have kept them separate from the main body of ducal players, three groups of instrumentalists would have sufficed to supply the music Messisbugo describes: six wind players, who were capable of changing from shawms (or shawms and trombones, whichever the term « i pifferi » refers to), to cornetts and trombones, to transverse flutes, recorders, wind-capped shawms (« dolzaine », « cornamuse » and crumhorns) or whatever winds were required; a string band of six viol players who could also double on other plucked and bowed strings; and a few virtuosi who could play keyboard instruments, lutes, or whatever additional instruments the musical requirements of the occasion dictated. Certainly sixteenth-century instrumentalists were trained to master more than one kind of instrument. If the Duke's chapel singers could perform madrigals, there seems to be no reason to suppose his dance musicians could not join in playing chamber music when they were asked to do so. No more than six winds or six viols are ever called on to perform in any one composition. In the final concerto at the first banquet, for example, six voices, six viols, and five winds (trombone, two recorders, a transverse flute and a « sordina ») were joined by five other instrumentalists (playing lira da braccio, lute, cittern or guitar, and two harpsichords or spinets).

The only composer Messisbugo names is Alfonso della Viola, instrumental virtuoso and madrigalist, whose reputation in music history rests mostly on the theatrical music he supplied for the Ferrarese court, now unfortunately mostly lost. With his theatrical bent, his prominent place on the program at the first two banquets,

---

[8] The trumpeters are listed in WEYLER, p. 87. Some sixteenth-century fanfares are published in modern edition (after a manuscript in the Royal Library in Copenhagen) in *Trompeterfanfaren, Sonaten und Feldstücke des 16.-17. Jahrhunderts*, ed. Georg Schünemann, *Das Erbe deutscher Musik*, vol. VII (Kassel, Bärenreiter 1936). Sabadino (GUNDERSHEIMER, p. 77) reports hearing more than fifty pairs of trumpeters (« più de cinquanta copie de trombetti ») at the festivities for Eleonora's wedding to Ercole I in 1473.

and his record of service to the Este family, Alfonso may well have been the man entrusted by the Duke with all of the musical arrangements for his and his family's evening parties.[9] Alfonso may have chosen the music, invented the scorings, rehearsed the musicians, and established the order of events. It is a tempting hypothesis, even if impossible to prove.

In addition to the regular members of the ducal musical establishment – if, indeed, I am correct in supposing all of the musicians to have come from among the Duke's salaried singers and players – a few other performers were called in to enliven the evenings. The Duchess Renée's pipe and tabor player, for example, accompanied some of the dancing at the first banquet (Appendix I, 7). The first concerto at the second banquet (Appendix II, 1) was sung by at least five singers, including Madonna Dalida, who is not otherwise mentioned in the admittedly incompletely published archival records of the Ferrarese court. That the lady was singled out for special mention, though, suggests she was not merely another professional singer, but a person of some note. She had, in fact, been the mistress of Ippolito II's uncle, Cardinal Ippolito I d'Este, who had died of overeating in 1520. Madonna Dalida Puti is recorded as a member of his household in the 1510's.[10] Perhaps, then, she was one of those well-born ladies distinguished as much for her musical as her other skills, and capable of participating with professional musicians in even the most important performances at court, a lady, in short, very much like the later and more famous " ladies of Ferrara ", who are remembered for their musicianship, though they were in the first place courtiers.[11] Their outstanding vocal ability, presumably, identified them as closer in spirit to the highly trained professional

---

[9] The fullest biographical information on Alfonso and his family may be found in ADRIANO CAVICCHI, *Della Viola*, in *Enciclopedia della Musica* (Milan, Ricordi 1963-64), vol. IV, p. 511. For an evaluation of Alfonso's madrigals, see Alfred EINSTEIN, *The Italian Madrigal* (Princeton University Press 1949), vol. I, pp. 300-07.

[10] I am grateful to Professor Lewis Lockwood for supplying me with information about Madonna Dalida Puti. She is mentioned as a singer in the Cardinal's entourage in MICHELE CATALANO, *Vita di Lodovico Ariosto* (Geneva, Olschki 1930), vol. I, p. 188.

[11] On the ladies of Ferrara, see ANGELO SOLERTI, *Ferrara e la corte estense nella seconda metà del secolo XVI*, in *I Discorsi di Annibale Romei* (Città di Castello, Lapi 1891); LUZZASCO, *Madrigali per cantar e sonare a uno, due e tre soprano (1601)*, ed. Adriano Cavicchi (Brescia and Kassel 1965); and ANTHONY NEWCOMB, *The Musica Secreta of Ferrara in the 1580's*, Ph.D. dissertation, Princeton University 1969.

madrigal singers of the Italian courts than to the amateur English madrigalists made famous by Thomas Morley.

The local inventor, M. Afranio, or Afranio degli Albonesi to give him his full name, was invited to both the first and third banquets (Appendix I, 10, and III, 5) to demonstrate his curious invention, the « fagotto » or Phagotus, a complicated bellows-blown bagpipe with two chanters and no drone, which was not widely adopted, but has nevertheless achieved some small notoriety in music history, partly because Afranio's nephew, Teseo, described and illustrated it in his book on the Chaldaic language, published in 1539, and partly because its name inevitably led some historians to assume that it was an early form of the bassoon.[12] If Teseo was correct, his uncle, a Ferrarese canon, played " divine songs and hymns " on his instrument – perhaps laude and other relatively simple sacred songs – rather than the " vain and amatory melodies " that might have seemed more appropriate for grand banquets. Teseo wrote, too, that his uncle could play either in one or two parts as desired, perhaps playing a drone on one chanter beneath a pious melody on the other, or moving his two voices partly in parallel motion, as on later wind instruments with double pipes.[13]

To go from the sublime to the ridiculous, another visitor from outside the ducal establishment was Angelo Beolco, the famous Paduan playwright and actor, whose brilliant characterization of his own creation, the bragging but cowardly, bawdy but lovable peasant, Ruzzante, gave him the nickname by which he is best known today.[14] From time to time, Ruzzante, the illegitimate son of the rector of the Faculty of Medicine at the University of Padua, organized and

---

[12] See ADAM CARSE, *Musical Wind Instruments* (London, Macmillan 1939; repr. 1965), pp. 181-82. On Afranio and his Phagotus, and on his nephew's book about him, see LUIGI-FRANCESCO VALDRIGHI, *Nomocheliurgografia antica e moderna* (Bologna, Forni 1967, repr. of various works originally published between 1884 and 1895), pp. 295-304; FRANCIS GALPIN, *The Romance of the Phagotum*, in « Proceedings of the Royal Musical Association », LXVII (1941), pp. 57-72; and WILLIAM A. COCKS, *The Phagotum: An Attempt at Reconstruction*, in « Galpin Society Journal », XII (1959), pp. 57-59.

[13] On double pipes and their playing technique, see ANTHONY BAINES, *Woodwind Instruments and Their History* (New York, Norton, rev. ed. 1963), pp. 194-208.

[14] The dialect plays along with translations into modern Italian appear in RUZZANTE, *Teatro*, ed. Lodovico Zorzi (Turin, Einaudi 1967). See also EMILIO LOVARINI, *Studi sul Ruzzante e la letteratura pavana*, ed. Gianfranco Folena (Padua, Antenore 1965).

rehearsed troupes of actors and actresses, who then gave performances not only in their native Padua, but also in Venice and, on more than one occasion, for the Este dukes in Ferrara. Ruzzante's dialect plays, which range in length and scope from simple comic monologues to full-fledged neo-classical comedies modelled on Plautus, contain a number of songs, some on Ruzzante's own texts and others taken from local popular traditions only partially preserved in the quodlibets of the frottola repertory.[15] Clearly, then, his actors had to display some musical talent, but perhaps it is a significant indication of their level of attainment that the « canzoni e madrigali alla pavana » sung by Ruzzante and his seven companions (Appendix II, 6) were the only unaccompanied songs performed at the Ferrarese banquets with more than one musician to a part, if we can assume, as I think we can, that polyphonic arrangements of popular or mock popular tunes were normally composed for four voices. Indeed, it is tempting to imagine that Ruzzante and his actors included in their repertory *Zoia zentil*, the « canzon di Ruzzante » set to music by the Netherlander, Adrian Willaert, who had been resident at the Ferrarese court earlier in the 1520's.[16]

Alfonso della Viola, or whoever planned the music for the two evenings, strove for contrast and variety not only in the tone colors he juxtaposed, but also in the kinds of compositions he scheduled. Almost every genre of secular music known to early sixteenth-century Italy was represented at the banquets. The lira da braccio player at the first and third banquets (Appendix I, 15, and III, 2) whom Messisbugo says sang after the fashion of Orpheus, doubtless declaimed *strambotti* in *ottava rima* or stanzas in *terza rima*, either improvised or semi-improvised for the occasion, or possibly drawn from the existing repertory of poetry intended or adaptable for recitation to the lute or lira: poems by one of the older *improvvisatori* of Ferrara

---

[15] On music in Ruzzante's plays, see LOVARINI, *Le canzoni popolari in Ruzzante e in altri scrittori alla pavana del secolo XVI* and his *Una poesia musicata del Ruzzante*, in LOVARINI, *Studi*, pp. 165-270.

[16] On *Zoia zentil* see LOVARINI, *Una poesia musicata*, and LODOVICO ZORZI, *Canzoni inedite del Ruzzante*, in « Atti dell'Istituto Veneto di Scienze, Lettere ed Arti », CXIX (1960-61), pp. 25-74. The canzone is published in modern edition in LOVARINI, *Una poesia musicata*, pls. 22-32 (which include a facsimile of the sixteenth-century edition), and in ERICH HERTZMANN, ed., *Volkstümliche italienische Lieder*, Das Chorwerk 8 (Wolfenbüttel, Möseler 1930), p. 8.

perhaps, like Pietro Bono, or even some passages from Ludovico Ariosto's epic, *Orlando Furioso*, published in its first version in Ferrara in 1516 and dedicated to Cardinal Ippolito I.[17] The musical settings for such verses were never written down. Their character can only be guessed at by considering the nature of the task involved, and especially the nature of the accompanying instrument.[18] The lira da braccio was best equipped to play simple chords, almost certainly arpeggiated and possibly supporting a single melodic line played on the top string. It may be, then, that Italian poet-musicians repeated the same series of chords above their declaimed part, or the same formulaic melody for each verse or even whole stanza of the poetry; the repeating chord progressions of much sixteenth-century Italian dance music and many variation sets – on the Passamezzo formulas, the Folia, the Ruggiero tune that originally set a stanza of *Orlando Furioso*, and so on – may have their origin in the improvisatory declamation of such lira players.

Dance music figured prominently at the first banquet (Appendix I, A, 7, 14 and 17). Messisbugo describes not only the social dancing by the guests, accompanied by the band of shawms, but also various theatrical dances, probably performed by younger members of the court as well as by professional musicians: the galliards, for example, played by a quartet of instrumentalists and danced by the two young couples who led the guests in to dinner; the Moresca miming rustics cutting grass, and the Moresca that ended the evening's entertainment; and the five couple dances – the « Comuna » (probably the bassadanza communa), the « Bassa di Spagna » (clearly related to the well-known cantus firmus), the « Reogarsa » and the « Brando » or branle – that were accompanied by pipe and tabor during the seventh

---

[17] On the lira da braccio, see EMANUEL WINTERNITZ, *Lira da braccio*, in *Die Musik in Geschichte und Gegenwart*, vol. VIII, pp. 935-54, and his *Musical Instruments and Their Symbolism in Western Art* (New York, Norton 1967), pp. 86-98. On improvvisatori, see EMILE HARASZTI, *La technique des improvisateurs de langue vulgaire et de latin au quattrocento*, in « Revue belge de musicologie », IX (1955), pp. 12-31; and NINO PIRROTTA, *Music and Cultural Tendencies in 15th-Century Italy*, in « Journal of the American Musicological Society », XIX (1966), pp. 127-61.

[18] On the playing technique of the lira da braccio, see BENVENUTO DISERTORI, *Pratica e tecnica della lira da braccio*, in « Rivista musicale italiana », XLV (1941), pp. 150-75; and H. M. BROWN, *Sixteenth-Century Instrumentation* (American Institute of Musicology, 1974), pp. 39-46.

course of the banquet.[19] Unfortunately no choreographic treatises from early sixteenth-century Italy survive to instruct us about the steps and patterns these young courtiers might have used – the manuscript treatises of the fifteenth century and the anthologies of the late sixteenth and seventeenth centuries preserve an entirely different repertory of dances;[20] moreover, no Moresca tunes were written down as dances before the middle of the century; no monophonic melodies come down to us in versions that the Duchess's pipe and tabor player might have read from directly; and, indeed, no Italian dance music for instrumental ensemble was published before 1553, when Francesco Bendusi issued his *Opera nova de balli*.[21] Still, the complete lack of primary sources need not discourage us completely from imagining the sound of this music. Ensemble versions of many dances could be reconstructed on the basis of the

---

[19] On the transition from fifteenth- to sixteenth-century French dances and the relationship between French and Italian dances, see DANIEL HEARTZ, ed., *Preludes, Chansons and Dances for Lute* (Neuilly-sur-Seine, Société de musique d'autrefois 1964), pp. xxxi-liv. The word « comuna » (or « commun ») often modified dance titles in the sixteenth century; see, for example, the index of H. M. BROWN, *Instrumental Music Printed Before 1600* (Cambridge, Mass. 1965), under « Branle », « Gaillarde », « Passamezzo », « Pavane », and so on. On the « Bassa di Spagna » (« Re di Spagna », or simply « La Spagna »), see OTTO GOMBOSI, ed., *Compositione di Meser Vincenzo Capirola* (Neuilly-sur-Seine, Société de musique d'autrefois 1955), pp. xxxvi-lxiii.

I am grateful to Professor Heartz for pointing out to me that a dance called « roegarze » – doubtless the same as Messisbugo's « Reogarsa » – is described in BALDESAR CASTIGLIONE, *Il libro de cortegiano* (Venice 1528), fol. d2 *v*, as having been danced after a *bassa danza* « con estrema gratia ». The French version of Castiglione (Paris 1544, fol. 64 *v*) translates the name of the dances as " Rovergoise ". So far as I know, the dance is otherwise unknown. It does not appear, for example, either in the list of fifteenth-century tunes printed in OTTO KINKELDEY, *Dance Tunes of the Fifteenth Century*, in DAVID G. HUGHES, ed., *Instrumental Music* (Cambridge, Mass. 1959), pp. 3-30; nor in BROWN, *Instrumental Music*.

[20] On fifteenth-century Italian dance treatises, see KINKELDEY, *Dance Tunes*, which includes references to earlier studies. On late sixteenth- and seventeenth-century dancing, see MABEL DOLMETSCH, *Dances of Spain and Italy from 1400 to 1600* (London 1954).

[21] A selection of dances from Bendusi's volume are printed in modern edition, ed. Helmut Mönkemeyer (Celle, Moeck 1965). The volume is listed as 1553[2] and described in BROWN, *Instrumental Music*. The only other volume of Italian dance music for instrumental ensemble. printed in the sixteenth century was GIORGIO MAINERIO, *Il primo libro de balli* (Venice 1578) listed by Brown as 1578[8] and published in a modern edition by Manfred Schuler in the series *Musikalische Denkmäler*, vol. V (Mainz, Schott 1961). A manuscript of Italian ensemble dances (London, The British Library, Royal Appendix MSS 59-62), tentatively dated about 1540, is briefly described – and a selection of dances printed in modern edition – in JOEL NEWMAN, ed., *Sixteenth-Century Italian Dances* (University Park and London, Pennsylvania State University 1966).

arrangements for lute and other plucked stringed instruments from the first part of the century; [22] and the nature of the music could be inferred from what we know about earlier and later music. It is difficult, for example, to see how a single pipe and tabor player could undertake a performance of the cantus-firmus dance, « la Bassa di Spagna », unless he elaborated each note of the foundation melody as a series of more or less ornate divisions; and a tentative version for shawms of the Moresca might easily be prepared from the tune published by Tielman Susato of Antwerp in 1551.[23]

The « canzoni » sung by four French boys at the first banquet (Appendix I, 16) must have been French chansons, either those of a sort just beginning to be published by Pierre Attaingnant in Paris at the very end of the 1520's – in which case, the sophisticated Ferrarese court was keeping up admirably with the latest European fashions – or else chansons by composers like Ninot le Petit, Antoine Bruhier, Jean Mouton, and Pierre de la Rue, which fit four unaccompanied voices more comfortably than most of the chansons published in the Petrucci anthologies of the early years of the century.[24] It is easier to imagine the choirboys embellishing the somewhat simpler textures of the Attaingnant chansons, by composers like Claudin de Sermisy, Pierre Certon and Clément Janequin. That they did ornament their music is explicitly stated, for the descriptive term « di gorga » (derived from the Italian word for " throat ") or more commonly « gorgia », later came to be used as a synonym for passaggi or divisions. So far as I know, this is the earliest use of the term to refer to the practice of vocal diminution, and, indeed, explicit references to vocal ornamentation are not common so early in the sixteenth century.[25] Presumably the boys added divisions that were not completely different in style from those Attaingnant himself published in his volumes of arrangements of chansons for keyboard and lute.[26]

---

[22] Those that were printed are listed and described in BROWN, *Instrumental Music*.

[23] TIELMAN SUSATO, *Danserye*, ed. F. J. Giesbert (Mainz, Schott 1936), vol. I, p. 11.

[24] On chansons between about 1500 and about 1530, see H. M. BROWN, *The Music of the Strozzi Chansonnier*, in « Acta musicologica », XL (1968), pp. 115-29.

[25] On the term « gorgia », see H. M. BROWN, *Embellishing Sixteenth-Century Music* (London, Oxford University Press 1975).

[26] Lute intabulations of Attaingnant chansons have been published in HEARTZ, *Preludes, Chansons and Dances*. Keyboard intabulations appear in ALBERT SEAY, ed.,

It is a great pity that Messisbugo did not set down the first lines or titles of the vocal pieces, concerti and instrumental music performed at the banquets. We know that Ruzzante and his troupe sang dialect songs, villotte or villanelle alla pavana, doubtless taken mostly from local tradition and never published, but we can partly imagine their style and character from the Paduan popular songs arranged by Filippo Azzaiolo and printed in the 1550's,[27] and from the popular songs, including one by Ruzzante himself, arranged by Adrian Willaert and others. But in the absence of specific guidance it is impossible to be certain about the remaining compositions played and sung on those two evenings. The phrase, « una musica di M. Alfonso della Viola », is simply too ambiguous for us to know without doubt what the Ferrarese musicians performed. Motets, for example, cannot entirely be ruled out, especially since we know they were sometimes sung at banquets later in the century.[28] Most of the a cappella music and the concerti, however, were probably set to Italian words by the first generation of madrigal composers, perhaps some by the major figures writing in the genre – Festa, Arcadelt, Verdelot and the young Willaert, who had, after all, been associated with the Este court – and some by the local composers, Maistre Jhan, Alfonso della Viola, and others.

The music need not have been composed especially for those particular banquets, nor for banquets in general. Any madrigal would have been appropriate, so long as its words were not very melancholy and its music not abstruse; but then most madrigals published in the 1530's – we should not forget that none had yet been printed at the time the banquets were given – were written in fairly simple textures, predominantly chordal or in lightly animated homophony alternating with clear points of imitation, which would have suited them well for performances on such festive occasions. Unfortunately

---

Pierre Attaingnant. Transcriptions of Chansons for Keyboard (1531) (American Institute of Musicology, 1961).

[27] Azzaiolo's three volumes of *villotte alla padoana*, first published in 1557, 1559 and 1569, are listed and described in EMIL VOGEL, *Bibliothek der gedruckten weltlichen Vocalmusik Italiens* (Hildesheim, Olms 1962, repr. of original ed. of 1892). The second volume of *villotte* has been published in modern edition, by Giuseppe Vecchi (Bologna, Palmaverde 1953).

[28] The wedding banquet of Duke Wilhelm V of Bavaria in 1568, for example, included some motets. See footnote 2 above.

a large enough cross-section of Alfonso della Viola's madrigals does not survive to enable us to establish criteria for determining which were most apt for banquets, and which could best be scored for combinations of voices with instruments. Nor do any antiphonal dialogues, of the sort Messisbugo describes at the second banquet (Appendix II, 3), come down to us with Italian texts from so early a date. But on the other hand, almost any of Alfonso's five-voiced madrigals, scattered throughout various sixteenth-century anthologies, might have been performed in Ferrara in 1529: *Fra le cose qua giù*, for example, in praise of an unknown lady, or *Che dolce più*, his setting of the first stanza of the thirty-first canto of *Orlando Furioso*, an appropriate hommage to Ferrara's greatest poet.[29] Indeed, it is tempting to speculate that the concerted madrigals by Alfonso performed in 1529 were later published, and thus still survive, but it is not likely that his printed five-voiced madrigals include the one that Bottrigari reported in 1594 as still being used by the famous Ferrarese concerto on special occasions: to entertain distinguished visitors, for instance.[30] The Este family would surely have wished to reserve such an extraordinary piece, performed only rarely and then under special circumstances, for themselves and their immediate circle rather than sharing it with the entire European music-buying public.

The purely instrumental ensembles at the two banquets might have played compositions in almost any genre current at the time. That vocal music constituted the major part of the instrumentalist's repertory is confirmed in a number of ways. The rubric " apt for voices or instruments " appears on too many printed volumes to have been merely a publisher's gimmick. Some manuscript anthologies containing motets and secular vocal music as well as dances and abstract instrumental compositions may have been prepared for bands of instrumentalists.[31] And many of the numerous anthologies of

---

[29] The two madrigals cited were published in the volume described by Alfred Einstein in his revision of VOGEL, *Vocalmusik*, 1962 repr., vol. II, p. 632, as 1542¹.

[30] See HERCOLE BOTTRIGARI, *Il Desiderio* (Venice 1594), facs. ed. by Kathi Meyer (Berlin, Martin Breslauer 1924), pp. 42 ff., and BOTTRIGARI, *Il Desiderio*, transl. into English by Carol MacClintock (American Institute of Musicology, 1962), pp. 52-53.

[31] I think in the first place of Copenhagen, Det Kongelige Bibliotek, MS Gl. Kgl. Samling, 1872-4°, which GOMBOSI, *Capirola*, p. lii, claims was prepared in Königsberg for the wind band of Duke Albrecht of Prussia, a plausible claim that is not, however,

sixteenth-century keyboard and lute music include a representative cross-section of every sort of music arranged for solo instrumental performance.[32] In addition to madrigals and motets, the Ferrarese instrumentalists might well have played some dances merely for the guests to listen to, and possibly even a few abstract instrumental pieces. The dances would have been in the cantus-oriented homophonic style of the sixteenth century rather than in intricate polyphony built around a cantus firmus in the manner of the fifteenth-century dances; and perhaps some were based on repeating chord patterns. The sorts of dances arranged for lute and issued by Joan Ambrosio Dalza in 1507 and Pietro Paulo Borrono in 1536, furnish models of what Italian musicians were playing in the first half of the century.[33] It may be, too, that by 1529 the Duke's band had begun to add to their repertory imitative ricercares in a style that resembles motets, even though such compositions did not appear in print for the first time until 1540, in Andrea Arrivabene's *Musica nova*.[34] It may be, too, that they still performed some older abstract instrumental pieces, like the series of carmina commemorating individuals – *La Alfonsina*, *La Bernardina*, and the like – that dated back to the first decade of the sixteenth century or even earlier.[35]

Even if it is possible to reconstruct only conjecturally the kinds of pieces performed at Ferrarese banquets in the first half of the sixteenth century, Messisbugo's descriptions make clear, at least by implication, the extent to which performing musicians re-arranged the music they received in the form of part books; at the very least they scored it for richly varying combinations of voices and instruments. Some of the compositions that look to us like unaccompanied

---

supported in JULIUS FOSS, *Det Kgl. Cantoris Stemmebøger A. D. 1541*, in « Aaborg for Musik », (Copenhagen 1923), pp. 24-40. See also HENRIK GLAHN, ed., *Udvalgte Satser af det Kongelige Kantoris Stemmebøger*, Dania Sonans 4 (Copenhagen, to be published).

[32] See the volumes listed in BROWN, *Instrumental Music*.

[33] Listed and described in BROWN, *Instrumental Music*, as 1508[2] and 1536[9]. The Dalza dances have been published in a modern edition by HELMUT MÖNKEMEYER, *Die Tabulatur*, vols. VI-VIII (Hofheim am Taunus, Hofmeister 1967).

[34] See H. COLIM SLIM, ed., *Musica Nova*, Monuments of Renaissance Music, 1 (Chicago and London 1964).

[35] Ghiselin's *La Alfonsina*, Josquin's *La Bernardina* and several other similar pieces were published by Petrucci at the beginning of the century in *Odhecaton, Canti B* and *Canti C*.

vocal music were, indeed, performed a cappella. But others were transformed into versions for solo players or singers, into purely instrumental music, or into colorful concerti, mixing instruments and voices together.

The Duke's chapel singers may have sung madrigals a cappella at both banquets. Messisbugo does not tell us what the group performed at the first banquet, but he does write that four unidentified musicians sang madrigals at the second. And on both evenings lighter madrigalian forms – « canzoni alla pavana in villanesco » or « canzoni e madrigali alla pavana » as Messisbugo calls them – were also performed without instrumental accompaniment, as well as the « canzoni », presumably French chansons, assigned to the choirboys. Evidently, then, unaccompanied singing of madrigals, villanelle, and chansons was by no means unknown at Italian courts – even for formal occasions – and usually they were performed with one singer to a part.

The presence of the Duchess's pipe and tabor player, and of M. Afranio with his Phagotus reminds us that secular monophony had never entirely disappeared from the musical scene, even well into the sixteenth century, even though it is very rarely preserved in any musical sources. And the lira player who declaimed in the manner of Orpheus recalls the lost quasi-improvisatory tradition of the Italian courtly poet-musicians of the fifteenth and sixteenth centuries. Messisbugo also causes us to remember that polyphonic madrigals could be arranged for solo singer and lute, even at the beginning of the genre's history. The young lady who played and sang divinely at the first banquet surely followed the same procedure as Adrian Willaert when he arranged most of Verdelot's first book of madrigals for solo voice and lute; she doubtless sang the top line and played an accompaniment by duplicating as literally as she could all the lower lines.[36]

Some of the purely instrumental music was unambiguously intended for the dance. Four, five or six shawms – or more likely several shawms supported by one or more trombones playing the

---

[36] *Intavolatura de li madrigali di Verdelotto da cantare et sonare nel lauto, intavolati per Messer Adriano* (Venice, [Ottaviano Scotto] 1536), listed and described in BROWN, *Instrumental Music*, as 1536[8].

bottom parts – accompanied the social dancing and the two Morescas. The association of shawms with dancing was by 1529 an old one, of course, and it may be that the guests thought the first banquet was over at the beginning of the ninth course because they assumed that social dancing would begin once the shawms had started up. The galliards that led the guests in to dinner, on the other hand, were accompanied by a mixed consort of soft instruments: recorder, harp, lute and « cetra », the last-named instrument possibly a guitar but more probably a cittern. Lute and harp were a common late fifteenth-century combination, in which the lute played the melody more or less embellished while the harp accompanied with chords or with an arrangement of the lowest lines of the piece. As the Morley *Consort Lessons* from the very end of the century show, the cittern is an ideal instrument for adding body to an accompaniment, almost in the manner of a Baroque realization.[37] If the Ferrarese instrumentalists were playing simple four-part galliards, the best sonorities would most likely have been produced if the recorder were given the melody, the harp some of the lower lines, and the cittern a chordal part perhaps derived from one of the lower lines, while the lute added a fast counter-melody either in the alto or tenor range. During the third course at the first banquet, a rather similar but simpler mixed consort supplied instrumental music. Again the recorder must have played the principal melody while the improbable combination of harp and harpsichord supplied a chordal accompaniment, doubtless worked out from a polyphonic version of whatever pieces they performed.

Besides the shawm band, other conventional groupings also supplied instrumental music for the two evenings. When cornetts were substituted for shawms in combination with trombones, a wind band resulted that could play virtually any sort of music to good effect. The Ferrarese court had access to at least six wind players who could form such a cornett-trombone band, but there seems to

---

[37] On lute and harp combinations, see H. M. BROWN, *Instruments and Voices in the Fifteenth-Century Chanson*, in *Current Thoughts in Musicology* (University of Texas Press, to be published). The Morley Consort Lessons have been reconstructed and published in modern edition by Sydney Beck (New York Public Library 1959). Messisbugo mentions both « cetra » and « citara ». It is by no means clear whether he intentionally distinguishes between two different instruments, or calls one instrument by two slightly different names.

have been no consistent proportion of one kind of instrument to the other; once (Appendix I, 1) three cornetts combined with three trombones, and once (Appendix II, 5) a single cornett joined five trombones, solutions that suggest that the players had mastered both instruments equally well. Particular scorings depended, I suppose, on the range of the voices and on the particular sonority the director sought; if we knew which pieces they had played, we could perhaps explain the discrepancy.

Once at each banquet the sound of softer instruments playing in whole consorts entertained the guests; viols at the first banquet (Appendix I, 13), and a quartet of flutes during the second while the drawing for the door prizes was being held (Appendix II, 9). Valdrighi reproduces a memorandum dated 1530 in which an anonymous Ferrarese takes some pains to distinguish transverse flutes from recorders, describing the former as blown in the middle instead of the top, « come si fano li nostri ».[38] If that report reflects sophisticated opinion of the time, transverse flutes must have been very new indeed in Italy when they were played at the Este's banquets.

The remaining four mixed consorts all included dolzaine or cornamuse, instruments whose exact nature is far from clear. The term « cornamusa », sometimes refers to a bagpipe, but it is more likely that Messisbugo refers to a soft straight wind-capped shawm, that is, an instrument of exactly the same type as a dolzaina, though no one knows how the two sorts differed. Praetorius lists five sizes of cornamusa, each with a range of nine notes upwards from b^b, d, c, B^b and F.[39] If the assumption that the two instruments are virtually the same is correct, then the ensemble that played during the fourth course at the first banquet is practically an unmixed consort; a

[38] LUIGI-FRANCESCO VALDRIGHI, *Cappelle, concerti e musiche di Casa d'Este*, in « Atti e memorie delle Rr. Deputazioni di storia patria per le provincie Modenesi e Parmensi », serie III, vol. II (1883), p. 462.

[39] On distinctions between « cornamusa », « dolzaina », and other wind-capped shawms, see H. M. BROWN, *Wind-cap instruments*, in *Grove's Dictionary of Music and Musicians*, 6th ed. (forthcoming). The « sordina » mentioned by Messisbugo is probably a *sordun* (see SYBIL MARCUSE, *Musical Instruments, A Comprehensive Dictionary* [New York, Doubleday 1964], article « sordone »). The ranges of *cornamuse* are given in MICHAEL PRAETORIUS, *Syntagma musicum*, vol. II: *De Organographia* (Wolfenbüttel 1619), facs. ed. Willibald Gurlitt (Kassel, Bärenreiter 1958), p. 24.

dolzaina and two cornamuse were supported by a viol which took over the bass line while a cittern added a proto-continuo part. Homogeneity of sound was also an important element of the band that played during the eighth course: three cornamuse, three recorders, and viol. If they did not play seven-part music, then either the three recorders alternated with the three cornamuse, each time with viol as bass, or else the recorders doubled the cornamuse, perhaps at the upper octave. And even the music for the eighth course at the second banquet did not mix sonorities wilfully; most likely the three top parts were performed on two dolzaine and crumhorn and the two bottom parts on tenor cornett and trombone. The second course at the first banquet, on the other hand, combined three quite distinct timbres. Surely the trombone played the bass, but whether the dolzaina or the flute took the highest part depended, of course, on the range and character of the melodic lines of the pieces they played, details we shall never know.

The musical highpoint of the first banquet was the brilliant concerted piece which ended the evening. At the more elaborate second banquet, ensembles mixing voices and instruments took a regular part. Thus the Ferrarese concerto, so famous later in the century, had already become a normal feature of musical entertainment at the ducal court by 1529. Messisbugo gives us invaluable details about the composition of these early concerti. In all of them, for example, except the antiphonal dialogue (Appendix II, 3), a consort of viols apparently doubled the singers, one of each to a part. In the dialogue, on the other hand, four instruments doubled the four singers of each chorus; presumably, then, each instrument took over one of the parts, though the lutenist surely took advantage of his ability to play chords. Since the viol and the trombone were probably the loudest instruments, perhaps they doubled the outer voices – viol on the superius and trombone on bass – with the flute playing an inner voice an octave higher, as was customary, and the lute a proto-continuo part devised from the vantage point of the other inner voice.[40]

---

[40] On the reinforcement of outer voices by viol and trombone; on the flute as an instrument for inner voices; and on proto-continuo parts, see BROWN, *Instrumentation*.

The very first concerto at the second banquet also made use of chordal instruments – harpsichord and lute – to accompany the main body of voices and viols, and in addition tenor and bass recorders doubled two of the voices, for reasons that might become clear if we knew the compositions they performed. The wording of Messisbugo's description of this ensemble is slightly ambiguous. Why should Madonna Dalida be said to have sung with four others, and Alfonso della Viola with five others? Perhaps Messisbugo singled out the two most prominent musicians from among the chorus of eleven, but possibly he intends to suggest that the two groups alternated in singing successive stanzas, or repetitions of the same stanza, and perhaps he meant to say that Madonna Dalida sang with four companions, and Alfonso and his group played five viols.[41]

The principle of doubling voices with viols, adding one or more chordal instruments, and then superimposing a further layer of wind or other melody instruments on some or all of the parts, obtains in all the other concerti. During the ninth course at the second banquet, for instance, the sound of the voice and viol ensemble, plus a keyboard, was filled out by four additional instruments; perhaps the lira played the top line adding a few chords beneath it, the trombone the bass, and the flute and recorder the inner voices. Similarly during the fourth course at the second banquet (Appendix II, 4), the five singers were supported by strings, an organ, and a wind band, in which the mute cornett must have doubled the top line, the two tenor recorders and the uncapped crumhorn the three inner voices, and the dolzaina the bass. The string ensemble, slightly more complex than usual, includes a violin playing with the viols – an early instance of this combination. Messisbugo does not make clear whether he reckons the violin among the five viols, or whether both violin and treble viol doubled the top line. That he singles out the largest viol for special mention tempts me to suppose that " The Ogress " doubled the bass line at sixteen-foot pitch, and thus Messisbugo records what may be the earliest-known use of the double

---

[41] The printed version of Messisbugo's description of this event differs from the manuscript version in Modena, Biblioteca Estense. The printed book describes the second group of singers as led by « Alfonso Santo », while the manuscript more plausibly refers to « Alfonso sudetto » (the " abovementioned Alfonso ", that is, della Viola). I am grateful to Pierluigi Petrobelli and Adriano Cavicchi for this information.

bass,[42] but, of course, he does not supply such precise information, and so my conjecture can never be proven.

Finally, the most complex concerto of all fittingly served as the grand finale of the first banquet, when six voices and six viols were complemented by five chordal instruments (lira, lute, cittern and two keyboards) and five winds (two recorders and flute probably playing the top lines and trombone and « sordina » the bottom lines.)

The lush, sensuous sonorities of that final concerto are a far cry from the thin, shrill sound of Renée's pipe and tabor player. Messisbugo evokes for us a rich assortment of tone colors between these two extremes, something, as it were, for every taste. At the very least his tour of two evenings of exemplary haute cuisine and all that goes with it evokes for us in a way few other documents could the elegant and sophisticated atmosphere in which secular music flourished in sixteenth-century Italian courts, and helps to correct what might otherwise be an overly monochromatic view of the " golden age of a cappella music ".

HOWARD MAYER BROWN

APPENDIX I [43]

A summary of the music performed at Belfiore on Saturday, 20 May 1529, for the banquet given by Ippolito II d'Este, Archbishop of Milan (later Cardinal of Ferrara), for his brother, Ercole II d'Este, Duke of Chartres (later Duke of Ferrara), his brother's wife, Renée of France, Francesco d'Este, and various other lords, ladies and gentlemen, fifty-four in all.

A. When the guests had gathered, a farce was performed and also « una divina musica di diverse voci e vari stromenti ». At 10 o'clock, when the farce had finished, the guests went into the garden, where an elaborately decorated table had been prepared. They were led by

---

[42] See ALFRED PLANYAVSKY, *Geschichte des Kontrabasses* (Tutzing, Hans Schneider 1970), pp. 15-19.

[43] In every case where ambiguity might arise in the translation I have given the original Italian. I have translated « flauto » as recorder, and « flauto mezzano » and « flauto grosso » as tenor and bass recorder. Messisbugo always describes the flute (that is, the transverse flute) as « flauto alla alemanna ». Violas da gamba are referred to as « violoni », « viole » (« viuole »), or « viole da arco ». For the original Italian, see the edition of Messisbugo cited in footnote 1 and also LLORENS, *Estudio*.

four instrumentalists (playing « cetra », lute, harp and recorder) and four dancers (two young couples) who danced « balli alla gagliarda ». The dancers continued while the guests washed their hands with perfumed water and ate the salad course. On the left side of the garden was a bower under which the musicians sat and played during the meal.

1. During the first course, three trombones and three cornetti played.

2. During the second course, three musicians played a dolzaina, a trombone and a flute.

3. During the third course, three musicians played harp, recorder and harpsichord.

4. During the fourth course, five musicians played dolzaina, viola da gamba, two « cornamuse » and a « cetra ».

5. During the fifth course, jesters (« buffoni ») « alla bergamasca e alla viniziana » clowned around the table (« andarono buffoneggiando intorno alla tavola »).

6. During the sixth course, the singers of the Duke sang – M. Giovan Michele, M. Gravio, M. Giannes del Falcone, and their companions.

7. During the seventh course, the pipe and tabor player (« il tamburino ») of Renée came out of the bower with couples who danced « la Comuna », « la bassa di Spagna », « la Reogarsa » and « il Brando » around the table.

8. During the eighth course, seven musicians played three recorders, three « cornamuse » and a viola da gamba, while two people did tricks (« facevano le bagatele »).

9. During the ninth course, the shawms played and everyone thought the banquet was over; but the top table cloth was taken up and the table newly laid.

10. During the tenth course, M. Afranio played his « fagotto ».

11. During the eleventh course, a richly dressed young lady came out of the bower and sang madrigals to the lute superbly well.

12. During the twelfth course, five people sang « certe canzoni alla pavana in villanesco ».

13. During the thirteenth course, five viols played.

14. During the fourteenth course, the shawms played a Moresca by torchlight in which rustics (« contadini ») pretended to cut the grass with scythes.

15. During the fifteenth course, someone came from the bower with a lira, singing in the style of Orpheus (« cantando al modo d'Orfeo »).

16. During the sixteenth course, four French boys sang embellished chansons (« cantarono quattro putti francesi canzoni di gorga »).

17. During the last course, and while the guests washed their hands with perfumed water, M. Alfonso della Viola conducted a composition (« fece una musica M. Alfonso della Viola ») with six voices, six viols, a lira, a lute, a « citara », a trombone, a bass recorder, a tenor recorder, a flute, a « sordina », and two keyboard instruments, one large and one small (« due stromenti da penna, un grande e un picciolo »). It was « tanto bene concertata », and thought by everyone to have been the best thing they had yet heard.

After the Archbishop had given gifts to all his guests, and as the clock struck 5, the shawms started up, and twenty-four musicians came out of the bower and danced a most beautiful Moresca, after which the guests went home.

APPENDIX II

A summary of the music performed on Sunday, 24 January 1529, at a banquet given by Ercole II d'Este, Duke of Chartres (later Duke of Ferrara), for his father, Ercole I d'Este, Duke of Ferrara; his aunt, Isabella d'Este, Marchioness of Mantua; his wife, Renée of France; his brother, Ippolito II d'Este, Archbishop of Milan (later Cardinal of Ferrara); Francesco d'Este; the French ambassador; two Venetian ambassadors; and other ladies and gentlemen from Ferrara and elsewhere, 104 in all.

A. In the great hall, Lodovico Ariosto's comedy, *La Cassaria*, was given. Afterwards the guests left the hall so that it could be prepared for the banquet; the most honored guests went to a room where they were entertained « con musiche e diversi ragionamenti ». When the trumpets sounded, the guests entered the great hall, were offered perfumed water to wash their hands, and ate the salad course.

1. During the first course, a composition by Alfonso della Viola was performed, sung by Madonna Dalida and four others (« nella quale cantò Madonna Dalida, da quattro altre voci accompagnata ») and by Alfonso with five companions, and played by five viols, a harpsichord with two stops (« uno gravacembalo da due registri »), a lute, and a bass and tenor recorder.

2. During the second course, four people sang diverse madrigals.

3. During the third course, a dialogue for eight voices was perfor-

med. It was divided into two choruses, each consisting of four voices, a lute, a viol, a flute and a trombone.

4. During the fourth course, another composition by Alfonso della Viola was performed by five of the Duke's singers, five viols with a violin (« cinque viuole da arco con uno rubecchino »), a viol called " The Ogress " as a bass (« una viola chiamata la orchessa per contrabasso »), a dolzaina as second bass, a crumhorn without a cap (« senza bussola ») played by M. Giovan Battista Leone, two tenor recorders, an organ with various stops (« uno organo a più registri ») and a mute cornett (« uno cornetto sordo »).

5. During the fifth course, five trombones and a cornett played together.

6. During the sixth course, Ruzzante and five companions and two ladies sang « canzoni e madrigali alla pavana », and they went around the table debating in dialect about rustic things (« contendendo insieme di cose contadinesche, in quella lingua, molto piacevoli »).

7. During the seventh course, the guests were entertained by jesters (« buffoni ») « alla veniziana e alla bergamasca », and rustics (« contadini ») « alla pavana » who went around the table clowning.

8. During the eighth course, music was played by two dolzaine, a crumhorn (« una storta »), a large cornett and a trombone.

9. During the last course, music was played by five viols and five voices, a quilled keyboard instrument (« stromento da penna »), a bass recorder, a lira, a trombone and a flute.

After the meal a pasty was brought forward which contained the names of all the guests. The names were drawn for various gifts while four flutes played.

Trumpets sounded to signal the guests to withdraw from the great hall so that it could be prepared for dancing. At 8.30 in the evening the shawms started up and the guests danced (except for the Duke and Duchess and the Marchioness of Mantua, who retired to their rooms). After a time a light supper was served, and dancing continued until dawn.

APPENDIX III

A summary of the music performed on 21 November 1532 in Mantua for a domestic meal (« cena domesticamente fatta ») given by Alfonso d'Este, Duke of Ferrara, for the Gran Commendatore di Leone and

Monsignor Granvela, secretaries of the Emperor, at which were present the Signoria, its secretariat and other gentlemen, eighteen in all.

1. During the first course, music for viols and voices was performed.

2. During the second course, someone played the lira.

3. Messisbugo does not mention music for the third course.

4. During the fourth course, trumpets (« trombe », by which he probably meant trombones) and cornetts played.

5. During the fifth course, the Reverend M. Afranio played his « fagotto ».

6. During the sixth course, vocal music was performed.

7. To end the meal a « divinissima musica di diversi stromenti » was performed.

[16]

Notes (and Transposing Notes) On the Transverse Flute In the Early Sixteenth Century

HOWARD MAYER BROWN

S URPRISINGLY LITTLE INFORMATION survives in treatises on music about the way transverse flutes were tuned and played in the first half of the sixteenth century.[1] Sebastian Virdung, in his not altogether enlightening little textbook, *Musica getutscht* (1511), included an illustration of a single transverse flute, but he did not describe the instrument or its playing technique in any detail.[2] In fact, he mentioned the flute in his text only in passing, where he described the field drums played by soldiers, usually with *Zwerchpfeiffen*. In this context, of course, *Zwerchpfeiff* means fife rather than transverse flute; Virdung and other sixteenth-century writers used the same word for both instruments. So it is not absolutely clear that Virdung even knew the transverse flute as an instrument suitable for soft chamber music.

Transverse flutes probably took part regularly in the performance of courtly secular music in the fifteenth and early sixteenth centuries—at least in northern Europe—although relatively few pictorial or archival documents of the time offer unambiguous testimony to prove that hypothesis. It is true that a number of fourteenth-century pictures and references in French and German literature show that the instrument was well known at that time in northern Europe.[3] A few of the pictures, such as

---

1. As various modern commentators have pointed out, among them Joscelyn Godwin, "The Renaissance Flute," *The Consort* 28 (1972): 70–81; Raymond Meylan, *La Flute* (Lausanne: Payot, 1974); Bernard Thomas, "The Renaissance Flute," *Early Music* 3 (1975): 2–10; David Munrow, *Instruments of the Middle Ages and Renaissance* (London: Oxford University Press, 1976), pp. 53–56; Anne Smith, "Die Renaissancequerflöte und ihre Musik, Ein Beitrag zur Interpretation der Quellen," *Basler Jahrbuch für Historische Musikpraxis* 2 (1978): 9–76; and Jane Bowers, "*Flaüste traverseinne* and *Flute d'Allemagne*—The Development of Flute Playing in France from the Late Middle Ages up through 1702," *Recherches sur la musique française classique* 19 (1979): 7–49.

2. Sebastian Virdung, *Musica getutscht* (1511), facs. ed. by Klaus Wolfgang Niemöller (Cassel and Basel: Bärenreiter, 1970). The most recent study of Virdung is Edwin M. Ripin, "A Reevaluation of Virdung's *Musica getutscht*," *Journal of the American Musicological Society* 29 (1976): 189–223, who draws attention to Virdung's shortcomings. The flute is illustrated in Virdung, fol. Biii[v], and "zwerch pfeiffen" are mentioned in fol. Civ[v].

3. For examples of transverse flutes in fourteenth-century art and literature, see, in ad-

those illustrating the Lieder of the Minnesänger in the so-called Manesse Manuscript, make it clear that the transverse flute played a role in the performance of secular music in a courtly atmosphere.[4] But fifteenth-century pictures offer no such assurances about the musical repertory entrusted to the instrument. Early in the century a few Franco-Flemish angels with transverse flutes appear among the crowds of angels that people the periphery of various illuminations in books of hours and Bibles.[5] A few fifteenth- or early sixteenth-century pictures show a flute (or rather a fife) being played with a drum by soldiers on military exercises, or at tournaments, as in fig. 1,[6] or by minstrels at dances or banquets, as in fig.

---

dition to the studies cited in note 1 above, Howard Mayer Brown, "Flute," *The New Grove Dictionary of Music and Musicians* (London: Macmillan, 1980), 6:664–81. Brown, "Trecento Angels and the Instruments They Play," *Modern Musical Scholarship*, ed. Edward Olleson (Stocksfield: Oriel Press, 1980), pp. 112–40, argues that the complete absence of transverse flutes in trecento paintings that show all instruments praising God strongly suggests that the instruments were unknown in Italy at the time.

4. Musicians playing transverse flutes to accompany dancing, and perhaps also singing, may be seen in *Die Manessische Lieder Handschrift*, facs. ed. (Frankfurt am Main: Insel Verlag, 1925–27), fols. 413ᵛ and 423ᵛ. See also the reproductions from this manuscript in Robert Haas, *Aufführungspraxis der Musik* (Wildpark-Potsdam: Akademische Verlagsgesellschaft Athenaion, 1931), opp. p. 80; Heirich Besseler, *Die Musik des Mittelalters und der Renaissance* (Potsdam: Akademische Verlagsgesellschaft Athenaion, 1937), p. 175; Karl Michael Komma, *Musikgeschichte in Bildern* (Stuttgart: Alfred Kröner Verlag, 1961), nos. 102, 103, and 105, and the studies cited in note 1, among other places.

5. See, for example, (1) the Annunciation in the *Belles Heures du duc de Berry* (illuminated by the Limbourg brothers in the first decade of the fifteenth century), now in New York, Metropolitan Museum MS 54.1.1, fol. 30, reproduced in Millard Meiss, *The Limbourgs and their Contemporaries*, 2 vols. (London: Thames and Hudson, 1974), 2: pl. 410; Meiss, *French Painting in the Time of Jean de Berry: The Late Fourteenth Century and the Patronage of the Duke*, 2 vols. (London: Phaidon, 1969), 2: pl. 779; Meiss, *French Painting in the Time of Jean de Berry: The Boucicaut Master* (London: Phaidon, 1968), pl. 126; and *The Belles Heures of Jean, Duke of Berry*, ed. Millard Meiss and Elizabeth H. Beatson (New York: George Braziller, 1974), fol. 30; (2) St. Jerome in his study, in the *Bible moralisée* painted by the Limbourg brothers, now in Paris, Bibliothèque nationale MS fonds fr. 166, fol. A, reproduced in Meiss, *Limbourgs*, 2: pl. 357; and (3) Christ in Glory in the *Heures de Turin* (now destroyed), painted by the Parement Master and his workshop, reproduced in Meiss, *French Painting . . . Late Fourteenth Century*, pl. 38. These paintings clearly reflect a continuation of the late fourteenth-century tradition of depicting music-making angels (including some playing transverse flute) in the margins of manuscripts, seen in such manuscripts as the *Belleville Breviary* and the *Hours of Jeanne d'Evreux* (both of which include flutes). For two other flute-playing angels of the late fourteenth century, see Meiss, *French Painting . . . Late Fourteenth Century*, pll. 95 and 180.

There is at least one flute-playing Spanish angel in a late fourteenth- or early fifteenth-century painting of the Virgin and Child by a follower of Juan Daurer. The painting, in the church of St. Maria del Puig in Pollensa, is reproduced in Chandler R. Post, *A History of Spanish Painting*, 14 vols. in 20 (Cambridge, Mass.: Harvard University Press, 1930–66), 3: pl. 309.

6. An engraving by Master MZ (probably Matthäus Zaisinger), showing a tournament in

NOTES (AND TRANSPOSING NOTES) ON THE TRANSVERSE FLUTE   7

2.[7] The tradition of depicting the transverse flute regularly as a chamber instrument seems to begin with the illuminations showing a trio of evidently upper-class people—a lady singing, a second person playing lute, and a third either flute or recorder—making music in a small boat. Such pictures illustrate the month of May in calendars that preface Flemish books of hours, such as that shown in fig. 3.[8] A single flute can be seen, too,

---

Munich in 1500, and reproduced in *Fifteenth Century Engravings of Northern Europe from the National Gallery of Art, Washington, D.C., December 3, 1967–January 7, 1968*, Exhibition Catalogue by Alan Shestack (Washington, D.C.: National Gallery of Art, 1967), pl. 153.

Other soldiers playing fife and drum on military exercises are shown in two Swiss manuscript illuminations from the last third of the fifteenth century, reproduced in Edmund Bowles, *Musikleben im 15. Jahrhundert* (Leipzig: VEB Deutscher Verlag für Musik, 1977), pll. 69 and 70; in another engraving dated 1500 by Master MZ, reproduced in *Fifteenth Century Engravings*, pl. 151; in an engraving dated 1499 by Master PPW of Cologne, reproduced in *Ausstellung Maximilian I. Innsbruck, 1. Juni bis 5. Oktober 1969* (Innsbruck: Verlagsanstalt Tyrolia, 1969), pl. 15; and in two early sixteenth-century woodcuts by Hans Burgkmair, reproduced in Georg Hirth, *Kulturgeschichtes Bilderbuch aus drei Jahrhunderten*, 3 vols. (Leipzig, 1882), 1:130 and 132.

7. A woodcut by Master CA (ca. 1500), reproduced in Sir Frank Crisp, *Mediaeval Gardens* (London, 1924; repr. New York: Hacker Art Books, 1966), fig. 110, and in *Die Musik in Geschichte und Gegenwart* 5: cols. 1555–56. It was originally published in Marsilio Ficino, *Das Buch des Lebens* (Strasbourg, 1509).

Master MZ also made an engraving of a ball in Munich in 1500, which shows several couples dancing to the accompaniment of two musicians playing fife and drum in a gallery. It is reproduced in Bowles, *Musikleben*, pl. 39; *Fifteenth Century Engravings*, pl. 152, and Robert Wangermée, *La musique flamande dans la société des XVe et XVIe siècles* (Brussels: Éditions Arcade, 1965), pl. 60. Bowles, *Musikleben*, p. 160, also reproduces a woodcut by Michael Wolgemut, showing four couples dancing outdoors to fife and drum. The woodcut was printed in *Der Schatzbehalter* (Nuremberg, 1491) and in Hartmann Schedel's *Weltchronik* (Nuremberg, 1493) among other places, and it was used as a model for a wall painting in the Knights' Hall in the Castle of Zvikov in Czechoslovakia. The wall painting is reproduced in Tomislav Volek and Stanislav Jares, *Dejiny Ceske Hudby v Obrazech* (Prague: Editio Supraphon, 1977), pl. 88, who also reproduce as pl. 92 a woodcut of a fife player accompanying a couple dancing in a tavern from a Czech book published in 1505. Soldiers playing fife and drum appear also in the margins of the Grimani Breviary of about 1500, now in Venice, Biblioteca Nazionale Marciana; the page showing fife and drum players is reproduced in *Le Bréviaire Grimani à la Bibliothèque Marciana de Venise*, ed. Salomone Morpurgo, Scato de Vries and Giulio Coggiola (Leiden: A. W. Sijthoff, 1903), pl. 22. In the early sixteenth century, Hans Burgkmair also made several woodcuts showing minstrels playing fife and drum at a dance, while street entertainers do acrobatic tricks, and for a court entertainment for Emperor Maximilian I. These are reproduced, among other places, in Hirth, *Kulturgeschichtliches Bilderbuch*, 1:490, 1:399 and 1:101 (Maximilian's *Mummenschanz* is also reproduced in Wangermée, *Musique flamande*, pl. 62).

8. From Munich, Bayerische Staatsbibliothek Cod. lat. 23,638, fol. 6ᵛ, an early sixteenth-century Flemish calendar, described and reproduced in Georg Leidinger, *Miniaturen aus Handschriften der kgl. Hof- und Staatsbibliothek in München*, vol. 2: *Flämischen Kalender* (Munich: Riehn und Tietze, s. d.), pl. 10. Note, however, that a drummer stands in the boat along with the musical trio (or quartet?). (Pl. 24 shows a couple dancing to fife and drum,

8　　　JOURNAL OF THE AMERICAN MUSICAL INSTRUMENT SOCIETY

FIGURE 1. Master MZ. The Tournament. Engraving. Washington, D.C. National Gallery of Art.

and pl. 25 people being led home from an evening entertainment by a fifer and a drummer.)

Other trios consisting of singer, lute and transverse flute in a boat appear in calendars of books of hours in the following manuscripts: (1) Brussels, Bibliothèque royale MS II.158, fol. 5ᵛ, the so-called *Heures de Notre Dame dites de Hennessy*, painted ca. 1540, and reproduced in Bowles, Musikleben, pl. 93, and Wangermée, *Musique flamande*, pl. 46; and (2) New York, Pierpont Morgan Library MS M.52, fol. 4, a Flemish Breviary, probably prepared for Queen Eleanor of Portugal, whose arms appear on the first folio.

Brussels, Bibliothèque royale MS IV.90, one of the recently recovered partbooks that belongs with the Tournai Chansonnier, shows a similar trio but with the third person playing recorder rather than flute. The page is reproduced in Wangermée, *Musique flamande*, pl. 48, and in my essay "Instruments and Voices in the Fifteenth-Century Chanson," in *Current Thoughts in Musicology*, ed. John W. Grubbs (Austin, Texas and London: University of Texas Press, 1976), pl. 9, where the problems of performing chansons with this combination are outlined. I also list there several other similar trios with recorder rather than flute; the list could easily be extended.

Shepherds are seen playing transverse flutes in two early fifteenth-century miniatures reproduced in Meiss, *Limbourgs*, 2: pll. 235 and 237, but they are illustrations of Virgil's *Eclogues*, and may well reflect ancient tradition, or the artist's conception of ancient tradition, rather than social reality.

Further illustrations of fifteenth-century transverse flutes are listed in Edmund Bowles,

NOTES (AND TRANSPOSING NOTES) ON THE TRANSVERSE FLUTE   9

FIGURE 2. Master CA. Woodcut from Marsilio Ficino, *Das Buch des Lebens* (Strasbourg: J. Grüninger, 1509).

among the instruments supplying music at banquets in Franco-Flemish paintings showing the prodigal son among whores;[9] and a series of paintings showing a trio of genteel ladies (one singing and the others playing flute and lute) seems to have been produced in quantity in Flanders during the first half of the sixteenth century. At least some of these pictures were for export to France where they were said to have hung traditionally

"A Checklist of Musical Instruments in Fifteenth Century Illuminated Manuscripts at the British Museum," *Notes* 29 (1973): 694–703, and Bowles, "A Checklist of Musical Instruments in Fifteenth Century Illuminated Manuscripts at the Bibliothèque Nationale," *Notes* 30 (1974): 474–91.

9. On paintings showing the prodigal son at banquets, with one person playing a transverse flute, see H. Colin Slim, *The Prodigal Son at the Whores': Music, Art and Drama* (Irvine, California: University of California, Irvine, 1976). One of the paintings is reproduced in Wangermée, *Musique flamande*, pl. 67. The paintings with the transverse flute seem all to date from the 1530's, 1540's, or even later.

FIGURE 3. Munich, Bayerische Staatsbibliothek, Cod. Lat. 23.638, fol. 6ᵛ. The month of May in a calendar from a sixteenth-century Flemish book of hours.

in inns and taverns.[10] The Flemish ladies are shown performing from legible notation real chansons such as Claudin de Sermisy's "Jouissance vous donneray," first published by Pierre Attaingnant in Paris in 1529.

10. This trio of ladies is reproduced widely. H. Colin Slim, "Paintings of Lady Concerts and the Transmission of 'Jouissance vous donneray'," *Imago Musicae* 1 (1984): 51–73, the most complete study of the ladies to date, compares in detail four versions of the painting: the best-known copy in the Harrach Gallery at Rohrau along with versions in Leningrad (Hermitage Museum), a private collection in Brazil, and one formerly in the Ducal Castle at Meiningen. He dates the paintings ca. 1520–1525. Slim includes an edition of Claudin's "Jouissance vous donneray" and cites previous studies of the paintings.

NOTES (AND TRANSPOSING NOTES) ON THE TRANSVERSE FLUTE   11

The numerous pictures from the first half of the sixteenth century showing flutes as chamber instruments began to appear at just about the same time as the only two surviving volumes of music in which a substantial number of compositions are singled out as especially appropriate for the instrument. In 1533, the Parisian music publisher Pierre Attaingnant issued two volumes of chansons, *Chansons musicales a quatre parties* and *Vingt et sept chansons musicales a quatre parties,* in which the title pages explain that the compositions marked with an "a" are better ("plus convenables") on flutes, those marked "b" better on recorders, and those marked "ab" equally appropriate for either instrument.[11] Anne Smith, who has recently published a list of the contents of the two volumes with the range and clef of each of the surviving parts, has also described in some detail a copy of Georg Forster's *Frische teutsche Liedlein* (Nuremberg, 1552), in which manuscript annotations single out some individual parts as especially good on the flute ("zwerch pfeiff gut," "gut zwerch," or some such), recorder ("gut flöt" or "gudt fleidt" or some such), bagpipe ("gut sackpfeiff" or something similar) and fiddle (if that instrument is meant by "gut leyren").

11. Attaingnant's two volumes are described, and the contents listed, in Daniel Heartz, *Pierre Attaingnant, Royal Printer of Music* (Berkeley and Los Angeles: University of California Press, 1969), pp. 250–53; Howard Mayer Brown, *Instrumental Music Printed Before 1600, A Bibliography* (Cambridge, Mass.: Harvard University Press, 1965), pp. 43–45; and Smith, "Renaissancequerflöte," pp. 64–67. These two volumes were neither the only music Attaingnant published in which transverse flutes were singled out for mention, nor the earliest chansons explicitly for flutes. Quite aside from volumes like the Arnt von Aich *Liederbuch* (RISM [1519]⁵), in which the music is described as "lustick zu syngen. Auch etlich zu fleiten, schwegelen und anderen musicalisch Instrumenten artlichen zu gebrauchen," Lawrence F. Bernstein, "The Bibliography of Music in Conrad Gesner's *Pandectae* (1548)," *Acta musicologica* 45 (1973): 119–63, lists two volumes of music for flutes (both now lost), after a mid-sixteenth-century bibliography: item 156, p. 148: "Viginti cantiunculae Gallicae 4. vocum, excusae Argentorati apud Petrus Schoeferus 1530. in 12. per transversum, maiori forma folii, chartis 16," (which he points out is the same as his item 285), and item 282, p. 158: "Quarante & quatre chansons a deux, ou duo, chose delectable aux fleustes. Petrus Attaignans excudebat Parisiis." Daniel Heartz, "*Au pres de vous*—Claudin's Chanson and the Commerce of Publishers' Arrangements," *Journal of the American Musicological Society* 24 (1971): 213–14, cites a royal privilege Attaingnant received in 1531 to protect his publications, including his "tablatures . . . des jeus de flustes."
    Another volume of music for transverse flute was published in 1558 by Simon Gorlier of Lyons, but it does not survive today. His *Livre de Tabulature de flutes d'Allemand* is described in Brown, *Instrumental Music,* p. 180.
    Attaingnant's three anthologies and those for flute published by Peter Schoeffer in Strasbourg and Simon Gorlier in Lyons, together with the increase in the number of pictures of lady concerts, boating parties, and flutes in mixed consorts, suggests that the flute enjoyed a great vogue from about 1520 on, both as an instrument to mix with other families of instruments and with voices, and as an instrument to play in unmixed consorts. On the possibility that conventions differed depending on the way the flute was used, see footnotes 25 and 46 below.

She has also published a list of the other music from the sixteenth and early seventeenth centuries in which transverse flutes are assigned particular parts.[12] Attaingnant's volumes of chansons appear to have been intended for quartets of flutes or recorders, an ensemble that apparently was cultivated more in France than in Germany during the first half of the sixteenth century, if François de Scépeaux, sieur de Vielleville and maréchal of France, is to be believed. Scépeaux wrote, after an evening of chamber music in Metz in 1554, that he could not understand why the instrument was called a German flute, "for the French play them better and more musically than any other nation; and they are never played *a 4* in Germany, as they normally are in France."[13]

The flute figures prominently, too, in the anthology of "plusiers singularités" (which includes the Lord's Prayer in a number of exotic languages; a fascinating series of architectural drawings of parts of the Cathedral at Reims, Notre Dame de Paris, the Sainte Chapelle, and various other buildings; a number of astronomical and astrological drawings; and a collection of musical instruments, shown alone and in whole and mixed consorts) compiled by François Merlin, *controlleur général* for the household of Marie Elizabeth, only daughter of Charles IX. It was written out between 1583 and 1587 in an exceptionally elegant calligraphic hand by Jacques Cellier, a resident of Reims. In the section on musical instruments, dated 1585, Cellier includes not only an "Accord de luth, violle, harpe, & flutte" (fig. 4), played by *putti*, but also an "accord de fluttes d'allemant" (fig. 5).[14] We should not, however, be so dazzled by the charm of the drawing

---

12. Smith, "Renaissancequerflöte," pp. 68–76.

13. *Nouvelle collection des mémoires pour servir à l'histoire de France, depuis le XIIIe siècle, jusqu'à la fin du XVIIIe*, vol. 9: *Mémoires de la vie de François de Scépeaux*, ed. Michaud and Poujoulat (Paris, 1838), p. 204. Scépeaux's evening in Metz involved making music with two singers (soprano and bass), and an ensemble consisting of harpsichord, lute, treble viol and flute, presumably a typical ensemble with single flute and other instruments and voices. In the original, Scépeaux's remark reads:

> Mais il l'entretenoit parfaicte et en prince; car avecques ung dessus et une basse-contre, il y avoit une espinette, ung joueur de luth, dessus de viole, et une fleute-traverse, que l'on appelle à grand tort fleuste d'allemand; car les Français s'en aydent mieulx et plus musicalement que toute aultre nation; et jamais en Allemaigne n'en fust joué à quatre parties, comme il se faict ordinairement en France.

14. Figs. 4 and 5 are taken from Paris, Bibliothèque nationale MS fonds fr. 9152, pp. 163 and 174. On the treatise of Merlin and Cellier, see Thurston Dart, "Some Sixteenth-Century French Drawings," *Galpin Society Journal* 10 (1957): 88–89 and pll. VI and VII; and Susi Jeans and Guy Oldham, "The Drawings of Musical Instruments in MS Add. 30342 at the British Museum," *Galpin Society Journal* 13 (1960): 26–31.

NOTES (AND TRANSPOSING NOTES) ON THE TRANSVERSE FLUTE   13

FIGURE 4. Paris, Bibliothèque Nationale, MS fonds fr. 9152, p. 174. "Accord de luth, violle, harpe, & flutte."

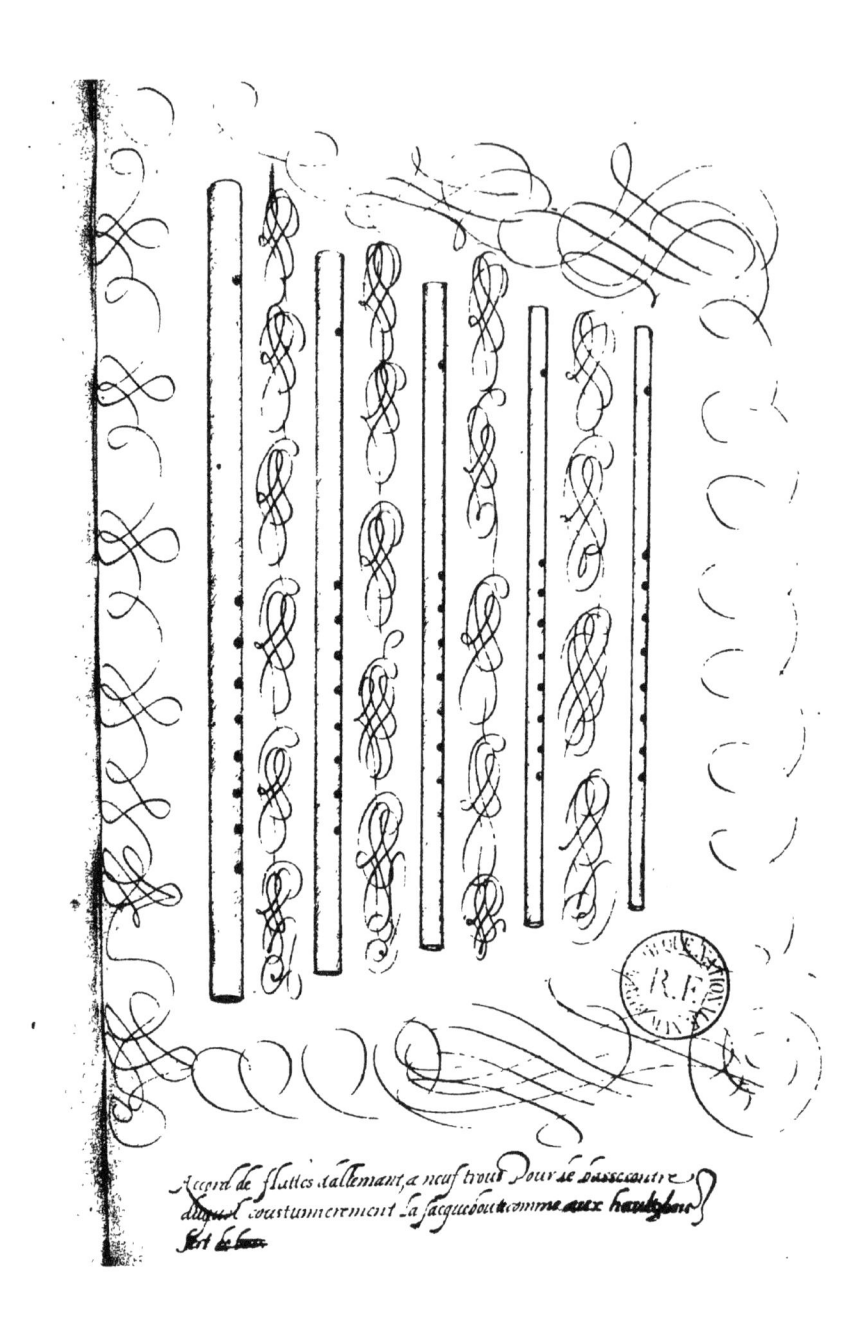

FIGURE 5. Paris, Bibliothèque Nationale, MS fonds fr. 9152, p. 174. "Accord de flutte d'allemant."

that we take what information Cellier has to give us absolutely literally. It seems improbable, for example, in the face of the overwhelming evidence to the contrary, that there could have been five different sizes of flute in common use in 1585, and quite unlikely that they should all have had the eight fingerholes depicted by Cellier. His statement, on the other hand, that consorts of flutes, like consorts of shawms ("hautbois"), often used as their bass a sackbut, seems entirely plausible, especially since that convention is mentioned by various later writers as well.

In short, either the flute was played in chamber ensembles more regularly in the sixteenth century than it had been before, or else it was more often described by writers and depicted by artists of the time. In either case, it would be good to know how it was used during that period so that we could have a clearer image of the sonority of a particular kind of music; and explaining tuning and transposition on the flute might help us to understand better the general (and presumably widespread) conventions of transposition. For information on these subjects, we are forced to turn to Martin Agricola, for he is the only writer to furnish details about performing on the flute before Philibert Jambe de Fer described the instrument in his treatise of 1556.[15] After Jambe de Fer, no other writer took up the instrument and its technique until the 1590s, when Zacconi included some information about it in his *Prattica di musica;*[16] and in the

15. Martin Agricola, *Musica instrumentalis deudsch* (Wittenberg, 1528/29) has been re-printed in quasi-facsimile in *Publikation älterer praktischer und theoretischer Musik-Werke,* vol. 20 (Leipzig: Breitkopf und Härtel, 1896) along with the fourth, revised edition of 1545. All references are to the Leipzig facsimile. The section on recorders and flutes (after both the 1529 and the 1545 editions) has been translated into English in William E. Hettrick, "Martin Agricola's Poetic Discussion of the Recorder and Other Woodwind Instruments," *The American Recorder* 21 (1980): 103–13, 23 (1982): 139–46, and 24 (1983): 51–60. The translation offered in William S. Hollaway, "Martin Agricola's *Musica instrumentalis deudsch:* Translation and Commentary," Ph.D. dissertation, North Texas State University, 1972, is not reliable.

Philibert Jambe de Fer, *Épitome musical des tons, sons et accordz, es voix humaines, fleustes d'alleman, Fleustes à neuf trous, Violes, & Violons* (Lyons, 1556) is reprinted in facsimile in François Lesure, "*L 'Épitome musical* de Philibert Jambe de Fer (1556)," *Annales musicologiques* 6 (1958/63): 341–86.

Hieronymus Cardanus, in his *De musica* written about 1546 and in his *De musica* completed in 1574, mentions the transverse flute (which he calls *fifola* or *fistula*); but he offers detailed information only about the recorder (which he calls *flautus* or *elyma*). Evidently, he did not know the flute well, for in one passage he claims that it has a range of only nine tones, while in another he explains how to play the upper register. See Cardanus, *Writings on Music,* translated and edited with an introduction by Clement A. Miller (American Institute of Musicology, 1973), esp. pp. 51, 113, 115 and 191.

16. Lodovico Zacconi, *Prattica di musica,* 2 vols. (Venice, 1592–1622) is reprinted in facsimile by Forni (Bologna: Forni, 1967). What meager information Zacconi gives on the transverse flute is to be found in the section on instruments, 1:212–19. He mentions only the transverse flute "in D."

following decades the flute was treated in varying amounts of detail by Aurelio Virgiliano,[17] Michael Praetorius,[18] Marin Mersenne[19] and Pierre Trichet.[20]

Modern writers have been quick to assume that the remarks by Praetorius, Mersenne, and the other late sixteenth- and seventeenth-century writers can be applied directly and without reservation to instruments and music of an earlier period. That assumption is not necessarily true and must be tested at every step along the way. In any case, we should exhaust what information we can glean from writers who lived during the first half of the century, before we try to apply statements printed almost a hundred years later to that music. Therefore, we first need to know what Agricola wrote—and what he meant—for he did offer important and fairly detailed information about the transverse flute, even if his exposition of the material is confusing and unclear (as he himself admitted in the introduction to the second and completely revised edition of his treatise[21]), so that his meaning has been misunderstood in the past.

Agricola published his *Musica instrumentalis deutsch* in 1528 or 1529 as an elementary instruction book both for his young students at the Protestant Latin school run by the city of Wittenberg and for laypeople and lovers of

---

17. Aurelio Virgiliano's *Il Dolcimelo*, surviving only in manuscript in Bologna, Civico Museo Bibliografico Musicale, is printed in facsimile by Marcello Castellani (Florence: Studio per Edizioni Scelte, 1979). Aurelio gives a fingering chart for the flute "in D" on p. 109, with indications of how the player can substitute one clef for another in order to transpose to any scale degree. On Aurelio's manuscript, see Imogene Horsley, "The Solo Ricercar in Diminution Manuals: New Light on Early Wind and String Techniques," *Acta musicologica* 33 (1961): 29–40.

18. Michael Praetorius, *Syntagma musicum*, vol. 2: *De Organographia* (Wolfenbüttel, 1619) is reprinted in facsimile by Wilibald Gurlitt (Cassel and Basel: Bärenreiter, 1958). The first and second parts of the volume are translated into English by Harold Blumenfeld as *The Syntagma Musicum of Michael Praetorius. Volume two. De Organographia. First and Second Parts* (2nd ed., New York: Bärenreiter, 1962), and by David Z. Crookes as *Michael Praetorius. Syntagma Musicum II. De Organographia. Parts I and II* (Oxford: Clarendon Press, 1986).

19. Marin Mersenne, *Harmonie universelle* (Paris, 1636) is reprinted in facsimile with an introduction by François Lesure, 3 vols. (Paris: Centre National de la Recherche Scientifique, 1963). The books on instruments are translated into English by Roger E. Chapman in Marin Mersenne, *Harmonie universelle. The Books on Instruments* (The Hague: Martinus Nijhoff, 1957).

20. Trichet's treatise, surviving only in manuscript in Paris, Bibliothèque Sainte-Geneviève, was completed after 1638 and before 1644 (the approximate date of Trichet's death). The treatise has been printed in a modern edition in François Lesure, "Le Traité des instruments de musique de Pierre Trichet," *Annales musicologiques* 3 (1955): 283–87 and 4 (1956): 175–248.

21. Agricola, *Musica*, 1545 edition, fol. A3, describes the first edition as "zutunckel und schwer zu verstehen" ("too obscure and hard to understand").

NOTES (AND TRANSPOSING NOTES) ON THE TRANSVERSE FLUTE 17

music in general.[22] Because he had such modest aims, happily for us, he explained many of the basic assumptions that sixteenth-century musicians took for granted, but that we need to have spelled out for us explicitly. In teaching a general audience about musical instruments, Agricola organized his treatise into three sections: one on winds, one on strings, and one on percussion instruments. When he came to publish his greatly expanded and reorganized second edition in 1545, even the overall organization was different. The 1545 edition contains five chapters: (1) on wind instruments; (2) on three kinds of fiddles (Italian, Polish, and small three-stringed *Geigen*); (3) on the lute and monochord (with special emphasis on placing the frets, that is, on establishing the temperament); (4) on the proportions of organ pipes and hammers; and (5) on miscellaneous instruments (harp, psaltery, xylophone and dulcimer).

Winds thus take pride of place in Agricola's treatment of musical instruments, and foremost among the wind instruments Agricola deals with recorders and flutes. Most of the space is given over to a brief description of the instruments and their playing technique. Each type is illustrated, and Agricola includes diagrams giving ranges and fingering. These diagrams are set up in the first place for recorders and flutes, but those for recorder include information about other instruments as well, especially shawms and crumhorns.

Agricola explains that there were three sizes of recorders—bass, tenor/alto, and discant—tuned, like most other winds, a fifth apart. The lowest notes of the three sizes are given in example 1; their almost fully chromatic ranges extend an octave and a sixth or seventh above their lowest notes. Fig. 6 shows Agricola's fingering chart for tenor recorder, taken from the 1530 printing of the first edition.[23] It shows at the bottom of the page a tenor recorder "in C" fingered for its note *g'* (an octave and a fifth above the lowest written note), and it gives the top of the tenor crumhorn's range and a special fingering for the ninth above the lowest note on the tenor shawm or *Bomhart*. But the main part of the diagram is taken up (reading from right to left) with vertical columns for the

22. Agricola, *Musica*, 1529 edition, fol. A2, writes that he has had his book published for "der jugent und allen andern auch leyen und ungelerten, die nur lesen künnen" ("youths and all others including laymen and the unlearned who only know how to read").

23. Agricola, *Musica*, 1530 edition (in Washington, Library of Congress), fol. B1ᵛ. The 1529 edition contains a mistake on this and the following page (see the Leipzig facsimile of 1896), as the editor, Robert Eitner, points out on pp. 287–88. The 1529 edition confused the fingering charts for discant and tenor/alto recorders, a mistake corrected during the press run in some copies.

A. As their bottom notes are written.

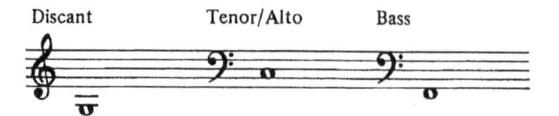

B. As their bottom notes would actually sound
    (if they were tuned to modern pitch standards):

EXAMPLE 1. Agricola's three sizes of recorder.

solmisation syllables of each note in the tenor recorder's range, the fingers that must be lifted up to produce the notes, the note names according to letters of the alphabet (C, D, E, F, and so on), the available accidentals (note that they are all to be solfeged as fa), their fingerings, and finally, in the left column, the clefs (F, C, and G) that serve as orientation for the reader.

It is important to note that what Agricola has to say about recorder fingerings has nothing to do with absolute pitches. We can never learn from such diagrams anything about absolute pitch levels, or what pitches instruments were actually tuned to.[24] Indeed, the greatest difficulty in associating surviving instruments with information given about them by sixteenth-century writers is that we can never be certain how the surviving instruments were said to be tuned.[25] Instead, what Agricola writes about is

24. On the difficulty of knowing for certain the absolute pitch levels used in the past, see Arthur Mendel, "Pitch in Western Music Since 1500, A re-examination," *Acta musicologica* 50 (1978): 1–93, who cites past studies of the subject.

On the pitches of surviving sixteenth-century flutes, see Rainer Weber, "Some Researches into Pitch in the 16th Century with Particular Reference to the Instruments in the Accademia Filarmonica of Verona," *Galpin Society Journal* 28 (1975): 7–10.

25. Thomas, "Renaissance Flute," pp. 2–10, makes the astute observation that Praetorius's plates seem to show flutes in larger sizes than would be appropriate for instruments tuned *g*, *d'* and *a'*. He suggests that flutes in the sixteenth century may regularly have sounded pitches approximating modern *f*, *c'* and *g'*. His suggestion that sixteenth-century flutists may therefore have transposed pieces in G-Dorian down a whole step is ingenious but, as he admits, it is not supported by any historical evidence.

Agricola (at least by implication in the 1545 edition of his treatise) and later writers (including Praetorius) all agree in stating that flutes were said to be in "g," "d'" and "a'" (some

NOTES (AND TRANSPOSING NOTES) ON THE TRANSVERSE FLUTE   19

FIGURE 6. Martin Agricola, *Musica instrumentalis deudsch* (from the 1530 printing of the first edition), fol. B1ʳ. Fingering chart for the tenor/alto recorder.

the relationship between the player's fingers and what he sees on the page. Thus Agricola tells us that every time a player of the tenor/alto recorder "in C" sees a *c* (an octave below middle *c'*), he is to play the lowest note of his instrument; every time he sees *c'* he is to play a note one octave above his lowest note; and so on. Similarly, every time a player of the bass recorder "in F" sees *f* (a fifth below middle *c'*), he is to play a note an octave above his lowest note; every time a player of the discant recorder "in G" sees a *g'* he is to play a note an octave above his lowest note; and so on. Understanding Agricola's tables in this way—as a diagram explaining how the player is to finger the notes he sees in the music before him—seems straightforward enough when it is applied to the recorders, but we shall see that the failure to understand Agricola's intentions has led to confusion apropos his treatment of transverse flutes.

In any case, applying Agricola's fingerings to a randomly selected German Lied of the early sixteenth century—Paul Hofhaimer's "Ach edler hort," the beginning of which is given as example 2[26]—shows that Agricola

---

writers omit one or more of the sizes). Therefore, whatever the actual pitches sounded, the lowest note on the flute "in D" must have been whatever the flutist saw as D in the written music before him (unless, of course, he was transposing using Agricola's tables, or some similar convention). In describing the scoring of particular pieces in *Syntagma musicum*, 3:153–54 and 156–57, Praetorius may have intended to refer only to flutes "in D," in which case his remark that flute parts in tenor clef go too low to balance other instruments makes better sense than it otherwise would. (Praetorius seems to be saying the same thing in his universal table in *Syntagma musicum*, 2:21, when he writes that "Diese Flötte [that is, a recorder in "D" or "C"], so wol auch die Querpfeiffe in diesen Thon, kan nicht allein zum Discant, wie ich es alhier eingesetzet, sondern auch zum Tenor ein Octave drunter, gebraucht werden," or, as Blumenfeld, p. 21, somewhat freely translates, "This recorder, and the cross flute in this register [*recte*: pitch] as well, may not only be used as a discant instrument [*recte*: on the discant part], as which I have set it down here, but also as a tenor [*recte*: on the tenor part], an octave lower").

That Praetorius lists three sizes of flute may only be an indication of his historicism. Already in 1556, Jambe de Fer asserted that flutes "in D" played treble parts; Zacconi in 1592 and Aurelio Virgiliano about 1600 both give ranges for the flute "in D" exclusively, and they do not mention other sizes; and Mersenne in 1636 gives fingerings for flutes "in G" and "in D" (although the treble part of his example of music for four flutes goes uncomfortably high if played on a flute "in D"). In short, there is little evidence that discant flutes "in A" were in common use at the end of the sixteenth and the beginning of the seventeenth centuries, especially since Praetorius's table of sizes can easily be explained away as evidence of his desire for historical completeness. Nevertheless, there still remains the problem of playing the E♭'s on a flute "in D" required by Praetorius in the pieces cited in *Syntagma musicum* 3. But that problem is the fit subject for a separate study, for whatever the solution, it will throw little light on the conventions of transposition in operation during the first third of the sixteenth century.

26. After Hans Joachim Moser, ed., *Einundneunzig Tonsätze Paul Hofhaimers und seines Kreises* (Stuttgart, 1929; reprint, Hildesheim: Georg Olms Verlagsbuchhandlung, 1966), pp. 24–25.

NOTES (AND TRANSPOSING NOTES) ON THE TRANSVERSE FLUTE   21

EXAMPLE 2. Paul Hofhaimer, "Ach edler hort," mm. 1–8.

expected recorders to sound an octave higher than notated. The first note of the bass part *(G)* is thus realized as a second above the lowest note of a bass recorder "in F," that is, *g* below middle *c'*, if the instrument is tuned to modern pitch standards. The first note of the tenor part *(bb)* is realized as a minor seventh and the first note of the alto part *(g')* as an octave and a fifth above the lowest note on the tenor/alto recorder "in C"; and the first note of the superius part (*d'*) as a fifth above the lowest note on the discant recorder "in G." If the instruments were tuned to pitches we could understand as approximating modern *f, c'* and *g'*, then the piece would sound on four recorders an octave higher than written.

In the 1529 edition of his treatise, Agricola's introduction to the fingering charts for flutes does not give their "normal" pitch, but in the 1545 edition of his treatise, he implies that whereas recorders are tuned to F, C and G, flutes are tuned to G, D and A.[27] It would be convenient if we could explain this difference as simply being caused by the fact that transverse flutes have no hole for the little finger of the lower hand (and, indeed, no thumb hole) and thus lack the lowest note of the recorders in corresponding sizes, even though such an explanation has, of course, no basis in fact. When the reader comes to apply the fingerings Agricola gives in 1529 for the three sizes of flute required for four-part music, however, he will be in for a rude surprise. Agricola's 1529 diagram (fig. 7) for the fingerings on a tenor/alto flute[28] shows *A* (a minor tenth below middle *c'*) as that instrument's lowest note. Thus, the first note of the tenor part in Hofhaimer's "Ach edler hort" (Example 2), written as *bb*, would be played as a minor ninth above the tenor/alto flute's lowest note, and the first note of the altus (*g'*) as an octave and a seventh above the lowest note. On a flute "in D," instead of *bb* and *g'* the two notes will sound *eb″* and *c‴*. If I am correct in assuming that Agricola is explaining the relationship between the written note and the player's fingers, in 1529 he regarded flutes as instruments that transposed not an octave above their written pitch, but an octave and a fourth above their written pitch.

If Agricola did not offer a convincing explanation of this curious state of affairs in his revised 1545 edition, he at least supplied further information which helps us to understand his interpretation of sixteenth-century conventions. In 1545, Agricola offered two sets of diagrams for transverse flutes. The first is described by him as "Sequuntur tres irregulares, harum Tibiarum Scalae, ad Epidiatess[aron] transpositae."[29] The diagram for tenor/alto flute "in D" is given as fig. 8. The second set of diagrams is described as "Sequuntur tres aliae, harum Fistularum, Scalae regulares."[30] The diagram for tenor/alto flute "in D" is given as fig. 9.

27. On this point, see Hettrick, "Agricola's Poetic Discussion," vol. 24, p. 60. I am grateful to Professor Hettrick for his help on this point.

28. Agricola, *Musica,* 1529 edition, fol. B6.

29. "There follow for these flutes three irregular scales, transposed up a fourth." The fingering chart for the tenor/alto flute is given in Agricola, *Musica,* 1545 edition, fol. D3ᵛ.

30. "There follow for these flutes three other, regular scales." The fingering chart for the tenor/alto flute is given in Agricola, *Musica,* 1545 edition, fol. D7.

NOTES (AND TRANSPOSING NOTES) ON THE TRANSVERSE FLUTE   23

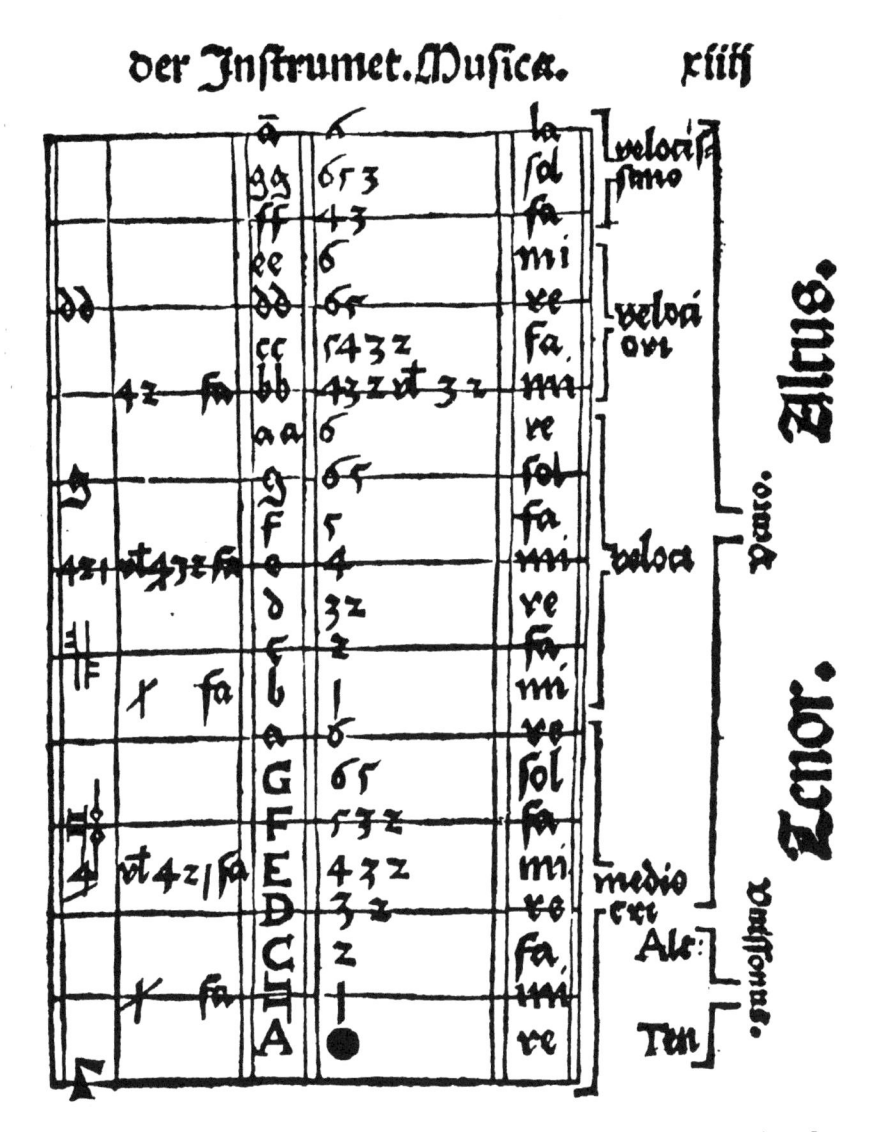

FIGURE 7. Agricola, *Musica instrumentalis deudsch* (1529), fol. B6. Fingering chart for the tenor/alto flute. Photograph courtesy of the New York Public Library.

To take matters up in the order in which Agricola presented them, the table of fingerings shown in fig. 8 (offering scales transposed "up a fourth") actually produces music sounding a fourth lower, or rather an octave and a fifth higher. But while this situation seems utterly bewildering at first glance, the explanation is actually rather simple and easy to understand.

24   JOURNAL OF THE AMERICAN MUSICAL INSTRUMENT SOCIETY

Das erſte Capitel.

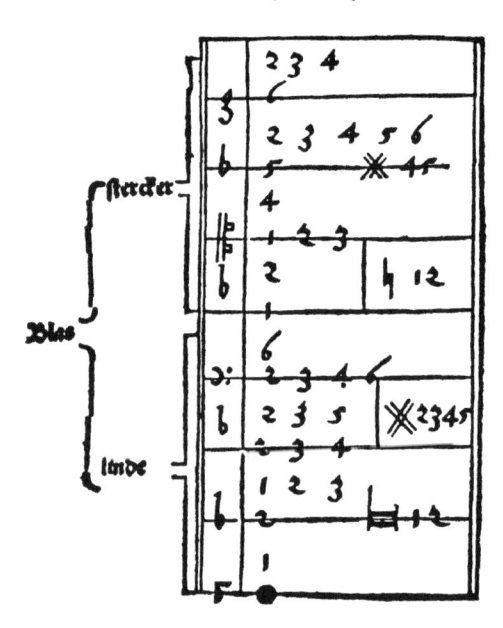

FIGURE 8. Agricola, *Musica instrumentalis deudsch* (1545), fol. D3ᵛ. Fingering chart for the tenor/alto flute transposed "ad Epidiatessaron." Photograph courtesy of the Herzog August Bibliothek Wolfenbüttel.

Comparing the fingering chart for tenor/alto flute playing "a fourth higher" (fig. 8) with Hofhaimer's "Ach edler hort" (example 2), we see that the first note in the tenor is to be played as an octave and a third higher than the lowest note, and the first note in the altus is to be played two octaves above the lowest note, producing on a flute "in D" the notes f'' and d''' rather than bb and g'. In other words, using the fingering chart to play this piece on four flutes would produce a performance in the D-Dorian rather than the G-Dorian mode, and thus the music is transposed, in one sense, a fourth lower, even though the actual notes sound an octave and a fifth higher than the notated pitches.

But from the player's point of view such a transposition makes sense if it is described as using a scale transposed up a fourth, for what a player will do is to imagine that his flute "in D" is actually a flute "in G" tuned a fourth higher. The flute, it should be emphasized, stays the same; it is still a flute sounding "d'''" as its lowest tone. But imagining it a fourth higher "in G"

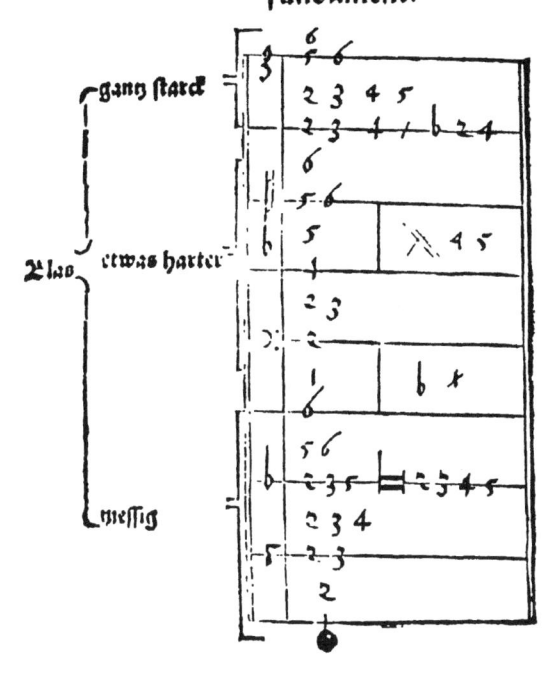

FIGURE 9. Agricola, *Musica instrumentalis deudsch* (1545), fol. D7. Fingering chart for the "untransposed" tenor/alto flute. Photograph courtesy of the Herzog August Bibliothek Wolfenbüttel.

means that from the player's point of view the first note of the tenor can easily be understood as sounding an octave and a third above the fundamental note, and the first note of the altus can easily be understood as two octaves above the fundamental. Clearly, then Agricola's first set of tables (fig. 7), from his 1529 edition, could have been described as presenting scales transposed a fifth higher, even though they create sounds an octave and a fourth higher (or "transposed a fifth lower") than the notation would suggest.[31]

31. In the remainder of this essay, I shall use the terms "transposed down a fourth" and "transposed down a fifth" to describe these procedures.

A part of the complication arises from the fact that Agricola seems to have regarded the flute at "untransposed" pitch as a two-foot, not a four- or eight-foot instrument, for his third set of tables (fig. 9) offers fingerings that will sound two octaves above notated pitch. Thus the tenor flutist would play the first note of Hofhaimer's "Ach edler hort" not a sixth above his lowest note, but an octave and a sixth above his lowest note. And the player of the alto line would first sound a note not an octave and a fourth above his fundamental but two octaves and a fourth above his fundamental. In other words, taking the two-octave transposition into account, the diagrams said to present music up a fourth (fig. 8) and up a fifth (fig. 7) actually present music *down* a fourth and fifth from the "normal, untransposed" version two octaves higher than notated. Agricola's first set of fingering charts will produce a performance of Hofhaimer's "Ach edler hort" in C-Dorian, his second in D-Dorian, and his third in G-Dorian.

We must suppose that sixteenth-century musicians did make use of this convention, if only because Agricola was not writing speculative theory, but describing as simply as he could to his students and the lay audience of sixteenth-century Germany his understanding of musical practices. But why did musicians make use of such an apparently confusing convention? The answer is not difficult to find, once the notion that the transverse flute was regarded as a two-foot instrument is understood. It would be very difficult to perform Hofhaimer's "Ach edler hort," for example, using Agricola's third "untransposed" fingering chart because the piece lies so high for all the instruments. The parts sound almost entirely in the second and third octaves of each instrument's range, and the highest notes are at the very top of Agricola's fingering chart (in the case of the altus), or very nearly so (for the other instruments). In other words the piece would sound unpleasantly shrill, with all the players using "vento velociori" or even breath pressure described as "auffs schnellst/velocissimo," to quote Agricola's characterization of the amount of wind necessary to play in the second and third octave.[32]

Therefore, the music needs to be brought down to a more comfortable range. Agricola's first transposition, from G-Dorian to C-Dorian, brings all the instruments down a fifth, within the comfortable part of their range, but the piece is still virtually unplayable at that pitch level, because the

---

32. See Agricola, *Musica,* 1529 edition, fols. B4ᵛ–B5ᵛ and 1545 edition, fols. D2ᵛ–D4 and D6ᵛ–D7ᵛ, for fingering charts where the amount of breath pressure is indicated for each segment of each instrument's range. Agricola also describes the amount of breath pressure necessary on fol. B4 of the 1529 edition.

discant flute "in A" has prominent B♭'s (written as F's), and the tenor/alto flutes "in D" both have prominent E♭'s (written as B♭'s), a minor ninth above their fundamentals. These are the least successful notes on the transverse flute, since they need to be half-holed,[33] and they can almost never be satisfactorily sounded exactly at pitch or with a tone quality in any way equivalent to that of the other notes. Quite aside from these impossible notes, moreover, all four flutists would need to play as stable scale degrees chromatic notes that are not wholly secure on their instruments. But if the composition is brought "down a fourth," transposed from G-Dorian to D-Dorian, using Agricola's second transposition tables (fig. 8), the piece fits relatively well on all the instruments, not only in terms of range, but also because the most awkward chromatic fingerings are no longer required on the principal destination notes of the song.

In short, Agricola supposed the transverse flute to be a two-foot instrument, playing two octaves above written notation. But since playing in that way meant that much of the secular polyphonic repertory of the early sixteenth century went too high for the instruments, forcing them either to play at the very top of their range or denying them access to the music because it went out of their range entirely, flutists had to transpose downwards much of the music they played in unmixed consorts, to make it fit the instruments better. In 1529, Agricola clearly thought that transposition "down a fifth" was the one most commonly used by flutists. At least that is the implication of the fact that he gave only the one fingering chart, without even warning the unsuspecting reader that transposition was involved.

In the revised edition of 1545, he introduced the third set of fingering charts—those for "untransposed" flutes—with a passage that explicitly declares the first two sets of diagrams to have been transposing tables:

> Volget noch ein ander, besser, und gemeine art, wie man die Claves nach Musicalischer weise, auff diesen Pfeiffen blasen und greiffen soll.

> Weiter mag ich nicht verschweigen
> Sondern noch ein arth anzeigen
> Der obgesagten fundament
> Auff Schweitzerpfeiffen jtzt genent,
> Welchs das gmeinst und leichst geacht
> Drumb hab ichs auch auff die ban bracht
> Las dir es aber nicht faul thun
> Das ich von zweien sage nun,

33. That is, the lowest hole must be only half covered by the finger (● ● ● ● ● ∅).

Und vom dritten gesagt jensmal[34]
Inn der Deudschen Instrumental,
Denn man kan alhie die Scalas
Transponirn, wie im gsang, merck das,[35]
Auch wie es auff Orgeln geschicht
Auff Lauten, wie ich dich bericht,
Und auff den andern so furtan
Derhalben lass fahrn den argwan.
Drumb hab ich sie beid dargestelt
Nim eine welche dir gefelt,
Idoch wil ich reden inn gmein[36]
Diese deucht mich die bequemst sein,
Wie du sie aber solt verstan
Wil ich inn figurn zeigen an,
Und lassen sie herfür draben
Du magst achtung darauff haben.[37]

> *(There follows a second, better and common way for one to finger and sound musical notes on these flutes.*
>
> *Moreover, I do not wish to keep secret, but rather to show still another kind of the regulations explained previously for [the instruments] now called Swiss pipes; this [set of regulations] is thought to be the most common and the easiest, and for that reason I have brought it into the discussion. But do not take it evil that I speak now of two [sets of regulations] and that I spoke earlier of a third in the* Musica instrumentalis deudsch *[of 1529], for here [i.e., with these two sets, or on flutes?] one can transpose the scales as in singing (note that!), and also as is done on organs, on lutes (as I have told you), and so forth; therefore, lay aside your mistrust. For that reason, I have shown you both sets; use whichever pleases you. Nevertheless, I wish to say that in general this [set of regulations] appears to me to be the most convenient. I wish to show you in diagrams how you should understand it, and let it come forth gradually; you ought to study it carefully.)*

The information Agricola offers is by no means exhaustive, but he seems to be saying that he prefers his third set of fingering charts simply because they are the least complicated. He implies, in other words, that he would transpose flute music by two octaves whenever he could, because that transposition is not only the most widespread and the easiest ("das gmeinst und leichst") but also, it seems to him, the most convenient ("Diese

---

34. The marginal comment here reads: "Anno 1529."

35. The marginal comment here reads: "Quemadmodum in cantu, ita in Instrumentis musicis, transpositio cantus fieri potest," that is, "How the transposition of a melody can be accomplished on musical instruments as in singing."

36. The marginal comment here reads: "Fundamentum, huius generis Tibiarum optimum," that is, "The best set of regulations for this kind of flute." I am grateful to Traute Marshall for advice about the translation of the passage by Agricola, and for correcting some of my mistakes.

37. Agricola, *Musica*, 1545 edition, fols. D5ᵛ–D6.

deucht mich die bequemst sein"). Agricola fails to give any reason why transposition should be necessary, but surely the most obvious explanation is the desire of instrumentalists to bring music which otherwise lay too high for them down within the ranges of their instruments, or simply to make the music fit better under the fingers. The latter reason seems to have impelled some sixteenth-century lutenists to transpose chansons and motets to diverse pitches, if Adrian le Roy can be taken as a reliable spokesman. In describing how to intabulate vocal music for the lute, Le Roy went to some pains to explain where compositions in particular modes best fit on the lute, that is, the relationship between notated pitch and the placement of the players' fingers on the strings. From Le Roy's explanation of the technique of intabulation, we can infer that chansons in Dorian mode, for example, were heard not only "in D" and "in G," but also in "E," "A" and "B."[38]

If my explanation of Agricola's practice is correct, then there is some circumstantial evidence to indicate that this convention of transposition was not limited to smaller German cities and to students at Latin schools. Indeed, transposition "down a fourth," set out in Agricola's second transposition table (fig. 8), but the first he gave in his new and improved edition of 1545, may have been more common than any other. At any rate, if flutists normally transposed the music they played "down a fourth," Philibert Jambe de Fer's statement in 1556 that music in flat keys was better for flutes than music in sharp keys can finally be seen to make sense.[39] Jambe de Fer's remark has puzzled modern commentators, for it appeared to be nonsense. The worst notes on keyless Renaissance flutes are those a minor second or a minor ninth above the fundamental note. Since they must be played by half covering the lowest hole, they can almost never be played in tune or with a satisfactory tone quality. On flutes in "G," "D," and "A,"

---

38. See Adrian le Roy, *Les Instructions pour le luth (1574)*, ed. Jean Jacquot, Pierre-Yves Sordes and Jean-Michel Vaccaro, 2 vols. (Paris: Centre National de la Recherche Scientifique, 1977), 1:5–45. Le Roy's procedure is briefly summarized in Howard Mayer Brown's review of this modern edition of Le Roy's treatise, in *Music and Letters* 60 (1979): 475–78. For a similar overview of the possibilities of transposition on the lute (chiefly by using the same fingerings on instruments tuned to various pitches), see the table of transposition prepared by George Bürscher, printed as a single leaf about 1571, and described and illustrated in Martin Staehelin, "Neue Quelle zur Mehrstimmigen Musik des 15. und 16. Jahrhunderts in der Schweiz," *Schweizer Beiträge zur Musikwissenschaft*, series 3, vol. 3 (1978): 82–83 and pl. 12.

39. Jambe de Fer, *Épitome*, ed. Lesure, pp. 48–49, writes apropos transverse flutes: "Le Jeu de b mol . . . est le plus plaisant, facile & naturel. . . . Le Jeu de ♮ quarré . . . n'est si usité, si plaisant, ne si facile."

therefore, Ab's, Eb's and Bb's could not be sounded securely. If, however, flutists normally transposed "down a fourth," the bad notes on the three sizes of instrument would be the relatively uncommon Db (on the bass), Ab (on tenor/alto) and Eb (on discant), a much better compromise than transposing the music "down a fifth," where the impossible notes would be the much more frequently needed Eb (on the bass), Bb (on tenor/alto) and F (discant). In short, Jambe de Fer's statement makes perfect sense if he is writing about consorts of flutes that sound a fourth lower than two octaves above written pitch. Moreover, whereas the transposition a fifth lower is much better for sharp keys (that is, music with finals on A and G), it would still cause greater difficulties than music in flat keys transposed "down a fourth," since in the transposition "down a fifth," the discant flute does not have a secure F.

The hypothesis that flutists more often transposed "down a fourth" rather than "down a fifth" receives some support from the conventions governing the transposition of other instruments in the early sixteenth century. Hans Gerle, for example, included in his *Musica und tabulatur* (second edition, 1546) a table of transposition for viols played in consort that is very similar to Agricola's transposing tables; and Gerle offered it for the same reason.[40] He explained that some of the music he wished to play went too high to fit comfortably on a treble viol with a top string tuned to "*a'*," a tenor/alto viol with a top string tuned to "*d'*," and a bass viol with a top string tuned to "a." Therefore, Gerle devised a table that made it simple to transpose such music down a fourth, so that it would fit better on the five-stringed instruments he preferred. Moreover, this sort of transposition may have become so common among instrumentalists that it was commercially feasible to build keyboard instruments that transposed down a fourth automatically.[41] If John Shortridge's hypothesis is correct (it has by no

40. Hans Gerle, *Musica und Tabulatur, auff die Instrument der kleinen und grossen Geygen, auch Lautten* (3rd, rev. ed., Nuremberg, 1546), fols. j2v–j3. On sixteenth-century conventions of transposition on viols, see Howard Mayer Brown, "Notes (and Transposing Notes) on the Viol in the Early Sixteenth Century," in *Music in Medieval and Early Modern Europe*, ed. Iain Fenlon (Cambridge: Cambridge University Press, 1981), pp. 61–78.

41. See John Shortridge, "Italian Harpsichord Building in the 16th and 17th Centuries," *U.S. National Museum Bulletin*, no. 225 (1960), pp. 95–107. Studies challenging Shortridge's position, or debating the issue, are listed in Brown, "Notes . . . on the Viol," p. 69, note 19.

It seems to me that the most serious drawback to supposing that such transpositions were common everywhere in the sixteenth century is the probability that transverse flutes were much less cultivated in Italy than elsewhere in western Europe. But Italians did play transverse flutes, and sometimes even in consort. Cristoforo da Messisbugo, *Banchetti, composizioni di vivande e apparecchio generale* (Ferrara, 1549), modern edition ed. Fernando Bandini (Venice: Neri Pozza Editore, 1960), for example, lists flutes among the instruments taking

means found universal agreement) many Italian harpsichords in the six-teenth century had automatic transposing keyboards, on which, for exam-ple, *c'* was sounded when the player depressed the key that looked to be *f'* a fourth above. If transposition down a fourth were so common for viol play-ers and flutists, it may be that harpsichord makers were encouraged to build such transposing instruments to accompany other instrumentalists, tnus saving the keyboard player the necessity of using his head.

Still another bit of evidence supports the hypothesis that consorts of flutes often transposed "down a fourth." Like Jambe de Fer's statement about the best keys for flutes, Pierre Attaingnant's criteria for deciding that some of the chansons he published were better for flutes and others better for recorders have never been understood.[42] He seems not to have decided between the two instruments on the basis of poetic content, range, or even mode, and no one has ever offered a convincing explanation of why some compositions were singled out as more appropriate for the one sort of in-strument and some for the other, whereas some compositions were said to be equally good for both.

Since the superius part book alone survives from the set of *Chansons mu-sicales*, it is not possible to reconstruct all the parts of all the chansons. But the majority can be identified, and Anne Smith has listed them all in the order in which they appear in the volumes, along with their ranges, clefs and modes.[43] Even though table 1 thus duplicates information already

---

part at various banquets he arranged in Ferrara in 1529–32; see Howard Mayer Brown, "A Cook's Tour of Ferrara in 1529," *Rivista italiana di musicologia* 10 (1975): 216–41. During the drawing for prizes at the banquet on 24 January 1529, a consort of flutes played; see Brown, *ibid.*, p. 240.

Flutists will understand that transposition "down a fourth" is actually a very easy and practical transposition, since three of the four players in a consort need only imagine that they are playing the next larger size of instrument. That is, the player of the discant flute "in A" can transpose "down a fourth" by using the fingerings of the tenor/alto flute "in D" (what modern players usually call "C fingerings"); players of the tenor/alto flute "in D" can trans-pose "down a fourth" by using the fingerings of the bass flute "in G" (what modern players usually call "F fingerings"); and players of the bass flute "in G" can transpose "down a fourth" by imagining that their parts are written in tenor rather than bass clef. I am grateful to Thomas MacCracken for pointing this fact out to me, for observing that shawm players in the sixteenth century also normally transposed their parts by imagining they were playing the next larger size of instrument, and for offering other good advice about the problem of transposition on wind instruments during the Renaissance.

42. Thomas, "Renaissance Flute," pp. 5–6, and Smith "Renaissancequerflöte," pp. 28–30, for example, both acknowledge the ambiguity of Attaingnant's criteria.

43. Smith, "Renaissancequerflöte," pp. 64–67. Since Smith has listed all the chansons, which are also listed in Brown, *Instrumental Music*, pp. 43–45, and in Heartz, *Attaingnant*, pp. 250–53, I have omitted from table 1 those chansons Attaingnant designated as suitable for both flutes and recorders by marking them "ab".

32   JOURNAL OF THE AMERICAN MUSICAL INSTRUMENT SOCIETY

TABLE 1
Chansons for Flutes or Recorders in Pierre Attaingnant's Anthologies[a]

A. Chansons best for flutes (marked "a" by Attaingnant)

In **Chansons musicales** *(1533)*

2. "J'aymeray qui m'aymera." Nicolas Gombert
    S: $d'-f''$ A: missing T: missing B: missing mode: G-Dorian
5. "Je l'ay aymé." [Pierre Certon]
    Certon, *Chansons polyphoniques . . . Livre I (1535–1539),* ed. Henry Expert and
    Aimé Agnel (Paris: Heugel, 1967), pp. 2–3.
    S: $d'-d''$ A: $g-bb'$ T: $f-g'$ B: $G-d'$ mode: G-Dorian
7. "Si par fortune." Pierre Certon
    Certon, *Chansons polyphoniques,* ed. Expert and Agnel, pp. 4–5.
    S: $d'-d''$ A: $g-a'$ T: $d-f'$ B: $Bb-d'$ mode: G-Dorian
8. "Desir m'assault." Pierre de Manchicourt
    S: $d'-d''$ A: missing T: missing B: missing mode: G-Dorian
10. "En espoir d'avoir mieulx." Nicolas Gombert
    Gombert, *Opera Omnia,* ed. Joseph Schmidt-Görg, vol. 11 (American Institute
    of Musicology, 1975), no. 9 (in D-Dorian).
    S: $d'-eb''$ A: $g-a'$ T: $f-f'$ B: $Bb-c'$ mode: G-Dorian
11. "Aultre que vous de moy ne jouyra"
    S: $c'-c''$ A: missing T: missing B: missing mode: F-Lydian
13. "Hors envieux retirez." Nicolas Gombert
    Gombert, *Opera Omnia,* ed. Schmidt-Görg, vol. 11, no. 17 (in D-Dorian).
    S: e'-f''   A: $a-bb'$ T: $d-f'$ B: $Bb-d'$ mode: G-Dorian
14. "Sur tous regretz." Jean Richafort
    Robert Eitner, ed., *Johann Ott: Ein hundert fünfzehn weltliche . . . Lieder,* 3 vols.
    (Leipzig: Breitkopf und Härtel, 1873–75), vol. 2, no. 78.
    S: $c'-c''$ A: $f-f'$ T: $c-eb'$ B: $G-bb$ mode: D-Dorian
17. "Vous l'ares s'il vous plaist." Adorno
    S: $d'-f''$ A: missing T: missing B: missing mode: G-Dorian
19. "Le printemps faict." Benedictus
    Tenor in The Hague, Koninklijke Bibliothek MS 74.H.7, no. 13.
    S: $d'-g''$ A: missing T: $d-g'$ B: missing mode: G-Dorian
20. "Si ung oeuvre parfait." Claudin de Sermisy
    S: $d'-c''$ A: missing T: missing B: missing mode: F-Lydian
25. "Veu le grief mal." Guillaume Le Heurteur
    Albert Seay, ed., *Pierre Attaingnant. Transcriptions of Chansons for Keyboard*
    (American Institute of Musicology, 1961), pp. 181–82.
    S: $g'-g''$ A: $d'-c''$ T: $a-a'$ B: $c-d'$ mode: D-Dorian
26. "Par trop aymer." Benedictus
    S: $g'-g''$ A: missing T: missing B: missing mode: D-Dorian

NOTES (AND TRANSPOSING NOTES) ON THE TRANSVERSE FLUTE   33

27. "La plus gorgiaze du monde"
    S: *g'–bb'*   A: missing T: missing B: missing   mode: G-Dorian
29. "Souvent amour me livre." Guillaume Le Heurteur
    Leta E. Miller, ed., *Thirty-Six Chansons by French Provincial Composers, 1529–1550* (Madison, Wisconsin: A-R Editions, 1981), pp. 50–51.
    S: *e'–c"*   A: *f–g'*   T: *e–d'*   B: *F–g*   mode: F-Lydian
30. "Si je ne dors je ne puis vivre." Jean Le Gendre
    S: *f'–e"*   A: missing T: missing B: missing   mode: G-Dorian

In Vingt et sept chansons musicales *(1533)*

3. "Parle qui veult." Claudin de Sermisy
    Sermisy, *Opera Omnia,* ed. Gaston Allaire and Isabelle Cazeaux, vols. 3 and 4 (American Institute of Musicology, 1974), vol. 4, no. 123.
    S: *f'–f"*   A: *b–a'*   T: *g–g'*   B: *A–d'*   mode: G Mixolydian
7. "Amours amours vous me faictes." Nicolas Gombert
    Gombert, *Opera Omnia,* ed. Schmidt-Görg, vol. 11, no. 10.
    S: *d'–f"*   A: *g–c"*   T: *g–f'*   B: *d–d'*   mode: G-Dorian
13. "Pren de bon cueur." Pierre de Manchicourt
    S: *f'–f"*   A: *a–bb'*   T: *g–g'*   B: *c–d'*   mode: G-Dorian
16. "Jectes moy sur l'herbette." Lupi
    S: *d'–g"*   A: *f–a'*   T: *d–g'*   B: *Bb–f'*   mode: G-Dorian
20. "Elle veult donc." Claudin de Sermisy
    Sermisy, *Opera Omnia,* ed. Allaire and Cazeaux, vol. 3, no. 47.
    S: *d'–d"*   A: *f–g'*   T: *f–f'*   B: *G–bb*   mode: G-Dorian
23. "Hayne et amour." Pierre Vermont
    S: *d'–f"*   A: *f–bb'*   T: *g–g'*   B: *Bb–c'*   mode: G-Dorian
24. "Pourquoy donc ne fringuerons nous." Passereau
    Anthology de la chanson parisienne au XVIe siècle, ed. François Lesure *et al* (Monaco: Oiseau Lyre, 1953), no. 4.
    S: *f'–f"*   A: *g–bb'*   T: *f–g'*   B: *c–d'*   mode: G-Dorian
26. "Je n'avoye point." Claudin de Sermisy
    Sermisy, *Opera Omnia,* ed. Allaire and Cazeaux, vol. 3, no. 76.
    S: *f'–f"*   A: *bb–a'*   T: *g–e'*   B: *G–bb*   mode: G-Dorian
28. "Si bon amour merite recompense." Jacotin
    S: *e'–d"*   A: *f–g'*   T: *f–f'*   B: *Bb–g*   mode: F-Lydian

B. Chansons best for recorders (marked "b" by Attaingnant)

In Chansons musicales *(1533)*

6. "De noz deux cuers." Jean Guyon
    Miller, ed., *Thirty-Six Chansons,* pp. 31–33.
    S: *d'–d"*   A: *e–a'*   T: *c–f'*   B: *A–c'*   mode: A-"Aeolian"

(continued)

TABLE 1 *(continued)*

9. "O desloialle dame." François Bourguignon
     S: *d'–d"*   A: missing   T: missing   B: missing   mode: G-Mixolydian
16. "Puis que j'ay perdu mes amours." Lupi
     Second livre (Paris: Attaingnant, 1536), no. 24.
     S: *c'–d"*   A: *g–g'*   T: *f–f'*   B: *A–c'*   mode: G-Mixolydian
22. "Eslongné suys de mes amours"
     S: *c'–d"*   A: missing   T: missing   B: missing   mode: G-Mixolydian

In Vingt et sept chansons musicales *(1533)*

18. "Troys jeunes bourgeoises." Guillaume Le Heurteur
     Howard Mayer Brown, ed., *Theatrical Chansons* (Cambridge, Mass.: Harvard
     University Press, 1963), no. 57.
     S: *f'–e"*   A: *f–a'*   T: *g–f'*   B: *G–a*   mode: G-Mixolydian
19. "Allez souspirs." Claudin de Sermisy
     S: *e'–c"*   A: *g–g'*   T: *f–e'*   B: *A–a*   mode: A-"Aeolian"

[a]Table 1 lists the chanson incipit; the composer's full name (in brackets if the attribution
does not appear in one of Attaingnant's anthologies); a single modern edition, if one exists,
or, in the case of the compositions from *Chansons musicales*, a sixteenth-century edition that
includes all the parts; the range of each voice; and the mode of each chanson (no distinction
is made between authentic and plagal forms of each mode). Smith, "Renaissancequerflöte,"
pp. 64–67, includes all the chansons in both volumes, and furnishes information about the
clef of each voice.
      An anthology of chansons from *Vingt et sept chansons* is published in modern edition as
Bernard Thomas, ed., *Pierre Attaingnant (1533), Fourteen Chansons for Four Recorders or Voices
ATTB* (London: London Pro Musica Edition, 1972). Three of the chansons from table 1B
(no. 6 from *Chansons musicales*, and nos. 18 and 19 from *Vingt et sept chansons*) are published
in a modern edition as Howard Mayer Brown, ed., *Chansons for Recorder* (New York: Associated Music, 1964).

published, it will nevertheless be helpful in seeking an explanation for Attaingnant's criteria for selection. Table 1 lists all the chansons for flutes or
recorders published by Attaingnant, arranged not in the order in which
they appear in his volumes, but grouped according to the categories devised by Attaingnant: section A, that is, names those chansons marked "a"
in Attaingnant's volumes, signifying they are better on flutes; and section
B names the chansons marked "b," better for recorders.
     Table 1 reveals, first of all, that virtually all the chansons singled out as
better for flutes were in fact composed in flat keys. There is only one exception among the twenty-one compositions: Claudin's "Parle qui veult" (*Vingt
et sept chansons*, no. 3) in G-Mixolydian. Moreover, the chansons for recorders are all in sharp keys. Without exception their finals occur on G or

A, and they lack any key signatures. The chansons appropriate for both kinds of instruments include some in flat and some in sharp keys. They evidently offer the instrumentalist some exceptions to the general rule coordinating accidentals with type of instrument.

In the second place, table 1 suggests some guidelines about the ranges most appropriate for the two kinds of instruments. Some of the superius parts in the chansons for flutes go as high as *f″* or *g″*, whereas those for recorders never ascend above *d″* or *e″*. Some of the alto parts in the chansons for flutes go as high as *bb′*, whereas those for recorders never ascend above *g′* or *a′*. And some of the bass parts in the chansons for flutes go as high as *d′* (and one as high as *f′*), whereas those for recorders never ascend above *c′*. Even though Agricola's fingering charts take the discant recorder up to *f″*, the tenor/alto up to *bb′*, and the bass up to *d′*, these were evidently not secure notes on recorders played in consort. Since Attaingnant took pains to avoid those notes, we may assume that his choice of an appropriate instrument related to some extent to range.

Table 1, in other words, does show that flutes were thought to be better in some modes than others, and that their ranges were somewhat different from those of recorders. But to understand Attaingnant's intentions better, we must look carefully at one chanson in each of his two principal categories.

Taking Claudin's "Elle veult donc" (the beginning is shown in example 3)[44] as a sample of chansons in category A, we can see immediately that the chanson could not be played "untransposed" on a consort of flutes tuned in "G," "D" and "A." The ranges of the superius and altus parts would necessitate playing in the very highest register of flutes treated as two-foot instruments. Moreover, the frequent Bb's in the superius part, and the frequent Eb's in the alto and tenor parts make the chanson nearly impossible to perform on two-foot flutes. Nor does transposing the chanson "down a fifth" from G-Dorian to C-Dorian make performance any easier, for while the range is more convenient for the consort of flutes, the discant flute will find it nearly impossible to play the written F's and difficult to play so many exposed written Bb's; and the tenor/alto flutes will find it impossible to play the written Bb's. Transposing the chanson "down a fourth," however, will not only bring the chanson down to a good range for all three sizes of flute—albeit a range higher than that we have hitherto supposed Renaissance flutes normally used—but will keep all principal pitches to the good

44. After Claudin de Sermisy, *Opera Omnia*, ed. Gaston Allaire and Isabelle Cazeaux, vol. 3 (American Institute of Musicology, 1974), pp. 74–76.

EXAMPLE 3. Claudin de Sermisy, "Elle veult donc," mm. 1–11.

notes on the instrument; this transposition avoids the impossible notes altogether.

In short, if flutes were really thought of as being in "G," "D" and "A" in relation to written music (and no evidence known to me contradicts that assumption), and if we must choose between "untransposed two-foot" performance or transposition "down a fourth or fifth"—the only transpositions Agricola explicitly mentions and hence the only transpositions documented as having been applied to flutes in the first half of the sixteenth century—then "Elle veult donc" can only have been played "down a fourth" on a consort of flutes. On the other hand, the designation of this chanson as "plus convenable à la fleuste d'allemant" implies that it is less apt for a consort of recorders, and it is not clear why that should have been thought to be true, especially since "Elle veult donc" is one of the chansons that does not go above d'' in the superius, g' in the tenor and alto, or bb in the bass. But then Attaingnant did not say that the chansons marked "a" were impossible to play on the recorder, only that they were more convenient on the flute.

Similarly, Claudin's "Allez souspirs" (the beginning is given as example 4),[45] marked with a "b" to signify that it is more convenient for recorders than flutes, fits an untransposed consort of recorders very nicely, all the parts coming comfortably within the range of each of the three sizes of instrument tuned in "F," "C" and "G." Like "Elle veult," "Alez souspirs" cannot be played on flutes as two-foot instruments sounding two octaves above written pitch, but it would not be impossible to play on a consort of flutes transposed either "down a fourth" or "down a fifth." In short, the chanson may be more comfortable on recorders, but it is not impossible on transposing flutes. And in like manner, all the chansons marked "ab" in Attaingnant's volumes fit recorder consorts as well as consorts of flutes transposed either "a fourth or a fifth down," though none could comfortably be played "at pitch," that is, two octaves above the written pitches.

So Attaingnant's enigmatic classification scheme, and Jambe de Fer's apparently meaningless remark about the propensity of flutes to play in flat keys can both be understood once we know the meaning of Agricola's bewildering fingering charts. And all three primary bits of evidence make good sense only if we suppose that consorts of flutes normally operated as transposing instruments, sounding music an octave and a fourth or fifth higher than written, that is, at transpositions a fourth or fifth below their regular two-foot pitches. Indeed, the evidence suggests that transpositions "down a fourth" must have been more common than transpositions "down

45. After Sermisy, *Opera Omnia*, 3:1–2.

EXAMPLE 4. Claudin de Sermisy, "Allez souspirs," mm. 1–18.

a fifth," which means that flutes, like viols and harpsichords in the early sixteenth century, often adjusted the written music to fit more comfortably on
their instruments, and in exactly the same way.[46] Praetorius, Mersenne and
the other late sixteenth- and seventeenth-century writers do not make any
reference to these practices. By then, older conventions may well have died
out and new ones have taken their place. Indeed, Jambe de Fer's statement
that the tenor/alto flute often played top parts[47] (Jambe de Fer does not
even mention the smallest flute "in A") already signals the passing of an old
order; and Mersenne seems to have known only two sizes of flute, those "in
G" and "in D." Moreover, Aurelio Virgiliano included information about
transposition to almost every pitch, so the special character of transpositions by fourth and fifth seems already to have been broken by the end of
the century, although in one passage of his encyclopedic work, Praetorius
at least implies that the easiest (and hence most common) intervals of
transposition were those of a fourth or fifth.[48] But the traditions and conventions of later times should not be allowed to obscure what happened in
the early sixteenth century. Indiscriminately mixing descriptions of standard practices written a hundred years apart may only serve to hide what
really happened, preventing us from ever knowing which conventions
changed, and which stayed the same.

The University of Chicago

46. No sixteenth- or seventeenth-century writer makes an explicit distinction between
the way flutes played in consort transposed, and the way a single flute playing with other
instruments and voices transposed. The conventions of transposition "down a fourth" and
"down a fifth," as I have explained them, clearly apply best to consorts of like instruments
(although I have suggested the possibility that such transpositions were common among viol
and keyboard players as well). But when a single transverse flute played in a mixed consort,
presumably it normally sounded one octave (according to Praetorius) or two octaves (according to Agricola) above written pitch. Agricola's statement that he preferred "untransposed" (that is, two-foot) flutes may possibly mean that he was more accustomed to hearing
the flute as a single instrument in a mixed consort than as one member of a family of four.

47. Jambe de Fer, *Épitome*, ed. Lesure, p. 53, explains apropos recorders that "la partie
du dessus ne se joue sus les tailles & haute contre comme en lautre;" that is, that treble parts
are not played on tenor/alto recorders, as is done on flutes. Thus, he reveals only indirectly
that he thought the flute "in D" the most appropriate instrument to play top parts.

48. Praetorius, *Syntagma musicum*, 2: fol. 9, complains that during church services, when
the organist transposes by a second or third, the cantor can easily cause a concerted composition to start on the wrong pitch, so that the instrumentalists cannot come in, because they
are not familiar with transposition by a second or a third. "Sintemahl," he writes, "es etlichen
sawer und schwehr gnug wird, einen Cantum *per Quartam* oder *Quintam* zu *transponieren,*
und machen also wol gar eine *Confusion,* oder doch sonsten erbärmliche Arbeit" (in Blumenfeld's somewhat free translation, p. 3: "To be sure, it is difficult and onerous enough for
some of them just to transpose a part by a fourth or a fifth, and even this simple transposition often engenders confusion and results in pitiful playing").

Part V
Notation

[17]

DIATONIC *FICTA*

Margaret Bent*

1. INTRODUCTION

This is a preliminary study of how what we call pitch was conceptualised in the fourteenth to sixteenth centuries. Its central concern is with vocally conceived, contrapuntally based polyphony around 1500, and our notational access to it. It does not deal directly with monophony (which only rarely compels a distinction between relative and fixed sounds) or with instrumental music and tablatures (which, for practical reasons, had to work with a preselected repertory of sounds). It attempts to combine some realities of performance with the testimony of contemporary theorists.[1]

Late-medieval and renaissance musicians had a much richer arsenal of words and concepts for what we, since only the eighteenth century, have subsumed under the umbrella terms pitch and rhythm. When we try to translate *sonus, vox, corda, nota, clavis, littera, punctus, locus, situs, gradus, phthongus, psophos,* and so on, as pitch, step, note and tone, we lose shadings of difference among the concepts of actual sounds, graphic or mnemonic representations of sound areas or of discrete sounds, sounds defined physically, and fixed or relative points defined in musically functional relationship to each other.

*See also some clarifications and refinements by the same author, in 'Diatonic *ficta* revisited: Josquin's *Ave Maria* in context', *Music Theory Online* (http://www.societymusictheory.org/mto/), September 1996, reprinted in her *Counterpoint, Composition, and Musica Ficta* (London and New York: Routledge, 2002), chapter 4, and the introduction to that volume, especially pp. 18–29.

[1]   I warmly thank Professor Harold Powers for many formative and stimulating conversations while these thoughts were taking shape. Professor Edward Lowinsky graciously engaged in a lively correspondence in which he gave me the benefit of his experience and reactions to a more informal statement of my hypothesis. Many other colleagues, students and friends have helped and encouraged this enterprise by their comments and criticisms; I beg to defer the pleasant duty of thanking them by name until I have the opportunity to present a more extended and fully documented study. Two summer seminars under the auspices of the National Endowment for the Humanities provided a congenial workshop for performing from original notation and exploring practical *ficta* applications. Earlier versions of this paper were read at New York University in November 1982, subsequently at other institutions, and in 1983 at Oxford and at the Annual Meeting of the American Musicological Society in Louisville.

Margaret Bent

This list avoids making a firm link between each of these terms and a
modern definition, because usage varies both between theorists and
over the late-medieval period. These distinctions have largely lost
their force for us, now that our letter names are inflexibly coupled, at
least for most theoretical purposes, to standard frequency and equal
temperament, even if there are still live traditions of pure intonation
for voices and strings.[2] A similar point can be made about durational
terms: the word 'rhythm' is almost totally absent from late-medieval
music theory, and its sixteenth-century application is confined to the
Greek poetic sense that was still primary for Mersenne in 1636.
What we now gather under this single term was likewise covered by a
variety of terms – *mensura, valore, proportio, relatio* – but with the
difference that our view of 'rhythm' remains more dependent on
context than does our view of 'pitch'. Indeed, the terms 'pitch' and
'rhythm' are not parallel for the musical dimensions they denote for
us; an isolated note has pitch, while without context it cannot have
rhythm but only duration. While we deal with pitch relationships on
many levels, our notions of pitch *per se* are more inflexibly coupled to
physically measurable standards than are our notions of duration;
hence the asymmetry of our tendency to treat pitch and rhythm as
comparable dimensions of music. For many modern musicians, the
isolated sounding of a specific frequency will evoke a pitch-label
letter (such as 'A') but cannot, without context, be defined as a note
value (such as a semibreve). During performances of the older
repertory we feel less bound to adhere rigidly to the metronome than
to the tuning fork. Our culture reveres the idea of 'absolute pitch',[3]
even if we may individually recognise its liabilities, but it has not
cultivated a comparable sense of absolute duration. For renaissance
vocal polyphony we cannot assume a fixed frequency anchorage as

[2] One fairly constant distinction is invoked by Calvin Bower to demonstrate that 'The
    translator has failed to distinguish between Guido's concept of qualitative pitch (*vox*) –
    sound defined by the intervals surrounding it – and discrete note (*nota*) – sound defined by
    a point on the system of a monochord and signified by a letter. Thus a subtle, but
    fundamental dualism of medieval musical thought has been obscured.' Review in *Journal of
    the American Musicological Society* (hereafter *JAMS*), 35 (1982), p. 164.
[3] Natasha Spender describes the faculty as a 'sensory and aesthetic life-enhancer' whose
    absence she finds analogous to colour blindness in an artist – an extreme statement of a
    common and wholly modern prejudice; the author finds no problem for her 'absolutist'
    acceptance of the modern phenomenon in the fact that 'a listener with absolute pitch
    would now be disoriented to hear a C major work in the pitch of Mozart's day'; s.v.
    'Absolute pitch', *The New Grove Dictionary of Music and Musicians*, ed. S. Sadie, 20 vols.
    (London, 1980).

2

Diatonic *ficta*

part of a note's definition, its 'A-ness'; the selection of frequency for a performance may be subject only to practical constraints. Nor can equal temperament or enharmonic equivalence underlie our presumptions about the equation of letter names with fixed points. While equal temperament may indeed serve to demonstrate examples of renaissance music without impairing their general sense except with respect to purity of intonation and slight distortion of interval size, this paper presumes that counterpoint was conceived without the notion of enharmonic equivalence between sharps and flats, without the danger of confusion between tritone and diminished fifth, and without the deceptive short cuts of keyboard-based thinking which can impoverish our intellectual understanding of this music.[4]

For a correct realisation of early vocal polyphony, its staff notation cannot be assumed to have the same connotations as ours, either for conveying the positions of tones and semitones, or for conveying pitch-points that can be transferred mechanically to the keyboard or into modern score. In many senses, we have now isolated and fixed the single note with respect to frequency and prescription; those things formerly depended on context, not only for purposes of construing musical function, as is the case for us, but also for their actual sounding realisation, in much the same way as did durations in mensural notation.

2. MEANINGS OF LETTERS

Alphabetical letters served to represent sounds in two different ways: as labels for separate points on the monochord and as names for moveable steps within adjacent areas of the gamut.

---

[4] Carl Dahlhaus has addressed a number of such questions. The following quotations from his 'Tonsystem und Kontrapunkt um 1500', *Jahrbuch des Staatlichen Instituts für Musikforschung preussischer Kulturbesitz 1969*, ed. D. Droysen (Berlin, 1970), pp. 7–17, are offered as samples rather than summaries of his important distinctions between counterpoint, tonal and tuning systems:
'Ein System ist . . . ein Inbegriff von Relationen, nicht von bloßen Bestandteilen.' '. . . Tonsysteme als Systeme von Tonrelationen [beruhen] auf Prinzipien, die nicht an einen bestimmten, immer gleichen Tonbestand gebunden zu sein brauchen. Form und Material sind nicht selten unabhängig voneinander.' 'Ein Tonsystem muß andererseits von der Stimmung oder Temperatur unterschieden werden, in der es erscheint oder sich verwirklicht. Eine Stimmung ist gleichsam die akustische Außenseite; und sie kann manchmal, wenn auch nicht immer, mit einer anderen vertauscht werden, ohne daß das

3

Margaret Bent

(1) Letters on monochord diagrams mark proportionally derived, non-equidistant points which carry no connotations of scale or musical function. They are like labels on a geometric diagram. The earliest medieval monochord treatises are quite inconsistent in their use of letter labels, and it was only by the time of Odo and Guido that some consistency of labelling began to result from the perceived convenience of aligning gamut letters with monochord points. Many early monochord tunings assign to those points letters which correspond neither to our usage, wherein letters connote fixed semitone positions (B–C, E–F), nor to the late-medieval gamut with its often similar results but different rationale. The choice of letters for monochord points was in principle arbitrary (as Prosdocimus and Ugolino show by their naming of the *ficta* positions: see below) but, because the sounds resulting from the points on the monochord and the norms for steps of the scale did approximately coincide more often than not, late-medieval theory usually brought them into alignment. The convenience of that alignment should not blind us to the fact that they are different in derivation and potentially different in meaning.[5]

Even the points on the monochord are norms that may be deviated from in actual practice: they represent relationships derived from one of several possible starting-points, where the principle of tuning successive adjacent simultaneities would have resulted in frequent shifting of a comma position that is static in any one 'demonstration' monochord tuning, and which would therefore yield an often inexact correspondence between an actual sound and its 'official' monochord position. This is surely what Prosdocimus meant in his striking passage on the infinity of sounds[6] and what theorists from

Tonsystem, dessen äußere Darstellung sie ist, aufgehoben oder auch nur in seiner musikalischen Bedeutung modifiziert wäre.'

5 See C. D. Adkins, 'The Theory and Practice of the Monochord,' Ph.D. dissertation (Iowa, 1963), especially the table facing p. 94, which documents from a wide range of theorists both before and after Guido the use of letters as monochord labels with the semitones between different letters from our scale.

6 'Reperiuntur etiam tamen alii diversi modi cantandi ab istis et etiam inter se, quos scribere foret valde difficile et forte impossibile, eo quod tales diversimodi cantandi quodammodo infiniti sint, et diversis diversimode delectabiles, qua propter insurgit diversitas componentium, et quia intelectus noster infinita capere non potest, cum non sit infinite capacitas sed finite, eo quod aliter in hoc intelectui divino adequaretur, quod non est dicendum. Pro tanto huiusmodi modi a scriptura relinquendi sunt, nec adhuc scribi possent propter sui infinitatem . . . Scire autem ubi hec signa [of *musica ficta*] dulcius cadunt auri tue dimitto, quia de hoc regula dari non potest, cum hec loca quodammodo infinita sint' (Prosdocimus, *Contrapunctus*, IV, V; ed. J. Herlinger, who very kindly made his

4

Diatonic *ficta*

Guido to Ornithoparcus meant when they confined to an elementary level the use of the monochord for picking out notes to be sung. It is inadequate beyond that elementary stage, presumably because it cannot supply for the inexperienced singer the component of aural and contrapuntal skill which he must bring to bear upon his reading of the notated pitches, just as, again, the metronome may have a role in rehearsal but will not be adhered to in a 'musical' performance.[7]

Prosdocimus tuned his monochord first according to *musica recta*, thus acknowledging an alignment between the notional content of monochord and scale, to produce the sounds normally available and normally needed. These were then labelled with the letters of their corresponding steps on the gamut, Gamma, A–G, a–g, aa–ee, with B♭ and B♮ for all except the lowest B. He then gave two methods of deriving the *ficta* pitches interspersed between the *rectas*. First he derived what we would call flats, with the minor semitone preceding the major, labelled H K I L M N O P Q R S T V(i.e., in order of derivation rather than of strictly left-to-right resulting position, H being the bridge) with no octave repetition of letters. Then he derived what we would call sharps, labelled X Y Z 1–9, ☉, ⦹. After discussing the shortcomings of each method he ended by combining them. These further points were nowhere explained or labelled as

work available to me in advance of publication). The above quotations embody the revisions of 1425 to the 1413 treatise. See also E. de Coussemaker, *Scriptorum de musica medii aevi nova series* (hereafter CS) (Paris, 1864–76), III, pp. 197–8.

[7] Guido recommends use of the monochord in his prologue to the Antiphoner: 'Duos enim colores ponimus, crocum scilicet & rubeum, per quos colores valde utilem tibi regulam trado, per quam aptissime cognosces de omni neuma & unaquaque voce, de quali tono sit, & de quali littera monochordi: si tamen, ut valde est opportunum, monochordum & tonorum formulas in frequenti habeas usu' (M. Gerbert, *Scriptores ecclesiastici de musica* (hereafter GS), Saint Blaise, 1784, II, 36a). But in the *Epistola Michaeli* he qualifies this advice: 'Ad inveniendum igitur ignotum cantum, beatissime Frater! prima & vulgaris regula haec est, si litteras, quas quaelibet neuma habuerit, in monochordo sonaveris, atque ab ipso audiens tamquam ab homine magistro dicere poteris. Sed puerulis ista est regula, & bona quidem incipientibus, pessima autem perseverantibus. Vidi enim multos acutissimos philosophos, qui sed quia in hac sola regula confisi sunt, non dico musici, sed neque cantores umquam fieri, vel nostros psalmistas puerulos imitari potuerunt (GS II, pp. 44b–45a). Translations of both passages in O. Strunk, *Source Readings in Music History* (New York, 1950), pp. 119, 123.

Ornithoparcus writes (in Dowland's English translation): 'The Monochord was chiefly invented for this purpose, to be judge of Musical voices and intervals: as also to try whether the song be true or false: furthermore, to shew haire-braind false Musitians their errors, and the way of attaining the truth. Lastly, that children which desire to learne Musicke, may have an easie meanes to it, that it may intice beginners, direct those that be forward, and so make of unlearned learned', *A Compendium of Musical Practice*, ed. G. Reese and S. Ledbetter (New York, 1973), I. 9.

5

Margaret Bent

inflections or alterations of their *recta* neighbours.[8] What Prosdocimus produced here (Figure 1) was in no sense an operational scale but rather an arsenal of pitches for demonstration purposes, preselected in the knowledge of musical functions – a selection from which, in practice, singers would need to depart infinitely. His use of the term *fictas musicas* for what we would call 'black notes' is further inconsistent with his clarification elsewhere that *musica ficta*, properly defined, embraces the whole 'accidental' system (see below) including the notes common to both *recta* and *ficta*. He used it here – as we do more generally – because there was simply no other way for him to designate those sounds that were residual after the *recta* ones had been set up. While this distinction was necessary for his discussion of monochord tuning, it had no place in the conceptualisation of hexachords for their principal purpose, namely as mnenonics for vocal performance.

Figure 1   Prosdocimus's monochord division showing superimpositions of *recta* and both *ficta* divisions (ratios only approximate here)

The monochord is the instrument of reference for medieval theory, and should not be mistaken for being merely a primitive form of our keyboard. It could never have been a practical performance instrument for polyphony.[9] Even if the string of a monochord was often about a yard long, there was no standard for its even approximate tension or frequency. And even if two monochords were tuned with true Pythagorean ratios, their resulting frequencies could be slightly different if those ratios were applied from a unison by a different route through the spiral of fifths.

---

[8]   *Parvus tractatulus de modo monachordum dividendi*; I again thank Professor Herlinger for access to the typescript of his new edition of this treatise. Ugolino's *Tractatus monochordi* (ed. A. Seay, *Corpus Scriptorum de Musica* (hereafter CSM), 7, III, pp. 227–53) assigns yet a different set of letters to his *recta* and *ficta* divisions. See also A. Hughes, 'Ugolino: the Monochord and *musica ficta*', *Musica Disciplina*, 23 (1969), pp. 21–39 and M. Lindley, 'Pythagorean Intonation and the Rise of the Triad', *R.M.A. Research Chronicle*, 16 (1980), pp. 4–61, for the systems of Prosdocimus and Ugolino, and n. 21 below.

[9]   Adkins ('Monochord') reviews the practical uses of the monochord in his chapter 7, but the pictorial evidence to which he refers does not weaken the general statement made here. It might be suggested that for purposes of theoretical demonstration it was symbolically important that the monochord remain essentially a monophonic instrument (despite later applications of the word to polychordal instruments). It precluded not only the checking of simultaneities, but also the efficient comparison of successive sounds.

Diatonic *ficta*

(2) The letters of the gamut, however, stand for steps on a ladder (*scala*), notated as graphically equidistant lines and spaces on the staff, a visual model of the ladder. These, in turn, stand for moveable points in a sound-area to be traversed: B fa and ♮ mi are two different routes between A and C.[10]

These two uses of the same series of alphabetical letters did roughly coincide in practice for much of the time. Especially in the later middle ages, as stated above, theorists tended to align them for most practical purposes, while usually keeping them separate in formal explanations. The similar musical results have blunted our sense of the different origins and function of labels on the monochord and letter-names in the *scala*, and have led us to assume that both can indeed merge into the convenient security of modern letter-names, with their more rigid coupling to frequency and temperament, even though post-renaissance music theory has of course respected comparable distinctions at many levels. It is for reasons such as this that we should beware of assuming that older concepts and terminology are inadequate to their purpose, and of being too hasty to resort to our own theoretical equipment.[11]

3. STAFF, HEXACHORDS, *clavis*

The lines and spaces of the staff represent points that look more equidistant than they sound; neither formerly nor now are they

---

[10] They are not, normally, mutually accessible; the only way to travel between two nearby stations may be to ride back to a junction where their lines intersect. A note's presence in the system does not guarantee that it will be accessible from all points.

Dahlhaus has noted that the unqualified letter-names also include 'altered' pitches: 'Zu Costeleys chromatischer Chanson', *Die Musikforschung*, 16 (1963), pp. 253–65, n. 37 and *passim*.

[11] The linking of monochord points by Prosdocimus and others with the corresponding 'places' of *musica recta* is a concession much less extreme than that of Johannes Boen's treatise of 1357 (ed. W. Frobenius, *Johannes Boens Musica und seine Konsonanzlehre*, Freiburger Schriften zur Musikwissenschaft, 1971), which fixes, as would be necessary on a keyboard, what would result if the system were restrained from the fluctuations which may occur in *a cappella* vocal practice. Despite a few such attempts to equate actual points with notional *recta* sounds, it remains clear that, except for such purposes as monochord demonstration in principle, we are indeed dealing with the *recta* 'scale' as a set of relationships rather than as a pre-tuned system. Until late fifteenth-century keyboard-influenced attempts at reconciling the systems, Boen was virtually alone in attempting to expound the monochord and the gamut in a single operation, as distinct from using the gamut letters to label the monochord. He resorted to some unusual vocabulary in so doing, e.g. *mansio* (= lunar mansion?), and *extorquere*, for the removal of sounds from those proper places.

7

Margaret Bent

spatially differentiated according to whether the steps are to be a tone or a semitone apart. The points on the monochord sound more equidistant than they look. Indeed, one single 'place' on the staff serves now for one sound, now for another, of what are two distinct points on the monochord, such as B♭, B♮. That much we have inherited, and the letter-name associated with a staff position may thus stand for different sounds at different times. But we name those differences in relation to letter-norms, F♯ as a modified F, B♭ as a modified B; late-medieval nomenclature, however, could express such differences neither for the monochord, where each point had an independent and indeed arbitrary label, nor on the scale, where the letter B served the whole area between A and C.[12]

A staff position represents a moveable step on the ladder, and the letter-name, *littera*, is a functional label for that moveable step. But the interval relationships among the several rungs on the ladder were articulated only by superimposing on it a network of overlapping hexachords or hexachord segments; hexachordal mutation is a means of negotiating the gamut. Any melodic progression conceivable within or necessitated by the understood rules and limits of late-medieval counterpoint could be solmised, by extension of the system. Hexachords provide a functional context for semitone locations which have been predetermined by musical considerations, but they do not in themselves determine what the sounds will be. The hexachordal *voces* are the means by which those sounds become practically accessible in vocal polyphony, just as, by analogy, fingering is the means by which small groups of notes are physically negotiated on instruments.

Hexachords articulate the scale of the letters by means of the *clavis*, often described as *vox* plus *littera*;[13] this clef or key yokes together letter-names of scale-positions and interval-specific hexachords for as long as is appropriate. The *clavis* functions like a key in a lock, or

---

12   See notes 8, 10 and 21. Only for the distinct purposes of tablature did letter-names thus indicate adjacency of keys by attaching genitive endings, as in *fis*; these endings often selected the 'wrong' enharmonic spelling of a note, showing that they were less tied to musical function than to keyboard designation.

13   'Clavis est littera localis per voces rectificata' (*clavis* is a letter of a place [on the staff] adjusted to it by means of *voces* [contextual hexachord members]), Adam von Fulda, GS III, p. 344. Du Cange gives *rectificata* = corrected (1332). 'A Key is a thing compacted of a Letter and a Voyce; . . . A Key is the opening of a Song, because like as a Key opens a dore, so doth it the Song' (Ornithoparcus, *Compendium*, I.3; see p. xxv for sources of these formulations in Guido and other earlier theorists).

8

Diatonic *ficta*

like gear-wheels, or indeed like fingered permutations of frets and strings, to make a system operative and to bring two or more different cycles into temporary functioning reconciliation. It has rich parallels with the theory and practice of medieval calendar determination.[14]

It is only when our modern staff lines are labelled by a clef that they take on letter identities and the semitone positions we have assigned to the letter series; similarly, then, it was only when yoked with hexachord syllables that the letters acquired unequivocal tone–semitone definition, even within the norms of *musica recta*. Only when

[14] F. Reckow, *Handwörterbuch der musikalischen Terminologie* (Wiesbaden, 1971–), s.v. 'Clavis', has shown the likely derivation of the musical term from computus terminology, and his brief statement invites amplification of the parallels. The church calendar, with its fixed and moveable feasts, depends on three periodic cycles lacking a common measure: the seven days of the week (A–G); the lunar month (29.15 days); the solar year (365.25 days). The weekday sequence is repeated only every twenty-eight years (not seven, due to the taking up of irregularities in bissextile (leap) years); the lunar month and solar year coincide only every nineteen years (again, with some adjustment of irregularities). The moveable feast of Easter, together with feasts whose dates are dependent upon that of Easter, touches all these cycles: Easter is the first Sunday after the full moon that occurs on or after the vernal equinox (March 21). These calculations were performed with a number of aids, including forms of the wheel diagrams and hands shared with music theory. J. Smits van Waesberghe, *Musikgeschichte in Bildern*, iii, *Musikerziehung* (Leipzig, 1969), pll. 57–8, has drawn attention to the existence of calendrical hands from as early as the so-called Guidonian hand (see pll. 55–84 on the musical hand in general), and there are some slightly later ones with even more significant musical analogy in that they link the seven-letter weekly cycle A–G with the permutations of the nineteen-year lunar cycle on which Easter depends and which gives rise to the so-called Golden Number – just as the musical hand links the seven-letter octave A–G with the permutating hexachord superstructures. The nineteen years of the lunar cycle, the nineteen places on the physical hand (knuckles and finger-tips), and the decision to confine the usable range of music to those nineteen positions on the Guidonian hand (excluding the later-added place for E la) present a striking analogy. Other calendrical hands show the A–G letters permutated with the so-called tabular of 'fnugo' letters, as does the musical hand with hexachords. See, for an example from a theorist also known to music history, W. E. van Wijk, *Le nombre d'or, . . . massa compoti d'Alexandre de Villedieu* (The Hague, 1936). The *sedes clavium* were fixed dates, the earliest dates on which a feast could occur. The *claves pasche* are a series of nineteen numbers (11–39) which, when added to the *sedes*, provide a ready means of calculating the date of Easter. They are a convenient shorthand, a summary means of regulating the disparate cycles, just as musical *claves* regulate the disparate systems of proportional monochord tuning, the octave cycle, the functional hexachords. In both systems, the respective irregularities of leap years and commas have to be absorbed.

While it is not necessary to bring in the Pythagorean doctrine of the music of the spheres in order to establish a connection between the methods of calendrical and musical calculation and terminology, it is nonetheless worth recalling that the proportionate speeds of planetary revolution were the same set of duple and triple geometric proportions as underlie Pythagorean tuning. Haar (*The New Grove Dictionary*, s.v. 'Music of the spheres') has called it a kind of celestial monochord. It is hardly surprising that computists and musicians found common ways and terms for reconciling and illustrating those parts of their subject matter that were explained by geometric proportion, with the non-proportional structures that were to be superimposed on them.

9

Margaret Bent

coupled with the superstructure of overlapping hexachords could letters convey the normal, customary relationships in *musica recta*. E–F was a semitone only by virtue of, or by being understood normally to have, the hexachord articulation mi–fa. The C clef, understood as the clef of C sol fa ut, did not even fix the semitone location; since C can be realised either as C fa in the G hexachord (with a semitone below it) or as C sol in the F hexachord (with a whole tone below it), the C clef leaves both possibilities open. C sol fa ut expresses the possible immediate intervallic contexts of a note but is not a label for a predetermined pitch. This is just another way of saying that B fa and B mi are both equally available in the *recta* system, and that neither of them has priority over, or is merely a modification of, the other. If the choice between these options is to be specified, a formula such as Tinctoris's 'fa of C sol fa ut' must be used.[15] *Musica recta* is not an arsenal of fixed pitches but denotes a set of relationships to a notional norm of pitch stability that is more like a flotilla at anchor than a Procrustean bed or a pre-tuned keyboard. The 'operation of *musica ficta*', that is, the substitution at any point, for contrapuntal reasons, of a tone for a semitone (or vice versa), could mean that the absolute frequency of the As, Bs, Cs that follow may not be the same as they were before, although the local interval relationships of small segments will remain intact. The taking of a *conjuncta* (substitution of a tone for a semitone or vice versa) anywhere in the system may change the actual pitches following that point without changing the relationships except at that point. The value of a semibreve may be changed by proportional operation or mensural change; the contextual relationships of that semibreve will continue to be observed after the point of change even if the absolute durations represented by the same symbol in the same context are different from before. Both for mensuration and for pitch, the values are achieved through local context and without reference to long-term absolutes.

It is in order to clarify that the *musica recta* relationships are in effect that medieval theory goes to the seemingly laborious lengths of tagging the hexachordal options onto every letter, even when those

---

[15] E.g., his *De natura et proprietate tonorum* (CSM 22, i), chapter 2. Indeed, the places on the so-called Guidonian hand itself embody all those options and do not in themselves assist in making choices between the possible articulations, any more than the unadapted hand copes with *musica ficta*. Such adaptation is only rarely documented, for example by Ugolino; see note 8 above.

Diatonic *ficta*

normal relationships are meant. It is not for octave definition,[16] which was effected by lower-case, upper-case or double letters, or by labelling them *graves*, *acutes* or *superacutes*. Some of the letter-plus-*voces* combinations indeed do not efficiently distinguish octaves: D la sol re, E la mi, F fa ut, G sol re ut are all repeated within the normal gamut.

Ramos's revolutionary step was to drop the hexachordal tags which identified the interval structures – even though he needed to use them subsequently in his treatise – and to propose the use of unqualified letters to denote the 'white-note' positions on the keyboard. His octave solmisation is in effect a redundant duplication of letter-names as applied to keyboard white notes, and neither he nor anyone else seems to have found it very useful. It is significant that he thus opened up the rift between the underlying concepts of vocal procedures and the practical confines of the keyboard by proposing this system in a chapter entitled 'combining a voice with an instrument in a subtle way'.[17]

For Guido of Arezzo, Bb was extra, *adiunctum vel molle*;[18] the soft hexachord seems to have taken on its equal status with the natural and hard only after Guido, surely as the first stage in the extension of the solmisation system that became necessary with the growth of polyphony and hence of contrapuntally necessitated consonances that were not called for in chant. When theorists from Ramos onwards sought, partly under the pressure to accommodate to the exigencies and compromises of the keyboard, to give Bb accidental status in accordance with its keyboard position, it was back to Guido that they appealed for authority, thus overleaping the period of late gothic counterpoint.

The other important development of the period around 1500 is likewise linked with this keyboard-prompted change in the status of Bb. It was no less than the breakdown of late-medieval solmisation and of the hegemony of the three-hexachord system. Instead of (or at least, in addition to) presenting the full *recta* gamut with F, G and C hexachords, theorists gave the scalar equivalents as two distinct forms, each representing only two and not three hexachord-types. The *scala ♮ duralis* gave equal access to the members of the hard and natural hexachords but a lower priority to the soft hexachord. In the

---

[16] A myth perpetuated in *The New Grove Dictionary*, s.v. 'Pitch'.

[17] Bartolomeo Ramis de Pareija, *Musica Practica* (Bologna, 1482), [Prima pars] chapter 7, 'Copulandi vocem cum instrumento modus subtilis'.

[18] *Micrologus*, ed. J. Smits van Waesberghe, CSM 4, chapter 8.10, p. 124.

11

Margaret Bent

absence of a signature, B♭ and B♮ thus lost their previously equal status and written B came to express a priority of B♮ over B♭. The *scala b mollis* included the natural and soft but not the hard hexachords. Depending on the absence or presence of a signature, B♭ or B♮ gained a priority over the other alternative if not excluding it. A third scale, the *scala ficta*, with two flats, was predisposed to the F and B♭ hexachords. The full implications of these changes in the status of B♭, of the way in which 'black notes' were thought of, and in the meaning of signatures, cannot be explored here, but it is the arguments of the more conservative theorists, with their more purely vocal orientation, that underlie most of the generalisations in this paper. A further important consequence of the break-down of the three-hexachord system was that full solmisation became impossible, and a 'lazy' short-cut solmisation was adopted, allowing 'fa super la' to be sung without mutation.[19] This means, in effect, that the entire rationale of medieval solmisation, namely to identify the semitone (as mi–fa) and give surrounding context to it, was eroded.

4. LINEAR OPERATION

Late-medieval notation operates on linear planes, symptomised by the persistent use of notation in separate parts for vocal polyphony, a presentation which is not designed for simultaneous visual control by one musician. This linear quality obviously applies to mensural notation, with its dependence on contextual evaluation, and I now believe it to be equally valid for the notation of pitch. In late-medieval terms, as already stated, a note may be identified in isolation as a semibreve, F, but the actual sounding pitch of the F in relation to other sounding pitches is as dependent on context as is the precise duration of the semibreve. The context dependency operates in two ways: visually, from the individual notated part (i.e., what the singer would do in monophony or expect to do in polyphony unless forced to do otherwise); and aurally, from the process of listening and adjusting to simultaneities that may require the singer to do something other than scrutiny of his own part would have led him to expect. Notation is representative rather than prescriptive and, although it is our only means of direct access to the composer's

[19] Specifically allowed by Listenius, *Musica* (Nuremberg, 1549), chapter 5, discussed and rejected by Aron, *Lucidario in musica* (Venice, 1545), book I, chapters 8, 10.

Diatonic *ficta*

intentions, is not in itself a complete or unambiguous record of those intentions.

Composing scores do not to my knowledge exist until the sixteenth century, and may not even have been common then; I do not believe that they ever existed in any significant sense for most preceding repertories.[20] We cannot know how composers composed. But it is likely that they conceived actual sounds, some essential or unambiguous, others perhaps open to variation, in some combination of successive and simultaneous thinking, which would then have been dictated or written as representative but incompletely prescriptive notation, to be realised as sounds by skilled performers. The composer could have used performance of successive stages as a memory crutch during the process of refining his aural conceptions.

What singers of the time did instead of depending on visual grasp of the musical entity was to make music by applying their knowledge of contrapuntal simultaneities, acceptable sounds, to the incompletely prescriptive notation.[21] No notation has ever been fully prescriptive, and the success of a notation depends in different ways on the kind of musical equipment to be presumed for those who realise it. Late-medieval singers were in a very real sense collaborators with the composer in making the music happen – realising it – within the limits of his intentions. Those limits included the possibility of different realisations, of different actual sounds at some but perhaps not all places which are underprescribed by our standards –

---

[20]   The few repertories that are not obviously for keyboard but for which score is characteristic (including organum and English discant) invite special consideration, but because they are not necessarily designed for or suited to use by one performer, they do not undermine the validity of the generalisation. The assumptions stated here and in what follows are shared with my '*Resfacta* and *Cantare Super Librum*', *JAMS*, 36 (1983), especially pp. 376–8. That article also stresses that, for Tinctoris, the process of composition included not only operation of the rules of counterpoint, but the weighing of choices and priorities between them.

[21]   For examples of theoretical statements documenting the role of the ear in counterpoint see R. L. Crocker, 'Discant, Counterpoint and Harmony', *JAMS*, 15 (1962), p. 4; this article presents many important insights about the nature of medieval counterpoint and stresses the importance of trying to conceive it in contemporary terms.

    To these references may be added a remarkable interpolation near the end of the revised version of Prosdocimus's *Contrapunctus*, ed. Herlinger, in which he says that the signs of *musica ficta* should be placed where they sound sweetly, that a choice between the discant and the tenor should be left to the ear, and that no rule can be given because the possibilities are infinite: 'Scire autem ubi hec signa dulcius cadunt auri tuo dimitto, quia de hoc regula dari non potest, cum hec loca quodammodo infinita sint.' If the 'variatio' sounds equally good in the tenor or the discant, it should be made in the discant. See below, section 9, on rules and priorities: this passage thus expresses a priority for applying *ficta* in a situation not otherwise discussed in this paper.

13

Margaret Bent

as indeed they do for many later repertories demanding initiatives from the performer. We do not expect a continuo player to avoid solecisms on a first play-through from a sparsely figured bass which does not include the solo part; we expect him to hear and adjust to what that part does. We expect performers of any repertory to complement the written notation by applying the stylistic assumptions and learned intuitions they share with the composer. I make the same presumptions for the vocal realisation of renaissance polyphony.

5. MEANINGS OF SIGNS

The signs we still call accidentals have become essentials of our notational system; a note is presumed 'white' on the piano unless it is marked to be 'inflected' or 'altered'. But we should not make the same assumption in a notational system where it was not essential to provide these signs; we cannot regard the non-provision by late-medieval musicians of all the accidentals (now so-called but then in a true sense) that we need as a failure by their standards. In their terms and for their purposes they were not misnotating musical pitch even if, for our purposes and our greater dependence on visual control, they were under-notating it. For us, sharps, flats and naturals raise, lower or restore a note from or to its normal or fixed place. Medieval musicians normally operated with only two signs, ♮ and ♭, hard and soft 'b', the signs of *musica ficta* or, more properly, the signs of mi and fa (not necessarily fictive); when present, these indicate where a semitone is to be sung. (These statements avoid comparing the different meanings of their and our signatures in relation to 'accidentals'.)

Signs do not necessarily raise or lower the notes before which they appear, there being no fixed standard but only a relative position for those notes. The signs express a relationship, not absolute pitches within a system. Most theorists explain the signs in a linear-intervallic-hexachordal context, going to considerable lengths of circumlocution to avoid saying that ♮ raises a note or that ♭ lowers it from a fixed place. Even where there is explicit reference to raising and lowering, this usually occurs either

(1) in a horizontal melodic context, so that the raising or lowering is explained rather in relation to the neighbours of the signed note than to its removal from a norm; or

14

Diatonic *ficta*

(2) in terms of vertical interval size, where the need for correction of the sound is stressed, but expressed rather in terms of adjusting the linear approach to it than of a decision to inflect one of the notes of the offending interval.

In both cases, theorists usually write of increasing or diminishing the [linear] ascent or descent rather than of raising or lowering individual notes.[22] As already mentioned, they refer to the *coniuncta*, the moment of change, at which the singer sings a semitone for a tone, or vice versa. Expressions of concern about the consequences for long-term frequency stability of such substitution are conspicuous only by their absence.

The signs may or may not result in what for us would be an alteration of pitch. If F–G becomes a semitone by the signalling of mi on F or fa on G, this could mean, in our terms, either F♯–G or F–G♭. In context we can usually work out which; but there are cases without context, in treatises, where it is not clear, and where the demonstration is not thereby impaired. Some kind of F goes to some kind of G, proceeding by a semitone. There was no normal terminology to distinguish whether our F–G♭ or F♯–G would occur (or even F♭–G♭♭), certainly nothing, either in terms of the letter-labels of the monochord or the scale-steps of the gamut, which conveyed a shifting of one note from its 'proper' place, leaving the other unaffected. Both F and G are in this case involved in the placing of a semitone where it does not occur on the hand, 'per se'.[23]

---

[22] Typical theoretical statements expressing ideas of raising or lowering in terms of linear context rather than of individual pitch inflection include J. de Muris (CS III, p. 73): 'on la sol la (A G A) the sol should be raised and sung as fa mi fa'; Prosdocimus (ed. Herlinger): '♭ augments the ascent and ♮ diminishes it. The two signs do not augment or diminish [intervals] except by a major semitone', *Contrapunctus* [v.4]. Contrast the terminology of Johannes Boen (n. 11 above); see also the citation from the 1375 Paris anonymous and other relevant passages cited in Bent, 'Musica Recta and Musica Ficta', *Musica Disciplina*, 26 (1972), p. 86 and *passim*.

[23] These phrases are typical of contemporary *ficta* definitions, e.g. Tinctoris, *Diffinitorium* (1472): 'ficta musica est cantus praeter regularem manus traditionem aeditus'; Prosdocimus, *Contrapunctus* [v]: 'ficta musica est vocum fictio sive vocum positio in *loco ubi esse non videntur [revised version from *: aliquo loco manus musicalis ubi nullo modo reperiuntur], sicut ponere mi ubi non est mi, et fa ubi non est fa . . .'; Ornithoparcus (*Compendium*, I.10), 'a Coniunct is this, to sing a Voyce in a Key which is not in it'.
To locate the notes on the monochord would involve a choice, but there is no standard monochord terminology that expresses or identifies any relationship between these notes and their neighbours, just as there are no functional names (such as F♯ and G♭) to distinguish the two possibilities. The two G♭s on the monochord, for example, are labelled by Prosdocimus N, R, by Ugolino O, P; the two F♯s X, 6 and S, 7 respectively. See also Dahlhaus 'Zu Costeleys chromatischer Chanson', p. 256: 'daß das 16.Jahrhundert für den Ton, daß wir "heses" nennen, weder einen Namen noch ein Zeichen hatte'.

15

Margaret Bent

Both the F and the G in this case count as *musica ficta*, not just the one
which, in our terms, is altered. A *ficta* hexachord starting on some
kind of D would be used in either case; the entire hexachord would
entail the use of *musica ficta*, not just the F♯ or the G♭. Furthermore,
this means that the boundary between *musica recta* and *musica ficta*
may not always be wholly clearcut. The moment at which the singer
begins to operate *musica ficta* may have no audible bearing on the
resulting sound; for example, when singing from C up to G via 'F♯',
he may mutate to the *ficta* hexachord either on D or E. (Similarly, the
point at which a fingering change occurs in playing such a progression may be neither audible nor musically significant.) The series of
letters is re-articulated by the operation of *musica ficta*, but individual
pitches are not thought of as being inflected. The resultant sounds
exist in their own right and are explained neither on the monochord
nor in functional solmisation as modifications of their *recta* 'neighbours'. There is no absolute pitch G or G fa, even assuming that we
know what the frequency of G was at the beginning of the piece. If a
new G is established by correct moment-to-moment operation of the
contrapuntal rules which are the common property of the composer
and the singer, the singer no more needs to keep track of where he was
in relation to the original frequency of G than he would need to keep
in mind what the original value of a semibreve beat was at the beginning of a piece which has required him to apply a series of proportional
relationships. In terms of both pitch and mensuration, the results of
conceptualising in our way and in theirs are often the same, just as
was the convenient alignment of two different letter-functions, but
that circumstance removes neither the importance of acknowledging
the differences nor the danger of misunderstandings.

6. WILLAERT EXAMPLE

Plate 1 gives the 'duo' form of Willaert's famous *Quidnam ebrietas* as
presented by Artusi, allegedly in a copy from the composer's
autograph.[24] To sing the first three staves of the tenor will make vivid

---

[24] *L'Artusi overo delle imperfettioni della moderna musica* (Venice, 1600; facsimile, Bologna, 1968),
Ragionamento Primo, ff. 21–21ᵛ. See J. S. Levitan, 'Adrian Willaert's Famous Duo
Quidnam ebrietas . . .', *Tijdschrift van de Vereniging voor Nederlandse Muziekgeschiedenis* (hereafter
TVNM), 15 (1938), pp. 166–233, and E. E. Lowinsky, 'Adrian Willaert's Chromatic
"Duo" Re-examined', *TVNM*, 18 (1956), pp. 1–36, where the piece is shown to have been a
four-part composition. The two parts given here sufficed to demonstrate the problems that
engaged theorists.

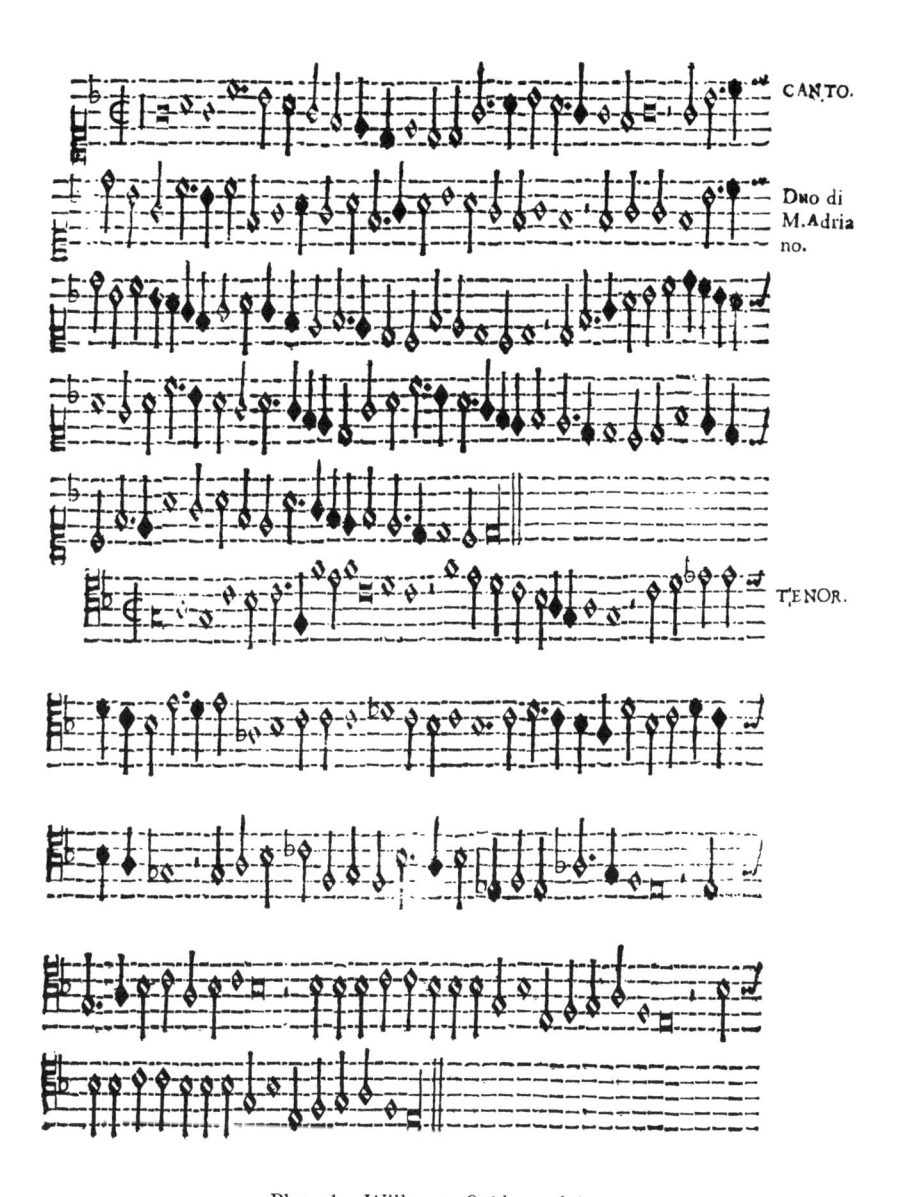

Plate 1   Willaert, *Quidnam ebrietas*

17

Margaret Bent

what their staff notation could do that ours cannot, simply following
these rules:

(1) ♭ indicates fa (and therefore has a semitone below it and a
whole tone above it) until the sign is superseded;

(2) all melodic leaps of fourths and fifths are to be sung perfect.[25]

The E at the end sounds two semitones below what E would have
been at the beginning. The trick of this piece is not that it 'modulates'
in our sense, but that it ends on a notated seventh which sounds an
octave;[26] it thus exercised theorists about its tuning implications.
Tuning or temperament only becomes an issue when pre-tuned
instruments are involved or have become the focal point for theoretical reference; for unaccompanied singers there is no reason why this,
and indeed all late-medieval and renaissance polyphony, should not
have been performed with pure intonation, Pythagorean in
principle, but probably with justly tempered thirds in practice. As
singing will demonstrate, there is no need either to transcribe it or to
rethink it enharmonically in equal temperament in order to achieve
the intended result. It uses its notational system completely normally and can be read easily, even though Willaert takes us abnor-
mally far round the spiral of fifths. We know also that this piece
exercised the members of the Papal chapel, who had difficulty
singing it. It is not the tenor on its own which is difficult but, with two
or more voices together, the unavoidable and unusual transition
from the point where they are nominally (or 'literally') together and
then move apart. This moment of the composition sounds much less
smooth than does the tenor alone, which indeed has to make a few
minor adjustments in response to the superius; singers of both parts
would also have been confounded by hearing abnormal combinations of hexachordal *voces*. The aspects of this piece that gave it
notoriety had to do with the problems posed by its unique composi-

---

[25] Both principles are widely documented, e.g. Ornithoparcus (*Compendium*, I.10, p. 25
[145]): 'Marking fa in b fa ♮ mi, or in any other place, if the Song from that shall make an
immediate rising to a Fourth, a Fift, or an Eight, even there fa must necessarily be marked,
to eschew a Tritone, a Semidiapente, or a Semidiapason, and inusuall, and forbidden
Moodes . . .' The example has leaps of those intervals; the principle is the same even where
theorists differ in their insistence on what needs to be notated. See n. 27 below.

[26] The term modulation is used in contemporary theory only to describe how an interval is
filled in melodically. It has no connotations of the kinds of change it has acquired in tonal
theory, and must join the ranks of words and concepts that are out of place if applied to
early music in a modern sense.

   The cleffing is indeed so contrived that the two finals are at the same place on their
respective staves.

Diatonic *ficta*

tional artifice, whether for tuning theories in the abstract or practical questions of coordination between singers, and not the normal notation that guides the tenor securely along its abnormal path.

What Willaert indicates are not 'individual inflections' but how to negotiate the points of interlock or conjunction between melodic segments. By our standards the notation is excessively economical; by his standards it is in some ways even over-explicit: the A♭ on stave 2 of the tenor, for example, is reassuring but not necessary if the melodic fifths are sung perfect. There is no need for each note to be related to an absolute pitch; it is not necessary to know exactly where we are in relation to an imagined fixed standard for the piece. To render this piece in modern notation requires either a forest of flats and double flats or enharmonic re-spelling, both of which would be cumbersome and hard to read, as well as doing violence to the artifice expressed so compactly by the notation in which it was conceived. (A similar point can be made about the awkwardness of rendering mensural syncopations and proportions in modern notation.)

This is an extreme but clear example of the difference between operating *musica ficta*, which we do when reading from Willaert's notation, and adding accidentals, as required by a modern notation which did not lie within the thought processes of composers of Willaert's time; but it is in this context that theorists' pleas for economy in the notation of *musica ficta* should be viewed.[27] Lowinsky has alerted us to several such special pieces;[28] their conceptual possibility, and the more plentiful existence of less extreme appli-

[27] Tinctoris's famous statement discouraging as asinine the notation of unnecessary signs is given below, section 9, as is the passage from Aron which, rather than indiscriminately encouraging notated signs, requires them explicitly for cases that could not be anticipated by the singers. Prosdocimus [*Contrapunctus*, v.2] criticises composers for using *ficta* where it is not necessary, and makes it clear in the revision (see n. 6 above) that it is the unnecessary notating of signs to which he objects.

[28] His study of the Willaert composition is cited in n. 24 above. It is hard to single out for mention here anything less than Lowinsky's complete body of writings, so masterfully has he laid out a terrain that must continue to attract further investigation. The reader not already familiar with Lowinsky's writings is referred to the listing under his name in *The New Grove Dictionary* and, even better, to the first few pages of his 'Secret Chromatic Art Re-examined', *Perspectives in Musicology*, ed. B. S. Brook, E. O. D. Downes and S. van Solkema (New York, 1972), pp. 91–135, where he reviews not only his own contributions, starting with *Secret Chromatic Art in the Netherlands Motet* (New York, 1946), but also scholarly responses to it and relevant contributions by other scholars. Particularly germane in the present context are his studies of the *Fortuna* settings by Josquin and Greiter, and the study by K. Levy, 'Costeley's Chromatic Chanson', *Annales musicologiques*, 3 (1955), pp. 213–63 (see also Dahlhaus, 'Zu Costeleys chromatischer Chanson').

19

Margaret Bent

cations of the same principles, should make us hesitate before claiming that 'added accidentals' in modern scores are a betrayal of the 'actual notes' written by the composer. It is we and not they who add accidentals. What they did was to 'operate *musica ficta*' in linear segments on the basis of heard simultaneities, redefining the relationships between the letter-names, untrammelled by our commitment to pitch constancy.

7. NATURAL AND ACCIDENTAL

The signs of *musica ficta* themselves are almost never called 'accidentals'.[29] Even as an adjective, 'accidental' refers only to the extension of a system, or a dependent or contingent sub-system, such as *musica ficta* is in relation to the 'natural' system of the 'Guidonian' hand of *musica recta*. *Musica ficta* cannot stand on its own. What is accidental in this application is the entire sub-system of *ficta* hexachords, not just the notes that are not also available by *musica recta*. Spataro refers to 'mi accidalmente in una naturale positione', meaning that, for example, the letters C, D, F or G have natural positions on the hand in association with other *voces*, but that mi falling on those letter-names would qualify as accidental; the mi would have its basis in a *ficta* hexachord.[30]

For Zarlino, who drew upon the basis of the Greater Perfect System rather than of the medieval gamut, the tuning of each *genus* in that system, whether diatonic, chromatic or enharmonic, was 'proper and natural'. The *genera* exist in their own right, without a hierarchy of dependence. There is no question of the chromatic *genus* being accidental to the diatonic. It is the entire synemmenon tetrachord in each case, not just its trite synemmenon (i.e. B♭ in the diatonic *genus*) that is considered accidental.[31]

These and other uses differ rather sharply from our own; the earlier view of the natural–accidental juxtaposition, rare in music

---

29   Marchettus lists them together with stems, dots, rests and ancillary markings in general in his ostentatiously Aristotelian *Pomerium*, ed. G. Vecchi, CSM 6, book I, part I. Heyden, *De arte canendi* (Nuremberg, 1540), p. 5, gives a different list of 'accidentia necessary to the art of singing': *scala, clavis, tactus, nota, punctum, pausa, mensura, tonus.*
30   Letter to Aron, 1531: cited by P. Bergquist, 'The Theoretical Writings of Pietro Aaron', Ph.D. Dissertation, Columbia (1964), p. 440 from Rome, Biblioteca Apostolica Vaticana, MS Vat. Lat. 5318, no. 86, f. 219ᵛ.
31   Zarlino, *Le Institutioni Harmoniche* (Venice, 1558), part III, chapter 72 (same chapter reference in edition of 1573).

Diatonic *ficta*

theory before the sixteenth century, was broader. Among other systems to which the terms are then applied are the ancestors, respectively, of what have become our most common uses, namely that

(1) accidental means outside the key signature, and

(2) accidentals mean black notes.

In the Roman singers' dispute of c.1540, Danckerts deals with the system that by then had more reality than the old *musica recta*: the scale of ♮ *duralis* (no signature) and the scale of ♭ *mollis* (flat signature). Though he avoids calling these systems 'natural', he refers to the need to feign 'accidentalmente . . . per b molle' when there is no signature.[32]

Theorists around 1500 began to adopt the terms natural and accidental for the systems of white and black ranks on the keyboard.[33] The fact that B♭ had natural status in a vocal-hexachordal context and accidental status on the keyboard led to heated discussion by Aron and others, and reflects the erosion of the fully operative three-hexachord system discussed above (Section 3, n. 17), as well as the emergence of the keyboard as an instrument of theoretical reference that would eventually supersede the monochord.

8. DIATONIC AND CHROMATIC

The terms 'diatonic' and 'chromatic' are used by medieval theorists only with reference to melodic entities, the tetrachords of the Greek *genera* which, like hexachords, are segments with identical interval content. Discussion of the *genera* stands somewhat apart from that of practical music where, as many theorists say, nothing good can be accomplished outside the diatonic *genus*. The diatonic semitone mi–fa (e.g., E–F) is distinguished from the chromatic (e.g. F–F♯), which

[32] L. Lockwood, 'A Dispute on Accidentals in Sixteenth-Century Rome', *Analecta Musicologica*, 2 (1965), pp. 24–40, especially pp. 28, 32.

[33] E.g. Aron, *Toscanello in musica* (Venice, 1529) book II, chapter 40: 'Che ne lo instrumento organico secondo il comune ordine, si ritrovano voci naturali di numero xxix, chiamati dal universale uso tasti bianchi: e accidentali di numero xviii, detti tasti negri, overo semituoni: per il qual ordine da noi sará diviso tasto per tasto: dimostrando ciascheduno intervallo del uno al altro cosi accidentali come naturali.' Aron's arguments in general for the accidental status of B♭ are to be found in the *Compendiolo* (Milan, post-1545), chapter 10; the *Libri tres de institutione harmonica* (Bologna, 1516), book I, chapter 15; and in the *Toscanello in musica* book II, chapter 5; also in the *Aggiunta* to that work.

Margaret Bent

is the characteristic and determining interval of the chromatic tetrachord, the chromatic *genus*. Despite theorists' statements about the undesirability of the chromatic, surviving music occasionally demands the chromatic semitone; if used, it has to be solmised disjunctly, i.e. without a pivotal mutation. The distinction between the two semitone types was functional: it was independent of the tuning system in which they were realised.[34]

Early theorists do not find it necessary to classify music as other than diatonic simply because it happens to require use of keyboard black notes. Haar is one of few scholars to have acknowledged the confined and purely melodic definition of 'chromatic' in sixteenth-century theory.[35] Others have continued to use the term loosely, thereby creating a misleading and primitive division between white and black notes, and prematurely imposing the concept of chromatic harmony. We do not confine our own use of 'diatonic' to white notes alone; not only our major scale is diatonic, let alone not only our C major scale. We use many scales and even modulations we call diatonic, while denying a comparable if different latitude to pre-tonal music. For Zarlino, only melodic progressions that sound chromatic because they use the chromatic semitone qualified as chromatic.[36] It is not the relationship of sounds to a pre-tuned system, nor even the use of sounds arrived at without reference to such a system, nor yet the way in which they are notated or designated, that allows them to be characterised as diatonic or chromatic, but only their strictly local melodic context. Even Vicentino describes his examples in four flats as transposed diatonic.[37] Diatonicism, in other words, is defined by the interval content of small melodic segments and is not affected by transposition. The famous prologue to Lasso's *Sibylline Prophecies* contains only four truly chromatic progressions.[38] The tenor of the Willaert 'duo' is

34 The relative sizes were reversed in Pythagorean (diatonic smaller than chromatic) and mean-tone (diatonic larger than chromatic) tunings. Dahlhaus has usefully separated consideration of the tuning system from the tonal system: 'am Tonsystem . . . änderte der Wechsel der Stimmungen nichts'.

35 J. Haar, 'False Relations and Chromaticism in Sixteenth-Century Music', *JAMS*, 30 (1977), pp. 391–418.

36 Zarlino, *Institutioni*, part III, especially chapters 76, 77.

37 N. Vicentino, *L'antica musica ridotta alla moderna prattica* (Rome, 1555), book III, chapter 14 (ff. 46ᵛ–47ᵛ).

38 Soprano, bars 4–5, 7–8; altus 18–19, 20–21. For a recent analysis of the prologue and references to earlier studies, see K. Berger, 'Tonality and Atonality in the Prologue to Orlando di Lasso's *Prophetiae Sibyllarum*: Some Methodological Problems in Analysis of Sixteenth-Century Music', *The Musical Quarterly*, 66 (1980), pp. 484–504.

Diatonic *ficta*

entirely diatonic in its progressions; it sounds diatonic by Zarlino's standards, and was never described as chromatic by the theorists who wrote about it at such length. Hence, diatonic *ficta*.

9. RULES AND PRIORITIES

Rules given by theorists for *ficta* and for counterpoint are closely related or complementary. If counterpoint treatises sometime dwell more on theoretical possibilities than on practical applications, this balance is often redressed by the same theorist's practical hints about *ficta*. Constant throughout the late middle ages and early renaissance is the prohibition of diminished or augmented perfect intervals. Tinctoris illustrates a diminished fifth and an augmented octave, even showing the offending intervals between upper parts supported by a tenor, which might be thought less problematic than having them at the bottom of the texture.[39] The late-medieval formulation of this rule prohibits the sounding of mi contra fa in vertical perfect intervals, something that can result from either the interval itself or the approach to it being wrong.[40]

Rules for *ficta* and counterpoint respond chronologically to changes in musical style; however, subtle shifts in their formulation and relative weighting are more common than drastic reversals. One rule that did change concerns the melodic tritone: Prosdocimus condones it as a direct leap when it is ancillary to a cadence, in order to maintain the progression to an octave from a major sixth. Melodic tritones came to be proscribed by the time of Tinctoris;[41] indeed, late fifteenth-century musical style gave much less opportunity to use the progressions demonstrated by Prosdocimus.

For the period around 1500, these are the two primary rules of counterpoint that may require fictive adjustment, and the present illustrations will be confined to them, namely:

(1) the prohibition of imperfect fifths or octaves sounding together;

---

39   Tinctoris, *Liber de arte contrapuncti*, II. xxxiv: 'Concordantiis perfectis que vel imperfecte vel superflue per semitonium chromaticum.'

40   See Bent, 'Musica Recta and Musica Ficta', p. 94.

41   Prosdocimus's well-known examples using tritones are given *ibid.*, pp. 91–2 and in the yet unpublished editions of Herlinger. The late-medieval tolerance of the melodic tritone did of course constitute a departure from earlier abhorrence of it; the reinstatement of this rule in the late fifteenth century is only one of a number of 'returns' to earlier positions – another being the reversion of B♭ to accidental status. Tinctoris's statements on the use of the tritone are given in this section.

Margaret Bent

(2) the discouragement of tritone melodic outlines, especially
unmediated ones.[42]

Armed with proper distinctions, we can approach the theorists for
help in establishing priorities; this they give more clearly than is
commonly acknowledged. While application of such statements of
priority does not solve all problems, it can considerably reduce the
number of apparently insoluble situations. For present purposes,
two well-known theoretical passages will be used to support the
general priority of the first of the above rules over the second. They
are from different types of treatises, fifty years apart in date, and
neither is even primarily devoted to counterpoint.

The first is from Tinctoris's *De natura et proprietate tonorum*:[43]

De formatione sexti toni.
Sextus autem formatur ex tertia specie diatessaron inferius, hoc est infra
ipsum diapente, ut hic probatur:
[example]
Praeterea uterque istorum duorum tonorum [the fifth or sixth] formari
potest ex quarta specie diapente quod, nisi exigente necessitate, fieri
minime debet. Necessitas autem quae eos ita formari cogit duplex est,
videlicet aut ratione concordantiarum perfectarum quae cantui composito
incidere possunt, aut ratione tritoni evitandi.
[Passage dealing with ♭ signatures omitted here]
Ut autem evitetur tritoni durities, necessario ex quarta specie diapente isti
duo toni formantur. Neque tunc ♭ mollis signum apponi est necessarium,
immo si appositum videatur, asininum esse dicitur, ut hic probatur:
[example with unsigned F–B progressions]
Notandum autem quod non solum in hiis duobus tonis tritonus est
evitandus, sed etiam in omnis aliis. Unde regula haec generaliter traditur,
quod in quolibet tono si post ascensum ad ♭ fa ♮ mi acutum citius in F fa ut
gravem descendatur quam ad C sol fa ut ascendatur, indistincte per ♭ molle
canetur, ut hic patet;
[examples from all 8 tones]
Non tamen ignorandum est quod in cantu composito ne fa contra mi in
concordantia perfecta fiat, interdum tritono uti necessarium sit, et tunc ad

---

[42]   Some statements by modern scholars indicate that the distinctions between these terms
       are still not clearly understood:
           (1) mi contra fa has sometimes been assumed to include relationships other than
       simultaneous vertical perfections (e.g. oblique false relations, melodic progressions), and
           (2) implicit assumptions of enharmonic equivalence have led to confusion between the
       tritone and the diminished fifth. Clearly it is impossible to avoid, all the time, melodic and
       harmonic tritones and diminished fifths.
[43]   Dated 1476; chapter 8. Ed. A. Seay, CSM 22, i, q.v. for music examples; translated A. Seay
       (Colorado Springs, 1976).

Diatonic *ficta*

significandum ubi fa evitandi tritoni gratia cantari deberet ibi mi esse
canendum, ♭ duri signum, hoc est ♭ quadrum, ipsi mi censeo
praeponendum, ut hic probatur;
[example with notated ♭ confirming tritone outline]
Denique sciendum quod non solum in tonis regularibus et vera musica
secundum exempla praemissa tritonum praedictis modis fugere ac eo uti
debemus, verum etiam in irregularibus tonis et musica ficta, ut hic patet:
[example with tenor avoiding and contrapunctus using melodic tritone]
Sumitur autem hic tritonus ipse, ut clarius quae de eo diximus intelligan-
tur, pro immediato aut mediato progressu, sive per arsin sive per thesin, de
una nota ad aliam ab illa tribus tonus distantem. Sed quamvis humana vox
tritono mediato possibiliter utatur eam tamen immediate uti, aut est
difficile aut impossibile, ut hic probatur:
[example of melodic tritones, direct and mediated]

In defining the sixth tone as using the third species of fourth (C–F)
and the third species of fifth (F–C via B♮), Tinctoris feels obliged to
introduce examples of two-part counterpoint in order to
demonstrate under what circumstances it is necessary to depart from
the interval species proper to the mode. He gives two two-part
examples, with tenors respectively in the fifth and sixth tone, each
provided with a B♭ signature evidently for the sole or principal
reason of ensuring that the Fs occurring as fifths with those Bs in the
added contrapunctus will sound as perfect fifths. There is not even,
here, a question of the modal interval structure being kept intact
with B♭ while the contrapunctus adjusts to it. Tinctoris describes
this as a situation of 'overriding necessity'. There are two such
necessities: one is the attainment of perfect concords (i.e. simultaneities), and the other is avoidance of the tritone (i.e., as a melodic
leap). After his two-part examples of vertical perfections, Tinctoris
gives melodic examples to demonstrate tritone avoidance (adding
that this applies not only to the fifth and sixth modes but also to all
the others). The example includes both direct and filled-in leaps that
would be tritones from F to B but for the use of B♭. Finally, in this
chapter, Tinctoris deals with conflicts between these two overriding
necessities and indicates how the priority between them is to be
resolved: 'In composed song, so that a fa against a mi not happen in a
perfect concord, occasionally it is necessary to use a tritone.' In such
cases, where B♭ would normally be sung but must be replaced by B♮
in order to achieve a perfect interval, he recommends the notation of
the ♮. In his examples, the tritone leaps thus tolerated all have at

Margaret Bent

least one intermediate note. He goes on to say that, while the human voice may possibly use a tritone in a scalewise progression, it is difficult or impossible in a leap. (While he does not directly tell us how to resolve a conflict involving an unmediated tritone, I believe it is implicit that even a direct tritone leap might have to be tolerated in favour of a vertical perfection.) This chapter provides a clear affirmation of the general priority of vertical perfection over both melodic tritones and 'modal purity'.

The other passage is from Aron's *Aggiunta* to the (Venice) 1529 edition of his 1523 *Toscanello in Musica*:[44]

Si muove fra alcuni de la musica desiderosi, dubbii & disputationi circa la figura del b molle & diesis, utrum se de necessita gli Compositori sono constretti a segnare ne gli canti da loro composti, dette figure, cioe b molle & diesis: overamente se il cantore è tenuto a dovere intendere, & cognoscere lo incognito secreto di tutti gli luoghi dove tal figure o segni bisogneranno. [lengthy discussion and examples of tritone avoidance] Ma perche io a te ho mostrato che sempre questi tre tuoni continuati luno dapoi laltro, debbono essere mollificati & temperati: pur che non tochino la quinta chorda, per due ragioni la nostra regola bisognera patire. La prima sara per necessita, & commodita: & la seconda per ragione intesa. Volendo adunque procedere da F grave infino a ♮ acuto, & subito dapoi per un salto de uno diapente discendere, sara dibisogno chel cantore alhora commetta & pronuntii quella durezza del nominato tritono per la commodita di quello intervallo, overamente voce posta nel luogo di hypáte mesôn chiamato E la mi: perche volendo satisfare al miglior commodo, è forza a lui preterire la regola. Onde osservando il precetto, accaderebbe grandissima incommodita, con differenti processi: come sarebbe dicendo fa nel ♮ mi acuto: con il qual fa, non mai rettamente discendera al vero suono di quella voce mi: come si vede nel terzo Agnus dei di Clama ne cesses [Josquin, *L'homme armé super voces musicales*]: al fine del controbasso la presente figura da Iosquino composta:

Example 1   (a) Bass only as given by Aron

Here Aron specifically addresses the question whether composers should notate the signs of B *molle* and *diesis*, or whether singers should be expected to recognise the 'hidden secret of all the places where these figures or signs are needed'. His view of signs has shifted

[44]   P. Aaron, *Toscanello in Musica* (English translation, P. Bergquist, Colorado Springs, 1970).

(b) modern score

significantly from that of Tinctoris, and includes a reference to the authority of Guido for the 'accidental' status of B♭, alleging that it is 'solely for the mitigation and temperament of the tritone', and that musicians understand that it should be used even where it is not notated. Many composers, he says, understood the rule but notated

Margaret Bent

the ♭ out of consideration for the carelessness of the singer. His long list of music examples, mostly from Petrucci prints, show where the composer has helped the singer in this way. Aron states his priority between rules as follows: although the melodic tritone should be avoided when the melody does not rise to the fifth degree (i.e. when F rises to B but not to C), the rule may be overridden for 'necessity and convenience' or for 'understood reason'. His example from the third Agnus of Josquin's Mass *L'homme armé super voces musicales* gives only the bass progression marked by a bracket above, describing it as rising from F to ♭ and immediately afterwards leaping down a fifth to E. It is not clear, without the other voices, why 'if he sings fa in the ♭ mi acute he cannot descend correctly to the proper pitch of the note mi', i.e. why all rules cannot be satisfied by singing, in our terms, B♭ and E♭. But as soon as we see the vertical context it becomes clear that both B♮ and E♮ are necessitated by the 'greater convenience' of the sustained notes of the *L'homme armé* cantus firmus at this point, and that the melodic tritone outline is the price paid for the greater good of the vertical perfection. In other words, Aron here subscribes to the same priority as Tinctoris: that in order to achieve vertical perfection there must sometimes be a concession with respect to melodic tritones.

Further evidence of the importance Aron attaches to vertical perfection is given a little later in the *Aggiunta*:

> it will now be considered whether the singer should or indeed can recognize at once the intent and secret of a composer, when singing a song he has not seen before. The answer is no, although among those who celebrate music there are some who think the contrary. They give the reason that every composer considers that his songs are to be understood by the learned and experienced, by a quick and perceptive ear, especially when imperfect fifths, octaves, twelfths and fifteenths occur . . . For it would be impossible for any learned and practiced man to be able to sense instantly an imperfect fifth, octave, twelfth or fifteenth without first committing the error of a little dissonance. It is true that it would be sensed more quickly by one than another, but there is not a man who would not be caught.

Therefore, Aron recommends that when such simultaneities occur in situations where correct anticipation and appropriate action would only be possible after an erroneous first attempt, the notes should be appropriately marked. The ensuing examples in his text are all such as would have been difficult or impossible to anticipate aurally

Diatonic *ficta*

without rehearsal. Aron clearly knows the harmonic context of these examples; although he cites individual parts from the part-books, we may have to score them, visibly or audibly, in order to take his point. There can be no doubt that Aron attached the greatest importance to the correction of vertical perfections in the performance of composed polyphony.

10. JOSQUIN EXAMPLE

With these considerations in mind, let us turn to the passage from Josquin's *Ave Maria* (Example 2), given here without the altus.[45] The rising sequence for soprano, tenor and bass (on the four-syllable units *Coelestia, terrestria, Nova replet laetitia*) is a stock-in-trade of contemporary counterpoint treatises. Hothby, Aron and others give or explain two-part examples of sequential counterpoint in an alternating chain of [perfect] fifths and sixths.[46]

This is exactly how the soprano and bass, respectively, relate to the tenor of Example 2. Any musician of the time would have thought it perverse in bar 3 for the simultaneously sounding B–F fifth between tenor and bass to have been anything but perfect; by singing 'B♭' the bass not only adjusts to the already-sounding tenor F but also avoids the linear tritone F–B, which would be tolerated

---

[45] (Edited in Josquin, *Werken*, ed. A. Smijers, Motets I.1.) Discussed by, amongst others, Carl Dahlhaus in 'Tonsystem und Kontrapunkt um 1500', pp. 15–16, with the rather different conclusion that 'der Tonsatz abstrakt konzipiert ist und daß sich Josquin über die Unentschiedenheit, wie er zu realisieren sei, hinwegsetzte, da sie ihm gleichgültig war'. Dahlhaus thus posits compositional indifference to the actual resulting sounds, and that abstractly conceived counterpoint may have lacked either prior aural imagination of sounds or indeed any musically acceptable realisation. However, the size of an interval (as major or minor) may be determined by the musical context so clearly at crucial points in the contrapuntal fabric that the composer neither needed to specify it nor the contrapuntally experienced singer to be told what to do. Such choices must surely have been a matter of structural if not also aesthetic concern to the composer, even if the conventions of performance did not necessitate, nor the nature of the notation permit, its full prescription. Dahlhaus seems here to approach the notation from a more conventional view based on fixed pitches and alterations although elsewhere ('Zu Costeleys chromatischer Chanson') recognising a principle he felicitously names 'relativ Fa-notation'. He there presents it as the special property of unusual pieces in which it is applied with extreme results, whereas I seek to bring that relative concept into play as a central and normal feature of renaissance notation.

[46] Hothby, *De arte contrapuncti*, ed. G. Reaney, CSM 26, p. 90; Aron, *Libri tres de institutione harmonica* (Bologna, 1516): this example is there explained only verbally. Similar passages by Vicentino and Lusitano are given by E. T. Ferand, 'Improvised Vocal Counterpoint in the Late Renaissance and Early Baroque', *Annales musicologiques*, 4 (1956), pp. 147–51. See also G. Monachus, *De preceptis artis musicae*, ed. A. Seay, CSM 11, p. 53.

29

Example 2   From Josquin, *Ave Maria a4*

Example 3   (a) Hothby, *De arte contrapuncti* Spetie tenore del contrapunto prima . . . contrapunto per 5 o 6 fugando; (b) Aron, *Libri tres de institutione harmonica*, III. 52

(a)

(b)

Diatonic *ficta*

only if it helped to achieve the greater good of a simultaneous perfection. The passage illustrates the satisfaction of both rules, irrespective of priorities between them. It is, moreover, carefully constructed with rhythmic overlaps (notably the soprano B at this point). The almost inevitable result is given in Example 4.

Example 4   = Example 2 with accidentals added as required by modern notation

That the soprano is forced to do something not demanded by that part alone is, far from being a problem, precisely what should happen when a seen expectation is tempered by a heard simultaneity. In the 'conventional' white-note reading of this passage, conversely, the bass is asked to perform something (the tritone outline) that he would not do, faced with his own part alone. It has been argued that Josquin's motet may date from the same decade as Tinctoris's dictum quoted above that to notate an obvious case of tritone avoidance (such as this?) was asinine. Any singer of the bass part who brought himself both to sing a diminished fifth with the tenor and, with the very same note, to produce a melodic tritone outline, would have committed a double error.

Margaret Bent

I believe that this solution can be defended independently of any possible textual or extra-musical significance; the extent to which passages such as this would have been heard as 'excursions' by contemporaries remains to be explored, as do many large and important questions of text and music relationship.[47] To say that the Josquin *Ave Maria* passage is out of place in a C major or Ionian piece and disturbs its tonal stability or betrays its diatonicism is to frame the problem in anachronistic terms. In addition, to recognise manuscript 'accidentals' as truly accidental allows the musical case to be built independently of notated signs. The sources of the *Ave Maria* contain very few;[48] since my argument assumes a strong aural initiative in achieving vertical perfections, it is only 'accidentally' touched by the presence or absence of such signs and the reliability of manuscripts containing them.

Example 5 gives all four parts of this passage, also in modern notation with added accidentals. The motet is mainly constructed out of different combinations of paired imitations and with the minimum of true four-part writing, which occurs only at the passages beginning homophonically at bars 40, 94 (tripla) and 143. Each of these punctuating passages is in some way unique within the piece. The first has just served as a *locus classicus* for demonstrating the application of contrapuntal rules. In this sequential passage, and at this point alone in the piece, the altus part can be diagnosed as a successively conceived addition to the texture, albeit neatly accommodated to the three primary parts of Example 2 (4).[49] Even if this

---

47   It may yet be demonstrated that the coincidence of the word *nova* with what we may anachronistically hear as a departure is significant, even though it does not fall within the kind of vocabulary supporting Lowinskian chromaticism. In urging that music must make sense independently of textual considerations that might have helped to shape it, I do not mean to underestimate considerations that cannot receive full treatment here.

48   Munich, Bayerische Staatsbibliothek, Mus. MS 19 marks the uncontroversial bass B♭s shown in bars 1 and 5. Munich, Bayerische Staatsbibliothek Mus. MS 3154 (on which Thomas Noblitt based his dating of the piece in the 1470s) has a B♭ signature in the bass part until beyond this passage. London, Royal College of Music MS 1070 has a B♭ before the bass B in bar 3. (I am grateful to Lawrence Earp for extracting these from the computerised data of the Princeton Josquin project.)

49   Manuscript accidentals in the altus: the late part-books Munich, Universitätsbibliothek, MS 8° 322–5 mark the B♭ shown in parentheses in bar 3. Observation of this 'fa'-sign might have further consequences quite disruptive for the basic counterpoint of the other parts. A performer studying his part alone might have sung this ♭ (whether or not notated, and whether or not we call it 'fa super la'). But on hearing the previously attacked B in the soprano (which also cannot be 'changed' without other consequences that are less readily defended than the version I propose), the altus is likely to sing B♮. The linear 'rounding-off' of this altus phrase with the ♭ was in any case an incompletely successful attempt to

Example 5

view of the status of the altus be contested, the present reading of it
can still be defended within fifteenth-century standards by invoking
the priority of vertical perfections over mediated linear tritones. To

rescue what has to be admitted, here alone in the motet, as a less elegant line, subservient
to the tight interlocking of the counterpoint between the other, primary, parts. I would
therefore choose to override it, but without insisting that this passage would always have
been solved in this way.

Margaret Bent

object that I have introduced a linear tritone where there was none before would assume the very correlation between notated pitches and keyboard-definable sounds that has been brought into question here. In the present example, the 'essential' piece of three-part counterpoint again takes priority both in its composition and its realisation, and the altus accommodates to this as best it may; there is no 'norm' from which this realisation is a departure. Irrespective of voice priority, this is a case of conflict between the claims of vertical perfection and mediated linear tritones; the former takes priority. The last three altus notes of bar 4 and the first four of bar 5 (marked in Example 5) then become intervallically identical to the passage quoted by Aron from Josquin's Mass *L'homme armé super voces musicales* (see above) and for similar though not identical reasons.

The example may be considered provocative. I have perpetrated for Josquin something that sounds not unlike what Lowinsky did, to mixed scholarly acclaim, for Clemens and Waelrant, composers about whom we perhaps have less deeply rooted prejudices than we do about Josquin. Despite some surface similarities of result, the reasons underlying my example, and my partial acceptance of Lowinsky's secret chromatic solutions, are patently different from his. The main thing that is wrong with the Secret Chromatic Art is that it is not chromatic; there was therefore no reason why it should have been secret. This reading is fully diatonic in its melodic progressions by any standards known to the sixteenth century.[50]

11. OBRECHT EXAMPLE

Van Crevel presented the passage from Obrecht's Kyrie *Libenter gloriabor* given here as Example 6, pointing out that to follow the sequence through exactly would result in a final cadence on F♭ as in Example 6(b).[51] What he actually printed, however, was a version which followed the sequence up to the first beat of bar 93 as in 6(a), but with E♭ and C♮ on the second beat of that bar in order to end on 'F♮'. As Lowinsky put it, 'van Crevel, afraid of his own courage,

---

[50] For those who prefer to define diatonic in terms of segments that can be transposed to piano white notes, this can be done for the last limb of the sequence starting on B♭ if played a minor third lower. See also Example 7.

[51] M. van Crevel, 'Verwante Sequensmodulaties bij Obrecht, Josquin en Coclico', *TVNM*, 16 (1941), pp. 119–21. Modern edition of Kyrie, ed. A. Smijers, *Van Ockeghem tot Sweelinck* (Amsterdam, 1939–56), II, 51.

Diatonic *ficta*

while holding fast to the possibility of the F♭ ending, proposed a compromise solution [ending in F major]'.[52] I agree with Lowinsky that van Crevel's printed version is musically unacceptable. But Lowinsky goes on to reject also van Crevel's (verbally indicated) 'spiralling' version, ending on 'F♭', on grounds that

(1) singers ending the Kyrie on F♭ would then 'have to accomplish the near miracle of beginning the Gloria on F' (which presumes that F is a frequency-determined constant for the performance);

(2) 'there is no poetic, emotional, or iconographic conceit that would justify so extreme a departure from the traditional harmonic conception at so early a time';

(3) 'there is no theoretical counterpart to such a modulation before 1505 (the year of Obrecht's death) that would conceptualize the use of C♭, F♭, and B♭♭';

(4) the 'secret chromatic' modulations proposed by Lowinsky and rejected by van Crevel are musically superior to the latter's Obrecht construction and historically more plausible. In fact, van Crevel admits the possibility of an 'F♭' ending which avoids the 'unmusical' twist objected to by Lowinsky when van Crevel makes the piece 'return home' to F, though Lowinsky, as stated above, objects to the F♭ ending because of its disjunction to the Gloria (which later invites a similar sequential spiral). In other words, Lowinsky objects to a spiral on grounds that are not strictly intra-musical, and he objects to a return to the same frequency on grounds of a harmonic wrench that is surely no worse than that which, by default, he seems to accept for bars 87–9, treating the notation as though it were exactly prescriptive, like a tablature. This passage surely must spiral, as in Example 6(b); the notated altus E♭ in 87 confirms what must happen, without changing what would have happened without it. Whether F or F♭ is used in bars 89–90 may depend on how the claims of exact sequence are balanced against those of the *recta* interval relationships.

Lowinsky objects that the singers would have to start the Gloria on F♭, not that 'F♭' at the end of the Kyrie makes that movement tonally incoherent. The objection disappears if we renounce frequency stability. The Gloria would start on the sound that is 'F' at that point (lower by one small Pythagorean semitone, and additionally subject to slight frequency difference from the starting point by

[52] Lowinsky, 'Secret Chromatic Art *Re-examined*', n. 63a.

Margaret Bent

reason of comma adjustment), and would then make its own spiral.

Tenor and bass are in strict canon with a suspended motive which invites a raised leading-note; the musical context allows the tenor to have the subsemitone but not the bass, which would thereby be unable to respect the higher priority of perfect simultaneous fifths. The superius and altus have the first three notes only of the tenor/ bass motive, a suspended lower returning note which, other considerations permitting, should be a subsemitone. As in the tenor, there is no reason for the superius not to take the subsemitone, falling as it does on the last beat of the modern bar. In the altus, however, this note always coincides with the superius entry a fifth higher, and produces a diminished fifth if the altus takes a subsemitone at these points. This choice for the altus (i.e., respecting the vertical perfection, even on a weak beat between upper parts, or raising the leading-note in an imitated motive) could be resolved differently in different performances. The bass, however, cannot 'raise' its leading notes; this would create not only diminished fifths at the bottom of the texture but also diminished octaves with the altus on all second beats or, if the altus adjusts its octaves to the bass, the effect of the diminished fifth between the lower parts will be worsened by the octave doubling of the bass by the altus. The case at no point depends on the maintenance of intervallically identical sequence laps, but rather on the independent determination, at each moment in the music, of how the priorities of vertical perfection and cadential subsemitones may be balanced.

Further, contemporary singers without commitment to constant frequency, having applied their *coniuncte* in bars 87–8, would then be in a position to read bars 89–96 as if nothing had happened. This would result in F♭ for bass and superius in 89–90, thus preserving the interval relationships proper to *musica recta* (or indeed to the mode), as signalled by the clef and signature. The 'minor triad' would be less likely to occur to a modern editor working with a transcription such as this, because it involves 'unnecessary' extra inflections of individual notes. I hope to have shown that this is immaterial to the operation of *musica ficta* or indeed, as in this case, to resuming the relationships implied by the clef. For the flats required by modern notation are mostly not even 'fictive' any more after the point of change in bar 88, as the nearly white-note transposition of this passage in Example 7 shows. This version, included to permit

Example 6   Obrecht, Kyrie *Libenter gloriabor*

Example 6 (*cont.*)

Margaret Bent

the reader of modern notation to test his prejudices about the sound
of the passage without the deterrent of excessive notated accidentals,
represents for bar 88 onwards something closer to the thought
processes of the renaissance singer. *Musica ficta* denotes neither the
sounds nor the symbols, but a process. The unsightly flats of
Example 6 are necessitated only by the difference between their
relative and our absolute pitch notation.

12. INTABULATIONS

Organ and lute intabulations of vocal polyphony tell the performer
where to put his fingers on an instrument which has been tuned prior
to performance and where, except for the adjustments possible on
fretted instruments,[53] a repertory of actual sounding pitches is
established at the outset, in a way that it never was or needed to be
for a-cappella vocal performance.[54] Keyboard tablatures were
treated as primary evidence for application of *musica ficta* by Apel[55]
while others have questioned the validity of this evidence on various
grounds, including chronological and geographical applicability.
Doubt has been cast upon the testimony of tablatures on grounds of
their inconsistency within and among themselves, and some have
wanted to discount them anyway as going too far, or not going far
enough. Despite the note-specificity of most tablatures, a glaring
need for some editorial decisions remains. Admirable work has been

---

[53] See, for example, E. Bottrigari, *Il Desiderio* (Venice, 1594), p. 5: 'Gli strumenti stabili, ma
alterabili [as distinct from those 'al tutto stabili'] sono tutti.quelli, che dapoi che sono
accordati dal sonator diligente, si possono alterare con l'accrescere, & minuire in qualche
parte, mediante il buon giudicio del sonatore toccando i loro tasti un poco più sù, un poco
più giù'.

[54] Most modern writers presume just such a repertory of available pitches, aligning the
gamut with the keyboard without recognising that vocal counterpoint and notation did not
need to be so anchored. This is true of Karol Berger's excellent study *Theories of Chromatic
and Enharmonic Music in Late 16th Century Italy* (Ann Arbor, 1980), from which a quotation
will serve to illustrate where his view of tonal materials differs from mine: 'Since steps
[relatively defined pitches] are defined by means of intervals . . . it is possible to discuss the
tonal system entirely in terms of intervals, that is, as a set of all intervals available to a
composer (that is, the gamut) and its pre-compositional organization. Octave equivalence
is basic to the sixteenth-century intervallic system; . . . the gamut consists of all intervals
possible within the octave . . . Certainly more than twelve, and possibly even all twenty-
one, different notes are used [notated] in practical sources. Although it can reasonably be
assumed that the musicians of the Renaissance were able to notate all the steps and
intervals they were using, it does not follow that all differently notated steps and intervals
were indeed different' (p. 98). For Prosdocimus on the infinity of sounds, see n. 21 above.

[55] *Accidentien und Tonalität in den Musikdenkmälern des 15. und 16. Jahrhunderts* (Berlin, 1936).

Example 7

Margaret Bent

done on the evidence of tablatures for performance practice of various kinds, notably embellishment and the 'use of accidentals': Howard Mayer Brown has argued that tablatures for fretted instruments indicate with greater precision and consistency than do organ tablatures the precise 'chromatic inflections' – a 'vast and largely unexplored repertory for the investigation of *musica ficta*'.[56] He believes that the practice of lutenists can be applied to vocal performance, noting that the counterpoint treatises of Gafurius and Burtius state or imply that their teachings can be applied both to instruments and to voices.[57]

But in subscribing to the much-explored view that intabulations are an important source of information for actual sounding notes in those repertories, we must remind ourselves that they are not so much transcriptions as arrangements (a point stressed by Dahlhaus); indeed, the quality that they most often compromise is precisely the contrapuntal voice-leading which invites or even compels a different logic of step-by-step progression in the vocally conceived original that was not committed in advance to a finite repertory of pre-tuned sounds. Neither modern notation nor tablature can provide the only, or the most correct, or even an accurate representation of what singers operating under a totally different set of constraints and options, i.e. with aurally determined contrapuntal procedures but without keyboard or even monochord anchorage, would have produced. The view of late-medieval vocal notation offered here is clearly different in principle from a system in which a symbol represents a single predetermined pitch. Renaissance intabulators encountered (perhaps without conscious rationalisation, because of the very large extent to which the two systems yield similar results) the same collisions of principle that we as editors do, and seem to have resolved them on a similarly cowardly and ad hoc basis. Modern notation is a kind of tablature every bit as

---

[56] 'Accidentals and Ornamentation in Sixteenth-Century Intabulations of Josquin's Motets', *Josquin des Prez*, ed. E. E. Lowinsky (London, 1976), pp. 475–522. 'While the character and extent of disagreement on the practical application of the rules of *musica ficta* on the part of sixteenth-century intabulators differed from that of modern scholars, who do not even agree on the existence and applicability of the rules, there was nevertheless a considerable difference of judgement and taste among the former' (p. 477 and *passim*).

[57] F. Gafurius, *Practica musicae* (Milan, 1496), book III, chapter 2: 'Species seu elementa contrapuncti in instrumentorum fidibus atque vocali concentu gravium atque acutorum sonorum commixtionem qua harmonica consurgit melodia proportionabiliter consequantur necesse est.' N. Burzius, *Musices opusculum* (Bologna, 1487), *Tractatus secundus*, sig. e. iij, speaks of *cantus*; instrumental reference is not specific at this point.

Diatonic *ficta*

confining as those of the sixteenth century. The keyboard with its fixed places, like modern staff notation with its fixed-point connotations, acted as a limitation upon the aurally determined contrapuntal thinking that is the necessary complement of vocal notation. It rendered Prosdocimus's infinity finite and forced the full notation of what need not, could not and should not be fully notated for voices. Many of the lute and keyboard arrangements fall short of the solutions demanded by the rules of counterpoint and *musica ficta* precisely because those arrangers, despite their different goal, were caught on the horns of the same dilemma that faces modern editors – namely that of finding a compromise between the ideal sound and a notational spelling that would look worryingly different from the vocally conceived original from which each is working. Because the process both of editing and of notated arranging is a written one, it encourages resolutions that avoid the visible anomaly even at the expense of an audible one.

With the important difference that the modern editor is trying to reproduce faithfully and the renaissance intabulator to arrange, both are trying to reconcile two superficially similar but fundamentally different notational systems possessing a large degree of overlap in practice and effect which masks the extent of their conceptual and potential difference. Keyboard tablatures are as accidental to this argument, and for the same reasons, as is modern notation; my main goal is to show why we must learn to acknowledge that early staff notation differs from both.

The problem of combining voices and instruments exercised theorists extensively from the late fifteenth century onwards, and they make it clear that certain compromises were necessary. Indeed, it is such theoretical testimony that provides almost our only evidence that theorists were aware of the collision of principle that I have here tried to sketch. Vicentino refers to the occasional need for an organist to effect a transposition during the course of a piece: '. . . & perche le voci sono instabili, molte fiate avviene ch'il Choro abassa un semitono, cantando dal suo primo principio, per seguire al fine: & inanzi che i Cantanti aggiungano al fine, qualche volta abbassano un tono; & acciò ch'il Discepolo cognosca il modo di poter sonare le compositioni un tono più basso . . .'[58] *Voci* here surely refer to the results of operating solmisation rather than to poor vocal intonation.

[58] N. Vicentino, *L'antica musica ridotta alla moderna prattica* (Rome, 1555); facsimile ed. E. E. Lowinsky (Kassel, etc., 1959, III. xiv, ff. 46ᵛ–47.

Margaret Bent

If the singers' wanderings were merely careless, Vicentino would surely have counselled them to improve their intonation or to match it to the organ rather than advising the organist to transpose.

Fixed-point instruments engender a different way of thinking from that induced by vocal counterpoint, and this in turn undoubtedly entailed different kinds of musical compromises. Theorists do more consistently present counterpoint as a vocal rather than as an instrumental skill. However, it is not very difficult for aurally alert modern musicians to play, for example on a fretted viol, vocal part-music of the fifteenth or sixteenth century, with appropriate linear adjustments at cadences and, the second time round, to correct or improve simultaneities noticed as unsatisfactory on the first reading. This may or may not involve signals between the performers, but in any case it can be done as simply as in vocal performance in the great majority of pieces. Very few, after all, require the kind of tonal spiralling which involves a change of frequency standard during a piece (which should be easier for renaissance singers not burdened with perfect pitch than for instrumentalists, even those equipped with Vicentino's suggestions). Even instrumentalists may have corrected perfect intervals, balanced priorities and matched imitative motives by exercising the same aural skills as singers.

An increasing body of evidence is suggesting that *a cappella* performance even of secular music in the fourteenth and fifteenth centuries may have been more common than hitherto thought; the problems that arise from combining voices and instruments may therefore have been avoided, in the same way and for the same reasons that groups of singers fastidious about intonation may prefer to sing unaccompanied. To combine voices with instruments of fixed tuning, keyboard or otherwise, will always cramp the style of what unaccompanied voices can do. Intabulations of *Fortuna, Ave Maria* and many other pieces which adopt less 'bold' versions than those resulting from the application of contrapuntal or other 'rules' therefore cannot be used as evidence that Lowinsky's and my readings of these pieces were not applied by sixteenth-century musicians, but rather that the intabulators faced the collision of principles at the point where the nominal and actual sounds, as understood in the different systems, diverged.[59]

---

[59]   J. van Benthem, '*Fortuna* in Focus: Concerning "Conflicting" Progressions in Josquin's *Fortuna dun gran tempo*', *TVNM*, 30 (1980), pp. 1–50, argues against Lowinsky's reading of

Diatonic *ficta*

13. TONAL COHERENCE

Our modern overriding concern with 'tonal coherence' in analysing music of any period is reflected, for renaissance music, principally in attempts to reconcile modal theories with musical realities, and in stronger assumptions about the notational prescription of precise pitch content than the evidence will bear.

Early theorists do not discuss long-term tonal coherence in the sense meant by most modern analysts of early music, other than in the context of mode which is obviously subject to at least the thin edge of the wedge of adjustment.[60] The work of Harold Powers has authoritatively disconnected modal assignments from the foreground of realised counterpoint and effectively confined them to background analysis and to precompositional intention in special sets of modally 'representative' works. He has essentially discredited the exercise of seeking modal classifications for works in which mode was not such an assumption.[61] Glareanus's exhaustive modal designations, despite their illustration from actual music, take no account of the need to disturb the official modal interval structures for

this piece ('The Goddess Fortuna in Music, with a Special Study of Josquin's *Fortuna d'un gran tempo*,' *The Musical Quarterly*, 29 (1943), pp. 45–77), on grounds which include the evidence of tablatures, the presence of 'mi–fa' false relations in other pieces by Josquin, and the unstated assumption that accidentals are a corruption of the text and should be kept to a minimum. That the result of Lowinsky's version is musically superior seems to me beyond question; the view of tonal materials here proposed helps to legitimate it against some arguments of its critics.

    While no attempt has been made to assemble tablature evidence for application to the present examples, it is perhaps worth pointing out that the Kleber tablature arrangement of Josquin's *Ave Maria* avoids the linear contrapuntal approach of the vocal model but does correct the vertical fifth – with F♯! The passage in the *L'homme armé* Agnus containing the problem illustrated by Aron is avoided altogether by Kleber. For modern transcriptions of both pieces see *Keyboard Intabulations of Music by Josquin des Prez*, ed. T. Warburton (Madison, 1980), pp. 32, 27.

60 *Pace* formulations such as 'used [*musica ficta*] as a "peccatum" . . . against the mode'; E♭ as a 'violation of the fifth mode': B. Meier, 'The Musica Reservata of Adrianus Petit Coclico and its relationship to Josquin', *Musica Disciplina*, 10 (1956), pp. 101, 103. See Howard Mayer Brown (in *Josquin des Prez*, ed. Lowinsky, p. 477): 'The idea that musicians of the time were guided by a desire to preserve the purity of the modes must be discarded once and for all. The profusion of accidentals incorporated into intabulations should lead those scholars who still advocate a policy of "utmost reserve" with respect to *musica ficta* to rethink their positions. Even so well-known a 'radical' in these matters as Edward Lowinsky would never gloss a reading as exuberantly as did some of the sixteenth-century lutenists.'

61 H. S. Powers, s.v. 'Mode', especially section III, *The New Grove Dictionary*; 'Modal Representation in Polyphonic Offertories', *Early Music History*, 2 (1982), pp. 43–86; 'Tonal Types and Modal Categories', *JAMS*, 34 (1980), pp. 428–70.

Margaret Bent

reasons of contrapuntal necessity. Aron's modal examples in the *Toscanello* are drawn from the same repertory as his *ficta* examples, but without overlap between the pieces chosen for the two purposes. He keeps the discussions separate and displays a totally different kind of musicianship in each. It appears that he too was, in a modal context, unconcerned with the actual intervallic realisation of the written notes. His assignments are abstractly analytical, and show none of the sensitivity to fictive intervallic adjustment that he displays in the *Aggiunta*. Finck assigns the fifth mode to Clemens's *Fremuit spiritu Jesu*, a piece which, in Lowinsky's 'secret chromatic' reading, discourages any linkage between modal designation and the prescription of actual sounds.[62]

One recurrent problem in modern discussions of mode and *ficta* in these repertories is the presumption that two such different ways of conceptualising pitch can somehow be reconciled on the common referential ground of the keyboard. Both the structure in principle of the gamut of *musica recta* and the intervallic structure of the modes as theoretical constructs were subject, in practice and when necessary, to adjustments which might create a 'departure' from the starting-point, temporary or for the rest of the piece. Analysis of a Romantic piece may reflect the abstract measure of the time signature as a musical reality yet not find it necessary to take account of rubato; the modal analyses of sixteenth-century theorists reflect a similar abstract background structure without taking account of the surface realisation. To alter the scale degree need not change the mode. The 'non-returning' sequential spiral at the end of the Obrecht Kyrie may be likened to a ritardando of pitch, the 'returning' Josquin to a 'repaid' rubato. Was it indeed as unmusical at that time to adhere, as if to a keyboard, to the starting pitch and implied interval structure of the opening of a piece, as it would be today to insist on constant metronomic measure for a performance? Did interpretations that stray from the white-note diatonicism to which we have grown accustomed sound different or special to them? It is hard for us to answer this until we have become used to thinking of sounds in a new way, to doing without the conventional dividing-lines we have applied between diatonic and chromatic, *recta* and *ficta*, not to mention abandoning our inherited faith in a pre-tuned white-note-

---

[62] H. Finck, *Practica musica* (Wittenberg, 1556), sig. Rr iiiᵛ.

Diatonic *ficta*

scalar modal chastity that is open to petty violation up to an ill-defined point. Modal theory does deal with some kind of long-term tonal coherence, but not necessarily such as can be equated with pitch stability – another distinction that has lost its force for us. This does not mean that there were no long-term tonal concerns, but that they were of a different kind from what we have learned to expect.[63] Notated 'pitches' await the musical realities of a contrapuntal context before they receive their actual definition in sound.

14. CONCLUDING REMARKS

If it is unrealistic to expect in one operation to abolish improper use of the words with which we customarily define *musica ficta*[64] – 'chromatic', 'inflection', 'alteration', 'added accidentals' – I hope at least to have injected more self-consciousness into such use. Once the prejudices in both directions have been dealt with, I believe we must learn to feel comfortable both with a different view of how counterpoint operated in practice, and with a more liberal approach to *musica ficta* than is currently considered respectable. If we are going to continue to enjoy the convenience of visual score control of early music, we must at least learn to recognise the nature of the compromises it represents, and learn to read it differently. There is no simple way of embodying choices or 'travelling' solutions in conventional modern notation. To put these repertories in score shifts to the editor or performer the onus of responding to aural realities and implementing consequences, even where these are not discernible from the individual parts, as they are not for the Josquin

---

[63] For statements reflecting the primacy that tonal organisation in its modern sense holds for much present-day scholarship, see Berger (*Theories*, p. 2): 'There can be little doubt that the organization of a sixteenth-century work is primarily tonal, that it is the organization of various pitches in certain specific ways, whereas organization of other values (temporal, timbral, dynamic) is of secondary importance.'

[64] See, for example, *Harvard Dictionary of Music*, 2nd rev. edn (Cambridge, Mass., 1969), s.v. 'Musica ficta': 'In the music of the 10th to 16th centuries, the theory of the chromatic or, more properly, non-diatonic tones . . .'; 'resulted from melodic modifications or from transpositions of the church modes'; '. . . disconcerting to find many long compositions completely lacking in any indication of accidentals'; '. . . the necessity for such emendations cannot be denied'; 'Matters were carried much too far in many editions published between 1900 and 1930 . . . no doubt historically accurate view of adding as few as possible.' And from *The New Grove Dictionary*: 'The term used loosely to describe accidentals added to sources of early music, by either the performer or the modern editor. More correctly it is used for notes that lie outside the predominantly diatonic theoretical gamut of medieval plainchant, whether written into the source or not.'

Margaret Bent

and Obrecht examples. This approach may not solve all problems, but to acknowledge the nature of the notation, to weigh priorities between rules, and sometimes to place the essentials of counterpoint above even notated accidentals does offer possible solutions for cases that have been considered intractable. It cuts through discussion about the duration, redundancy and cancellation of accidentals as inflections; through the presumption that additions should be kept to a minimum; through the identification of 'cautionary' signs that demand a reversal of their normal meaning, or of deliberately unsigned code notes; and indeed through the assumption that signatures are binding in the same way as their modern counterparts. It should disqualify counter-arguments couched in terms of absolute frequency, pitch stability, tonal coherence, modal purity, 'diatonic' supremacy, resistance to added accidentals as departing from the 'actual written notes', and tablature evidence for such notes as prescriptive for vocal performance. I have had to oversimplify here many issues that will eventually need careful and lengthy working out; but neglect of some primary musical facts has led us to tolerate the aural dissonance of intolerable intervals before we will accept the merely graphic dissonance of an intolerable-looking modern score.

Princeton University

'High' clefs in composition and performance

Andrew Johnstone

NOT for the first time in this journal, Andrew Parrott has recently defended his practice of performing a 4th lower than their written notation the compositions Monteverdi printed in 1610 in the 'high' clefs known as *chiavi alte* or *chiavette*. The debate had been reopened by Roger Bowers, who argued that the result of thus transposing those compositions (the *Missa In illo tempore*, the vesper psalm *Lauda Jerusalem*, and the two Magnificats) is just too low for comfort, and that they ought to be performed no more than a major 2nd lower than they are written.[1]

The difference of opinion stemmed partly from a difference of method. On the one hand, Parrott had presented, and has now reiterated, a compelling array of historical evidence from musical and theoretical sources, evidence that establishes 4th-lower performance as a general rule for 'high'-clef music from which Monteverdi's could not be exempt. On the other hand, Bowers presented analytical evidence from within Monteverdi's mass and vespers that was seemingly incompatible with most of the historical evidence. He assumed, however, that Parrott had no support from Italian theorists (p.533); as Parrott has subsequently pointed out, some important Italian theoretical sources have been brought to light by Patrizio Barbieri that confirm the case for transposition by a 4th. Bowers further assumed that the 'high'-clef movements ought to be transposed with the object of aligning their vocal ranges with those of the other movements, which are in normal clefs or *chiavi naturali* (p.528). Yet, as Jeffrey Kurtzman has succinctly put it, 'compositions in *chiavi alte* that have been transposed downwards often have sounding ranges a bit lower than the sounding ranges of untransposed pieces in *chiavi naturali*, even though

the original notation of pieces in *chiavi alte* looks higher.'[2] This paradoxical situation has a history reaching back to the early 16th century. By reviewing modern interpretations of the two standard clef combinations, by exploring their origins, and by amplifying the available evidence that shows how each relates to the other, this article will explain why low tessitura is indeed something to be expected of music notated in the apparently 'high' clefs.

Recent scholarship on clefs has not been helped by the universal editorial habit of transcribing into bass or treble clefs voice-parts originally notated in other clefs. No apology is made for the original, correct clefs that are used here. Information about the original cleffing of individual works has been obtained from a mixture of primary and secondary sources which are detailed in appendix 2. In the text, tables and endnotes, printed editions are identified by *RISM* numbers, and manuscripts by *New Grove* library sigla. It should be noted that editions and manuscripts are cited with the purpose only of showing that a work exists in a particular form of notation; most of the works referred to have more primary sources than those given here.

Modern interpretations of the standard clef combinations

For the chorus parts of his *Missa In illo tempore* and Vespers of 1610, Monteverdi used two clef combinations that were then standard in Continental vocal polyphony, and had been so for two or three generations. Each configures four voice-types in a similar manner, with the tenor lying a 5th higher than the bass, the alto a 3rd higher than the tenor, and the soprano a 5th higher than the alto (ex.1).

Ex.1 The standard clef-combinations of 16th- and early 17th-century vocal polyphony

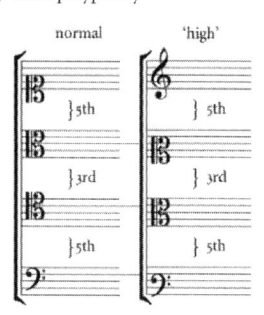

Ex.2 Kiesewetter's method for reading and transposing the 'high' clefs

Bowers's remark that there is 'common agreement' that these two combinations represent 'a single pitch-level diversely notated' (p.528) alludes to a notorious musicological red herring that requires some explanation. Because the 'high' clefs *look* as if they are related to the normal clefs by the interval of a 3rd, the idea that they imply transposition by that interval has proved much more seductive to modern interpreters than the rule, stated most famously by Praetorius in 1619, of transposing by a 4th or a 5th.[3] Transposition by a 3rd is not without historical precedents, for 'high'-clef pieces are known to have been once so performed in Italy, Germany and the Netherlands. But this *alla terza* practice dates from no earlier than the mid-17th century, when lower pitch standards were being introduced, composers were abandoning the 'high' clefs, and 16th-century normal-clef pieces were actually being transposed higher.[4] Nor has the practice ever been cited in support of modern theories of transposition by a 3rd.

The source of those theories can be traced to an essay on 'high'-clef pieces published by Rafael Georg Kiesewetter in 1847 (see appendix 1a). Finding himself on the horns of a dilemma that will be all too familiar to many of his readers today, Kiesewetter is torn between historical evidence for transposition by a 4th and the preference of contemporary performing groups for other transpositions. He yields to the latter, pointing out that, to save the bother of writing out a transposed version, a 'high'-clef score can simply be read as if it were in the normal

clefs (which were perfectly familiar to singers of Kiesewetter's time) and imagining an appropriate sharp or flat signature to preserve the position of each tone and semitone. A sharp signature thus transposed the 'high'-clef notation down a minor 3rd, while a flat one transposed it down a major 3rd (ex.2).

It was Kiesewetter's convenient transposition method, and not his erudite historical references, that would be seized on by later writers.[5] Knud Jeppesen's statement that the 'high'-clef combination 'was used to indicate that the particular composition could be performed a minor or a major 3rd lower than noted' shows that the 19th-century method ended up being mistaken for a genuine 16th-century one.[6] Until a strong historical case for transposition by a 4th or a 5th was made by Arthur Mendel in 1947, the debate seems to have fixed on the 3rd as the only possible degree of transposition. Those objections to it that were raised were motivated by a humanistic tendency to regard any degree of transposition as detrimental to the individual affective qualities of the modes.[7] (Ironically, a 17th-century expression of that very tendency, to be discussed below, provides irrefutable evidence that transposition by a 4th or a 5th was normal practice in Italy at that time.)

Despite Mendel's conclusion that there was 'not a shred of evidence' for it,[8] transposition by a 3rd went on to form the basis of Siegfried Hermelink's influential theory of clefs and modes which Harold Powers has subsequently developed into the

Ex.3 Hermelink's theory that the standard clef-combinations result from a ten-line staff: (a) normal clefs; (b) 'high' clefs

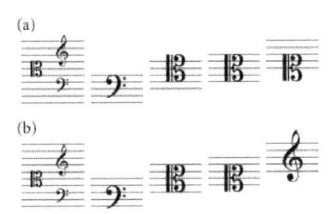

doctrine of 'tonal types'.[9] Hermelink believed that the 5th–3rd–5th configuration of voices resulted from drafting polyphony on a ten-line staff encompassing F to e'' (the limits of the Guidonian system plus F), a process described or at least hinted at by the 16th-century German theorists Venceslaus Philomathes, Auctor Lampadius and Heinrich Faber.[10] When the four voices were so drafted, the bass confined itself to the lowest five lines of the staff, and the soprano to the highest five, while the tenor and alto occupied medial portions of it. Once the voice-parts were fair-copied on to their own discrete five-line staffs, those staffs turned out bearing the four standard clefs (ex.3a). According to Hermelink, in cases where the Guidonian limits had to be exceeded, the overall compass of the 'usual' ten-line staff could be redefined as, say, D to c'' (a 3rd lower) or, much more typically, A to g'' (a 3rd higher). This would yield different sets of clefs for the individually copied voice-parts, but would amount to little more than a change of note nomenclature because the entire range (or 'Klangraum') would still be a 21st, and the relative ranges of the four voice-types would remain precisely similar (ex.3b).[11]

There is no evidence, however, that professional composers ever worked on ten-line staffs,[12] and Hermelink had to use constructed examples to illustrate his claim that 'high'-clef notation had originated in staff redefinition. Nor does his argument ring true that certain (actually fortuitous) clef changes in Palestrina's works prove that the 'low' and 'high' clef-combinations are related by a minor 3rd: the clef changes he cites occur in the plainsong-based masses *In minoribus duplicibus*

and *In maioribus duplicibus* (PW xxiii), and in the 'Vergine' madrigal cycle (*RISM* P761, of which nos.1–8 form a tonary), and they result from Palestrina's notating in natural and octave-transposed positions modes not specifically chosen by him but predetermined by context. Applying the Praetorius rule—to transpose 'high'-clef pieces without a flat signature to the lower 5th—to the liturgically contiguous Kyrie and Gloria of the *Missa In maioribus duplicibus* produces a result far preferable to the chromatic modulation adduced by Hermelink (ex.4).[13]

The substantive difference between normal and 'high'-clef notation postulated by Hermelink's 'Tonart-typen' (and to some extent, in consequence, by Powers's 'tonal types') thus needs re-examining. And evidence to be discussed shortly will show that in certain circumstances the two forms of notation are not mutually exclusive but interchangeable. This is not only because they were never related in the way Hermelink claimed; it is also because individual pieces were occasionally notated in *both* forms.

Origins of the standard clef-combinations

'Probably', says Bowers, 'the rationale informing contemporary deployment of this dual system of configurations will be understood much more fully when determination has been made of the manner in which that system came to be distilled during the 16th century' (pp.537–8, n.5). Hermelink's implausible theory therefore needs to be replaced with a new one.

The 5th–3rd–5th configuration was arrived at gradually over a long period. Medieval polyphony had distinguished only three voice-types: the tenor, whose range was determined by the *cantus prius factus* (when there was one), the contratenor, whose range was the same as the tenor's, and the superius, whose range was somewhat higher than the tenor's. The first Renaissance innovation was the addition, in Dufay's time, of the 'contratenor bassus' or bass. Next, the superius settled at roughly an octave above the tenor. Finally, by shifting its range upwards by about a 3rd, the contratenor evolved into the alto.

A factor influencing these developments (and even perhaps influenced by them) was the growing

Ex.4 *Missa In maioribus duplicibus*: conclusion of Kyrie (based on Mass II, *LU*, p.19) and opening of Gloria (based on ad libitum Gloria I, *LU*, pp.86–7): (a) as notated by Palestrina; (b) as interpreted according to Praetorius; (c) as interpreted by Hermelink (who does not quote the Gloria intonation)

importance of imitation as a formal basis for composition. With clefs separated by a 7th, the tenor and superius could jointly paraphrase a *cantus prius factus* in some form of canon at the octave—as, for example, in Heinrich Isaac's alternatim masses.[14] When the bass and contratenor participated in the imitation, they often did so at the same pitch as the tenor, with the result that all the voices entered on the same pitch-class. This procedure is particularly common in the works of Antoine Brumel—whose *Lauda Sion* (*RISM* 1503/1, no.13), for example, follows it exclusively—and Josquin, who followed it to open both sections of the Agnus Dei of his *Missa Pange lingua* (*I-Rvat* Ms. Cappella Sistina 16, ff.36v–46; ex.5a). That work, however, is chiefly characterized by a different type of imitation which would dominate 16th-century style: the fugue. Increasing use of the fugal answer obliged the contratenor to occupy a higher range between the tenor and superius, turning it into the new-style alto. It is thus clear from the famous opening of Josquin's

Pange lingua Kyrie that the normal clef-combination was a symptom of distributing fugal entries evenly among the voices (ex.5b).

The 'high' clef combination passed through similar developmental stages, existing in both contratenor and alto versions. It too was symptomatic of the rise of imitation, but its use was governed by considerations of mode and *cantus prius factus* setting that are easiest to account for by looking first at the tenor alone, in its traditional role as the plainchant-bearing voice.

A five-line staff with a C4 clef will accommodate chants falling within the range *c* to *f'*—almost all chants, that is, of the 1st, 3rd, 4th, 6th and 8th modes. But it will not accommodate chants whose ranges extend below *c* or above *f'*. The composer could solve this problem in two different ways: either adjust the chant to fit the clef, or adjust the clef to fit the chant. The first solution—transposition—reflected the practical necessity of singing extreme chants at a moderate pitch.

Ex.5 Josquin, *Missa Pange lingua*: (a) Agnus Dei (imitation with contratenor scoring); (b) Kyrie (fugue with alto scoring)

(a)

(b)

Ex.6 Chant ranges and their standard notations for polyphonic tenor parts. Rarely used notes are shown in parentheses. The chant ranges are from B. Meier, *The modes of classical vocal polyphony*, trans. E. S. Beebe (New York, 1988), p.41.

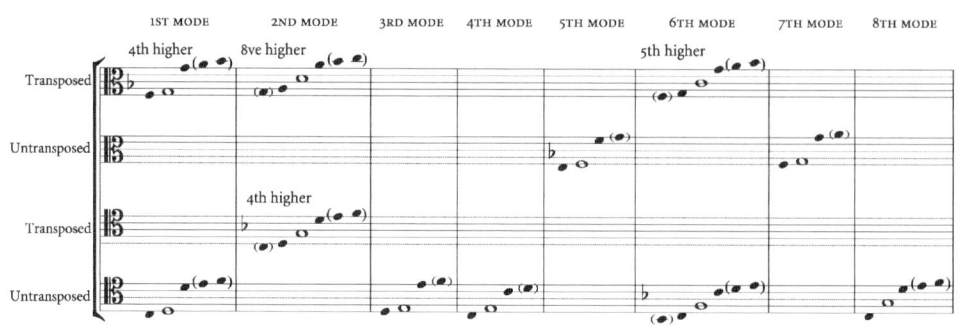

The second—clef change—preserved those extreme chants in their 'natural' written positions, leaving it to the performers to make the necessary pitch adjustment.

The results of these solutions are shown in ex.6. Written transposition was generally adopted for the 2nd mode, which extends as low as *G*. Placed a 4th higher, with final *g* and a signature of one flat, it sits comfortably in the C4 clef. Clef change was meanwhile the preferred solution for the 5th and 7th modes. In certain cases, transposition and clef change were combined, yielding alternative notations for the 1st mode (a 4th higher with flat signature and final *g*) and the 2nd mode (an octave higher with final *d′*). The 6th mode could likewise appear in the C3 clef, but here the method of transposition was more subtle: to avoid diminished 5ths below pitch-class F, polyphonic pieces in the 6th mode invariably had a signature of one flat already, so transposition up a 5th, with final *c′*, was effected by taking the flat signature away.

In certain modes, therefore, there was a choice of notations, and making that choice clearly depended on the range of the chant that was being set. Before leaving ex.6 we should observe that, for the 1st, 2nd and 6th modes, notation in the C3 clef would have been chosen for chants with *lower* rather than higher ranges.

Having changed the clef of the tenor, the diligent composer who wished to preserve the 5th–3rd–5th configuration of the whole ensemble would have to change the clefs of the other voices too. This produced the standard 'high' combination of F3-C3-C2-G2, but very often a greater adjustment was made to the bass part, placing it in the C4 clef, just a 3rd lower than the tenor. While the resulting 3rd–3rd–5th configuration is occasionally to be met with in a normal-clef version (F3-C4-C3-C1), its 'high'-clef version (C4-C3-C2-G2) is ubiquitous, and hints strongly, as we shall presently see, at the intended function of the 'high' clefs.

The desirability of consistently co-ordinating the voices with the tenor—whatever its clef—seems to have dawned slowly on composers of the high Renaissance, and this (at least partly) explains why early 16th-century polyphony exhibits such bewilderingly varied clef-combinations. For example, in the anonymous cycles of mass propers in *D-Ju* Ms.35 and the Lyons *Contrapunctus* (1528/1) the clef of the chant-bearing tenor varies from piece to piece, depending on the mode, while the clefs of the other voices remain, with a few exceptions, the same. It took at least 40 years of music printing to achieve the standardization that would characterize the Palestrina style, and charting the progress of that standardization presents certain methodological difficulties. Even if all the published vocal ensemble music of the first four decades of the 16th century had survived intact, and if it were all easily available, a comprehensive survey would still have to confront many confusing issues: clef changes during a piece (most often in the contratenor/alto part); sets of four partbooks that have pieces for more than four voices crammed into them; individual voice-parts that could or should have been printed in another clef (or even in another partbook); and the curious practice of anthologizing *voci pare* works suitable for men's voices alongside *voce piena* works suitable for mixed voices (resulting in the not infrequent appearance of tenor parts in superius partbooks). Furthermore, given that music publishers habitually pillaged material from earlier printed editions, reliable dating of individual works (and even collections) is often impossible. The following brief observations are therefore sketchy, and are based on a restricted selection of sources that must be regarded as no more than roughly representative of the period.

The 45 four-part items in Ottaviano Petrucci's *Odhecaton* (1501/1) are cast in no fewer than 20 different clef combinations. Yet about half the items have a superius part whose clef is a 7th higher than the tenor's (as in the standard combinations), while just over half have a new-style alto part. Significantly, the most frequent combination is the standard normal one, which appears 11 times.

With the first book of Petrucci's *Motetti de la corona* series (1514/1), the ratio of 26 motets to 11 clef combinations remains similar. But only four items have an old-style contratenor, while 15 are in the standard combinations (12 normal and three 'high'). That this trend appears to continue with the second book (1519/1) is partly because nearly half the items it contains are by Jean Mouton (whose entire output marks him out as probably the first composer for whom the 5th–3rd–5th configuration was the norm).[15] Only two of its 25 motets have old-style contratenors, 16 have normal clefs, and five have standard 'high' ones. The cleffing of the third book (1519/2), however, is less forward-looking: just two of its 16 items are standard (one normal and one 'high'), just two have identical cleffing (the *voci pare* combination F4-C4-C4-C4), the contratenor is back in force, and within nearly half of the pieces changes of clef occur in one or two of the voices.

While the 'high' clefs appear but infrequently in Petrucci's anthologies, they are much more in evidence by the time of Pierre Attaingnant's first motet book (1534/3) where they emerge on an equal footing with the normal clefs, each standard

combination being applied to ten of the 25 items.[16] And in Antonio Gardano's first book of *Motetti del frutto a quatro* (1539/13) the standard 'high' clefs actually predominate, being used for all except four of the 24 pieces. While this is unusual, other features of the collection are increasingly typical: it is ordered by clef, signature and final; it makes restricted use of the old-style contratenor (which appears only in no.6, in the *secunda pars* of no.20, and in no.22); and *voci pare* pieces are banished to anthologies of their own. Gardano thus appears to have intended each of his partbooks to contain exclusively material suited to its designated voice-type, and that impression is confirmed by his *Motetti del frutto … cum quinque vocibus* (1538/4). Here, apparently for the first time in an Italian printed motet anthology, the second tenor and second alto parts are gathered together in a fifth book not designated for any particular voice-type but simply labelled 'quintus'.[17]

Single-composer motet collections first appeared in 1539, with Attaingnant publishing one devoted to Pierre de Manchicourt, and Girolamo Scotto publishing two devoted to Jachet of Mantua, three to Adrian Willaert and two to Nicolas Gombert. Table 1 divides the clef-combinations used in those publications into three groups; the non-standard group includes occasional *voci pare* works, works with contratenor, and five-part works whose fifth voice does not duplicate one of the other four (a Gombert idiosyncrasy). Manchicourt, the youngest of the four composers, seems far more at home with the 'high' clefs than the others do. But other sources, printed and manuscript, of motets by all three older composers tell quite a different story.

Dual notation

We have seen that certain modes offered 16th-century musicians a choice of notations. This is evinced by a small but significant number of pieces that survive in two forms of notation that are almost invariably a 4th or a 5th apart.[18]

Willaert's motet *Veni Sancte Spiritus*, for example, was copied into the Medici Codex (*I-Fl* Ms.acq. e doni 666) with standard 'high' clefs, final *g* and a signature of one flat. Scotto, however, printed it with normal clefs and final *d* (ex.7).

Table 1   Clef-combinations in the single-composer motet books of 1539

Work	Printer	RISM	Standard clefs		Non-standard clefs	Total
			normal	'high'		
Jachet, *Motecta quatuor vocum. . .*	Scotto	J9	10	0	13	23*
———, *Motecta quinque vocum. . .liber primus*	Scotto	J6	14	1	11	26
Willaert, *Musica quatuor vocum. . .liber primus*	Scotto	W1106	9	0	17	26
———, *Motetti. . .libro secondo a quattro voci*	Scotto/Antico	W1108	9	6	6	21
———, *Musica quinque vocum. . .liber primus*	Scotto	W1110	15	0	8	23
Gombert, *Musica quatuor vocum. . .*	Scotto	G2977	8	1	13	22†
———, *Musica. . .quinque vocum. . .*	Scotto	G2981	2	1	20	23
Manchicourt, *Liber decimus quartus. . .*	Attaingnant	M269	3	12	4	19

* A further item, no.6, is by Claudin de Sermissy.
† A further item, no.8, is by Nicholas Payen.

Nor was this exceptional: three other motets by Willaert, one by Gombert and no fewer than seven by Jachet also have concordances a 4th higher than in Scotto's prints. (See table 2 for details of these and similar works from the period.) This suggests that during Girolamo Scotto's first year as manager of the family press he, or his editor, viewed the 'high' clefs with some suspicion.[19] Indeed, the only Scotto print from 1539 to make much use of the standard 'high'-clef combination—Willaert's second book of four-voice motets—happens also to be the only one that was not typeset by Scotto but printed from woodblocks prepared for him by Andrea Antico.

In 1545 Gardano reissued Willaert's four-voice motets in a markedly different two-volume edition (W1107 and W1109).[20] Ten motets that had been admitted to Scotto's edition but are absent from Gardano's all have contratenor or *voci pare* scorings and non-standard clef combinations,[21] while eight that are new to Gardano's edition include three normal-clef and four 'high'-clef items.[22] And though Gardano retained Scotto's normal notation in *Veni Sancte Spiritus* (W1109 no.8), he exchanged it for his preferred 'high' notation in the motets *Surgit Christus* (see table 2) and *Ioannes apostolus*. With the second of these items we encounter our second form of dual notation, whose written pitches differ by a 5th (see table 3).

Though they are not concordances in the same sense as the works listed in tables 2 and 3, the motets

and related imitation masses listed in table 4 similarly illustrate the phenomenon of dual notation. In most cases the clefs of the models are normal, while those of the masses are 'high'. This apparent preference for 'high' clefs in masses is corroborated by five masses based on items listed in table 3 that all follow the 'high' rather than the normal version of their model: Berchem, *Missa Altro non è el mio amor'* (1547/3 f.17); Gaspar de Albertis, *Missa Dormendo un giorno* (A664 no.3); Francisco Guerrero, *Missa Dormendo un giorno* (G4870 no.6); Clemens non Papa, *Missa Quam pulchra es* (C2683); and Palestrina, *Missa Quam pulchra es* (P677 no.4).

In addition to the examples of dual notation listed in tables 2, 3 and 4, whose differing notated pitches are transmitted in separate sources, a number of 16th- and early 17th-century publications have been cited by Mendel, Parrott and Barbieri that contain pieces simultaneously notated at two pitch levels. These are anthologies of madrigals that include an arrangement or intabulation of each piece for keyboard or lute (1584/12, 1586/2, 1589/11, 1591/12, [1595]/6), and two posthumous editions of Palestrina's *Canticum canticorum* motets that are supplied with a 'bassus ad organum' (P725; P727, illus.1). In the vast majority of the madrigals, and in all of the motets, the instrumental parts for 'high'-clef works with a flat signature are a 4th lower, while those for 'high'-clef works without signature are a 5th lower.[23]

Ex.7 Dual notation for Willaert's *Veni Sancte Spiritus*: (a) *I-Fl* Ms.acq. e doni 666; (b) W1106

Table 2   Works with concordances notated a 4th apart

Work	'Lower' notation (without signature)	'Higher' notation (with flat signature)
Carpentras, *Lamentations* ('Incipit')	1557/7 no.1*	G1572 no.1[†]
Elimot/Hotinet Barra, *Nuptiae factae sunt*	I-CFm Ms.LIX, f.55v	I-Fl Ms.Acq. e doni 666, ff.72v–74r
Verdelot, *Hesterna die* (*prima pars*)	1549/15 no.9	1549/12 no.2
————, *Con l'angelico riso*	1540/20 no.13	US-Cn Case Ms.-VM 1578.M91 no.III 1
————, *Piove da gli occhi*	1540/20 no.19	US-Cn Case Ms.-VM 1578.M91 no.III 14
Jachet, *Alma Redemptoris mater*	J6 no.15	J14 no.10
————, *Audi dulcis amica mea*	J9 no.2	1538/5 no.22
————, *Descendi in ortum*	I-Rbv Ms.Vall.S.Borr.E.II.55–60 no.40	1534/10 no.17
————, *Mirabile mysterium*	J6 no.7	J14 no.15
————, *O Dei electe . . . Ambrosi*	J6 no.8	J14 no.20
————, *Plorabant sacerdotes*	J6 no.13	J14 no.16
————, *Repleatur os meum*	J6 no.14	1540/7 no.9
————, *Salvum me fac*	J6 no.14	1538/4 no.8
————, *Si ignoras o pulchra*	J6 no.9	J14 no.9
Festa, *Regina caeli*	I-Rvat Ms.Cappella Giulia XII 4, f.64v	I-Fl Ms.Acq. e doni 666, ff.141v–143r
Willaert, *Ave Maria*	W1106 no.1	I-TVd Ms.8, ff.122v–124r
————, *O gemma clarissima*	W1106 no.9	I-Bc Ms.Q19, ff.109v–110r
————, *Surgit Christus*	W1106 no.25	W1109 no.16
————, *Veni Sancte Spiritus*	W1106 no.11	I-Fl Ms.acq. e doni 666, ff.62v–66r
Gombert, *Salvum me fac*	G2977 no.9	1538/5 no.25

* With a signature of one flat.
[†] With a signature of two flats.

Certain critics have assumed that works existing in dual notation were actually sung at two different pitch levels, a symptom of this assumption being the habit of always referring to the C3 clef as 'alto' regardless of whether it appears in a normal- or 'high'-clef context. Colin Slim thus proposed that Gardano renotated Scotto's version of Willaert's *Surgit Christus* to make it 'available for performance by a more diverse performing group'.[24] Concerning Mouton's *Peccata mea* (a work whose earliest sources are in 'low' clefs that take the bassus part down to C—see table 3), Edward Lowinsky complained that a concordance in normal clefs 'robs the work of an essential element of its character and sonority by transposing it a 5th higher'.[25] Likewise, Kenneth Kreitner has argued for the literal interpretation of similar works in 'low' notation by Ockeghem and Tinctoris.[26]

The existence of normal-clef concordances for *Peccata mea* suggests, however, that 'low'-clef notation was a copyist's artifice that could be used to emblematize doleful texts, and that 'low'-clef works were actually performed at the pitch level represented by the normal clefs.[27] Nor is *Peccata mea* the only 'low'-clef work with differently notated concordances: the sole manuscript source of Josquin's *Absalon fili mi* is in 'low' clefs with final Bb (GB-Lbl Ms.Royal 8 G.vii, ff.56v–58r), while its two printed sources are extraordinarily a 9th higher with final c' (1540/7 no.24; 1559/2 no.10). That this motet was actually performed at neither of the extreme pitch levels represented by these sources, but at the medial pitch level represented by the normal clefs, is apparent from a lute intabulation (1558/20, ff.30r–31v) and an anonymous *Missa Absalon fili mi* (I-Bsp Ms.31, ff.110v–118r), in both of which the final is f.

Table 3   Works with concordances notated a 5th apart

Work	'Lower' notation (with flat signature)	'Higher' notation (without signature)
Mouton, *Peccata mea, Domine**	1519/1 no.17	M4017 no.20
de Silva, *Omnis pulchritudo Domini*	*I-Bc* Ms.Q27(1), ff.49*v*–50*r*	*I-Fl* Ms.Acq. e doni 666, ff.122*v*–125*r*
Verdelot, *Gaudeamus omnes*	1549/12 no.4	1549/15 no.2
————, *In te Domine speravi*	*I-Bc* Ms.Q27(1), ff.51*v*–52*r*	*US-Cn* Case Ms.-VM 1578.M91 no.II 2
————, *Altro non è el mio amor' ch'el proprio inferno*	[*c.*1538/20] no.6	1538/21 no.2
————, *Dormendo d'un giorno*	[*c.*1538/20] no.18	1540/7 no.42
Willaert, *Iohannes apostolus*	W1106 no.21	W1107 no.7
Lupi, *Quam pulchra es*	1538/8 no.13	1532/11 no.9
Arcadelt, *Qual Clitia sempre al maggior lun' intento*	1539/23 no.33	1539/22 no.25
————, *Perche la vit'e breve*	*I-Fn*, Mss.Magliabecchi XIX 130 no.8	1564/15 no.11
Ruffo, *Ben mille nott'ho gia*	*I-Fn*, Mss.Magliabecchi XIX 130 no.4	R3065 no.15
Clemens, *Missa Misericorde*	*B-Bc* Ms.27087, ff.151*v*–172*r*	C2667

* Both forms of notation have a signature of two flats: in the 'lower' form, which has the final *c*, notes of pitch-class A are flatted with accidentals.

Table 4   Models and imitation masses notated a 5th apart

Work	'Lower' notation (with flat signature)	'Higher' notation (without signature)
Bauldeweyn, *Quam pulchra es*	—	1519/3 no.15
Gombert, *Missa Quam pulchra es*	1532/6 no.2	—
Jachet, *Aspice Domine quia facta est*	J6 no.6	—
Palestrina, *Missa Aspice Domine*	—	P660 no.5
Jachet, *Spem in alium*	J9 no.19	—
Palestrina, *Missa Spem in alium*	—	P664 no.1
Willaert, *Si rore Aonio*	W1110 no.5	—
Lassus, *Missa Si rore aenio*	—	*D-Mbs* Ms.24, ff.1–37
Sermisy/Sandrin, *O combien est malheureux*	—	1542/15 no.8
Clemens, *Missa Or combien es*	1570/1 no.3	—
Lupi, *Spes salutis pacis*	1538/5 no.24	—
Clemens, *Missa spes salutis*	—	1570/1 no.4
Manchicourt, *Non conturbetur cor vestrum*	*E-MO* Ms.768, f.124*v*	—
————, *Missa Non conturbetur cor vestrum*	—	*NL-L* Ms.1441, f.153*v*
Maillard, *Eripe me de inimicis meis*	M184, f.13	—
Palestrina, *Missa Eripe me*	—	P667 no.5

Further evidence that 'high'-clef notation was not meant to be taken literally is provided by the clef-combination Scotto used for his version of Willaert's *Ioannes apostolus*: F4-F3-C4-C2. Though typical of the pieces listed in table 3, this combination would soon disappear from 16th-century usage, and it has been classed as non-standard in table 1 above. It occurs, however, in all Scotto's 1539 motet collections: twice in each of Jachet's two books, three times in each of Willaert's

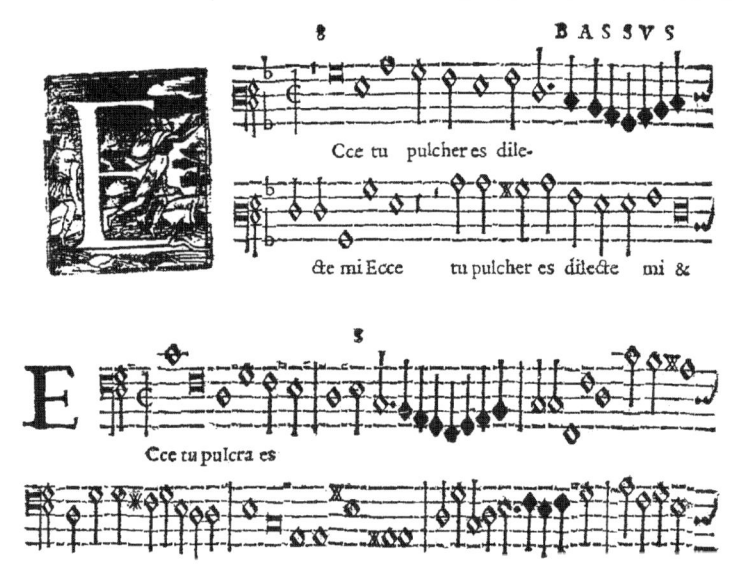

1 Vocal and instrumental bass parts from a posthumous print of Palestrina's *Canticum canticorum* motets (P727). The instrumental bass parts for all the 'high'-clef items with a flat signature in this print are a 4th lower than the vocal bass, while those without signature are a 5th lower. (By permission of The British Library, D.205.e)

three books, twice in Gombert's four-part book and three times in his five-part book.[28] Because it is invariably accompanied by a flat signature, and because each of its clefs lies exactly a 5th lower than the corresponding 'high' clef, this special combination produces a form of notation whose appearance is in all other respects identical to standard 'high'-clef notation for the 3rd–3rd–5th configuration (ex.8).

Presumably, therefore, Scotto used this and the other 'lower' equivalents of 'high'-clef notation in 1539 to spell out unambiguously transpositions that were still establishing themselves as conventional for the performance of 'high'-clef works. Meanwhile, the more extensive use of 'high' clefs in contemporary and later publications—Gardano's particularly—suggests that, more and more, composers and printers were delegating the responsibility for such transpositions to performers.

Dual notation raises the question of why 'high' notation was necessary at all, if it could always have been converted into normal notation. Often

this conversion could not be made without the use of ledger lines, of course, and this brings us back to Hermelink and his observation that the limits of the two standard clef-combinations place each modal final and ambitus in slightly different relationships. (Compare, for example, the two transposed forms of the 2nd mode shown in ex.6.) Hermelink held that such differences in ambitus produce 20 discrete 'Tonart-Typen' that are more subtly characterized than the four traditional pairs of authentic and plagal modes. Arguably, this neo-modal system overstresses negligible differences of ambitus that were never very rigorously observed in practice. But those differences do explain why a 16th-century composer, copyist or printer might have preferred one form of notation to the other.

That 'high' clefs can have been used for no reason other than that they provided a neater way of notating *lower* vocal ranges than those accommodated by the normal clefs is nicely illustrated by Palestrina's 'high'-clef *Missa Eripe me*, which is

Ex.8 Dual notation for Willaert's *Ioannes apostolus*: (a) W1107; (b) W1106

Ex.9 (a) Opening of Maillard's motet *Eripe me de inimicis meis*; (b) Opening from Palestrina's *Missa Eripe me* based on a normal-clef motet by Jean Maillard with no known 'high'-clef concordances (see table 4). Despite the close resemblance of certain passages (ex.9), the two forms of notation conceal slight discrepancies between the voice-ranges of the model (ex.10a) and those of the mass (ex.10c). Converting the mass's voice-ranges into normal clefs reveals that the tenor, alto and soprano lie a little lower than in the model, and would have required ledger lines if the notation of the model had been retained (ex.10b).

Transposition and 'high' clefs

Though 'high'-clef notation was in use by 1500, it was not until much later that theorists associated it with specific transpositions. This was because transposition *per se* could not take place without reference to a pitch standard, and before such standards were established the pitch-level at which a piece was notated hardly mattered because choirs would sing it at whatever pitch suited them. How they agreed upon suitable pitches before the 16th century is a complete mystery, however, and the pitches they took can now only be guessed at. For modern performers of the polyphony of Josquin's time and earlier, therefore, the only possible approach to the pitch question is a purely empirical one that historical research will probably never be able to corroborate.[29]

Our knowledge of 16th-century pitch standards is dominated by evidence from Venice,[30] the centre of European woodwind-instrument making and a

byword for standardization in manufacturing generally. In that context the preference for normal-clef notation evident in Scotto's 1539 motet books strongly suggests that in Venice those clefs were by then associated with a vocal pitch standard, and were thus beginning to be regarded as *naturali* or normal. Scotto might even have been trying to impose a Venetian uniformity on vocal notation by abolishing the 'high' clefs altogether—an ideal that would not be achieved until early in the 18th century.

Though the foremost theorists of the mid-16th century, Vicentino and Zarlino, are frustratingly taciturn on the questions of pitch and transposition, it can be inferred from the general pattern of clefs

Ex.10 Comparison of the ranges of Maillard, *Eripe me de inimicis meis* and Palestrina, *Missa Eripe me*: (a) the motet; (b) the mass if it had been notated like the motet; (c) the mass as Palestrina notated it

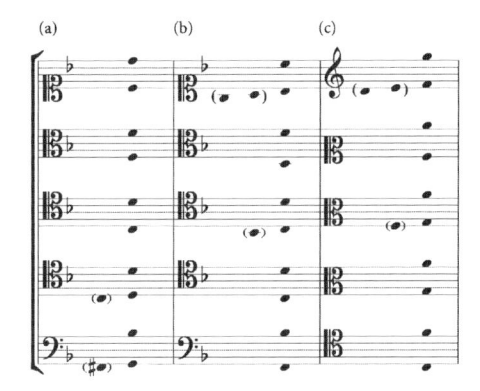

Table 5   Clef usage and transposition in Palestrina's works

Clef of bass part	Performed at pitch	With flat signature, performed a 4th lower than written		Without signature, performed a 5th lower than written		Others	Total
	F_4	C_4	F_3	C_4	F_3		
Masses	16	6	23	22	14	11*	92
Motets & hymns	81	25	107	102	44	28	387
Magnificats	10	2	3	9	3	8	35
Madrigals	39	6	35	37	7	10	134
Total	146	39	168	170	68	57	648

* Includes the four masses with movements in different clefs.

and signatures in the works of Palestrina that he habitually composed with specific transpositions in mind (see table 5). The bass parts of his 'high'-clef works with flat signature tend to be placed in the F3 clef, so that transposition by the usual 4th gives them a lowest limit of E—only a semitone lower than the lowest limit of the normal clefs. Meanwhile, the bass parts of his 'high'-clef works without flat signature tend to be placed in the C4 clef, so that transposition by the usual 5th takes them no lower than F—the same as the lowest limit of the normal clefs. And the bass parts of nearly half the works that are in the F3 clef without flat signature are also suitable for 5th-lower transposition because they too have a lowest written limit of c. Nor did Palestrina often exceed that limit in his remaining F3 bass parts without flat signature: the *Missa O admirabile commercium* (P681 no.3), for example, contains just one B, the *Missa Ascendo ad Patrem* (P687 no.3) one B and one B♭, and the

Missa Tu es Petrus a6 (*I-Rvat* Ms.Ottoboniani latini 2927, on his own motet) just two As.

Palestrina thus appears to have used the 3rd–3rd–5th configuration purposefully to avoid excessive lowness of the bass when 5th-lower transposition was effected. That configuration is not, therefore, a variant form of the 5th–3rd–5th one with a *higher* bass part, but a variant form with *lower* tenor, alto and soprano parts (ex.11). And its usual association with 'high' rather than normal notation can mean nothing other than that, with 'high' notation, a significant downwards transposition was expected.

As Barbieri has pointed out, the Italian theorists' silence on the transposition question was decisively broken in the early years of the 17th century. Years before Praetorius published it, the classic transposition formula was prescribed by Adriano Banchieri, first in 1601 and again in 1610 (see illus.2 and appendix 1b).[31] In 1631 it was reiterated by Silverio Picerli (appendix 1c), and in 1640 the humanist

Ex.11 Palestrina's notational schemes and their ranges when conventionally transposed in performance

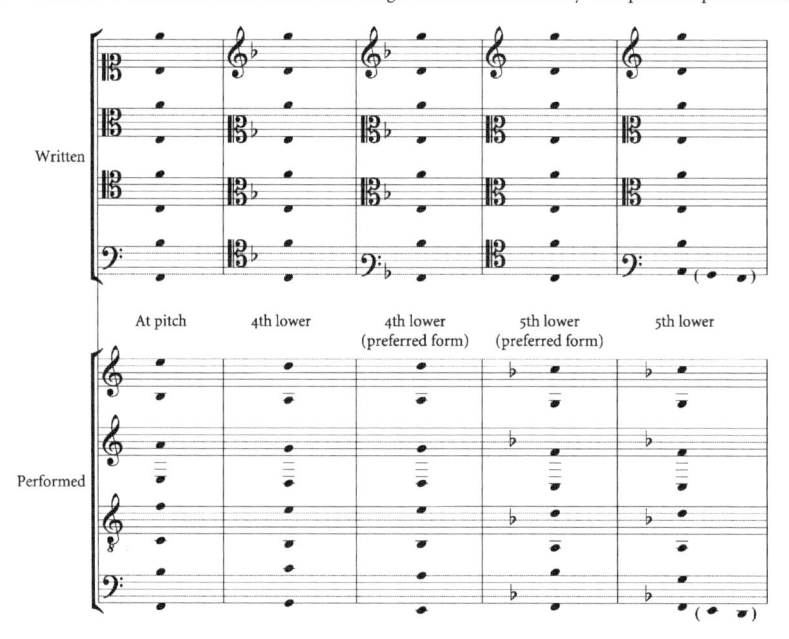

2 Adriano Banchieri's written-out examples of 'high'-clef transpositions (see appendix 1b). The transposed section of the soprano part of the first example is incomplete, and the initial clef of the tenor part of the second section should be C2. (By permission of The British Library, Hirsch IV 1468)

Giovanni Battista Doni reported that it was then usually applied in Rome (appendix 1d). In a chapter entitled 'Dell'inutile osservanza de' Tuoni hodierni' ('The uselessness of observing the modern modes') Doni actually complained that the usual transpositions obscure a mode's defining features, and proposed a new gamut extending from *C* to *c‴* that would accommodate all Glarean's 12 modes polyphonically in their natural positions.

Doni's music examples (illus.3) show that the Italians were by then applying 4th-lower transposition to 'high'-clef pieces *without* flat signature—an expedient recommended by Praetorius for works in certain modes. To write out that transposition, a signature of one sharp had to be used, and resistance to this new-fangled notational device was so prolonged in certain quarters that the 'high' clefs continued to be used in preference to it. In the *Saggi di contrappunto* penned by

Bernardo Pasquini in 1695, examples in *chiavi trasportate*—whether or not they have a flat signature—are marked 'si suona e si canta alla 4.a bassa' (*D-Bsb* Ms.P.Landsberg 214, p.33).

In the mass he published in 1610 Monteverdi retained the 'high' clefs and *c'* final of its model, Gombert's motet *In illo tempore loquente Iesu* (1539/3 no.1). In other words, then, the mass is in Glarean's Hypoionian, one of the modes Praetorius deemed suitable for transposition to the lower 4th. Indeed, by taking the bass part of the mass down to *G* (that of the motet goes no lower than *c*), Monteverdi signalled that he expected it to be transposed a 4th lower in the manner illustrated by Doni—just as it appears, in fact, in two later sources.[32]

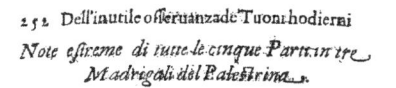

3 Giovanni Battista Doni's comparison of the ranges of three madrigals by Palestrina. (See appendix 1d.) *Vergine pura* and *Vergine chiara* are in normal clefs and sung *come sta* (i.e. at written pitch); *Vergine saggia*, which is in 'high' clefs, is transposed a 4th or a 5th lower. (By permission of The British Library, Hirsch I 149)

Appendix 1:   Readings

(a) R. G. Kiesewetter, *Galerie der alten Contrapunctisten* ... (Vienna, 1847), pp.viii–xi. The authorities Kiesewetter cites are R. Rodio, *Regole di musica* (Naples, 1609), G. B. Martini, *Esemplare o sia saggio fondamentale pratico di contrappunto sopra il canto fermo: parte prima* (Bologna, 1774) and G. Paolucci, *Arte prattica di contrappunto* (Venice, 1765–72).

Vorrede *über die Nothwendigkeit, viele Compositionen der alten Meister für unsere Zeit in andere Tonlagen zu versetzen* ...

... wir wissen jetzt (was Autoren in der Literatur berühmten Namens, ein *Rocco Rodio*, ein *P. Martini, Paolucci* u. A. auch mit Bestimmtheit *bezeugen*): dass solche Compositionen von den Capellsängern *nur tiefer intonirt* wurden, und zwar nach beliebiger *Uebereinkunft*, oder (wie weiland *Ab. Baini*, der Geschichtschreiber des grossen *Palestrina*, es ausdrückt) *al commodo delle loro voci*: Sie waren in der *Versetzung* irgend eines Gesanges, vom Blatte, *aus dem Stegreif in jede beliebige Tonlage*, ungemein geübt. — Am *gewöhnlichsten* geschah, bei den oben gezeigten *chiavette*, die Intonation in der *Unterquarte*, und es verdient in dieser Beziehung hier angemerkt zu werden, dass — seit der Einführung einer beständigen *Orgelbegleitung* in den Capellen, *diese* Versetzung, in den für sie gedruckten Auflegstimmen, gewöhnlich *nur in dem für den Organisten* gedruckten *Bassus ad Organum*, mit der einfachen Formel: *a la quarta bassa,* — oder *per quartam deprimitur*, angezeigt wurde. Für die *Sänger* war die Sache so gleichgiltig, dass man es für überflüssig gehalten zu haben scheint, sie hiervon auch nur zu benachrichtigen.

Unsre *heutigen Sänger* darf man nicht mit der Zumuthung einer *improvisirten* höheren oder tieferen *Intonation* in Versuchung führen wollen; für sie müssen die *Parte* im eintretenden Falle vorbereitet, das ist *vollständig*, und zwar *in eine moderne Tonleiter, umgeschrieben* werden.

Dem Gesagten zufolge sollte nun die *Umschreibung* der in den *chiavette* geschriebenen Compositionen für uns in die *Unterquarte* geschehen: da findet es sich aber, dass für *unsern Chor* die Stimmen wieder *zu tief* gehalten sein würden: die *Alten* besetzten zu ihrer Zeit die *Discant-* und *Alt-Partie* mit *Männern*, die im Falset oder als *Alti naturali* (oder *Tenorini*) sangen, und also in der Höhe beschränkt waren; wir mit *Knaben* oder *Weibern*, denen hinwieder die tiefe Lage allzu unbequem wäre. Nun würden zwar *Discantisten* und *Altisten*, wie solche *unser Chor* dermal zur Verfügung hat, eine solche Composition sogar *im Tone der Schrift*, ohne sich sehr wehe zu thun, zur Noth ausführen können; allein, der verständige und gewissenhafte Anordner darf nicht

einzelne Stimmen des Chores berücksichtigen wollen auf Kosten der Andern, und auf die Gefahr des Misslingens des Ganzen: Gewiss ist es, dass der *Bass*, gesungen von sogenannten *Baritonisten* (an welchen es freilich nirgends mangelt), durch die *hohe Tonlage* seine Bedeutsamkeit und seinen Ernst einbüssen würde; die eigentlichen (*Sarastro-*) *Bassisten* würden zur Noth ihr Trompetenregister ziehen, die unglücklichen *Tenoristen* aber, beständig in der höheren und höchsten Stimmlage angestrengt, müssten vollends *verzweifeln*, und würden ganz zuverlässig durch arges Schreien, in dessen Folge durch das unausbleibliche Sinken der Stimmen, den Chor herabziehen und so die Ausführung zu Grunde richten.

Alles wohl erwogen, und nachdem ich Mancherlei versucht, habe ich endlich gefunden, dass (*im Allgemeinen*) die Versetzung *solcher* Compositionen *in die Unterterz* (statt Unterquarte) einem Chor *unsrer Sänger* noch am besten zusagt; und ich machte bald die Entdeckung, dass sich *diese Versetzung, ohne an dem Original einen Notenkopf zu verrücken*, wie mit einem Zauberschlag bewerkstelligen lässt: Setze ich *neben die chiavette* des Originals *unsre gewöhnlichen und gewohnten* (Sopran-, Alt-, Tenor- und Bass-) *Schlüssel*, mit der *Vorzeichnung*, welche der neu entstandenen Tonleiter (*der Unterterz*) unserm modernen System gemäss gebührt; — so habe ich zugleich das *unversehrte Original*, und zugleich dieselbe Composition (ad libitum) *in die Unterterz versetzt*, und zwar *in einer für jeden Musiker unsrer Zeit verständlichen Partitur*, vor Augen. ...

Diese Versetzung, die ich in der Regel allgemein anwende, habe ich in den meisten Fällen *auch für die Ausführung* der Composition als die passendeste befunden. Wie denn aber keine Regel ohne Ausnahme ist, so habe ich *für den Zweck der Ausführung*, oder zu angenehmerer Ansicht der Partitur (auch wohl, um den nicht immer mit Adepten der Musik besetzten Chor nicht in einer *allzu chromatischen* Vorzeichnung auf eine vielleicht gefährliche Probe zu stellen) niemals ein Bedenken getragen, manches Tonstück nur *um Eine Tonstufe*, ein anderes wieder wohl gar um die *ganze Quarte* herabzusetzen. (Ja zuweilen ist es mir glaublich geworden, dass manches in den *ordinären Schlüsseln* geschriebene Stück, wegen besonders *tiefer Haltung der Stimmen*, schon von den damaligen Capell-Sängern übereinkömmlich *sogar höher intonirt* wurde.) Die Aufgabe ist endlich immer die: das *Vermögen der Sänger*, dann das gehörige *Verhältniss* (den Abstand) *der Stimmen unter einander* zu beobachten. Diesem letzteren Theil der Aufgabe ist oft nicht leicht zu entsprechen, weil man (in Folge der damaligen Organisation der Capellen) häufig den *Alt* beträchtlich tiefer geführt findet, als wir ihn heut zu Tage zu führen pflegen: und dennoch muss im Conflict die vorzüglichere Sorge dem *Tenor* zugewendet werden.

Preface on the necessity, in our time, of transposing many works by the old masters to other registers . . .

. . . we now know (as such reputable authors as Rocco Rodio, Padre Martini, Paolucci *et al.* have indubitably testified) that chapel choirs sang such compositions at a lower pitch and however they found it convenient, or (as the late abbé Baini, biographer of the great Palestrina, puts it) *al commodo delle loro voci*; they were immensely skilled at spontaneously transposing any composition, at sight, into the required key. Transposition to the lower 4th was most usual with the above-mentioned *chiavette*, and in this connection it should be noted that, since the introduction of organ continuo in the chapels, this transposition, in printed editions of the part-books, was usually only printed in the organ part, and indicated by the simple phrase *a la quarta bassa*, or *per quartam deprimitur*. Singers were so indifferent to this matter that it seems to have been unnecessary to notify them of it. One simply must not lead our present-day singers astray by placing upon them the unreasonable demand of an extempore higher or lower transposition; the parts must be meticulously prepared for them one by one, and that means writing them out in a modern scale.

In accordance with the above, the writing out of those compositions that use *chiavette* ought to involve transposition to the lower 4th: here, however, we find that the voice-parts lie too low for our own choirs; in the time of the old masters the soprano and alto parts were sung by men, with falsetto or *haute contre* (tenorini) voices, whose upper reaches were therefore limited. The choirs of today, with their boy trebles or female sopranos, conversely find the lower reaches uncomfortable. Indeed, the sopranos and altos of our choirs would, at a pinch, be able to sing such compositions in the written key without doing themselves too much damage, but the understanding and conscientious director cannot give preference to one section of the choir over another, nor risk the breakdown of a performance. The bass part, sung by so-called baritones (which are never in short supply) would certainly have to relinquish some of its *gravitas* because of the

high tessitura; the true (Sarastro-type) basses would be forced to pull out their trumpet stop [so to speak], while the hapless tenors, stretched to breaking point in their highest and loudest register, would become quite desperate, their shrieking would bring about an inevitable wilting of the voices and would pull down the whole choir, and so the performance would be razed to the ground.

All things being equal, and after having weighed the matter, I have ultimately found that (in general) performing such compositions as these a 3rd lower (rather than a 4th) is best for a choir of today; and I have made the discovery that this transposition, as if by magic, keeps the notes in their original places on the staff. If I place next to the original *chiavette* our familiar and usual soprano, alto, tenor and bass clefs, with the signature of the resulting scale a 3rd lower as befits our modern system, I have before my very eyes both the unaltered original and the composition transposed (*ad lib.*) to the lower 3rd, in a score comprehensible to all musicians of our time. [See ex.2 above.]

I have also found this transposition, which I generally tend to use, to be in most instances the most suitable in actual performance. But, as no rule is without its exceptions, for the purpose of the performance, or to improve the appearance of the score (even to avoid placing in jeopardy those choirs not adept enough to cope with an all-too chromatic key signature), I have never had any scruples about transposing many a composition down just one step, and others down by an entire 4th. (Indeed, of late, I have even come to realize that, because of the particularly low range, many pieces in the normal clefs were by common consent sung higher by the old chapel choirs.) The task in hand never changes: first to consider the singers' ability, then to observe an appropriate disposition of the parts. This last part of the task is often hard to perform because (as a result of the way chapel choirs were formerly constituted) one often finds that the alto part is considerably lower than would be usual today; nonetheless, in cases of conflict, particular attention has to be paid to the tenor.

(b) A. Banchieri, *Cartella overo regole utilissime à quelli che desiderano imparare il canto figurato* (Venice, 2/1610), pp.13–15. The wording differs slightly from the first edition (Venice, 1601).

D[ISCEPOLO]. Signor Maestro ... hora nell'ultimo mi è nato un dubbio, & è quando le note sono inferiori a F. fa ut Grave, & E. la mi Sopracuto sono voci Instrumentali, & non a voci humane appropriate, tuttavia ho veduto cantare per la Chiave di G. sol re ut, si per b. molle, come per b. quadro, & passar E. la mi di tre & quattro voci, in tal guisa, come stà questo negotio.

M[AESTRO]. Questo dubbio è facile da ponere in chiarezza (notate). Tutti li canti per la Chiave di G. sol re ut, è d'avertire se sono per b. molle, ò pure per b. quadro; quando sono per b. molle si trasportano intentionalmente una Quarta bassa, & quando sono per b. quadro, si trasportano similmente una Quinta bassa, mutando tutte le Chiavi alle parti . . .

D. Signor Maestro non capisco molto questo trasportare, & ciò non essend' io per ancora instrutto, se non alla parte del Soprano, credo però così voglia egli inferire, ogni fiata che il Soprano nelle compositioni sarà per la chiave di G. sol re ut in b. molle sì trasporta nel cantare mentalmente tutte le parti una Quarta bassa, che riescono nella chiave di C. sol fa ut in b. quadro; quando poi la chiave sarà di G. sol re ut per b. quadro si trasportano tutte le parti una Quinta bassa, che riesce in C. sol fa ut per b. molle. Ma a che fine gli Compositori non usano tutti gli suoi componimenti per le chiavi di C. sol fa ut, senza havergli a trasportare, che così facendo s'impareria il cantare con maggiore facilità, & prestezza,

M. Di già ve l'ho accennato, che s'usano gli canti per le chiavi di G. sol re ut per gl'istromenti, atteso che sonando così all'alta rendono maggiore vivezza di armonia, sì che sia necessario saper leggere tutte le chiavi, & con la pratica trasportargli mentalmente, sì come gli soprascritti essempi ve l'hanno significato.

D[ISCIPLE]. Master . . . now at the last moment a doubt has come to me: when the notes are lower than *F* in the lowest part and [higher than] *e''* in the highest they are instrumental parts and unsuited to human voices, and yet I have witnessed singing in the clef of *G'*, both with B♭ and with B♮, going beyond *e''* by three or four notes . . . [An example in staff notation shows that those notes are *f''*, *g''*, *a''* or *f''*, *g''*, *a''*, *b''♭*.]

M[ASTER]. This doubt is easy to clear up. Listen carefully. When considering any song with the clef of G it must be noted whether it has B♭ or B♮; when it has B♭ it is mentally transposed down a 4th, and when it has B♮ it is similarly transposed down a 5th, changing the clefs in all the parts, as we see here in these two examples [illus.2].

D. Master, I do not understand a great deal about this transposing, because up to now I have been trained only in the soprano part, but I believe the following is to be inferred: that in singing any composition where the soprano has the clef of G2 with B♭, all the parts are mentally transposed down a 4th, so that the clef becomes

that of C with B♮; and that when the clef is that of G with B♮ the parts are all transposed down a 5th, so that the clef is now that of C with B♭. But why do composers not notate all their compositions with the clefs of C so that they will not have to be transposed? If they did, singing would be easier to learn and could be learned more quickly.

M. I have already alluded to the reason. Compositions are notated with the clefs of G for instruments, because playing high in that way they produce a more vivacious harmony. So one needs to be able to read all the clefs, and, with practice, mentally to transpose them, as the above examples intimated.

(c) S. Picerli, *Specchio secondo di musica* (Naples, 1631), p.192.

Per conoscer dal Basso in che ordine si canta la compositione, si deve avertire, che regolarmente all'hora si canta principalmente per b molle, quando nel principio della compositione dopò la chiave è posto esso b molle; all'hora poi si canta principalmente per b quadro quando la chiave di f fa ut vi appare nella linea di mezzo, ò quella di C sol fa ut nella seconda linea di sopra, alle quali ordinariamente corrisponde nel Canto la chiave di G sol re ut, o di b quadro; & all'hora si canta principalmente per natura, quando vi appare la chiave di f fa ut nella prima, ò nella seconda linea di sopra. Ma vi bisogn' havere un'altro avertimento, che, quando la compositione si canta per b quadro . . . o per la chiave di G sol re ut, la compositione si trasporta mentalmente, ò in scritto, una quarta, ò quinta sotto . . . Ma si trasporta una quarta sotto, quando si canta co 'l b molle, & una quinta, quando si canta senza b molle.

In order to tell from the bass in which order the composition is sung, it must be noted that as a rule one sings mainly with B♭ when a B♭ is placed after the clef at the beginning of the composition; and that one sings mainly with B♮ when what appears there is the clef of F on the middle line or that of C on the second line down; to these, in singing, the clef of G, or of B♮, normally corresponds; and one sings mainly according to nature when the clef of F appears there on the top line or the second line down. But another thing needs to be noted: when sung with B♮ . . . or with the clef of G, the composition is transposed down a 4th or a 5th, mentally or in writing . . . But one transposes down a 4th when one sings with B♭ and a 5th when one sings without B♭.

(d) G. B. Doni, *Annotazioni sopra il compendio de' generi e de' modi della musica* (Rome, 1640), pp.250–51.

Pare una grande stravaganza, che i concenti segnati dal Compositore più gravi, trasportati poi, si cantino per ordinario più acuti di quelli che non si trasportano; mà si cantano semplicemente, come stanno. Per essempio questo Madrigale del Palestrina, anzi del Petrarca, *Vergine pura* si canta à Roma, & nel resto d'Italia, come stà. Or supponendo, che si canti, come si fà, nel Tuono Dorio, & più commodo à tutte le parti, doverebbe quest' altro *Vergine saggia* (il quale perche è segnato all'alta, come dicono, & riuscirebbe troppo scommodo, se si cantasse, come stà) nel trasportarsi alla quinta bassa, ch'è la maniera più consueta di trasportatione, cantarsi nel medesimo Tuono di *Vergine pura*: il che se succeda, si giudichi dall'estreme note grave, & acuta, di tutto il Madrigale, & di ciascuna Parte negl'essempii, che seguono. . . . La quale diversità di Tuoni sarebbe comportabile, & lodevole, se facesse il Concento più acuto, e più grave, dove il soggetto lo richiede tale, come succedeva ne' Tuoni antichi. Mà il male è, che il più delle volte si canteranno, non dico più gravi quelli, ch'il Compositore hà segnati più acuti; mà in Tuono grave, e rimesso quel soggetto, che richiede più tosto la Melodia più tesa, vivace, & allegra; & per il contrario in Tuono più acuto & sforzato, quelle parole, che richiederebbono il contrario.

It seems very odd that pieces notated lower by the composer, which are then transposed, are usually sung higher than those which are not transposed but sung simply as they are written. For example, this madrigal by Palestrina—or rather, by Petrarch—*Vergine pura*, is sung in Rome and the rest of Italy as it stands. Now, supposing it is sung (as indeed it is) in the Dorian mode [i.e. the 3rd mode, Glarean's Phrygian], the most comfortable for all the parts, this other one, *Vergine saggia* (which, since it is notated *all'alta*, as they say, and would be too uncomfortable if sung as it stands), when transposed down a 5th—the commonest kind of transposition—would have to be sung in the same mode as *Vergine pura*: let whether this happens be judged on the basis of the lowest and highest notes of the whole madrigal and of each of its parts in the following examples [illus.3]. . . . This difference of modes would be tolerable, and praiseworthy, if it made the piece higher and lower where the subject requires it to be, as happened in the ancient modes. But the trouble is that more often than not those pieces which the composer notated as higher will be sung, not only low, but in a low mode, and a subject requiring the melody to be more taut, lively and cheerful will instead be placid; and,

contrariwise, those words that would require the opposite will be in a higher and more strained mode.

Appendix 2:   Sources

All primary musical sources referred to in the text and tables are tabulated below. The 'Collation' column shows either a library siglum, indicating the location of a primary source from which information has been directly obtained, or another abbreviation, indicating a secondary source from which information has been derived. Library sigla are those used in *New Grove*; abbreviations for secondary sources are as follows:

B   P. Barbieri, '*Chiavette* and modal transposition in Italian practice (*c*.1500–1837)', *Recercare*, iii (1991), pp.5–75, at pp.47–52

CMM   Corpus mensurabilis musicae (American Institute of Musicology, 1949–)

iv	*Clemens non Papa: Opera omnia*, ed. K. P. Bernet Kempers
vi	*Nicolas Gombert: Opera omnia*, ed. J. Schmidt-Görg
xxi	*Jacobi Arcadelt: Opera omnia*, ed. A. Seay
xliii	*Jean Mouton: Opera omnia*, ed. A. C. Minor
liv	*Jachet of Mantua: Opera omnia*, ed. G. Nugent
lv	*Pierre de Manchicourt: Opera omnia*, ed. L. J. Wagner
lviii	*Elziarii Geneti (Carpentras): Opera omnia*, ed. A. Seay
lxv	*Heinrich Isaac: Opera omnia*, ed. E. R. Lerner

G   R. E. Gerken, *The polyphonic cycles of the proper of the mass in the Trent codex 88 and Jena choirbooks 30 and 35* (diss. Indiana U., 1969)

Ha   J. Haar, '*Altro non è il mio amor*', in *Words and music: the scholar's view*, ed. L. Berman (Cambridge, MA, 1972), pp.93–114, at pp.97, 109

Hg   J. Haar, 'A gift of madrigals to Cosimo I: the Ms. Florence, Bibl. naz. centrale, Magl, XIX, 130', *Rivista italiana di musicologia*, i (1966), pp.167–89, at pp.177, 189

J   C.C. Judd, *Reading Renaissance music theory: hearing with the eyes* (Cambridge, 2000), pp.73–5, 79

Lmc   E. E. Lowinsky, *The Medici codex . . . : historical introduction and commentary* (Chicago, 1968), pp.114–5, 166, 205

Lnd   E. E. Lowinsky, 'A newly discovered sixteenth-century motet manuscript at the Biblioteca Vallicelliana in Rome', *Journal of the American Musicological Society*, iii (1950), pp.173–232, at p.219

LW   Orlando di Lasso: Sämtliche Werke, neue Reihe, ed. S. Hermelink *et al.* (Kassel, 1956–)

MME Monumentos de la Música Española (Madrid etc., 1941–)

   li *Francisco Guerrero: Missarum liber quartus*, ed. J. M. Llorens

MRM Monuments of Renaissance music (Chicago, 1964–)

   v *The Medici codex* (facs. edn)

NJE New Josquin edition, ed. W. Elders *et al.* (Amsterdam, 1989–)

P A. Parrott, 'Transposition in Monteverdi's vespers of 1610: an "aberration" defended', *Early music*, xii (1984), pp.490–516, at p.496

PW Pierluigi da Palestrina's Werke, ed. F. X. Haberl *et al.* (Leipzig, 1862–1907)

RRMR Recent researches in the music of the Renaissance (New Haven etc., 1964–)

   xcv *Modulorum Ioannis Maillard: the five- six- and seven-part motets part I*, ed. R. H. Rosenstock

S H. C. Slim, *A gift of madrigals and motets* (2 vols., Chicago, 1972), i, pp.127–30

TLM Treize livres de motets parus chez Pierre Attaingnant en 1534 et 1535, ed. A. Smijers and A. T. Merritt (Paris, 1934–63)

Z Adrian Willaert: Sämtliche Werke, i, ed. H. Zenck (Leipzig, 1937), pp.xii, xv

Manuscripts

Library siglum, Ms. number	Collation
B-Bc, Ms.27087	*B-Bc*
D-Bsb, Ms.P.Landsberg 214	*D-Bsb*
D-Ju, Ms.35	G
D-Ju, Ms.36	CMM lxv/1
D-Mbs, Ms.24	LW ix
D-Mbs, Ms.31	CMM lxv/1
E-MO, Ms.768	CMM lv/6
GB-Lbl, Ms.Royal 8 G.vii	NJE xiv
I-Bc, Ms.Q19	Z
I-Bc, Ms.Q27(1)	Lmc, S
I-Bsp, Ms.31	NJE xiv
I-CFm, Ms.LIX	Lmc
I-Fl, Ms.Acq. e doni 666	MRM v
I-Fn, Mss.Magliabecchi XIX 130	Hg
I-Rbv, Ms.Vall.S.Borr.E.II.55–60	Lnd
I-Rvat, Ms.Cappella Giulia XII 4	Lmc
I-Rvat, Ms.Cappella Sistina 16	NJE iv
I-Rvat, Ms.Ottoboniani latini 2927	PW xxiv
I-TVd, Ms.8	Z
NL-L, archieven van de Kerken Ms.1441	CMM lv/3
US-Cn, Case Ms.-VM 1578.M91	S

Printed anthologies

RISM	*Collation*
1501/1	J
1503/1	*GB-Lbl*
1514/1	J
1519/1	*GB-Lbl*
1519/2	*GB-Lbl*
1519/3	*GB-Lbl*
1528/1	*GB-Lbl*
1532/6	CMM vi/3
1532/11	GB-LbL
1534/3	TLM i
1534/10	TLM vii
1538/4	*GB-Lbl*
1538/5	*GB-Lbl*
1538/8	*D-Mbs*
[*c.*1538]/20	*D-Mbs*
1538/21	*D-Mbs*
1539/3	*D-Mbs*
1539/13	*GB-Lbl*
1539/22	*D-Mbs*
1539/23	*D-Mbs*
1540/7	*D-Mbs*
1540/20	*D-Mbs*
1542/15	*GB-Lbl*
1547/3	Ha
1549/12	*D-Mbs*
1549/15	*GB-Lcm*
1557/7	*D-Mbs*
1558/20	NJE xiv
1559/2	NJE xiv
1564/15	CMM xxi/7
1570/1	*D-Mbs*
1584/12	P
1586/2	B
1589/11	B
1591/12	B
[1595]/6	B

Single-composer printed collections

RISM	Collation	RISM	Collation
A664	*D-Mbs*	P664	PW xii
C2667	*D-Mbs*	P667	PW xiii
C2683	CMM iv/7	P677	PW xv
G1572	CMM lviii/2	P681	PW xvii
G2977	*D-Mbs*	P687	PW xxi
G2981	*D-Mbs*	P725	B
G4870	MME li	P727	*GB-Lbl*
J6	CMM liv/5	P761	PW xxix
J9	*D-Mbs*	R3065	Hg
J14	*GB-Lbl*	W1106	*GB-Lbl*
M184	RRMR xcv	W1107	*GB-Lbl*
M269	CMM lv/1	W1108	*D-Mbs*
M4015	*GB-Lbl*	W1109	*GB-Lbl*
M4017	*GB-Lbl*	W1110	*GB-Lbl*
P660	PW xi		

Andrew Johnstone is a lecturer in music at Trinity College, Dublin. He is working on a book about modes and vocal scoring in the Renaissance and Baroque periods.

I am grateful to Paul Raspé, librarian of the Conservatoire Royal de Bruxelles, and my colleague Thomas McCarthy, both of whom collated primary sources. I would also like to thank my wife, Siobhán Donovan, and John C. Barnes for their kind assistance in translating respectively the German and Italian readings.

1 A. Parrott, 'Transposition in Monteverdi's vespers of 1610: an "aberration" defended', *Early music*, xii (1984), pp.490–516, at p.511 n.2; R. Bowers, 'An "aberration" reviewed: the reconciliation of inconsistent clef-systems in Monteverdi's Mass and Vespers of 1610', *Early music*, xxxi (2003), pp.527–38; Parrott, 'Monteverdi: onwards and downwards', *Early music*, xxxii (2004), pp.303–17. Parrott's view has been adopted by Jeffrey Kurtzman in *The Monteverdi vespers of 1610: music,*

context, performance (New York, 1999), pp.404–11.

2 Kurtzman, *The Monteverdi vespers*, p.411.

3 M. Praetorius, *Syntagma musicum*, iii (Wolfenbüttel, 1619), pp.80–81.

4 P. Barbieri, '*Chiavette* and modal transposition in Italian practice (*c*.1500–1837),' *Recercare*, iii (1991), pp.5–75, at pp.52–7; M. A. Mendel, 'Pitch in the 16th and early 17th centuries—part III, *Musical quarterly*, xxxiv (1948), pp.336–57, at pp.352–3; R. Rasch, 'Modes, clefs and transposition in the early seventeenth century', *Théorie et analyse musicales, 1450–1650 / Music theory and analysis: proceedings of the International Conference, Louvain-la-Neuve, 23–25 September 1999*, ed. A.-E. Ceulemans and B. Blackburn (Louvain-la-Neuve, 2001), pp.403–32, at pp.426–31.

5 H. Bellermann, *Der Contrapunkt* (Berlin, 1862), pp.65–8; M. Haller, *Kompositionslehre für den polyphonen Kirchengesang* (Regensburg, 1891), p.10.

6 K. Jeppesen, *Counterpoint*, trans. G. Haydon (New York, 1939), p.58.

7 Mendel, 'Pitch in the 16th and early 17th centuries', pp.339–40, 346.

8 Mendel, 'Pitch in the 16th and early 17th centuries', p.357.

9 S. Hermelink, *Dispositiones modorum: die Tonarten in der Musik Palestrinas und seiner Zeitgenossen* (Tutzing, 1960); H. Powers, 'Tonal types and modal categories in Renaissance polyphony', *Journal of the American Musicological Society*, xxxiv (1981), pp.428–70.

10 Hermelink, *Dispositiones modorum*, pp.33–7; J. A. Owens, *Composers at work: the craft of musical composition, 1450–1600* (New York, 1997), pp.17–19, 26–9, 38–41. Other German music

theorists of the period often gave examples on ten- or 11-line staffs, but with the purpose of illustrating how the voice-ranges in modal polyphony overlap with one another: see S. Gissel, 'Zur Modus bestimmung deutscher Autoren in der Zeit von 1550–1650: eine Quellenstudie', *Die Musikforschung*, xxxix (1986), pp.201–17.

11 Hermelink, *Dispositiones modorum*, pp.40–43.

12 S. Hermelink, 'Die Tabula compositoria: Beiträge zu einer Begriffstimmung', *Festschrift Heinrich Besseler zum sechzigen Geburtstag* (Leipzig, 1961), pp.221–30; Owens, *Composers at work*, pp.5, 61, 97.

13 Hermelink, *Dispositiones modorum*, pp.93–5.

14 See particularly the *Missa Paschale a6* (*D-Ju* Ms.36) and the *Missa Solenne a6* (*D-Mbs* Ms.31).

15 There being no up-to-date complete edition of Mouton's motets, the following rough analysis of their cleffing is based on J. M. Shine, *The motets of Jean Mouton* (diss. New York U., 1953): standard 'low' combination, about 40 per cent; standard 'high' combinations, about 20 per cent; standard combinations with contratenor instead of alto, about 10 per cent; canonic works with certain voice-parts not notated, about 10 per cent; other combinations, about 20 per cent. Though the standard 'high' combination is the basic one for about half of Mouton's masses, statistics are impossible to compile because of the frequent clef changes within individual voice-parts that occur in Petrucci's edition (*RISM* M4015) but which are not indicated in the critical edition

(*Jean Mouton: Opera omnia*, ed. A. C. Minor, Corpus Mensurabilis Musicae, xliii (AIM, 1967)).

16 On clef-combinations in the French repertory, see U. Hertin, *Die Tonarten in der französischen Chanson der 16. Jahrhunderts* (Jannequin, Sermisy, Costeley, Bertrand) (Munich, 1974); H. M. Brown, 'Theory and practice in the sixteenth century: preliminary notes on Attaingnant's modally ordered chansonniers', *Essays in musicology: a tribute to Alvin Johnson*, ed. L. Lockwood ([Philadelphia], 1990), pp.75–100; M. Egan-Buffet, *Les chansons de Claude Goudimel: analyses modales et stylistiques* (Ottawa, 1992), pp.22–69.

17 The second alto part of no.17 is in the tenor book, and the corresponding tenor part is in the quintus book: ironically, this, the only item in the collection to distribute the parts inconsistently, is by Gardano himself.

18 The examples that follow are all by Continental composers, but dual notation is often encountered in the English Catholic repertory (where transposition by a major 2nd also occurs): see M. Hofman and J. Morehen, *Latin music in British sources, c.1485–c.1610* (London, 1987).

19 On Girolamo Scotto and his dealings with Antonio Gardano, see J. A. Bernstein, *Print culture and music in sixteenth-century Venice* (New York: 2001), pp.123–6, 147–80.

20 On Joshua Rifkin's view that Gardano's edition was compiled independently of Scotto's, see A. Smith, 'Willaert's motets and mode', *Basler Jahrbuch für historische Musikpraxis*, xvi (1992), pp.117–65, at pp. 117–8.

21 Not included in w1107 or w1109: w1106 nos.1, 7, 13, 14, 18, 22, 23; w1108 nos.4, 5, 15.

22 New items with standard clefs: w1109 nos.1, 11 and 20 (F4-C4-C3-C1); w1107 nos.11 and 12; w1109 no.12 (F3-C3-C2-G2); w1109 no.17 (C4-C3-C2-G2). Sole new item with non-standard clefs: w1107 no.13 (F3-C3-C3-C2).

23 Mendel, 'Pitch in the 16th and early 17th centuries', p.356; Parrott, 'Transposition in Monteverdi's vespers of 1610', pp.496–7; Barbieri, '*Chiavette* and modal transposition', pp.47–51. Facsimiles of 1586/2 no.4, by Palestrina, are given by Parrott and Barbieri, and at the beginning of *Pierluigi da Palestrina's Werke*, ed. F. X. Haberl *et al.* (Leipzig, 1862–1907), xxx, on unnumbered pages.

24 H. C. Slim, *A gift of madrigals and motets*, 2 vols. (Chicago, 1972), i, p.128.

25 E. E. Lowinsky, *The Medici codex . . .: historical introduction and commentary* (Chicago, 1968), p.184.

26 K. Kreitner, 'Very low ranges in the sacred music of Ockeghem and Tinctoris', *Early music*, xiv (1986), pp.467–79.

27 Perversely, 'low' notation was sometimes associated with texts that were not doleful, and 'high' notation with texts that were: see Barbieri, '*Chiavette* and modal transposition', p.11.

28 J9 nos.20, 21; J6 nos.1, 3; w1106 nos.17, 19, 21; w1108 nos.16, 18, 20; w1110 nos.5, 7, 10; G2977 nos.13, 23; G2981 nos.3, 5, 11.

29 See, for example, D. Fallows, 'The performing ensembles in Josquin's sacred music', *Tijdschrift van de vereniging voor nederlandse muziek geschiedenis*, xxxv (1985), pp.32–66.

30 B. Haynes, *A history of performing pitch: the story of 'A'* (Lanham, MD, 2002), pp.58–69.

31 For a facsimile of the somewhat differently worded version of this passage that appears in the first edition (Venice, 1601), see Barbieri, '*Chiavette* and modal transposition', p.42.

32 Kurtzman, *The Monteverdi vespers*, p.410.

Part VI
Perspective

[19]

Sight-readings: notes on *a cappella* performance practice

Donald Greig

In his lucid and perceptive essay, 'The English *a cappella* Renaissance' (*Early music*, xxi (1993), pp.452–71), Christopher Page outlines a broad consensus of critics, performers and musicologists who sustain the well tended tradition of English *a cappella* performance of early music. He goes so far as to suggest that the performers of this group constitute a 'class', the characteristics of which are that they are English, often Oxbridge (certainly well educated), good sight-readers, quick learners and possessed of vocal abilities which lend themselves to the performance of medieval and Renaissance repertory. Although I would not claim to fulfil all the conditions of Page's taxonomy, I do regularly perform with several of the groups included in the discography in the appendix to his essay.

Page's essay confronts a particular conjunction of critic, performer and musicologist. I intend here to supplement his arguments by drawing on my experience as a performer and on the specific musical education he sketches. This article is also an expression of my desire to find answers to questions continually raised during the performing process.

Page proposes what he tentatively calls the 'English discovery' theory:

> It begins from the premiss that English singers performing *a cappella* are currently able to give exceptional performances of medieval and Renaissance polyphony from England and the Franco-Flemish area because the ability of the best English singers to achieve a purity and precision instilled by the discipline of repeated *a cappella* singing in the choral institutions is singularly appropriate to the transparency and intricate counterpoint of the music. From that premiss we proceed to the theory that, in certain respects, and especially in matters relating to accuracy of tuning and ensemble, these performances represent a particularly convincing postulate about the performing priorities of the original singers. (p.454)

The model which Page sets up is a sort of unconscious of the English early-music world, a set of drives and desires which are rarely overtly expressed but which underlie and motivate a particular aspect of the performance of early music. Concerning the thesis that a 'good' performance of a particular form of music provides us with important clues as to its original performance, I contend that any similarities are mostly a happy coincidence, and that the particular skills of the British early-music singer can prevent a full appreciation of the demands of the

Donald Greig is a freelance singer and has lectured in semiology and film studies. His e-mail address is dgreig@sv.span.com.

1 The choir gallery of the Sistine Chapel (photo © Nippon Television Network Corporation)

music and inhibit forms of expression yet to be explored. I suggest too that modern *a cappella* performance may tell us more about current cultural conditions than about the original performance. This is not to say that I dispute the validity of the *a cappella* argument, that I line up on the side of those who support the idea of the *a cappella* heresy;[1] rather, I have a fundamental distrust of the performer's instinct (clouded by subjective notions of musical satisfaction and pleasure) which might tell me that a piece 'works' in one way and not in another. Performers do, though, have their own perspective; their arguments, as long as they take into account this dangerous and often misleading instinct, may well have an increasing part to play in the debate.

I hope to offer a corrective to one of the dominant myths of the English *a cappella* renaissance, a myth which Page is at pains to refute but which, through the act of elucidation, reconstructs itself. It is that the choral institutions of England (the cathedral choirs

and Oxbridge colleges) are somehow responsible for the *a cappella* renaissance. Page demonstrates that 'an influential forum of scholars, critics and performers in England has felt a pervasive desire to direct a good deal of medieval and Renaissance music … towards the best voices to emerge from the chapels attached to the Oxbridge colleges' (p.468). An élitist stance cannot be attributed to Page, but the approach fails to provide an account of other educations and trainings which, to my mind, have an equal and corrective value to the (often narrow) cathedral/college approach.

The history of the *a cappella* renaissance, which Page's essay has inititated, will need a full account of the membership of this 'class' and the various educations which have contributed to it. A limited account might well be seen retrospectively as paralleled by the dominance of all-male groups over the movement, and for the virtual exclusion of women from its critical history. It is refreshing to follow the

2 The Tallis Scholars perform from the choir gallery of the Sistine chapel, 9 April 1994
(photo © Nippon Television Network Corporation)

success of the all-women group Anonymous 4, just as it is not surprising to see the somewhat phobic reaction of some sections of the British music press to that success.[2]

It is well known that English *a cappella* choirs are excellent sight-readers: the reason generally cited is their training in the choral institutions of Britain.[3] There is little doubt that the rapid turnover of repertory in these institutions is a major contributor to the development of what has become a prerequisite skill for the professional singer of early music in Britain today. That is not to say that such skills can be learnt only in these institutions: British early-music groups also contain a number of people who have received their musical training outside the Oxbridge and cathedral systems. Of these, many of whom received their education at music college or non-Oxbridge universities,[4] the great majority are women. The reasons for this are cultural and, to

some extent, political. Women do not enjoy full access to choir schools (where girls remain the exception), the cathedral institutions or the five main Oxbridge choirs.[5] The situation has, admittedly, changed somewhat over the last 20 years. Within the Oxbridge system there now exist several choral scholarships for women, and there has been a gradual correlative decline in the all-men choir (as opposed to the all-male choir of boys and men). There are, though, still no women lay clerks, where the restriction cannot be on voice range alone, since other vocal groups accept female altos. This limitation on the education of women is not based on ability but on a combination of tradition, taste and, probably, prejudice. There is no feeling in the groups in which I work that the women are in any way inferior to the men in sight-reading ability, musical ideas, interpretation or knowledge. Indeed, one of the great pleasures that such groups afford is their collective nature and the assumption of equality of singers.

It would be disingenuous to discount the training in the cathedral and Oxbridge systems, just as it would be misleading to suggest that it is this training ground alone which is responsible for the high standards of the *a cappella* renaissance. What is clear is that all the singers involved have had some experience of *ensemble* singing, and that is a major resource. However, we must not limit our search for the training of the early-music *a cappella* performer to education alone, but must also view the experience gained while singing within these groups as part of the learning process. Groups have achieved their positions through a process of evolution that includes the ongoing development of the skills of their singers. Group styles were not laid down in stone when the group first performed but have developed over a period; much of that development is due to an increasing familiarity with the repertory and the particular demands it makes upon singers.

Many groups have devoted themselves to a particular musical period[6] and have maintained a certain continuity of personnel. In this concentrated world of rehearsals, concert-giving and recording, the sight-reading skills of each singer have been refined to a level where it is not just a transmission that can be given at sight but an interpretation.[7] What is at work here is not some mystical synchronicity but the development of a series of sub-codes of expression, a development of a sense of the use of *ficta*, and an appreciation of the likely movement of lines, not only intervallically, but also in their interaction with other lines and their potential for shaping. In short, singers who perform much music from the Renaissance (or who concentrate on any other period of music, for that matter) are likely to develop an ear for that music, or what has been usefully termed a 'learned instinct'.

It is easy to characterize the short rehearsal time and large discographies of English groups as evidence of a cursory knowledge and appreciation of the music, but this saturation in a variety of music from a single period is a vital component in the development of the singer's assimilation of its conventions. The high turnover of repertory, characteristic of both cathedral institutions and of the early-music *a cappella* groups in Britain, leads directly to a more complete appreciation of styles and idioms of spe-

cific periods. The experience of a member of one of the busier English groups might well be paralleled with that of, say, a singer in the Sistine Chapel in the 16th century.[8]

I am not suggesting that limited rehearsal is by any means ideal. It is a circumstance thrust upon these groups for primarily economic reasons. The question must be asked, though, whether it is as a direct result of the ability of English groups to work quickly that subsidy is not forthcoming or whether an economic determinism operates to produce this particular response. Groups cannot ask for large subsidies when the time allotted to any project is figured in hours rather than weeks. Specialist early-music singers tend to work on a session basis; that is, they are paid for each rehearsal, concert and recording session, and receive no salary, pension, or share in any royalties. The reasons are legion, and include labour relations in Britain, freelance tax status, unionization of performers and the individual history of each group.[9] Many of the calls for new ways of working may prove incompatible with this economic reality, in which there is a strong pressure to perform more concerts on fewer rehearsals.

Certainly the current situation among British early-music *a cappella* groups has produced wonderful results and a community of singers familiar and comfortable with the demands and rewards of singing early music. The question remains, though, as to what are the effects of the reliance on sight-reading in the performance of this repertory. The most obvious problem is that the repertory covered by these different groups is historically and geographically vast: ranging from 1100 to 1600, spread across several nations, split between sacred and secular, written for a variety of acoustics and occasions, it is, from any perspective, stunningly heterogeneous. And, as an obvious correlative, the original singers who performed this music could not share anything like the unities shared by the current group of British early-music singers. Yet the success of the monopolization of this repertory through *a cappella* performance leads us to a homogenization of a period of music (and, of course, of the valorization of the term 'early music'), a homogeneity made possible only by the success of a particular contemporary mode of performance.

There is an adage that a good sight-reader makes a bad memorizer of music, and *vice versa*. This opposition between memory and reading is initially attractive. What it means is that the sight-reader will always be reliant on the score, but that the memorizer can throw it away after a couple of runthroughs (having presumably learnt the music by rote). But it is a dangerous opposition as well, for it denies the role of memory in sight-reading. Let us be clear that no one sight-reads a piece in concert, barring extraordinary circumstances such as a singer falling ill at the last minute and parts having to be redistributed. Sight-reading, then, takes place in the rehearsal space and can really only be said to happen on the very first run-through. This may be of a very high level of accuracy, but as soon as the piece is sung a second time we are already dealing with a level of accretion of memory: this second runthrough is different from and more assured than the first. Memory is at work here, though the primary aim is not towards performance *from* memory, as is admitted by the use of scores in concert. A great deal of the rehearsal time is spent in discussion of *ficta*, possible speeds, time changes, whether to vocalize or not, balance, dynamics, meaning of text—in short, interpretation. The modern score is thus something of an *aide-memoire* to the sight-reader, the repository of interpretative marks and the site of the notes to be sung.[10]

The musical education of the early-music singer is geared towards modern transcription, and sightreading training is based exclusively on modern notation. It is no surprise, then, that we find an almost universal preference for transcriptions over the reproduction of the original notation. There is, however, no reason why singers should not learn earlier systems of notation and learn them very quickly. (Indeed, I have witnessed several almost miraculous conversions to some systems of original notation.) For notation is simply a codification, a representation in graphical form of acoustic intent. There is no reason why a crotchet should be represented by a black blob with a tail affixed, as opposed to, say, the image of a club on a playing card. Musical notation is a coherent, self-contained system in which the signs employed are inevitably arbitrary.[11] I remain suspicious of arguments which suggest that there are major differences between performances from original notation and performances from modern transcriptions.[12] From a linguistic point of view there is a primary level of arbitrariness of the musical sign such that all reading of music is context-dependent. It is only our usage of these signs, their fixity through convention, that leads us to consider (to use Margaret Bent's example) an F♯ dotted minim as possessing a fixed signified. We are therefore talking about a secondary level of arbitrariness, of context-dependency (and here we begin to talk about the more obvious graphical differences between original and modern notation), which means that even in modern notation there is a relativity which Bent does not stress.

The early-music performer, particularly the performer of music from before 1400, often quickly recovers this (seeming) context-dependency of original notation through working with extreme transpositions (e.g. down a 4th, down a major 6th, etc.). Similarly, the more one gets to know a piece (in rehearsal), the more one understands the relativity of note-values and often removes editorial beaming. Indeed, the more one rehearses a piece the more one comprehends its textual nuances. Which is, ultimately, to say that it is in the increase of rehearsal time that the development of the skills of the earlymusic singer might best be served.

We must not, then, look at the level of the signs themselves for any hints as to the differences of performance of the 'original' early-music singer and his contemporary counterpart. It is valid, however, to discuss broader differences in the organization of the scores. Modern transcriptions do not maintain the tradition of the separation of the individual parts on the page, but use a system of vertical alignment that maintains the real space/time of the parts. Whatever the historical reasons for the development of this system, it is its maintenance which concerns us here. Its continued use also marks the centrality of sightreading to the performance of early music, bringing with it the benefits of instant location for the singer within a harmonic world and an immediate transcription (visual representation) of that world. Consider, for example, two singers who have 16 bars rest: a singer working from a partbook would be involved in a complex system of cross-referencing to establish the note on which to enter; a singer using a modern score, however, follows with ease the unfolding counterpoint and can see, in advance, the harmony which his or her note will realize.

The original singer was not as helpless as this scenario suggests, nor, for that matter, is the contemporary singer as hidebound by the text. The former would have been able to hear the other parts and have relied upon them as a reference system. The modern performer also has this system at his/her disposal, but has no need to rely on it. It is not simply a question of bad habits, but of the tendency, or degree, to which these contrasting performers would have been reliant on the respective realms of written representation and acoustic memory.

I suggest that singers brought up on partbooks and choirbooks would have a far more acoustic relationship with the music than their modern counterparts, in that their appreciation and understanding of harmony and counterpoint was primarily an aural one rather than the visually aided one of the modern sight-reader. This approach would have been supported within a culture in which the everyday notation of information would, by comparison with the 20th century, have been severely limited. Much information which today we jot down on a pad of paper, enter into the Filofax or note on the Dictaphone would have had to be committed to memory. Studies have shown the major role that memory played in medieval culture;[13] the development of the ability to fix acoustic memory would have been a major tool for the singer.

Together with this reliance on memory as the site of the musical text, improvisation and elaboration were required skills of the singer. It has been suggested that such skills were already central to the music collected in the Winchester Troper,[14] and as late as the 16th century there was a tradition of improvised polyphony in the Sistine Chapel.[15] This is a broad sweep, from the 11th to the 16th centuries—perhaps too broad to make for a convincing argument—and it supports an even broader assertion about musical performance. What seems clear, though, is that, by contrast with the logocentric 20th century, the status of the written note or the written musical text was not afforded the same primacy by the original performers of early music.[16]

The correlative to this is the different educations that these two sets of performers would have enjoyed. Their respective methods of learning the chant repertory will serve as an illustration. Aside from the fortunate few who learn a fair proportion of the plainchant repertory as choirboys (and I use the gendered term knowingly),[17] most singers come to plainchant as a new notational system to be learnt. For the original early-music performer, the chant repertory would have been learnt by rote across a ten-year period. (Although with the gradual influence of the Guidonian hexachord system the learning time was ultimately reduced to two years.)[18] This difference in musical education reveals something of the dialectic at work in the figuring of graphic representation and memorial systems. We can see Guido's hexachord system as a midway point between complete reliance on acoustic memory and logocentric reliance on graphic representation. A full study of this might well include theories of linguistics and cognition, of the neurological processes of learning and memory, which would throw light on the sites of the brain used in the activities of improvisation and reading.[19]

The suggestion implicit here is that there is a world of difference between the original performer and his/her contemporary counterpart. This contention does not seem surprising, yet it is an argument which slips by in Christopher Page's article and which must be addressed,[20] for any differences in the process of realization of the same piece of music by the respective performers begins to tell us much about differences in the performers themselves.

This discussion of sight-reading alerts us to the role of vision in performance. Music, an acoustic medium, is never performed and rarely received 'blind' (after all, one pays to 'see' a group perform), and an account of performance practice is incomplete without an account of the role of looking within the performance space.

In *a cappella* performance we are dealing with at least two looks and sometimes three—the look of the audience, the look of the performer and the look of the conductor. There are variations of this simple model (performer to audience, audience to performer, performer to conductor, performer to performer etc.) and there is a history of the organization of the look and looking in performance. In this section I shall consider the different functions of the look that might be deduced from a comparison between original performers of early music and their contemporary counterparts and the implications of those differences for aspects of ensemble. I shall use as a model for this discussion a hypothetical (sacred) performance of a Palestrina Mass in the Sistine Chapel in the 16th century and a real (secular) performance of music by Palestrina in a concert by the Tallis Scholars in the same venue.[21]

In the earlier performance the singers are grouped around the music desk in front of a single copy of the music. The immediate focus of the singer's look is the music itself, though one can only surmise as to the direction of the singer's individual look. The choir is placed in a gallery situated some six feet above the ground and effectively hidden from view by a wooden screen which surrounds the singers at a height of some five to six feet. The choir desk itself is above eye-level; thus the look of the singer is already away from the listeners, inclined towards the ceiling of the chapel. There are, therefore, several physical constraints on any visual contact with the congregation. The congregation would have had the experience of hearing a sourceless sound, concomitant with the general theory that the choir would have been acting as representatives of angels.[22] Everything about this performing space is geared towards the invisibility of the choir, towards a carefully maintained balance between their actual presence and a suggestion of their absence.[23] This organization of the performance space has several advantages, not least of which is that it leaves the singers free to look at each other and thereby encourages communication.[24] For music so reliant upon ensemble this is of obvious benefit.

The contrast with the modern performance space is informative. A group faces the audience and acknowledges their applause with, appropriately, nothing other than the look. Once the music begins, however, there is a shift towards a hesitant acknowledgement of the audience, though the look of the singers is directed mainly to the music. Christopher Page notes the direction of the look in a publicity shot for the Tallis Scholars, commenting that the 'eyes down' approach promotes an image of 'the essentially literate and punctilious nature of trained musicianship in Britain' (p.459). This is certainly true, but what is also at work here (aside from the fact that performance which relies on sight-reading will always, of necessity, produce singers who have to look at their copies) is an ambivalence in the look of the performer. To use another opposition, that between the orchestral player and the vocal soloist, the former never acknowledges the audience while performing and the latter is in a state of constant address to the audience. The early-music performer of sacred music is caught somewhere between the two as a transmitter of music and expression but also as reader and contemplator of sacred text (and the adjective can apply to both words and music).

This difference of the organization of the look is not simply cosmetic; rather, it is one of context, the former being a sacred context and the latter secular, though in both cases the music sung is the same. The issue of the look also pertains to the way that the music was performed or, more accurately, to the organization of the performance. That is to say, singers grouped around a single source have much scope for visual cues, clues and directions, whereas in a modern concert the look between performers is reduced to a single relay through the conductor to the audience.

Good ensemble singing is always a compromise between the individual expression of single lines balanced with the need for synchronization of those lines. There is no such thing as a metronomic performance of this music, just as there is no one tuning system in operation at any one time. These may be the aims of many early-music groups, but there is, nevertheless, a recognition of the limitations of strict tempos and an accommodation of flexibility. Singers achieve this mainly through listening to other parts, but also through the (anachronistic) presence of the conductor. For a group hidden away from view there is not only the acoustic aid to ensemble singing but also the visual aid of nods, of body movement, of conducting (by any singer) and even of touching (*tactus*).[25] This might seem a small advantage, but think, for a moment, of the lack of physical movement that singing entails. The singer of classical music is encouraged to be still at all times ('look over the heads of the audience to the back'), to avoid the expression of the voice through the body ('keep your head still') and to reduce the physical effort of singing in favour of a position of repose ('don't raise your shoulders when you breathe'). This is a matter of degree; yet contrast *any* performer of pop music with *any* singer of classical repertory and the distinction is clear. Compare, too, the movements of singers and those of any instrumentalist. The latter, by virtue of the physical manipulation of the instrument, is immediately giving a series of visual indications about the attack of any note, be it through fingering, bowing or striking. With singers, the most obvious clue is the shape of the mouth as it forms the consonants and vowels. But if the mouth is visible only to the audience and not to fellow singers then the visual cues must be provided by a third party, which in most cases is the conductor. Clearly there is a delimitation of a whole set of sub-codes of expression and timing caused by performance by the contemporary singer of early music in *a cappella* form, a delimitation which, we can assume, was not present in many earlier contexts.[26]

There is a general rule that the more performers there are, the greater the need for the conductor. This is simply because the only physical clue that is left for the performers who look out at the audience rather than among themselves—breathing—is reduced in direct proportion to the increase in numbers. This is at least one of the reasons why the smaller early-music *a cappella* groups perform with no conductor (Gothic Voices, Hilliard Ensemble, Orlando Consort) and why larger groups rely upon (and are often promoted through) a conductor (Peter Phillips—the Tallis Scholars; Harry Christophers—The Sixteen; Andrew Parrott—the Taverner Consort).

For the singers in the Sistine Chapel, hidden from view, there would be little need for a conductor. It seems that pieces would have been started by the senior singer of the relevant part and that tempos would have been conveyed by visual or physical cues. The role of the *maestro di cappella*, who would himself have been a singer, seems to have been basically administrative.[27] It is unlikely that any individual would stand in front of the choir desk and conduct. (In no illustrations of singers at choir desks is anyone shown doing this; in the Sistine Chapel it would have been physically impossible.)[28] Thus there would be no focus for the singers other than the primary one of the music itself.

There is further study to be done here on the role of the conductor in early-music performance. An historical survey might well show that the development of the conductor is matched by a general movement towards the aggrandizement of the individual over the group (well supported by the rise of humanism), which culminates in the 20th century's seeming inability to comprehend the notion of collective activity. This is sustained by marketing strategies which focus on an individual—the conductor. The responsibility of the singer has become displaced and refound in the role of the conductor. The reality of singing *a cappella* music is not so much that of an individual determining the shape of individual lines (musical direction) but of the collective activity of the various singers.

I have not drawn a distinction between these two modes of delivery of Renaissance music to illustrate some loss of authenticity which we face by virtue of performing such music in concert. To return modern-day performance of medieval and Renaissance music to its original sacred context is obviously impossible. However, we may have much to learn from performing this music in the original venues with due attention to the organization of the performers within that space. If the original acoustics can be re-created then performing music in the venues for which it was intended may tell us much about, for example, the limits of tempos.[29]

Similarly, the use of choirbooks and the organization of performers around one score may well promote a more acoustic relationship with the music and aid ensemble. Unquestionably, the current text-based approach cannot be seen as without affect; a certain pressure has already been exerted by musicologists upon performers to develop the kind of skills with which their original counterparts would have been familiar.[30] However, it is primarily the acoustic relationship with the music in which I place my own performing faith, and not necessarily in learning its original codification.[31]

In either event, an approach which foregrounds the apparatus of ensemble offers a subversion of the conventional codes of the concert hall and reveals the gap between the original performance of this music and the cosmetic niceties of the modern concert hall. Here we begin to address some of the cultural constraints of the reception of this music and begin to draw attention to cultural determinants which may, ultimately, be both responsible for this efflorescence and, at the same time, place limitations on *a cappella* performance. It is in this context that I shall next consider the critical perception of *a cappella* performance.

I have already touched upon representations of the performer of early music. A series of complementary discourses—press releases, codes of concert performance, publicity photos, cultural codes—accrete around the figure of the singer an image which may be some way from the reality which any one singer feels. The primary image in this constellation is that of the 'scholar', of the student who has graduated to become a learned person. Some performers did indeed begin their careers as choral scholars, and the epithet is also valid for some who are editors and scholars in their own right. The Tallis Scholars is the clearest example of the appropriation of the term: I do not know why the name was chosen, but, given that the group originally consisted of several choral scholars and dedicated itself to Renaissance music, it is not difficult to see its attractions. Yet today a specific knowledge of Tallis or his contemporaries is not a prerequisite for membership, nor is prior experience as a choral scholar. The connection is still made in much publicity material, though, and the link with further education is one found in other early-music groups.[32]

But the image of the scholar is not promoted simply through the written word. As Christopher Page noted of the publicity shot of the Tallis Scholars, the visual discourses involved in the promotion of the group also play on the image of scholarliness in the 'eyes down' approach. The lack of engagement with the camera is an assurance of the performer's engagement with the music, of a concentration which must not be disturbed by such petty concerns as the presence of an audience. The implication is that the performance is much the same as that achieved in rehearsal and that the presence of the audience cannot in any way influence the true transmission of the scholarly work.

Other groups' publicity photos often use a particular architectural space to connote this image of scholarliness and provide the reassurance of historical research. A recurring motif is an arch, against which the performers are often set.[33] The primary connotation is of sacredness, for the (usually Gothic) arches are often part of the exterior of a church. But there is a secondary level of meaning in the suggestion of collegiate life, of life in the quad.

This image of performer as scholar brings certain assurances: that the performance is well researched; that the performer is true to the music rather than to his/her muse; that the performer is subservient to the music. In short, it is implicit that authenticity is respected even if does not achieve primacy. (That so many publicity photos are taken in informal dress is an admission that the performers are individuals and that their individuality is not completely subsumed within the scholarly enterprise.) The inclusion of old buildings is a literal and metaphorical background, an admission that the past is at work in the present and an invocation of a historicity lacking in countries such as the USA and Japan, where such groups enjoy particular success.

The arch functions also as metaphor. It forms an entrance: we are accorded admission by the performers, who are the guardians of the portal and guarantors that the account of the past to be found beyond is a truthful one. The image is both an invitation and a contract: as such, the look of the performers is direct to camera.

The arch is not so much a door as a window offering a view of the past and the world of early music. The performance is transparent, uninterrupted by surplus noise and undisturbed by excesses of expression or opinion. This helps explain the sobriety of these photographs,[34] where the performers are involved in the *serious* business of revealing fundamental truths about the music. This is paralleled in the dress codes: in many groups the standard seems to be tails (a convention borrowed from the 19th-century orchestra) or, in the cathedral choirs, the full cassock.[35] Both photographic codes and dress codes work to efface individual expression and thereby connote an image of a collective effort whose primary aim is true to an academic project. Both photographs and dress are assurances of a noise-free signal, of an accurate transmission of data shorn of individual expression and conflict of ideas. In short, the photographs are a coded guarantee of authenticity. This guarantee is now, more than ever, a marketing ploy exploited by recording companies rather than by groups themselves; authenticity, as an academic argument, no longer holds centre stage.

So far, then, I have discussed the training of the personnel, the working methods of the groups, the discourse of the look within the modern performance space, and the marketing of those groups. But the sum of all these parts still does not explain the groups' extraordinary success both in concert and as recording artists. Christopher Page has noted the nostalgic tug of English *a cappella* performance of early music, its ability to 'turn the memories and dreams of a social class into sound'. But nagging questions still remain, as so often when one is attempting to trace the rhythms of popularity—questions of pleasure. We must therefore address the *a cappella* renaissance as a cultural production of the 20th century.

A cappella performance has an appeal which goes beyond the dictates of musicological research. Something ultimately elusive and evasive is at work. I do not propose to write a history of *a cappella* performance, but we might note a few historical pointers. *A cappella* literally means 'as in the chapel': from this we might deduce that there is something about the voice which inclines towards the realm of the sacred. And—to take only one of the sites of this performance, the Sistine Chapel—there is something about the Christian myth that alerts us to the close association of the problematic of sexual difference with the voice itself, a problematic which finds its most 'vocal' expression in the troubling figure of the castrato. I shall offer a few observations on the particular conjunction of the voice, the body, and sexual difference and, in so doing, outline something of the contribution that psychoanalysis might have to offer to this debate.

The opposition between body and voice is central

to Roland Barthes's essay 'The grain of the voice'.[36] The essay, inspired by Barthes's personal search for an explanation of his own predilection for the voice of Panzera over that of Fischer-Dieskau, is an attempt to render music criticism more scientific, to rescue it from 'the poorest of linguistic categories: the adjective'.[37] The argument is dense and challenging: some understanding of the semiotic and post-structuralist project will assist the reader.[38] The focus becomes the elaboration of a theoretical abstraction which Barthes terms the 'grain of the voice'. This is located at the point where one can perceive the body of the performer in the action of performance, the moment of utterance glimpsed behind or through what is heard. 'The "grain" is the body in the voice as it sings, the hand as it writes, the limb as it performs.'[39] What is being established here is a kind of image of the performer which the listener him/herself perceives and, perhaps, constructs; 'the image of the body (the figure) given me'.[40] The relationship to the performer is more than simply acoustic and more than visual: it is a relationship which is also real at the psychic level. In this context Barthes can talk of an erotic relationship to the performer (and this does not mean a sexual one):

> If I perceive the 'grain' in a piece of music and accord this 'grain' a theoretical value (the emergence of the text in the work), I inevitably set up a new scheme of evaluation which will certainly be individual—I am determined to listen to my relation with the body of the man or woman singing or playing and that relation is erotic—but in no way 'subjective' ...[41]

Barthes's essay has a double value. On the one hand it establishes that the relationship to the voice is always more than acoustic, that what is also involved is a relationship with the perceived body of the performer. In this respect it alerts us to a psychic reality that is at play in the appreciation of all musical groups. On the other hand, it points us towards a reconsideration of the metaphors in the critical discourses that define these groups. For he demonstrates that between the actuality of performance and the critical discourse which purports to describe that reality lies a gap which speaks for the presence of the Unconscious. Hence, through an examination of the most frequently used metaphors we can begin to locate something of the intrinsic and specific pleasure of the *a cappella* text.

To characterize the specific sound of English *a cappella* performance Page employs the Middle English word *clanness*:

clanness is the quality of something that is pure (like a pearl) or of fine and precise workmanship (like an elaborate goblet). *Clanness* can characterize the vessels used in the Eucharist or the goblets which serve men and women of exalted dignity in their banquets; it blurs the edges of earthly things with a nimbus of heaven, in other words, and yet it can make what is celestial seem clearer to human sense. ... I believe many English singers of the *a cappella* renaissance have captured this quality. (pp.466/468)

Page's account of reviews in (mainly) French and Spanish journals and newspapers supports his reading and confirms that, for many, the perception of British *a cappella* performance is, above all, 'clean' and 'clear'. In reviews of the Tallis Scholars the most common adjectives used to describe the sound include 'pure', 'blend', 'clear' and 'vibrato-free' or 'vibrato-less'.[42] It is evident, particularly in the neologistic tendencies of the last two words and in Page's own recourse to Middle English, that the struggle for appropriate terms for description of this mode of performance marks a series of assumptions about singing. Singing is often 'impure', works towards distinction and difference, is 'unclear', and, crucially, employs vibrato. It is not my concern here to question the various reports or contest the observation that singers sing without vibrato (though, for the record, it is a question of degree).[43] What concerns me is the sense that the perception of *a cappella* performance always tends towards a denial of the physical presence of the singers themselves, a sense that there is a perception of the voice as the mark of the denial of the body itself, that the 'grain of the voice' is denied or repressed in *a cappella* performance. Further, we move to a broader outline of the perception of corporeality at work in these observations and the implications that this has for the issue of sexual difference within the early music *a cappella* renaissance.

Let us analyse these adjectives more closely. 'Vibrato-free' is a term that marks the denial of the body in the voice, a denial of the production of sound or of the inflection of sound by the body (the chest, lungs—the volume of the body); the voice is (impossibly!) not produced at all, but emanates, as it were, from the space above the vocal chords, from the throat or head alone. 'Clear'—as synonyms such as 'unblemished', 'transparent' and 'cleansed' suggest—is concerned with images of non-materiality, or of materiality purged to a degree that negates the terrestrial and corporeal. 'Blend' (a word much used by practitioners within the *a cappella* tradition) is concerned with reduction, of diminution of many to one, with a disavowal of the production of sound by many to the implicit origination of sound from one, non-identifiable source: unanimity here confirms anonymity. 'Pure' connotes images of innocence, of virginity, of the non-corporeal production of sound.

The figure around which all these adjectives cohere and the metaphor they promote and sustain is that of the angel. The angel is the sacred figure in a secular society, the representative of heaven on earth. The angel is also often portrayed as the musical expression of the word of God. In the same way, singers of sacred music fulfil this function, and there is often a conflation between the metaphoric role assigned to singers with the connotations that the particular vocal delivery suggests. There is nothing new about this conflation: through a nice historic irony, the same deliberate confusion is found in Bede's anecdotal account of Gregory the Great's pun made between Angles (the English) and angels.[44]

Clearly, critical accounts of *a cappella* performances do not bother to separate the connotations of sacredness from the actuality of the performance, but that is not to say that the performances do not also play on this expectation. It is interesting that another aspect of angels also finds its way into the reception of *a cappella* performance—their asexuality. For angels do not possess gender, do not bear the marks of sexual difference, marks which must be borne on the body. We begin to see that the very negation of sexual difference, which I suggest is characteristic of reviews of *a cappella* groups, is also a negation of the materiality of the performer.[45]

We must first, though, return to the particular organization of sexual difference within the Catholic church. Though the following discussion is necessarily limited to the performance of sacred *a cappella* music my conclusions still have resonance for any form of *a cappella* music. I am struck by the lack of *a cappella* groups of mixed gender within the world of popular music, as if the foregrounding of sexual difference (so obviously the domain of pop music) already answers the questions posed by the voice.[46]

Catholicism is a fundamentally patriarchal institution. The terms of its organization are a clear indication of the empowerment of men over women; the heightened evaluation of the mother figure of Mary testifies to its reliance on the male Oedipal drama as psychic support to its status as myth.[47]

The exclusion of women from employment as musicians within the church alerts us to a hierarchy which is evidence of an idealization of an all-male environment. The need for an extension of vocal range was achieved by the most drastic expression of the law—the exercise of castration. There are, of course, examples of women as composers and performers even within this sacred environment,[48] but the suspicion remains that the hierarchy demands the complete segregation of the sexes, that sexual difference in this context represents a form of corruption. If this is true, then we are confronting head-on what Lacanian psychoanalysis[49] has termed the Symbolic order. The Symbolic is the realm of the law in all its forms—juridical, paternal, linguistic, economic, scientific, religious. It is a pre-existent order, a defined realm into which every human subject must enter and find or be given its place. This ordering, so clearly expressed in the overdetermination of the all-male performance of sacred music in the 16th century, has already been subverted by the modern secularization of its music. It may well be seen that the real *a cappella* renaissance has been the introduction of female voices into this realm, and that this new vocal product may well be a text which has only become possible in a post-modern culture.

What, then, of the secular context in which this music is performed today? More importantly, what of the psychic implications of the introduction of the figure of woman into the performance? I have already pointed to what I consider to be a denial of the materiality of the performers, amounting almost to a denial of sexual difference itself. The problematic of sexual difference in psychoanalysis is centred around the Oedipus, around the moment when the child first begins to realize that sexual difference exists. This realization initiates the painful and confusing process of (re-)identification and realignment along the axis of sexual difference (represented by the parents), which leads to the organization of his/her sexuality. This moment, in the fictional account of the child's development, marks the movement from the Imaginary realm to the Symbolic order. The Imaginary is crystallized by the stage described as the Mirror Phase—Lacan's account of the child's realization of him/herself as a unified body/image—and refers to the child's comprehension of him/herself as a complete body. There is no sexual difference in the Imaginary: the realm is characterized by a primary identification with the mother, a period of oneness and plenitude with her. The Symbolic order ruptures this primary narcissism and marks the necessary development of the child to a speaking subject.

Guy Rosolato has traced this particular well worn path in terms of the child's aural development and has theorized the particular play between the Imaginary and the Symbolic in terms of the voice.[50] In the realm of the Imaginary, the mother's voice (identifiable by the child as early as ten weeks) is warm, all-enveloping, reassuring maternal signifier. The cries of the child, answered by the mother, are responsible for the creation of an 'acoustic mirror', an extension in auditory terms of the Mirror Phase and responsible for granting to the child the sense of a coherent ego upon which all future identifications can be built.[51] The voice plays a central role in the development and articulation of the child's sense of space in the exchange of the cries of demand issued by the child and the answering maternal voice. In Rosolato's scenario, the cries of the child also initiate the presence of the mother, whose voice effects a 'unison' which becomes, for the child, the mark of pleasure. The mother's voice becomes the primary model for all future auditory pleasure. The voice also plays its part in the moment of accession to the Symbolic, for this moment, crystallized by the presence of the father as initiator of the Oedipal struggle, is achieved through the action of the father's voice as voice of interdiction, the voice of the law.

Rosolato sees at play in the voice an oscillation between the two realms. He suggests that this oscillation is found not only in vocal music but in all music, for it is this original drama, played across the parental voices and the bodies that they represent, which provides the model for harmony itself.

The harmonic and polyphonic display can be seen as a succession of tensions and resolutions, of unisons and dissonances of tiered parts which interact to form chords and ultimately to resolve into the simplest unity. It is therefore the complete dramatization of the separation and reunion of bodies which underlies harmony itself.[52]

This represents a particularly fortuitous conjunction for the study of the *a cappella* text, and it is easy to hear the echo of the Oedipus. This approach suggests that the presence of female voices in *a cappella* performance provides the final term of an Oedipal triangle such that the religious connotations of the original text are displaced and relocated in the secular context.[53] (Barthes's comments on the Oedipus as central to all narrative prefigure this observation of the universality of certain textual pleasures through recourse to this central issue within psychoanalysis.)[54] The inclusion of women in *a cappella* performance of sacred music marks a surprisingly radical textual strategy when viewed from this perspective.

This drama is also replayed in the (historical) movement from the male castrato to the contempo-

rary soprano, a drama played out across this troubled line of sexual differentiation. I contend that the denial of gender which the male castrato or prepubescent boy represents is found, displaced, in the image of woman in the early-music scene. Sexual difference, which (within a patriarchal society at least) is represented by the image of woman, is effaced by and replaced with a form of sexual neutrality. This neutrality can be located in a series of discourses which concern the representations of *a cappella* singers, most notably those of critical reviews and publicity; it finds its clearest expression in the varied employment of images of unity, non-difference and non-corporeality. Significantly, women's voices in modern early-music performance are often described as being like boy's voices (this is often offered as a compliment), yet it is quite clear that they are the voices of adults. It may be true that they employ less vibrato than equivalent voices in opera, but this is also true of male singers, who are never spoken of in these same gendered terms. It is as if the introduction of sexual difference into this realm of all-male performance produces a defensive response within accounts of that same performance that represents an attempt to return that difference to neutrality, to in-difference.

As a coda I shall add a few comments on the historical rise of the CD as a condensation of the foregoing discussion. The two histories of the efflorescence of English *a cappella* groups and the ascendance of the CD as *the* recording format go virtually hand in hand. The CD will be seen within a history of industrial design as the quintessential product of the 1980s—clean, shiny, a beautiful object in itself which creates a perfect, pure sound. It is the ultimate fetish object which allows the listener the ideal state of disavowal of the body of the performer.[55] The particular ideology of sound of the 80s was one of purity and cleanliness, of static-free, interference-reduced, pristine brilliance. It is precisely this ideology which the English *a cappella* groups represent. It remains to be seen whether this sound and the ideology that sustains it can be maintained in the face of demands for a new performance practice or whether the current recording/performance practice will in turn make its own demands.

I wish to thank the following people for their generous help and invaluable suggestions, observations and comments: Tessa Bonner, Sally Dunkley, Paula Higgins, Daniel Leech-Wilkinson, Christopher Page and David Pascoe.

1 For a brief but excellent account of the history of the *a cappella* debate see C. Page, 'The English *a cappella* heresy', *Companion to medieval and Renaissance music*, ed. T. Knighton and D. Fallows (London, 1992), pp.23–9. The article is of added interest in that many of the ideas prefigure Page's later essay.

2 If an admission that all male groups constitute the norm against which all comers must be judged then look no further than Anthony Pryer's review of *On Yoolis Night: medieval carols and motets* by Anonymous 4 in *Musical times*, cxxxv (June 1994). He writes 'The four anons are all women (is this a political statement?) ...' I have yet to see an all-male group be accused of making a political statement through their existence: the comment alerts us to a particularly desperate state of affairs.

3 '... many insular musicians ... possess a remarkable ability to produce an accurate performance virtually at sight, a skill acquired by many singers during years of preparing services under pressure in cathedrals and Oxbridge chapels' (Page, 'The English *a cappella* renaissance', p.464–5). The point is made elsewhere by Howard Mayer Brown and quoted by Page in a footnote '... the training the various choral foundations provide explains more than anything else the extraordinary high standards of ensemble singing in Britain today, since many collegiate choral scholars and boy singers go on to take up professional singing careers.' (p.471, n.8) and in 'Pedantry or liberation', *Authenticity and early music*, ed. N. Kenyon (Oxford, 1988), p.41.

4 An informal poll of singers in The Sixteen and the Tallis Scholars revealed that, of the total number of 'core' singers, half were Oxbridge and half were redbrick/music college.

5 These five are generally recognized as King's College, Cambridge, St John's, Cambridge, Christ Church, Oxford, Magdalen, Oxford, and New College, Oxford.

6 There are many exceptions to this rule, but the dominant image is of many of these groups as early-music specialists. The Hilliard Ensemble, The Sixteen and the Taverner Consort all regularly perform modern repertory.

7 I use an opposition suggested by Daniel Leech-Wilkinson in his contribution to 'The limits of authenticity: a discussion', *Early music*, xii (1984), pp.13–16.

8 The list of music cited in J. Lionnet, 'Performance practice in the Papal Chapel in the 17th century', *Early music* xv (1987), pp.4–15, is not dissimilar to the amount of music performed by the Tallis Scholars in a calendar year.

9 Some may be surprised to learn that, with very few exceptions, specialist early-music singers cannot survive on early music alone. (And it still comes to many singers as a surprise that it is a surprise.) All work as singers in other fields—as teachers, choral conductors, performers of much later music, 'session singers'—which perpetuates a system wherein time spent must be rewarded by payment. In a world where you are only as good as your last concert and where you can be dropped from any group there is bound to be an underlying current of standardization and repetition of successful formulae achievable by short-cuts, a situation which is further complicated by the imperatives of the recording industry.

10 '... the musical sign, which is a graphic element, is neither music, nor its reflection, but a solely mnemonic device' (Siohan, 'La musique comme signe', *Colloque sur le signe et les systèmes de signes*, Royaumont, 12–15 April 1962, EPHE 6th section, 9, typescript summary, p.22, cited in J.-J. Nattiez, *Music and discourse* (Princeton, NJ, 1990), p.71).

11 I am borrowing here from the structural linguistics of Ferdinand de Saussure, the founder of semiology, who proposed the idea of the arbitrary nature of sign in language, where there is no relationship between the sign and its referent other than that found in the

interdependence of the terms used. See F. de Saussure *Course in general linguistics* (London, 1974) as well as the accounts of Saussure's work in R. Barthes, *Elements of semiology* (London, 1976) and J. Culler, *Saussure* (London, 1976). For a full discussion of the problems of the Saussurian concept of the sign with regard to a semiology of music see Nattiez, *Music and discourse*, pp.3–37.

12 See M. Bent 'Editing early music: the dilemma of translation', *Early music*, xxii (1994), pp.373–92, for further comments on the problems of 'translating' original manuscripts into modern notation.

13 See M. Carruthers, *The book of memory* (Cambridge, 1990), and L. Treitler, 'Homer and Gregory: the transmission of epic poetry and plainchant', *Musical quarterly*, lx (1974), pp.333–72.

14 See S. Rankin, 'Winchester polyphony: the early theory and practice of organum', *Music in the medieval English liturgy: Plainsong and Medieval Music Society centennial essays*, ed. S. Rankin and D. Hiley (London, 1993): 'In performance, a thinking (and listening) musician must have been faced by situations which stimulated more than one appropriate response, and had to make decisions in favour of one "procedure" instead of another, or between a "rule of behaviour" and a musical response naturally suggested by a unique melodic contour.' (p.96); 'these written-down organa themselves provide evidence of a continuing ad hoc practice at Winchester' (p.99).

15 See Lionnet, 'Performance practice in the Papal Chapel in the 17th century': 'For solemn feasts, the whole Mass setting was sung, and the singers *improvised* the counterpoint on the chant of the Offertory and a number of antiphons, particularly the one preceding the Magnificat at Vespers. *The papal singers were very proud of their skill in improvisation, a common practice in Rome throughout this period*.' (pp.4–5) (my emphasis).

16 The closest equivalents today to the original performers are jazz musicians, for whom the musical text, or 'chart', is only a sketch to be completed during performance, not during rehearsal. It seems to me that it is the acoustic relationship to the music that we must try to recover; calls for performance from original performing materials might well be misplaced. This is not to say that the project is not worth while, for it will inevitably aid the particular acoustic relationship between performers for which I argue. This argument is made, in passing, by Margaret Bent: 'There has been a deep reluctance to assume that the near-absence of early scores might mean that its first creators and performers managed quite well without them, and hence that we had better do so too if we are to master their musical language and the essentials of their musical thinking processes.' Bent, 'Editing early music', p.373.

17 Few Catholic choral institutions employ girls as choristers (Brompton Oratory is the exception which proves the rule), though there are some which use women in the choir.

18 '[Guido's] new learning method reduces the time for learning the chant repertory to two years (previously ten were required). A boy can learn a new chant in three days.' (D. Hiley, *Western plainchant: a handbook* (Oxford, 1993), p.467.)

19 Leo Treitler has suggested certain directions for work in the field of memory as related to improvisation ('Homer and Gregory', pp.344–7). It would also be interesting to apply the kind of historical approach found in Michel Foucault's work to the various musicological discourses from the 12th century to the present day to see whether it is possible to talk of musical *épistèmés* with regard to musical performance and cognition. See M. Foucault, *The order of things* (London, 1970), and M. Foucault, *Madness and civilisation* (New York, 1965). For a clear definition of *épistèmé* see an interview with Raymond Bellour in *Les livres des Autres*, 10/18 (Paris, 1978), pp.11–25.

20 In his outline of Page's 'discovery theory', quoted in full above, it is the final term of his argument which conceals this particular point: 'we proceed

to the theory that, in certain respects, and especially in matters relating to accuracy of tuning and ensemble, these performances represent a particularly convincing postulate about the performing priorities of the original singers.' Page, 'The English *a cappella* renaissance', p.454.

21 The performance took place in the Sistine Chapel on 9 April 1994 as a celebration concert for the completion of the restoration of Michelangelo's frescoes. The concert, sponsored by Nippon Television Network Corporation in collaboration with RAI, was broadcast live in Italy and one week later in Japan. The real benefit of this event was that afforded to the singers of singing from the original choir gallery.

22 'The main restriction placed on the musical performance of the papal singers was that they should sing without any instruments. The pope represented Christ on earth and thus the *cappella* was regarded as the angelic choir around God's throne. Since there are no biblical references to the

employment of instruments by the angels …' Lionnet, 'Performance practice in the Papal Chapel in the 17th century', p.5.

23 Even today there is an almost universal set of rules for the performance of sacred music in the cathedrals of Britain. These are drummed into children in the cathedral institutions and may be summarized as follows: look at the conductor; if there is no conductor then look straight ahead; do not look at the congregation (or, when television cameras are present, do not look at the camera).

24 When in the Sistine Chapel we were fortunate enough to be allowed into the choir gallery to perform the verse sections of the *Miserere* by Allegri. The four singers could not be seen from the main body of the chapel and could thus look at each other for signs and gestures to aid ensemble singing.

25 I am indebted to Andrew Parrott for this point and for the accompanying reference. See J. S. van Waesberghe 'Singen und Dirigieren der Mehrstimmigen Musik in Mittelalter', *Melanges offerts à René Crozet*, ii, ed. P. Gallais and Y.-J. Riou (Poitiers, 1966), pp.1,345–54. Waesberghe offers an analysis of several sources from the 12th to the 15th centuries, including several sculptures and drawings. 'The physical/psychological accord of the singing groups is quite obvious in [the miniatures from] both periods. In the first period [*c*.12th–14th centuries] pictures show that the singers looked each other in the eye during performance; furthermore, the written and pictorial evidence demonstrates that the "director" or precentor, who often sang as well, guided and corrected the collective singing with gestures, with pressure of the hand [*Handdruch*] or by whispering into the singer's ear … In the second period [*c*.15th century] "looking into each other's eyes" disappears, but the physical/psychological rapport is maintained … often a singer would beat time on another singer's shoulder with his hand or fingers, or would put his arm around the neck of another singer …' (p.1,349) Many thanks to Julian Podger for help with the article and for the translation.

26 See, for example, J. Dyer 'A thirteenth-century choirmaster: the *Scientia ars musicae* of Elias Salomon', *Musical quarterly*, lxvi (1980), pp.83–111. Dyer describes some of the methods by which singers would have communicated during performance, including the very public means of whispering musical directions into the ear of another singer. The *rector* would have been the main controlling force, but it is not just his beat which dictates ensemble: 'the *rector* is indispensable to Salomon's idea for a successful performance, for the others must follow the articulation and observe the *pausae* just as he indicates them with his right hand. *Moreover, all four singers must have visual contact with each other.*' (p.97) (my emphasis).

27 See Lionnet, 'Performance practice in the Papal Chapel in the 17th century', and R. Sherr, 'Performance practice in the Papal Chapel in the 16th century', *Early music*, xv (1987), pp.452–62. Dyer and Waesberghe present evidence that the same system was in operation much earlier: 'In an ideal situation, according to Salomon, the *rector* ought to be one of the four performers.' (Dyer, 'A thirteenth-century choirmaster', p.101.)

28 The choir desk is mounted on the balustrade of the balcony, some 16 feet above the floor of the chapel.

29 The performance in the Sistine Chapel told us little about this issue, as the original carpet and tapestries are no longer present. This led to a very 'swimmy' acoustic; though, when singing from the gallery, the clarity of voices was markedly improved. The Tallis Scholars have also performed music from the Eton Choirbook in Eton College Chapel. We could not understand how such intricate music could have been written for such a building until it was revealed that the original wooden roof had been replaced by a stone one, resulting in the present bathroom acoustic. Any recreation of original performance spaces might well be a costly enterprise!

30 'We may reasonably hope that the next generation of early-music singers will advance on the present in not needing full instructions on the opera-

tion of *ficta* ... Scholars and performers need to learn the language(s). This means learning to read fluently directly from, and in the first instance to sing from, original notation in facsimile.' (Bent, 'Editing early music', pp.382, 391.) '... it will be a significant achievement when the finest professional groups regularly give their concerts at their favoured pitch and in their favoured voicing from a full size reproduction choirbook on a great lectern in the midst of their singers.' (B. Turner, 'The editor: diplomat or dictator?', *Companion to medieval and Renaissance music*, p.254.) 'Modern performance practice of pre-1600 music could benefit substantially from the restoration of solmization as a living practice.' (R. Wegman, '*Musica ficta*', *Companion to medieval and Renaissance music*, p.274.)

31 Attempts to become familiar with original notation are currently being undertaken by the various singers of the Clerks' Group, who are to work on Ockeghem's *Missa Prolationem* from original manuscripts and will record the results for ASV in 1995. Other work is also taking place in developing the more acoustic relationship with music and performance through working with jazz ensembles. The Hilliard Ensemble have been working with Jan Garbarek, a noted jazz saxophonist, and continue to perform a series of concerts over the coming year. The Orlando Consort begin a collaboration with The Perfect Houseplants in 1995 with the intention of developing a working knowledge of modes, particularly through its application in plainsong, and, at the same time, with the aim of learning improvisation techniques. This project has only been made possible through funding from the Arts Council of Great Britain. We may have to wait a long time for these practices to become a standard part of the education of early-music singers.

32 The Sixteen makes explicit reference to its Oxbridge credentials. Until quite recently publicity for the Tallis Scholars did the same.

33 The Hilliard Ensemble, Gothic Voices, the Tallis Scholars, the Orlando Consort and the Gabrieli Consort have all used publicity photos with this particular architectural backdrop.

34 See Page's analysis of the photographs of instrumental groups with their altogether more 'wacky' approach. The clearest and most brilliant example to my mind is that of Charles Daniels on his ten-speed bike in a publicity photo for the Gabrieli Consort.

35 'Subtle clues to the changing status of early music ... will inevitably reflect itself in the choice of concert dress as early music performers exchange their down-home, artsy, or Bohemian garb for tuxedos and evening gowns.' (P. Higgins, 'From the ivory tower to the marketplace: early music, musicology, and the mass media', *Current musicology*, no.53 (1993).)

36 R. Barthes, 'The grain of the voice', *Image, music, text*, selected and trans. S. Heath (London, 1977), originally published as 'Le grain de la voix', *Musique en jeu*, no.9 (1972).

37 Barthes, 'The grain of the voice', p.179.

38 Barthes's essay alludes to the work of Jacques Lacan in its easy appropriation of the term 'Imaginary', employs Julia Kristeva's opposition of pheno- and geno-text to postulate the theoretical opposition of pheno-song and geno-song and assumes an understanding of Kristeva's notion of *significance*. All this should be set within the context of Barthes's own work, which is too rich and varied to be summarized satisfactorily in a footnote. See *Structuralism and since*, ed. J. Sturrock (Oxford, 1979), T. Hawkes, *Structuralism and semiotics* (London, 1977), and, for a specific account of Barthes's contribution to the field of music criticism see B. Engh, 'Loving it: music and criticism in Roland Barthes', *Musicology and difference: gender and sexuality in music scholarship*, ed. R. A. Solie (Berkeley, CA, 1993), pp.66–79.

39 Barthes, 'The grain of the voice', p.189.

40 Barthes, 'The grain of the voice', p.189.

41 Barthes, 'The grain of the voice', p.188.

42 I take as my source a collection of reviews of concerts given by the Tallis Scholars in America over the past seven years, though I am convinced that this sample is valid for Europe as well.

43 It is actually impossible to sing without vibrato and, I would suggest, it is often a question of the speed rather than the degree of vibrato that is being noted.

44 I am indebted to Christopher Page for furnishing me with the exact details of this reference.

45 It is also interesting that the word *clanness* which Page uses is defined by him using exactly the same sacred/secular opposition we have seen repeated in reviews of the Tallis Scholars in America.

46 I am grateful to Rex Brough, something of an expert in the vagaries of popular music, for confirmation that there are remarkably few mixed-gender, *a cappella* pop groups.

47 For an audacious de(con)struction of the Christian myth see Ernest

Jones's various essays on this subject, in particular 'Psycho-analysis and the Christian religion' and 'A psycho-analytic study of the Holy-Ghost concept', *Essays in applied psychoanalysis*, ii (London, 1952), pp.198–211, 358–73.

48 See J. Bowers, 'The emergence of women composers in Italy, 1566–1700', *Women making music: the Western art tradition, 1150–1950*, ed. J. Bowers and J. Tick (London, 1986), pp.116–67; and A. B. Yardley. '"Ful weel she soong the service dyvyne": the cloistered musician in the Middle Ages', *ibid.*, pp.15–38. Despite the strong tradition of performance of sacred music by both women and men, there seem to be almost no examples of *polyphony* performed by both sexes together in a *sacred* context.

49 For a fuller account of Lacan and the *École freudienne* see A. Lemaire, *Jacques Lacan* (London, 1977), J. Rose, Introduction to *Feminine sexuality* (London, 1982), and J. Rose, 'The imaginary', *The talking cure* (London, 1981).

50 See G. Rosolato, 'La voix: entre corps et langage', *Revue française de psychanalyse*, no.38 (Jan 1974), pp.75–94. This article was first brought to my attention by the account in M.-A. Doane, 'The voice in the cinema', *Yale French studies*, no.60 (1980), pp.43–50.

51 See also D. Anzieu, 'L'enveloppe sonore du soi', *Nouvelle revue de psychanalyse*, no.13 (Spring, 1976).

52 Rosolato, 'La voix', p.82 (my translation).

53 For Rosolato both the sacred and the voice are concerned with the search for origins and the idealization of origins. He suggests that they are indissolubly linked at the psychic level, which explains the strong tradition of sacred vocal music: 'Vocal music has always been bound up with prayer, with religious or sacred celebration which glorifies a historic or mythic past, and also with tradition, from Vedic chant to the Liturgy of the Mass ...' (p.89). However, Rosolato wants to extend the notion of the sacred to include any sys-tems which tell of this process of idealization and which lead towards a fore-grounding of the voice itself. (Hence, for him, the essay is always also about opera.) The notion of the sacred he establishes goes some way to explaining the recent popular success of sacred music in a secular context. For Rosolato the sacred/secular opposition is not at all clear-cut. Note, also, how close we are to the nostalgia of which Page writes: 'We can detect a nostalgic aspect of musical pleasure, an inclination towards an origin.'(p.88)

54 'Doesn't every narrative lead back to Oedipus? Isn't storytelling always a way of searching for one's origin, speaking one's conflicts with the Law, entering into the dialectic of tenderness and hatred?' R. Barthes, *The pleasure of the text*, trans. R. Howard (New York, 1975).

55 Note that within Freudian psycho-analysis, fetishism describes the (male) child's disavowal of sexual difference itself: see S. Freud, 'Fetishism', *On sexuality* (Harmondsworth, 1977), pp.351–7.

[20]

For whom do the singers sing?

Bonnie J. Blackburn

1 *The Chevalier Philip Hinckaert, the Virgin and Child and St Philip* (Cambridge, Fitzwilliam Museum, PD.19-1961)

'O MATER dei memento mei' pleads the donor as he kneels before the Virgin and Child, permanently recording his devotion and his prayer to Mary, Intercessor with Christ the Judge (see illus.1). Donor portraits bridge time and space: the donor as a painted figure speaks to the living Virgin, and the donor as a living being is present before the painted image of the Madonna. The record is permanent, but is renewed each time the donor kneels before his painting, adding new prayers to that of his painted counterpart. After death, his portrait reminds his family to pray for his soul to be released from purgatory. What about the painter? His hand created the image, his brush painted the words

'O mater Dei memento mei'. No matter if this was a commercial transaction: the portrait could also be regarded as a prayer on his behalf, presenting his artistry as a gift to the Virgin.

This painting represents the Chevalier Philip Hinckaert, *maître d'hôtel* to Philip the Fair, duke of Burgundy, between 1493 and 1504. As in most such portraits, he kneels at a prie-dieu, his prayer-book in front of him. But here the book is closed and covered with a cloth, which perhaps indicates that the painting was made or finished after his death in 1505.[1] Pensively, the Chevalier stares into space; he does not look at the Virgin. Nor, indeed, could he: though she is standing on the same pavement, her physical presence is an illusion, for he is meditating, and his plea, the tiny rhyming couplet 'O mater dei memento mei', is a silent prayer.

A banderole with 'O mater dei memento mei' is not uncommon in donor portraits; it is very likely what the donor would have said every time he knelt to pray or passed an image of the Virgin. But it had uncommon significance for Philip Hinckaert and his family: his ancestor, the Chevalier Gerrelin, was nicknamed Hinckaert because he was lame (Middle Flemish: *hinckaerdt*); he prayed to the Virgin for help: 'O mater dei memento mei', and was cured when a vision of the Virgin appeared to him saying 'Marche droit, Hinckaert'. The family then assumed this name and the prayer as motto, and incorporated a wooden leg in their heraldry; it appears between the initials P and G on the back wall in the painting, together with the stylized leather thong that bound it to Hinckaert's leg. (P and G evidently stand for Philip and Gertrude, his second wife, whom he married in 1494.)

At the beginning of the music manuscript Brussels 228 Margaret of Austria is portrayed kneeling in prayer in her private chamber; a banderole records her words: 'Memento mei'. She too prays to the Virgin and Child, but they are in a different frame: across the page in the space before the soprano initial (illus.2).[2] Such portraits, similar to donors' portraits, figure frequently in the musical manuscripts that

emerged from the atelier of Petrus Alamire and other musical copyists of what has been called the Netherlands court complex. But while Philip Hinckaert prays in the stillness of his private meditation, Margaret also listens to the music that joins her to the Virgin and Child, both visually and aurally: a setting of the prayer 'Ave sanctissima Maria', probably by Pierre de La Rue.[3]

The counterpart in music of the great flowering of devotional painting and illuminated books of hours in the late 15th century is the prayer motet. Motets with personal addresses to Christ, Mary and the saints start to proliferate at this time. It is unlikely that those cast in the first person singular were sung in services: with the notable exception of the Credo, in liturgical texts, except for those taken from Scripture, it is the collective form that rules, for example in the Salve Regina: 'Ad te clamamus ... ad te suspiramus ... advocata nostra' ('To thee we cry ... to thee we sigh ... our advocate'). There are many motet settings of prayers in the first person plural such as *Ave Maria gratia plena* or *Sub tuum praesidium confugimus*. Many other texts, including liturgical ones, begin with a general invocation, but close with words such as 'ora pro nobis Deum' or 'miserere nobis'. Sometimes a motet text even refers to the choir of singers, as in Obrecht's commemoration of his father, *Mille quingentis*, or Josquin's *Illibata dei virgo*. It seems entirely appropriate for a choir to sing such prayers collectively, not only on behalf of themselves and the listeners, but of all mankind. But a polyphonic setting of a first person singular prayer seems an anomaly.[4]

For whom do the singers sing? This is not a question that is asked very often, and it is probably one that singers themselves rarely think about. If it is chant, the easy answer would be 'for the glory of God'. Often the answer will be that the singers sing for themselves, for the sheer love of singing. Sometimes it is just a job: they sing for their supper. The question becomes more pressing in the case of sacred music: do the words matter to the singer? Is it necessary to be a believer in order to sing a confession of faith, as we must do when we sing the Ordinary of the Mass? Of course the answer, for many people, is 'No'. Yet I suspect that many will sing what they might not be willing to say.[5]

Bonnie J. Blackburn is affiliated with Wolfson College, Oxford, and is General Editor of the series Monuments of Renaissance Music.

The singers who stand before the Brussels manuscript, open at *Ave sanctissima Maria*, are singing on behalf of Margaret of Austria, whether she is present in person or only in the illumination. Although it mostly contains chansons, the manuscript opens with a motet, as if to underline the common devotional practice of beginning any activity, whether rising from bed in the morning or setting out on a journey, with a prayer. Margaret's manuscript begins with this prayer to the Virgin:

Ave sanctissima Maria, mater dei, regina celi, porta paradisi, domina mundi. Tu es singularis virgo pura; tu concepisti Jesum de spiritu sancto; tu peperisti Creatorem et Salvatorem mundi, in quo ego non dubito. Ora pro me Jesum dilectum tuum et libera me ab omnibus malis.

Hail most holy Mary, Mother of God, Queen of Heaven, Gate of Paradise, Mistress of the World. Thou art a singularly pure virgin; thou didst conceive Jesus through the Holy Spirit; thou didst bear the Creator and Saviour of the World, in whom I do not doubt. Pray for me to Jesus, thy beloved, and deliver me from all evil.

It is a personal prayer, cast in the first person singular, the kind of prayer with which books of hours are filled. Margaret, kneeling at her prie-dieu, with her prayer-book in front of her, probably said this prayer and many similar ones at her private devotions or while Mass was celebrated. To set such a prayer to music for six voices (La Rue's setting is a triple canon, 6 ex 3) seems surprising, and raises anew the question for whom the singers sing: while they all sing for Margaret, or whoever else is listening, they also are singing for themselves: 'Pray for *me* to Jesus.'[6]

The question for whom the singers sing takes another turn when we consider the case of indulgenced prayers. 'Ave sanctissima Maria' is one of these; according to the rubrics in many books of hours (though not officially confirmed) it was composed by Pope Sixtus IV (1471–84), who accorded an indulgence of 11,000 years to those reciting it before an image of the Virgin *in sole*—against the golden rays of the sun—as in the miniature in Margaret's manuscript.[7] Will a singer singing this prayer receive the same indulgence? If he fulfils the necessary conditions, it should not matter if the prayer is said or sung. The tenor singing with intent should gain his indulgence, while the bass who has only dinner on his mind will not. And the listeners? If they are truly

contrite and confessed, the normal conditions necessary for receiving an indulgence, will they too benefit? Since it was possible to obtain indulgences for attending services in particular churches on certain days, or merely gazing on the Host at the Elevation, hearing a sung prayer should confer the same benefit as saying or singing it. Thus the singers pray not only for themselves but also for the listeners.

Do indulgences matter? Modern Catholics say little of the subject, and Protestants have always despised the whole business. Judging from books of hours, indulgences did matter, for they are frequently mentioned in rubrics. But scepticism attached to them even in the 15th century, and especially to the sometimes extravagant number of years in purgatory remitted. The compiler of one of the popular devotional books of the time, Bernardino de' Busti, remarked that his *Thesaurus spiritualis* contained 'many prayers privileged by various popes with indulgences, which, if I may say so without prejudice to the truth, have been revoked a thousand times, or in the future will be revoked; nevertheless, because of their wonderful contents they should not be neglected, for those who say them devoutly will obtain many favours from God.'[8]

Many indulgenced prayers are too long to be suitable as motet texts, but a few shorter ones were set frequently. In addition to 'Ave sanctissima Maria', two others stand out because they were to be said before well-known images: 'Salve sancta facies' before Veronica with the image of Christ's face on her cloth and 'O Domine Jesu Christe adoro te' before the Man of Sorrows or Image of Pity (sometimes in the context of the Mass of St Gregory). Many books of hours display these images and the accompanying prayers, not infrequently with a rubric specifying the amount of the indulgence and the name of the pope according it. Books of hours were often made to order, and while certain items were standard (the Office of the Virgin,

---

2 *(overleaf)* An opening from the manuscript Brussels, Bibliothèque Royale Albert 1ᵉʳ, Ms. 228, ff.1v–2r, showing Pierre de La Rue's canonic *Ave sanctissima Maria*. The illuminated initial on the verso depicts the Virgin and Child; that on the recto shows Margaret of Austria kneeling in prayer.

3 The Master of St Veronica, *St Veronica with the Sudarium* (London, National Gallery)

Vigils of the Dead, the seven Penitential Psalms, and the two long Marian prayers 'O intemerata et in aeternum benedicta' and 'Obsecro te sancta virgo Maria'), others were variable, especially the suffrages to saints and prayers to God the Father, Christ, and Mary. If a man or woman (and many books of hours were owned by women) could specify which prayers should be included in a Book of Hours, so might those with musical establishments tell their singers (and composers) what prayers they wished to have sung—during Mass (sometimes overriding the prescribed texts, as Galeazzo Maria Sforza evidently intended with the *motetti missales*), during private devotions, or at any time of the day when music was wanted. It is very difficult to know where and when these prayer motets were sung. But

the fact that they start proliferating in the late 15th century is a sure indication that there was a need for them. And it is likely that the greatest demand was at courts with chapels, where sacred and secular often flowed together in easy interchange.[9] These chapels most likely had the appropriate images, perhaps at dedicated altars.

Some images were in such great demand in the 15th century that painters specialized in them. This is the case with the Cologne painter known as the 'Master of St Veronica'. Illus.3 shows one of his many paintings. According to the most popular of her several legends, Veronica was the woman who held her cloth to Christ's face when he stumbled under the weight of the cross on the way to Calvary, leaving an imprint of his suffering face.[10] A cloth with the likeness of Christ turned up in Rome in the 8th century; it was the most precious relic kept in St Peter's during the 14th and 15th centuries, and the culmination of pilgrimages in Jubilee years.

For many pilgrims, viewing the image may have meant no more than being able to tick off one more relic on their list of things to see in Rome. But the purpose of images is to transport the spectator in his imagination, to make him vicariously a participant in the actual event: he should empathize with Veronica's compassion, imagine the weight of the Cross, and look with horror and pity on Christ's bloody and sweaty face. To help the viewer fix his thoughts, he recites a prayer. In the case of the Veronica veil, two prayers are often mentioned in the books of hours: the short 'Ave facies preclara', which seems not to have been set to music, and the much longer 'Salve sancta facies', for which we have one setting by Obrecht, another attributed to Josquin, and a third by an anonymous composer in the Segovia manuscript. Howard Brown discusses these in a recent article, tracing the history of the devotion to Veronica and her cloth.[11] According to a German devotional book of 1520, the prayer was written by Pope John XXII, who gave an indulgence of 10,000 days for reciting it before an image of the Veronica;[12] it does not need to be the relic in St Peter's—any image will do. Hence the proliferation of images of the Veronica in art.

Strictly viewed, the musical settings of *Salve sancta facies* would not have gained the indulgence, because none of them sets the complete text, a long rhymed *prosa* with up to 12 stanzas. The Segovia anonymous set only the first stanza; the setting attributed to Josquin (an *unicum* of Bologna Q20) comprises the first four—the length commonly found in books of hours. Obrecht sets eight stanzas, but combines them, rather surprisingly, with the text and melody of the Corpus Christi responsory *Homo quidam fecit cenam magnam*. Reinhard Strohm has plausibly suggested that the motet was written for a guild of cloth-workers or wool-weavers who sponsored a 'table of the poor'; Veronica, of course, was their patron saint.[13] If so, the motet was almost certainly sung before an image of the Veronica.

Images have not always been accepted by the Church, for there is the danger that they, like music, may appeal to the senses rather than the intellect. Augustine valued intellectual above corporeal vision, and was famously worried about the sensual appeal that music had for him. Thomas Aquinas, writing at a time when images had ceased to be a problem, approved of them, since he thought that 'the sense of devotion … is more efficaciously aroused by things seen than by things heard'.[14] In his *Complexus effectuum musices* Tinctoris appears to turn Aquinas's position around when he states that 'Music stirs the feelings to devotion', the sixth of his effects of music—citing in his support a different passage in Augustine's *Confessions* (book 10): 'I am inclined … to favour the custom of singing in church, so that through the delights of the ears the weaker spirit may attain to a mood of devotion.'[15] As his 11th effect Tinctoris claims that 'music uplifts the earthly mind'. Here he quotes St Bernard: 'The jubilation of praise elevates the eyes of the heart.'[16] Music adds one more dimension to praying before an image: vision and sound are fused, intensifying the experience of meditation.

No image could wrench the eyes of the heart more than the Passion. The image shown in illus.4 is not one of those: it is, in fact, a visual example of a meditation, commonly known as the Mass of St Gregory. According to the legend, one day as Pope Gregory was celebrating Mass in the Roman church of Santa Croce in Gerusalemme, there appeared to him a vision of Christ on the altar, showing the wound on his side and surrounded by the instruments of the

Passion: the so-called Image of Pity or Man of Sorrows. Only he sees the vision; his assistants and the bystanders are oblivious to it. Then, according to Bernardino de' Busti and numerous books of hours, Gregory, moved by the devotion and compassion he experienced, decreed that anyone who devoutly said a certain three prayers before an image of the Man of Sorrows, together with five Pater nosters and five Ave Marias, providing he had confessed all his sins and was contrite, should receive an indulgence of 14,000 years. The prayers normally follow in the manuscripts that contain this image, as they do in this early 16th-century Book of Hours.

This indulgence is probably the one most frequently found in devotional books, with increasing numbers of years and prayers. If we are to believe Busti, successive popes from Nicholas V onwards doubled and redoubled the indulgences; Pius II added two more prayers, and Paul II a sixth and a seventh. The apex is reached in a breviary printed in Venice in 1522, where Innocent VIII is said to have added two more prayers and doubled all previous indulgences: this would come to 112,000 years. But we should not believe Busti. As Eamon Duffy has recently shown, five of the prayers already existed in England by the early 9th century.[17] But no matter: Busti's view was that of his time, and the prayers were presumed efficacious. Moreover, they were short and easily memorized. Busti gives them in the following form:[18]

ORATIO PRIMA

O Domine Iesu Christe: adoro te in cruce pendentem: coronam spineam in capite portantem: deprecor te ut tua crux liberet me ab angelo percutiente.

O Lord Jesus Christ, I adore thee hanging on the cross, wearing the crown of thorns upon thy head: I beseech thee that thy cross may deliver me from the angel that smiteth.

ORATIO SECUNDA

O Domine Iesu Christe: adoro te in cruce vulneratum: felle et aceto potatum: deprecor te ut tua vulnera sint remedium anime mee.

O Lord Jesus Christ, I adore thee wounded on the cross, given gall and vinegar to drink: I beseech thee that thy wounds may be the salvation of my soul.

ORATIO TERTIA

O Domine Iesu Christe: adoro te in sepulchro positum: mirrha et aromatibus conditum: deprecor te ut tua mors sit vita mea.

O Lord Jesus Christ, I adore thee laid in the sepulchre,

embalmed with myrrh and spices: I beseech thee that thy death may be my life.

ORATIO QUARTA

O Domine Iesu Christe: pastor bone: iustos conserva: peccatores iustifica: omnibus fidelibus miserere: et propitius esto mihi peccatori.

O Lord Jesus Christ, good shepherd, save the just, justify sinners, have mercy on all the faithful, and be well disposed to me, the sinner.

ORATIO QUINTA

O Domine Iesu Christe: propter illam amaritudinem tuam quam pro me in cruce pendens sustinuisti: maxime quando nobilissima anima tua egressa est de corpore tuo sanctissimo: miserere anime mee in egressu suo.

O Lord Jesus Christ, for the sake of that bitterness of thine that thou didst sustain for me, hanging on the cross, above all when thy most noble soul departed from thy most holy body: have mercy on my soul in its departure.

ORATIO SEXTA

O Domine Iesu Christe: adoro te descendentem ad inferos: liberantemque captivos: deprecor te ne permittas me illuc introire.

O Lord Jesus Christ, I adore thee descending into hell and liberating the captives: I beseech thee not to permit me to enter there.

ORATIO SEPTIMA

O Domine Iesu Christe: adoro te ascendentem in celum: sedentemque ad dexteram patris: deprecor te miserere mei. Amen.

O Lord Jesus Christ, I adore thee ascending into heaven, and sitting on the right hand of the Father: I beseech thee, have mercy on me. Amen.

The Prayers of St Gregory, either singly or as a cycle, were set to music a number of times in the course of the 15th and 16th centuries. The best known is the setting (of the first five) attributed to Josquin, *O Domine Jesu Christe adoro te*. Sombre and restrained, set for low voices and largely chordal, this is music ideally suited to the eyes of the heart.[19] Cycles were also composed by Gombert, Senfl, Heinrich Finck, Maistre Jan and Willaert, and single prayers by Brumel, Mouton, Renaldo, Manchicourt, Maillard, Victoria, Felis and Giovanni Gabrieli, as well as several anonymous settings. Brumel's setting may in fact be part of a cycle that is only partially preserved; the fourth of the prayers, 'O domine Jesu Christe pastor bone', appears under his name in Bologna Q19 and, as Barton Hudson realized, anonymously and with a changed text pleading for recovery from illness, in

4 The Mass of St Gregory, accompanying the prayers of St Gregory (Oxford, Bodleian, Ms. Douce 112, f.139r)

142
Ex.1 Josquin, *Ave Maria … virgo serena*, end

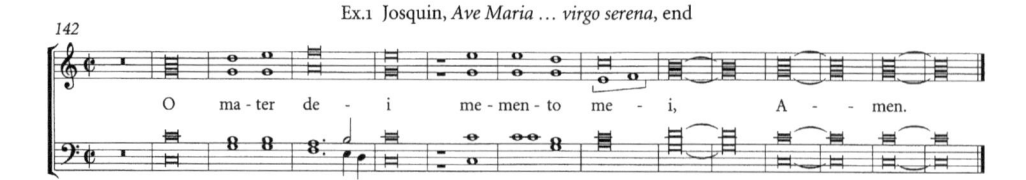

O   ma-ter   de -   i   me-men-to   me -   i,   A -   - men.

Florence Panc. 27. But in the latter manuscript the fifth prayer follows, and stylistically it forms a pair with Brumel's.[20]

O Domine is the earliest musical setting of the cycle of prayers. It appears in only one source, Petrucci's collection of Passion motets, *Motetti B* (1503). The tone is penitential, as befits the text, though the composer has not chosen the mode most often associated with such texts, Phrygian. Instead he opted for Dorian, using frequent B♭s, often appearing as the root of a chord; the harmonic movement gravitates towards A, on which the second and third prayers end (the fourth prayer closes on F). The text comes to the fore: even when the setting is not chordal, at least two of the voices deliver the same words simultaneously. Only in the longer final prayer does the music become more expansive, with imitations more widely spaced and a melismatic Amen that sinks down sequentially to the final cadence.

Here is truly a prayer motet: solemn, reverent, unostentatious, and with the text clearly understandable. Not a word is missing in any voice. Therefore the same benefit will accrue to each singer singing the prayers as if he were saying them—and perhaps even more, if we believe with Tinctoris that 'music stirs the feelings to devotion'. To sing these prayers with devotion requires attention not just to the music and the declamation of the text, but entry into the most heightened state of belief, contemplating the unfathomable divine mystery. The first three prayers evoke graphic images: Christ hanging on the cross, with the crown of thorns; the wounds that pour forth blood; and the deposition and burial. It is likely that these prayers would be sung or said in sight of these images: the Crucifix, universal in Catholic churches; an image of the Man of Pity, where the wounds are prominent, as in illus.4 (devotion to the wounds was

widespread at the time); and a Pietà. And if these images are not contemplated directly, then a mental image can be formed. Moreover, the first three prayers evoke not only sight but the senses of touch (the pain of the thorns), taste (gall and vinegar), and smell (myrrh and spices).[21] The fourth prayer is more general, turning away from images and sensations to Christ's role in the Redemption. The fifth prayer is the culmination of the series (the sixth and seventh prayers are clearly later additions), the most emotive and personal of the prayers: the sinner beseeches mercy on his soul at the moment of death 'for the sake of that bitterness of thine that thou didst sustain for *me*'.

'O mater dei memento mei' intones the singer in long notes at the end of Josquin's *Ave Maria … virgo serena* (see ex.1),[22] perhaps gazing on a painting of the Virgin, on the altar or in his choirbook, perhaps re-creating her image in his mind, perhaps thinking of nothing more than dinner. And since he is singing a four-part motet he is not alone: three other singers utter the same prayer. Some may pray for themselves or for the listeners, others merely sing. Those singing the motet for the first time may be taken by surprise on suddenly finding themselves giving voice to a prayer, for Josquin has inserted a personal prayer at the end of a text on the five joys of the Virgin, beginning *Ave cuius conceptio*. This text, which celebrates the five main events of the Virgin's life, differs from the ordinary five 'Joys of the Virgin' because it begins with the Conception. It seems not to pre-date the 15th century, and is associated with the increasing devotion to the Virgin's Conception and the cult of St Anne.[23] So far as I can determine, it appears almost exclusively in French books of hours, sometimes in conjunction with an Office or Mass of the Conception.[24] Although not always explicitly stated, this feast is often to be understood as the Immaculate Conception, a doctrine not officially sanctioned until 1477 (by Sixtus IV), and a matter of long-standing and continuing controversy between the Franciscans (pro) and Dominicans (contra).[25]

Josquin's motet to the Virgin, with its attached prayer, may have served as a model for a poetic prayer (see appendix) to the Virgin by Jean Molinet, based on the same five feasts as in Josquin's text.[26] While Josquin prefaced the text with two lines from the sequence 'Ave Maria ... virgo serena', and added the prayer at the end, Molinet wrote a *dizain* on each of the feasts, embedding the prayer 'O mater dei memento mei' in an acrostic in each of them.[27]

Like the artist who painted the words 'O mater dei

memento mei' on the portrait of Philip Hinckaert, Josquin and Molinet offer their artistry to the Virgin together with their prayer. Time and space of another kind govern sung and poetic prayers: singing or saying the work of a deceased author also allows his prayer to be heard once more, spoken from beyond the grave. Thus every time we sing *Ave Maria ... virgo serena* we also sing for Josquin.[28] Jean Molinet said as much for himself in another 'Oroison a la Vierge Marie', including the lines:

> Fais nous tel grace en la fin de nos jours
> Que moy, liseur de ceste oration,
> Et le facteur aions grace a tousjours.[29]

Appendix

Molinet, 'Ung dictier des cinq festes Nostre Dame'

Josquin, *Ave Maria ... virgo serena*

Ave Maria, gratia plena
Dominus tecum, Virgo serena.

CONCEPTION

O quelle offense oultrageuse et acherbe,
Maledicte Eve apporta en ce monde!
Terreur en vint du serpent qui enherbe
De son venin maint bon coeur net et monde;
Justice en fit Dieu qui nos pechiés monde;
Mes pour avoir paix, Madame saincte Anne,
Mente odorant, conchut la douce manne,
Tout purement, sans tache originelle,
Medecine aspre au pecheur qui se danne,
Implorant grace et gloire supernelle.

Ave cuius conceptio,
solemni plena gaudio,
Celestia, terrestria,
Nova replet letitia.

NATIVITÉ

On estimoit humain lignage mort,
Malleureux, ort et pollut par orgoeul;
Terriblement l'ennemy qui nous mort
Depopuloit tout le poeuple a son voeul;
Icelle dame Anne en fit le recoeul,
Mere devint et Marie descherge,
Membre divin, du filz de Dieu concherge;
Tous ses parens feste moult solennelle
Menerent lors, alumans maint beau cherge,
Implorant grace et gloire supernelle.

Ave cuius nativitas
Nostra fuit solemnitas,
Ut lucifer lux oriens,
Verum solem preveniens.

ANNUNCIATION

On presenta au temple la tres bonne
Marie, fleur flourissant comme lis;
Terrigene eur, d'honneur l'adresse et bonne
Delaissier volt et tous mondains delis;

Ave pia humilitas,
Sine viro fecunditas,
Cuius annunciatio
Nostra fuit salvatio.

Illec ung angle, issu des cieux pollis,
Messagier vray, bon salut luy aporte,
Mentionnant que Dieu veult qu'elle porte,
Tousjours estant vierge perpetuelle,
Messias vif, ouvrant du ciel la porte,
Implorant grace et gloire supernelle.

PURIFICATION

O admirabile effect, la basse lune   Ave vera virginitas,
Maine le hault soleil qui le regarde,   Immaculata castitas,
Terrestre fille est dessus toutes l'une,   Cuius purificatio
De qui Dieu fit sa mere et bonne garde;   Nostra fuit purgatio.
Icelle offrit son effant, qui le garde,
Meismes es bras Simeon, en plain choeur;
Menant grand joie il dit: 'j'ay sans rancoeur
Total salut, car lumiere eternelle
Me rend clarté; j'en seray, de bon coeur,
Implorant grace et gloire supernelle.'

ASSUMPTION

Or estes vous roÿne et dominés,   Ave preclara omnibus
Maistresse en court de pardurable tour;   Angelicis virtutibus,
Terre vous est scabelle et vous regnés   Cuius fuit assumptio
Dessus les cieux, ou fut vostre retour;   Nostra glorificatio.
Je vous requiers, dame de noble atour,
Me secourir au besoing soir et main;
Mendiant suis, grand pecheur inhumain,
Tout vostre serf, o Vierge maternelle,
Mettés mon fait en vostre seure main,
Implorant grace et gloire supernelle.

Princes mondains, triumphans par vaillance,   O mater dei
En temps de guerre horrible et criminelle,   Memento mei,
Servés la Vierge, acquerés bienvoeullance,   Amen.
Implorant grace et gloire supernelle.

Portions of this paper were read at the 23rd Conference on Medieval and Renaissance Music, Southampton, 8 July 1996, and at the Annual Meeting of the American Musicological Society, Baltimore, 9 November 1996. My thanks to Leofranc Holford-Strevens for a critical reading and for improving my translations, and to Nicholas Rogers, archivist at Sidney Sussex College, Cambridge, for helpful suggestions.

1 See the description in A. Arnould and J. M. Massing, *Splendours of Flanders* (Cambridge, 1993), p.42, with reference to earlier literature. Little is known about Hinckaert.

2 Brussels, Bibliothèque royale Albert Ier, Ms.228, ff.1v–2.

3 On this prayer and its numerous musical settings, see B. J. Blackburn, 'The Virgin in the sun: music and image for a prayer attributed to Sixtus IV', *Encomium musicae: essays in honor of Robert J. Snow*, ed. D. Crawford (in press).

4 The musical expression of personal prayers is not new, of course; one has only to recall the 'pious' trouvère songs and other vernacular lyrics of the 12th and 13th centuries. But the polyphonic setting of non-liturgical Latin prayers in the first person singular is new in the 15th century. (My thanks to

Christopher Page for reminding me of the monophonic precedents.)

5 Harold Copeman has considered some of these questions and others (including the difficult question of singing anti-Semitic texts) in *Singing the meaning: a layman's approach to religious music* (Oxford, 1996).

6 Two main traditions of this text are set out in Blackburn, 'The Virgin in the sun'; of the 36 settings examined there, most follow what must be the original form of the prayer, in the first person singular. Several change 'dubito' to 'dubitamus' and 'me' to 'nos'; yet others have a mixed form, retaining 'dubito' but changing the last lines to

'Ora pro nobis' and 'libera nos'.

7 As demonstrated in Blackburn, 'The Virgin in the sun', this is a prayer on the Immaculate Conception, and this particular form of the image, with Mary standing on a crescent moon (the 'mulier amicta sole' of the Apocalypse), became the standard way to represent the Immaculate Conception.

8 'In hoc libro ponuntur multe orationes a summis pontificibus diversis indulgentijs privilegiate. Que licet ut ita dicam sine veri preiudicio essent milies revocate: vel in futurum revocarentur: tamen propter eorum mirabilem continentiam non debent dimitti. Quia illas devote dicentes multas gratias a deo impetrabunt': Bernardino de' Busti, *Thesaurus spiritualis cum quamplurimis alijs additis noviter impressus* ([Lyons]: Nicolaus Wolff, 1500), f.50*v*.

9 The names of the composers of prayer motets are suggestive in this regard, pointing clearly to Milan and Ferrara. In Petrucci's motet volumes the following prayer motets are written (or contain passages) in the first person singular:

Motetti A (1502)
  Josquin, *Ave Maria … Virgo serena*
  Compère, 2.*p.* of *Crux triumphans* (with 'nostra'): *Jesus nomen dignum*
  Gaspar [van Weerbeke], *Ave domina sancta Maria* (a version of *Ave sanctissima Maria*)
  Anon., *Ave vera caro Christi*
  Gaspar, *Christi mater ave*
  [Gaspar], *Mater digna dei*
Motetti B (1503)
  Josquin, *O Domine Jesu Christe adoro te*
  Gaspar, *Anima Christi sanctifica me*
  Anon., *Adoro te devote latens*
  Compère, *Officium de Cruce* (*In nomine Jesu*), last section, *Hora completorii*
Motetti C (1504)
  [Josquin], *O bone et dulcis domine Jesu*
  Anon., *Respice me infelicem*
  Anon., *Miserere mei deus quoniam in te anima mea*
  Anon., *Magnus es tu domine*
Motetti Libro quarto (1505)
  Mouton, *O Maria virgo pia*
  Ghiselin, *Miserere domine*

Ghiselin, *O gloriosa domina*
Ninot, *O bone Jesu*
Motetti a 5 (1508)
  Regis, *Clangat plebs*
  Diniset, *Ave sanctissima Maria*

10 A recent book on this theme is E. Kuryluk, *Veronica and her cloth* (Cambridge, MA, and Oxford, 1991). There are many earlier studies.

11 H. M. Brown, 'On Veronica and Josquin', *New perspectives on music: essays in honor of Eileen Southern*, ed. J. Wright with S. A. Floyd (Warren, MI, 1992), pp.49–61.

12 Nicolaus Salicetus, *Liber meditationum ac orationum devotarum. Qui Anthidotarius anime dicitur* (Nuremberg, 1520), f.87. All such attributions and especially the claims of indulgences differ from source to source and are untrustworthy.

13 R. Strohm, *Music in late medieval Bruges* (Oxford, 1985), pp.143, 145.

14 Thomas Aquinas, *In IV libros sententiarum*, lib. 3, dist. 9, q. 1, a. 2, sol. 2, ad 3. Quoted in Blackburn, 'The Virgin in the sun', n.44. Devotional images are the subject of H. van Os, *The art of devotion in the late Middle Ages in Europe, 1300–1500*, trans. M. Hoyle (London, 1994), which illustrates the three types discussed in this article and many others.

15 Johannes Tinctoris, *Complexus effectuum musices*, in *Opera theoretica*, ed. A. Seay, Corpus Scriptorum de Musica, xxii (American Institute of Musicology, 1975), p.169. See now Egidius Carlerius and Johannes Tinctoris, *On the dignity and the effects of music: two fifteenth-century treatises*, trans. and annot. J. D. Cullington, ed. R. Strohm and J. D. Cullington, Institute of Advanced Musical Studies Study Texts, ii (London, 1996), pp.54, 70, from which the translation is taken.
  Christopher Page has called attention to Tinctoris's unsignalled borrowings from Augustine in the *Complexus*, and suggests that it is quite possible he knew them through Aquinas's *Summa theologiae*, which incorporates the relevant passages from the *Confessions*; see C. Page, 'Reading and reminiscence: Tinctoris on the beauty of music', *Journal of the American Musicological Society*, il (1996), pp.1–31, esp. pp.11–16.

Like Augustine, Tinctoris stresses the effect music has on him personally.

16 'Oculos cordis attollit iubilus laudis': Tinctoris, *Complexus effectuum musices*, ed. Seay, p.172; Tinctoris, *On the dignity and the effects of music*, ed. Strohm and Cullington, pp.56, 94. Tinctoris gives the source in St Bernard as *Super cantica*; Cullington and Strohm did not find the exact wording, but point out similar phrases involving 'iubilus cordis'.

17 In the Book of Cerne. By the 10th century they had become part of the *Adoratio Crucis* on Good Friday. See E. Duffy, *The stripping of the altars: traditional religion in England c.1400–c.1580* (New Haven and London, 1992), pp.238–43. For the *Adoratio Crucis* see K. Young, *The drama of the medieval church* (Oxford, 1933), i, pp.112–48.

18 Many books of hours contain these prayers, sometimes in a different order, and sometimes beginning 'Domine Jesu Christe' or even 'Adoro te, domine'. Before the 1470s only the first five prayers commonly appear in devotional books.

19 Josquin des Prez, *Werken*, ed. A. Smijers, *Motetten*, ii (Amsterdam and Leipzig, 1924), no.10. (The last word of the *prima pars* is incorrectly given as 'penitente' in the edition; it is 'percutiente'.) Certain technical aspects of the motet cast doubt on the attribution; I shall take up the question elsewhere.

20 Bologna, Civico Museo Bibliografico Musicale, Ms. Q19, ff.93*v*–94, published in Antoine Brumel, *Opera omnia*, v, ed. B. Hudson, Corpus Mensurabilis Musicae, v/5 (American Institute of Musicology, 1972), pp.86–8; Florence, Biblioteca Nazionale Centrale, Ms. Panc. 27, ff.86*v*–88, with the text 'O Domine Jesu Christe, te supplices exoramus ut N. servum tuum languescentem et molesta febre pressum, ab omni egretudinis gravamine incolumen per merita tue passionis sanitatisque munere letum reddere digneris.' The *secunda pars* bears the normal text of the fifth prayer, beginning 'O domine Jesu Christe propter illam amaritudinem'.

  The setting attributed to Mouton is of the fourth prayer and appears only in the late source Rhau, *Symphoniae jucundae* (1538[8]), no.41; the petition is made for 'nobis peccatoribus'. Renaldo's setting of the second prayer, in Bologna Q19, ff.44v–45, has a slightly different (and grammatically incorrect) text: 'O domine yhesu christe: te suplices exoramus ut in cruce vulneratum felle et acceto potatum deprecor te ut tua vulnera sint remedium anime mee.'

21 The phrase that Tinctoris applies to the works of his admired contemporaries, 'perfumed with such sweetness', interpreted in musical terms by Rob C. Wegman ('Sense and sensibility in late-medieval music: thoughts on aesthetics and authenticity', *Early music*, xxiii (1995), pp.299–312), has received a rich metaphorical explanation in Page, 'Reading and reminiscence'. Indeed, Pierre d'Ailly's treatise on the spiritual senses, *Compendium contemplationis* (discussed on pp.28–30), covers not only spiritual hearing and spiritual sight, which (following Aristotle) are associated with memory and understanding, but also spiritual olfaction, awakening the desire for God.

22 The alto sings what appears to be a litany tone, different from the common litany invocation but matching the setting of the words 'Sancta Maria virgo virginum' in the superius and tenor of Noel Bauldewyn's six-part motet of the same name, recently identified by Bernadette Nelson in a Spanish manuscript, Barcelona, Biblioteca de Catalunya, M.1967. See her article 'Pie memorie', *Musical times*, cxxxvi (July 1995), pp.338–44, where she called attention to the likeness (p.340 and n.25; the incipit is given in her ex.1).

23 There are other settings by Brumel (*Opera omnia*, v, pp.3–6); Andreas de Silva, *2.p.* of *Ave ancilla trinitatis*, which also concludes 'O mater dei memento mei', unrelated musically to Josquin (*Opera omnia*, ed. W. Kirsch, Corpus Mensurabilis Musicae, xlix (American Institute of Musicology, 1970–), i, pp.61–8); and Nicholas Ludford (ed. N. Sandon, Antico Edition RCM 127). A single voice from an anonymous English five-part setting is discussed in N. Sandon, 'The Manuscript London, British Library Harley 1709', *Music in the medieval English liturgy: Plainsong*

and Mediaeval Music Society centennial essays, ed. S. Rankin and D. Hiley (Oxford, 1993), pp.355–79, esp. pp.371–5. This same manuscript includes a rare English setting of the prayers of St Gregory, beginning 'Adoro te'; see ibid., pp.367–70.

24 The text is related only tangentially to the Office of the Recollectio, for which Dufay composed the plainchant. At the time Michel de Beringhen, a canon at Cambrai Cathedral, endowed this feast in 1457, six Marian feasts were celebrated, including the Visitation. Beringhen wished to add this new collective feast, evidently to bring the number up to the Marian seven. Barbara Haggh discovered that the new text was composed by Gilles Carlier and the music by Dufay; see her preliminary report, 'The celebration of the "Recollectio Festorum Beatae Mariae Virginis", 1457–1987', *Atti del XIV congresso della Società Internazionale di Musicologia, trasmissione e recezione delle forme di cultura musicale*, ed. A. Pompilio, D. Restani, L. Bianconi, and F. A. Gallo, 3 vols. (Turin, 1990), iii, pp.559–71. Pomerium, under the direction of Alexander Blachly, has recently recorded the First Vespers (Archiv 447 773-2).

25 This is discussed in Blackburn, 'The Virgin in the sun'. The Dominicans speak of Mary's 'sanctification' in the womb, holding that as a human being she was not exempt from Original Sin. Herein lies the explanation for the changed text of *Ave cuius conceptio* in some sources. In Petrucci's *Motetti A*, Glareanus and several manuscript sources the first two lines read 'Ave celorum domina, Maria plena gratia' instead of 'Ave cuius conceptio, Solemni plena gaudio' (the same is true of Brumel's setting of *Ave cuius conceptio* in *Motetti C*; Cappella Sistina 42 has the correct text). Petrucci's editor, Petrus Castellanus, was a Dominican, and in his church, SS. Giovanni e Paolo in Venice, it is not likely that a motet referring to the Immaculate Conception would have been sung.

26 Molinet and Josquin may well have been acquainted. Josquin is named first in Molinet's *Déploration* on Ockeghem, and Josquin set it to music. At the time of Molinet's death in 1507 his

son Augustin was a canon at Josquin's church, Notre Dame de Condé; see N. Dupire, *Jean Molinet: la vie—les œuvres* (Paris, 1932), p.16. In 1494 Molinet himself held a canonry at Condé, as well as at Saint-Géry in Cambrai (ibid., p.17). His main prebend, however, was as canon of Nôtre-Dame de La Salle in Valenciennes.

27 Published in *Les Faictz et dictz de Jean Molinet*, ed. N. Dupire, 3 vols. (Paris, 1936–9), ii, pp.450–2. Since the three sources all date from the early 16th century (Molinet died in 1507), this may be a late work, although the mention of war in the envoi could put it back to the 1480s or earlier. See N. Dupire, *Étude critique des manuscrits et éditions des poésies de Jean Molinet* (Paris, 1932), 15, 34, 46. Since Dupire published his book one source has been destroyed (Tournai, in a fire of 1940) and another discovered: Brussels, Bibliothèque royale, Ms. IV 541 (dated 1568); see J. Lemaire, *Meschinot, Molinet, Villon: témoignages inédits. Étude du Bruxellensis IV 541, suivie de l'édition de quelques ballades* (Brussels, 1979). Dupire remarks that the lines of the poem end in rebuses, but the edition does not make clear what they are. Both Molinet and Josquin, by using the words 'sans tache originelle' and 'immaculata' respectively, align themselves with the Franciscan position on the Immaculate Conception.

28 And not only in this motet but in Pierre de La Rue, *Missa de Septem doloribus* (*Opera omnia*, ed. N. St John Davison, J. E. Kreider, and T. H. Keahey, Corpus Mensurabilis Musicae, xcvii/3 (Neuhausen–Stuttgart, 1992), no.14). In Osanna II La Rue quotes the superius of Josquin's final passage (a 12th lower) with the words 'O mater dei memento mei. Amen' (in Cappella Sistina 36), inserted in the middle of the sequence text 'Salve virgo generosa', which is used at this point in the Mass.

29 'Intercede for us at the end of our days so that I, the reader of this prayer, and the author may ever find mercy' (ll. 130–32); *Les Faictz et dictz*, ed. Dupire, ii, p.480. The Brussels manuscript mentioned in n.27 places these verses at the end of the poem.

Series Bibliography

Adorno, T.W. (1967), 'Bach Defended against His Devotees', in T.W. Adorno, *Prisms*, London, pp. 133–46.

Aldrich, Putnam (1957), 'The "Authentic" Performance of Baroque Music', in Putnam Aldrich, *Essays on Music in Honor of Archibald Thompson Davison by His Associates*, Cambridge, MA: Department of Music, Harvard University, pp. 161–71.

Bank, J.A. (1972), *Tactus, Tempo, and Notation in Mensural Music from the 13th to the 17th Century*, Amsterdam: Annie Bank.

Blades, James and Montagu, Jeremy (1976), *Early Percussion Instruments: From the Middle Ages to the Baroque*, London: Oxford University Press.

Boulez, Pierre (1990), 'The Vestal Virgin and the Fire-Stealer: Memory, Creation, and Authenticity', *Early Music*, **18**, pp. 355–58.

Brett, Phillip (1988), 'Text, Context and the Early Music Editor', in Nicholas Kenyon (ed.), *Authenticiy and Early Music*, Oxford: OUP.

Brown, Howard Mayer *et al.*, 'Performing Practice', in *The New Grove Dictionary of Music and Musicians* (2nd edn).

Brown, H.M. and Sadie, S. (eds) (1989), *Performance Practice* (2 Vols), The New Grove Handbooks in Music, London: Macmillan.

Butt, John (2002), *Playing with History: The Historical Approach to Musical Performance*, Cambridge: Cambridge University Press.

Careri, E. (1993), *Francesco Geminiani 1687–1762*, Oxford: Oxford University Press.

Copeman, Harold (1990), *Singing in Latin or Pronunciation Explor'd*, Oxford: Harold Copeman.

Covey-Crump, Rogers (1992), 'Vocal Consort Style and Tunings', in John Paynter *et al.* (eds), *Companion to Contemporary Musical Thought*, Vol. II, London and New York: Routledge, pp. 1020–50.

Dart, Thurston (1954), *The Interpretation of Music*, London: Hutchinson's University Library.

Davies, S. (1987), 'Authenticity in Musical Performance', *British Journal of Aesthetics*, **27**, pp. 39–50.

Davies, S. (1988a), 'Transcription, Authenticity and Performance', *British Journal of Aesthetics*, **28**, pp. 216–27.

Davies, S. (1988b), 'Authenticity in Performance: A Reply to James O. Young', *British Journal of Aesthetics*, **29**, 373–76.

Donington, R. (1963), *The Interpretation of Early Music*, London: Faber, and New York: St Martin's Press; rev. 1989.

Dreyfus, Laurence (1983), 'Early Music Defended against Its Devotees: A Theory of Historical Performance in the Twentieth Century', *Musical Quarterly*, **69**, pp. 297–322.

Druce, Duncan (1992), 'Historical Approaches to Violin Playing', in John Paynter *et al.* (eds), *Companion to Contemporary Musical Thought*, Vol. II, London and New York: Routledge, pp. 993–1019.

Dulak, Michelle (1993), 'The Quiet Metamorphosis of "Early Music"', *Repercussions: Critical and Alternative Viewpoints on Music and Scholarship*, **2**, pp. 31–61.

Garratt, James (2002), *Palestrina and the German Romantic Imagination: Interpreting Historicism in Nineteenth-Century Music*, Cambridge: Cambridge University Press.

Goehr, Lydia (1992), *The Imaginary Museum of Musical Works: An Essay in the Philosophy of Music*, Oxford: Clarendon Press.

Greenberg, Noah (1966), 'Early Music Performance Today', in Jan LaRue (ed.), *Aspects of Medieval and Renaissance Music: A Birthday Offering to Gustave Reese*, New York: W.W. Norton, pp. 314–18; reprint edn, New York: Pendragon Press, 1978.

Grout, Donald Jay (1957), 'On Historical Authenticity in the Performance of Old Music', in *Essays on Music in Honor of Archibald Thompson Davison by His Associates*, Cambridge, MA: Department of Music, Harvard University, pp. 341–47.

Harper, John (1991), *The Forms and Orders of Western Liturgy from the Tenth to the Eighteenth Century: A Historical Introduction and Guide for Students and Musicians*, Oxford: Clarendon Press.

Haskell, Harry (1988), *The Early Music Revival: A History*, London: Thames and Hudson.

Haynes, Bruce (2007), *The End of Early Music: A Period Performer's History of Music for the Twenty-First Century*, Oxford: Oxford University Press.

Higgins, P. (1993), 'From the Ivory Tower to the Marketplace: Early Music, Musicology, and the Mass Media', *Current Musicology*, **53**, pp. 109–23.

Hudson, R. (1994), *Stolen Time: The History of Tempo Rubato*, Oxford: Oxford University Press.

Jackson, Roland (1988), *Performance Practice, Medieval to Contemporary: A Bibliographic Guide*, Music Research and Information Guides 9, Garland Reference Library in the Humanities 790, New York and London: Garland.

Kenyon, Nicholas (ed.) (1988), *Authenticity and Early Music: A Symposium*, Oxford and New York: Oxford University Press.

Kenyon, Nicholas (1997), 'Time to Talk Back to Treatises!', *Early Music,* **25**, pp. 555–57.

Kerman, Joseph, Dreyfus, Laurence, Kosman, Joshua, Rockwell, John, Rosand, Ellen, Taruskin, Richard and McGegan, Nicholas (1992), 'The Early Music Debate: Ancients, Moderns, Postmoderns', *Journal of Musicology*, **10**, pp. 113–30.

Kivy, Peter (1995), *Authenticities: Philosophical Reflections on Musical Performance*, Ithaca, NY and London: Cornell University Press.

Lawson, Colin and Stowell, Robin (1999), *The Historical Performance of Music: An Introduction*, Cambridge: Cambridge University Press.

Le Huray, Peter (1990), *Authenticity in Performance: Eighteenth-Century Case Studies*, Cambridge: CUP.

Leech-Wilkinson, D., Taruskin, R. and Temperley, N. (1984), 'The Limits of Authenticity: A Discussion', *Early Music*, **12**, pp. 3–25.

Leppard, R. (1988), *Authenticity in Music*, London: Faber and Faber.

MacClintock, Carol (ed.) (1979), *Readings in the History of Music in Performance*, Bloomington, IN and London: Indiana University Press.

Marcuse, Sibyl (1975), *A Survey of Musical Instruments*, New York: Harper and Row.

Mertin, Josef (1986), *Early Music: Approaches to Performance Practice*, trans. Siegmund Levarie, New York: Da Capo.

Morrow, Michael (1978), 'Musical Performance and Authenticity', *Early Music*, **6**, pp. 233–46.

Neumann, F. (1982), *Essays in Performance Practice*, Epping: University of Rochester Press.

Neumann, F. (1989), *New Essays on Performance Practice*, Ann Arbor, MI and London: University of Rochester Press.

Philip, Robert (1992), *Early Recordings and Musical Style*, Cambridge: Cambridge University Press.

Philip, Robert (2004), *Performing Music in the Age of Recording*, New Haven, CT and London: Yale University Press.

Potter, John (1998), *Vocal Authority: Singing Style and Ideology*, Cambridge: Cambridge University Press.

Remnant, Mary (1978), *Musical Instruments of the West*, London: B.T. Batsford.

Rosen, Charles (2000), 'The Benefits of Authenticity', in Charles Rosen, *Critical Entertainments*, Cambridge, MA and London: Harvard University Press, pp. 201–21.

Sachs, Curt (1953), *Rhythm and Tempo: A Study in Music History*, New York: W.W. Norton.

Sadie, S. (1990), 'The Idea of Authenticity', in J.A. Sadie (ed.), *Companion to Baroque Music*, London: OUP, pp. 435–46.

Saint-Saëns, Camille (1915a), 'The Execution of Classical Works: Notably Those of the Older Masters', *Musical Times*, **56**, pp. 474–78.

Saint-Saëns, Camille (1915b), *On the Execution of Music, and Principally of Ancient Music; a Lecture by M. Camille Saint- Saëns, Delivered at the ... Panama-Pacific International Exposition. Done into English with Explanatory Notes by Henry P. Bowie*, trans. Henry P. Bowie, San Francisco, CA: The Blair-Murdock Company.

Segerman, Ephraim (1996a), 'A Re-examination of the Evidence on Absolute Tempo before 1700 – I', *Early Music*, **24**, pp. 227–48.

Segerman, Ephraim (1996b), 'A Re-examination of the Evidence on Absolute Tempo before 1700 – II', *Early Music*, **24**, pp. 681–89.

Sherman, Bernard D. (1997), *Inside Early Music: Conversations with Performers*, New York and Oxford: Oxford University Press.

Stevens, Denis (1972), 'Some Observations on Performance Practice', *Current Musicology*, **14**, pp. 159–63.

Stevens, Denis (1980), *Musicology: A Practical Guide*, London: Schirmer Books.

Strahle, G. (1995), *An Early Music Dictionary: Musical Terms from British Sources, 1500–1740*, Cambridge: CUP.

Taruskin, Richard (1982), 'On Letting the Music Speak for Itself', *Journal of Musicology*, **1**, pp. 338–49.

Taruskin, Richard *et al.* (1984), 'The Limits of Authenticity: A Discussion', *Early Music*, **12**, pp. 1–25.

Taruskin, Richard (1988), 'The Pastness of the Present and the Presence of the Past', in Nicholas Kenyon (ed.), *Authenticity and Early Music: A Symposium*, Oxford and New York: Oxford University Press, pp. 137–207.

Taruskin, Richard (1995), *Text and Act: Essays on Music and Performance*, New York and Oxford: Oxford University Press.

Vinquist, Mary and Zaslaw, Neal (eds) (1970), *Performance Practice: A Bibliography*, New York: W.W. Norton, 1970. Supplements in *Current Musicology* (1971), **12**, pp. 129–49 and (1973), **15**, pp. 126–36.

Walls, Peter (2002), 'Historical Performance and the Modern Performer', in John Rink (ed.), *Musical Performance: A Guide to Understanding*, Cambridge: CUP, pp. 17–34.

Walls, Peter (2003), *History, Imagination and the Performance of Music*, Woodbrige, Suffolk and Rochester, NY: Boydell.

Williams, Peter (1992), 'Performance Practice Studies: Some Current Approaches to the Early Music Phenomenon', in John Paynter *et al.* (eds), *Companion to Contemporary Musical Thought*, Vol. II, London and New York: Routledge, pp. 931–47.

Winternitz, Emanuel (1979), *Musical Instruments and Their Symbolism in Western Art: Studies in Musical Iconology* (2nd edn), New Haven, CT and London: Yale University Press.

Wistreich, Richard (2002), 'Practising and Teaching Historically Informed Singing – Who Cares?', *Basler Jahrbuch für historische Musikpraxis*, **26**, pp. 17–29.

Wray, Alison (1992), 'Authentic Pronunciation for Early Music', in John Paynter *et al.* (eds), *Companion to Contemporary Musical Thought*, Vol. II, London and New York. Routledge, pp. 1051–64.

Young, J.O. (1988), 'The Concept of Authentic Performance', *British Journal of Aesthetics*, **28**, pp. 228–38.

Name Index

Abano, Petrus de 88
Agazzari, Agostino 196–7, 200
Agricola, Martin 299, 300–304 *passim*, 306–7,
    309–14 *passim*, 319, 321
Agustino 58
Aich, Arnt von 127, 129 *passim*, 132, 133
Alba, Duke of 113
Albertis, Gaspar de 382
Albonesi, Afranio degli 271, 279, 285, 288
Albonesi, Teseo 271
Aldrovandino, Isabetta 148
Alessandrini, Rinaldo xiv, 137–43
Alfonso V of Aragon 227
Almela, Diego Rodriguez de 120
Almire, Petrus 422
Altaemps, Duke Giovanni Angelo 223
Amadino, Ricciardo 221
Amanditis, Virgilius de 204
Anchieta, Juan de 55, 110, 112
Anchin, Jean d' 39
Andrieu, F. 85
Anerio, Felice 221, 223
Anerio, Giovanni Francesco 197
Anglés, Higinio 149
Animuccia, Giovanni 204, 208, 216
Anne, Saint 430
Anthony of Padua, Saint 36
Antico, Andrea 97, 100, 382
Antonelli, Abundio 197
Apel, Willi 366
Aquinas, Thomas 427
Arcadelt, Jacob (Jacques) 276
Arévelo, Rodrigo Sánchez de 112
Ariosto, Ludovico 226, 286
Aristotle 88
Arnulph of Saint Gilles 17
Aron, Pietro 36, 347, 352, 354–5 *passim*, 360,
    372
Arrivabene, Andrea 278
Arthur, King 107
Artusi, Giovanni Maria 137, 342
Attaingnant, Pierre xvii, 275, 294, 295, 296, 315,
    318–19 *passim*, 321, 381

Augustine, Saint 427
Azzaiolo, Filippo 275

Bach, Johann Sebastian 147, 152, 168
Baldini, Signor 184
Banchieri, Adriano 140, 221, 390
Barbieri, Patrizio 207, 375, 382, 390
Barthes, Roland 412, 415
Basin, Pierrequin 32
Bassano, Giovanni 22, 207
Bastianelli, Signor 184
Battre, H. 40, 41, 42
Bavaria, Duke Albrecht of 248
Baxandall, Michael 190
Behaim, Michel 248
Bellucio (Bellucius), Cesare 186–7, 199, 204
Bendusi, Francesco 274
Bent, Margaret xvii, 327–74, 407
Berchem, Jachet de 382
Bermudo, Juan 22, 119, 152
Bernáldez, Andrés 227–8
Bernard, Saint 427
Bernhard, Christoph 139, 142
Binchois, Gilles 42, 53, 61, 84, 125, 152
Blackburn, Bonnie J. xviii, 421–34
Blanc, Tirant lo 112
Boetticher, W. 158
Borrono, Pietro Paulo 278
Botto, Louis 170
Bottrigari, Hercole 277
Bourgois, Louis 41, 42
Bovicelli, Giovanni Battista 11, 198, 207
Bowers, Roger 44, 57, 375, 376, 377
Bradshaw, Murray 221
Brancadori, Domenico 204
Bridgman, Nanie 35
Brown, Howard Mayer xiii, xiv, xvii, 99, 120,
    263–88, 289–323, 368, 426
Brudieu, Joan 231
Bruhier, Antoine 275
Brumel, Antoine 158, 161, 379, 428
Buckel, Coppin 32
Buglhat, Giovanni de 264